D1091641

Glencoe

Understanding Psychology

With Features From TIME

**Glencoe
McGraw-Hill**

New York, New York   Columbus, Ohio   Woodland Hills, California   Peoria, Illinois

Author

Richard A. Kasschau, Ph.D., is Professor of Psychology at the University of Houston. Dr. Kasschau is a member of the American Educational Research Association, the American Psychological Association, and the American Psychological Society. He has written extensively for magazines, newspapers, and professional journals, and has a dozen books to his credit. An award-winning and distinguished teacher who has taught psychology for 35 years, Dr. Kasschau has won the University of Houston's Teaching Excellence Award twice in the last 15 years.

A Division of The McGraw·Hill Companies

Copyright © 2001 by The McGraw-Hill Companies, Inc. All rights reserved. Except as permitted under the United States Copyright Act of 1976, no part of this publication may be reproduced or distributed in any form or by any means, or stored in a database or retrieval system, without the written permission of the publisher.

Send all inquiries to
Glencoe/McGraw-Hill, 8787 Orion Place, Columbus, Ohio 43240-4027

ISBN 0-07-820338-4 (Student Edition)
ISBN 0-07-820339-2 (Teacher's Wraparound Edition)

Printed in the United States of America

5 6 7 8 9 10 027/043 04 03 02

Senior Consultant-Writers

Ronald Foore, Ed.D.
Booker T. Washington Magnet High School
Tulsa, Oklahoma

Jim Matiya
Carl Sandburg High School
Orland Park, Illinois

Academic Consultants

Martha Alcock, Ph.D.
Capital University
Columbus, Ohio

Shirley DeLucia, Ed.D.
Capital University
Columbus, Ohio

Maureen Hester, Ph.D.
Holy Names College
Oakland, California

Judith R. Levine, Ph.D.
State University of New York at Farmingdale
Farmingdale, New York

Joel Stellwagen, Ph.D.
Hinsdale South High School
Darien, Illinois

Educational Reviewers

Jerry Agner
Marion Harding High School
Marion, Ohio

Lynn Erven
Lake Forest High School
Lake Forest, Illinois

Dale Kinney
Ralston High School
Omaha, Nebraska

Patrick Mattimore
South San Francisco High School
San Francisco, California

Nathan McAlister
Highland Park High School
Topeka, Kansas

Gale Ow
Lowell High School
San Francisco, California

Table of Contents

Table of Contents

v

Table of Contents

psychology.glencoe.com

Visit the *Understanding Psychology* Web site!

- **Chapter Overviews** provide you with a quick preview or review of the chapter.

- **Student Web Activities** take you into the real world of psychology.

- **Self-Check Quizzes** help you prepare for the Chapter Test.

Use our Web site for additional resources. All essential content is covered in the Student Edition.

TIME
REPORTS

Profiles In Psychology

Table of Contents

Table of Contents

Psychology and You

More About...

Table of Contents

Table of Contents

Figure 13.9 Distribution of IQ Scores

This normal curve displays intelligence by IQ tests. The average IQ score is 100. *About how many people score at least 145 on IQ tests?*

- Mentally handicapped
- Borderline
- Slow learner
- Low average
- High average
- Above average
- Superior
- Gifted

55 70 80 90 100 110 120 130 145

50%
95%
99%

Table of Contents

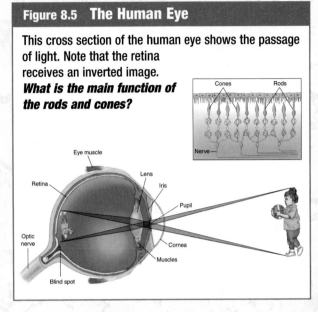

Figure 8.5   The Human Eye

This cross section of the human eye shows the passage of light. Note that the retina receives an inverted image.
What is the main function of the rods and cones?

Reading for Information

Think about your textbook as a tool that helps you learn more about the world around you. It is an example of nonfiction writing—it describes real-life events, people, ideas, and places. Here is a menu of reading strategies that will help you become a better textbook reader. As you come to passages in your textbook that you don't understand, refer to these reading strategies for help.

✔ BEFORE YOU READ

Set a Purpose
- Why are you reading the textbook?
- How does the subject relate to your life?
- How might you be able to use what you learn in your own life?

Preview
- Read the chapter title to find what the topic will be.
- Read the subtitles to see what you will learn about the topic.
- Skim the photos, charts, graphs, or maps. How do they support the topic?
- Look for vocabulary words that are boldfaced. How are they defined?

Draw From Your Own Background
- What have you read or heard about concerning new information on the topic?
- How is the new information different from what you already know?
- How will the information that you already know help you understand the new information?

✓ AS YOU READ

Question
- What is the main idea?
- How do the photos, charts, graphs, and maps support the main idea?

Connect
- Think about people, places, and events in your own life. Are there any similarities with those in your text-book?
- Can you relate the textbook informa-tion to other areas of your life?

Predict
- Predict events or outcomes by using clues and information that you already know.
- Change your predictions as you read and gather new information.

Visualize
- Pay careful attention to details and descriptions.
- Create graphic organizers to show relationships that you find in the information.

LOOK FOR CLUES AS YOU READ

- **Comparison-and-Contrast Sentences:**

  Look for clue words and phrases that signal comparison, such as *similarly, just as, both, in common, also,* and *too.*

  Look for clue words and phrases that signal contrast, such as *on the other hand, in contrast to, however, differ-ent, instead of, rather than, but,* and *unlike.*

- **Cause-and-Effect Sentences:**

  Look for clue words and phrases such as *because, as a result, therefore, that is why, since, so, for this reason,* and *consequently.*

- **Chronological Sentences:**

  Look for clue words and phrases such as *after, before, first, next, last, during, finally, earlier, later, since,* and *then.*

✓ AFTER YOU READ

Summarize
- Describe the main idea and how the details support it.
- Use your own words to explain what you have read.

Assess
- What was the main idea?
- Did the text clearly support the main idea?
- Did you learn anything new from the material?
- Can you use this new information in other school subjects or at home?
- What other sources could you use to find more information about the topic?

How to Think Like a Psychologist

Why Study Psychology?

Many people begin their study of psychology without a clear definition or understanding of the subject. They may have images of a laboratory where scientists run rats through mazes, or they may assume that it deals only with abnormal emotional disturbances. These, however, are only small parts of the study of psychology. Psychology provides tools to help us gain insight into our own behavior, as well as our relationships with others.

What to Expect

As you begin your study of psychology, you will find that it is different from any of your other classes. This is because psychology is connected to both the social sciences—such as history or economics—and the natural sciences—such as biology and chemistry. As a social science, psychology explores the influences of society on individual behavior and group relationships. As a natural science, psychology looks for biological explanations for human behavior. You will learn more about the social and biological aspects of human behavior as you draw from the course material to gain insight into your life and the lives of those around you.

Your study of psychology can help you gain insights into explaining your and others' behavior.

PET scan of a human brain

How Do Psychologists Think?

In your study of psychology, you will learn to think like a scientist. Scientists constantly question their own assumptions and look for alternative evidence and conclusions.

Scientists—including psychologists—use the **scientific method** as a problem-solving tool. It teaches them to think critically by encouraging open-mindedness, intellectual curiosity, and evaluation of reasons. Using the scientific method will help you think critically and be objective when applying principles to everyday issues, people, and problems.

How to Think Like a Psychologist

The Scientific Method

The scientific method consists of five steps that help the scientist integrate theory and research, as well as compare empirical—or factual—data with common sense ideas. Using the scientific method will help you think like a psychologist.

The Scientific Method

1. **Ask a question or identify a problem.**
   - Develop the habit of questioning assertions and asking for evidence.
   - Consider and question information, do not automatically accept it.

2. **Form a hypothesis.**
   - Remember that the goal is never to prove the hypothesis but rather to confirm or fail to confirm it.

3. **Test the hypothesis—collect data.**
   - Use the hypothesis to make predictions.
   - Test the predictions by experiments or observations.

4. **Analyze the results of your test.**
   - Ask questions about how the "facts" were obtained— was the information collection and research process adequate?
   - It does not matter who says something is true or false; what matters is the evidence—the facts and reasoning on which the idea is based.

5. **Draw conclusions.**
   - Modify your hypothesis according to the results gained from the testing of your hypothesis.

UNIT 1

Approaches to Psychology

Contents

▶ **Psychology is the study of the human mind and human behavior.**

Why It's Important

What do you expect to learn in this introductory psychology course? You may learn more about yourself. You may learn more about others. This unit will explain why psychologists study human behavior. Psychologists attempt to explain and predict why people behave, feel, and think as they do. They attempt to learn ways in which people can improve the quality of life.

These excerpts describe two experiments. The first experiment, related in *The Story of Psychology*, took place in an ancient time, when humans were just beginning to question the origin of their own thoughts. The second excerpt appeared in *History of Psychology* and details the attempts of one scientist to change the behavior of a wild boy.

Reader's Dictionary

Assyrians: people of an empire in the Middle East, c. 650 B.C.

spontaneously: arising naturally, without external influence

Phrygians: people of an ancient country located in Anatolia, or present-day Turkey

innate: existing in an individual from birth

inarticulate: incapable of understandable speech

erratic: strange; not normal

An EXPERIMENT in the SEVENTH CENTURY B.C.

BY MORTON HUNT

A most unusual man, Psamtik I, King of Egypt. During his long reign, in the latter half of the seventh century B.C., he not only drove out the Assyrians, revived Egyptian art and architecture, and brought about general prosperity, but found time to conceive of and conduct history's first recorded experiment in psychology.

The Egyptians had long believed that they were the most ancient race on earth, and Psamtik, driven by intellectual curiosity, wanted to prove that flattering belief. Like a good psychologist, he began with a hypothesis: If children had no opportunity to learn a language from older people around them, they would spontaneously speak the primal, inborn language of humankind—the natural language of its most ancient people—which, he expected to show, was Egyptian.

To test his hypothesis, Psamtik commandeered two infants of a lower-class mother and turned them over to a herdsman to bring up in a remote area. They were to be kept in a sequestered cottage, properly fed and cared for, but were never to hear anyone speak so much as a word. The Greek historian Herodotus, who tracked the story down and learned what he calls "the real facts" from priests of Hephaestus in Memphis, says that Psamtik's goal "was to know, after the indistinct babblings of infancy were over, what word they would first articulate."

The experiment, he tells us, worked. One day, when the children were two years old, they ran up to the herdsman as he opened the door of their cottage and cried out *"Becos!"* Since this meant nothing to him, he paid no attention, but when it happened repeatedly, he sent word to Psamtik, who at once ordered the children brought to him. When he too heard them say it, Psamtik made inquiries and learned that *becos* was the Phrygian word for bread. He concluded that, disappointingly, the Phrygians were an older race than the Egyptians.

We today may smile condescendingly; we know from modern studies of children brought up under conditions of isolation that there is no innate language

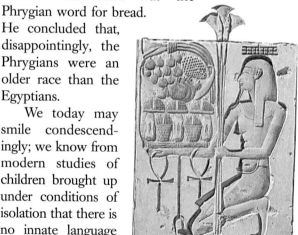

and that children who hear no speech never speak. Psamtik's hypothesis rested on an invalid assumption, and he apparently mistook a babbled sound for an actual word. Yet we must admire him for trying to prove his hypothesis and for having the highly original notion that thoughts arise in the mind through internal processes that can be investigated.

THE WILD BOY OF AVEYRON

BY DAVID HOTHERSALL

In 1799 [Phillipe] Pinel was asked to examine a wild boy, believed to be about twelve years old, who had been found by three hunters in the woods of Saint-Serin near Aveyron in southern France. From reports of hunters who had caught glimpses of him, it was believed that he had lived in the woods for some years. He was virtually naked, covered with scars, dirty, and inarticulate. Apparently he had survived on a diet of acorns and roots. He walked on all-fours much of the time and grunted like an animal. News of the capture of this wild boy caused a sensation in Paris. The newly formed Society of Observers of Man arranged for him to be brought to the capital for study. . . . Taken to Paris in 1800 and exhibited in a cage, the wild boy sat rocking back and forth and was completely apathetic. He was a great disappointment to the hordes of curious spectators. . . .

After examining the boy, Pinel concluded that far from being a noble savage, the boy was an incurable idiot. Despite this conclusion, one of Pinel's assistants, Jean-Marc-Gaspard Itard (1744–1835), undertook to care for the wild boy and to try to educate him. First he gave him a name, Victor, and then made a working assumption that Victor's behavior was due to his social isolation rather than the result of brain damage or some other organic condition. Itard had five aims:

1st Aim—To interest him in social life by rendering it more pleasant to him than the one he was then leading, and above all more like the life which he had just left.

2nd Aim—To awaken his nervous sensibility by the most energetic stimulation, and occasionally by intense emotion.

3rd Aim—To extend the range of his ideas by giving him new needs and by increasing his social contacts.

4th Aim—To lead him to the use of speech by inducing the exercise of imitation through the imperious law of necessity.

5th Aim—To make him exercise the simplest mental operations upon the objects of his physical needs over a period of time, afterwards inducing the application of these mental processes to the objects of instruction. (Itard, 1894)

So Itard undertook Victor's rehabilitation. With the assistance of a Madame Guerin, Itard succeeded, after truly heroic efforts, in teaching Victor to pay attention, to keep clean and to dress himself, to eat with his hands, to play simple games, to obey some commands, and even to read and understand simple words. However, despite all their efforts, Victor never learned to talk. At times he showed signs of affection, but often, and especially under stress, his behavior was erratic, unpredictable, and violent. Victor learned simple discriminations, but when they were made more difficult, he became destructive, biting and chewing his clothes, sheets, and even the chair mantlepiece. After working with Victor for five years, Itard gave up hope of ever attaining his goals. Victor's background and the "passions of his adolescence" could not be overcome. Victor lived with Madame Guerin until 1828, when he died at the age of forty.

Analyzing the Reading

1. What was Psamtik's hypothesis? Why was it invalid?
2. Why was Psamtik's experiment important even though his hypothesis was flawed?
3. **Critical Thinking** Do you think Itard's experiment was worthwhile? Why or why not?

Introducing Psychology

PSYCHOLOGY JOURNAL

Think about your personal reasons for studying psychology. Write an entry in your journal of at least 100 words describing what you hope to gain from this experience. ■

PSYCHOLOGY
Online

Chapter Overview
Visit the *Understanding Psychology* Web site at psychology.glencoe.com and click on **Chapter 1—Chapter Overviews** to preview the chapter.

Reader's Guide

■ Main Idea
Through the study of psychology, people can discover psychological principles that have the potential to enrich the lives of humans.

■ Vocabulary
- physiological
- cognitive
- psychology
- hypothesis
- theory
- basic science
- applied science
- scientific method

■ Objectives
- Describe the range of topics that are covered in an introductory psychology course.
- Cite the goals and scientific basis of psychology.

EXPLORING PSYCHOLOGY

Addicted to the Internet

It's 4 A.M. and "Steve" is engulfed in the green glare of his computer screen, one minute pretending he's a ruthless mafia lord masterminding a gambling empire, the next minute imagining he's an evil sorcerer or an alien life form.

Steve, a college student, is playing a Multiple User Dungeon (MUD) game—a fictional game modeled after Dungeons and Dragons that is played by sending online messages to other players. But as he continually logs on for hours, Steve finds himself sleeping through classes, forgetting his homework, and slipping into "Internet addiction" . . .

—from the *APA Monitor,* June 1996

From a psychologist's point of view, Steve is demonstrating complex behavior. Steve stays on his computer from midnight until morning, often ignoring **physiological**, or physical, needs such as sleep and hunger. He engages in this behavior because of **cognitive**, or private, unobservable mental, reasons. For example, Steve may go online because he likes the intellectual challenge of outwitting the other players. Or Steve's behavior may be motivated by emotions—he goes online to avoid the pressures of college life. There may also be subconscious, emotional, and behavioral reasons. For instance, does the Internet reinforce his behavior? Does this Internet use reflect a weak self-concept? Learning about psychology can help you gain a better understanding of your own behavior, knowledge about how psychologists study human and animal behavior, and practical applications for enriching your life.

physiological: having to do with an organism's physical processes

cognitive: having to do with an organism's thinking and understanding

GAINING INSIGHT INTO BEHAVIOR

Reading Check
What insights might you gain from studying psychology?

Psychology can provide useful insight into behavior. For example, suppose a student is convinced that he is hopelessly shy and doomed forever to feel uncomfortable in groups. Then he learns through social psychology that different kinds of groups tend to have different effects on their members. He thinks about this. He notes that although he is miserable at parties, he feels fine at meetings of the school newspaper staff and in the group he works with in the biology laboratory (in technical terms, he is much more uncomfortable in unstructured social groups than in structured, task-oriented groups). Realizing that he is uncomfortable only in some groups brings him relief. He is not paralyzingly shy; he just does not like unstructured groups. He is not alone in his feelings—and thinking about his feelings helps him gain confidence in himself.

ACQUIRING PRACTICAL INFORMATION

Most of the chapters in this book include material that has a practical application in everyday life. You will learn concrete and detailed ways to carry out a number of useful procedures psychologists have developed.

For example, Chapter 9 describes the systematic way of dispensing rewards and punishments that psychologists call shaping. You will definitely find this useful if you ever have to train a puppy. (You give the puppy a treat after it obeys a command.) You may find yourself wondering how you are shaping the behavior of people around you. Perhaps you have two friends who are always happy to join you for a soda or a movie but who never bring any money along. You have loaned them money many times, and just as many times, they have failed to pay you back. You know they can afford to pay their share, and you have repeatedly told them so. They are good friends, however, so you end up paying their way again and again. In doing so, you are rewarding or reinforcing an undesirable behavior pattern. Is that what you really want to do?

Chapter 10 includes a description of several mnemonic devices, or memory aids, that help you retain information. The poem beginning "Thirty days has September," which helps many people remember the number of days in

| Figure 1.1 | **Psychology and You** |

Studying psychology may help you gain a better understanding of human behavior. *What is psychology?*

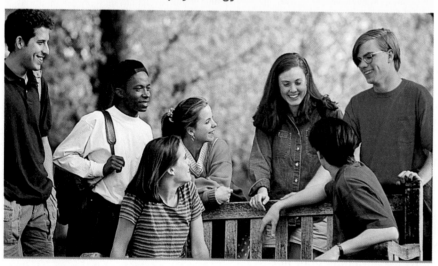

each month, is an example. With mnemonic devices, you usually associate each item on a list with something easier to remember, such as a picture, rhyme, or phrase. Although this may require time and effort, memory experts have shown that it is worth the trouble.

In reading about child development in Chapter 3, you may recall similar experiences you had in your own childhood. Chapter 16, on disturbance and breakdown, may help you understand difficult periods in your own life and in the lives of those around you.

OVERVIEW OF PSYCHOLOGY

Psychology is the scientific study of behavior and mental processes. Such study can involve both animal and human behaviors. When applied to humans, psychology covers everything that people think, feel, and do. Psychologists differ in how much importance they place on specific types of behavior. For example, some psychologists believe that you should study only behavior that you can see, observe, or measure directly. Steve's behavior of logging on and remaining on the Internet for hours at a time is an observable behavior. Some psychologists believe that our thoughts, feelings, and fantasies are also important, even though these processes are not directly observable. Steve may log on because he feels intimidated by others or by schoolwork, but psychologists cannot directly observe that these are the reasons that Steve is engaging in this behavior.

While psychologists may differ on which types of behavior are important, they do agree that the study of behavior must be systematic. The use of a systematic method of asking and answering questions about why people think, act, and feel as they do reduces the chances of coming to false conclusions. Consider the story of the blind men and the elephant. A long time ago, three very wise, but blind, men were out on a journey when they came across a sleeping elephant. Because they could not see the elephant, they did not know what was blocking their way, so they set about to discover what they could about the obstacle.

As it happened, each man put his hands on a different section of the elephant, examining it in great detail and with much thought. The first man, having felt the elephant's trunk, described a creature that was long, wormlike, and quite flexible. "No, no! You must be mistaken," said the second man who was seated astride the elephant. "This creature is wide, very round, and does not move very much." The man who was holding one of the elephant's tusks added his description of a small, hard, pointed creature.

Why You Overreact

Your friend makes a simple comment about your hair or clothes, and you blow up, getting violently angry and feeling deeply hurt. Why? Emotions occur as the result of a physical stimulation paired with some social or personal event. If an emotional event occurs, but you do not have a physical reaction—such as a pounding heart or a tense stomach—you will not feel that emotion in the usual sense. Yet consider the following situation: You just drank two cans of caffeinated soda. Your heart is beating hard, and your stomach is tense. Then your friend makes a critical comment. When you hear the comment, you get angry—but you get angrier than usual because your body is already stimulated. On the other hand, if you are very tired, you might not react to an emotional event.

psychology: the scientific study of behavior that is tested through scientific research

Figure 1.2   Test Your Intuitions

Test your intuitions about behavior by answering true or false to the statements below. *Turn to page 12 to check your answers.*

1. The behavior of most lower animals—insects, reptiles and amphibians, most rodents, and birds—is instinctive and unaffected by learning.

2. For the first week of life, a baby sees nothing but a gray-blue regardless of what he or she "looks at."

3. A child learns to talk more quickly if the adults around the child habitually repeat the word he or she is trying to say, using proper pronunciation.

4. The best way to get a chronically noisy child to settle down and pay attention is to punish him or her.

5. Slow learners remember more of what they learn than fast learners.

6. Highly intelligent people—"geniuses"—tend to be physically frail and socially isolated.

7. On the average, you cannot predict from a person's grades at school and college whether he or she will do well in a career.

8. Most stereotypes are completely true.

9. In small amounts, alcohol is a stimulant.

10. The largest drug problem in the United States, in terms of the number of people affected, is marijuana.

11. Psychiatry is a subdivision of psychology.

12. Most mentally handicapped people also have psychological disorders.

13. A third or more of the people suffering from severe psychological disorders are potentially dangerous.

14. Electroshock therapy is an outmoded technique rarely used in today's mental hospitals.

15. The more severe the disorder, the more intensive the therapy required to cure it; for example, schizophrenics usually respond best to psychoanalysis.

16. Nearly all the psychological characteristics of men and women appear to be inborn; in all cultures, for example, women are more emotional and sexually less aggressive than men.

17. No reputable psychologist "believes in" such irrational phenomena as ESP, hypnosis, or the bizarre mental and physical achievements of Eastern yogis.

Each of these men was correct in his description of what he felt, but in order to understand the elephant fully, they needed to combine their accumulated knowledge. The study of human behavior is similar. Many different approaches are necessary to understand the complex richness of human behavior.

We each like to think we understand people. We spend time observing others (and ourselves) and form conclusions about people from our daily interactions. Sometimes the conclusions we draw, however, are not accurate because we are not systematic in our "study."

The Goals of Psychology

As psychologists go about their systematic and scientific study of humans and animals, they have several goals. Overall, psychologists seek to do four things—describe, explain, predict, and influence behavior.

Description   The first goal for any scientist or psychologist is to describe or gather information about the behavior being studied and to present what is known. For example, we described Steve's behavior at college.

PSYCHOLOGY *Online*

Student Web Activity
Visit the *Understanding Psychology* Web site at psychology.glencoe.com and click on **Chapter 1— Student Web Activities** for an activity about the study of psychology.

Explanation Psychologists are not content to simply state the facts. Rather, they also seek to explain why people (or animals) behave as they do. Psychologists propose these explanations as hypotheses. A **hypothesis** is an educated guess about some phenomenon. It is a researcher's prediction about what the results of a study are expected to be. As research studies designed to test each hypothesis are completed, more complex explanations called theories are constructed. A **theory** is usually a complex explanation based on findings from a large number of experimental studies. Theories change as new data improves our understanding, and a good theory becomes the source of additional ideas for experiments. Theories allow us to describe, explain, and predict observed behavior.

Prediction The third goal of psychologists is to predict, as a result of accumulated knowledge, what organisms will do and, in the case of humans, what they will think or feel in various situations. By studying descriptive and theoretical accounts of past behaviors, psychologists can predict future behaviors.

Influence Finally, some psychologists seek to influence behavior in helpful ways. These psychologists are conducting studies with a long-term goal of finding out more about human or animal behavior. They are doing **basic science,** or research. Other psychologists are more interested in discovering ways to use what we already know about people to benefit others. They view psychology as an **applied science** and are using psychological principles to solve more immediate problems.

Psychologists who study the ability of infants to perceive visual patterns are doing basic research. They may not be concerned with the implication their findings might have on the design of a crib. Psychologists studying rapid eye movement in sleep research are also involved in basic science. If they discover that one individual has a sleep disturbance, they will try to understand and explain the situation, but they may not try to correct it. That is a job for applied scientists, such as clinical psychologists, industrial/organizational psychologists, counseling psychologists, or engineering psychologists.

An example of a psychologist involved in applying psychological principles rather than discovering them is a consultant to a

hypothesis: an assumption about behavior that is tested through scientific research

theory: a set of assumptions used to explain phenomena and offered for scientific study

basic science: the pursuit of knowledge about natural phenomena for its own sake

applied science: discovering ways to use scientific findings to accomplish practical goals

Figure 1.3	Gaining Perspective

Psychology involves gaining new perspectives on your own and others' behavior. Upon examination, René Magritte's painting *The Human Condition* becomes more and more complex. *How does your perspective of this painting change upon closer examination of it?*

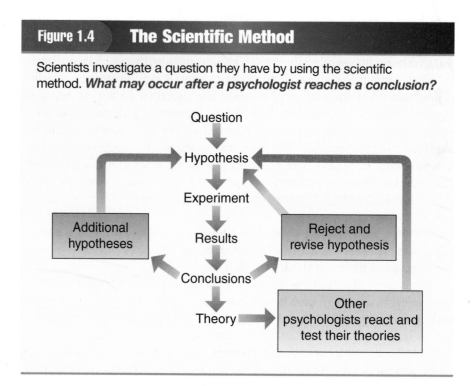

Figure 1.4   The Scientific Method

Scientists investigate a question they have by using the scientific method. *What may occur after a psychologist reaches a conclusion?*

Answers to Figure 1.2
All of the statements in Figure 1.2 are false. As you read the different chapters in *Understanding Psychology,* you will learn more about the correct answers to these statements and the research that psychologists have conducted to demonstrate why these statements are false.

toy manufacturer. A toy manufacturer tries to develop toys that appeal to children. The manufacturer may apply, or use, psychological principles when designing those toys. The distinction between basic and applied science is important. Why? Because the transfer of findings from basic to applied science can be tricky. The following example illustrates this.

Psychologists doing basic research have found that babies raised in institutions such as orphanages become seriously delayed in their physical, intellectual, and emotional development. Wayne Dennis (1960), among others, traces this to the fact that these babies have nothing to look at but a blank, white ceiling and white crib cushions, and are handled only when they need to be fed or changed. However, we have to be very careful not to apply this finding too broadly. Because children who lack stimulation tend to develop poorly does not mean that by providing them with maximum stimulation, they will grow up emotionally sound and intellectually superior. Quite the contrary, most babies do best with a medium level of stimulation (White, 1969). Even more significantly, social interaction seems much more important than visual stimulation. Normal development is more likely to result from long-term interactions with a responsive caregiver (Rice, Cunningham, & Young, 1997). Basic science provides specific findings—what happens in one study conducted at one time and in one place.

THE SCIENTIFIC BASIS OF PSYCHOLOGY

To ensure that data is collected accurately, psychologists rely on the **scientific method** (see Figure 1.4). In psychology, facts are based on data. The data is obtained from methods such as experiments, surveys, and case

scientific method: a general approach to gathering information and answering questions so that errors and biases are minimized studies. This means that psychologists reach their conclusions by identifying a specific problem or question, formulating a hypothesis, collecting data through observation and experimentation, and analyzing the data.

The scientific basis of psychology goes back many years. Today people are very sophisticated about scientific procedures, but that has not always been true. In 1879 Wilhelm Wundt is credited with setting up the first psychology laboratory in Leipzig, Germany. He proposed that psychological experience is composed of compounds, much like the compounds found in chemistry. Psychology, he claimed, has two kinds of elements—sensations and feelings. Wundt tried to test his statements by collecting scientific data. Although Wundt's methods proved cumbersome and unreliable, the importance of Wundt's work is the procedure he followed, not the results he obtained. He called the procedure "introspection," and in psychology it led to what we now call the scientific method. Whereas in Wundt's "introspection" an individual observes and analyzes his or her own mental experiences, the scientific method developed as an objective method of observation and analysis.

Preserved brain

Although psychologists use the scientific method to demonstrate and support many theories, many questions about behavior remain unanswered. Psychological theories are continually reviewed and revised. New theories and technological developments are constantly generating new questions and new psychological studies.

Reading Check
What is the scientific method?

SECTION **1** **Assessment**

1. **Review the Vocabulary** What is the difference between a hypothesis and a theory?

2. **Visualize the Main Idea** In a graphic organizer similar to the one below, list and describe the goals of psychology.

Goals of Psychology

3. **Recall Information** Why do psychologists use the scientific method?

4. **Think Critically** How might a psychologist doing basic science and a psychologist practicing applied science differ in their approach to the issue of "Internet addiction"?

5. **Application Activity** Use the four goals of psychology to outline how a psychologist might approach the following question: Why are you sitting here in psychology class when there are other things you could be doing?

A Brief History of Psychology

Reader's Guide

■ Main Idea
Psychology involves sets of questions, theories, methods, and possible answers that have been passed on and changed from generation to generation.

■ Vocabulary
- structuralist
- introspection
- functionalist
- psychoanalyst
- behaviorist
- humanist
- cognitivist
- psychobiologist

■ Objectives
- Explain important trends in the history of psychology.
- Identify various approaches to the study of psychology.

EXPLORING PSYCHOLOGY

The Science of Skull Bumps

S.S. . . . was sent to the State Prison for five years for assault and battery, with intent to kill, . . . Before his mind became deranged, he exhibited great energy of passion and purpose, but they were all of a low character, their sole bearing being to prove his own superiority as an animal. . . . The drawing shows a broad, low head, corresponding with such a character. The moral organs are exceedingly deficient, . . . If the higher capacities and endowments of humanity were ever found coupled with such a head as this, it would be a phenomenon as inexplicable as that of seeing without the eye, or hearing without the ear.

—from "Mathew B. Brady and the Rationale of Crime: A Study in Daguerreotypes," *Library of Congress Quarterly Journal,* Madeleine B. Stern

In the 1800s Marmaduke B. Sampson wrote the account above to explain why crime occurs. According to Sampson, the behavior of S.S. was the direct result of the shape of his head. Phrenology—the practice of examining bumps on a person's skull to determine that person's intellect and character traits—became an important practice in the United States in the mid-1800s. Although this pseudoscience may appear ridiculous to us, modern scientists credit phrenology for encouraging study into the role of the brain in human behavior. Phrenology may have inspired scientists to consider the brain, instead of the heart, as responsible for human behavior.

THE ORIGINS OF PSYCHOLOGY

Psychology has come a long way since the days of studying bumps on skulls. In the fifth and sixth centuries B.C., the Greeks began to study human behavior and decided that people's lives were dominated not so much by the gods as by their own minds: people were rational.

These early philosophers attempted to interpret the world they observed around them in terms of human perceptions—objects were hot or cold, wet or dry, hard or soft—and these qualities influenced people's experience of them. Although the Greek philosophers did not rely on systematic study, they did set the stage for the development of the sciences, including psychology, through their reliance on observation as a means of knowing their world.

In the mid-1500s, Nicolaus Copernicus (1473–1543) published the idea that Earth was not the center of the universe, as was previously thought, but revolved around the sun. Later, Galileo Galilei (1564–1642) used a telescope to confirm predictions about star position and movement based on Copernicus's work. The individuals of the Renaissance were beginning to refine the modern concept of experimentation through observation.

Seventeenth-century philosophers popularized the idea of *dualism,* the concept that the mind and body are separate and distinct. The French philosopher René Descartes (1596–1650) disagreed, however, proposing that a link existed between mind and body. He reasoned that the mind controlled the body's movements, sensations, and perceptions. His approach to understanding human behavior was based on the assumption that the mind and body influence each other to create a person's experiences. Exactly how this interaction takes place is still being studied today.

As one psychologist has expressed it, "Modern science began to emerge by combining philosophers' reflections, logic, and mathematics with the observations and inventiveness of practical people" (Hilgard, 1987). By the nineteenth century, biologists had announced the discovery of cells as the building blocks of life. Later, chemists developed the periodic table of elements, and physicists made great progress in furthering our understanding of atomic forces. Many natural scientists were studying complex phenomena by reducing them to simpler parts. It was in this environment that the science of psychology was formed.

HISTORICAL APPROACHES

The history of psychology is a history of alternative perspectives. As the field of psychology evolved, various schools of thought arose to compete and offer new approaches to the science of behavior.

Structuralism

In 1879 in Leipzig, Germany, Wilhelm Wundt (1832–1920) started his Laboratory of Psychology. Because of his efforts to pursue the study of human behavior in a systematic and scientific manner, Wundt is generally acknowledged as establishing modern psychology as a separate,

Figure 1.5 Phrenology

This 1893 advertisement endorsed the "science" of phrenology. *How did phrenology lead to psychology?*

Heads and Faces tell the Story.

MEN AND WOMEN

Differ in character as they do in appearance and temperament! No two are alike. You can understand these SIGNS OF CHARACTER, and

IF YOU WANT SOMETHING

that will interest you more thoroughly than any book you ever read, send for a copy of

HEADS AND FACES;
How to Study Them.

A new Manual of Character Reading for the people, by Prof. Nelson Sizer, the Examiner in the phrenological office of Fowler & Wells Co., and H. S. Drayton, M.D. The authors know what they are writing about, Prof. Sizer having devoted nearly fifty years exclusively to the reading of character, and he here lays down the rules employed by him in his professional work, showing that it is not "BUMPS" but diameters that are considered. Contains 200 large pages, 250 portraits. 110,000 sold.
We will send it carefully by mail, postpaid, on receipt of price, 40 cents, in paper, or $1 in cloth binding. Address

FOWLER & WELLS CO., Pubs.,
23 E. 21st Street, New York.

structuralist: a psychologist who studied the basic elements that make up conscious mental experiences

introspection: a method of self-observation in which participants report their thoughts and feelings

formal field of study. Although he was trained in physiology—the study of how the body works—Wundt's real interest was in the study of the human mind. Wundt was a **structuralist,** which means that he was interested in the basic elements of human experience. In his laboratory, Wundt modeled his research on the mind after research in other natural sciences he had studied. He developed a method of self-observation called **introspection** to collect information about the mind. In carefully controlled situations, trained participants reported their thoughts, and Wundt tried to map out the basic structure of thought processes. Wundt's experiments were very important historically, not so much because he advanced our understanding of the mind, but because his work attracted many students who carried on the tradition of psychological research.

Functionalism

William James (1842–1910) taught the first class in psychology at Harvard University in 1875. James is often called the "father of psychology" in the United States. It took him 12 years to write the first textbook of psychology, *The Principles of Psychology* (1890). James speculated that thinking, feeling, learning, and remembering—all activities of the mind—serve one major function: to help us survive as a species. Rather than focusing on the structure of the mind as Wundt did, James focused on the functions or purposes of the conscious mind and the goals or functions or purposes of behaviors. **Functionalists** study how mental processes help animals and people adapt to their environment. Although James was not particularly interested in experimentation, his writings and theories are still influential. In Chapter 12 you will learn more about James's ideas on motivation and emotion.

Did You Know?

Studying Scientists Some researchers study how scientists do science. Their findings point out flaws:

- Scientists are not always objective. They sometimes ignore data that does not support their theories rather than impartially examining all available evidence.
- Some scientists are not all that open-minded. Critics accused Isaac Newton, Charles Darwin, and Albert Einstein of intolerance.
- The best scientists are not always the brightest. Studies demonstrate that no strong relationship between scientists' IQs and their contributions exists.

Inheritable Traits

Sir Francis Galton (1822–1911), a nineteenth-century English mathematician and scientist, wanted to understand how heredity influences a person's abilities, character, and behavior. (*Heredity* includes all the traits and properties that are passed along biologically from parent to child.) Galton traced the ancestry of various eminent people and found that greatness runs in families. He therefore concluded that genius or eminence is a hereditary trait. This conclusion was like the blind men's ideas about the elephant. Galton did not consider the possibility that the tendency of genius to run in distinguished families might be a result of the exceptional environments and socioeconomic advantages that also tend to surround such families. He also raised the question: Wouldn't the world be a better place if we could get rid of the less desirable people? Galton encouraged "good" marriages to supply the world with talented offspring. Later, scientists all over the world recognized the flaws in Galton's theory. A person's heredity and that person's environment interact to produce intelligence.

functionalist: a psychologist who studied the function (rather than the structure) of consciousness

Figure 1.6   **Sir Francis Galton**

Galton declared that the "most fit" humans were those with high intelligence. He assumed that the wealthiest people were also the most intelligent. *What factors did Galton fail to take into account in his studies?*

The data Galton used were based on his study of biographies. Not content to limit his inquiry to indirect accounts, however, he went on to invent procedures for directly testing the abilities and characteristics of a wide range of people. These tests were the primitive ancestors of the modern personality tests and intelligence tests.

Although Galton began his work shortly before psychology emerged as an independent discipline, his theories and techniques quickly became central aspects of the new science. In 1883 he published a book, *Inquiries into Human Faculty and Its Development,* that is regarded as the first study of individual differences. Galton's writings raised the issue of whether behavior is determined by heredity or environment—a subject that remains a focus of controversy today.

Gestalt Psychology

A group of German psychologists, including Max Wertheimer (1880–1943), Wolfgang Köhler (1887–1967), and Kurt Koffka (1886–1941), disagreed with the principles of structuralism and behaviorism. They argued that perception is more than the sum of its parts—it involves a "whole pattern" or, in German, a *Gestalt.* For example, when people look at a chair, they recognize the chair as a whole rather than noticing its legs, its seat, and its other components. Another example includes the perception of apparent motion. When you see fixed lights flashing in sequence as on traffic lights and neon signs, you perceive motion rather than individual lights flashing on and off (see Figure 1.8). Gestalt psychologists studied how sensations are assembled into perceptual experiences. This approach became the forerunner for cognitive approaches to the study of psychology.

CONTEMPORARY APPROACHES

Many ideas taken from the historical approaches to psychology are reflected in contemporary approaches to the study

"HAVE A COUPLE OF DREAMS, AND CALL ME IN THE MORNING."

Figure 1.7   **Dream Analysis**

Freud believed that dreams can represent past, present, or future concerns or fears. Most contemporary psychologists, though, disagree with the symbols Freud found in dreams. *How do you think the psychologist in the cartoon plans to help his patient?*

Figure 1.8   Gestalt Psychology

Artist Giuseppe Arcimboldo (1527–1593) played with perceptual images in his painting *Autumn.*

An electric sign in which the bulbs go on and off in turn, with the appropriate timing, gives the impression of motion. *How do these two images represent the ideas of Gestalt psychology?*

of psychology. The most important approaches to the study of psychology today are the psychoanalytic, behavioral, humanistic, cognitive, biological, and sociocultural approaches.

Psychoanalytic Psychology

While the first psychologists were interested in understanding the conscious mind, Sigmund Freud (1856–1939), a physician who practiced in Vienna until 1938, was more interested in the unconscious mind. He believed that our conscious experiences are only the tip of the iceberg, that beneath the surface are primitive biological urges that are in conflict with the requirements of society and morality. According to Freud, these unconscious motivations and conflicts are responsible for most human behavior. He thought that they were responsible for many medically unexplainable physical symptoms that troubled his patients.

Freud used a new method for indirectly studying unconscious processes. In this technique, known as *free association,* a patient said everything that came to mind—no matter how absurd or irrelevant it seemed—without attempting to produce logical or meaningful statements. The person was instructed not to edit or censor the thoughts.

Freud's role, that of **psychoanalyst,** was to be objective; he merely sat and listened and then interpreted the associations. Free association, Freud believed, revealed the operation of unconscious processes. Freud also believed that dreams are expressions of the most primitive unconscious urges. To learn more about these urges, he used *dream analysis—* basically an extension of free association—in which he applied the same technique to a patient's dreams (Freud, 1940) (see Figure 1.7).

While working out his ideas, Freud took careful, extensive notes on all his patients and treatment sessions. He used these records, or case studies, to develop and illustrate a comprehensive theory of personality (Ewen, 1993). Freud's theory of personality will be discussed in Chapter 14.

In many areas of psychology today, Freud's view of unconscious motivation remains a powerful and controversial influence. Modern psychologists may support, alter, or attempt to disprove it, but most have a strong opinion about it. The technique of free association is still used by psychoanalysts, and the method of intensive case study is still a major tool for investigating behavior. (A *case study* is an analysis of the thoughts, feelings, beliefs, experiences, behaviors, or problems of an individual.)

psychoanalyst: a psychologist who studies how unconscious motives and conflicts determine human behavior

Behavioral Psychology

The pioneering work of Russian physiologist Ivan Pavlov (1849–1936) charted another new course for psychological investigation. In a now-famous experiment, Pavlov rang a tuning fork each time he gave a dog some meat powder. The dog would normally salivate when the powder reached its mouth. After Pavlov repeated the procedure several times, the dog would salivate when it heard the ring of the tuning fork, even if no food appeared. It had been conditioned to associate the sound with the food.

Profiles In Psychology

Mary Whiton Calkins

1863–1930

"What we most need to know about any man is surely this: whether he is good or bad."

Mary Whiton Calkins, a female pioneer in psychology, contributed greatly to the field of psychology despite numerous obstacles. In the 1800s, North American universities barred women from Ph.D. programs. Despite this, Harvard's William James admitted Calkins into his graduate seminar. When Calkins joined the seminar, all the other students dropped it in protest, so James tutored her alone.

Calkins taught and studied, petitioning Harvard to admit her as a Ph.D. candidate. Harvard refused and, instead, held an informal examination for Calkins. Calkins completed the requirements for the doctoral degree and outperformed all her male counterparts on the examination. When Radcliffe University offered her the doctoral degree, she refused to accept the compromise.

Calkins served as a full professor of psychology at Wellesley College and became the first female president of both the American Psychological Association (APA) and the American Philosophical Association.

Quick Lab

Why do you do what you do?

Throughout the course of a day, you perform many activities. Why?

Procedure

1. Observe and keep careful notes of your behavior on a particular day.

2. You may want to make a chart listing each action, such as "woke to the alarm clock's ring," "ate breakfast," and "yelled at little brother."

Analysis

1. Beside each behavior you have noted, list what caused your behavior. For example, "I woke up at 7:00 A.M. because school starts at 8:00 A.M., and I hate being late. I ate breakfast because I was hungry."

2. Next, list the psychological approach that would best explain your behavior. For example, waking to the alarm clock's ring may fall under behaviorism or functionalism.

See the Skills Handbook, page 622, for an explanation of designing an experiment.

behaviorist: a psychologist who analyzes how organisms learn or modify their behavior based on their response to events in the environment

humanist: a psychologist who believes that each person has freedom in directing his or her future and achieving personal growth

cognitivist: a psychologist who studies how we process, store, retrieve, and use information and how cognitive processes influence our behavior

The conditioned reflex was a response (salivation) provoked by a stimulus (the tuning fork) other than the one that first produced it (food) (see Chapter 9 for a complete explanation). The concept was used by psychologists as a new tool, as a means of exploring the development of behavior. Using this tool, they could begin to account for behavior as the product of prior experience. This enabled them to explain how certain acts and certain differences among individuals were the result of learning.

Psychologists who stressed investigating observable behavior became known as **behaviorists.** Their position, as formulated by psychologist John B. Watson (1878–1958), was that psychology should concern itself only with the *observable* facts of behavior. Watson further maintained that all behavior, even apparently instinctive behavior, is the result of conditioning and occurs because the appropriate stimulus is present in the environment.

Although it was Watson who defined and solidified the behaviorist position, it was B.F. Skinner (1904–1990) who introduced the concept of reinforcement. (*Reinforcement* is a response to a behavior that increases the likelihood the behavior will be repeated.) Skinner attempted to show how his laboratory techniques might be applied to society as a whole. In his classic novel *Walden Two* (1948), he portrayed his idea of Utopia—a small town in which conditioning, through rewarding those who display behavior that is considered desirable, rules every conceivable facet of life.

Humanistic Psychology

Humanistic psychology developed as a reaction to behavioral psychology. In the 1960s, **humanists** such as Abraham Maslow, Carl Rogers, and Rollo May described human nature as evolving and self-directed. It differs from behaviorism and psychoanalysis in that it does not view humans as being controlled by events in the environment or by unconscious forces. Instead, the environment and other outside forces simply serve as a background to our own internal growth. The humanistic approach emphasizes how each person is unique and has a self-concept and potential to develop fully. This potential for personal growth and development can lead to a more satisfying life.

Cognitive Psychology

Since 1950, cognitive psychology has benefited from the contributions of people such as Jean Piaget, Noam Chomsky, and Leon Festinger. **Cognitivists** focus on how we process, store, and use information and how this information influences our thinking, language, problem solving, and creativity. They believe that behavior is more than a simple response to a stimulus. Behavior is influenced by a variety of mental processes, including perceptions, memories, and expectations.

Reading Check
How do cognitive psychologists differ from behaviorists?

Biological Psychology

This viewpoint emphasizes the impact of biology on our behavior. **Psychobiologists** study how the brain, the nervous system, and hormones and genetics influence our behavior. PET scans and CAT scans (explained in Chapter 6) are the newest tools used by psychobiologists. Psychobiologists have found that genetic factors influence a wide range of human behaviors. Recently, psychobiologists have discovered a link between chemicals in the brain (neurotransmitters) and human behavior. For example, researchers found that autistic children share a genetic defect in regulating the neurotransmitter serotonin. Serotonin plays an important role in brain functioning. In many ways, our behavior is the result of our physiological makeup.

psychobiologist: a psychologist who studies how physical and chemical changes in our bodies influence our behavior

Sociocultural Psychology

The newest approach to psychology involves studying the influence of cultural and ethnic similarities and differences on behavior and social functioning.

Figure 1.9	Contemporary Approaches to Psychology

Modern psychologists use many different approaches to study the same behavior. Each viewpoint offers additional information to understanding behavior and reflects a different view of human nature. *What other questions might a cognitivist study?*

Approach	What influences our behavior?	Sample research question
Psychoanalytic Psychology	Unconscious motivations influence our behavior	How have negative childhood experiences affected the way I handle stressful situations?
Behavioral Psychology	Events in the environment (rewards and punishments) influence our behavior	Can good study habits be learned?
Humanistic Psychology	Individual or self-directed choices influence our behavior	Do I believe I can prepare for and pass the test?
Cognitive Psychology	How we process, store, and retrieve information influences our behavior	How does caffeine affect memory?
Biological Psychology	Biological factors influence our behavior	Do genes affect your intelligence and personality?
Sociocultural Psychology	Ethnicity, gender, culture, and socioeconomic status influence our behavior	How do people of different genders and ethnicities interact with one another?

For example, a sociocultural psychologist considers how our knowledge and ways of thinking, feeling, and behaving are dependent on the culture to which we belong. Think about how much you are like other people of your culture—you share cultural perspectives and behaviors. Psychologist Leonard Doob (1990) illustrated the cultural implications of a simple, reflexive behavior—a sneeze. Doob asks, "Will [the person who senses the urge to sneeze] try to inhibit this reflex action? What will he say, what will bystanders say, when he does sneeze? What will they think of him if he fails to turn away and sneezes in their faces? Do they and he consider sneezing an omen and, if so, is it a good or bad omen?" To answer such questions, we would have to understand the cultural context in which the sneeze occurred, as well as the cultural beliefs associated with the sneeze.

Sociocultural psychologists also study the impact and integration of the millions of immigrants who come to the United States each year. The character of the U.S. population is rapidly changing. By the year 2010, Americans of Hispanic origin will make up almost 14 percent of the population, while those of African American and Asian or Pacific Islander descent will make up almost 19 percent (U.S. Census Bureau, 1998). Psychologists study the attitudes, values, beliefs, and social norms and roles of these different ethnic groups. They also study methods to reduce intolerance and discrimination.

The sociocultural approach is also concerned with issues such as gender and socioeconomic status and is based on the idea that these factors impact human behavior and mental processes. For instance, how might you be different if you had been born female instead of male, or male instead of female? Would you be different if you had been born in poverty, or into an extremely wealthy family?

SECTION 2 Assessment

1. **Review the Vocabulary** Using your own words, describe the structuralist, functionalist, behaviorist, and humanist approaches to the study of psychology.

2. **Visualize the Main Idea** Use a graphic organizer similar to the one below to list the different historical approaches to the study of psychology.

3. **Recall Information** Identify some issues that sociocultural psychologists might research.

4. **Think Critically** With which approach to psychology do you most agree? Why?

5. **Application Activity** Consider the following question: Why are you sitting here in psychology class when there are other things you could be doing? Compare how the various approaches to the study of psychology would address this question differently.

The Four Humors

Period of Study: Around A.D. 150

Introduction: Hippocrates (460–375 B.C.), often referred to as the "father of medicine," became one of the first people to claim that illness had natural, not supernatural, causes. Hippocrates associated the four elements—earth, air, fire, and water—with four humors in the body. He associated earth with phlegm (mucus), air with blood, fire with yellow bile, and water with black bile. Humans with balanced humors were healthy; an imbalance among the humors resulted in sickness. Galen (A.D. 130–200) extended Hippocrates' theory to include characteristics of human personalities.

Hypothesis: Galen identified four personality characteristics called *melancholic, sanguine, choleric,* and *phlegmatic.* Galen associated these four characteristics with the four humors of the body. Each humor was thought to give off vapors that rose to the brain. An individual's personality could be explained by the state of that person's humors.

Method: If a person had excess phlegm, that person was probably dull, pale, and cowardly. Cheerful and generous personalities resulted from the dominance of blood. Laziness and gloominess were associated with cold and dryness (black bile). If a person had too much choler (yellow bile) in his system, he was probably a violent or vengeful person. The perfect personality resulted when none of the four humors dominated.

At that time, treatment of a psychological disorder involved restoring a balance among the humors. Doctors often gave patients poisonous herbs to eat. This caused vomiting, a sign that the imbalanced humor was leaving the patient's body. Balancing the diet could also balance the humors.

Results: The theories of Hippocrates and Galen proved unfounded, and their prescribed treatments for various disorders

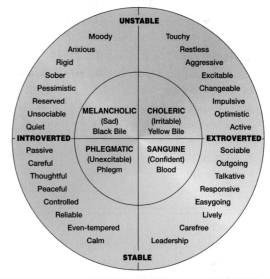

A Personality Wheel

Humor	Principal Source	Temperament	Characteristic
Phlegm	Brain	Phlegmatic	Sluggish, unemotional
Blood	Heart	Sanguine	Cheerful
Yellow bile	Liver	Choleric	Quick-tempered, fiery
Black bile	Spleen	Melancholic	Sad

did not prove reliable. The relationship between your physical makeup and your personality is not yet firmly established. Your mental state can make the symptoms of some diseases more distressing, or factors such as stress can make you more liable to getting sick. However, the dominance of, say, black bile in your system does not lead to depression. Galen's notion, though, that a healthy personality is a balanced one may indeed be sound.

Analyzing the Case Study

1. According to Galen's hypothesis, how are a person's physical and mental states related?
2. How did Galen treat psychological disorders?
3. **Critical Thinking** How can Galen's original theory be used today as a prescription for a healthy personality?

Psychology as a Profession

■ Main Idea

Psychologists are trained to observe, analyze, and evaluate behavior patterns, to develop theories of behavior, and to apply what they have learned to influence behavior.

■ Vocabulary

- psychologist
- clinical psychologist
- counseling psychologist
- psychiatry
- developmental psychologist
- educational psychologist
- community psychologist
- industrial/organizational psychologist
- experimental psychologist

■ Objectives

- Explain the work of a psychologist.
- Summarize the careers and specialized fields in psychology.

EXPLORING PSYCHOLOGY

The Thoughts of a Patient

Everything seems to be contradictory. I don't seem to know what else to tell you, but that I am tearful and sad—and no kick out of Christmas. And I used to get such a boot out of it. . . . It's an awful feeling. . . . I don't get a bit of a kick out of anything. Everything seems to get so sort of full of despair. . . . I feel so sort of what I call "empty"—nothing in back of you like when you're feeling yourself. . . . You go to bed and you dread each day when you feel low like that. . . . And I try to keep saying to myself, like you say, that I haven't been that bad that I should have to punish myself. Yet my thinking doesn't get cheerful. When it doesn't get cheerful it makes you wonder will it all end in suicide sometime. . . .

—from *The Encyclopedia of Behavior* by Robert M. Goldenson, 1970

The thoughts above are the reflections of a patient. The patient is suffering from depression—an emotional state of dejection and sadness, ranging from mild discouragement to feelings of utter hopelessness and despair. Some psychologists conduct research to collect information and form theories about disorders such as depression. Other psychologists apply that information in the form of therapy to help people cope with depression. What else do people in the field of psychology do? Let's start by defining a psychologist.

WHAT IS A PSYCHOLOGIST?

Psychologists are people who have been trained to observe, analyze, evaluate, and treat behavior. They usually have a doctorate degree in psychology. There are many different fields of psychology. The principal ones are described in this section.

As the field of psychology expanded, it divided into a number of subfields. Clinical and counseling psychology are the most popular. **Clinical psychologists** help people deal with their personal problems. They work mainly in private offices, mental hospitals, prisons, and clinics. Some specialize in giving and interpreting personality tests designed to determine whether a person needs treatment and, if so, what kind. (About one-half of all psychologists specialize in clinical psychology.) **Counseling psychologists** usually work in schools or industrial firms, advising and assisting people with the problems of everyday life. They help people adjust to the challenges of life.

People often confuse the terms *psychologist* and *psychiatrist*. These are different professions. **Psychiatry** is a specialty of medicine. After a student of psychiatry completes medical school, he or she continues training in psychiatric medicine and learns to treat people with disturbed behavior. A psychiatrist is a medical doctor who can prescribe medication to patients. Sometimes a psychiatrist works with a psychologist in testing, evaluating, and treating patients. In most states a doctorate is required to be a clinical or counseling psychologist.

School psychologists, educated in principles of human development, clinical psychology, and education, help young people with emotional or learning problems. A large number of specialists study personality, social psychology, or developmental psychology. These psychologists are usually involved in basic rather than applied science. Psychologists who study personality investigate its development, study personality traits, or may create personality tests. Social psychologists study groups and how they influence individual behavior. Some are particularly interested in public opinion and devote much of their time to

psychologist: a scientist who studies the mind and behavior of humans and animals

clinical psychologist: a psychologist who diagnoses and treats people with emotional disturbances

counseling psychologist: a psychologist who usually helps people deal with problems of living

psychiatry: a branch of medicine that deals with mental, emotional, or behavioral disorders

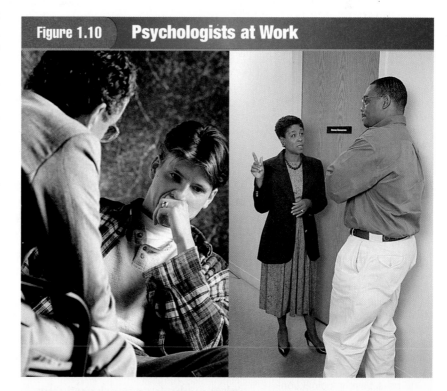

Figure 1.10 **Psychologists at Work**

All psychologists, no matter what their area of expertise, are interested in theories about behavior and mental processes. *Can you name the type of psychologist at work in each photo?*

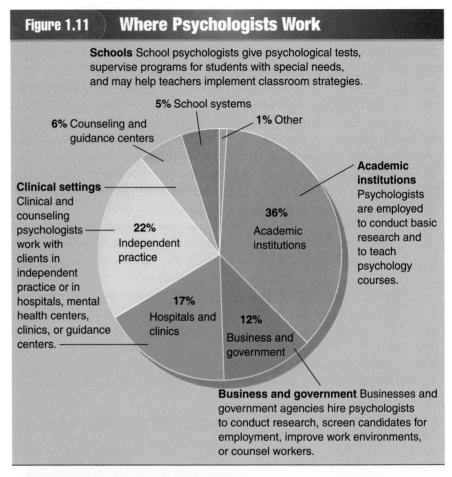

Figure 1.11 Where Psychologists Work

Schools School psychologists give psychological tests, supervise programs for students with special needs, and may help teachers implement classroom strategies.

5% School systems

1% Other

6% Counseling and guidance centers

Academic institutions Psychologists are employed to conduct basic research and to teach psychology courses.

Clinical settings Clinical and counseling psychologists work with clients in independent practice or in hospitals, mental health centers, clinics, or guidance centers.

22% Independent practice

36% Academic institutions

17% Hospitals and clinics

12% Business and government

Business and government Businesses and government agencies hire psychologists to conduct research, screen candidates for employment, improve work environments, or counsel workers.

Most psychologists in the United States are engaged in clinical psychology. *Why do businesses and government agencies hire psychologists?*

developmental psychologist: a psychologist who studies the emotional, cognitive, biological, personal, and social changes that occur as an individual matures

educational psychologist: a psychologist who is concerned with helping students learn

community psychologist: a psychologist who may work in a mental health or social welfare agency

industrial/organizational psychologist: a psychologist who uses psychological concepts to make the workplace a more satisfying environment for employees and managers

conducting polls and surveys. **Developmental psychologists** study physical, emotional, cognitive, and social changes that occur throughout life.

Educational psychologists deal with topics related to teaching children and young adults, such as intelligence, memory, problem solving, and motivation. Specialists in this field evaluate teaching methods, devise tests, and develop new instructional devices. A **community psychologist** may work in a mental health or social welfare agency operated by the state or local government or by a private organization. A community psychologist may help design, run, or evaluate a mental health clinic. **Industrial/organizational psychologists** are employed by business firms and government agencies. Industrial psychologists study and develop methods to boost production, improve working conditions, place applicants in jobs for which they are best suited, train people, and reduce accidents. Organizational psychologists study the behavior of people in organizations such as business firms.

Environmental psychologists work in business settings or within the government to study the effects of the environment on people. They may look at the effects of natural disasters, overcrowding, and pollution on the population in general as well as individuals and families. *Psychobiologists* study the effect of drugs or try to explain behavior in terms of biological factors, such as electrical and chemical activities in the nervous system. *Forensic psychologists* work in legal, court, and correctional systems. They assist police by developing personality profiles of criminal offenders or help law-enforcement officers understand problems like abuse. *Health psychologists* study the interaction between physical and psychological health factors. They may investigate how stress or depression leads to physical ailments such as ulcers, cancer, or the common cold.

Figure 1.12　Divisions of the APA

The divisions of the American Psychological Association (APA) represent the many areas in which a psychologist may specialize. *Under which divisions might the work of a clinical psychologist fall?*

1. Society for General Psychology
2. Society for the Teaching of Psychology
3. Experimental Psychology
4. There is no Division 4
5. Evaluation, Measurement, and Statistics
6. Behavioral Neuroscience and Comparative Psychology
7. Developmental Psychology
8. Society for Personality and Social Psychology
9. Society for the Psychological Study of Social Issues - SPSSI
10. Psychology and the Arts
11. There is no Division 11
12. Society of Clinical Psychology
13. Consulting Psychology
14. Society for Industrial and Organizational Psychology
15. Educational Psychology
16. School Psychology
17. Counseling Psychology
18. Psychologists in Public Service
19. Military Psychology
20. Adult Development and Aging

21. Applied Experimental and Engineering Psychology
22. Rehabilitation Psychology
23. Society for Consumer Psychology
24. Theoretical and Philosophical Psychology
25. Experimental Analysis of Behavior
26. History of Psychology
27. Society for Community Research and Action: Division of Community Psychology
28. Psychopharmacology and Substance Abuse
29. Psychotherapy
30. Psychological Hypnosis
31. State Psychological Association Affairs
32. Humanistic Psychology
33. Mental Retardation and Developmental Disabilities
34. Population and Environmental Psychology
35. Psychology of Women
36. Psychology of Religion
37. Child, Youth, and Family Services

38. Health Psychology
39. Psychoanalysis
40. Clinical Neuropsychology
41. American Psychology-Law Society
42. Psychologists in Independent Practice
43. Family Psychology
44. Society for the Psychological Study of Lesbian, Gay, and Bisexual Issues
45. Society for the Psychological Study of Ethnic Minority Issues
46. Media Psychology
47. Exercise and Sport Psychology
48. Peace Psychology
49. Group Psychology and Group Psychotherapy
50. Addictions
51. Society for the Psychological Study of Men and Masculinity
52. International Psychology
53. Clinical Child Psychology (Division 12, Section I)
54. Society of Pediatric Psychology (Division 12, Section V)

Source: American Psychological Association, 1999.

experimental psychologist: a psychologist who studies sensation, perception, learning, motivation, and emotion in carefully controlled laboratory conditions

Reading Check
How does developmental psychology differ from educational psychology?

Finally, some psychologists are **experimental psychologists.** These psychologists perform research to understand how humans (and animals) operate physically and psychologically. Experimental psychologists do everything from testing how electrical stimulation of a certain area of a rat's brain affects its behavior, through studying how disturbed people think, to observing how different socioeconomic groups vote in elections. Experimental psychologists supply information and research used in psychology.

The American Psychological Association (APA), founded in 1892, is a scientific and professional society of psychologists and educators. It is the major psychological association in the United States and is the world's largest association of psychologists. The APA is made of 52 divisions, each representing a specific area, type of work or research setting, or activity. Some divisions are research-oriented, while others are advocacy groups. Together they are a cross section of the diverse nature of psychology (see Figure 1.12). The APA works to advance the science and profession of psychology and to promote human welfare.

What psychologists think about, what experiments they have done, and what this knowledge means form the subject of *Understanding Psychology.* Psychology is dedicated to answering some of the most interesting questions of everyday life: What happens during sleep? How can bad habits be broken? Is there a way to measure intelligence? Why do crowds sometimes turn into mobs? Do dreams mean anything? How does punishment affect a child? Can memory be improved? What causes psychological breakdowns? In trying to answer such questions, psychologists tie together what they have discovered about human behavior, thoughts, and feelings in order to look at the total human being. The picture is far from complete, but some of what is known will be found in the chapters that follow.

SECTION 3 Assessment

1. **Review the Vocabulary** Describe the work of a clinical psychologist, a counseling psychologist, a developmental psychologist, and a community psychologist.

2. **Visualize the Main Idea** Use a graphic organizer similar to the one below to name several specialty fields of psychology.

   Specialty Fields of Psychology

3. **Recall Information** How might the work of environmental psychologists differ from that of industrial/organizational psychologists?

4. **Think Critically** If you decided to continue in the field of psychology, what type of psychologist would you want to be? Why?

5. **Application Activity** Create a pamphlet that answers some basic questions concerned with psychology as a profession, for example: What is psychology? What is the difference between psychiatry and clinical psychology? What kinds of jobs can I get with a psychology degree?

Summary and Vocabulary

Psychologists study human behavior to attempt to explain and predict why people behave and feel as they do.

Section 1 Why Study Psychology?

Main Idea: Through the study of psychology, people can discover psychological principles that have the potential to enrich the lives of humans.

- Psychology is the scientific study of behavior and mental processes.
- The goals of psychology are description, explanation, prediction, and influence.
- Psychologists rely on the scientific method when researching an issue.
- Psychology can provide insight into behavior and has practical applications in everyday life.

Section 2 A Brief History of Psychology

Main Idea: Psychology involves sets of questions, theories, methods, and possible answers that have been passed on and changed from generation to generation.

- Historical approaches to psychology include structuralism, functionalism, inheritable traits, and Gestalt psychology.
- Psychoanalytic psychology involves interpretation of unconscious thoughts.
- Behaviorists investigate observable behavior.
- Humanists believe that human behavior is self-directed.
- Cognitive psychologists focus on mental processes and rationally motivated behavior.
- Psychobiologists are interested in the physiological basis of behavior in humans and animals.
- Sociocultural psychology is a modern influential movement on how to view human behavior from a political and cross-cultural point of view.

Section 3 Psychology as a Profession

Main Idea: Psychologists are trained to observe, analyze, and evaluate behavior patterns, to develop theories of behavior, and to apply what they have learned to influence behavior.

- Psychiatrists and clinical psychologists both treat people with psychological disorders. Psychiatrists are medical doctors, whereas clinical psychologists are trained in psychology.
- There are many specialty fields in psychology, including clinical, developmental, industrial/organizational, experimental, and community psychology.

Chapter Vocabulary

physiological (p. 7)

cognitive (p. 7)

psychology (p. 9)

hypothesis (p. 11)

theory (p. 11)

basic science (p. 11)

applied science (p. 11)

scientific method (p. 12)

structuralist (p. 16)

introspection (p. 16)

functionalist (p. 16)

psychoanalyst (p. 19)

behaviorist (p. 20)

humanist (p. 20)

cognitivist (p. 20)

psychobiologist (p. 21)

psychologist (p. 25)

clinical psychologist (p. 25)

counseling psychologist (p. 25)

psychiatry (p. 25)

developmental psychologist (p. 26)

educational psychologist (p. 26)

community psychologist (p. 26)

industrial/organizational psychologist (p. 26)

experimental psychologist (p. 28)

Self-Check Quiz
Visit the *Understanding Psychology* Web site at
psychology.glencoe.com and click on **Chapter 1—
Self-Check Quizzes** to prepare for the Chapter Test.

Reviewing Vocabulary

Choose the letter of the correct term or concept below to complete the sentence.

a. psychobiologist
b. hypothesis
c. structuralist
d. functionalist
e. behaviorist
f. theory
g. clinical psychologist
h. developmental psychologist
i. experimental psychology
j. industrial/ organizational psychology

1. Psychologists who do research in memory, perception, and learning are involved in _____.

2. A(n)_____ wants to learn how various mental processes help people adapt to their environment.

3. A psychologist who focuses on studying objectively verifiable phenomena is known as a(n)_____.

4. The type of psychologist who usually works in a mental health clinic, mental hospital, or prison is called a(n) _____.

5. _____ is concerned with using psychological concepts to make the workplace a more satisfying environment for employees.

6. A(n) _____ would study the influence of biological factors on behavior and mental processes.

7. An educated guess, or _____, predicts what the results of testing will be.

8. A(n) _____ would attempt to describe the basic elements of human experience.

9. A belief or set of beliefs that is used to explain observed facts and to predict new facts is called a(n) _____.

10. A(n) _____ charts changes in behavior as people grow older, trying to understand the factors that influence those changes.

Recalling Facts

1. What is psychology?
2. What are the steps of the scientific method?
3. What are four goals of psychology?
4. What method of study did Wundt develop to collect information about the mind?
5. Using a graphic organizer similar to the one below, compare and contrast functionalism and behaviorism.

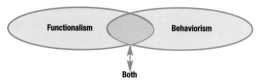

Critical Thinking

1. **Synthesizing Information**   Write your own definition of psychology. Is your definition different from one you would have written before reading the chapter? Put the definition in your Psychology Journal and read it at the end of the course to see if you still agree with it.

2. **Demonstrating Reasoned Judgment**   Do you think human behavior is free or determined? Defend your answer using theories from the different approaches to psychology.

3. **Making Comparisons**   Consider the issue of fear of the dark. How would the work of a psychologist involved in basic science and a psychologist involved in applied science differ in regard to the study of this issue?

4. **Making Inferences**   Do you think that humanistic psychology presents an optimistic view of the world? Explain.

5. **Drawing Conclusions**   Why do you think it is important to study the history of psychology?

CHAPTER 1 Assessment

Psychology Projects

1. **Why Study Psychology?** Imagine that you are a psychologist and a patient has arrived at your office to discuss a problem. (Create a problem—such as stress or shyness—for the assignment.) Using the four goals of psychology, outline a possible plan to help the patient. Your plan should meet all the goals.

2. **A Brief History of Psychology** Create a chart that explains the differences in the study of psychology between Sigmund Freud and B.F. Skinner. Your chart should include motivations of behavior, reward structures, and procedures for diagnosis and treatment. You may illustrate your text with cartoons or drawings to clarify certain points.

3. **Psychology as a Profession** Create an advertisement for your new psychology clinic. In the advertisement, describe the services of the different types of psychologists that work at your clinic. You should include at least six types of psychologists, such as clinical, environmental, social psychologists, and so on. When creating your ad, keep in mind the types of problems that people might want to bring to the clinic. You may want to create a magazine, newspaper, or Internet ad.

Technology Activity

Use the Internet or the computerized card catalog in your local or school library to find information on careers in psychology. Choose one field of psychology and detail the education, experience, and qualities needed for a job in that field. Present your research in an informational pamphlet.

Psychology Journal

Review the journal entry that you wrote at the beginning of the chapter on your reasons for studying psychology. Based on what you have learned from studying the chapter and classroom discussions, assess the ideas you presented in the original entry. Ask yourself:

- Are any of the ideas based on misconceptions, false premises, or faulty reasoning?
- What ideas would you revise or delete?
- What other ideas for studying psychology would you now include?

Write a new entry in your journal. Describe the three biggest benefits you feel you can derive from studying psychology. Provide reasons to justify your choices.

Building Skills

Identifying Cause-and-Effect Relationships
Review the cartoon and answer the questions that follow.

1. How might this girl have "learned" to avoid the intended bad consequences of pulling the string?
2. Which approach to psychology might this cartoon illustrate?

 See the Skills Handbook, page 624, for an explanation of identifying cause-and-effect relationships.

 Practice and **assess** key social studies skills with **Glencoe Skillbuilder Interactive Workbook CD-ROM, Level 2.**

CHILD PSYCHOLOGIST

Jean Piaget

He found the secrets of human learning hidden behind the seemingly illogical notions of children

By SEYMOUR PAPERT

JEAN PIAGET, THE PIONEERING SWISS philosopher and psychologist, spent much of his professional life listening to children, watching children and poring over reports of researchers around the world who were doing the same. He found, to put it most succinctly, that children don't think like grownups. After thousands of interactions with young people often barely old enough to talk, Piaget began to suspect that behind their cute and seemingly illogical utterances were thought processes that had their own kind of order and their own special logic. Einstein called it a discovery "so simple that only a genius could have thought of it."

Piaget's insight opened a new window into the inner workings of the mind. By the end of a wide-ranging and remarkably prolific research career that spanned nearly 75 years—from his first scientific publication at age 10 to work still in progress when he died at 84—

Piaget had developed several new fields of science: developmental psychology, cognitive theory and what came to be called genetic epistemology. Although not an educational reformer, he championed a way of thinking about children that provided the foundation for today's education-reform movements. It was a shift comparable to the displacement of stories of "noble savages" and "cannibals" by modern anthropology. One might say that Piaget was the first to take children's thinking seriously.

JEAN PIAGET: A towering figure of 20th-century psychology

Others who shared this respect for children—John Dewey in the U.S., Maria Montessori in Italy and Paulo Freire in Brazil—fought harder for immediate change in the schools, but Piaget's influence on education is deeper and more pervasive. He has been revered by generations of teachers inspired by the belief that children are not empty vessels to be filled with knowledge (as traditional pedagogical theory had it) but active builders of knowledge—little scientists who are constantly creating and testing their own theories of the world. And though he may not be as famous as Sigmund Freud or even B.F. Skinner, his contribution to psychology may be longer lasting. As computers and the Internet give children more autonomy to explore ever larger digital worlds, the ideas he pioneered become ever more relevant.

Piaget grew up near Lake Neuchâtel in a quiet region of French Switzerland. His father was a professor of medieval studies and his mother a strict Calvinist. He was a child prodigy who soon became interested in the scientific study of nature. When, at age 10, his observations led to questions that could be answered only by access to the university library, Piaget wrote and published a short note on the sighting of an albino sparrow in the hope that this would influence the librarian to stop treating him like a child. It worked. Piaget was launched on a path that would lead to his doctorate in zoology and a lifelong conviction that the way to understand anything is to understand how it evolves.

After World War I, Piaget became interested in psychoanalysis. He moved to Zurich and then to Paris to study logic and abnormal psychology. Working with Theodore Simon in Alfred Binet's child-psychology lab, he noticed that Parisian children of the same age made similar errors on true-false intelligence tests. Fascinated by their reasoning processes, he began to suspect that the key to human knowledge might be discovered by observing how the child's mind develops.

The core of Piaget is his belief that looking carefully at how knowledge develops in children will clarify the nature of knowledge in general. Whether this has in fact led to deeper understanding remains, like everything about Piaget, controversial. But for those who still see Piaget as the giant in the field of cognitive theory, the difference between what the baby brings and what the adult has is so immense that the new discoveries do not significantly reduce the gap but only increase the mystery. ∎

PSYCHOANALYST

Sigmund Freud

He opened a window on the unconscious and changed the way we view ourselves

By PETER GAY

MORE THAN ANY OTHER EXPLO-RER of the psyche, Sigmund Freud has shaped the mind of the 20th century. The very fierceness and persistence of his detractors are a wry tribute to the staying power of Freud's ideas.

His fundamental idea—that all humans are endowed with an unconscious in which potent sexual and aggressive drives, and defenses against them, struggle for supremacy, as it were, behind a person's back—has struck many as a romantic, scientifically unprovable notion. His contention that the catalog of neurotic ailments to which humans are susceptible is nearly always the work of sexual maladjustments, and that erotic desire starts not in puberty but in infancy, seemed to the respectable nothing less than obscene. His dramatic evocation of a universal Oedipus complex, in which (to put a complicated issue too simply) the little boy loves his mother and hates his father, seems more like a literary conceit than a thesis worthy of a scientifically minded psychologist.

Freud first used the term *psychoanalysis* in 1896, when he was already 40. He had been driven by ambition from his earliest days and encouraged by his doting parents to think highly of himself. After an impressive career in school, he enrolled in 1873 in the University of Vienna and drifted from one philosophical subject to another until he hit on medicine. As he pursued his medical researches, he came to the conclusion that the most intriguing mysteries lay concealed in the complex operations of the mind. By the early 1890s, he was specializing in "neurasthenics" (mainly severe hysterics); they taught him much, including the art of patient listening. At the same time he was beginning to write down his dreams, increasingly convinced that they might offer clues to the workings of the unconscious, a notion he borrowed from the Romantics. He saw himself as a scientist taking material both from his patients and from himself, through introspection. By the mid-1890s, he was launched on a full-blown self-analysis, an enterprise for which he had no guidelines and no predecessors.

The book that made his reputation in the profession—although it sold poorly—was *The Interpretation of Dreams* (1900), an indefinable masterpiece—part dream analysis, part autobiography, part theory of the mind, part history of contemporary Vienna. The principle that underlay this work was that mental experiences and entities, like physical ones, are part of nature. This meant that Freud could admit no mere accidents in mental procedures. The most nonsensical notion, the most casual slip of the tongue, the most fantastic dream, must have a meaning and can be used to unriddle the often incomprehensible maneuvers we call thinking. ∎

—For the complete text of this article and related articles from TIME, please visit www.time.com/teach

POST-FREUDIAN ANALYSIS

Other psychologists continued the work that Freud began, though not always in ways that he would have approved.

CARL JUNG A former disciple of Freud's, Jung shared his mentor's enthusiasm for dreams but not his obsession with the sex drive. Jung said humans are endowed with a "collective unconscious" from which myths, fairy tales and other archetypes spring.

ALFRED KINSEY A biologist who knew little about sex and less about statistics, Kinsey nonetheless led the first large-scale empirical study of sexual behavior. The Kinsey reports shocked readers by documenting high rates of what some considered atypical sexual behavior.

B.F. SKINNER A strict behaviorist who avoided all reference to internal mental states, Skinner believed that behavior can best be shaped through positive reinforcement. Contrary to popular misconception, he did not raise his daughter in the "Skinner box" used to train pigeons.

FROM TOP TO BOTTOM: STEPHAN BRETSCHER, ARCHIVE PHOTOS, JAMES F. COYNE

ANALYZING THE ARTICLES

1. What was Piaget's contribution to psychology?
2. **CRITICAL THINKING** How might the ways we think about children and ourselves be different today if Piaget and Freud had not proposed their theories?

CHAPTER 2

Psychological Research Methods and Statistics

For the next seven days, observe how statistics are used in the media. In your journal, describe the examples you find. ■

104,957
101,228
23,951
208,000
199,704
96,760
3,954
81,410

105,001
102,111
23,952
207,500
199,357
96,813
3,953
81,320
8,362
72,548
17,735
20,858
8,834
5,435
11,571

105,322
102,040
23,983
207,750
199,697
97,038
3,961
81,480
8,378
72,662

PSYCHOLOGY Online

Chapter Overview
Visit the *Understanding Psychology* Web site at psychology.glencoe.com and click on **Chapter 2—Chapter Overviews** to preview the chapter.

What Is Research?

Reader's Guide

■ Main Idea
Psychologists must first decide how to approach the research issue. Then psychologists conduct the research in one of a variety of ways to test a hypothesis, solve a problem, or confirm previous findings.

■ Vocabulary
- sample
- naturalistic observation
- case study
- survey
- longitudinal study
- cross-sectional study
- correlation
- hypothesis
- variable
- experimental group
- control group

■ Objectives
- Describe the process of psychological research.
- Name the different types of psychological research.

EXPLORING PSYCHOLOGY

Do You Act This Way?
There are some chimps who, far more than others, constantly seem to try to ingratiate themselves with [win over] their superiors. Melissa, for one, particularly when she was young, used to hurry toward and lay her hand on the back or head of an adult male almost every time one passed anywhere near her. If he turned toward her, she often drew her lips back into a submissive grin as well. Presumably Melissa, like the other chimps who constantly attempt to ingratiate themselves in this way, is simply ill at ease in the presence of a social superior, so that she constantly seeks reassurance through physical contact. . . . There is much controversy as to how the human smile has evolved. It seems fairly certain, though, that we have two rather different kinds of smiles, . . . We smile when we are amused and we smile when we are slightly nervous, on edge, apprehensive. . . .

—from *In the Shadow of Man* by Jane Goodall, 1988

Jane Goodall observed the behavior of chimpanzees in Tanzania, Africa, to obtain data. She observed the behavior of chimps over a period of 30 years and provided much information about the animals' lives. Whereas Goodall used the research methods of naturalistic observation and case study, other psychologists use methods such as conducting experiments and surveys.

Psychologists collect information somewhat like most people do in everyday life—only more carefully and more systematically. When you turn on the television and the picture is out of focus, you experiment with different knobs and dials until you find the one that works. When you ask a number of friends about a movie you are thinking of seeing, you are conducting an informal survey. Of course, there is more to doing scientific research than turning dials or asking friends what they think. Over the years psychologists, like other scientists, have transformed these everyday techniques for gathering and analyzing information into more precise tools.

PRE-RESEARCH DECISIONS

sample: the small group of participants, out of the total number available, that a researcher studies

Researchers must begin by asking a specific question about a limited topic or hypothesis. The next step is to look for evidence. The method a researcher uses to collect information partly depends on the research topic. For example, a social psychologist who is studying the effects of group pressure is likely to conduct an experiment. A psychologist who is interested in personality might begin with intensive case studies. Whatever approach to gathering data a psychologist selects, however, he or she must make certain basic decisions in advance.

Profiles In Psychology

Jane Goodall

1934–

"Every individual matters. Every individual has a role to play. Every individual makes a difference."

Jane Goodall, a British zoologist, became known for her work with chimpanzees in the wild. In 1960 she began her research at what is now Gombe Stream National Park in Tanzania. By living among the chimpanzees, she won their trust, observing their daily activities and writing detailed reports. She wrote, "The most wonderful thing about fieldwork, whether with chimps, baboons or any other wildlife, is waking up and asking yourself, 'What am I going to see today?'"

Goodall discovered while doing 30 years of research that chimps hunt and eat larger animals and make and use tools more than any other species except humans. Goodall also witnessed the first known instance in which one group of chimps systematically killed another group, although the first group's survival was not threatened. This discovery surprised naturalists and suggested that behaviors like hunting, using tools, and warfare are not uniquely human.

Samples

Suppose a psychologist wants to know how the desire to get into college affects the attitudes of high school juniors and seniors. It would be impossible to study every junior and senior in the country. Instead, the researcher would select a **sample**, a relatively small group out of the total *population* under study—in this case, all high school juniors and seniors.

A sample must be *representative* of the population a researcher is studying. For example, if you wanted to know how tall American men were, you would want to make certain that your sample did not include a disproportionately large number of professional basketball players. Such a sample would be *nonrepresentative*; it would probably not represent American men in general.

There are two ways to avoid a nonrepresentative sample. One is to take a purely *random sample* so that each individual has an *equal chance* of being represented. For example, a psychologist might choose every twentieth name on school enrollment lists for a study of schoolchildren in a particular town. Random sampling is like drawing names or numbers out of a hat while blindfolded.

The second way to avoid a nonrepresentative sample is to deliberately pick individuals who represent the various subgroups in the population being studied. For example, the psychologist doing research on schoolchildren might select students of both sexes, of varying ages, of all social classes, and from all neighborhoods. This is called a stratified sample. In a *stratified sample*, subgroups in the population are represented proportionately in the sample. For example, if about 30 percent of schoolchildren in the United States are ages 5–8, then in a stratified sample of schoolchildren in the United States, 30 percent of those studied will be ages 5–8.

✔️ *Reading Check*
How does a random sample differ from a stratified sample?

METHODS OF RESEARCH

The goals of research are to describe behavior, to explain its causes, to predict the circumstances under which certain behaviors may occur again, and to control certain behaviors. Psychologists use various methods of research to accomplish each of these goals.

Naturalistic Observation

Researchers need to know how people and animals behave naturally, when they are not conscious of being observed during an experiment. To obtain such information, a psychologist uses **naturalistic observation.** The cardinal rule of naturalistic observation is to avoid disturbing the people or animals you are studying by concealing yourself or by acting as unobtrusively as possible. Otherwise you may observe a performance produced because of the researcher's presence.

naturalistic observation: research method in which the psychologist observes the subject in a natural setting without interfering

Case Studies

A **case study** is an intensive study of a person or group. Most case studies combine long-term observations with diaries, tests, and interviews. Case studies can be a powerful research tool. Sigmund Freud's theory of personality development, discussed in Chapter 14, was based on case studies of his patients. Jean Piaget's theory of intellectual development, described in Chapter 3, was based in part on case studies of

case study: research method that involves an intensive investigation of one or more participants

Did You Know?

A Polling Fiasco One of the greatest polling fiascos of all time occurred when the *Literary Digest* predicted the winner of the presidential election of 1936. (A poll is a type of survey in which citizens' votes are recorded.) The *Literary Digest* mailed out 10,000,000 ballots and had 2,300,000 returned. Based on the results, the magazine predicted that Alfred M. Landon would win by a comfortable margin. Instead, Franklin D. Roosevelt received over 60 percent of the popular vote, representing one of the largest majorities in American presidential history.

survey: research method in which information is obtained by asking many individuals a fixed set of questions

his own children. By itself, however, a case study does not prove or disprove anything. The results cannot be generalized to anyone else. The researcher's conclusions may not be correct. Case studies, though, provide a wealth of descriptive material that may generate new hypotheses that researchers can then test under controlled conditions with comparison groups.

Surveys

The most practical way to gather data on the attitudes, beliefs, and experiences of large numbers of people is through surveys. A survey may consist of interviews, questionnaires, or a combination of the two. Interviews allow a researcher to observe the participant and modify questions if the participant seems confused by them. On the other hand, questionnaires take less time to administer and the results are more uniform because everyone answers the same questions. Questionnaires also eliminate the possibility that the researcher will influence the participant by unconsciously frowning at an answer he or she does not like. Of course, there is always a danger that participants will give misleading answers in order to make themselves "look good."

Longitudinal Studies

longitudinal study: research method in which data is collected about a group of participants over a number of years to assess how certain characteristics change or remain the same during development

When conducting longitudinal studies, a psychologist studies the same group of people at regular intervals over a period of years to determine whether their behavior and/or feelings have changed and if so, how. Longitudinal studies are time-consuming and precarious; participants may disappear in midstudy. Longitudinal studies, however, are an ideal way to examine consistencies and inconsistencies in behavior over time. A good example was the New York Longitudinal Study begun in 1956. Psychologists followed 133 infants as they grew into adulthood, discovering that children are born with different temperaments (Thomas, Chess, & Birch, 1968).

Cross-Sectional Studies

cross-sectional study: research method in which data is collected from groups of participants of different ages and compared so that conclusions can be drawn about differences due to age

An alternative approach to gathering data is cross-sectional studies. In a cross-sectional study, psychologists organize individuals into groups on the basis of age. Then, these groups are randomly sampled, and the members of each group are surveyed, tested, or observed simultaneously. Cross-sectional studies are less expensive than longitudinal studies and reduce the amount of time necessary for the studies.

In 1995 researchers conducted a cross-sectional study in which they showed three-, four-, six-, and seven-year-olds a picture of a serious-looking woman. The psychologists then asked the participants what they thought the woman was thinking about. The psychologists found that the older children seemed to have a clearer picture of mental processes. From this discovery, the psychologists proposed that as children mature, their understanding of mental processes improves (Flavell, Green, & Flavell, 1995).

Correlations and Explanations

A researcher may simply want to observe people or animals and record these observations in a descriptive study. More often, however, researchers want to examine the *relationship* between two sets of observations—say, between students' grades and the number of hours they sleep.

Scientists use the word **correlation** to describe how two sets of data relate to each other. For example, there is a *positive correlation* between IQ scores and academic success. High IQ scores tend to go with high grades; low IQ scores tend to go with low grades. On the other hand, there is a *negative correlation* between the number of hours you spend practicing your tennis serve and the number of double faults you serve. As the hours of practice increase, errors decrease. In this case, a high rank on one measure tends to go with a low rank on the other (see Figure 2.1).

It is important to keep in mind that a correlation describes a relationship between two things. It does not mean, though, that one thing causes the other. In some cases, a third factor exists that may account for the positive correlation. Correlations do not identify what causes what. For example, although you might detect a positive correlation between sunny days and your cheerful moods, this does not mean that sunny days cause good moods.

correlation: the measure of a relationship between two variables or sets of data

Experiments

Why would a researcher choose experimentation over other research methods? Experimentation enables the investigator to *control* the situation and to decrease the possibility that unnoticed, outside variables will influence the results.

| Figure 2.1 | A Correlational Study |

These charts display possible correlations between different variables. *How does time spent studying psychology correlate to the final grade in a psychology course?*

hypothesis: an educated guess about the relationship between two variables

variable: any factor that is capable of change

experimental group: the group to which an independent variable is applied

control group: the group that is treated in the same way as the experimental group except that the experimental treatment (the independent variable) is not applied

Every experiment has a **hypothesis,** or an educated guess, about the expected outcome—the researcher has some evidence for suspecting a specific answer. In a hypothesis, a psychologist will state what he or she expects to find. The hypothesis also specifies the important variables of the study.

In designing and reporting experiments, psychologists think in terms of **variables,** conditions and behaviors that are subject to change. There are two types of variables: independent and dependent. The *independent variable* is the one experimenters change or alter so they can observe its effects. The *dependent variable* is the one that changes in relation to the independent variable. For example, the number of hours you study (the independent variable) affects your performance on an exam (the dependent variable).

Participants who are exposed to the independent variable are in the **experimental group.** Participants who are treated the same way as the experimental group, except that they are not exposed to the independent variable, make up the **control group** (see Figure 2.2). A control group is necessary in all experiments. Without it, a researcher cannot be sure the experimental group is reacting to what he or she thinks it is reacting to—a change in the independent variable. By comparing the way control and experimental groups behaved in an experiment (statistically), the researchers can determine whether the independent variable influences behavior and how it does so.

The results of any experiment do not constitute the final word on the subject, however. Psychologists do not fully accept the results of their own or other people's studies until the results have been *replicated*—that is, duplicated by at least one other psychologist with different participants. Why? Because there is always a chance that the studies may have hidden flaws.

Ethical Issues

Ethics are the methods of conduct, or standards, for proper and responsible behavior. The American Psychological Association (APA) published a set of ethical principles that govern psychologists' research. These principles are as follows:

- Using recognized standards of competence and ethics, psychologists plan research so as to minimize the possibility of misleading results. Any ethical

Figure 2.2   Experimental Research

Psychology is an experimental science. Psychologists follow the same general procedures when conducting experimental research. *What are the dependent and independent variables of this experiment?*

Step 1: Ask Research Question:
Does watching violence on TV lead to aggressive behavior?

Step 2: Form a Hypothesis:
People who watch violent TV programs will engage in more acts of violence than people who don't.

Step 3: Determine Variables:
People watch violent TV programs (independent variable); people engage in aggressive acts (dependent variable).

Step 4: Experiment (Testing):
a. Participants (randomly assigned to groups)

Experimental group spends four hours a day watching violent programs

Control group spends four hours a day watching nonviolent programs

b. Measure aggressive behavior (dependent variable) of experimental and control groups

Step 5: Compare Measurements

Step 6: Interpret Results and Draw Conclusions

problems are resolved before research is started. The welfare and confidentiality of all participants are to be protected.

- Psychologists are responsible for the dignity and welfare of participants. Psychologists are also responsible for all research they perform or is performed by others under their supervision.

- Psychologists obey all state and federal laws and regulations as well as professional standards governing research.

- Except for anonymous surveys, naturalistic observations, and similar research, psychologists reach an agreement regarding the rights and responsibilities of both participants and researcher(s) before research is started.

- When consent is required, psychologists obtain a signed, informed consent before starting any research with a participant.

- Deception is used only if no better alternative is available. Under no condition is there deception about (negative) aspects that might influence a participant's willingness to participate.

- Other issues covered include sharing and utilizing data, offering inducements, minimizing evasiveness, and providing participants with information about the study.

Recently the use of animals in research has caused much concern and debate. Researchers have attempted to balance the rights of animals with the need for advancing the health of humans through research. While some people oppose subjecting animals to pain for research purposes, others point to the enormous gains in knowledge and reduction in human suffering that have resulted from such research.

PSYCHOLOGY *Online*

Student Web Activity
Visit the *Understanding Psychology* Web site at psychology.glencoe.com and click on **Chapter 2—Student Web Activities** for an activity about psychological research.

SECTION 1 Assessment

1. **Review the Vocabulary** Explain how a psychologist might select a sample for a survey.

2. **Visualize the Main Idea** In a chart similar to the one below, list and describe the advantages and disadvantages associated with each method of research.

Research Method	Description	Advantages	Disadvantages

3. **Recall Information** What pre-research decisions must a psychologist make?

4. **Think Critically** Why should psychologists question the results of an experiment that they have conducted for the first time?

5. **Application Activity** Suppose you wanted to find out whether there was a correlation between hours spent watching television and test grades in psychology class. Design a plan using one or more of the methods of research to help you study this correlation.

Problems and Solutions in Research

Reader's Guide

■ Main Idea
The investigation of psychological issues is a painstaking process. Psychologists must recognize and resolve errors while doing research.

■ Vocabulary
- self-fulfilling prophecy
- single-blind experiment
- double-blind experiment
- placebo effect

■ Objectives
- Summarize the methodological hazards of doing research.
- Examine experimental procedures psychologists use to avoid bias.

EXPLORING PSYCHOLOGY

Was She Doomed?

One young woman died of fear in a most peculiar way: When she was born, on Friday the 13th, the midwife who delivered her and two other babies that day announced that all three were hexed and would die before their 23rd birthday. The other two did die young. As the third woman approached her 23rd birthday, she checked into a hospital and informed the staff of her fears. The staff noted that she dealt with her anxiety by extreme hyperventilation (deep breathing). Shortly before her birthday, she hyperventilated to death.

—from *Introduction to Psychology* by **James W. Kalat, 1999**

Once an expectation is set, we tend to act in ways that are consistent with that expectation. How did the woman in the excerpt above die? Technically, when people do not breathe voluntarily, they breathe reflexively—the amount of carbon dioxide in the blood activates breathing. By breathing so deeply for so long (hyperventilating), the woman exhaled so much carbon dioxide that she did not have enough left in her bloodstream to trigger the breathing reflex. When she stopped breathing voluntarily, she stopped breathing altogether and died. In effect, the woman believed in the Friday the 13th hex and unintentionally fulfilled its prediction.

This is what we mean by a self-fulfilling prophecy. A **self-fulfilling prophecy** involves having expectations about a behavior and then acting in some way, usually unknowingly, to carry out that behavior.

In everyday life, we consciously or unconsciously tip off people as to what our expectations of them are. We give them cues, such as nodding

self-fulfilling prophecy:
a situation in which a researcher's expectations influence that person's own behavior, and thereby influence the participant's behavior

and raising our eyebrows. People pick up on those cues and act as expected. Psychologists must be aware of such cues when conducting experiments. They must not allow their expectations to influence the results. The results must be unbiased. Science is a painstaking, exacting process. Every researcher must be wary of numerous pitfalls that can trap him or her into mistakes. In this section, we will look at some of the most common problems psychological researchers confront and how they cope with them.

AVOIDING A SELF-FULFILLING PROPHECY

Sometimes an experimenter's behavior may unwittingly influence the results. The experimenter may unintentionally raise an eyebrow or nod when posing a question, thus influencing the person being studied. One way to avoid this self-fulfilling prophecy is to use the single-blind or double-blind technique. Suppose a psychologist wants to study the effects of a particular tranquilizer. She might give the drug to an experimental group and a placebo (a substitute for the drug that has no medical benefits) to a control group. The next step would be to compare their performances on a series of tests. This is a **single-blind experiment.** The participants are "blind" in the sense that they do not know whether they have received the tranquilizer or the placebo. What does it mean, then, if the participants taking the placebo drug report that they feel the effects of the tranquilizer? It means that their expectations have played a role—that they felt the effects because they believed they were taking a tranquilizing drug, not because of the drug itself.

The researcher also may not know who takes the drug or the placebo. She may, for example, ask the pharmacist to number rather than label the pills. *After* she scores the tests, she goes back to the pharmacist to learn which participants took the tranquilizer and which took the placebo. This is a **double-blind experiment.** Neither the participants nor the experimenter knows which participants received the tranquilizer. This eliminates the possibility that the researcher will unconsciously find what she expects to find about the effects of the drug. The researcher remains unbiased.

THE MILGRAM EXPERIMENT

In the 1960s Stanley Milgram wanted to determine whether participants would administer painful shocks to others merely because an authority figure had instructed them to do so. Milgram collected 2,000 male

---

More About...

The Hawthorne Study

In 1939 a group of industrial psychologists set out to determine how to increase workers' productivity at a General Electric plant in Hawthorne, Illinois (Roethlisberger & Dickson, 1939). The participants were eight assembly line workers. In the first experiment, the psychologists gradually increased the lighting in the room (the independent variable) and observed the effect on productivity (the dependent variable). Productivity improved as the lighting was increased. In a second experiment, the participants were permitted to take rest breaks. This also increased the productivity of the workers. Next, the psychologists reduced the lighting levels, and again productivity increased. The psychologists found that no matter what they did, productivity increased. Why? The psychologists soon recognized that the participants realized they were receiving special attention. This motivated the workers to work harder, thus increasing their productivity.

The results of the experiment in Hawthorne generated studies in human relations and management that apply to work situations today.

single-blind experiment: an experiment in which the participants are unaware of which participants received the treatment

double-blind experiment: an experiment in which neither the experimenter nor the participants know which participants received which treatment

Figure 2.3   Single-Blind and Double-Blind Experiments

Researchers must take measures during experimentation to guard against seeing only what they expect to see. *Why would a researcher conduct a double-blind experiment?*

	Experimenter	Participants	Organizer of Experiment
Single-Blind Experiment	aware	unaware	aware
Double-Blind Experiment	unaware	unaware	aware

participants, including college students and adults in different occupations. Milgram told the group of paid volunteers that he was studying the effects of punishment on learning. Milgram introduced each volunteer to a "learner"—actually someone posing as a learner. The volunteer watched the learner attempt to recite a list of paired words that he supposedly had memorized earlier. Each time the learner made a mistake, the volunteer, or "teacher," was ordered to push a button to deliver an electric shock to the learner. The shocks, mild at first, would increase with each mistake to a painful and dangerous level of 450 volts.

The volunteers at this point did not realize that the shocks were false because the learners displayed distress and pain, screaming and begging for the electric shocks to stop. Although the task did not seem easy for them, most of the volunteers delivered a full range of the electric shocks to the learners. (Sixty-two percent of the volunteers pushed the shock button until they reached maximum severity.)

The results implied that ordinary individuals could easily inflict pain on others if such orders were issued by a respected authority. Later, Milgram informed the volunteers that they had been deceived and that no shocks had actually been administered. This was a good example of a single-blind experiment because the participants were unaware that they were not administering a shock. Critics raised the following questions, though. How would you feel if you had been one of Milgram's participants? Did Milgram violate ethical principles when he placed participants in a position to exhibit harmful behavior? Was the deception Milgram used appropriate? Did the information gained outweigh the deception? Before the start of any experiment today, the experimenter is required to submit a plan to a Human Subjects Committee that can either approve or reject the ethics of the experiment.

Milgram's hypothesis and experiment has been applied in similar studies. In Milgram's original study, more than half of the participants (26 of 40, or 65 percent) administered the highest level of shock. Researchers at Swarthmore College hypothesized that Milgram's findings were due, in part, to the fact that his participants were mostly

Reading Check

Why can the Milgram experiment be classified as a single-blind experiment?

middle-aged, working-class men. Most had probably served in the military during World War II and thus had experience taking orders and obeying authority. Young, liberal, highly educated Swarthmore students would obey less. Yet, surprisingly, 88 percent of the Swarthmore undergraduates administered the highest level of shock!

THE PLACEBO EFFECT

When researchers evaluate the effects of drugs, they must always take into account a possible placebo effect. The **placebo effect** is a change in a patient's illness or physical state that results solely from the patient's knowledge and perceptions of the treatment. The placebo is some sort of treatment, such as a drug or injection, that resembles medical therapy yet has no medical effects.

In one study (Loranger, Prout, & White, 1961), researchers divided hospitalized psychiatric patients into two experimental groups and a control group. They gave the experimental groups either a "new tranquilizer" or a "new energizer" drug. The control group received no drugs at all. After a six-week period, the researchers evaluated the experimental groups. Fifty-three to eighty percent of the experimental groups reported that they had indeed benefited from the drugs. Yet all the drugs administered during the experiment were placebos. The participants had reacted to their own expectations of how the drug given to them would affect them. Neither the researchers nor the patients were aware that the drugs were placebos until after the experiment.

People spend millions of dollars a year on herbal remedies such as these, which have not been proven to cure their ills.

placebo effect: a change in a participant's illness or behavior that results from a belief that the treatment will have an effect, rather than the actual treatment

---

SECTION 2 Assessment

1. **Review the Vocabulary** Explain how psychologists try to avoid the self-fulfilling prophecy.

2. **Visualize the Main Idea** Use a diagram similar to the one below to outline an experiment discussed in this section.

   Hypothesis:_____
   ▼
   Independent   Dependent
   Variables:_____ Variables: _____
   ▼
   Results:_____
   ▼
   Conclusions:_____

3. **Recall Information** What questions about the Milgram experiment did critics raise? How are today's experiments restricted in regards to ethics?

4. **Think Critically** How can the expectations of the participants bias the results of an experiment? How can the expectations of the experimenter bias the results of an experiment?

5. **Application Activity** Describe a single-blind experiment you might set up. Explain your hypothesis and the participants' tasks.

The Case of Clever Hans

Period of Study: 1911

Introduction: A horse, Clever Hans, grew famous throughout Europe for his startling ability to answer questions. Taught by his owner, Mr. von Osten, Hans seemed to be able to add, subtract, multiply, divide, spell, and solve problems, even when his owner was not around. Oskar Pfungst decided to investigate the humanlike intelligence of the horse.

Hypothesis: Two different hypotheses are involved in this case. First, Mr. von Osten, believing that horses could be as intelligent as humans, hypothesized that he could teach Hans some problem-solving abilities. Pfungst, on the other hand, believed that horses could not learn such things and, while investigating this theory, developed a hypothesis that Hans, the horse, was reacting to visual cues to answer questions.

Method: Mr. von Osten, a German mathematics teacher, started by showing Hans an object while saying "One" and at the same time lifting Hans's foot once. Von Osten would lift Hans's foot twice for two objects, and so on. Eventually Hans learned to tap his hoof the correct number of times when von Osten called out a number. For four years, von Osten worked with Hans on more and more complex problems, until Hans was able to answer any question given him.

Upon hearing of the amazing horse, Pfungst grew skeptical and investigated. Pfungst soon discovered that Hans responded correctly to questions only when the questioner had calculated the answer first. Then Pfungst realized that Hans's answers proved wrong when the horse could not see the questioner. To test his hypothesis, Pfungst fitted the horse with blinders. The horse failed to answer the questions. Eventually Pfungst realized that the questioner would unknowingly give Hans clues as to the right answer. For example, after asking a question, the questioner would lean forward to watch Hans's foot. This was a cue for Hans to start tapping. Pfungst observed that "as the experimenter straightened up, Hans would stop tapping, he found that even the raising of his eyebrows was sufficient. Even the dilation of the questioner's nostrils was a cue for Hans to stop tapping." (Pfungst, 1911) Questioners involuntarily performed these actions, but Hans responded to the visual signals.

Results: Von Osten believed that he had been teaching the horse how to solve problems and answer questions, when in fact he had been teaching Hans to make simple responses to simple signals. Pfungst had uncovered errors in Von Osten's experiments. Von Osten had practiced a self-fulfilling prophecy—he had unintentionally communicated to Hans how he expected the horse to behave. Pfungst had learned the truth by isolating the conditions under which Hans correctly and incorrectly answered questions. He had carefully observed the participant's reactions under controlled conditions.

Analyzing the Case Study

1. How did Mr. von Osten test his hypothesis?

2. What errors did von Osten make while testing his hypothesis?

3. **Critical Thinking** If Pfungst had not come along and found the truth, how could we discover today how Hans answered the questions?

Statistical Evaluation

Reader's Guide

■ Main Idea
Psychologists must collect and evaluate evidence to support their hypotheses.

■ Vocabulary
- statistics
- descriptive statistics
- frequency distribution
- normal curve
- central tendency
- variance
- standard deviation
- correlation coefficient
- inferential statistics

■ Objectives
- Recognize types of descriptive statistics.
- Describe inferential statistics.

EXPLORING PSYCHOLOGY

When Statistics Lie

Long ago, when Johns Hopkins University had just begun to admit women students, someone not particularly enamored of [happy with] coeducation reported a real shocker: Thirty-three and one-third percent of the women at Hopkins had married faculty members! The raw figures gave a clearer picture. There were three women enrolled at the time, and one of them had married a faculty man.

—from *How to Lie With Statistics* by Darrell Huff, 1954

A lthough people may use statistics to distort the truth (such as in the example above), people may also use statistics honestly to support their hypotheses. In order to allow statistics to validly support a hypothesis, psychologists must collect meaningful data and evaluate it correctly.

How many times have you been told that in order to get good grades, you have to study? A psychology student named Kate has always restricted the amount of TV she watches during the week, particularly before a test. She has a friend, though, who does not watch TV before a test but who still does not get good grades. This fact challenges Kate's belief. Although Kate hypothesizes that among her classmates, those who watch less TV get better grades, she decides to conduct a survey to test the accuracy of her hypothesis. Kate asks 15 students in her class to write down how many hours of TV they watched the night before a psychology quiz and how many hours they watched on the night after the quiz. Kate collects additional data. She has her participants check off familiar products on a

Baseball Statistics

Let's look at how statistics are used in one of our most popular sports, baseball. A batting average is the number of hits per official "at bats" (walks do not count). If a player has a batting average of .250, it means that on average he or she gets a hit every fourth time at the plate.

The earned run average represents the number of runs a pitcher allows per 9 innings of play. Consider the pitcher who pitches 180 innings in a season and allows 60 runs. On the average, this pitcher allows one run every 3 innings (180 innings divided by 60 runs). One run every 3 innings equals 3 runs every 9 innings, so the earned run average is 3. The next time you watch your favorite sport, think about the part that statistics plays in it.

list of 20 brand-name items that were advertised on TV the night before the quiz. Kate also asks her participants to give their height.

When the data are turned in, Kate finds herself overwhelmed with the amount of information she has collected. Her data are presented in Figure 2.4. How can she organize it all so that it makes sense? How can she analyze it to see whether it supports or contradicts her hypothesis? The answers to these questions are found in **statistics,** a branch of mathematics that enables researchers to organize and evaluate the data they collect. We will explore the statistical procedures that help psychologists make sense out of the masses of data they collect.

statistics: the branch of mathematics concerned with summarizing and making meaningful inferences from collections of data

descriptive statistics: the listing and summarizing of data in a practical, efficient way

DESCRIPTIVE STATISTICS

When a study such as Kate's is completed, the first task is to organize the data in as brief and clear a manner as possible. For Kate, this means that she must put her responses together in a logical format. When she does this, she is using **descriptive statistics,** the listing and summarizing of data in a practical, efficient way, such as through graphs and averages.

Figure 2.4	Kate's Data			
Before	**After**	**Grade***	**Products**	**Height**
0.0	1.5	5	2	71
0.5	2.5	10	4	64
0.5	2.5	9	6	69
1.0	2.0	10	14	60
1.0	2.5	8	10	71
1.0	1.5	7	9	63
1.5	3.0	9	7	70
1.5	2.5	8	12	59
1.5	2.5	8	9	75
1.5	3.0	6	14	60
2.0	3.0	5	13	68
2.5	2.5	3	17	65
2.5	3.5	4	10	72
3.0	3.0	0	18	62
4.0	4.0	4	20	67

Kate's data show the number of hours of television watched before and after the quiz, the grade on the quiz, the number of products recognized, and participants' height in inches. *How much television did the two students with the best grades watch the night before the quiz?*

* Highest grade possible is 10.

Figure 2.5   A Frequency Distribution

A frequency distribution shows how often a particular observation occurs. *How many students watched three or more hours of television the night before the quiz?*

Hours	Frequency Before*	Frequency After*
0.0	1	0
0.5	2	0
1.0	3	0
1.5	4	2
2.0	1	1
2.5	2	6
3.0	1	4
3.5	0	1
4.0	1	1
Total	15	15

*Number of students

Distributions of Data

One of the first steps that researchers take to organize their data is to create frequency tables and graphs. Tables and graphs provide a rough picture of the data. Are the scores bunched up or spread out? What score occurs most often? Frequency distributions and graphs provide researchers with their initial "peek" at the data.

Kate is interested in how many hours of TV her participants watched the night before and the night after the quiz. She uses the numbers of hours of TV viewing as categories, and then she counts how many participants reported each category of hours before and after the quiz. She has created a table called a frequency distribution (see Figure 2.5). A **frequency distribution** is a way of arranging data so that we know how often a particular score or observation occurs.

What can Kate do with this information? A commonly used technique is to figure out percentages. This is done simply by dividing the frequency of participants within a category by the total number of participants. So, before the quiz, about 13 percent of her participants (2 divided by 15) watched TV for 2.5 hours. On the night after the quiz, 40 percent of her participants watched 2.5 hours of TV (6 divided by 15). You are familiar with the use of percentages; test grades are often expressed as percentages (the number of correct points divided by the total number of questions times 100). Sometimes frequency distributions include a column giving the percentage of each occurrence.

frequency distribution: an arrangement of data that indicates how often a particular score or observation occurs

Figure 2.6   A Frequency Polygon

This graph shows the number of hours of TV watched the night before the quiz and the night after the quiz. *How do the two lines compare?*

— Hours of TV watched before quiz   — Hours of TV watched after quiz

Figure 2.7   **A Normal Curve**

The maximum frequency lies in the center of a range of scores in a perfect normal curve. The frequency tapers off as you reach the edges of the two sides. *Where is the mean located in a normal curve?*

It is often easier to visualize frequency information in the form of a graph. Since Kate is most interested in how much TV her classmates watched, she decides to graph the results. Kate constructs a histogram. *Histograms* are very similar to bar graphs except that histograms show frequency distribution by means of rectangles whose widths represent class intervals and whose areas are proportionate to the corresponding frequencies.

Another kind of graph is the frequency polygon or frequency curve. Figure 2.6 is a frequency polygon. It shows the same information presented in a different way. Instead of boxes, a point is placed on the graph where the midpoint of the top of each histogram bar would be. Then the points are connected with straight lines.

Frequency polygons are useful because they provide a clear picture of the shape of the data distribution. Another important feature is that more than one set of data can be graphed at the same time. For example, Kate might be interested in comparing how much TV was watched the night before the quiz with the amount watched the evening after the quiz. She can graph the "after quiz" data using a different kind of line. The comparison is obvious; in general, her participants watched more TV on the night after the quiz than on the night before the quiz.

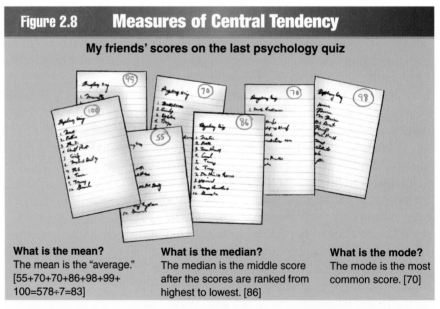

Figure 2.8   **Measures of Central Tendency**

My friends' scores on the last psychology quiz

What is the mean?
The mean is the "average."
[55+70+70+86+98+99+
100=578÷7=83]

What is the median?
The median is the middle score after the scores are ranked from highest to lowest. [86]

What is the mode?
The mode is the most common score. [70]

It is often useful to summarize a set of scores by identifying a number that represents the center, average, or most frequently occurring number of the distribution. *If your score matched the median on the last psychology quiz, how did you do in comparison to your classmates?*

Imagine that Kate could measure how much TV everyone in Chicago watched one night. If she could graph that much information, her graph would probably look something like Figure 2.7. A few people would watch little or no TV, a few would have the TV on all day, while most would watch a moderate amount of TV. Therefore, the graph would be highest in the middle and taper off toward the tails, or ends, of the distribution, giving it the shape of a bell.

This curve is called the **normal curve** (or bell-shaped curve). Many variables, such as height, weight, and IQ, fall into such a curve if enough people are measured. The normal curve is symmetrical. This means that if a line is drawn down the middle of the curve, one side of the curve is a mirror image of the other side. It is an important distribution because of certain mathematical characteristics. We can divide the curve into sections and can predict how much of the curve, or what percentage of cases, falls within each section.

normal curve: a graph of frequency distribution shaped like a symmetrical, bell-shaped curve; a graph of normal distribution

Measures of Central Tendency

Most of the time, researchers want to do more than organize their data. They want to be able to summarize information about the distribution into statistics. For example, researchers might want to discuss the average height of women or the most common IQ test score. One of the most common ways of summarizing is to use a measure of **central tendency**— a number that describes something about the "average" score. We shall use Kate's quiz grades (refer back to Figure 2.4) in the examples that follow.

The *mode* is the most frequent score. In a graphed frequency distribution, the mode is the peak of the graph. The most frequently occurring quiz grade is 8; that is, more students received an 8 than any other score. Distributions can have more than one mode. The data for height presented in Figure 2.4 have two modes: 60 and 71. Distributions with two modes are called "bimodal."

When scores are put in order from least to most, the *median* is the middle score. Since the median is the midpoint of a set of values, it divides the frequency distribution into two halves. Therefore, 50 percent of the scores fall below the median, and 50 percent fall above the median. For an odd number of observations, the median would be the exact middle value.

The *mean* is what most people think of as an "average" and is the most commonly used measure of central tendency. To find the mean, you add up all the scores and then divide by the number of scores you added. The mean equals the sum of the scores on variable *X* divided by the total number of observations. For the quiz grades, the sum of the scores is 96, and the number of scores is 15. The mean equals 96 divided by 15, giving us a mean quiz grade of 6.4.

The mean can be considered the balance point of the distribution, like the middle of a seesaw, since it does reflect all the scores in a set of data. If the highest score in a data set is shifted higher, the mean

central tendency: a number that describes something about the "average" score of a distribution

Reading Check
What is the difference between the mean and the mode?

| Figure 2.9 | Standard Deviation |

Two distributions with the same mean and different standard deviations are shown. *What information does the standard deviation supply?*

Transforming Scores

Suppose you take the ACT and score a 26. Then you take the SAT and get a 620. The college you want to go to will accept either test score. Which score should you send? (Which score is better?) To make a comparison between two scores that have different distributions, different means, and different variabilities, you must transform the scores.

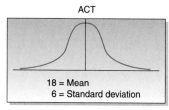

ACT

18 = Mean
6 = Standard deviation

SAT

500 = Mean
100 = Standard deviation

If you look at the distributions of the ACT and SAT, you will find that the ACT has a mean of 18 and a standard deviation of 6. So you take your score on the ACT (26) and subtract the mean from it (26−18) to get 8; 8 is 1.33 standard deviations above the mean (8/6). Do the same for your SAT score [620−500 = 120; so 620 is 1.2 standard deviations above the mean (120/100)]. So which score would you submit to the college of your choice? (The correct answer is your ACT score because 1.33 is greater than 1.2.)

What we just did was to make a standard score. A standard score is a transformed score that provides information about its location in a distribution.

variance: a measure of difference, or variance

standard deviation: a measure of variability that describes an average distance of every score from the mean

will shift upward also. If we change the highest quiz grade from 10 to 20, the mean changes from 6.4 to 7.1.

Measures of Variance

Distributions differ not only in their "average" score but also in terms of how "spread out" or how variable the scores are. Figure 2.9 shows two distributions drawn on the same axis. Each is symmetrical, and each has the same mean. However, the distributions differ in terms of their variance. Measures of **variance** provide an index of how spread out the scores of a distribution are.

Two commonly used measures of variance are the range and the standard deviation. To compute the *range,* subtract the lowest score in a data set from the highest score. The highest quiz grade is 10 and the lowest is 0, so the range is 10. The range uses only a small amount of information, and it is used only as a crude measure of variance.

The **standard deviation** is a better measure of variance because, like the mean, it uses all the data points in its calculation. It is the most widely used measure of variance. The standard deviation is a measure of distance. It is like (but not exactly like) an "average" distance of every score to the mean of the scores. This distance is called a "deviation" and is written: $X - \overline{X}$. Scores above the mean will have a positive deviation, and scores below the mean will have a negative deviation. The size of the "average" deviation depends on how variable, or spread out, the distribution is. If the distribution is very spread out, deviations tend to be large. If the distribution is bunched up, deviations tend to be small. The larger the standard deviation, the more spread out the scores are (see Figure 2.9).

Correlation Coefficients

A **correlation coefficient** describes the direction and strength of the relationship between two sets of observations (recall the discussion of correlations in Section 1). The most commonly used measure is the Pearson correlation coefficient (r). A coefficient with a plus (+) sign indicates a *positive correlation.* This means that as one variable *increases,* the second variable also *increases.* For example, the more you jog, the better your cardiovascular system works. A coefficient with a minus (−) sign indicates a *negative correlation;* as one variable *increases,* the second variable *decreases.* For example, the more hours a person spends watching TV, the fewer hours are available for studying. Correlations can take any value between +1 and −1 including 0. An r near +1 or −1 indicates a strong relationship (either positive or negative), while an r near 0 indicates a weak relationship.

Generally, an r from ±0.60 to ±1.0 indicates a strong correlation, from ±0.30 to ±0.60 a moderate correlation, and from 0 to ±0.30 a weak correlation. A correlation of ±1.0 indicates a perfect relationship between two variables and is very rare.

correlation coefficient: describes the direction and strength of the relationship between two sets of variables

To get an idea of how her data look, Kate draws some scatterplots. A *scatterplot* is a graph of participants' scores on the two variables, and it demonstrates the direction of the relationship between them. Figure 2.10 illustrates the different kinds of correlations Kate looks at. Note that each point represents one person's score on two variables.

INFERENTIAL STATISTICS

The purpose of descriptive statistics is to describe the characteristics of a sample. Psychologists, however, are not only interested in the information they collect from their participants, but they also want to make generalizations about the population from which the participants come. To make such generalizations, they need the tools of inferential statistics. Using **inferential statistics,** researchers can determine whether the data they collect support their hypotheses, or whether their results are merely due to chance outcomes.

inferential statistics: numerical methods used to determine whether research data support a hypothesis or whether results were due to chance

Probability and Chance

If you toss a coin in the air, what is the probability that it will land with heads facing up? Since there are only two possible outcomes, the probability of heads is 0.50. If you toss a coin 100 times, you would expect 50 heads and 50 tails. If the results were 55 heads and 45 tails, would you think the coin is fair? What if it were 100 heads and zero tails?

When a researcher completes an experiment, he or she is left with lots of data to analyze. The researcher must determine whether the findings from the experiment support the hypothesis (for example, the coin is fair) or whether the results are due to chance. To do this, the researcher must perform a variety of statistical tests, called measures of statistical significance. When researchers conclude that their findings are statistically significant, they are stating, at a high level of confidence, that their results are not due to chance.

Statistical Significance

For many traits in a large population, the frequency distribution follows a characteristic pattern, called the normal curve (see Figure 2.7). For example, if you measured the heights of 500 students chosen at random from your high school, you would find very few extremely tall people and very few extremely short people. The majority of students

Figure 2.10   A Scatterplot

When there is little or no relationship between two variables, the points in the scatterplot do not seem to fall into any pattern. *What conclusions can you draw from this scatterplot?*

Do some people really have psychic powers?

A well-known psychic sometimes begins his performance by saying the following: "Think of a number between 1 and 50. Both digits must be odd numbers, but they must not be the same. For example, it could be 15 but it could not be 11. Please choose a number and I will tell you what number you are thinking of."

Procedure

1. Develop a hypothesis that explains how the psychic is performing this feat. (Hint: The psychic uses statistics, not magic.)
2. Try out the psychic's act on several of your classmates and record their responses.

Analysis

1. Based on the psychic's directions, decide which numbers can be used and which numbers will most likely be used.
2. How do your observations support or contradict your hypothesis?

See the Skills Handbook, page 622, for an explanation of designing an experiment.

would fall somewhere in the middle. Suppose Kate wants to know if her classmates watch more TV than the "average American." Since daily TV viewing is probably normally distributed, she can compare her results to the normal distribution if she knows the population's mean number of TV viewing hours.

When psychologists evaluate the results of their studies, they ask: Could the results be due to chance? What researchers really want to know is whether the results are so extreme—or so far away from the normal curve—that they are more likely due to chance.

The problem is that this question cannot be answered with a yes or no. This is why researchers use some guidelines to evaluate probabilities. Many researchers say that if the probability that their results were due to chance is less than 5 percent (0.05), then they are confident that the results are not due to chance. Some researchers want to be even more certain, and so they use 1 percent (0.01) as their level of confidence. When the probability of a result is 0.05 or 0.01 (or whatever level the researcher sets), we say that the result is *statistically significant*. It is important to remember that probability tells us how likely it is that an event or outcome is due to chance, but not whether the event is *actually* due to chance.

When does a statistically significant result *not* represent an important finding? Many statistical tests are affected by sample size. A small difference between groups may be magnified by a large sample and may result in a statistically significant finding. The difference, however, may be so small that it is not a meaningful difference.

SECTION 3 | Assessment

1. **Review the Vocabulary** What is the difference between a frequency distribution and a histogram? Between a normal curve and a scatterplot?

2. **Visualize the Main Idea** Using an organizer similar to the one at right, list and describe the measures of central tendency.

3. **Recall Information** What is the importance of the normal curve?

4. **Think Critically** What does correlation tell you about the relationship of two variables?

5. **Application Activity** Conduct a class or family survey on an issue, then display your findings in a frequency distribution, frequency polygon, or scatterplot. What conclusions can you reach from your results?

Psychologists learn about what they do not know by carefully and systematically collecting information. They then must describe and analyze their research findings through various statistical measurements and interpret their results.

Section 1 | What Is Research?

Main Idea: Psychologists must first decide how to approach the research issue. Then psychologists conduct the research in one of a variety of ways to test a hypothesis, solve a problem, or confirm previous findings.

- Researchers begin their research by asking a specific question about a limited topic; determining the validity of a claim, hypothesis, or theory; and choosing an unbiased sample.
- Psychologists use several methods of research to accomplish their research goals. These methods include naturalistic observation, case studies, surveys, and experiments.
- Psychologists follow a set of ethical principles that govern their research.

Section 2 | Problems and Solutions in Research

Main Idea: The investigation of psychological issues is a painstaking process. Psychologists must recognize and resolve errors while doing research.

- In a self-fulfilling prophecy, an experimenter has expectations about a participant's behavior and then acts in some way, usually unknowingly, to influence that behavior.
- In single-blind experiments, the participants do not know which participants have received the treatment.
- Researchers can avoid a self-fulfilling prophecy by using the double-blind technique in their experiments.
- When researchers evaluate the effects of drugs, they must always take into account a possible placebo effect.

Section 3 | Statistical Evaluation

Main Idea: Psychologists must collect and evaluate evidence to support their hypotheses.

- Researchers use descriptive statistics to organize data in a practical, efficient way.
- Descriptive statistics include distributions of data, measures of central tendency, measures of variance, and correlation coefficients.
- Researchers use inferential statistics to make generalizations about the population from which the participants come.
- Researchers perform a variety of statistical tests, called measures of statistical significance, to determine whether findings from their experiment support the hypothesis or whether the results are due to chance.

Chapter Vocabulary

sample (p. 36)
naturalistic observation (p. 37)
case study (p. 37)
survey (p. 38)
longitudinal study (p. 38)
cross-sectional study (p. 38)
correlation (p. 39)
hypothesis (p. 40)
variable (p. 40)
experimental group (p. 40)
control group (p. 40)
self-fulfilling prophecy (p. 42)
single-blind experiment (p. 43)
double-blind experiment (p. 43)
placebo effect (p. 45)
statistics (p. 48)
descriptive statistics (p. 48)
frequency distribution (p. 49)
normal curve (p. 51)
central tendency (p. 51)
variance (p. 52)
standard deviation (p. 52)
correlation coefficient (p. 52)
inferential statistics (p. 53)

Self-Check Quiz
Visit the *Understanding Psychology* Web site at
psychology.glencoe.com and click on **Chapter 2—
Self-Check Quizzes** to prepare for the Chapter Test.

Reviewing Vocabulary

Choose the letter of the correct term or concept below to complete the sentence.

a. variance
b. sample
c. longitudinal study
d. control group
e. single-blind experiment
f. double-blind experiment
g. placebo effect
h. statistics
i. normal
j. frequency distribution

1. _____ is a branch of mathematics that helps researchers organize and evaluate data.

2. In a(n) _____, only the participants of the experiment do not know whether they are in the experimental group or the control group.

3. Measures of _____ indicate how spread out the scores of a distribution are.

4. A bell-shaped curve is a(n) _____ curve.

5. In an experiment, the _____ includes the participants who are not exposed to experimental variables.

6. The _____ is a change in a patient's physical state that results from the patient's perceptions of the treatment.

7. Researchers use a(n) _____ to arrange data so that they know how often a particular observation occurs.

8. Researchers generally select a(n) _____, which is a relatively small group of the total population that is being studied.

9. In a(n) _____, neither the participants nor the experimenter knows whether the participants are in the experimental group or the control group.

10. In a(n) _____, a researcher studies a group of people over a period of years.

Recalling Facts

1. What are two ways that a researcher can avoid a biased sample?

2. When do researchers use naturalistic observation?

3. How does a self-fulfilling prophecy present a problem for researchers?

4. Using a graphic organizer similar to the one below, identify and explain the kinds of descriptive statistics.

DESCRIPTIVE STATISTICS

5. Why do researchers use inferential statistics? How do inferential statistics describe data differently than descriptive statistics?

Critical Thinking

1. **Synthesizing Information** How could you attempt to disprove the following hypothesis? You can raise blood pressure by making a participant anxious.

2. **Analyzing Statements** Explain the following statement: "Correlation does not imply causation."

3. **Making Inferences** What correlation would you expect between students' grades and class attendance?

4. **Applying Concepts** How are statistics used within your classroom? Within your school?

5. **Analyzing Information** Various kinds of statistics are used in sports. Provide examples of statistics from various sports.

Psychology Projects

1. **What Is Research?** Choose a traffic intersection near your home or school that has a stop sign. Design a study to assess whether or not motorists stop at the posted sign. Consider the research questions you need to answer, such as how to determine whether motorists comply with the sign, the number of vehicles, and the time of day. Conduct your study and record your observations.

2. **Statistical Evaluation** Collect heights from 20 women and 20 men. Create a frequency distribution for each group, and divide them into 5-inch intervals before counting. Graph your data for men and women separately as frequency polygons on the same axis. Compute means, medians, modes, ranges, and standard deviations for women and men separately. How are the two distributions alike and different?

Technology Activity

Does smoking cause lung cancer? Some scientists cite animal studies as proving that it does. Representatives of the tobacco industry state that animal studies cannot be generalized to humans. Search the Internet to find arguments and data from each side of this debate. Use that information to support both viewpoints in an essay.

Psychology Journal

For each of the examples of statistics you listed in your journal (at the beginning of the chapter), indicate whether you feel that enough information was provided to evaluate the validity of any reported claims. What other information should have been provided? How might additional information change the reported conclusions?

Building Skills

Interpreting Graphs Review the graphs, then answer the questions that follow.

1. What does each of the graphs illustrate?
2. Which age group owns or uses the most cellular phones?
3. How has the number of cellular subscribers changed since 1988?
4. Do most cell-phone owners talk on the phone while driving? How often do they use their phones while driving?
5. What arguments might these statistics be used to support or refute?

Practice and **assess** key social studies skills with **Glencoe Skillbuilder Interactive Workbook CD-ROM, Level 2.**

See the Skills Handbook, page 628, for an explanation of interpreting graphs.

Cell-Phone Use

Cellular subscribers

55.2

(in millions)

'88 '98

Talk on the phone while driving

Fewer than half of trips 15%

Most trips 11%

Never 11%

Very few trips 54%

About half of trips 9%

Own or use a car phone (by age group)

16-20	21-24	25-34	35-44	45-54	55-64	65+	All ages
26%	28%	32%	36%	39%	23%	16%	30%

Sources: National Highway Traffic Safety Administration; Cellular Telecommunications Industry Association.

UNIT 2

The Life Span

Contents

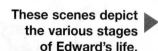

These scenes depict the various stages of Edward's life.

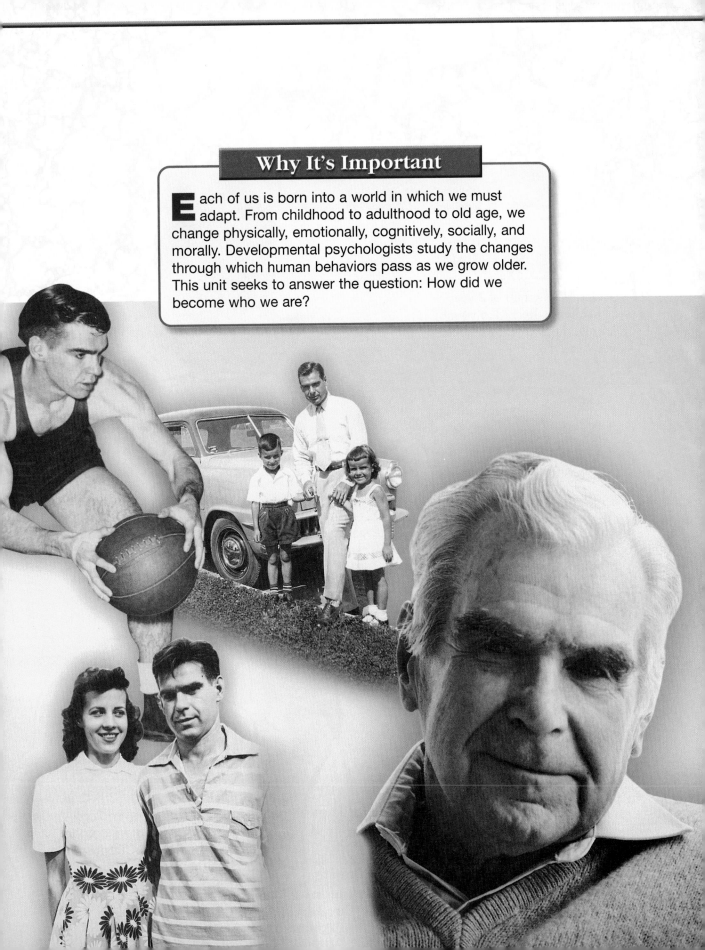

Why It's Important

Each of us is born into a world in which we must adapt. From childhood to adulthood to old age, we change physically, emotionally, cognitively, socially, and morally. Developmental psychologists study the changes through which human behaviors pass as we grow older. This unit seeks to answer the question: How did we become who we are?

Infancy and Childhood

PSYCHOLOGY JOURNAL

Observe a group of 2-year-old children. Record in your journal the two-word sentences you hear. ■

PSYCHOLOGY
Online

Chapter Overview
Visit the *Understanding Psychology*
Web site at psychology.glencoe.com
and click on **Chapter 3—Chapter
Overviews** to preview the chapter.

Physical, Perceptual, and Language Development

Reader's Guide

■ Main Idea
Infants are born equipped to experience the world. As infants grow physically, they also develop perceptions and language.

■ Vocabulary
- developmental psychology
- grasping reflex
- rooting reflex
- maturation
- telegraphic speech

■ Objectives
- Describe the physical and perceptual development of newborns and children.
- Discuss the development of language.

EXPLORING PSYCHOLOGY

What Do Babies See?

Propped against my knees in the delivery room, my son, minutes old, peered at me with wide, unblinking eyes. He looked so intent. So serious. So thoughtful. What could earth's freshest arrival possibly be thinking about? Maybe he was wondering who all the giants looming over him might be, especially the pair with the goofy grins who kept counting his fingers and toes over and over. Maybe his head still ached from the incredibly narrow trip out of my womb. Maybe he was asking himself, "Hey, who turned on the lights?" It's hard to know how the world appears to a new baby. But in recent years, researchers have deduced plenty about what infants sense, remember, prefer, and need. And such knowledge is more than academic for new parents.

—from *Parent* magazine, Paula Spencer, 1999

D o you remember anything from when you were a baby? Less than 15 years ago, you were probably only two feet tall and just taking your first step. Just a year or two after that, you spent your days intently playing. Most of those events from your life are long forgotten, but you changed faster and learned more in early childhood than you ever will again.

In this chapter you will learn about **developmental psychology**— the specialized study of how an individual's physical, social, emotional, moral, and intellectual growth and development occur in sequential inter-related stages throughout the life cycle.

developmental psychology: the study of changes that occur as an individual matures

NATURE AND NURTURE

✓ Reading Check
What is the argument of nature versus nurture?

Developmental psychologists study the following main issues: (1) continuity versus stages of development, (2) stability versus change, and (3) nature versus nurture. On the question of nature versus nurture, psychologists ask: How much of development is the result of inheritance (heredity), and how much is the result of what we have learned? Some psychologists believe that most of our behaviors are the result of genetics or inheritance. Others believe that most of our behaviors are the result of experience and learning. Separating biological and environmental causes of behavior is very complicated. Usually behavior develops as a result of both heredity and environment.

grasping reflex: an infant's clinging response to a touch on the palm of his or her hand

rooting reflex: an infant's response in turning toward the source of touching that occurs anywhere around his or her mouth

NEWBORNS

Development begins long before an infant is born. Expectant mothers can feel strong movement and kicking—even hiccuping—inside them during the later stages of pregnancy. It is common for a fetus (an unborn child) to suck its thumb, even though it has never suckled at its mother's breast or had a bottle.

More About...

Reflexes

The *rooting* and *sucking* reflexes, present in all human infants, gradually decline in strength. The *grasping* reflex disappears during the first six months in those infants where it is present at birth. The Moro, or *startle,* reflex is quite unusual. An infant lying on its back when startled by a loud noise out of sight above his or her head will show a very complex response. The arms will spread out at right angles to the body and grasp upwards, and the legs will spread outward.

Now consider this situation. What would happen if someone ran a thumbnail right up the center bottom of your foot? Your toes would curl, and your foot would withdraw. Before her first birthday, an infant will do exactly the opposite—the toes flare outward, and the foot presses against the stimulus. This is called the *Babinski* reflex. Pediatricians use the shift in the Babinski from infantlike to adultlike form around the first birthday as a sign of normal neurological development.

Capacities

Newborns have the ability at birth to see, hear, smell, and respond to the environment. This allows them to adapt to the new world around them. Psychologists have found that birth puts staggering new demands on a baby's capacity to adapt and survive. He goes from an environment in which he is totally protected from the world to one in which he is assaulted by lights, sounds, touches, and extremes of temperature. The newborn is capable of certain inherited, automatic, coordinated movement patterns, called reflexes, that can be triggered by the right stimulus (see Figure 3.1). Infants are born with many such reflexes. The **grasping reflex,** for example, is a response to a touch on the palm of the hand. Infants can grasp an object, such as a finger, so strongly that they can be lifted into the air.

Also vital is the **rooting reflex.** If an alert newborn is touched anywhere around the mouth, he will move his head and mouth toward the source of the touch. In this way the touch of his mother's breast on his cheek guides the infant's mouth toward her nipple. The sucking that follows contact with the nipple is one of the infant's most complex reflexes. The infant is able to suck, breathe air, and swallow milk twice a second without getting confused.

Figure 3.1　Newborn Reflexes

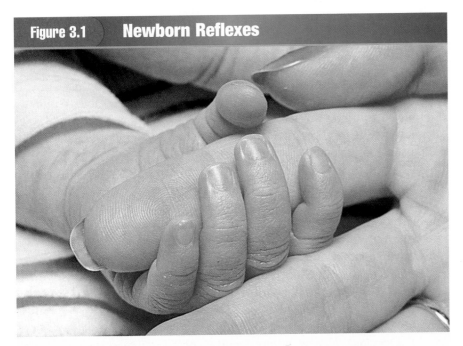

Reflexes are important in determining the health of an infant. In the grasping reflex, newborns close their fingers tightly around objects placed in their hands. *What seems to be the purpose of these reflexes?*

How do we measure the capabilities of newborn infants who cannot speak or understand the questions of curious psychologists? One reasonable way to answer these questions is to take advantage of the things infants *can* do. What they can do is suck, turn their heads, look at things, cry, smile, and show signs of surprise or fright. The vigor of an infant's sucking, the patterns of eye movements, and expressions of pleasure and displeasure are all closely tied to how the infant is being stimulated. By measuring these behaviors while stimulating the infant in different ways, we can infer how the infant perceives the world.

PHYSICAL DEVELOPMENT

Infants on average weigh 7.5 pounds at birth. Some infants can weigh as much as 20 or 25 pounds by the end of the first year. At birth, 95 percent of infants are between 5.5 and 10 pounds and are 18 to 22 inches in length. In the space of two years, the grasping, rooting, searching infant will develop into a child who can walk, talk, and feed herself or himself. This transformation is the result of both maturation and learning.

Did You Know?

SIDS Infants have been known to quietly and mysteriously die in their sleep. Physicians call this "sudden infant death syndrome," or SIDS. SIDS takes more lives in the first year than any other cause of infant death. We do not know why SIDS happens. One theory suggests that it results from a failure in the infant's central nervous system in learning how to turn a reflex into a voluntary action. That is, the infant fails to learn to keep passages open for breathing. There is no known way to predict or prevent SIDS. Recent studies report a decreased incidence of SIDS when the infant is positioned on the sides or back to sleep instead of on the stomach.

Maturation

To some extent an infant is like a plant that shoots up and unfolds according to a built-in plan. She will begin to lift her head at about 3 months, smile at 4 months, and grasp objects at 5 to 6 months. Crawling appears at 8 to 10 months. By this time the infant may be able to pull herself into a standing position, although she will fall if she lets go. She will begin to walk 3 or 4 months later, tentatively at first, but gradually acquiring a sense of balance.

maturation: the internally programmed growth of a child

Psychologists call internally programmed growth **maturation.** Maturation is as important as learning or experience, especially in the first years. (*Learning* is a relatively permanent change in behavior resulting from responses that change as a result of experience.) Unless a child is persistently underfed, severely restricted in her movements, or deprived of human contact and things to look at, she will develop more or less according to this schedule. Purely as a matter of efficiency, it is worth a parent's time to wait until infants reach *maturational readiness* before pushing them into mastering new skills. No amount of coaching will push a child to walk or speak before she is physiologically ready.

The process of maturation becomes obvious when you think about walking. An infant lacks the physical control walking requires. By the end

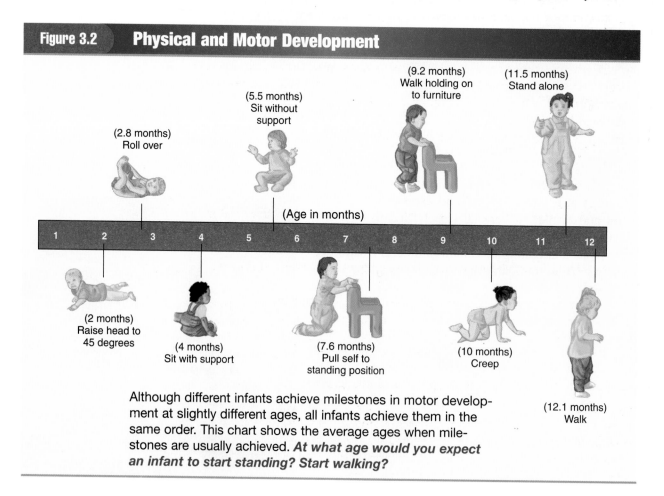

Figure 3.2   Physical and Motor Development

(2 months) Raise head to 45 degrees

(2.8 months) Roll over

(4 months) Sit with support

(5.5 months) Sit without support

(7.6 months) Pull self to standing position

(9.2 months) Walk holding on to furniture

(10 months) Creep

(11.5 months) Stand alone

(12.1 months) Walk

(Age in months)

1 2 3 4 5 6 7 8 9 10 11 12

Although different infants achieve milestones in motor development at slightly different ages, all infants achieve them in the same order. This chart shows the average ages when milestones are usually achieved. *At what age would you expect an infant to start standing? Start walking?*

of the first year, however, the nerves connected to the child's muscles have grown. He or she is ready to walk.

By recording the ages at which thousands of infants first began to smile, to sit upright, to crawl, and to try a few steps, psychologists have been able to develop an approximate timetable for maturation (see Figure 3.2). This schedule helps doctors and other professionals spot problems and abnormalities. If a child has not begun to talk by the age of 2½, a doctor will recommend tests to determine if something is wrong.

One of the facts to emerge from this effort, however, is that the maturational plan inside each child is unique. On the average, infants start walking at 12 to 13 months. Some, though, are ready at 9 months, and others delay walking until 18 months. Each infant also has his or her own temperament. Some infants are extremely active from birth, and some are quiet. Some are cuddly and some stiff. Some cry a great deal while others hardly ever whimper. Although no two infants are exactly alike and no two mature according to the same timetable, most infants progress through the same sequential steps. Identifying similarities and differences in growth patterns is the challenge for developmental psychologists.

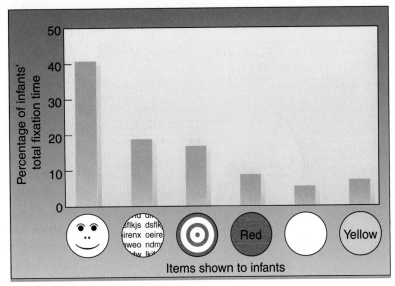

Figure 3.3 **The Visual Preferences of Infants**

Three- or four-month-old infants show a strong preference for faces and patterns, suggesting that infants are born with and develop visual preferences. *How do researchers measure the capabilities of infants?*

PERCEPTUAL DEVELOPMENT

Besides grasping and sucking, newborns look at their bodies and at their surroundings. Newborns have mature perception skills. Robert Fantz (1961) showed infants different faces to discover their preferences. He discovered that infants prefer looking at human faces and patterned materials the most (see Figure 3.3).

Two experimenters (Gibson & Walk, 1960) devised the visual cliff to determine whether infants had depth perception. The visual cliff is a platform, part of which has a checkerboard pattern. The other part consists of a sheet of glass with the checkerboard pattern a few feet below it. It creates the illusion of a clifflike dropoff (see Figure 3.4). Whereas very young infants seemed unafraid, older infants (6 months and older) who were experienced at crawling refused to cross over the cliff. The older infants had explored the world, apparently finding that dropoffs are dangerous. Also, researchers found that there were changes in the heart rates of very young infants even if they would crawl farther, implying that newborns are born with some perceptual capabilities.

Figure 3.4   **The Visual Cliff**

Infants display the ability to perceive three-dimensional space. Infants' heart rates increased as they approached the perceived dropoff of the visual cliff. *Why do you think researchers measured the infants' heart rates during this experiment?*

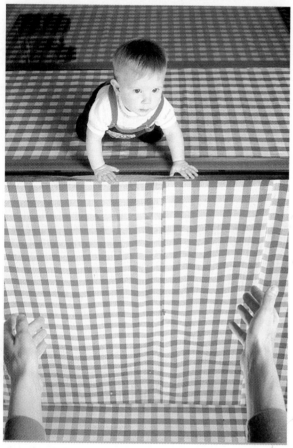

THE DEVELOPMENT OF LANGUAGE

Language and thought are closely intertwined. Both abilities involve using symbols. We are able to think and talk about objects that are present and about ideas that are not necessarily true. A child begins to think, to represent things to himself, before he is able to speak. The acquisition of language, however, propels the child into further intellectual development (Piaget, 1926). We have been able to learn a good deal about the acquisition of language from animals.

Can Animals Use Language?

Psychologists believe that chimpanzees must develop at least as far as 2-year-old humans because, like 2-year-olds, they will look for a toy or a bit of food that has disappeared. They can represent the existence of that toy or bit of food in their minds. Can they be taught to "talk" about it? Allen and Beatrice Gardner raised a baby chimp named Washoe in their home and—since chimps are very good with their hands—taught her to use the American Sign Language for the deaf. At 3½ years of age, Washoe knew at least 87 signs for words like "food," "dog," and "toothbrush." By age 5, Washoe used more than 160 signs.

Several chimpanzees have been taught to "talk" in other ways. Chimpanzees have been trained on special typewriters connected to computers. One chimpanzee, Panzee, used a special computer keyboard with symbols to communicate with humans (see Figure 3.5).

The chimps use only aspects of the human language. Chimps use words as symbols but do not apply grammatical rules. The ability to arrange symbols in new combinations to produce new meanings is especially well developed in the human brain. The rules for such organization of symbols are called *grammar.* Grammatical rules are what make the sentence "the rhinoceros roared at the boy" mean the same thing as "the boy was roared at by the rhinoceros." It may be in our ability to use such grammatical rules that we surpass the simpler language of the chimpanzee.

How Children Acquire Language

Some psychologists argue that language is reinforced behavior, while others claim it is inborn. Some people claim there is a "critical period," or a window of opportunity, for learning a language. For example, songbirds learn their song more easily during an early sensitive period of life. Humans may also have a sensitive period early in life in which acquisition of language is easier.

The example of Washoe shows that there are several steps in learning language. First, one must learn to make the signs—whether by hand or by mouth. Then, one must give them meaning. Finally, one must learn grammar. Each child takes these steps at his or her own rate (see Figure 3.6). During the first year of life, the average child makes many sounds. Crying lessens, and the child starts making mostly cooing sounds, which develop into a babble that includes every sound humans can make—Chinese vowels, African clicks, German rolled *r*'s, and English *o*'s.

Late in the first year, the strings of babbles begin to sound more like the language that the child hears—French babies babble French sounds, Korean babies babble Korean sounds. Children imitate the speech of their parents and their older brothers and sisters, and are greeted with approval whenever they say something that sounds like a word. In this way children learn to speak what becomes their native language even though they could just as easily learn any other.

The leap to using sounds as symbols occurs sometime in the second year. The first attempts at saying words are primitive, and the sounds are incomplete: "Ball" usually sounds like "ba," and "cookie" may even sound like "doo-da." The first real words usually refer to things the infant can see or touch. Often they are labels or commands ("dog!" "cookie!").

By the time children are 2 years old, they have a vocabulary of at least 50 words. Toward the end of the second year, children begin to express themselves more clearly by joining words into two-word phrases. From about 18 months to 5 years of age, children are adding approximately 5 to 10 words a day to their vocabulary (Carey, 1978).

At age 2, though, a child's grammar is still unlike that of an adult. Children use what psychologists call **telegraphic speech**—for example, "Where my apple?" "Daddy fall down." They leave out words but still get the message across. As psychologists have discovered, 2-year-olds already understand certain rules (Brown, 1973). They keep their words in the same order adults do. Indeed, at one point they overdo this, applying grammatical rules too consistently. For example, the usual rule for forming the past tense of English verbs is to add "ed." Many verbs, however, are irregular, such as "go"/"went." At first children learn the correct form of the verb: "Daddy went yesterday." Once children discover the rule for forming past tenses, they replace the correct form with sentences like

telegraphic speech: the kind of verbal utterances in which words are left out, but the meaning is usually clear

✓ **Reading Check**
At what age do children start to use sounds as symbols?

Figure 3.5	How Animals Talk

Panzee, the chimpanzee, used the computer keyboard to type requests and answer questions. *Which aspects of human language do chimps use?*

Figure 3.6 The Flowering of Language

Between the ages of 2 and 5, the typical child learns an average of 10 words a day—nearly 1 word every hour awake! *When should new parents expect to hear their baby's first word?*

Age	Language Abilities	Example
1 year	Babbling begins and increases; by year's end, infant masters sounds of own language and usually says his first word	baba mama
2 years	Infant will progress to saying dozens of words; begins to speak in paired words; to ask a question, child issues a declaration in a rising tone; to negate something, child uses nouns with a negative word	Allgone ball. More ball. Jenny go? No ball.
3 years	Child acquires more grammatical knowledge; says appropriate sentences; uses simple declaratives; produces correct negative sentences; average size of vocabulary is about 400 words	I eating. I'm eating. Don't go.
4 years	Child uses more grammatical rules and future tense; asks questions in adult form; average vocabulary is over 1,000 words	Will Jenny go? I can't go. Why is Jenny crying?
5 years	Child uses more complex clauses; joins two or more ideas in one sentence	I see what you did.

Source: Adapted from *Developmental Psychology* by Howard Gardner, 1963.

"Daddy *goed* yesterday." "Goed" is a positive error because it indicates the child is applying rules. When the correct form appears, the child has shifted from imitation through *overgeneralization* to rule-governed language. By the age of 4 or 5, children have a vocabulary of several thousand words. Their ability to use words will continue to grow with their ability to think about and understand things.

SECTION 1 Assessment

1. **Review the Vocabulary**   Describe two reflexes that infants display.

2. **Visualize the Main Idea**   Using a flow-chart similar to the one below, list the steps involved in learning language.

Learning Language

3. **Recall Information**   What questions do developmental psychologists raise concerning nature versus nurture?

4. **Think Critically**   How does human language acquisition differ from the acquisition of human language by an animal?

5. **Application Activity**   Interview a younger sibling, cousin, or friend (5 years old or younger). Use what you have learned about the development of language to describe that child's use of language.

Too Late for Words: *The Case of Genie*

Period of Study: 1981

Introduction: In 1970 an unusual and unfortunate discovery was made in California. A 13-year-old girl known as "Genie" had spent all 13 years of her life locked in a room isolated from the world. Her parents had kept her harnessed to a potty-chair, which allowed only small movements of her hands and feet. At night Genie was put in a type of straitjacket and forcefully placed in a wire cage. Her parents refused to communicate with her in any way and demanded Genie's siblings avoid any form of communication with her as well.

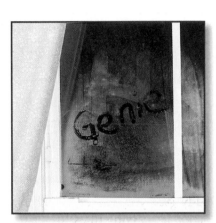

Genie was discovered by a combined effort of people in social services and the police. When she was discovered, she had no bowel or bladder control, could not chew solid food, had severely damaged posture from years of sitting, and she could not speak or understand language. Nursing Genie back to physical health became the top priority. Then psychologists were to be called upon to evaluate her mental and emotional conditions, as well as to begin teaching her how to communicate.

Hypothesis: The unfortunate case of Genie provided psychologists with some clues in defining whether language can be learned at any point in time or if there is a specific stage of development in which humans need to learn language and communication skills. The function of language has been traced to the left hemisphere of the brain. However, it is undetermined if a "window" exists in early childhood that allows for language to be learned easily.

Method: Placed in a hospital, Genie was described as being "a pitiful, malformed, incontinent, unsocialized, and severely malnourished creature" (Pines, 1981). Genie was given various tests that were designed to measure social maturity and school-level placement. She scored at a level equal to that of a normal 1-year-old child. As time passed, Genie learned to recognize her written name. After 7 months passed, she began to develop spoken use of the phrases "stopit" and "nomore," one-word utterances similar to what toddlers use. One-word use progressed to two-word use; however, Genie's development was slower than that of a toddler with similar language skills.

Results: Genie made limited progress in language development. After 7 years had passed, she had learned as much language skill as a normal child learns in 2 to 3 years. When she was 24 years old, she had the language skills of a 5-year-old. Even though Genie learned much about language, she could not fully understand grammar or the use of pronouns and was unable to control the pitch of her voice. Perhaps Genie's window for learning language had passed; thus her brain could only understand language in a simplified form. However, the physical, emotional, and mental abuse that Genie sustained during her first 13 years of life undoubtedly played key roles in her development as a whole.

Analyzing the Case Study

1. Why, when found, was Genie unable to speak coherently or understand language?

2. Describe Genie's ability to learn to properly use language. How much progress in language development did Genie make? Explain.

3. **Critical Thinking** What conclusions can you draw from this case about a "window of opportunity" to learn language? Are the results conclusive? Explain.

Cognitive and Emotional Development

Reader's Guide

■ **Main Idea**
As the thought processes of children develop, they begin to think, communicate and relate with others, and solve problems.

■ **Vocabulary**
- schema
- assimilation
- accommodation
- object permanence
- representational thought
- conservation
- egocentric
- imprinting
- critical period

■ **Objectives**
- Summarize the cognitive-development theory.
- Discuss how children develop emotionally.

EXPLORING PSYCHOLOGY

What Is She Thinking?

At [2 years and 4 months old] L. heard water running in the bathroom upstairs. She was with me in the garden and said to me: *"That's daddy up there."* At [2 years and 5 months old] L. went with her uncle to his car and saw him drive off along the road. She then went back into the house, and went straight to the drawing-room, where he had been earlier, and said: *"I want to see if uncle C. has gone."* She went in, looked all round the room and said: *"Yes, he's gone."*

—from *Plays, Dreams and Imitation in Childhood* by **Jean Piaget**, 1962

P sychologist Jean Piaget (1896–1980) chronicled the development of thought in his own daughter ("L."). From the stories Piaget described above, it is obvious that children think differently from adults in many ways. Children form their own hypotheses about how the world works.

COGNITIVE DEVELOPMENT

If you have a younger brother or sister, you may remember times when your parents insisted that you let the little one play with you and your friends. No matter how often you explained hide-and-seek to your 4-year-old brother, he spoiled the game. Why couldn't he understand that he had to keep quiet or he would be found right away?

This is a question Swiss psychologist Jean Piaget set out to answer more than 60 years ago. According to him, intelligence, or the ability to understand, develops gradually as the child grows. The sharpest, most inquisitive 4-year-old simply cannot understand things a 7-year-old grasps easily. What accounts for the dramatic changes between the ages of 4 and 7?

Piaget spent years observing, questioning, and playing games with babies and young children—including his own. He concluded that young children think in a different way than older children and adults; they use a different kind of logic. A 7-year-old is completely capable of answering the question "Who was born first, you or your mother?" but a 4-year-old is not (Chukovsky, 1963). Intellectual development involves quantitative changes (growth in the *amount* of information) as well as qualitative changes (differences in the *manner* of thinking).

How Knowing Changes

Understanding the world involves the construction of **schemas,** or mental representations of the world. Each of us constructs intellectual schemas, applying them and changing them as necessary. We try to understand a new or different object or concept by using one of our preexisting schemas. In the process of **assimilation,** we try to fit the new object into this schema. In the process of **accommodation,** we change our schema to fit the characteristics of the new object.

For example, suppose an infant encounters a new block. The block fits his schema for other blocks he has encountered before. He may fit it into his stacking schema. The infant has stacked blocks before and can easily assimilate the new block into the existing schema. Suppose the infant then encounters an open box. He may at first try to fit the box into his stacking schema but finds that a block just falls inside the box. Now the stacking schema must be altered to accommodate this new object.

Assimilation and accommodation work together to produce intellectual growth. When events do not fit into existing schemas, new and grander schemas have to be created. The child begins to see and understand things in new ways.

Object Permanence An infant's understanding of things lies totally in the here and now. The sight of a toy, the way it feels in her hands, and the sensation it produces in her mouth are all she knows. She does not imagine it, picture it, think of it, remember it, or even forget it. When an infant's toy is hidden from her, she acts as if it has ceased to exist. She does not look for it. Instead, she grabs whatever else she can find and

More About...

Imaginary Playmates

There's nothing new about imaginary playmates—children have always had them. Our understanding about the role of imaginary playmates in the development of children, though, has grown. Dr. Jerome L. and Dr. Dorothy G. Singer studied a group of 3- and 4-year-olds, and found a number of differences between children with imaginary playmates and those without. For example:

- More than half of the children have imaginary playmates.
- Children with imaginary playmates are less aggressive and more cooperative than other children.
- They are rarely bored and have a rich vocabulary, far advanced for their age.
- They watch fewer hours of television than other children.
- They have a greater ability to concentrate.

Above all, imaginary playmates seem to fill a gap in children's lives and are especially important to children who are first-born or who have no brothers and sisters. They are an adaptive mechanism that helps children get through the boring times in life.

schema: a specific plan for knowing the world

assimilation: the process of fitting objects and experiences into one's schemas

accommodation: the adjustment of one's schemas to include newly observed events and experiences

Reading Check
How are assimilation and accommodation different?

PSYCHOLOGY Online

Student Web Activity
Visit the *Understanding Psychology* Web site at psychology.glencoe.com and click on **Chapter 3—Student Web Activities** for an activity about infancy and childhood.

plays with that, or she may simply start crying. At 7 to 12 months, however, this pattern begins to change. When you take the infant's toy and hide it under a blanket—while she is watching—she will search for it under the blanket. However, if you change tactics and put her toy behind your back, she will continue to look for it under the blanket—even if she was watching you the whole time.

You cannot fool a 12- to 18-month-old quite so easily. A child this age watches closely and searches for the toy in the last place she saw you put it. Suppose you take the toy, put it under the blanket, conceal it in your hands, and then put it behind your back. A 12-month-old will act surprised when she does not find the toy under the blanket—and keep searching there. An 18- or 24-month-old will guess what you have done and walk behind you to look (see Figure 3.7). She knows the toy must be somewhere (Ginsburg & Opper, 1969).

This is a giant step in intellectual development. The child has progressed from a stage where she apparently believed that her own actions created the world, to a stage where she realizes that people and objects are independent of her actions. Piaget called this concept **object permanence.** This concept might be expressed in this way: "Things continue to exist even though they cannot be seen or touched." It signifies a big step in the second year of life.

object permanence: a child's realization that an object exists even when he or she cannot see or touch it

representational thought: the intellectual ability of a child to picture something in his or her mind

Representational Thought The achievement of object permanence suggests that a child has begun to engage in what Piaget calls **representational thought.** The child's intelligence is no longer one of

---

Figure 3.7 | Showing Object Permanence

A child that lacks object permanence will reach for a visible toy but not for one that is hidden behind a barrier—even if the child has seen someone place the toy behind the barrier. The child below, however, displays object permanence. *At what age should a child begin to understand the concept of object permanence?*

action only. Now, children can picture (or represent) things in their minds. At 14 months of age, Piaget's daughter demonstrated this. When she was out visiting another family, she happened to witness a child throwing a temper tantrum. She had never had a tantrum herself, but the next day she did—screaming, shaking her playpen, and stamping her feet as the other child had. She had formed so clear an image of the tantrum in her mind that she was able to create an excellent imitation a day later (Ginsburg & Opper, 1969). To Piaget, this meant that his daughter was using symbols. Soon she would learn to use a much more complex system of symbols—spoken language.

conservation: the principle that a given quantity does not change when its appearance is changed

egocentric: a young child's inability to understand another person's perspective

The Principle of Conservation

More complex intellectual abilities emerge as the infant grows into childhood. Between the ages of 5 and 7, most children begin to understand what Piaget calls **conservation,** the principle that a given quantity does not change when its appearance is changed. For example, if you have two identical short, wide jars filled with water and you pour the contents of one of these jars into a tall, thin jar, a child under 5 will say that the tall jar contains more water than the short one. If you pour the water back into the short jar to show the amount has not changed, the child will still maintain that there was more water in the tall container. Children under 5 do not seem to be able to think about two dimensions (height and width) at the same time. That is, they do not understand that a change in width is made up for by a change in the height of the tall glass (see Figure 3.8). This happens because children are **egocentric.** Egocentric thinking refers to seeing and thinking of the world from

Profiles In Psychology

Jean Piaget
1896–1980

"[T]he child no longer tends to approach the state of adulthood by receiving reason and the rules of right action ready-made, but by achieving them with his own effort and personal experience; in return society expects more of its new generations than mere imitation: it expects enrichment."

Born in Switzerland, Jean Piaget sought to answer one question in his life work: How does knowledge grow? He studied his three children and thousands of other children to answer this question. Piaget spent his time watching children play and playing with them. He told them stories and listened to their stories, asking them questions about why things are as they are. He invented problems for them to solve and asked them what they dreamt about.

What did Piaget discover? He discovered that knowledge builds as children grow. Children develop logic and think differently at different ages. Psychologists regard Piaget's discovery as revolutionary and insightful. Piaget's theory challenged the behaviorists' view that the environment determines behavior. Piaget stressed a child's active role in gaining knowledge. For these contributions, many consider Piaget the greatest child psychologist of the twentieth century.

your own standpoint and having difficulty understanding someone else's viewpoint and other perspectives. By age 7, the same child will tell you that the second jar contains the same amount of water as the first.

Piaget's Stages of Cognitive Development   Piaget described the changes that occur in children's understanding in four stages of cognitive development (see Figure 3.9). During the *sensorimotor stage*, the young infant uses schemas that primarily involve his body and sensations. The *preoperational stage* emerges when the child begins to use mental images or symbols to understand things. By the third, *concrete operations stage*, children are able to use logical schemas, but their understanding is limited to concrete objects or problems. In the *formal operations stage,* the person is able to solve abstract problems. According to Piaget, a person's development through these four stages depends on both the maturation of his or her nervous system and on the kinds of experiences he or she has had. Everyone goes through the stages in the same order, but not necessarily at the same age.

EMOTIONAL DEVELOPMENT

While the child is developing his ability to use his body, to think, and to express himself, he is also developing emotionally. He begins to become attached to specific people and to care about what they think and feel.

Figure 3.8	Tasks to Measure Conservation

The concept of conservation can be used to show that children think less logically than adults do. Children in the preoperational stage do not understand that the property of a substance remains the same although its appearance may change. *How is conservation related to egocentric thinking?*

Type of conservation	First display	Second display	Child is asked
Length	The child agrees that the sticks are of equal length.	The experimenter moves one stick over.	*Which stick is longer?* Preconserving child will say that one stick is longer. Conserving child will say that they are the same length.
Substance amount	The child acknowledges that the two balls have equal amounts of clay.	The experimenter rolls out one of the balls.	*Do the two pieces have the same amount of clay?* Preconserving child will say that the long piece has more clay. Conserving child will say that the two pieces have the same amount of clay.

Figure 3.9   Piaget's Stages of Cognitive Development

Piaget stressed the active role of the child in gaining knowledge. He also stressed the differences in the way a child thinks during different stages of maturity. *At which of Piaget's stages do children lack the concept of conservation?*

Stage	Approximate Age	General Characteristics
Sensorimotor	Birth–1½ years	Behavior consists of simple motor responses to sensory stimuli; lacks concept of object permanence
Preoperational	1½ years–7 years	Lacks operations (reversible mental processes); exhibits egocentric thinking; lacks concept of conservation; uses symbols (such as words or mental images) to solve simple problems or to talk about things that are not present
Concrete operations	7–11 years	Begins to understand concept of conservation; still has trouble with abstract ideas; classification abilities improve; masters concept of conservation
Formal operations	11 years–onward	Understands abstract ideas and hypothetical situations; capable of logical and deductive reasoning

Experiments With Animals

Experiments with baby birds and monkeys have shown that there is a maturationally determined time of readiness for attachment early in life. If the infant is too young or too old, the attachment cannot be formed, but the attachment itself is a kind of learning. If the attachment is not made, or if a different attachment is made, the infant will develop in a different way as a result.

Imprinting   Konrad Lorenz became a pioneer in the field of animal learning. Lorenz discovered that baby geese become attached to their mothers in a sudden, virtually permanent learning process called **imprinting.** A few hours after they struggle out of their shells, goslings are ready to start waddling after the first thing they see that moves. Whatever it is, they usually stay with it and treat it as though it were their mother from that time on. Usually, of course, the first thing they see is the mother goose. Yet Lorenz found that if he substituted himself or some moving object like a green box being dragged along the ground, the goslings would follow that. Lorenz's goslings followed him wherever he went and ran to him when frightened (see Figure 3.10). Goslings are especially sensitive just after birth, and whatever they learn during this critical period, about 13 to 16 hours after birth, makes a deep impression that resists change. A **critical period** is a time in development when an animal (or human) is best able to learn a skill or behavior. If geese have been imprinted with a human being instead of a goose, they will prefer the company of human beings to other geese. Imprinting is important for survival purposes.

imprinting: inherited tendencies or responses that are displayed by newborn animals when they encounter new stimuli in their environment

critical period: a specific time in development when certain skills or abilities are most easily learned

Figure 3.10

The Process of Imprinting

Konrad Lorenz was the first moving object these goslings saw after they hatched, so they became imprinted on him. **How is imprinting related to survival?**

Surrogate Mothers

An American psychologist, Harry Harlow, studied the relationship between mother and child in a species closer to humans, the rhesus monkey. His first question was: What makes the mother so important? He tried to answer this question by taking baby monkeys away from their natural mothers as soon as they were born. (This is described further in Chapter 12.) Harlow raised the monkeys with two surrogate, or substitute, mothers. Each monkey could choose between a mother constructed of wood and wire and a mother constructed in the same way but covered with soft, cuddly terry cloth. In some cages, the cloth mother was equipped with a bottle; in others, the wire mother was.

The results were dramatic. The young monkeys became strongly attached to the cloth mother, whether she gave food or not, and for the most part ignored the wire mother. If a frightening object was placed in the monkey's cage, the baby monkey would run to the cloth mother for security, not to the wire mother. It was the touching—physical contact comfort—that mattered, not the feeding. Harlow called this contact comfort or tactile touch. He concluded that the monkeys clung to their mothers because of the need for contact comfort.

Human Infants

Is there a critical period when infants need to become attached to a caregiver, as Lorenz's experiments suggest? Some psychologists would answer this question with a firm "yes." Infants begin to form an attachment to their mothers (or to a surrogate mother) at about 6 months, when they are able to distinguish one person from another and are beginning to develop object permanence. This attachment seems to be especially strong between the ages of 6 months and 3 years. By 3 years, the child has developed to the stage where he is able to remember and imagine his mother and maintain a relationship with her (in fantasy) even if she is absent.

When an attachment bond to one person has been formed, disruption can be disturbing to the infant. (Attachment is a deep, caring, close, and enduring emotional bond between an infant and caregiver.) For example, when a 1-year-old child encounters a stranger, that child may display anxiety even when the mother is present. If the mother remains nearby, this *stranger anxiety* will pass. *Separation anxiety* occurs whenever the child is suddenly separated from the mother. If the separation persists, the child may develop psychological disorders.

Mary Ainsworth studied attachment in families with John Bowlby (Ainsworth & Bowlby, 1991). Ainsworth devised a technique called the

This monkey went to the cloth surrogate mother for comfort and reassurance.

Strange Situation to measure attachment. In this technique, mothers and children undergo a series of episodes that sometimes involved the mother leaving and coming back into the room when a stranger was present and when a stranger was not present. From her research, she found there were three patterns of attachment in children: *secure attachment, avoidant attachment,* and *resistant attachment.* Psychologists have since identified a fourth attachment, called *disorganized attachment.*

Infants who demonstrate secure attachment balance the need to explore and the need to be close. They welcome the mother back when she leaves and are free of anger. In avoidant attachment, the infants avoid or ignore the mother when she leaves and returns. The infants with resistant attachment are not upset when the mother leaves but reject her or act angrily when she returns. The infants with disorganized attachment behave inconsistently. They seem confused and act in contradictory ways. They may not be upset when the mother leaves but then they avoid her when she returns. This attachment seems to be the least secure attachment. (Mothers who are sensitive and responsive tend to have securely attached infants. However, there is a complex interplay between caregivers and infants.)

Quick Lab

How do children exhibit attachment?

How do children show emotional attachment to their parents or caregivers?

Procedure
1. Observe a 1- or 2-year-old child with a parent or caregiver for signs of emotional attachment. A day care center, a pediatrician's waiting room, or a play area in a shopping mall are good places to observe.
2. Watch for the following: How often does the child make contact with his or her parent? Does the child move away and explore? How does the child respond to unfamiliar people or objects?

Analysis
1. Does the child exhibit separation anxiety? What were the signs?
2. In a short paragraph, assess the emotional attachment of the child you observed.

See the Skills Handbook, page 622, for an explanation of designing an experiment.

SECTION 2 | Assessment

1. **Review the Vocabulary** Why do infants construct schemas?

2. **Visualize the Main Idea** Using Piaget's stages, create a time line that tracks the cognitive development of a child. See the example below.

Sensorimotor

Birth | 1 year | 2 years

• Child displays simple motor responses to sensory stimuli.

3. **Recall Information** What does it mean when people say children are egocentric?

4. **Think Critically** How might a child who displays avoidant attachment react when placed alone in a strange room?

5. Application Activity Design your own test for object permanence. Use several objects and test a younger sibling, cousin, or your pet dog or cat to see if they search for hidden objects. Describe the results of your experiment.

Parenting Styles and Social Development

Reader's Guide

■ Main Idea
Children face various social decisions as they grow and progress through the stages of life.

■ Vocabulary
- authoritarian family
- democratic/authoritative family
- permissive/laissez-faire family
- socialization
- identification
- sublimation
- role taking

■ Objectives
- Describe theories of social development.
- Outline Kohlberg's stages of moral reasoning.

EXPLORING PSYCHOLOGY

A Day in the Life of a Preschool Teacher

"Hey you two—just pretend to eat, remember? If you put those spoons in your mouth, you'll pick up germs. Just pretend to use them."

That afternoon, the same two boys engaged in a mock karate battle on the playground. Hitting and kicking is forbidden in my class, regardless of whether it hurts anyone or not. To listen to them protesting the time-out, you'd think they'd never heard the rule.

"We weren't fighting!"

"You were kicking." I said sternly. "We don't kick here."

"But we weren't kicking!" they protested. "We were pretend-kicking, just like pretend-eating."

—from "Little People's Logic" by Sarah Starr

The story above comes from a preschool teacher. She concluded that children do not necessarily draw the conclusions you intend them to. The children involved in the "pretend-eating" and "pretend-kicking" did not follow the teacher's logic. The teacher explained the difference between acceptable "pretend-eating" and "pretend-fighting" by stating, "Sometimes people get hurt even when you pretend to fight." Children learn the rules for behavior in society through experiences such as this one.

PARENTING STYLES

The way in which children seek independence and the ease with which they resolve conflicts about becoming adults depend in large part on the parent-child relationship. Diana Baumrind (1971, 1973) observed and interviewed nursery school children and their parents. Follow-up observations when the children were 8 or 9 led to several conclusions about the impact of three distinct parenting styles on children.

In **authoritarian families** parents are the "bosses." They do not believe that they have to explain their actions or demands. In fact, such parents may believe the child has no right to question parental decisions.

In **democratic** or **authoritative families** children participate in decisions affecting their lives. There is a great deal of discussion and negotiation in such families. Parents listen to their children's reasons for wanting to go somewhere or do something and make an effort to explain their rules and expectations. The children make many decisions for themselves, but the parents retain the right to veto plans of which they disapprove.

Figure 3.11   Parents and Children

Diana Baumrind's research focused on European-American children, but parenting styles may differ across cultures and groups. *According to research on European-American children, which parenting style seems to lead to more confident children?*

In **permissive** or **laissez-faire families** children have the final say. The parents may attempt to guide the children but give in when the children insist on having their own way. Or the parents may simply give up their child-rearing responsibilities—setting no rules about behavior, making no demands, voicing no expectations, virtually ignoring the young people in their house.

Psychologists (Maccoby & Martin, 1983) later identified a fourth parenting style: *uninvolved parents.* These parents were typically very self-centered in their child rearing and seemed uncommitted to their role and quite distant from their child.

Effects of Parenting Styles

Numerous studies suggest that adolescents who have grown up in democratic or authoritative families are more confident of their own values and goals than other young people. This seems to come from two features—the *establishment of limits* on the child and *responding* to the child with warmth and support (Bukatko & Daehler, 1992). The children of democratic families are more likely to want to make their own decisions with or without advice. There are several reasons for this: First, the child is able to *assume responsibility gradually.* He or she is not denied the opportunity to exercise judgment (as in authoritarian families) or given too much responsibility too soon (as in permissive families). Second, the child is more likely to *identify with parents* who love and respect him or her than with parents who treat him or her as incompetent or who seem

authoritarian family: parents attempt to control, shape, and evaluate the behavior and attitudes of children in accordance with a set code of conduct

democratic/authoritative family: adolescents participate in decisions affecting their lives

permissive/laissez-faire family: children have the final say; parents are less controlling and have a nonpunishing, accepting attitude toward children

Nature vs. Nurture

Do you think that the way parents treat their children influences how those children will turn out? Judith Rich Harris does not think so (Harris, 1998). Harris argues that other than the genes parents contribute to their children, virtually nothing they do or say makes a difference in what kind of adult the child becomes. Harris further proposes that a child's natural, genetic tendencies make her parents behave a certain way.

Harris claims that peer groups, not parents, teach children how to behave in the world. So the only influence parents are able to have over their children, then, is by supplying the environment in which their children meet other peers. For example, parents should live in a good neighborhood so their children associate with the "right" peers.

Many psychologists passionately criticize Harris's theory. Critics claim that there is a very strong relationship between parenting styles and the social development of children. They argue that although two children may share the same parents, they may be treated differently by them and, thus, turn out differently.

indifferent. Finally, through their behavior toward the child, democratic parents *present a model of responsible, cooperative independence* for the growing person to imitate.

Although the style parents adopt in dealing with their children influences adolescent development, it would be wrong to conclude that parents are solely responsible for the way their children turn out. Children themselves may contribute to the style parents embrace, with consequences for their own personal development. Parents may adopt a laissez-faire attitude simply because they find that style the easiest way to cope with a teenager who insists on having his or her own way. Adolescents experiencing rapid physical and emotional changes may force their parents to make major adjustments in their parenting style.

CHILD ABUSE

Child abuse includes the physical or mental injury, sexual abuse, negligent treatment, or mistreatment of children under the age of 18 by adults entrusted with their care. Accurate statistics are difficult to compile, since many incidents of child abuse go unreported. In 1996 about 3 million cases of child abuse were reported. After investigation, an estimated 1 million children were confirmed as victims of actual abuse or neglect situations (American Humane Association, 1999).

Child abuse is viewed as a social problem resulting from a variety of causes. Many abusive parents were themselves mistreated as children, suggesting that these parents may have learned an inappropriate way of caring for children. Such parents tend to use the harsh physical discipline that they saw their own parents using. Many abusive parents have little patience with their children. Often they have unrealistic expectations for them.

Overburdened and stressed parents are more likely to abuse their children. Low-birthweight infants and those children who are hyperactive or mentally or physically disadvantaged experience a higher than normal incidence of abuse. One reason for this higher incidence may be that such children are less responsive and more difficult to care for, thus making greater demands on and providing fewer rewards for the parents (Belsky, 1984; Pianta, Egelands, & Erikson, 1989). Social-cultural stresses such as unemployment and lack of contact with family, friends, and groups in the community are other factors associated with child abuse.

The most effective way of stopping child abuse is to prevent future incidents. Parent education for abusive parents allows them to learn new ways of dealing with their children. By providing information about resources and a support system for these families, communities may reduce the incidence of child abuse.

Abuse has many developmental effects for its victims. It may rob children of their childhood and create a loss of trust and feelings of guilt, which in turn may lead to antisocial behavior, depression, identity confusion, loss of self-esteem, and other emotional problems. Every state and most counties have social services agencies that provide protective services to children. They have legal authority to investigate reported incidents of child abuse.

SOCIAL DEVELOPMENT

Learning the rules of behavior of the culture in which you are born and grow up is called **socialization.** To live with other people, a child has to learn what is considered acceptable and unacceptable behavior. This is not as easy as it sounds. Some social rules are clear and inflexible. Other social rules leave room for individual decisions, so that sometimes there seems to be a "gray area" between right and wrong. Some rules change from situation to situation. Some apply to certain categories of people. For example, some rules for boys in our society are different from the rules for girls. We tend to encourage boys to express aggression but not fear; traditionally, girls have been raised to express emotions but not ambitions. Of course, the rules for feminine behavior have changed over the years.

Learning what the rules are—when to apply and when to bend them—is, however, only one dimension of socialization. Every society has ideas about what is meaningful, valuable, worth striving for, and beautiful. Every society classifies people according to their family, sex, age, skills, personality characteristics, and other criteria. Every culture has notions about what makes individuals behave as they do. In absorbing these notions, a child acquires an identity as a member of a particular society, a member of different social categories, a member of a family—and an identity as an individual. This is a second dimension of socialization.

Finally, socialization involves learning to live with other people and with yourself. Anyone who has seen the shock of a 2-year-old's face when another child his age takes a toy he wants, or the frustration and humiliation a 4-year-old experiences when she discovers she is unable to hit a baseball on the first try, knows how painful it can be to discover that other people have rights and that you have limitations.

Figure 3.12 Socializing

Socialization involves the way children learn to relate to other people. *What are the three dimensions of socialization?*

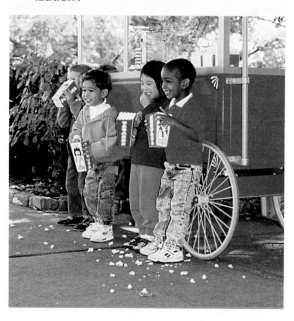

Reading Check
What is an effective way of stopping child abuse?

socialization: the process of learning the rules of behavior of the culture within which an individual is born and will live

Freud's Theory of Psychosexual Development

Sigmund Freud believed that all children are born with powerful sexual and aggressive urges. In learning to control these impulses, children acquire a sense of right and wrong. The process—and the results—are different for boys and girls.

According to Freud, in the first few years of life, boys and girls have similar experiences. Their erotic pleasures are obtained through the mouth, sucking at their mother's breast. Weaning the child from nursing is a period of frustration and conflict—it is the child's first experience with not getting what he wants. Freud called this the *oral stage* of development (see Figure 3.13). Later the anus becomes the source of erotic pleasure, giving rise to what Freud called the *anal stage*. Through toilet training the child learns to curb freedom and establish social control.

A major conflict comes between the ages of 3 and 5, when children discover the pleasure they can obtain from their genitals. As a consequence, they become extremely aware of the differences between themselves and members of the opposite sex. In this *phallic stage,* according to Freud, the child becomes a rival for the affections of the parent of the opposite sex. The boy wants to win his mother for himself and finds himself in hostile conflict with his father. The girl wants her father for herself and tries to shut out her mother. These struggles take place on an unconscious level. Generally, the child and the parents do not have any clear awareness that it is going on. In this process, which is called **identification** with the aggressor, the boy takes on all his father's values and moral principles. Thus, at the same time that he learns to behave like a man, he internalizes his father's morality. His father's voice becomes a voice inside him, the voice of conscience. The girl also goes through this process and begins to identify with her mother. She feels her mother's triumphs and failures as if they were her own, and she internalizes her mother's moral code.

Freud believed that at about age 5 children enter a *latency stage*. Sexual desires are pushed into the background, and children explore the world and learn new skills. This process of redirecting sexual impulses into learning tasks is called **sublimation.** Ideally, when one reaches the *genital stage* at adolescence, one derives as much satisfaction from giving pleasure as from receiving it. For Freud, personality development is essentially complete as we enter adolescence. Today relatively few psychologists believe that sexual feelings disappear in childhood.

identification: the process by which a child adopts the values and principles of the same-sex parent

sublimation: the process of redirecting sexual impulses into learning tasks

Figure 3.13	Freud's Stages of Psychosexual Development

According to Freud, there is often conflict between child and parent. The conflict occurs because the child wants immediate gratification of needs while the parent restricts that gratification in some way. *At what stage do children compete with their parents?*

Oral Stage
Infant's pleasure seeking focused on the mouth.
Ages: first 18 months of life

Anal Stage
Infant's pleasure seeking centered on functions of elimination.
Ages: 1½ years – 3 years

Phallic Stage
Infant's pleasure seeking focused on the genitals.
Ages: 3 – 6 years

Latency Stage
Sexual thoughts repressed; child focuses on developing social and intellectual skills.
Ages: 6 years to puberty

Genital Stage
Sexual desires are renewed; individual seeks relationships with others.
Ages: puberty through adulthood

Erikson's Theory of Psychosocial Development

Erik Erikson takes a broader view of human development than Freud in terms of both time and scope. Although he recognizes the child's sexual and aggressive urges, he believes that the need for social approval is just as important. Erikson studied what he called *psychosocial* development. (Psychosocial development refers to life periods in which an individual's goal is to satisfy desires associated with social needs.) Although he believes that childhood experiences have a lasting impact on the individual, he sees development as a lifelong interactive process between people (see Figure 3.14).

Erikson argues that we all face many "crises"—as we grow from infancy to old age, as we mature and people expect more from us. Each of these crises represents an issue that everyone faces. The child—or adolescent or adult—may develop more strongly in one way or another, depending on how other people respond to his or her efforts.

For example, the 2-year-old is delighted with his newfound ability to walk, to get into things, to use words, and to ask questions. The very fact that he has acquired these abilities adds to his self-esteem, and he is eager to use them. If the adults around him applaud his efforts and acknowledge his achievements, he begins to develop a sense of autonomy, or independence. However, if they ignore him except to punish him for going too far or being a nuisance, the child may begin to doubt the value of his achievements. He may also feel shame because the people around him act as if his new desire for independence is bad.

Reading Check
How does Erikson's view of development differ from Freud's?

Learning Theories of Development

Both Freud and Erikson stress the emotional dynamics of social development. Their theories suggest that learning social rules is altogether different from learning to ride a bicycle or to speak a foreign language. Many psychologists disagree. They believe children learn the ways of their social world because they are rewarded for conforming and because they copy older children and adults in anticipation of future rewards. In other words, social development is simply a matter of conditioning and imitation. (See Chapter 9 for a discussion of these concepts.)

The Cognitive-Developmental Approach

Theorists who emphasize the role of cognition or thinking in development view the growing child quite differently. Learning theory implies that the child is essentially passive—a piece of clay to be shaped. The people who administer rewards and punishments and serve as models do the shaping. Cognitive theorists see the *child* as the shaper. Taking their cue from Jean Piaget, they argue that social development is the result of the child's acting on the environment and trying to make sense out of his experiences. The games children play illustrate this.

Games and Play Children's games are serious business. When left to their own devices, youngsters spend a great deal of time making up rules. This enables them to learn for themselves the importance of agreeing on a structure for group activities. A child can relax and enjoy himself without fear of rejection as long as he does not break the rules. The world of play thus becomes a miniature society, with its own rules and codes. Games also teach children about aspects of adult life in a nonthreatening way. In young children's games, it is the experience of playing, not winning, that counts.

Much of the children's play involves **role taking.** Youngsters try on such adult roles as mother, father, teacher, storekeeper, explorer, and rock star. Role taking allows them to learn about different points of view firsthand. Suppose a child plays a mother opposite another child who plays a whiny, disobedient baby. When she finds herself totally frustrated by the other child's nagging, she begins to understand why her mother gets mad. You are unable to cook even a pretend meal when the baby keeps knocking over the pots and pans.

role taking: children's play that involves assuming adult roles, thus enabling the child to experience different points of view

Moral Development   Lawrence Kohlberg's studies show just how important being able to see other people's points of view is to social development in general and to moral development in particular. Kohlberg (1968) studied the development of moral reasoning—deciding what is right and what is wrong—by presenting children of different ages with a series of moral dilemmas. For example: In Europe, a woman was near death from

---

Figure 3.14   **Erikson's Stages of Psychosocial Development**

According to Erikson, a child encounters a psychosocial challenge at each stage. If the child successfully resolves the issue, the child develops a positive social trait and progresses to the next stage. *What issues concern a child in the first year of life?*

Stage 8: Ego integrity versus despair
Ages: older adult
Have I lived a full life?

Stage 7: Generativity versus stagnation
Ages: middle adult
Will I succeed in life?

Stage 6: Intimacy versus isolation
Ages: young adult
Shall I share my life with someone or live alone?

Stage 5: Identity versus role confusion
Ages: early teens
Who am I?

Stage 4: Industry versus inferiority
Ages: 6 – 12
Am I successful or worthless?

Stage 3: Initiative versus guilt
Ages: 3 – 6 years
Am I good or bad?

Stage 2: Autonomy versus shame and doubt
Ages: 1 – 3 years
Can I do things myself or must I rely on others?

Stage 1: Trust versus mistrust
Ages: early infancy
Is my world predictable and supportive?

---

cancer. One drug might save her, a form of radium that a druggist in the same town had recently discovered. The druggist was charging $2,000, ten times what the drug cost him to make. The sick woman's husband, Heinz, went to everyone he knew to borrow the money, but he could get together only about half of what it cost. He told the druggist that his wife was dying and asked him to sell it cheaper or let him pay later. But the druggist said "No." The husband got desperate and broke into the man's store to steal the drug for his wife. Should the husband have done that? Why?

What interested Kohlberg was how the children arrived at a conclusion. He wanted to know what sort of reasoning they used. After questioning 84 children, Kohlberg identified six stages of moral development (see Figure 3.15). He then replicated his findings in several different cultures.

Stages of Moral Development In stage one, children are totally egocentric. They do not consider other people's points of view and have no sense of right and wrong. Their main concern is avoiding punishment. A child in this stage will say that the man should steal because people will blame him for his wife's death if he does not, or that he should not steal because he might go to prison.

Children in stage two have a better idea of how to receive rewards as well as to avoid punishment. Youngsters at this level interpret the Golden Rule as "help someone if he helps you, and hurt him if he hurts you." They are still egocentric and premoral, evaluating acts in terms of the consequences, not in terms of right and wrong.

In stage three, children become acutely sensitive to what other people want and think. A child in this stage will say that the man in the story should steal because people will think he is cruel if he lets his wife die, or that he should not steal because people will think he is a criminal. In other words, children want social approval in stage three, so they apply the rules other people have decreed literally and rigidly.

In stage four, a child is less concerned with the approval of others. The key issue here is "law and order"—a law is seen as a moral rule and is obeyed because of a strong belief in established authority. For example, a woman may stay married because she gave her "word," or a driver may obey the speed limit when no police are around. Moral thinking here, as at stage three, is quite rigid.

In the remaining two stages, people continue to broaden their perspective. The stage-five person is primarily concerned with whether a law is fair or just. He believes that laws must change as the world changes, and they are never absolute. The important question is whether a given law is good for society as a whole. Stage six involves an acceptance of ethical principles that apply to everyone, like the Golden Rule: "Do unto others as you would have them do unto you." Such moral "laws" cannot be broken—they are more important than any written law.

Critics point out a gender bias in Kohlberg's theory (Gilligan, 1977). Whereas girls might argue that both stealing and letting Heinz's wife die are wrong, boys might logically argue that life has greater value than

Figure 3.15

Kohlberg's Stages of Moral Development

Kohlberg investigated why people make the moral decisions they make. Each stage of his theory is cognitively more complex than the last. *Why would a child in the first stage choose to listen to her parents?*

Level	Stage	Orientation	Example
Pre-conventional	1	Obedience and punishment	I don't steal cookies because mommy would get mad at me.
	2	Instrumental relativist	For a cookie, I will clean my room.
Conventional	3	"Good boy/Nice girl"	I don't misbehave because my teacher doesn't like it.
	4	"Law and order"	I don't steal because it's against the law.
Post-conventional	5	Social contract	I don't steal because society has made a law against stealing. (The law benefits society.)
	6	Universal ethics principle	I don't steal because it is wrong.

property. Using these arguments, Kohlberg would place boys at higher levels of moral development. Girls are taught to be empathetic, whereas boys are taught the goal of justice.

To reach the highest levels of moral development, a child must first be able to see other people's points of view. Yet this understanding is no guarantee that a person will respect the rights of others. Thus, the development of thinking or cognitive abilities influences moral development.

SECTION 3 Assessment

1. **Review the Vocabulary** Describe Freud's theory of socialization.

2. **Visualize the Main Idea** Describe parenting styles using a chart similar to the one below.

Parenting Style	Role of Parents	Role of Children

3. **Recall Information** What are the functions of children's games? How do these games illustrate the cognitive-developmental approach?

4. **Think Critically** What questions might you ask a child to determine what stage of moral development he or she is in?

5. **Application Activity** Go to a public place where you can observe children, such as a playground, park, or shopping mall. Note the behaviors between parents and child and among the children as they play together. Record and analyze your observations. Describe the different parenting styles you observed.

Summary and Vocabulary

Developmental psychology is the study of the changes that occur as people grow up and grow older. It covers the entire life cycle, from conception to death.

Section 1 — Physical, Perceptual, and Language Development

Main Idea: Infants are born equipped to experience the world. As infants grow physically, they also develop perceptions and language.

- Some psychologists believe that most behaviors are the result of genetics—nature. Others believe that most behaviors are the result of experience and learning—nurture.
- The newborn is capable of certain inherited, automatic, coordinated movement patterns, called reflexes, which are triggered by the right stimulus.
- Infants experience rapid physical growth through maturation and learning.
- Depth perception increases in older infants.
- There are several steps involved in learning language.

Section 2 — Cognitive and Emotional Development

Main Idea: As the thought processes of children develop, they begin to think, communicate and relate with others, and solve problems.

- Children's knowledge of the world changes through the processes of assimilation and accommodation.
- Piaget described the changes that occur in children's understanding in four stages of cognitive development.
- Infants begin to develop emotionally by attaching to specific people, usually their mother.

Section 3 — Parenting Styles and Social Development

Main Idea: Children face various social decisions as they grow and progress through the stages of life.

- There are four basic parenting styles—authoritarian, democratic or authoritative, permissive or laissez-faire, and uninvolved.
- Socialization is the process of learning the rules of behavior of one's culture.
- Freud's theory of psychosexual development suggests that all children are born with powerful sexual and aggressive urges, and in learning to control these impulses, children acquire a sense of right and wrong.
- Erikson's theory of psychosocial development suggests that the need for social approval is important.
- The cognitive-developmental theories of development suggest that social development is the result of the child trying to make sense out of his experiences.
- Kohlberg suggested that humans progress through six stages of moral reasoning.

Chapter Vocabulary

developmental psychology (p. 61)
grasping reflex (p. 62)
rooting reflex (p. 62)
maturation (p. 64)
telegraphic speech (p. 67)
schema (p. 71)
assimilation (p. 71)
accommodation (p. 71)
object permanence (p. 72)
representational thought (p. 72)
conservation (p. 73)
egocentric (p. 73)
imprinting (p. 75)
critical period (p. 75)
authoritarian family (p. 79)
democratic/authoritative family (p. 79)
permissive/laissez-faire family (p. 79)
socialization (p. 81)
identification (p. 82)
sublimation (p. 82)
role taking (p. 84)

Self-Check Quiz
Visit the *Understanding Psychology* Web site at
psychology.glencoe.com and click on **Chapter 3—
Self-Check Quizzes** to prepare for the Chapter Test.

Reviewing Vocabulary

Choose the letter of the correct term or concept below to complete the sentence.

a. rooting reflex
b. maturation
c. democratic/ authoritative families
d. telegraphic speech
e. schemas
f. object permanence
g. egocentric
h. socialization
i. sublimation
j. developmental psychology

1. _____ is the awareness that objects exist even when they cannot be perceived.
2. In _____, adults develop a parenting style in which children participate in decisions affecting their lives.
3. Because of the _____, a newborn who is touched anywhere around the mouth will move her head and mouth toward the source of the touch.
4. Seeing and thinking of the world only from one's own standpoint is called _____ thinking.
5. _____ is internally programmed growth.
6. Children at around age 2 use _____, in which words are left out but the message gets across.
7. The process of redirecting sexual impulses into learning tasks is _____.
8. To understand the world, children construct _____, or mental representations of the world.
9. The study of changes that occur as an individual matures is _____.
10. Learning the rules of behavior of one's culture is called _____.

Recalling Facts

1. Describe capacities newborns display.
2. How does the maturation process explain why a 4-month-old infant cannot be taught to walk?
3. Describe the process by which children learn to talk.
4. Define socialization and explain why it is so important to development.
5. Using a diagram similar to the one below, list and explain Kohlberg's stages of moral development.

Critical Thinking

1. **Demonstrating Reasoned Judgment** Do you think development is the result of heredity or the result of experience and learning or both? Why?
2. **Making Inferences** Should young children be treated as "little adults"? Based on what you have learned about development, do you think that is reasonable? Why or why not?
3. **Applying Concepts** Young children are egocentric. Provide some examples of children's egocentric thinking.
4. **Analyzing Concepts** What do you assume might happen when a boy plays with action-figure dolls? How does this behavior fit into the learning theories of development?
5. **Evaluating Information** Determine how well your beliefs agree with those of your parents. How important do you think your early social training was for what you believe?

CHAPTER 3 Assessment

Psychology Projects

1. **Physical, Perceptual, and Language Development** Investigate recent findings about the role of heredity and environment on a child's development. Present your information in an oral report.
2. **Social Development** How are sex roles communicated to people in American society? Look through magazines and newspapers, watch television commercials, and listen to the radio. Present your findings in an illustrated, captioned poster.
3. **Cognitive Development** Using information from the chapter as well as from other sources, present 10 ideas that people can use with children to increase their language and intellectual development. Explain how these 10 suggestions will increase a child's language and intellectual development.

Technology Activity

Use the Internet and computer software catalogs to find examples of computer software that parents and other adults can use with infants and small children. Explain what aspect of the child's development—physical, language, emotional, intellectual, and social—the software addresses.

Psychology Journal

Reread your journal entry about the sentences spoken by 2-year-olds. What sorts of words are used and in what context? Can you specify the grammatical rules children of this age use in combining words? Write your answers in your journal.

Building Skills

Interpreting a Graph Doctors often record infants' and young children's weight and height on growth charts similar to the one for girls here. The measurements are presented in the form of percentiles. For example, a 30-month-old girl who weighs 28.7 pounds falls into the 50th percentile. This means that half of all 30-month-old girls weigh less than that child and half weigh more. Review the growth chart, then answer the questions that follow.

1. Into what percentiles does an 18-month-old girl fall who weighs about 28 pounds and is 34 inches high?
2. Into what percentile would a 9-month-old girl fall who weighs 22 pounds?
3. How do growth charts illustrate that a child's physical development is unique?

 Practice and **assess** key social studies skills with **Glencoe Skillbuilder Interactive Workbook CD-ROM, Level 2.**

 See the Skills Handbook, page 628, for an explanation of interpreting graphs.

TIME REPORTS

Is It More Than Boys Being Boys?

Two books examine the emotional development of boys

By HARRIET BAROVICK

UNTIL KIP KINKEL OPENED FIRE ON his schoolmates in Springfield, Ore., in May, everyone thought he was just a regular kid. A little angry, maybe, with a gruesome sense of humor. Mostly, just a boy. But even before the frantic second-guessing over the tragedy began came two books to suggest that boys being boys—or what the world tries to make of boys—may have been a big part of the problem. Michael Gurian, a Spokane, Wash., therapist and author of *A Fine Young Man,* and Harvard psychiatry professor William Pollack, author of *Real Boys: Rescuing Our Sons from the Myths of Boyhood,* argue that boys are in crisis from emotional undernourishment. Though our culture views them as testosterone-driven demons, boys are much more fragile than many adults realize. And that's about all they agree on; where they clash is on the origin of the difficulties and how to avert them.

Both grapple with a universal truth: boys have complicated relationships with their mothers. Pollack, who is alarmed by what he calls the "silent crisis" of "normal" boys, says we live in a confused society in which mothers are afraid to cling to their sons. On the one hand, we ask 1990s boys to be sensitive and expressive, and on the other, we saddle them with the culture's outdated notions of masculinity. The result is what Pollack calls the ever present "boy code"—a stoic, uncommunicative, invulnerable stance that does not allow boys to be the warm, empathic human beings they are. The "gender straitjacketing" starts, Pollack says, during the early years, when boys suffer their first and most momentous trauma: premature separation from their well-meaning mothers. Fearful that maintaining a close connection will result in the shaming of their sons (name calling from peers, disapproval from adults), mothers disconnect, usually by the time their boys are five or six. When boys feel ashamed of their dependence on Mom, when they are discouraged from emotional expression, they withdraw, creatively and psychically. They become lost.

Not exactly, insists the anthropologically oriented Gurian, who focuses on adolescent boys. Boys—who are just being who they are—are making a natural, and critical, separation.

IRON JOHNNIES: Boys, says Gurian, love the rough and tumble but need attention, too.

And by the way, moms cling too much. Boys are more independent than girls at ages 5 and 6. To suggest something is wrong with this is to "pathologize" boys. Indignant about society's ignorance of male biology, Gurian says we're basing our expectations on female models.

One of the biggest problems for boys in our culture, says Gurian, is that adults, especially female ones, need to be educated about "what a boy is." Evolved from hunter-gatherer primates whose main purpose was survival, boys' uniquely fragile brains are not equipped to handle emotive data in the same way girls' are. So boys are by their nature emotionally insecure. At the same time, their several daily surges of testosterone "hardwire" them to be dominant and physically aggressive and to solve problems quickly. It is the job of parents—in particular, fathers or male mentors—to help them resolve this contradiction and channel their natural attributes productively.

Gurian concedes that a solid relationship with Mom is important during infancy and early childhood. But by age 10 or so, boy raising should largely be a man's game, where values such as honor, compassion, integrity and respect for women are handed down with discipline and understanding. The ability to talk about feelings is worth striving for, but boys don't come to it naturally. Besides, there are other, equally important ways of achieving intimacy.

So is there any agreement at all on how to help avert crises? Sort of. Both advise boy-specific nurturing techniques, like engaging in action-oriented activity that will lead to conversation instead of asking direct "How do you feel?" questions.

What Gurian and Pollack both bitterly lament—and convincingly illustrate—is the peculiar pain, and the potential loneliness, of being a boy in America today. Especially acute are the adolescent years, when boys look hulking and powerful but are in fact needy and terrified. The statistics are scary: adolescent boys are five times as likely to commit suicide as adolescent girls; adolescent boys are 1.5 times as likely as girls to be victims of violent crime; boys are more likely to be diagnosed with attention deficit disorder and mental illnesses; and boys commit violent crime at a higher rate than adults.

Sure, Gurian says, boys can't process emotional trauma as well as girls can, and without proper guidance can go haywire. And Pollack says misdirected rage is a response to emotional repression and to society's message that anger is an acceptable male emotion. The latter argument—like Pollack's overall idea—seems more expansive and more convincing. But either way, we clearly ought to be paying more attention. ■

Surviving Your Teens

Reviving Ophelia chronicles the traumas of troubled girls

By **ELIZABETH GLEICK**

IN THE LAND OF POPULAR PSYCHOLOGY books, nothing works so well as a bunch of case studies, paired with a lot of enthusiastic word of mouth. The No. 1 paperback best seller, Mary Pipher's *Reviving Ophelia: Saving the Selves of Adolescent Girls*, has the combination just right. Dozens of troubled teenage girls troop across its pages: composite sketches of Charlottes, Whitneys and Danielles who have faced traumatic psychological issues ranging from bulimia to enduring their parents' bitter divorce. There's a girl here for everyone: either the girl the reader once was or the sullen one now lolling about the reader's house listening to Hole.

PHENOMENON: Best-selling author Mary Pipher

"The book put a name and a face on something I was already sensing," says Annette Davis, a San Jose, California, mother of two, who has given copies of the book to her children's teachers. "It wasn't just about my daughter, though. It was about me. It spoke to something in my experience in adolescence and some of the pain I still carry around."

Thanks to readers like Davis, who are buying the book by the dozens to give to friends and showing up to hear Pipher, a Lincoln, Nebraska, clinical psychologist, speak, *Reviving Ophelia* has become a phenomenon. Originally rejected by 13 publishers, the hard-cover book was published in 1994 by Putnam. The book really took off, though, when the paperback came out last March.

Certainly the premise of *Reviving Ophelia* (which takes its title from the doomed Hamlet heroine) is a familiar one. Pipher believes adolescence is an especially precarious time for girls, a time when the fearless, outgoing child is replaced by the unhappy and insecure girl-woman. "Something dramatic happens to girls in early adolescence," Pipher writes. "Just as planes and ships disappear mysteriously into the Bermuda Triangle, so do the selves of girls go down in droves." She decided to write the book because her own practice was increasingly occupied by girls—mostly white and middle class, she says—coping with such problems as eating disorders, depression, substance abuse and self-mutilation.

Pipher's view—and what, no doubt, helps make her work so popular—is that, for the most part, the culture, not the parents, are to blame. Pipher points out that girls enter junior high school faced with daunting magazine and movie images of glossy, thin, perfect women. She argues that pop culture is saturated with sex; violence against women is rampant; and drugs and alcohol are far more accessible than they were during her 1950s girlhood in a small Nebraska town.

Pipher does offer commonsensical, unthreatening solutions. She suggests that parents immerse themselves in their daughters' life and take the trouble to learn about the pressures at school. And through therapy she tries to teach the girls to turn their pain outward: to write their angry thoughts in journals, rather than cut, starve or kill themselves; to get involved in charity work when they feel shunned by classmates; and to remind themselves daily of the ways in which they are valuable and unique. ■

—For the complete text of this article and related articles from TIME, please visit www.time.com/teach

ANALYZING THE ARTICLES

1. What is the "boy code"? Do you think such a code exists?
2. **CRITICAL THINKING** According to the books reviewed, what are the crises that adolescent males and females encounter? Are those crises really so different?

Adolescence

PSYCHOLOGY JOURNAL

According to psychologist Erik Erikson, building an identity is a task that is unique to adolescence. Write in your journal two paragraphs that argue in favor of Erikson's point of view. ■

PSYCHOLOGY Online

Chapter Overview
Visit the *Understanding Psychology*
Web site at psychology.glencoe.com
and click on **Chapter 4—Chapter
Overviews** to preview the chapter.

Physical and Sexual Development

Reader's Guide

■ Main Idea

All adolescents experience dramatic changes in their physical size, shape, and capacities, as well as biological development related to reproduction.

■ Vocabulary

- initiation rites
- puberty
- menarche
- spermarche
- asynchrony

■ Objectives

- Describe the physical changes that characterize adolescence.
- Describe research related to the sexual attitudes and roles of adolescents.

EXPLORING PSYCHOLOGY

The Nature of Adolescence

Of all the periods in human life in which the instinctual processes are beyond question of paramount importance, that of puberty has always attracted most attention. Adolescents are excessively egotistic, regarding themselves as the center of the universe and the sole object of interest, and yet at no time in later life are they capable of so much self-sacrifice and devotion. . . . On the one hand they throw themselves enthusiastically into the life of the community and, on the other, they have an overpowering longing for solitude. They oscillate between blind submission to some self-chosen leader and defiant rebellion against any and every authority.

—from *The Ego and the Mechanisms of Defense* by Anna Freud, 1946

A s Anna Freud described above, adolescent development is complicated. Adolescence is the transition period between childhood and adulthood, and while we all have an idea about what adolescence is, defining it precisely is difficult. Some define it in psychological terms: a time period of mixed abilities and responsibilities in which childlike behavior changes to adultlike behavior. In some societies, adolescence is not recognized as a separate stage of life; individuals move directly from childhood to adulthood.

In our own society, however, adolescence is looked upon as a time of preparation for adult responsibilities (Hall, 1904). There are many

initiation rites: ceremonies or rituals in which an individual is admitted to new status or accepted into a new position

initiation rites, or rites of passage, that mark admission into adulthood. These rites include informal celebrations such as birthdays—at 16 or 18 or 21—as well as more formal events such as bar mitzvahs and bat mitzvahs, graduation from high school or college, and even weddings. Many of the new burdens of adulthood are assumed just when young people are undergoing complex physical and emotional changes that affect them both personally and socially. The end of adolescence and the beginning of adulthood is often blurry because it varies for each person.

Because so much is happening in these years, psychologists have focused a great deal of attention on the period of adolescence. We will concentrate on some of the major changes adolescents encounter.

THEORIES OF ADOLESCENCE

The contradictory views of society at large are reflected not just in the behavior of adolescents but in the theories of psychologists. Controversy concerning the nature of adolescent experience has raged since 1904, when G. Stanley Hall presented his pioneering theory of adolescence. Hall saw the adolescent as representing a transitional stage in our evolutionary development from beast to human. Being an adolescent for Hall was something like being a fully grown animal in a cage, an animal that sees freedom but does not know quite when freedom will occur or how to handle it. Thus, the adolescent was portrayed as existing in a state of great "storm and stress," as a marginal being, confused, troubled, and highly frustrated.

Through the years many psychologists and social scientists have supported Hall's theories, but there have been others who strongly disagreed. The latter theorists regard adolescence as a period of growth that is in no way discontinuous with the period of childhood that precedes and the period of young adulthood that follows.

One major proponent of this theory was Margaret Mead. In a series of classic anthropological studies in the late 1920s and early 1930s, Mead (1935) found that in some cultures, adolescence is a highly enjoyable time of life and not at all marked by storm and stress. She proposed that adolescent storm and stress was a by-product of an industrialized society. Mead proposed that culture might play a role in development.

Other studies conducted since then have tended to support Mead. They point to a relative lack of conflict in the lives of adolescents and a continuous development out of childhood that is based on individual reactions to their culture. In 1988 a report indicated that

Figure 4.1 Adolescence

Adolescents are stuck somewhere between childhood and adulthood. Most adolescents remain closely tied to their parents but spend more and more time with their peers. *Why has adolescence been characterized as a time of "storm and stress"?*

adolescence may be a difficult time period, but only 11 percent of adolescents encounter serious difficulties. Only 32 percent have sporadic problems, while 57 percent enjoy basically positive, healthy development during the teenage years (Peterson, 1988).

Reading Check
How do Hall's and Mead's theories of adolescence differ?

Although adolescence may not be as crisis-ridden as some psychologists think, few would deny that there is at least some stress during that period. Great physical, mental, and emotional changes occur during adolescence. As psychologist Robert Havighurst (1972) pointed out, every adolescent faces challenges in the form of developmental tasks that must be mastered. Among the tasks that Havighurst lists are the following:

1. Accepting one's physical makeup and acquiring a masculine or feminine gender role
2. Developing appropriate relations with age-mates of both sexes
3. Becoming emotionally independent of parents and other adults
4. Achieving the assurance that one will become economically independent
5. Deciding on, preparing for, and entering a vocation
6. Developing the cognitive skills and concepts necessary for social competence
7. Understanding and achieving socially responsible behavior
8. Preparing for marriage and family
9. Acquiring values that are harmonious and appropriate

Although the tasks present a challenge, adolescents generally handle it well. Most face some stress but find ways to cope with it. There are, of course, exceptions. A small percentage of young people experience storm and stress throughout their adolescent years. Another small group confronts the changes all adolescents experience with no stress at all. Perhaps the only safe generalization is that development through adolescence is a highly individualized and varied matter.

The pattern of development a particular adolescent displays depends upon a great many factors. The most important of these include the individual's adjustment in childhood, the level of adjustment of his or her parents and peers, and the changes that occur during adolescence. This time period is marked by major physical, social, emotional, and intellectual changes. It is to these changes that we now turn.

PHYSICAL DEVELOPMENT

Sexual maturation, or **puberty,** is the biological event that marks the end of childhood. Hormones trigger a series of internal and external changes. These hormones produce different growth patterns in boys and girls. The beginning of puberty varies. Some girls may start to mature physically as early as 8, while boys may start to mature at 9 or 10 years of age. Thirteen is the average age of puberty, plus or minus a year. Just before puberty, boys and girls experience a growth spurt.

puberty: sexual maturation; the end of childhood and the point when reproduction is first possible

The growth spurt is a rapid increase in weight and height (see Figure 4.2). It generally begins in girls between the ages of 10 and 14 and in boys between 11 and 16. (The growth spurt generally lasts two years. Soon after the growth spurt, individuals reach sexual maturity.) At about the age of 10, girls rather suddenly begin to grow. Before this growth spurt, fat tissue develops, making the girl appear chubby. The development of fat tissue is also characteristic of boys before their growth spurt. Whereas boys quickly lose it, progressing into a "string bean" or lean and lanky phase, girls retain most of this fat tissue and even add to it as they begin to spurt.

Once their growth spurt begins, females can grow as much as 2 to 3.5 inches a year. During this period, a girl's breasts and hips begin to fill out, and she develops pubic hair. Between 10 and 17—often between 12 and 13—she has her first menstrual period, or **menarche.** Another 12 to 18 months will pass before her periods become regular and she is capable of conceiving a child. Yet most societies consider menarche the beginning of womanhood.

At about 12, boys begin to develop pubic hair and larger genitals. Normally, between 12 and 13 they achieve their first ejaculation, or **spermarche.** Though their growth spurt begins 24 to 27 months later than that of girls, it lasts about 3 years longer. Once their growth spurt begins, boys grow rapidly and fill out, developing the broad shoulders and thicker trunk of an adult man. They also acquire more muscle tissue than girls and develop a larger heart and lungs. Their voices gradually deepen, and hair begins to grow on their faces and later on their chests.

The rate and pattern of sexual maturation varies so widely that it is difficult to apply norms or standards to puberty. In general, however, girls begin to develop earlier than boys and for a year or two may tower over male age-mates.

This period of adolescent growth can be an awkward one for both boys and girls because of **asynchrony**—the condition of uneven growth or maturation of bodily parts. For example, the hands or feet may be too large or small for the rest of the body. As the adolescent grows older, however, the bodily parts assume their correct proportions.

Reactions to Growth

In general, young people today are better informed than they were two or three generations ago. Most do not find the signs of their sexual maturation upsetting. Nevertheless, the rather sudden bodily changes that occur during puberty make all adolescents somewhat self-conscious. This is particularly true if they are early or late to develop.

menarche: the first menstrual period

spermarche: period during which males achieve first ejaculation

asynchrony: the condition during adolescence in which the growth or maturation of bodily parts is uneven

Figure 4.2   Average Annual Gains in Height

Increases in height during the growth spurt can be dramatic; a boy may experience a yearly increase of 4–6 inches (10.16–15.24 cm), while a girl may increase 3–5 inches (7.62–12.7 cm) in height. *When does the growth spurt occur in girls? In boys?*

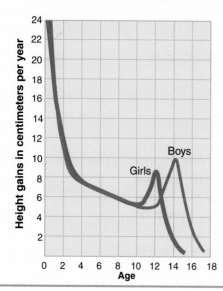

Figure 4.3 | **Rates of Physical Development**

Rapid physical changes occur during adolescence. Normally the changes that occur in adulthood are gradual. *Why do you think there are psychological reactions to physical growth?*

Adolescents usually want to be accepted by their peers. They conform to ideals of how a male or female their age should act, dress, and look. For both young men and women, there is a strong correlation between having a negative body image and feelings of depression (Rierden, Koff, & Stubbs, 1988). Adolescents are very aware of these rapid physical changes. They are very concerned that they measure up to what is "right" and what is "ideal." As you can imagine, very few ever measure up to these expectations. Most adolescents mention physical appearance when they discuss what they do not like about themselves. Most, especially girls, tend to evaluate themselves in terms of their culture's body ideal. Youths of both sexes are particularly sensitive about any traits they possess that appear to be sex-inappropriate. For example, boys tend to be very shy about "underdeveloped" genitalia, lack of pubic hair, or "fatty breasts," whereas girls are likely to be disturbed by "underdeveloped" breasts or dark facial hair.

Individual differences in growth significantly affect the personality of young adolescents. For example, research indicates that boys who mature early have an advantage. They become heroes in sports and leaders in formal and informal social activities. Other boys look up to them; girls have crushes on them; adults tend to treat them as more mature. As a result, they are generally more self-confident and independent than other boys. Some late-maturing boys may withdraw or rebel (Downs, 1990). The effects of late maturation for boys may last a long time.

Variations in the rate of development continue to have an effect on males even into their thirties. Those who matured earlier have been found to have a higher occupational and social status than those who matured later. The correlation weakens, however, as males enter their forties (Jones, 1965).

With girls the pattern is somewhat different. Girls who mature early may feel embarrassed rather than proud of their height and figure at first. Some begin dating older boys and become bossy with people their own

Reading Check
How do female and male growth spurts differ?

Figure 4.4   **Sexual Growth**

During puberty, boys and girls begin to produce higher levels of hormones. Those hormones spark sexual development. *How have sexual attitudes changed in the past 30 years?*

age. Late-maturing girls tend to be less quarrelsome and may get along with their peers more easily. In their late teens, girls who matured early may be more popular and have a more favorable image of themselves than girls who matured slowly.

Why does physical growth have such powerful psychological effects? According to one widely held theory, the psychological reactions to physical growth may be the result of a self-fulfilling prophecy. For example, the boy who believes he does not meet his culture's physical ideal may think less of himself and not pursue success as doggedly as the next person. His belief actually helps bring about the failure he feared.

SEXUAL DEVELOPMENT

As we noted earlier, adolescence is accompanied by puberty, which is when individuals mature sexually. The physical changes that occur are accompanied by changes in behavior. Adolescence is also the time when an individual develops attitudes about sex and expectations about the gender role he or she will fill. Early sexual maturity and cultural patterns of sexual behaviors have changed from one generation to the next generation. For example, the average age of marriage is 24 years, about three or four years later than it was in the 1950s and about 12 years after sexual maturation (Children's Defense Fund, 1997).

Sexual Attitudes

Attitudes affect the way we feel about sex and the way we respond sexually. Around the world there are wide variations in what children are told about appropriate sexual behavior and how they respond. In some societies children are kept in the dark about sex until just before they are married, whereas in others preadolescent children are encouraged to engage in sexual play in the belief that such play will foster mature development.

Although middle- and upper-class females who attend college seem to be more sexually active than college females were 30 years ago, in general in the United States sexual behavior in other social categories is about the same today as it was then. In terms of attitudes, however, there has been a change.

The increase of sexual awareness and activity of today's teens has raised many questions over the role of family, religion, and government in providing information and guidance about sex. The Youth Risk Behavior Surveillance Report (1997) claims that approximately 1 million pregnancies occur each year among adolescents, along with 3 million cases of sexually transmitted diseases. The teen birthrate has fallen steadily since 1991, but teen-related pregnancies and births continue to be societal issues. Studies show that children of teenage mothers are more likely to become teenage parents themselves, to do poorly in school, and to serve time in prison.

Fear of sexually transmitted diseases and the AIDS epidemic have also impacted sexual attitudes. The occurrence of AIDS is just beginning to decline in the United States. At first associated only with homosexual sex and intravenous drug use, AIDS was ignored by many Americans. Education efforts at increasing condom use have been successful, though. The use of condoms has more than doubled between 1982 and 1990 for young people (Centers for Disease Control and Prevention, 1997).

Many teens are examining the risks of sexual behavior and deciding that the only safe choice is abstinence from sexual intercourse. *Abstinence* is a choice to avoid harmful behaviors including premarital sex and the use of drugs and alcohol. By choosing abstinence some teens hope to avoid unwanted pregnancies, sexually transmitted diseases, and loss of self-respect.

SECTION 1 Assessment

1. **Review the Vocabulary** What do menarche and spermarche have to do with physical development?

2. **Visualize the Main Idea** Create two flowcharts similar to the one below to characterize physical changes in a male and female adolescent and possible reactions to those changes.

Physical Change = Puberty
↓
Early Maturer
↓
Possible Reactions

3. **Recall Information** According to Margaret Mead, how does one's culture influence adolescent development?

4. **Think Critically** What are the problems with defining the start and end of adolescence? Why do these problems exist?

5. **Application Activity** Think back over the stages of your life from childhood to the present. Which were the best and worst years of your life and why? Compare your responses to your classmates, and as a class debate whether adolescence is a time of "storm and stress."

Case Studies

Early Maturation

Period of Study: 1992

Introduction: In 1986 a 9-year-old Brazilian girl, Maria Eliana Jesus Mascarenhas, amazingly gave birth to a healthy 7-pound daughter.

How can a 9-year-old girl bear children? Maria suffered from a hormone imbalance that produced premature puberty, also known as *precocious puberty.* (Sexual development normally begins around age 11 in girls.) For reasons unknown, this disorder tends to affect females more than males. Children who start puberty prematurely are tall for their age because of the growth spurt triggered by hormones. However, since their skeleton matures and growth stops at an earlier age than normal, they never achieve their full height potential as adults.

There are also countless psychological difficulties for the child and parents who encounter this disorder. At the time of her child's birth, doctors estimated that Maria's body matched those of normal 13- or 14-year-old girls. This case inspired psychologists to study the influence of psychological factors on the maturation of females in general.

Hypothesis: Psychological factors, including stressors revolving around family, social relationships, and school, will cause an earlier menarche in some females (Rice, 1992a).

Method: Researchers conducted a longitudinal study on a group of 16-year-old girls. Psychologists assessed the living conditions in which the participants grew up, including the absence of a father, mother, or both; family conflict; and parental marital difficulty.

Results: The study found that females who grow up in conditions of family stress experience behavioral and psychological problems that stimulate earlier pubertal onset, leading to reproductive readiness, as in Maria's case. These stressful conditions caused a slower metabolism, resulting in weight gain and triggering early menarche.

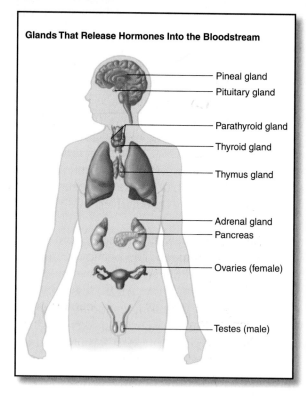

Glands That Release Hormones Into the Bloodstream

- Pineal gland
- Pituitary gland
- Parathyroid gland
- Thyroid gland
- Thymus gland
- Adrenal gland
- Pancreas
- Ovaries (female)
- Testes (male)

Further studies have indicated that girls who experience precocious puberty may go through periods of moodiness or irritability, while boys may become aggressive. These children may also become self-conscious about their bodies. Treatment for precocious puberty is usually aimed at changing the hormonal imbalance in the body through drug therapy. Psychologically, the behavior of children usually improves, becoming more age-appropriate, as their bodies return to normal development.

Analyzing the Case Study

1. How was a 9-year-old child able to give birth?
2. What are the psychological causes of precocious puberty?
3. **Critical Thinking** What considerations might a psychologist take into account when treating a child suffering from precocious puberty?

Personal Development

Reader's Guide

■ **Main Idea**
The transition from childhood to adulthood involves changes in patterns of reasoning and moral thinking, as well as the development of one's identity.

■ **Vocabulary**
• rationalization
• identity crisis
• social learning theory

■ **Objectives**
• Describe the cognitive and ideological changes that characterize adolescence.
• Outline the process by which adolescents find a personal identity.

EXPLORING PSYCHOLOGY

The Tattoo

"I had this tiny butterfly in a circle of roses tattooed on my left shoulder. No one else knew it was there, but I did, and whenever I thought about it I felt happy, like a different person. My mother was furious when she found out I'd had it done, but I think it's really pretty." (Barbara, age 19)

—from *Adolescence: The Survival Guide for Parents and Teenagers* by Elizabeth Fenwick and Dr. Tony Smith, 1994

During adolescence, a sense of identity and self-esteem are very important and depend very much on friends. Barbara's butterfly tattoo served as a statement of identity and made her happy and confident. Also during adolescence, many changes are occurring in ways of thinking and feeling. Becoming an adult involves much more than becoming physically mature, although that is an important part of the process. The transition from childhood to adulthood also involves changes in patterns of reasoning and moral thinking, and adjustments in personality and sexual behavior.

COGNITIVE DEVELOPMENT

During adolescence, the thinking patterns characteristic of adults emerge. Jean Piaget described this as "formal operations" thinking (Piaget & Inhelder, 1969). From about age 11 or 12, most people's thinking becomes more abstract. For example, the adolescent can consider the

Reading Check
How does an adolescent's thinking differ from that of a child?

answer to a hypothetical question like "What would the world be like if people lived to be 200?" He or she can entertain such hypothetical possibilities in a way that a young child cannot. This ability expands the adolescent's problem-solving capacity. A teenager who discovers that her car's engine has a knock can consider a number of possible causes and systematically test various adjustments and auto parts until she finds the root of the problem. This is the same ability that a scientist must have to conduct experiments.

With comprehension of the hypothetical comes the ability to understand abstract principles and deal with analogies and metaphors. Not only is this capacity important for studying higher-level science and mathematics, but it also leads the adolescent to deal with abstractions in his or her own life such as ethics, conformity, and phoniness. It allows for introspection—examining one's own motives and thoughts. One adolescent noticed, "I found myself thinking about my future, and then I began to think about why I was thinking about my future, and then I began to think about why I was thinking about why I was thinking about my future."

These new intellectual capacities also enable the adolescent to deal with overpowering emotional feelings through **rationalization.** After failing a test, for example, an individual may rationalize that it happened "because I was worried about the date I might be going on next week." An 8-year-old is too tied to concrete reality to consider systematically all the reasons why he or she might have failed.

Do all adolescents fully reach the stage of formal operations thinking at the same age? As you might suspect, just as there are variations in physical maturity, so there are variations in cognitive maturity. In general, the rate of mental growth varies greatly both among individual adolescents and among social and economic classes in this country. One study showed that less than half of the 17-year-olds tested had reached the stage of formal operations thinking (Higgins-Trenk & Gaite, 1971).

Differences have also been noted among nations. Formal operations thinking is less prevalent in some societies than in others, probably because of differences in the amount of formal education available. People who cannot read and write lack the tools to separate thought from concrete reality, and hence they cannot reach, or do not need to reach, more advanced levels of thinking (Dasen & Heron, 1981).

The change in thinking patterns is usually accompanied by changes in personality and social interactions as well. For example, adolescents tend to become very idealistic. This is because, for the first time, they can imagine the hypothetical—how things might be. When they compare this to the way things are, the world seems a sorry place. As a result, they can grow rebellious.

rationalization: a process whereby an individual seeks to explain an often unpleasant emotion or behavior in a way that will preserve his or her self-esteem

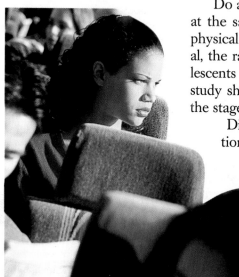

Figure 4.5   Introspection

Adolescents display an egocentrism—the tendency to be overly concerned with the sudden changes in their lives. Usually this period of intense introspection decreases as adolescents become young adults. *Why does formal operations thinking bring about introspection in adolescents?*

Some adolescents even develop a "messiah complex" and believe they can save the world from evil. In addition, the adolescents of each generation typically become impatient with what they see as the adult generation's failures. They do not understand why, for example, a person who feels a job compromises his or her principles does not just quit. (In other words, adolescents tend to be somewhat unrealistic about the complexities of life. Yet at the same time, their idealism can help keep older adults in touch with ways in which the world could be improved.)

Dr. David Elkind (1984) described some problems adolescents develop as a result of immaturity and abstract thought processes:

- **Finding fault with authority figures:** Adolescents discover that people they admired for years fall short of their ideals and let everyone know it.
- **Argumentativeness:** Adolescents practice building their own viewpoints by arguing any problem that presents itself.
- **Indecisiveness:** Aware of many choices, adolescents often have trouble making even simple decisions.
- **Apparent hypocrisy:** Adolescents have difficulty understanding an ideal and living up to it.
- **Self-consciousness:** Adolescents assume that everyone is thinking about the same thing they are—themselves!
- **Invulnerability:** Adolescents begin to feel special, that their experiences are unique, and that they are not subject to the same rules that govern everyone else. This special feeling of invulnerability underlies adolescent risk-taking behavior and self-destructive behavior.

MORAL DEVELOPMENT

Besides experiencing physical and cognitive changes, some adolescents, though by no means all, also go through important changes in their moral thinking. You will recall that according to Lawrence Kohlberg (whose theory was reviewed in Chapter 3), moral reasoning develops in stages. Young children in the early stages of their moral development are very egocentric. They consider an act right or wrong depending on whether or not it elicits punishment (Stage 1) or on whether it has positive or negative consequences for themselves (Stage 2). At later stages they judge an action by whether or not it is socially approved (Stage 3) or is sanctioned by an established authority (Stage 4).

Many people never get beyond Stage 4, and their moral thinking remains quite rigid. For those who do, however, adolescence and young adulthood are usually the periods of the most profound development. Individuals who progress to Stage 5 become concerned with whether a

More About...

Teenagers and Work

By high school graduation, more than 80 percent of students have had some kind of job. Most take low-skilled jobs that provide an opportunity to make some extra money. While most people tend to believe that any kind of job experience is good, especially for economic necessity, research indicates that such work can, in fact, be harmful.

One reason for this is that students who work evenings or weekends have less time to study. If you work, you need to set time aside for schoolwork. Another reason is that students gain a false impression of the workplace from their work experience. The jobs they take tend to be low paying, boring, and unchallenging.

Finally, working while still in school can create false ideas about money. Most students work to pay for luxury items, such as brand-name clothes or concert tickets. There is a danger that they will experience "premature affluence" because what they earn is spending money and they do not have to pay for necessities such as food and rent. Realizing that spending money may, in fact, be less available when you take a full-time job will help you avoid this trap.

How does the media portray adolescents?

Many television shows feature teenagers as the main characters. How are these teenagers featured? What are their concerns and how do they handle problems?

Procedure

1. Watch a television show that features teenagers as the main characters.

2. List the problems or issues a teenager in the show faced.

3. Explain why the problems existed and how the teenager attempted to solve the problems.

Analysis

1. In a report, describe other ways the teenager might have solved the problems or issues that he or she faced.

2. Which of the developmental tasks of adolescence was the teenager in the television show mastering?

3. How well did he or she master these tasks?

See the Skills Handbook, page 622, for an explanation of designing an experiment.

law is fair or just. They believe that the laws must change as the world changes and are never absolute. For example, an individual who has progressed to Stage 5 might ignore a law to save a human life. Individuals who reach Stage 6 are also concerned with making fair and just decisions. However, they differ from Stage 5 individuals in that they formulate absolute ethical principles, such as the Golden Rule, that they have worked through for themselves. They believe such moral laws apply to everyone, cannot be broken, and are more important than any written law.

Reaching higher levels of moral thinking involves the ability to abstract—to see a situation from another's viewpoint. That is why such moral development tends to occur in adolescence, when individuals gain the capacity for formal operations thinking. Not all adolescents who display such thinking simultaneously show higher levels of moral reasoning, though. In fact, only about 1 in 10 do (Kohlberg & Tunel, 1971). Thus, formal thought, while necessary for higher moral development, does not guarantee it. Interestingly, by the mid-1980s, Kohlberg began to question whether differentiating between Stages 5 and 6 was necessary. He concluded that only one stage—combining the key features of both stages—adequately identified the most advanced form of moral development and thinking.

Overall, psychologists agree that a person's moral development depends on many factors, especially the kind of relationship the individual has with his or her parents or significant others. Evidence shows that during high school, adolescent moral development does not progress much. During college, however, when the individual is away from home more and experiencing different cultures and ideas, more pronounced changes in moral development occur.

IDENTITY DEVELOPMENT

The changes adolescents undergo affect many facets of their existence, so it is hardly surprising that cumulatively they have a shaping influence on personality. Psychologists who have studied personality changes in adolescence have focused on the concept of identity. One psychologist in particular, Erik Erikson, has shown that the establishment of identity is key to adolescent development. His theory of how individuals arrive at an integrated sense of self has inspired a great deal of argument.

Erikson's Theory of the Identity Crisis

According to Erikson, building an identity is a task that is unique to adolescence. Children are aware of what other people (adults and peers) think of them. They know the labels others apply to them (good, naughty, silly, talented, brave, pretty, etc.). They are also aware of their biological drives and of their growing physical and cognitive abilities. Children may dream of being this or that person and act out these roles in their play. Yet they do not brood about who they are or where they are going in life. Children live in the present; adolescents begin to think about the future.

To achieve some sense of themselves, most adolescents must go through what Erikson termed an **identity crisis**—a time of inner conflict during which they worry intensely about their identities. Several factors contribute to the onset of this crisis, including the physiological changes and cognitive developments we have described, as well as awakening sexual drives and the possibility of a new kind of intimacy with the opposite sex. Adolescents begin to see the future as a reality, not just a game. They know they have to confront the almost infinite and often conflicting possibilities and choices that lie ahead. In the process of reviewing their past and anticipating their future, they begin to think about themselves. The process is a painful one, full of inner conflict, because they are torn by the desire to feel unique and distinctive on the one hand and to "fit in" on the other. Only by resolving this conflict do adolescents achieve an integrated sense of self.

identity crisis: a period of inner conflict during which adolescents worry intensely about who they are

According to Erikson, adolescents face a crisis of identity formation versus identity confusion. The task of adolescents is to become a unique individual with a valued sense of self in society. This issue is never completely resolved. The issue surfaces many times during a lifetime.

Adolescents need to organize their needs, abilities, talents, interests, background, culture, peer demands, and so on, to find a way to express themselves through an identity in a socially acceptable way. Identity forms when the adolescent can resolve issues such as the choice of an occupation, a set of values to believe in and live by, and the development of a sexual identity. The adolescent question is "Who am I?"

Role confusion is normal. It may be the reason why some adolescents' lives seem so chaotic. It also may explain why some adolescents are extremely self-conscious. Confusion is represented by childish behavior to avoid resolving conflicts and by being impulsive in decision making.

Good Looks Are Overrated

Often our opinions of ourselves relate to our looks. Many people actually think that they are better looking than what others rate them. Also, any social advantages, such as popularity, seem to decline as people mature. This may be because plain people work harder to develop social skills, while their better-looking peers do not receive the automatic attention they once did. Having good looks is not the only way to earn self-respect. Researchers studied a group of boys from age 10 to early adulthood, finding that those with consistently high self-esteem were not necessarily the best looking. The most confident boys were the ones whose parents had set high standards yet showed respect for the boys' own decision making.

Erik Erikson

1902–1994

"Healthy children will not fear life if their elders have integrity enough not to fear death."

Born of Danish parents, Erikson never knew his father. Erik's father left his mother before he was even born. His mother married a German-Jewish pediatrician. Erikson felt that he did not belong. Mocked in synagogues because of his fair features and ostracized by non-Jews because of his faith, the development of an identity became one of the greatest concerns of Erikson's life.

Erikson traveled to Rome as an art student to study the works of Michelangelo, and this experience inspired him to study psychoanalysis with Anna Freud (Sigmund Freud's daughter). The success of therapy convinced Erikson to become an analyst.

Although Erikson never formally attained a degree in psychology, he taught at such prestigious institutions as Harvard and Yale. His work with the Sioux and Yurok Native American groups convinced Erikson that development is a lifelong process. His major contribution to the field of psychology was his identification of a life cycle consisting of eight distinct stages (see Chapter 3).

Marcia's View of the Identity Crisis

Erikson's theory finds support in the work of another psychologist, James Marcia. According to Marcia (1966), Erikson is correct in pointing to the existence of an adolescent identity crisis. That crisis arises because individuals must make commitments on such important matters as occupation, religion, and political orientation. Using the categories of "crisis" and "commitment," Marcia distinguished four attempts to achieve a sense of identity (see Figure 4.6): (1) *identity moratorium adolescents,* who are seriously considering the issues but have not made a commitment on any of the important matters facing them; (2) *identity foreclosure adolescents* have made a firm commitment about issues based not on their own choice but on the suggestion of others; (3) *identity confused or diffused adolescents,* who have not yet given any serious thought to making any decisions and have no clear sense of identity; and (4) *identity achievement adolescents,* who considered many possible identities and have freely committed themselves to occupations and other important life matters.

These categories must not be too rigidly interpreted. It is possible for an individual to make a transition from one category to another, and it is also possible for the same individual to belong to one category with respect to religious commitment and to another with respect to political orientation or occupational choice. Marcia's main contribution is in clarifying the sources and nature of the adolescent identity crisis.

Although Erikson and Marcia insist that all adolescents experience an identity crisis, not all psychologists agree. The term "crisis" suggests that adolescence is a time of nearly overwhelming stress. It also implies that the adolescent transition to maturity requires a radical break with childhood experience. As we noted earlier, many psychologists believe that

Figure 4.6 Adolescent Identity Categories

Progress in the search for one's identity can be divided into four categories. *In which category would you place someone who is not actively concerned with his or her identity and is waiting until later to decide the issue?*

	Exploring identity issues	Not exploring identity issues yet
Decisions already made	Identity Achievement	Identity Foreclosure
Decisions not yet made	Identity Moratorium	Identity Diffusion

Source: Adapted from Kalat, 1999.

adolescence is not so strife-ridden and constitutes a relatively smooth transition from one stage of life to the next.

One of the reasons Erikson may have arrived at his view is that he focused his study on disturbed adolescents who sought clinical psychiatric treatment. When adolescents attending school are selected at random and studied, critics point out that most show no sign of crisis and appear to be progressing rather smoothly through adolescence (Haan & Day, 1974).

Social Learning View

Psychologists and social scientists seeking an alternative to Erikson's theory have offered several other explanations for adolescent identity formation. A.C. Peterson (1988), for example, argues that crisis is not the normal state of affairs for adolescents. When crises develop—as they do in a little more than 20 percent of all adolescent boys (Offer & Offer, 1975)—the cause is generally a change in the external circumstances of an individual's life rather than a biological factor. Thus, a divorce in the family or a new set of friends may trigger teenage rebellion and crisis, but no internal biological clock dictates those events.

Human development, in Albert Bandura's view, is one continuous process. At all stages, including adolescence, individuals develop by interacting with others. Because of Bandura's emphasis on interaction in understanding adolescence and all other phases of human development, his approach is usually referred to as the **social learning theory** of development (Bandura, 1977).

Margaret Mead also stressed the importance of the social environment in adolescent identity formation. On the basis of her studies in Samoa (1973), for example, she concluded, like Bandura, that human development is more a continuous process than one marked by radical discontinuity. In that remote part of the world, adolescents are not expected to act any differently than they did as children or will be expected to act as adults. The reason is that children in Samoa are given a great

Reading Check
What is the major criticism of Erikson's theory?

social learning theory: Bandura's view of human development; emphasizes interaction

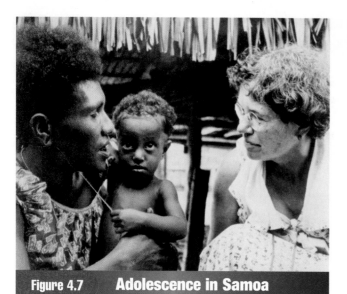

Figure 4.7   Adolescence in Samoa

The Samoa that Mead saw is now gone. Once a place in which most young people came of age with relative ease has become a place where young people experience great difficulty in terms of finding a place in their society, to the point where they currently have one of the highest suicide rates in the world. *How did Mead characterize adolescence? Why did she characterize it this way?*

deal of responsibility. They do not suddenly go from being submissive in childhood to being dominant later in life. Mead also pointed out that in Samoa, as in other nonindustrial societies, children have gender roles similar to those of adults and therefore do not experience the onset of sexuality as an abrupt change or a traumatic experience. The identity crisis, then, is by no means a universal phenomenon.

Personality development in adolescence is a complex phenomenon. It involves not only how a person develops a sense of self, or identity, but how that person develops relationships with others and the skills used in social interactions. No one theory can do justice to all that is involved in the process of personality development. Erikson's emphasis on the adolescent's need for his or her own identity is an important contribution. In adolescence, self-esteem is influenced by the process of developing an identity. (Self-esteem refers to how much one likes oneself. Self-esteem is linked to feelings of self-worth, attractiveness, and social competence.) By focusing on individual psychology, however, Erikson tended to ignore the influence of society. The studies of Bandura and Mead provide needed correctives. To arrive at a balanced picture of personality change and identity formation in adolescence, we must call upon all viewpoints.

SECTION 2 | Assessment

1. **Review the Vocabulary**   Describe the social learning theory.

2. **Visualize the Main Idea**   Use a chart similar to the one below to describe the characteristics of each category of Marcia's identity theory.

Identity Status	Characteristics

3. **Recall Information**   What is an example of rationalization and a reason it might occur?

4. **Think Critically**   What factors may help adolescents in their search for an identity? How might adolescents discover occupations, religions, or political orientations that are right for them?

5. **Application Activity**   Select one of Dr. David Elkind's adolescent problems and characterize that problem in a cartoon or fictional dialogue.

Social Development

■ **Main Idea**

Adolescents undergo many changes in their social relationships, adjusting to new relationships with parents and the influence of peers.

■ **Vocabulary**

- clique
- conformity
- anorexia nervosa
- bulimia nervosa

■ **Objectives**

- Describe the role of family and peers during adolescence.
- Discuss difficulties that some adolescents encounter.

EXPLORING PSYCHOLOGY

Peer Pressure

Consider the following situation: "You are with a couple of your best friends on Halloween. They're going to soap windows, but you're not sure whether you should or not. Your friends say you should, because there's no way you could get caught. What would you really do?"

—adapted from *Developmental Psychology* by T.J. Berndt, 1979

The situation above was presented to participants from the third, sixth, ninth, and twelfth grades. The participants had to determine what they would do in the situation. The results demonstrated that conformity to peer pressure rose steadily from the third to the ninth grade, then declined with twelfth graders.

Adolescents experience various changes in their social relationships. No longer a child though not yet an adult, the teenager must find a new role in the family—one that parents are not always ready to accept. He or she must also adjust to new, often more intense relationships with peers.

THE ROLE OF THE FAMILY

Families in the United States experienced marked changes in the past several decades. With many marriages ending in divorce, fewer and fewer American families have the pre-1970s norm of a wage-earning father working outside the house and a mother working within the home. Regardless of these changes, one of the principal developmental tasks for adolescents is becoming independent of their families. Unfortunately, the means of achieving this status are not always clear, either to the adolescents or to their parents. First, there are mixed feelings on both sides. Some parents have built their lifestyles around the family and are reluctant to let the child go. Such parents know they will soon have to find someone else on whom to shift their emotional dependence. Also, parents whose children are old enough to leave home sometimes have to wrestle with their own fears of advancing age. Many parents worry about whether their children are really ready to cope with the harsh realities of life—and so do adolescents. At the same time that young people long to get out on their own and try themselves against the world, they worry a lot about failing there. This internal struggle is often mirrored in the adolescent's unpredictable behavior, which parents may interpret as "adolescent rebellion." Against this background of uncertainty, which is almost universal, there are various family styles of working toward autonomy (see Chapter 3).

Reading Check
How does the role of the family change during adolescence?

More About...

Are Boys in Trouble?

Many researchers claim that today's boys are in trouble and it is time to pay attention to how we are raising them. Why? Let us just look at the numbers. Males die in greater numbers in infancy than females. Boys are far more likely than girls to be told they have learning disabilities, to be sent to the principal's office, to be suspended from high school, or to commit crimes. In adolescence boys kill themselves five times more often than girls do. In adulthood they are being jailed at increasing rates, abandoning families, and are more likely to be the victims of or commit violence.

Some psychologists seek to explain these numbers by proposing that the way we parent and educate boys does not allow them to fully develop the capacity for emotional depth and complexity. As a result, boys are less capable than girls of meeting the challenges of adolescence successfully. In effect, we are not training boys correctly. Their traditional survival qualities, such as physical strength and dominant personalities, no longer assure their survival or success.

THE ROLE OF PEERS

Adolescents can trust their peers not to treat them like children. Teenagers spend much of their time with friends—they need and use each other to define themselves. High schools are important as places for adolescents to get together, and they do get together in fairly predictable ways. Most schools contain easily recognizable and well-defined groups. These groups are arranged in a fairly rigid hierarchy—everyone knows who belongs to which group and what people in that group do with their time. Early in adolescence the groups are usually divided by sex, but later the sexes mix. Groups usually form along class lines. Some school activities bring teenagers of different social classes together, but it is the exception rather than the rule that middle-class and lower-class adolescents are close friends.

Besides class, what determines whether an adolescent will be accepted by a peer group? Many studies have shown that personal characteristics are very important. For example, in the 1970s, well-liked peers tended to be well-groomed, good-looking, outgoing, neat, fun, and adept at making others feel accepted. Unpopular peers were seen by others as irresponsible, sloppy, childish, shy, and lonely, among other negative characteristics (Hartup, 1970; Horrocks & Benimoff, 1967). These characteristics are changing, though. Today many peer groups adopt very distinct styles to express themselves.

Belonging to a **clique** (a group within a group) is very important to most adolescents and serves several functions. Most obviously, perhaps, it fulfills the need for closeness with others. In addition, it gives the adolescent a means of defining himself or herself, a way of establishing an identity. The group does this by helping the individual achieve self-confidence, develop a sense of independence from family, clarify values, and experiment with new roles. For instance, members of cliques may imitate one another's clothing, speech, or hairstyles. By providing feedback, clique members not only help define who an individual is but also who he or she is not: group membership separates an adolescent from others who are not in his or her group.

Of course, there are drawbacks to this kind of social organization. One of the greatest is the fear of being disliked, which leads to **conformity**—the "glue" that holds the peer group together. A teenager's fear of wearing clothes that might set him or her apart from others is well known. Group pressures to conform, however, may also lead young people to do more serious things that run contrary to their better judgment.

Despite their tendency to encourage conformity, peer groups are not always the dominant influence in an adolescent's life. Both parents and peers exercise considerable influence in shaping adolescent behavior and attitudes. Peers tend to set the standards on such matters as fashion and taste in music. In addition, their advice on school-related issues may also be considered more reliable than parental counsel (Berndt, 1992).

When it comes to basic matters, however, involving marriage, religion, or educational plans, adolescents tend to accept their parents' beliefs and to follow their advice (Offer & Schonert-Reichl, 1992). Only in a few areas touching basic values—for example, drug use or sexual behavior—are there differences. Even here the differences are not fundamental and

clique: a small, exclusive group of people within a larger group

 Reading Check
Why do adolescents join cliques?

conformity: acting in accordance with some specified authority

| Figure 4.8 | **The Rebellious Teen** |

Adolescence is often described as a time of children's rebellion against parents. This rebellion is usually aimed at the controls parents exercise over the adolescents' behavior. *Who replaces parents as a source of emotional support for adolescents?*

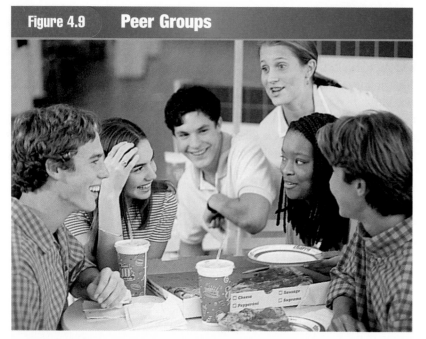

Figure 4.9   Peer Groups

As individuals progress from childhood to adolescence, peers become very important. *Why are adolescents so heavily influenced by peers?*

represent only a difference in the strength with which the same basic belief is held. For example, adolescents may have more liberal views on premarital sex than their parents do.

Peer groups, then, do not pose a threat to parental authority. Even though parents spend less time with their adolescent children as the latter mature, their influence is still strong. Adolescents of both sexes tend to choose friends with values close to those of their parents, and these peer groups are of immense help in making the transition from dependent child to independent adult. Thus, generational conflict is not nearly so pronounced as some would have us believe.

On the other hand, psychologist Judith Rich Harris claims that peer groups, not parents, teach children how to behave in the world (Harris, 1998). So, the only influence parents are able to have over their children, then, is by supplying the environment in which their children meet other peers. She argues, for example, that parents should live in a good neighborhood so their children associate with the "right" peers. Many psychologists passionately criticize Harris's theory. Critics claim that there is a very strong relationship between parenting styles and the social development of children.

DIFFICULTIES DURING ADOLESCENCE

As we have seen in this chapter, adolescence is a time of transition. There are many developmental tasks to be mastered, but adolescence is not distinct from other periods of life in this respect. As Erikson (1968) pointed out, every stage of life brings with it unique challenges that are specific to that stage, whether it is old age, early childhood, or adolescence.

Given the great array of profound changes the adolescent must cope with involving his or her mind, body, emotions, and social relationships, it is natural and normal that most adolescents should experience some *temporary* psychological difficulties. The great majority, however, adjusts fairly quickly. Although some studies show that mental illness and suicide are relatively rare among adolescents, the rates of both have been increasing over the past several decades. The occurrence of teenage suicide has tripled over the past 20 years—and this figure may be underestimated

Student Web Activity
Visit the *Understanding Psychology* Web site at psychology.glencoe.com and click on **Chapter 4— Student Web Activities** for an activity about adolescent development.

because medical personnel sometimes label a death as an accident to protect the victim's family.

The illusion of invulnerability—"Others may get caught, but not me!"—is a part of adolescent egocentrism. This illusion may lead adolescents to do things with their peers they would not do alone. This troubled minority often "acts out" problems in one of several ways. Acts of juvenile delinquency—running away from home, teen pregnancies, alcohol and drug abuse, and underachievement at school—are typical (see Figure 4.10). Juveniles were involved in 17 percent of all violent crime arrests and 35 percent of all property crime arrests in the United States in 1997 (Snyder, 1997). Repeat offenders and the fact that many offenders are not caught make these data hard to interpret, though. Most of us outgrow these tendencies as we mature.

Unfortunately, troubled adolescents do not simply "outgrow" their problems but carry them into later life if they are not treated. Adults, therefore, should be concerned about troubled teenagers. It is important to note, however, that unusual behavior should be seen as a more intense form, or a more extreme degree, of normal behavior. It should be considered just a different *kind* of behavior. For example, teenagers who experiment with drugs—or even become drug abusers—need understanding. By not labeling the teenaged drug abuser "strange" or "abnormal," we can begin to understand his or her psychological needs.

Did You Know?

Reporting Suicides Publicizing teen suicides does not seem to prevent more suicides. In fact the opposite seems to occur—publicizing suicides seems to encourage more suicides. Psychologists are trying to understand why this happens.

Teenage Depression and Suicide

According to Kathleen McCoy (1982), the phenomenon of teenage depression is much more widespread than most parents or educators

Figure 4.10	Arrests Per 100,000 Juveniles Ages 10–17

The juvenile arrest rate for all offenses reached its highest level in the last two decades in 1996 before declining in 1997. *What factors contribute to juvenile delinquency?*

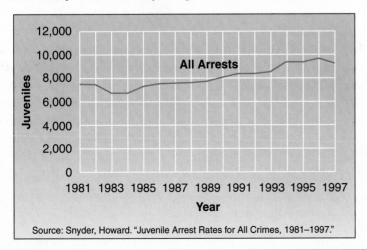

Source: Snyder, Howard. "Juvenile Arrest Rates for All Crimes, 1981–1997."

suspect. To many grownups who see adolescence as the best years of life, depression and youth may seem incompatible. What events trigger depression in adolescents? One major event is the loss of a loved one through separation, family relocation, divorce, or death. The adolescent may experience grief, guilt, panic, and anger as a reaction. If the teenager is not able to express these feelings in a supportive atmosphere, depression may result.

Another form of loss that causes depression is the breakdown of the family unit, often as a result of separation and divorce. Family members may be in conflict with each other and thus unable to communicate well. Adolescents may be therefore deprived of the emotional support they need.

Unlike depressed adults, who usually look and feel sad or "down," depressed teenagers may appear to be extremely angry. They often engage in rebellious behavior such as truancy, running away, drinking, using drugs, or being sexually promiscuous. Often, depressed teenagers appear intensely hyperactive and frantic, traits that are frequently mistaken for normal behavior in teenagers. McCoy urges parents and educators to be aware of the warning signals of teenage depression and suicide. One warning signal is a change in the intensity and frequency of rebellious behavior. Others are withdrawal from friends, engaging in dangerous risk taking, talking about suicide, and excessive self-criticism. Frequently, the greatest danger of suicide occurs after a depression seems to be lifting.

The best way to deal with teenage depression is to communicate with the teenager about his or her problems. Sometimes a caring, listening parent or a responsive, sensitive friend can help the youth deal with his or her concerns. In other cases, parents and their teenage child may need professional help. This is particularly true when few channels of communication are open.

anorexia nervosa: a serious eating disorder characterized by a fear of gaining weight that results in prolonged self-starvation and dramatic weight loss

Figure 4.11   Anorexia

Anorexia develops over time as a way of coping with emotional stress or pain, unhappiness, or other problems a person may have. *How is anorexia nervosa treated?*

Eating Disorders

Eating disorders such as anorexia nervosa and bulimia nervosa affect many teenagers and young adults, especially females. Adolescents who develop eating disorders do not get the calories or the nutrition they need to grow. A serious eating disorder, **anorexia nervosa,** is characterized by refusing to eat and not maintaining weight. People suffering from this disorder have an intense fear of gaining weight or amassing fat. Anorexics have a distorted body image—they see themselves as fat even though they are thin.

When faced with the pressures of adolescence, some people develop abnormal eating patterns. Some psychologists suggest that anorexia represents a female's refusal to grow up. Girls who develop anorexia typically miss menstrual cycles. Other psychologists propose that anorexia is an attempt by teenagers to assert control over their lives at a time when so much seems beyond their control. Treatment for anorexics involves a focus on encouraging weight gain and dealing with psychological problems. Another serious disorder, **bulimia nervosa,** is characterized by binge eating followed by purging—vomiting, using laxatives, or rigorous dieting and fasting—to eliminate the calories taken in during the binge. People suffering from bulimia nervosa are excessively concerned about body shape and weight. Bulimics usually engage in this behavior in private.

Some psychologists suggest that bulimia may result from a teen's feeling of alienation during adolescence or a need to find approval from others. Some bulimics also experience depression, anxiety, and mood swings. Treatment involves therapy and the use of antidepressant drugs.

Culture and Body Image

"You've gained weight" is a traditional compliment in Fiji. Dinner guests in the South Pacific are supposed to eat as much as possible. A nicely rounded body is the norm for men and women. All that changed, though, with the arrival of TV. Now, girls in Fiji dream of looking like American stars on TV—skinny. In fact, eating disorders are more common in industrialized countries, suggesting that cultural factors play a major role in body image. Meanwhile, in Fiji, the percentage of girls with eating disorders has increased, and in a 1998 survey 69 percent of the girls stated that they had been on a diet. How does today's culture affect you? What is your ideal body image? Why?

bulimia nervosa: a serious eating disorder characterized by compulsive overeating usually followed by self-induced vomiting or laxative abuse

SECTION 3 Assessment

1. **Review the Vocabulary** What are the symptoms of anorexia nervosa and bulimia nervosa?

2. **Visualize the Main Idea** Using a graphic organizer similar to the one at right, identify and describe three difficulties that adolescents might encounter.

Difficulty:

Causes:

Treatment:

3. **Recall Information** How does the influence of parents over their children change during adolescence?

4. **Think Critically** Why do adolescents form cliques? Do you think cliques serve a positive or negative purpose? Explain your answers.

5. **Application Activity** Create an informational pamphlet on a problem some teens encounter, such as eating disorders or depression. Include statistics and treatment suggestions.

Gender Roles and Differences

Reader's Guide

■ **Main Idea**
Females and males have physical and psychological gender differences. Our beliefs about what we think it means to be male or female influence our behavior.

■ **Vocabulary**
• gender identity
• gender role
• gender stereotype
• androgynous
• gender schema

■ **Objectives**
• Explain the difference between gender identity and gender role.
• Describe gender differences in personality and cognitive abilities.

EXPLORING PSYCHOLOGY

Boys Will Be Boys . . .

On the Oceanside playground I watched four boys from Miss Bailey's classroom start to climb up the "dirt pile" at the edge of the grassy playing field. As they climbed and compared the gripping power of their shoes, Matt suggested that they have a "falling contest; see who can fall the farthest," which they proceeded to do. . . .

In gestures of intimacy that one rarely sees among boys, girls stroke or comb their friends' hair. They notice and comment on one another's physical appearance such as haircuts or clothes, and they borrow and wear one another's sweatshirts or sweaters.

—from *Gender Play: Girls and Boys in School* by Barrie Thorne, 1993

Many people just take for granted the differences between boys and girls, claiming that "boys will be boys," or something similar. Pick up a magazine, turn on the TV, or look outside your window—gender stereotypes are everywhere. Some parents dress baby girls in pink and boys in blue, give them gender-specific names, and expect them to act differently.

The first question asked of new parents is "Is the baby a boy or a girl?" Your gender greatly influences how you dress, move, work, and play. It can influence your thoughts and others' thoughts about you. Are there significant psychological differences between males and females? Do children learn gender identities or are they born different?

GENDER ROLES

Gender identity and gender roles are two different, though closely related, aspects of our sexual lives. **Gender identity** is one's physical and biological makeup. It is your awareness of being male or female. Thus, if one has a vagina, one's gender identity is female; if a penis, male. Gender identity includes genetic traits we have inherited and may include some gender-linked behaviors as well. Between the ages of 2 and 3, most children learn to label themselves as boys or girls. By the age of 5, most children have learned the thoughts, expectations, and behaviors that accompany their gender role (Biernat & Wortman, 1991).

A person's **gender role** is defined partly by genetic makeup but mainly by the society and culture in which the individual lives. The gender role is a standard of how a person with a given gender identity is supposed to behave and includes the traditional behaviors that society expects of people because they are male or female. For example, in the United States, men were traditionally viewed as dominant, competitive, and emotionally reserved; women were viewed as submissive, cooperative, and emotionally responsive. These traits were considered appropriate for the different sexes. Today young people have a much broader view of what is appropriate behavior for males and females.

Gender roles vary from one society to another, and they can change over time within a given society. Gender roles give social meaning to gender identity. However, not all societies agree on the roles the sexes should assume. Indeed, anthropologists have found that some societies reverse the roles that Americans traditionally give to men and women, while others assign to both sexes what we might consider "masculine" or "feminine" roles. Not only do gender roles vary among societies, but they also may change radically within a society, as we are witnessing today in the United States and Canada.

Sometimes gender roles become so rigid that they become **gender stereotypes.** Gender stereotypes are oversimplified or prejudiced opinions and attitudes concerning the way men or women should behave. These stereotypes—that men should be rugged and women sensitive—have their roots deep in a time in our history when a division of labor was necessary for survival. Today, however, modern technology and birth control have freed women from duties associated with child rearing and childbearing for a large part of their lives. Sharp gender-role divisions are no longer necessary or appropriate, especially in the labor force. New concepts of what it means to be "masculine" and "feminine" are more widely accepted.

Given these changing standards of acceptable gender roles, psychologist Sandra Bem argues that people should accept new **androgynous** roles—that is, roles that involve a flexible combination of traditionally male and female characteristics. She began her research by asking college students how desirable they considered various characteristics for a man and for a woman. Not surprisingly, she found that traits such as ambition, self-reliance, independence, and assertiveness were considered to be desirable for men. It was desirable for women to be affectionate, gentle, understanding, and sensitive to the needs of others.

gender identity: the sex group (masculine or feminine) to which an individual biologically belongs

gender role: the set of behaviors that society considers appropriate for each sex

gender stereotype: an oversimplified or distorted generalization about the characteristics of men and women

 Reading Check
How do gender roles differ from gender stereotypes?

androgynous: combining or confusing traditionally male and female characteristics

These and other traits were then listed in a questionnaire called the Bem Sex Role Inventory. Bem asked people to rate how each of these traits applied to them on a scale from one (never or almost never true) to seven (always or almost always true). In one early report, Bem (1975) described the results for 1,500 Stanford undergraduates: about 50 percent stuck to "appropriate" sex or gender roles (masculine males or feminine females), 15 percent were "cross-sexed typed" (women who described themselves in traditionally male terms or men who checked feminine adjectives), and 36 percent were considered "androgynous," in that they checked off both male and female characteristics to describe themselves.

In later studies, Bem found that the people whose responses indicated androgynous preferences were indeed more flexible. Such women were able to be assertive when it was required, as could traditional males, but traditional females could not. Such people were also able to express warmth, playfulness, and concern, as could traditional females, but traditional males could not. In our complex world, Bem argues, androgyny should be our ideal: there is no room for an artificial split between "a woman's world" and "a man's world."

Androgyny is becoming an accepted ideal in our culture. One consequence of this shift is that adolescents who are developing into adults have more choices in the way they define themselves in life. In some ways, this shift toward more freedom in gender roles has resulted in greater personal responsibility. No longer limited by rigid gender-role stereotypes, young people are challenged to define themselves according to their talents, temperaments, and values. At the same time, not all people within the culture accept the more androgynous gender roles. Older people, especially, may still define themselves and others in terms of more traditional and rigid gender-role standards.

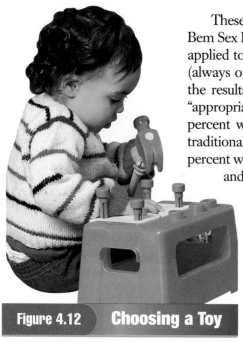

Figure 4.12 **Choosing a Toy**

Between the ages of 3 and 5, children gain ideas about which toys, clothes, or activities are appropriate for their gender. *When do children start labeling themselves as male or female?*

GENDER DIFFERENCES

Psychologists have found that most people do see differences between genders. Are these differences, though, real or imagined? Are these differences the result of cultural stereotypes, or do they show up in the actual behaviors of boys and girls?

Gender Differences in Personality

Are there differences between the sexes? Studies have found that besides the obvious physical differences, differences between males and females do exist. It is important to note that these differences, though, exist between groups of males and females. Individuals may or may not exhibit these differences.

One study (Mednick & Thomas, 1993) found that males are more confident than females, especially in academic areas or in tasks stereotyped as "masculine," such as math and science. Even when they achieve the same grades as men, women perceive themselves as less competent than males. The self-confidence of females rises, though, when they perform tasks in which they receive clear and direct feedback on their performance and on which they complete alone.

Many studies have also found that aggression is one of the areas with the most significant differences between genders. (*Aggression* refers to hostile or destructive behavior.) Females engage in more verbal aggressive acts, while males participate in more physical aggression (Turner & Gervai, 1995). Some researchers propose that women also think differently about aggression (Kendrick, 1987). The women studied said they feel guilty or have more anxiety about the dangers involved in aggressive behavior.

Differences in aggressive behavior can be observed by watching children at play. Whereas males are more likely to use mock fighting and rough and tumble play, females tend to use indirect forms of aggression such as talking about or rejecting, ignoring, or avoiding the target of aggression (Bjorkqvist, Lagerspetz, & Kaukianen, 1992).

What causes this physical aggression in boys? Studies on identical twins show that men have lower levels of a neurotransmitter, serotonin, than women (Berman, Tracy, & Coccaro, 1997). Lower levels of serotonin have been associated with higher levels of aggression. Boys are encouraged, also, to use aggression. Starting at an early age, society encourages boys to be competitive and to settle conflicts through aggression.

Another gender difference can often be detected in male and female communication styles. Although many popular stereotypes portray women as the "talkers," studies have demonstrated that men actually talk more than women and interrupt women more while they are talking. Women talk more, though, when they have power in a relationship. Females are more likely to use *hedges* in speech, such as "kind of" or "you know." Women also use more *disclaimers*, such as "I may be wrong" or "I'm not sure." Finally, women use more *tag questions* at the end of sentences, such as "Okay?" (Lakoff, 1973; McMillan et al., 1977).

As far as nonverbal communication goes, women are more likely to show submission and warmth, whereas men display more dominance and status. More women than men, though, are sensitive to nonverbal cues (Briton & Hall, 1995).

Gender Differences in Cognitive Abilities

You may have heard someone claim that females are better than males at verbal skills, while males excel at spatial and mathematical skills. Janet Hyde and Marcia Linn (1988) examined 165 studies on verbal ability, finding that no measurable differences in verbal skills exist between males and females. If differences exist, they are relatively small. When researchers examined mathematical ability, they discovered no significant differences between male and female abilities.

Figure 4.13	Gender in the Media

The media often targets specific genders using stereotypes in their advertisements. This may help children form their ideals of what it means to be a male or female. *How might this doll advertisement reinforce gender stereotypes?*

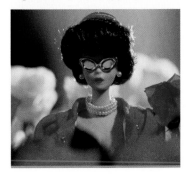

Figure 4.14 **Gender and Personality**

Girls are often described as concerned, sensitive, and nurturing; boys are viewed as controlling, aggressive, and independent. *How does this cartoon depict gender differences?*

When researchers examine specific topics and age trends, some differences do appear. For example, males and females perform about the same in problem solving until high school. At that point, males outperform females. Men also tend to do better than females on tests of spatial ability; however, women are better at tracking objects (see Figure 4.15).

In conclusion, there are very few cognitive differences between males and females. The studies mentioned above should not limit the participation of males and females in specific areas, or be used as a basis for discrimination. The studies fail to reflect individual differences of ability and do not reflect an individual's motivations, past history, and ambitions.

ORIGINS OF GENDER DIFFERENCES

How do differences in gender develop? How gender differences develop is one of the many questions that falls into the nature versus nurture issue. While some argue that differences between sexes are biological, others propose that we learn gender differences from our environment. Today most psychologists agree that nature and nurture interact to influence gender differences.

Biological Theory

The biological theory of gender role development emphasizes the role of anatomy, hormones, and brain organization. Supporters of this theory point out that regardless of what parents do, boys seem to prefer trucks, while girls prefer to play with dolls.

Supporters of this idea claim that differences in gender are the result of behaviors that evolved from early men and women. That is, men and women adopted certain behaviors throughout time in an attempt to survive. For example, men increased their chances of finding a mate and reproducing by adopting dominant and aggressive traits, while women increased their chances of raising children by being concerned, warm, and sensitive. Therefore, certain genetic or biological traits were formed in men and women (Archer, 1997).

Psychoanalytical Theory

According to Sigmund Freud, when a child identifies with a parent of the same sex, gender identity results. Little boys identify with their fathers, while girls identify with their mothers. This identification process occurs when children are between 3 and 5 years of age. Critics argue that identification seems to be the result, rather than the cause, of gender typing (Maccoby, 1992).

Social Learning Theory

The social learning theory emphasizes the role of social and cognitive processes on how we perceive, organize, and use information. For example, children learn their gender roles by observing and imitating models, such as their parents, friends, peers, and teachers. These models respond to and reward certain behaviors in boys and different behaviors in girls.

For example, parents may buy rugged toy trucks for boys and soft dolls for girls. Parents may punish a girl for being outspoken and reward her for completing household chores. Parents may encourage a boy's high ambitions and independence. In effect, these parents are rewarding or discouraging behaviors, depending on whether these behaviors match traditional male and female gender roles.

Cognitive-Developmental Theory

The cognitive-developmental theory proposes that children acquire gender roles by interacting with their environment and thinking about those experiences. As they do this, children learn different sets of standards for male and female behavior (Bem, 1981).

To learn about gender, a child must first see himself or herself as male or female. Then the child begins to organize behavior around this

Figure 4.15   Test Yourself

Test A: Which two figures on the right are the same as the figure on the left? (Answers at bottom.)

Test B: Cover the bottom box. Carefully study the top box for 1 minute. Then cover the top box, uncover the bottom box, and follow the instructions below.

Now note each item that remains in its original spot and each item that has been moved.

Source: Shepard & Metzler, 1971.

Answer to Test A: Figures 1 and 3 are the same as the figure on the left.

When it comes to spatial abilities, some argue that women are better than men at tracking objects and that men are better at forming "mental maps." In these tests, most men would find Test A easier, while most women find Test B easier. *How might biological theories explain gender differences of spatial ability?*

concept. The child may begin to acquire preferences consistent with his or her perceived gender. For example, a boy watches a football game and then engages in rough play with another boy. Eventually that boy forms a gender schema. A **gender schema** is a mental representation of behavior that helps a child organize and categorize behaviors. For instance, a girl develops a schema of how a female should act and then behaves in accordance with that schema. The girl begins to play with dolls when she perceives that this behavior fits in with her notion of what kinds of toys girls play with. When she acts appropriately with the schema, her self-confidence rises. When she fails to act in accordance with her schema, she feels inadequate.

gender schema: a set of behaviors organized around how either a male or female should think and behave

CHANGING GENDER ROLES

The roles of women and men in society are changing. For example, before the 1960s in the United States, few women sought careers. Most women grew up expecting to marry and quit work to raise children. By the mid-1980s, though, this had changed. Most women had jobs outside the home. For women and men, work provides income, as well as a sense of accomplishment.

Despite the fact that more women are in the workforce, studies have shown that, in general, women do not advance as quickly as men and women occupy lower levels of leadership positions. Industrial/organizational psychologists propose that the inequality in the workplace may be the result of several factors. Companies may discriminate against women. Many women interrupt their careers for child care and in doing so miss opportunities for promotion and salary increases. Also, men and women may differ in their ambition. That is, women may have been taught by society to set different goals.

SECTION 4 **Assessment**

1. **Review the Vocabulary** What is a person's gender schema?

2. **Visualize the Main Idea** Using an organizer similar to the one below, list and characterize three theories explaining the origins of gender differences.

   Origins of Gender Differences

   I. _____

   II. _____

3. **Recall Information** According to the social learning theory, how do children learn gender roles?

4. **Think Critically** Why might many people disagree with or oppose biological theories of gender differences?

5. **Application Activity** Review a TV program, movie, Internet site, or advertisement. Analyze the gender roles portrayed, then answer the following question: What role does the media play in the development of gender stereotypes?

Summary and Vocabulary

Adolescence is the transition period between childhood and adulthood.

Section 1 | **Physical and Sexual Development**

Main Idea: All adolescents experience dramatic changes in their physical size, shape, and capacities, as well as biological development related to reproduction.

- In his theory of adolescence, G. Stanley Hall portrayed the adolescent as existing in a state of great "storm and stress." Other psychologists and social scientists, such as Margaret Mead, regard adolescence as a relatively smooth continuous development out of childhood and into adulthood.
- The onset of puberty marks the end of childhood; both boys and girls experience a growth spurt just before puberty.
- The rate and pattern of sexual maturation varies so widely that it is difficult to apply norms or standards to puberty.

Section 2 | **Personal Development**

Main Idea: The transition from childhood to adulthood involves changes in patterns of reasoning and moral thinking, as well as the development of one's identity.

- During adolescence, most people reach the stage of formal operations thinking in which thinking becomes abstract and less concrete.
- According to Erik Erikson, building an identity is a task that is unique to adolescence; most adolescents must go through an identity crisis, a time of inner conflict during which they worry intensely about their identities.

Section 3 | **Social Development**

Main Idea: Adolescents undergo many changes in their social relationships, adjusting to new relationships with parents and the influence of peers.

- One of the principal developmental tasks for adolescents is becoming independent of their families.
- Belonging to a peer group fulfills the need for closeness with others and gives the adolescent a means of establishing an identity.
- Parents and peers exercise influence in shaping adolescent behavior and attitudes.

Section 4 | **Gender Roles and Differences**

Main Idea: Females and males have physical and psychological gender differences. Our beliefs about what we think it means to be male or female influence our behavior.

- During adolescence, individuals develop attitudes about gender and expectations about the gender role they will fill.
- Most psychologists agree that nature and nurture interact to influence gender differences.
- The roles of men and women in society are changing.

Chapter Vocabulary

initiation rites (p. 94)
puberty (p. 95)
menarche (p. 96)
spermarche (p. 96)
asynchrony (p. 96)
rationalization (p. 102)
identity crisis (p. 105)
social learning theory (p. 107)
clique (p. 111)
conformity (p. 111)
anorexia nervosa (p. 114)
bulimia nervosa (p. 115)
gender identity (p. 117)
gender role (p. 117)
gender stereotype (p. 117)
androgynous (p. 117)
gender schema (p. 122)

Self-Check Quiz
Visit the *Understanding Psychology* Web site at
psychology.glencoe.com and click on **Chapter 4—
Self-Check Quizzes** to prepare for the Chapter Test.

Reviewing Vocabulary

**Choose the letter of the correct term or concept
below to complete the sentence.**

a. puberty
b. asynchrony
c. gender identity
d. gender role
e. identity crisis

f. social learning theory
g. clique
h. conformity
i. gender stereotypes
j. anorexia nervosa

1. Belonging to a(n) _____ is important to most adolescents and serves several functions.

2. A person's physical and biological makeup is his or her _____.

3. According to Erik Erikson, adolescents go through a(n) _____, a time of inner conflict in which they worry about their identities.

4. _____ is an eating disorder in which an individual refuses to eat and loses weight.

5. The biological event that marks the end of childhood is _____.

6. Albert Bandura's belief that individuals develop by interacting with others is referred to as the _____ of development.

7. Feet that are too large for the body is an example of _____, or the condition of uneven growth or maturation of bodily parts.

8. A person's _____ is the standard of how a person with a given gender identity is supposed to behave.

9. Oversimplified or prejudiced opinions and attitudes concerning the way men or women should behave are called _____.

10. An adolescent's fear of being set apart from others leads to _____ among peer group members.

Recalling Facts

1. Describe G. Stanley Hall's theory of adolescence. Does the research of Margaret Mead support his position? Explain.

2. When Sandra Bem discusses androgyny, is she talking about gender role or gender identity?

3. Explain what Jean Piaget means by "formal operations" thinking. How does this change in cognitive ability affect an adolescent?

4. Use a chart similar to the one below to explain the identity formation theory of each of the following: Erik Erikson, James Marcia, Albert Bandura, and Margaret Mead.

Psychologist/Social Scientist	Theory of Identity Formation

5. How does the biological theory of gender development explain the differences in gender?

Critical Thinking

1. **Evaluating Information** Write five words or phrases that, in your opinion, characterize adolescence. Then ask an adult to also write five words or phrases. What are the similarities and the differences? What are some reasons for the differences?

2. **Analyzing Information** Which of the developmental tasks of adolescence do you think is the most difficult? Explain your answer.

3. **Demonstrating Reasoned Judgment** Do you think an individual with an androgynous gender role is healthier than one with a traditional gender role? Why do you think so?

4. **Making Inferences** Erikson and Marcia insist that all adolescents experience an identity crisis. Do you agree? Explain your answer.

5. **Synthesizing Information** Identify three different cliques in your school. How would you characterize the people who belong to each group? What do you think keeps groups together?

Psychology Projects

1. **Physical and Sexual Development** It has often been said that American culture is preoccupied with youthfulness. Find as many examples as you can of this in newspapers, magazines, radio, television, and popular music. Pay particular attention to advertising that emphasizes the marketing of youthful values. Cut out examples as evidence and compile a bulletin-board display.

2. **Personal Development** Work with a partner to develop a skit of a situation that illustrates the conflict that Erik Erikson believes teenagers face in trying to be unique on the one hand and to fit in on the other hand. Present your skit to the class and discuss ways that teenagers can resolve this conflict.

3. **Gender Roles and Differences** Review magazines and newspapers from the past 50 years to find examples of traditional gender roles and nontraditional roles. Clip or photocopy your examples and display them in a montage titled "Gender Roles—The Last 50 Years." What do the pictures say about gender roles in this country in the past 50 years?

Technology Activity

During adolescence, young people begin to better understand abstract principles and often tend to become idealistic. Find out about issues that are facing your lawmakers today. Then find the E-mail addresses of your representatives and send an E-mail to them, expressing your views and your wishes for the way they should address the issues. Share any responses.

Psychology Journal

Reread the journal entry that you wrote at the beginning of this chapter. Other social scientists have suggested that building an identity is a lifelong process and that changes to the identity occur at different times. Write a journal entry that argues that building an identity is a lifelong process. Support your argument with evidence from the chapter as well as evidence from your own experience. Finally, reread both entries and write a short summary explaining whether you think one position is more valid than the other.

Building Skills

Interpreting a Graph Review the graphs below, and then answer the questions that follow.

Practice and **assess** key social studies skills with **Glencoe Skillbuilder Interactive Workbook CD-ROM, Level 2.**

1. What is the major cause of death for people between the ages of 5 and 24?

2. How do the causes of death for the 5–24 age group compare to that of the 25 and older age group?

3. How do some of the thought processes of adolescents help explain the leading causes of death in young people?

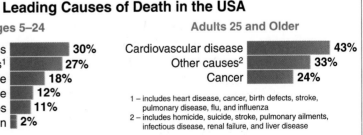

Leading Causes of Death in the USA

Young People Ages 5–24

Motor vehicle crashes	30%
Other causes[1]	27%
Homicide	18%
Suicide	12%
Other injuries	11%
HIV infection	2%

Adults 25 and Older

Cardiovascular disease	43%
Other causes[2]	33%
Cancer	24%

1 – includes heart disease, cancer, birth defects, stroke, pulmonary disease, flu, and influenza
2 – includes homicide, suicide, stroke, pulmonary ailments, infectious disease, renal failure, and liver disease

Source: National Center for Health Statistics, Centers for Disease Control and Prevention, 1995.

See the Skills Handbook, page 628, for an explanation of interpreting graphs.

Marya Hornbacher grew up in a comfortable, middle-class American home. At an early age, she remembers crying her heart out because she thought she was "fat." By age nine, she was secretly bulimic; by age 15, anorexic. In this excerpt, taken from her memoirs *Wasted* (1998), Marya describes her illness.

Reader's Dictionary

virulence: extreme bitterness
cacophony: a harsh sound
belie: to show to be false or wrong

WASTED

BY MARYA HORNBACHER

I became bulimic at the age of nine, anorexic at the age of fifteen. I couldn't decide between the two and veered back and forth from one to the other until I was twenty, and now, at twenty-three, I am an interesting creature, an Eating Disorder Not Otherwise Specified. My weight has ranged over the past thirteen years from 135 pounds to 52, inching up and then plummeting back down. I have gotten "well," then "sick," then "well," then "sicker," and so on up to now; I am considered "moderately improved," "psychologically stabilized, behaviorally disordered," "prone to habitual relapse." I have been hospitalized six times, institutionalized once, had endless hours of therapy, been tested and observed and diagnosed and pigeonholed and poked and prodded and fed and weighed for so long that I have begun to feel like a laboratory rat. . . .

I am not here to spill my guts and tell you about how awful it's been, that my daddy was mean and my mother was mean and some kid called me Fatso in the third grade, because none of the above is true. I am not going to repeat, at length, how eating disorders are "about control," because we've all heard it. It's a buzzword, reductive, categorical, a tidy way of herding people into a mental quarantine and saying: *There*. . . . The question is really not *if* eating disorders are "neurotic" and indicate a glitch in the mind—even I would have a hard time justifying, rationally, the practice of starving oneself to death or feasting only to toss back the feast—but rather why; why this glitch, what flipped this switch, why so many of us? Why so easy a choice, this? Why now? Some toxin in the air? Some freak of nature that has turned women against their own bodies with a virulence unmatched in history, all of a sudden, with no cause? The individual does not exist outside of society. There are reasons why this is happening, and they do not lie in the mind alone.

This book is neither a tabloid tale of mysterious disease nor a testimony to a miracle cure. It's simply the story of one woman's travels to a darker side of reality, and her decision to make her way back. On her own terms.

My terms amount to cultural heresy. I had to say: I will eat what I want and look as I please and laugh as loud as I like and use the wrong fork and lick my knife. I had to learn strange and delicious lessons, lessons too few women learn: to love the thump of my steps, the implication of weight and presence and taking of space, to love my body's rebellious hungers, responses to touch, to understand myself as more than a brain attached to a bundle of bones. I have to ignore the cultural cacophony that singsongs all day long, Too much, too much, too much. . . .

I wrote this book because I believe some people will recognize themselves in it—eating disordered or not—and because I believe, perhaps naively, that they might be willing to change their own behavior, get help if they need it, entertain the notion that their bodies are acceptable, that they themselves are neither insufficient nor in excess. I wrote it because I disagree with much of what is generally believed about eating disorders, and wanted to put in my two cents, for whatever it's worth. I wrote it because people often dismiss eating disorders as manifestations of vanity, immaturity, madness. It is, in some ways, all of these things. But it is also an addiction. It is a response, albeit a rather twisted one, to a culture, a family, a self. I wrote this because I want to dispel two common and contradictory myths about eating disorders: that they are an insignificant problem, solved by a little therapy and a little pill and a pat on the head, a "stage" that "girls" go through—I know a girl whose psychiatrist told her that her bulimia was just part of "normal adolescent development"—and, conversely, that they must belie true insanity, that they only happen to "those people" whose brains are incurably flawed, that "those people" are hopelessly "sick."

An eating disorder is not usually a phase, and it is not necessarily indicative of madness. It is quite maddening, granted, not only for the loved ones of the eating disordered person but also for the person herself. It is, at the most basic level, a bundle of deadly contradictions: a desire for power that strips you of all power. A gesture of strength that divests you of all strength. A wish to prove that you need nothing,

that you have no human hungers, which turns on itself and becomes a searing need for the hunger itself. It is an attempt to find an identity, but ultimately it strips you of any sense of yourself, save the sorry identity of "sick." It is a grotesque mockery of cultural standards of beauty that winds up mocking no one more than you. It is a protest against cultural stereotypes of women that in the end makes you seem the weakest, the most needy and neurotic of all women. It is the thing you believe is keeping you safe, alive, contained—and in the end, of course, you find it's doing quite the opposite. These contradictions begin to split a person in two. Body and mind fall apart from each other, and it is in this fissure that an eating disorder may flourish, in the silence that surrounds this confusion that an eating disorder may fester and thrive. . . .

There were numerous methods of self-destruction available to me, countless outlets that could have channeled my drive, perfectionism, ambition, and an excess of general intensity, millions of ways in which I could have responded to a culture that I found highly problematic. I did not choose those ways. I chose an eating disorder. I cannot help but think that, had I lived in a culture where "thinness" was not regarded as a strange state of grace, I might have sought out another means of attaining that grace, perhaps one that would not have so seriously damaged my body, and so radically distorted my sense of who I am.

Analyzing the Reading

1. Why did the author write this?
2. According to the author, how do eating disorders rob the sufferer of an identity?
3. **Critical Thinking** What underlying causes of her disorder does the author reveal?

Adulthood and Old Age

PSYCHOLOGY JOURNAL

You have probably heard the saying "You can't teach an old dog new tricks." In your journal, express this statement in your own words. Then, write whether you believe this saying is true, somewhat true, or false. ■

PSYCHOLOGY Online

Chapter Overview
Visit the *Understanding Psychology* Web site at psychology.glencoe.com and click on **Chapter 5—Chapter Overviews** to preview the chapter.

Reader's Guide

■ Main Idea
Adulthood is a time of transition—it involves shifting priorities and outlooks on life from adolescence and throughout the remainder of life.

■ Vocabulary
- menopause
- generativity
- stagnation

■ Objectives
- Characterize the physical changes that take place during adulthood.
- Describe the social and emotional changes that occur during adulthood.

EXPLORING PSYCHOLOGY

Questions

I remember sitting in a restaurant in Nags Head, North Carolina, . . . A woman I barely knew came over to me. She shook my shoulder, got right in my face and said "Hey, hey. Did you just find out that life ain't fair? Hmmm?" All I could do was nod. I had lived to be forty years old. I was a child of an upper-middle-class family, blessed with good health, a good education, and endless possibilities. Now I was confronting age-old questions: Where am I going with the rest of my life?" "Who am I?" I vaguely remembered asking these questions as a teenager but had forgotten the answers, if I ever knew them. After that I forgot to ask the questions.

—from *Awakening at Midlife* by Kathleen A. Brehony, 1996

L ike the author above, many people face questions and adjustment in adulthood. What is adulthood like? For one thing, it is a period when opposite factors affect lives. There is change and sameness, success and failure, crisis and stability, joy and sadness. Adulthood can be a time when a person matures fully into what he or she is, or it can be a time when life closes in and what was once possibility is now limitation. How each of us reacts depends on circumstances and our general outlook on life.

PHYSICAL CHANGES

Reading Check
What physical changes occur as we age?

One theory of aging claims that our bodies age as a result of breakdowns in our body's cells. With time our body's cells become less able to repair themselves. Thus aging is the result of normal wear and tear on our bodies. Another theory says that our bodies age because our cells have preset biological "clocks" that limit the number of times cells can divide and multiply. After cells have reached that limit, they begin to die and aging occurs.

In general, young adults are at their physical peak between the ages of 18 and 30 (see Figure 5.1). This is the period when we are the strongest, healthiest, and have the quickest reflexes. For most adults, the process of physical decline is slow and gradual—not at all noticeable, even month to month. For example, a 20-year-old manages to carry four heavy bags of groceries, while a 40-year-old finds it easier to make two trips. What is lost physically may be replaced by experience. A 60-year-old racquetball player who is well versed in the game's strategies can compete with a faster, less experienced 30-year-old player.

In middle age, appearance changes. The hair starts to turn gray and perhaps to thin out. The skin becomes somewhat dry and inelastic, and wrinkles appear. In old age, muscles and fat built up over the years break down so that people often lose weight, become shorter, and develop more wrinkles, creases, and loose skin. Some physiological changes occur as we become older, while behavioral factors and lifestyles can affect psychological health.

With time the senses require more and more stimulation. During their 40s, most people begin having difficulty seeing distant objects, adjusting to the dark, and focusing on printed pages, even if their eyesight has always been good. Many experience a gradual or sudden loss of hearing in their later years. In addition, reaction time slows. If an experimenter asks a young person and an older person to push a button when they see a light flash on, the older person will take about 20 percent longer to do so.

More About...

The Cohort Effect

Suppose you were asked to measure the performance of trains at various points along a busy route. How would you go about it?

You might adopt a longitudinal approach. You would board a train and stay with it for its entire journey, recording your observations along the way. Alternatively, you might employ a cross-sectional strategy. You would ask observers stationed at key points to report on the performance of various trains that pass by.

Psychologists who study the behavior of people as they progress through adulthood and old age face a similar task. Since this "journey" can last decades, few researchers adopt a purely longitudinal approach. Instead, most conduct cross-sectional studies in which they can measure different age groups, or cohorts, together at one time.

Unfortunately, people from different cohorts usually have different experiences in a number of important areas, including access to education, nutrition, career opportunities, and social values. Their different backgrounds make it difficult to determine how age affects human abilities, attitudes, and even health.

Health Problems

Some of the changes we associate with growing older are the result of the natural processes of aging. Others result from diseases and from simple disuse and abuse. Good health reflects a life of making choices, which involve exercise, diet, and lifestyle. A person who eats sensibly, exercises, avoids cigarettes, drugs, and alcohol, and is not subjected to severe emotional stress will look and feel younger than someone who neglects his or her health.

Three of the most common causes of death in later adulthood—heart disease, cancer, and cirrhosis of the liver—may be encouraged by the fast-moving lifestyle of young adults. Drug abuse—likely to peak in late adolescence or young adulthood and drop sharply after that—is a problem. Other contributing factors are inadequate diet and violent deaths. The deaths may result from accidents, a tendency—especially among males—to push the physical limits, and a social environment that encourages risk taking among young adults (Miedzian, 1991). All three of these contributing factors are psychological, although their ultimate effects have biological consequences.

Menopause

Between the ages of 45 and 50, every woman experiences a stage called the *climacteric,* which rep-

Figure 5.1   How Our Bodies Age

When young adults reach their 20s, they have reached the level of highest physical ability and capacity. *What are some theories as to why our bodies age?*

Ages

20s

Early Adulthood: Most of us reach our peaks in our 20s. Our immune systems, senses, and mental skills operate at maximum efficiency.

30s

40s

Middle Adulthood: In our 30s and 40s, we may become less active and start to gain weight. By our late 40s, our heart rates, lung capacity, muscle strength, and eyesight slightly decrease.

50s

60s

Late Adulthood: In our 50s and 60s, we experience a gradual bone loss and a further decrease in lung output. Our skin wrinkles and our joints deteriorate. Sensory organs become less sensitive. Our hearts become less efficient.

70s

80s

Old Age: Our muscle strength, bone density, speed of nerve connections, and heart and lung output further decrease.

90s

resents all of the psychological and biological changes occurring at that time. A woman's production of sex hormones drops sharply—a biological event called **menopause.** The woman stops ovulating (producing eggs) and menstruating and therefore cannot conceive children. However, menopause does not cause any reduction in a woman's sexual drive or sexual enjoyment. Many women experience little or no discomfort during menopause. The irritability and severe depression some women experience during the climacteric, however, appear to have an emotional rather than physical origin.

One study shows that the negative effects of menopause are greatly exaggerated. Women are also undergoing environmental changes in roles and relationships at this time. Half of the women interviewed said they felt better, more confident, calmer, and freer after menopause than they had before. They no longer had to think about their periods or getting pregnant. Their relations with their husbands improved, and they enjoyed sex as much as or more than they had before. Many said the worst part of menopause was not knowing what to expect (Neugarten et al., 1963).

menopause: the biological event in which a woman's production of sex hormones is sharply reduced

Men do not go through any biological change equivalent to menopause. The number of sperm a man's body produces declines gradually over the years, but men have fathered children at an advanced age. It appears as if men go through psychological changes related to expectations about work, the death of parents, illness, and aging in general.

Marriage and Divorce

About 90 percent of adults in the United States will marry at some time in their lives. Forty to sixty percent of new marriages, though, end in divorce. What makes a marriage last? Researchers who have performed longitudinal studies on married couples have proposed that success or failure largely depends on two factors: how couples handle conflicts and how often couples share intimate and happy moments.

Although happily married couples seem to argue just as much as unhappy couples, they argue more constructively. They listen to each other and focus on solving the problem. They also show respect for each other's views. Unhealthy ways of dealing with conflict include ignoring or denying conflict, exaggerating issues, and having ugly verbal fights.

Sexual Behavior

Is there sex after 40? Studies have shown that sexual activity does not automatically decline with age. Indeed, as sex researchers William Masters and Virginia Johnson point out, there is no physiological reason for stopping sexual activity with advancing age (1970). Most older people who have an available partner maintain quite vigorous sex lives. Those who are inactive cite boredom with a partner of long standing, poor physical condition or illness (such as heart disease), or acceptance of the stereotype of loss of sex drive with aging (Mulligan & Moss, 1991).

COGNITIVE CHANGES

People are better at learning new skills and information, solving problems that require speed and coordination, and shifting from one problem-solving strategy to another in their mid-20s than they were in adolescence (Baltes & Schaie, 1977). These abilities are considered signs of intelligence and are among the skills that intelligence tests measure.

At one time many psychologists thought that intellectual development reached a peak in the mid-20s and then declined. The reason was that people do not score as high on intelligence

Figure 5.2   Marriage

Many people, like this couple in India, marry in young adulthood. It is an Amish tradition for the father to adjust the height of this "courting candle." His daughter must return from her date before the candle burns down to the first rung. *How are conflicts resolved in happy marriages?*

tests in middle age as they did when they were younger. Further investigation revealed that some parts of these tests measure speed, not intelligence (Bischof, 1969). As indicated earlier, a person's reaction time begins to slow after a certain age. Intelligence tests usually "penalized" adults for this.

Even with a decline in speed, people continue to acquire information and to expand their vocabularies as they grow older. The ability to comprehend new material and to think flexibly improves with years and experience. This is particularly true if a person has had higher education, lives in a stimulating environment, and works in an intellectually demanding career. One researcher studied more than 700 individuals who were engaged in scholarship, science, or the arts. Although the patterns varied from profession to profession, most of the participants reached their peaks of creativity and productivity in their 40s (Dennis, 1966), but in the humanities, such as history, foreign languages, and literature, most reached their peaks later in their 60s.

Did You Know?

Arranged Marriages   While most American couples marry for love, people in many other parts of the world follow the tradition of having marriages arranged. Arranged marriages often prove more lasting than ones based on love because the society usually disapproves of breaking up an arranged union. Some researchers also believe that the union lasts longer because each person enters the union without expectations of personal happiness. Such arranged marriages usually provide strong family ties and, therefore, support on both sides.

SOCIAL AND PERSONALITY DEVELOPMENT

An individual's basic character—his or her style of adapting to situations—is relatively stable over the years. Researchers are also convinced, however, that personality is flexible and capable of changing as an individual confronts new tasks. A number of researchers have given the same attitude and personality tests to individuals in late adolescence and again 10 or 15 years later. Many of the participants believed that they had changed dramatically, but the tests indicated that they had not. The degree of satisfaction they expressed about themselves and about life in general in their middle years was consistent with their earlier views. Confident young people remained confident; self-haters, self-hating; passive individuals, passive—unless something upsetting had happened to them, such as a sudden change in economic status (Kimmel, 1980).

Despite the stability of character, people do face many changes in their lifetimes and adjust accordingly. Adults encounter new developmental tasks, just as adolescents do. They too must learn to cope with problems and deal with new situations. Learning the skills needed to cope with change seems to occur in stages for both adult males and females.

Levinson's Theory of Male Development

Daniel Levinson proposed a model of adult development for men (see Figure 5.3). Notice the similarity between Levinson's eras and the last three of the eight stages of Erikson's psychosocial theory, which was discussed in Chapter 3. Between these eras, Levinson identified important transition periods at ages 30, 40, 50, and 60 that last approximately 5 years.

Reading Check
In what ways does intelligence increase as we grow older?

Figure 5.3   Levinson's Theory of Male Development

This model shows the developmental sequence of a man's life that Levinson proposed. The scheme emphasizes that development is an ongoing process that requires continual adjustment. *According to Levinson, what happens during the "age-thirty crisis"?*

Age		Era
70		Late Adult Era
65	Late Adult Transition	
60	Culmination of Middle Adulthood	Middle Adult Era
55	Age 50 Transition	
50	Entering Middle Adulthood	
45	Midlife Transition	
40	Settling Down	Early Adult Era
33	Age 30 Transition	
28	Entering the Adult World	
22	Early Adult Transition	
17		
(Age)	Childhood and Adolescence	

Entering the Adult World   From about age 22 to age 28, the young man is considered, both by himself and by society, to be a novice in the adult world—not fully established as a man, but no longer an adolescent. During this time, he must attempt to resolve the conflict between the need to explore the options of the adult world and the need to establish a stable life structure.

The Age-Thirty Crisis   Levinson's data reveal that the years between 28 and 30 are often a major transitional period. The thirtieth birthday can truly be a turning point; it could be called the "age-thirty crisis." During this transitional period, the tentative commitments that were made in the first life structure are reexamined, and many questions about the choices of marriage partner, career, and life goals are reopened, often in a painful way. The man feels that any parts of his life that are unsatisfying or incomplete must be attended to now, because it will soon be too late to make major changes.

Settling Down   The questioning and searching that are part of the age-thirty crisis begin to be resolved as the second adult-life structure develops. Having probably made some firm choices about his career, family, and relationships, the man now begins actively carving out a niche in society, concentrating on what Levinson calls "making it" in the adult world.

Levinson found that near the end of the settling-down period, approximately between the ages of 36 and 40, there is a distinctive

BOOM phase—"becoming one's own man." Now it is time to become fully independent. During this period, the man strives to attain the seniority and position in the world that he identified as his ultimate goal at the beginning of the settling-down period.

The Midlife Transition At about age 40, the period of early adulthood comes to an end and the midlife transition begins. From about age 40 to age 45, the man begins again to ask questions, but now the questions concern the past as well as the future. He may ask: "What have I done with my life?" "What have I accomplished?" "What do I still wish to accomplish?" During this transition, he begins to develop yet another life structure that will predominate during the period of middle adulthood.

Often a successful midlife transition is accompanied by the man's becoming a mentor to a younger man. This event signals the attainment, in Erik Erikson's terms, of generativity. By **generativity,** Erikson means the desire to use one's wisdom to guide future generations—directly, as a parent, or indirectly. The opposite—**stagnation**—can also occur. A man may choose to hang on to the past, perhaps by taking part in the same sports. On the other hand, he may become preoccupied with his health or bitter about the direction his life has taken. Generativity or stagnation occurs for both men and women.

Middle Adulthood The late 40s is a time when true adulthood can be achieved. The man who finds satisfactory solutions to his life crisis reaches a period of stability. He understands and tolerates others, and he displays a sensitivity and concern for other people as people. He is able to strike a balance between the need for friends and the need for privacy.

For the man who is not as fortunate, this period can be a time of extreme frustration and unhappiness. Instead of generativity, there is stagnation; instead of change and improvement, there is a mood of resignation to a bad situation. The job is only a job. The individual may feel cut off from family and friends, and the future holds no promise. By avoiding this life crisis, he is only inviting a later appearance of it, at age 50, with a more crushing force (Rogers, 1979). Keep in mind that Levinson's eras and transitions are based on averages from many individual interviews. Nobody's life is likely to match Levinson's divisions exactly.

Female Development

While there have been far more studies conducted among men than among women, some researchers have focused their attention on women's midlife development. While many men experience a crisis at midlife, married women at midlife may be facing fewer demands in their traditional task as mother. For many, this means greater personal freedom. As a result, they may be reentering the workforce, going back to college, or starting or renewing careers outside the home. Rather than a time of crisis, it is a time of opportunity for those who opted to have a family first. Evidence generally does not support the existence of a midlife crisis for most women in today's world (Berger, 1994).

Student Web Activity
Visit the *Understanding Psychology* Web site at psychology.glencoe.com and click on **Chapter 5— Student Web Activities** for an activity about adult development.

generativity: the desire, in middle age, to use one's accumulated wisdom to guide future generations

stagnation: a discontinuation of development and a desire to recapture the past

Quick Lab

Do men and women go through the same stages of development?

The latest studies show that just as during adolescence, men and women also go through stages of development during adulthood. Are their experiences the same?

Procedure

1. Prepare a list of interview questions that address a person's attitude about work, family relationships, and importance of physical attractiveness.

2. Arrange to interview, separately, a man and a woman who are middle-aged; explain the purpose of your interview to them.

Analysis

1. What differences in attitudes or feelings did you detect between the man and the woman?

2. Based on your interview, do you think men and women go through different stages of adult development? Explain. As a class compare your conclusions.

See the Skills Handbook, page 622, for an explanation of designing an experiment.

The "Empty Nest" Syndrome   A significant event in many women's lives is the departure from home of the last child. Contrary to popular belief, this event need not be traumatic. In fact, many women find that the period after the children are grown is one of the happiest of their lives. If they have not already done so, they reorganize their lives by focusing on new interests and activities (Grambs, 1989).

Of course, not all women experience the same sense of new freedom. Psychologists have found that a stable marriage makes a difference. If a woman has a warm relationship with her husband, she may find the adjustment easier because of his support. If the woman is widowed or divorced, the transition can be much more difficult.

Depression in Midlife   Depression can affect people of all ages, but it is most common among middle-aged women. During the early years of a woman's life, she may derive a sense of personal worth from her roles of daughter, lover, wife, and mother. These relationships change as children grow, parents die, or marriages fail. Some women begin to experience a sense of loss and personal worthlessness. The onset of menopause can trigger depression. Those who have defined themselves as childbearers now view themselves as useless when they lose their ability to produce and care for children. Other women welcome this time of life. Some women in their 50s find that the nature of their marriage changes when they no longer have to focus their attention on the needs of their children.

SECTION 1 Assessment

1. **Review the Vocabulary**   What is menopause? What physical reactions does it cause?

2. **Visualize the Main Idea**   Use a flow-chart similar to the one below to summarize Levinson's theory of male development.

Levinson's Theory of Male Development

3. **Recall Information**   How do generativity and stagnation affect a person's mid-life transition?

4. **Think Critically**   How do the intelligence abilities of young adults and older adults differ?

5. **Application Activity**   Create a comparison chart of challenges faced by adults and adolescents. Include illustrations and real-life examples.

Old Age

Reader's Guide

■ Main Idea
As we age, our priorities and expectations change to match realities, and we experience losses as well as gains.

■ Vocabulary
- decremental model of aging
- ageism
- senile dementia
- Alzheimer's disease

■ Objectives
- Identify changes that occur in health and life situation during old age.
- Summarize how people physically, mentally, and socially adjust to old age.

EXPLORING PSYCHOLOGY

Be Suspicious

Be suspicious if you are told ill health is what you can expect at your age. Remember the man of 104 who, when he complained of a stiff knee, was told, "After all, you can't expect to be agile," and replied, "My left knee's 104, too, and that doesn't hurt."

—from *Say Yes to Old Age: Developing a Positive Attitude Toward Aging* by Alex Comfort, 1990

Many people believe that experiencing problems in old age is inevitable. In one big-city newspaper, the photograph of a man celebrating his ninetieth birthday was placed on the obituary page. Is this only one newspaper editor's view on aging? Perhaps, but unfortunately, many people tend to regard old age as being just one step away from the grave. Indeed, some would rather die than grow old.

The fear of growing old is probably one of the most common fears in our society. We are surrounded with indications that aging and old age are negative—or at best something to ridicule. Birthday cards make light of aging; comedians joke about it. Advertisements urge us to trade in older products for the newer, faster model. We encourage older workers to retire—whether or not they want to retire—and replace them with younger people. Many do not even want to use the word *old* and instead refer to "golden agers" and "senior citizens."

ATTITUDES TOWARD AGING

decremental model of aging: idea that progressive physical and mental decline are inevitable with age

Many of our attitudes about aging are based on a **decremental model of aging**, which holds that progressive physical and mental decline is inevitable with age. In other words, chronological age is what makes people "old." In fact, there are great differences in physical condition among the elderly, depending on their genetic makeup and environment. Many of us know people who are 80 and look and act 50, and vice versa. The prevalence of the decremental view in our society can be explained in part by ignorance and a lack of contact with older people. The result is a climate of prejudice against the old. A researcher coined the word **ageism** to refer to this prejudice. As with racism and sexism, ageism feeds on myths rather than facts.

ageism: prejudice or discrimination against the elderly

Young people tend to believe that the old suffer from poor health, live in poverty, and are frequent victims of crime. The elderly seldom see these as personal problems, though; interestingly, they tend to think of them as problems for other older people (Harris, 1978). Such beliefs, however, affect stereotypes of the elderly.

The notion that the aged withdraw from life and sit around doing nothing is also very common. This, too, is a false picture. There are many musicians and actors who are good examples of active older individuals, and many less well-known older people follow their lead. The majority of older Americans work or wish to work either for pay or as volunteers. Stereotypes perpetrate widespread misconceptions about older people.

One misconception is the notion that older people are inflexible or senile. Actually, rigidity is more a lifelong habit than a response to aging. The older person who tends to be rigid was probably rigid as a young adult. Senility, which affects only 10 percent of the aged, usually results from some disease rather than from the natural process of aging.

Figure 5.4	Views of Growing Older

Despite the negative attitudes associated with growing older, many people find their forties, fifties, and older years rewarding periods of life. *How does this cartoonist view the process of aging?*

CHANGES IN HEALTH

Most people over 65 are in reasonably good health. Physical strength and the senses do decline, of course. For the most part, the health of an older person is related to his or her health when younger. Good health in adolescence and adult life carries over into old age. Eating habits and exercise influence patterns of health and disease. Today's emphasis on healthy lifestyles will also lead to physical wellness into old age.

All people, young and old, are subject to disease, though. About 40 percent of the elderly have at least one chronic disease (a permanent disability as opposed to an acute or temporary disability more common with younger people). The four most prevalent chronic diseases are heart disease, hypertension, diabetes, and arthritis. In general, the major causes of death among the old are heart disease, cancer, and strokes. Most older people, though, believe their health is good. Nearly three-fourths of the noninstitutionalized people aged 65 to 74 years old and two-thirds of those 75 and older rate their health as good (U.S. Bureau of the Census, 1995).

The quality of health care for the elderly remains by and large inferior to that of the general population. The reasons for this are numerous. The elderly in the lower socioeconomic class tend not to take care of themselves or to seek out treatment when needed. Some doctors may prefer to administer to younger patients with acute diseases rather than to older patients with long-term chronic conditions that can only be stabilized, not cured. Some doctors hold stereotypical views of the aged that can lead to misdiagnosis and improper treatment.

For the 1 million old people who are no longer able to care for themselves, there are institutions (but only 15 percent of males and 25 percent of females live in nursing homes). Too many of these nursing homes, however, have inadequate facilities. As more and more people each year reach late adulthood, it is paramount that there be a general overhaul of health care treatment and facilities for the elderly.

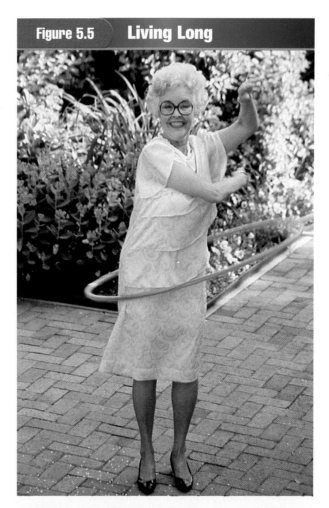

Figure 5.5 Living Long

A larger percentage of people in our society are living to more advanced ages. As a result, the elderly exert an increasing influence. *How does a person's health change with age?*

CHANGES IN LIFE SITUATION

For younger people, transitions in life—graduation, marriage, parenthood—are usually positive and create a deeper involvement in life. In late adulthood, transitions—retirement, widowhood—are often negative and

Reading Check
What major changes in life situation affect older people?

reduce responsibilities and increase isolation. Perhaps the most devastating transition is the loss of a spouse. Over 50 percent of women and 20 percent of men are widowed by the age of 65. By the age of 80, one-third of men and 7 out of 10 women are alone. Across the entire age spectrum, there are six widows for every widower (U.S. Census Bureau, 1998). All too often, the person loses not just a spouse but the support of friends and family, who cannot cope with the widowed person's grief or feel threatened by the survivor's new status as a single person.

The symptoms of depression are very common in older adults. Many older people have suffered because of life challenges such as aging and loss of spouses and friends. Symptoms such as weight changes, feelings of worthlessness, extreme sadness, inability to concentrate, and thoughts of death and suicide are often cited. Depression is caused by many factors, such as genetic predisposition, family heritage, an unhealthy lifestyle, poor nutrition, lack of exercise, loneliness, and stress.

On the positive side, older people continue to learn and develop skills more than ever before. Some people attend night school, local adult education classes, or learn about computers. It has become clear that in older adults some abilities such as nonverbal tasks and problem solving may decline, but other abilities remain normal and some improve with age.

More About...

Growing Old

America's old people may not be given much respect because they often lack status. Many occupy the lower rungs of the economic ladder and go without adequate medical care. In Japan that situation rarely develops because the able-bodied continue to work or to help their families in the home. In addition, they are guaranteed a minimum income, receive free annual health examinations, and are eligible for completely free medical care after age 70.

The Japanese also fully integrate the elderly into their daily lives. In Japan 75 percent of the old live with their children, as opposed to only 25 percent in the United States. For those who do live alone, the Japanese have established programs to assure that they receive daily visits or calls. To encourage the active involvement of all older citizens in social activities, the government subsidizes Elders Clubs and sports programs. Through these programs the aged supply each other with mutual support and gain a sense of self-pride.

CHANGES IN SEXUAL ACTIVITY

Just as young people tend to think sexual activity diminishes at midlife, they often believe it ceases altogether in old age. Yet the majority of people over the age of 65 continue to be interested in sex, and healthy partners enjoy sexual activity into their 70s and 80s. One psychologist commented that "Sexy young people mature into sexy middle-aged and elderly people" (Allgeier, 1983). As with so many human behaviors, the best predictor of future behavior is past behavior. For the elderly with an available partner, the frequency and regularity of sexual activities during earlier years are the best overall predictor of such activities in later years. The reasons some do not engage in sexual activity apparently are related to poor health or the death of a spouse, rather than to a lack of interest or to sexual physiology and functioning. Societal attitudes are another factor that discourages sexual expression by the elderly. Old people are not supposed to be interested in sex or be sexually active. Sexual relationships in old age—and even displays of affection—are often considered silly, improper, or even morally wrong.

People who grow old in this atmosphere may give up sexual activity because they are "supposed to." On a more personal level, older people often encounter opposition from family and friends if they want to remarry after the death of a spouse. Children and family, too, find the idea of love and sex in old age ridiculous or even vaguely disgusting. A change in our ideas may enable a large segment of our population to continue to enjoy a guilt-free, healthy sex life in old age.

ADJUSTING TO OLD AGE

Many of the changes the elderly face make their adjustment to everyday life more difficult because they represent a loss of control over the environment. When older people are unable to maintain what they value most—good health, recognition in the community, visits from family and friends, privacy, leisure and work activities—the quality of their life suffers dramatically, along with their self-image.

The loss of control is usually gradual, and it may involve both physical changes (becoming sick or disabled) and external circumstances (moving to a nursing home). Losing a husband is terrible enough, but the burden is only made worse by the further losses of friends and one's house. Those who experience a loss of control often develop a negative self-concept. They can regain their sense of control and a more positive self-image if they are helped to make the best of the options available to them. People with assertive personalities are often better at coping with life changes than more passive individuals because they are better able to demand and get the attention they need.

In order to help old people adjust, society must make some basic changes. Older people are beginning this process themselves by supporting organizations such as the AARP (American Association of Retired Persons). These groups speak out and lobby on social issues of importance to them. Since the population over 65 is constantly growing, social policy will have to take the elderly into consideration more and more (see Figure 5.6). Attitudes toward old people are already slowly changing. Eventually a time will come when old age will be considered the culmination of life, not simply the termination.

PSYCHOLOGY and You — Retirement and You

The average age in North America continues to creep upward. That is bad news for the smaller number of children being born and growing up now as they plan for their own retirement. Today's retirees can count on Social Security for funds—but will those funds be there when you retire? Social Security is not a personal retirement program; it is a tax-supported benefit. What workers pay in as a salary tax is paid right back out to today's retirees as a benefit.

As the number of older people increases and the number in the workforce does not, one of two things has to happen. Taxes have to go up to continue supporting Social Security at its current levels. A more likely scenario, however, is a decrease in Social Security benefits. Today's workers—this means you—need to be finding other funding sources for their retirement.

CHANGES IN MENTAL FUNCTIONING

As people age, there are also changes in many of the mental functions they use, although there is much less decline in intelligence and memory than people think. If you compare measures of intellectual ability for a

Figure 5.6   **Percentage of Older Population**

The number of elderly in the United States is rapidly growing. *How have life expectancy rates changed since 1950?*

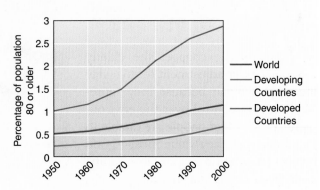

group of elderly people with similar measures for younger people, you might see a difference—namely that older people do not score as well on intellectual tests. However, the older group of people will most likely be less educated and less familiar with test taking than younger people. Furthermore, there are many different types of mental skills and abilities that combine to produce intellectual functioning, and these abilities do not develop at the same rate or time across the life span. Factors such as physical health, vision, hearing, coordination, the speed or timing of intelligence testing, and attitudes in the testing situation all affect intelligence test scores.

John Horn (1982) has proposed two types of intelligence: *crystallized* and *fluid* intelligence. Crystallized intelligence refers to the ability to use accumulated knowledge and learning in appropriate situations. This ability increases with age and experience. Fluid intelligence is the ability to solve abstract relational problems and to generate new hypotheses. This ability is not tied to schooling or education and gradually increases in development as the nervous system matures. As people age and their nervous systems decline, so does their fluid intelligence. Thus, older people may not be as good at problems that require them to combine and generate new ideas. A decline in the nervous system affects reaction time, visual motor flexibility, and memory (see Figure 5.7). Elderly people have difficulty retrieving information from memory. If they are asked to recognize a familiar name or object, they cannot do so as well as younger people.

Senile Dementia

A small percentage of people develop senile dementia in old age. **Senile dementia** is a collective term that describes conditions characterized by memory loss, forgetfulness, disorientation of time and place, a decline in the ability to think, impaired attention, altered personality, and

senile dementia: decreases in mental abilities experienced by some people in old age difficulties in relating to others. Dementia has many causes—some forms are treatable, whereas others are not at this time.

Alzheimer's Disease The most common form of senile dementia is Alzheimer's disease. **Alzheimer's disease** is an affliction more commonly seen among the elderly. About 4 million people have this disease, and it is the fourth leading cause of death among U.S. adults.

Alzheimer's is a neurological disease marked by a gradual deterioration of cognitive functioning. Early signs of the disease include frequent forgetting, poor judgment, increased irritability, and social withdrawal. Eventually Alzheimer's patients lose their ability to comprehend simple questions and to recognize friends and loved ones. Ultimately they require constant supervision and custodial care often from trained professionals. Rarely do patients die from the disease itself, but their weakened state leaves them vulnerable to a variety of other potentially fatal problems.

The causes of Alzheimer's are complex and still not completely understood. Genetic susceptibility plays a role. Other causes may involve life events. At present there is no cure for the disease. Many patients and their caretakers (usually their families) are offered supportive therapy that helps them learn to accept the relentless progression of the disease and the limitations it imposes on its victims.

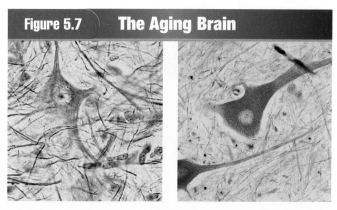

Figure 5.7   The Aging Brain

At left is a microscopic image of neurons (nerve cells) in the cerebellum (brain) of a young adult. At right is an image of neurons in an older adult. Notice that the branching of the dendrites decreases, reducing the connections between neurons. *What effects do aging neuron connections have on older people?*

Alzheimer's disease: a condition that destroys a person's ability to think, remember, relate to others, and care for herself or himself

---

SECTION **2**   ## Assessment

1. **Review the Vocabulary** Describe the decremental model of aging. Is this an accurate model of aging? Explain.

2. **Visualize the Main Idea** Use a graphic organizer similar to the one below to list and define the two types of intelligence.

   Types of Intelligence

3. **Recall Information** How do life transitions in late adulthood differ from those in early adulthood?

4. **Think Critically** How might a person differentiate between Alzheimer's disease and changes in mental processes as a result of aging?

5. **Application Activity** Create a "to-do" list that will help you successfully adjust to old age.

Reader's Guide

■ **Main Idea**

Death is inevitable. Most people face death by going through stages or an adjustment process.

■ **Vocabulary**
- thanatology
- hospice

■ **Objectives**
- Identify the stages of dying.
- Describe the services of hospices.

EXPLORING PSYCHOLOGY

Thinking About Death

Goodbye Papa, it's hard to die
When all the birds are singing in the sky
Now that the spring is in the air
Little kids are everywhere
Think of me and I'll be there.

—from "Seasons in the Sun" by Terry Jacks

Dying and death are popular subjects for many poets and song-writers. Why does death mystify us? Death is inevitable. Death is not just biological. When a person dies, there are legal, medical, psychological, and social aspects that need attention. It is not very easy to even define death anymore because there are medical advances that cloud this issue.

Biological death becomes entangled with social customs. These customs include cultural attitudes toward death, care of the dying, the place of death, and efforts to quicken or slow down the dying process. Death also has social aspects, including the disposal of the dead, mourning customs, and the role of the family. These social and cultural aspects of death are intertwined with our own thoughts and values about dying and death. Death may sound simple, but culturally it may be complex and confusing.

ADJUSTING TO DEATH

Once terminally ill patients have been informed of their condition, they must then cope with their approaching death. Elisabeth Kübler-Ross (1969) did some pioneering work on how the terminally ill react to their impending death. Her investigations made a major contribution in establishing **thanatology**—the study of dying and death. Based on interviews with 200 dying patients, she identified five stages of psychological

thanatology: the study of dying and death

adjustment. The first stage is *denial*. People's most common reaction to learning that they have a terminal illness is shock and numbness, followed by denial. They react by saying, "No, it can't be happening to me," or "I'll get another opinion." They may assert that the doctors are incompetent or the diagnosis mistaken. In extreme cases, people may refuse treatment and persist in going about business as usual. Most patients who use denial extensively throughout their illness are people who have become accustomed to coping with difficult life situations in this way. Indeed, the denial habit may contribute to the seriousness of a condition. For example, a person might refuse to seek medical attention at the onset of the illness, denying that it exists.

During the second stage, *anger,* the reaction of dying people is "Why me?" They feel anger—at fate, at the powers that be, at every person who comes into their life. At this stage, they are likely to alienate themselves from others, for no one can relieve the anger they feel at their shortened life span and lost chances.

During the stage of *bargaining,* people change their attitude and attempt to bargain with fate. For example, a woman may ask God for a certain amount of time in return for good behavior. She may promise a change of ways, even a dedication of her life to the church. She may announce that she is ready to settle for a less threatening form of the same illness and begin to bargain with the doctor over the diagnosis. For example, if she submits gracefully to some procedures, might she be rewarded by being spared the next stage of the illness? This stage is relatively short and is followed by the stage of *depression.*

During depression, dying people are aware of the losses they are incurring (for example, loss of body tissue, loss of job, loss of life savings). Also, they

Profiles In Psychology

Elisabeth Kübler-Ross

1926–

"If you have lived fully, then you have no regrets, because you have done the best you can. If you made lots of goofs— much better to have made lots of goofs than not to have lived at all."

As a young woman, Dr. Kübler-Ross visited a concentration camp in Maidanek, Germany, during World War II. There she spoke to a young Jewish woman who had just lost her entire family in a gas chamber. This woman was supposed to be the last one in the chamber, but there was not room, so she was spared. When Kübler-Ross asked how Nazi leader Adolf Hitler could commit such atrocities, the woman replied that there is a Hitler in every human. Kübler-Ross came to understand that depending on the circumstances, anyone could do horrible things.

After that experience Kübler-Ross sought to understand humans and human death. This eventually led her to develop a theory on the stages of dying. As a result of her studies, many people have been able to come to terms with death and help others die in peace.

are depressed about the loss that is to come: they are in the process of losing everybody and everything. Kübler-Ross suggests that it is helpful to allow such people to express their sadness and not to attempt to cover up the situation or force them to act cheerfully.

Finally, patients *accept* death. The struggle is over, and they experience a sense of calm. In some cases, the approach of death feels appropriate or peaceful. They seem to become detached intentionally so as to make death easier.

Not all terminal patients progress through the stages that Kübler-Ross describes. Some people may go through the stages but in different order, or they may repeat some stages. Critics note that individuals are unique and sometimes do not follow predictable patterns of behavior. For example, a person may die in the denial stages because he or she is psychologically unable to proceed beyond it or because the course of the illness does not grant the necessary time to do so. Kübler-Ross notes that patients do not limit their responses to any one stage; a depressed patient may have recurring bursts of anger. She notes, too, that all patients in all stages persist in having hope. Even the most accepting and realistic patients leave open the possibility that they may live after all.

Reading Check
Why do some people criticize Kübler-Ross's stages of dying?

Most people have trouble dealing with the thought of their own death, and they also find it difficult to deal with the death of others. What should we do when a loved one is approaching death? Like all people, dying people need respect, dignity, and self-confidence. Dying people need support and care. They require open communication about what is happening (what to expect in terms of their illness) and legal and financial arrangements. What should we do after a loved one has died? Our society has developed certain standards that provide guidance on this point. For instance, in the 1800s, a widow or widower was expected to grieve for a long time. Today society encourages people to try to get back to their normal lives (Stroebe et al., 1992). How long a person grieves depends on the person who is grieving.

Hospices

The discussion of death is one of the few taboos left in twentieth-century America. The breakdown of extended families and the rise of modern medicine have insulated most people in our society from death. Many people have no direct experience with death, and partly as a result, they are afraid to talk about it. In 1900 the average life span was less than 50 years, and most people died at home in their own beds. Today, most Americans live until at least 75, and they die in nursing homes and hospitals. Elaborate machines may prolong existence long after a person has stopped living a normal life.

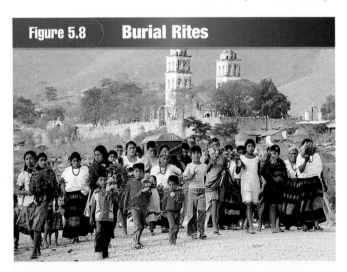

Figure 5.8 **Burial Rites**

The ceremonies associated with death in many cultures, like the Mexican culture, help people start and work through the grieving process. *How might funeral ceremonies force people to confront and accept the death of a loved one?*

A movement to restore the dignity of dying revolves around the concept of the **hospice**—usually a special place where terminally ill people go to die. The hospice is designed to make the patient's surroundings pleasant and comfortable—less like a hospital and more like a home. Doctors in hospices do not try to prolong life but to improve the quality of life. A key component of hospice care is the use of tranquilizers and other drugs to ease discomfort and relieve pain. The patient in a hospice leads the most normal life he or she is able to do and is taken care of as much as possible by family members. If it can be arranged, a patient may choose to die at home.

Another form of hospice service is becoming part of the mainstream of the health care system of the United States. This program features care for the elderly at home by visiting nurses, aides, physical therapists, chaplains, and social workers. Medicare now includes arrangements for providing and financing these hospice services. Many other insurance policies also include provisions for in-home hospice care and "respite care." Growing rapidly in recent years, home-based hospice care is now a more frequently used service than inpatient hospice care in the United States.

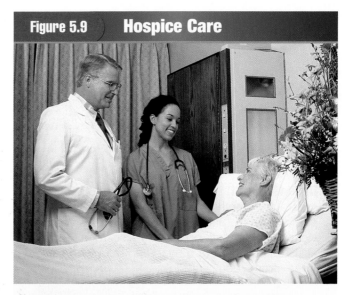

Figure 5.9   Hospice Care

The staff of a hospice responds to the unique needs of the terminally ill by providing physical and emotional care. *How does hospice care help a person die with dignity?*

hospice: a facility designed to care for the special needs of the dying

---

SECTION 3 | Assessment

1. **Review the Vocabulary**   Explain why thanatology is a subfield of psychology.

2. **Visualize the Main Idea**   Using a diagram similar to the one below, list Kübler-Ross's stages of dying.

Stages of Dying

5. _____
4. _____
3. _____
2. _____
1. _____

3. **Recall Information**   What do people go through during the denial stage of dying?

4. **Think Critically**   Do you think that Kübler-Ross's stages of dying apply to other types of losses (such as in sports or a romantic breakup)? Explain.

5. **Application Activity**   Research to find information on hospices and nursing homes. Evaluate the services these institutions provide and determine what services you would want if you needed to spend time in one of these places.

Case Studies

Psychologically *Able to Decide?*

Period of Study: 1960–ongoing

Introduction: In April 1999, a Michigan court jury sentenced Dr. Jack Kevorkian, a pathologist, to 10 to 25 years in prison. The conviction was based on Kevorkian's role in the assisted suicide of a 52-year-old man who suffered from Lou Gehrig's disease.

Kevorkian provided his "patient" with lethal drugs. The doctor claimed he had used this "method" in about 130 other cases. Kevorkian argued that the assisted suicides he performed were methods of euthanasia. Euthanasia is allowing a terminally ill patient to die naturally without life support, or putting to death a person who suffers from an incurable disease (Rice, 1995). The Michigan jury who sentenced Kevorkian ruled that Kevorkian was guilty of murder because he had injected the lethal drugs directly into his patient. (The Lou Gehrig's disease sufferer was unable to take the drugs himself.)

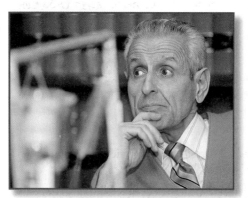

The controversy surrounding Kevorkian and assisted suicide are the most well-known examples regarding not only euthanasia but also an individual's right to die. Opinions and feelings vary on this sensitive topic. For those who believe a terminally ill individual does have the right to die, it is important to determine if that person is psychologically able to make that final decision.

Hypothesis: How do you assess the psychological competence of a terminally ill person who desires death? This question must be resolved in a case-by-case manner and according to the varied laws of each state. Medical doctors and psychologists must rely on the information gathered from past and present cases of those who were granted permission by either physicians or the court system to terminate life-support systems.

Method: When a person is assessed for psychological competence, psychologists look for signs of depression, mental illness, and negative effects from any medication administered to them. If the terminally ill person does not show positive signs of these, the case is turned over to a physician, lawyer, or court system, or any combination of these. From there, it is the legal decision of these authorities to allow the ill individual to follow through with the decision. This is the procedure used in adult cases. However, when the situation involves a child or teenager, the process is much more complex and emotionally difficult.

Results: Unfortunately experts cannot determine if a person who has opted to end life has made a psychologically sound decision. For this reason, among others, many people oppose the idea that a person can terminate his or her own life. Those who support euthanasia believe that ill individuals no longer feel the pain and anguish their disease or condition has caused. They argue that it is unfair for others to grant or deny the choice of death because they have not experienced the pain and anguish of a terminally ill condition themselves.

Analyzing the Case Study

1. What is euthanasia? Why is it controversial?
2. Why was Dr. Kevorkian convicted of murder?
3. **Critical Thinking** How might you use Kübler-Ross's stages of dying to help you determine whether a person is psychologically able to terminate his or her life?

Summary and Vocabulary

Much of people's fear of aging is rooted in stereotypes of what it means to grow older. The positive side of aging adult life is one of the best-kept secrets in our society.

Section 1 | Adulthood

Main Idea: Adulthood is a time of transition—it involves shifting priorities and outlooks on life from adolescence and throughout the remainder of life.

- For most adults, the process of physical decline is slow and gradual.
- The adulthood years are a time when lifestyle may set the stage for problems that will show up then or in later life.
- Good physical and mental health seem to be the key factors affecting sexual activity in adulthood.
- The ability to comprehend new material and to think flexibly improves in early adulthood, and overall intelligence improves with age.
- An individual's basic character remains relatively stable throughout life.

Section 2 | Old Age

Main Idea: As we age, our priorities and expectations change to match realities, and we experience losses as well as gains.

- The idea that progressive physical and mental decline is inevitable with age has resulted in a climate of prejudice against the old.
- The health of older people, for the most part, is related to their health when younger.
- In late adulthood, life transitions are often negative and reduce responsibilities and increase isolation.
- The frequency and regularity of sexual activities during earlier years is the best overall predictor of such activities in later years.
- Crystallized intelligence, or the ability to use accumulated knowledge and learning in appropriate situations, increases with age; fluid intelligence, or the ability to solve abstract relational problems and to generate new hypotheses, decreases with age.

Section 3 | Dying and Death

Main Idea: Death is inevitable. Most people face death by going through stages or an adjustment process.

- Elisabeth Kübler-Ross identified five stages of psychological adjustment to death: denial, anger, bargaining, depression, and acceptance.
- A hospice is a special place where terminally ill people go to die; it is designed to make the patient's surroundings pleasant and comfortable.

Chapter Vocabulary

menopause (p. 131)

generativity (p. 135)

stagnation (p. 135)

decremental model of aging (p. 138)

ageism (p. 138)

senile dementia (p. 142)

Alzheimer's disease (p. 143)

thanatology (p. 144)

hospice (p. 147)

Self-Check Quiz
Visit the *Understanding Psychology* Web site at
psychology.glencoe.com and click on **Chapter 5—
Self-Check Quizzes** to prepare for the Chapter Test.

Reviewing Vocabulary

Choose the letter of the correct term or concept below to complete the sentence.

a. climacteric
b. menopause
c. generativity
d. stagnation
e. decremental model of aging

f. ageism
g. senile dementia
h. Alzheimer's disease
i. thanatology
j. hospice

1. During _____, a woman's production of sex hormones drops sharply.

2. The study of dying and death is _____.

3. Prejudice against the old is referred to as _____.

4. An adult who chooses to hang on to the past is experiencing _____.

5. _____ is a neurological disease marked by a gradual deterioration of cognitive functioning.

6. A(n) _____ is a special place where terminally ill people go to die.

7. Between the ages of 45 and 50, every woman experiences a stage called the _____, which represents all of the psychological and biological changes occurring at that time.

8. The desire to use one's wisdom to guide future generations is called _____.

9. According to a(n) _____, progressive physical and mental decline is inevitable with age.

10. _____ is characterized by memory loss, forgetfulness, disorientation of time and place, a decline in the ability to think, impaired attention, altered personality, and difficulties in relating to others.

Recalling Facts

1. Using a graphic organizer similar to the one below, identify three midlife issues faced by adult women.

2. Describe how the "decremental model of aging" leads to ageism.

3. What is crystallized intelligence? What is fluid intelligence? Which type of intelligence increases with age?

4. List Kübler-Ross's five stages of psychological adjustment to death. What behaviors would you expect of someone at each stage?

5. What is a hospice designed to do? What types of people might live in a hospice?

Critical Thinking

1. **Making Inferences** Why do you think some men experience the age-thirty crisis? Do you think that some women might experience the age-thirty crisis? Explain.

2. **Analyzing Information** Do you think an individual's personality basically remains the same throughout the individual's life, or is it capable of change during adulthood? Explain your answer.

3. **Drawing Conclusions** Do you think that people of other cultures necessarily experience a "midlife crisis"? Why do you think so?

4. **Synthesizing Information** Dying and death have only recently become topics that are discussed openly. Given this growing openness, what changes do you see being made to make the adjustment to the prospect of dying less severe? What other changes do you think still need to be made?

5. **Demonstrating Reasoned Judgment** Some people believe that dying people should not be told they are dying. Do you agree? Why or why not?

Building Skills

Interpreting Graphs Review the graphs, then answer the questions that follow.

Living Arrangements of Americans 65 and Older, 1997

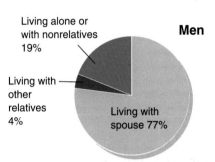

Men

Living alone or with nonrelatives 19%

Living with other relatives 4%

Living with spouse 77%

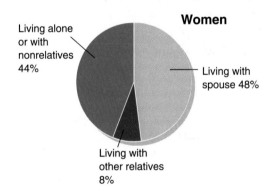

Women

Living alone or with nonrelatives 44%

Living with spouse 48%

Living with other relatives 8%

Source: U.S. Bureau of the Census, 1997.

1. With whom do most Americans 65 and older live?
2. Do more men or women of this age group live with a spouse? How can you explain this difference?
3. How might living arrangements impact a person's adjustment to old age?

Practice and **assess** key social studies skills with **Glencoe Skillbuilder Interactive Workbook CD-ROM, Level 2.**

See the Skills Handbook, page 628, for an explanation of interpreting graphs.

Psychology Projects

1. **Adulthood** Interview an adult who is more than 50 years old. Ask this person to describe himself or herself physically, socially, intellectually, and emotionally at the ages of 20, 30, 40, and 50. Before the interview, list specific questions that would provide this information. Ask which age was his or her favorite and why.

2. **Old Age** Explore the way that elderly adults are depicted in art and in the media. Bring in examples of art, literature, and newspaper or magazine articles that depict or describe the elderly. Present your findings to the class and explain whether they depict the elderly fairly.

3. **Dying and Death** Rituals surrounding death vary around the world. Research customs and rituals surrounding death in other countries or cultures. Present your findings in a pictorial essay.

4. **Aging and Society** With plastic surgery and cosmetics, many of the visible signs of aging can be camouflaged. Should men with gray hair dye their hair? Should women get face-lifts? Discuss the double-standard for aging men and women and its implications about the underlying values of society in a brief essay.

Technology Activity

Locate Web sites on the Internet that address issues of middle adulthood and late adulthood. (The Web site for the AARP is one such site.) Find out what kinds of information these sites offer. Evaluate the sites in terms of how they might benefit the lives of adults in middle and old age.

Psychology Journal

Reread the entry in your journal that you wrote about the saying "You can't teach an old dog new tricks." Think about this statement in light of adult development and learning. What evidence is there that this statement is incorrect? Using what you have learned, write an entry in your journal that presents evidence supporting both sides of the issue.

UNIT 3

The Workings of Mind and Body

Contents

Sketching of the human ▶
brain and body

Why It's Important

Psychology is the study of what the nervous system does. Your nervous system interacts with your genes and environment to produce your behaviors. Your thoughts, emotions, memories, intelligence, and creativity are based on biological processes that take place within and between cells.

Body and Behavior

PSYCHOLOGY JOURNAL

Ask yourself why it is important for psychologists to study the brain and nervous system. Write your answer to this question in your journal and justify your response. ■

PSYCHOLOGY
Online

Chapter Overview
Visit the *Understanding Psychology*
Web site at psychology.glencoe.com
and click on **Chapter 6—Chapter
Overviews** to preview the chapter.

The Nervous System: The Basic Structure

Reader's Guide

■ Main Idea
Learning about the nervous system helps us know how messages that are sent to the brain cause behavior.

■ Vocabulary
- central nervous system (CNS)
- spinal cord
- peripheral nervous system (PNS)
- neurons
- synapse
- neurotransmitters
- somatic nervous system (SNS)
- autonomic nervous system (ANS)

■ Objectives
- Identify the parts of the nervous system.
- Describe the functions of the nervous system.

EXPLORING PSYCHOLOGY

Have You Experienced the Runner's High?

It's almost like running is this great friend we both share . . . Anyway, that's what I'd like to talk to you about . . . running as a friend, a companion, a lover even . . . in other words, the relationship of running. "WHAT!?" many of you will be saying, "I thought that I was going to learn how to improve my 10k time." Go read *Runner's World* for that. You see, I don't view running as what I DO or who I AM, but as this thing, this force, that changes me over time. . . .

—from "Running and Me: A Love Story" by Joan Nesbit, 1999

Why does the writer above love running so much? One of the reasons may be that people who do a lot of running for exercise, especially long-distance running, often talk of an effect called a "runner's high." The longer they run, the more tired they get, of course; but at some point, the runners will "push through the wall" and "get their second wind." Why does this happen? Endorphins, which are neurotransmitters, produce the euphoria of a runner's high. As the body deals with a very physically stressful situation—running—the runner's body reacts to stress. So, in effect, running really does change you. In this section, you will learn how your nervous system can produce a runner's high.

HOW THE NERVOUS SYSTEM WORKS

The nervous system is never at rest. There is always a job for it to do. Even when you are sleeping the nervous system is busy regulating your body functions. The nervous system controls your emotions, movements, thinking, and behavior.

Structurally, the nervous system is divided into two parts—the **central nervous system [CNS]** (the brain and the **spinal cord**) and the **peripheral nervous system [PNS]** (the smaller branches of nerves that reach the other parts of the body) (see Figure 6.1). The nerves of the peripheral system conduct information from the bodily organs to the central nervous system and take information back to the organs. These nerves branch out from the spinal column and are about as thick as a pencil. Those in the extremities, such as the fingertips, are invisibly small. All parts of the nervous system are protected in some way: the brain by the skull and several layers of sheathing, the spinal cord by the vertebrae, and the peripheral nerves by layers of sheathing. The bony protection of the spinal cord is vital. An injury to the spinal cord could prevent the transmittal of messages between the brain and the muscles, and could result in paralysis.

central nervous system (CNS): the brain and spinal cord

spinal cord: nerves that run down the length of the back and transmit most messages between the body and brain

peripheral nervous system (PNS): nerves branching out from the spinal cord

Figure 6.1   The Nervous System

Central Nervous System

Brain   Spinal cord

Peripheral Nervous System

Somatic:
controls voluntary
muscles

Autonomic:
controls involuntary
muscles

Sympathetic:
expends energy

Parasympathetic:
conserves energy

The nervous system is divided into two parts: the central nervous system (CNS) and the peripheral nervous system (PNS). *What are the two main parts of the central nervous system?*

Figure 6.2   **Anatomy of Two Neurons**

Photomicrograph of neuron

The human body contains billions of neurons. The neuron receives messages from other neurons on its dendrites. The messages are then transmitted down the axon and sent out through the axon terminals. The myelin sheath is wrapped around the axon to protect it. *What is the function of the dendrites?*

Neurons

Messages to and from the brain travel along the nerves, which are strings of long, thin cells called **neurons** (see Figure 6.2). Chemical-electrical signals travel down the neurons much as flame travels along a firecracker fuse. The main difference is that the neuron can "burn" over and over again, hundreds of times a minute.

Transmission between neurons or nerve cells occurs whenever the cells are stimulated past a minimum point and emit a signal. The neuron is said to "fire." The firing of neurons occurs in line with the all-or-none principle, which states that when a neuron fires, it does so at full strength. If a neuron is not stimulated past the minimum, or threshold level, it does not fire at all.

Basic Parts of a Neuron   Neurons have three basic parts: the cell body, dendrites, and the axon (see Figure 6.2). The cell body contains the nucleus and produces the energy needed to fuel neuron activity. The *dendrites* are short, thin fibers that stick out from the cell body. Dendrites receive impulses, or messages, from other neurons and send them to the cell body. The *axon* is a long fiber that carries the impulses away from the cell body toward the dendrites of another neuron. Axons can be very short to several feet in length.

A white, fatty substance called the *myelin sheath* insulates and protects the axon for some neurons. In cases of multiple sclerosis, the myelin sheath is destroyed, and as a result, the behavior of the person is erratic and unco-ordinated. The myelin sheath also speeds the transmission of impulses. Small fibers, called *axon terminals,* branch out at the end of the axon. Axon terminals are positioned opposite the dendrite of another neuron.

The Neuron Connection   If you look closely at Figure 6.2, you can see that there is a space between the axon terminals of one neuron and the dendrites of another neuron. This space between neurons is called the **synapse.** The synapse is a junction or connection between the neurons (see Figure 6.3). A neuron transmits its impulses or message to another neuron across the

neurons: the long, thin cells of nerve tissue along which messages travel to and from the brain

Reading Check
What are the three basic parts of a neuron?

synapse: the gap that occurs between individual nerve cells

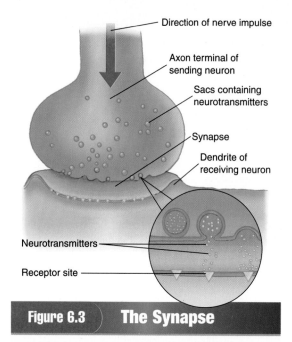

- Direction of nerve impulse
- Axon terminal of sending neuron
- Sacs containing neurotransmitters
- Synapse
- Dendrite of receiving neuron
- Neurotransmitters
- Receptor site

Figure 6.3 **The Synapse**

Neurons do not touch one another. Instead, a neuron sends its messages across a gap called a synapse by releasing neurotransmitters. These neurotransmitters are received by the dendrite of another neuron. *How many neurons are involved in sending a message to the brain to raise your arm to answer a question?*

neurotransmitters: the chemicals released by neurons, which determine the rate at which other neurons fire

somatic nervous system (SNS): the part of the peripheral nervous system that controls voluntary movement of skeletal muscles

autonomic nervous system (ANS): the part of the peripheral nervous system that controls internal biological functions

synapse by releasing chemicals called **neurotransmitters.** These neurotransmitters open chemical locks or excite the receptors. The neurotransmitters can excite the next neuron or stop it from transmitting (inhibition). The neurotransmitters are like the valves in a water system that allow flow in only one direction. There are many different neurotransmitters; for example, norepinephrine, which is involved with memory and learning, and endorphin, which inhibits pain. The oversupply or undersupply of certain neurotransmitters has been linked to certain diseases. For instance, an undersupply of acetylcholine—a neurotransmitter involved with movement and memory—is associated with paralysis and Alzheimer's disease. An oversupply of dopamine—involved with learning, emotional arousal, and movement—is linked to schizophrenia, while an undersupply is linked to Parkinson's disease. An undersupply of norepinephrine and serotonin may result in depression.

Neuron Activity The intensity of activity in each neuron depends on how many other neurons are acting on it. Each individual neuron is either ON or OFF, depending on whether most of the neurons acting on it are exciting it or inhibiting it. The actual destination of nerve impulses produced by an excited neuron, as they travel from one neuron to another, is limited by what tract in the nervous system they are on. Ascending tracts carry sensory impulses to the brain, and descending tracts carry motor impulses from the brain. There are different types of neurons. The *afferent* neurons, or sensory neurons, relay messages from the sense organs (including eye, ear, nose, and skin) to the brain. The *efferent* neurons, or motor neurons, send signals from the brain to the glands and muscles. The *interneurons* carry impulses between neurons in the body.

Voluntary and Involuntary Activities

Some of the actions that your body makes in response to impulses from the nerves are voluntary acts, such as lifting your hand to turn a page (which actually involves many impulses to many muscles). Others are involuntary acts, such as changes in the heartbeat, in the blood pressure, or in the size of the pupils. The term **somatic nervous system (SNS)** refers to the part of the peripheral nervous system that controls voluntary activities. The term **autonomic nervous system (ANS)** refers to the part of the nervous system that controls involuntary activities, or those that ordinarily occur "automatically," such as heartbeat, stomach activity, and so on.

The autonomic nervous system itself has two parts: sympathetic and parasympathetic nervous systems. The sympathetic nervous system prepares the body for dealing with emergencies or strenuous activity. It speeds up the heart to hasten the supply of oxygen and nutrients to body tissues. It constricts some arteries and relaxes others so that blood flows to the muscles, where it is most needed in emergencies and strenuous activity (such as running, thereby sometimes producing a runner's high). It increases the blood pressure and suspends some activities, such as digestion. In contrast, the parasympathetic nervous system works to conserve energy and to enhance the body's ability to recover from strenuous activity. It reduces the heart rate and blood pressure and helps bring the body back to its normal resting state.

All of this takes place automatically. Receptors are constantly receiving messages (hunger messages, the need to swallow or cough) that alert the autonomic nervous system to carry out routine activities. Imagine how difficult it would be if you had no autonomic nervous system and had to think about it every time your body needed to digest a sandwich or perspire.

Figure 6.4 **Voluntary and Involuntary Activities**

Climbing stairs is a voluntary activity. When the pupils of your eyes get smaller after they are exposed to brighter light, this is an involuntary activity. *What other involuntary activities take place in your body?*

SECTION 1 Assessment

1. **Review the Vocabulary** List and describe the parts of the neuron.

2. **Visualize the Main Idea** In a diagram similar to the one below, list the divisions of the nervous system.

3. **Recall Information** What is the difference between afferent and efferent neurons? What are interneurons?

4. **Think Critically** Marty runs in marathons. Explain the functions of Marty's sympathetic nervous system and the parasympathetic nervous system during and after the race.

5. **Application Activity** Put your pen or pencil down and then pick it up again. Identify and describe the parts of the nervous system that caused those movements to happen.

Studying the Brain

Reader's Guide

■ Main Idea
There are many parts in the human brain that work together to coordinate movement and stimulate thinking and emotions, resulting in behavior.

■ Vocabulary
- hindbrain
- midbrain
- forebrain
- lobes
- electroencephalograph (EEG)
- computerized axial tomography (CAT)
- positron emission topography (PET)
- magnetic resonance imaging (MRI)

■ Objectives
- Identify the structure and functions of the human brain.
- Discuss the different ways psychologists study the brain.

EXPLORING PSYCHOLOGY

Origins of Thoughts

Early Greeks were not impressed with the brain. They suggested that the brain's main function was to cool the blood. They were much more impressed by the heart. They proposed that the heart was the source of feelings and thoughts. Hippocrates, however, observed the effect of head injuries on people's thoughts and actions and noted, "[F]rom the brain, and from the brain only, arise our pleasures, joys, laughter and jests, as well as our sorrows, pains, griefs and tears. Through it, in particular, we think, see, hear. . . . Eyes, ears, tongue, hands and feet act in accordance with the discernment [judgment] of the brain."

—adapted from *Psychology* by Peter Gray, 1999

Greek physician Hippocrates was right. In the 24 centuries since his observations, many attempts have been made to explain how the mass of soggy gray tissue known as the human brain could create the theory of relativity, the Sistine Chapel ceiling, and the energy crisis. The mind, however, remains a mystery to itself.

THE THREE BRAINS

hindbrain: a part of the brain located at the rear base of the skull that is involved in the basic processes of life

The brain is composed of three parts: the hindbrain, midbrain, and forebrain (see Figure 6.5). The **hindbrain,** located at the rear base of the skull, is involved in the most basic processes of life. The hindbrain includes the *cerebellum, medulla,* and the *pons.* The cerebellum, located at the base of the spinal cord, helps control posture and balance. The medulla controls breathing and a variety of reflexes, while the pons functions as a bridge to interconnect messages between the spinal cord and brain. The pons is also involved in producing chemicals needed for sleep.

The **midbrain** is a small part of the brain above the pons that integrates sensory information and relays it upward. The medulla and pons extend upward into the midbrain. The medulla, pons, and midbrain compose most of

Figure 6.5   The Parts of the Brain

Corpus callosum

Forebrain

Cerebral cortex

Thalamus

Hypothalamus

Pituitary gland

Cerebellum

Pons

Medulla

Spinal cord

Hindbrain   Midbrain

The brain is the largest, most complex part of the nervous system. *What are the functions of the cerebellum?*

the brain stem, and the reticular activating system (RAS) spans across all these structures. The RAS serves to alert the rest of the brain to incoming signals.

The **forebrain,** covering the brain's central core, includes the *thalamus,* which integrates sensory input. The thalamus is a relay station for all the information that travels to and from the cortex. All sensory information with the exception of smell enters the thalamus. All information from the eyes, ears, and skin enters the thalamus and then is sent to the appropriate areas in the cortex. Just below the thalamus is the *hypothalamus.* It controls functions such as hunger, thirst, and sexual behavior. It also controls the body's temperature so when we are warm, we begin to sweat and when we are cold, we shiver.

The "higher" thinking processes—those that make us unique—are housed in the forebrain. The outer layer of the forebrain consists of the *cerebral cortex.* The inner layer is the *cerebrum.* The cerebral cortex and cerebrum surround the hindbrain and brain stem much like the way a halved peach surrounds the pit. The cerebral cortex gives you the ability to learn and store complex and abstract information, and to project your thinking into the future. Your cerebral cortex allows you to see, read, and understand this sentence. The cortex, or bark, of the cerebrum is the site of the conscious thinking processes, yet it is less than a half-inch thick.

The *limbic system,* found in the core of the forebrain, is composed of a number of different structures in the brain that regulate our emotions and motivations. The limbic system includes the hypothalamus, amygdala, thalamus, and hippocampus. The amygdala controls violent

midbrain: a small part of the brain above the pons that integrates sensory information and relays it upward

forebrain: a part of the brain that covers the brain's central core emotions such as rage and violence. The hippocampus is important in the formation of memories. If the hippocampus is damaged, it would be difficult to form new memories. Covering all these parts is the cerebrum.

Reading Check
What are the three parts of the human brain?

lobes: the different regions into which the cerebral cortex is divided

The Lobes of the Brain

The cerebrum is really two hemispheres, or two sides. The cerebral hemisphere is connected by a band of fibers called the *corpus callosum*. Each cerebral hemisphere has deep grooves that form regions, or **lobes** (see Figure 6.6). The occipital lobe is where the visual signals are processed. Damage to this area can cause visual problems. The parietal lobes are concerned with information from the senses from all over the body. The temporal lobes are concerned with hearing, memory, emotion, and speaking. The frontal lobes are concerned with organization, planning, and creative thinking.

Some areas of the cortex receive information from the skin senses and from muscles. The amount of brain tissue connected to any given body part determines the sensitivity of that area, not its size. For example, the highly developed sense of touch in the hand involves a much larger brain area than that of the relatively insensitive calves. The part of the cortex that receives information is called the somatosensory cortex. The motor cortex sends information to control body movement. The motor cortex is also divided according to need. The more sophisticated the movements have to be (such as those used in speaking), the bigger the brain area involved.

The association areas mediate between the other areas and do most of the synthesizing of information. For example, association areas turn sensory input into meaningful information. Different neurons are activated when we see different shapes and figures. The association areas receive this input and then arrange the information so that we see something meaningful like our friend's face.

Left and Right Hemispheres There is much concern that information about properties of the left and right hemispheres is misinterpreted. Popular books have oversimplified the properties of the two hemispheres. In reality, the left and right sides complement and help each other. So be aware of this as we list the properties of each hemisphere. The two hemispheres in the cortex are roughly mirror images of each other. (Each of the four lobes is present in both hemispheres.) The corpus callosum carries messages back and forth

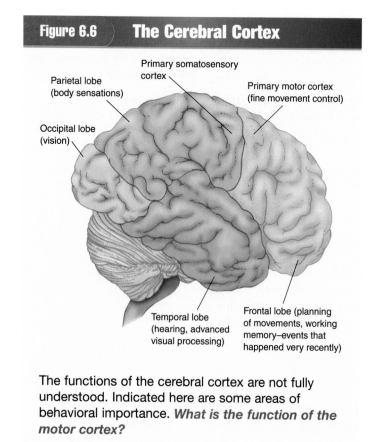

Figure 6.6 The Cerebral Cortex

Parietal lobe (body sensations)

Primary somatosensory cortex

Primary motor cortex (fine movement control)

Occipital lobe (vision)

Temporal lobe (hearing, advanced visual processing)

Frontal lobe (planning of movements, working memory–events that happened very recently)

The functions of the cerebral cortex are not fully understood. Indicated here are some areas of behavioral importance. *What is the function of the motor cortex?*

Figure 6.7   **Functions of the Brain's Hemispheres**

The idea of whether we are "right-brained" or "left-brained" has been exaggerated. We constantly use both hemispheres of the brain, since each hemisphere is specialized for processing certain kinds of information. *In what areas does the right hemisphere specialize?*

Front

Left   Right

Back

Verbal: speaking, understanding language, reading, writing

Mathematical: adding, subtracting, multiplying, calculus, physics

Analytic: analyzing separate pieces that make up a whole

Nonverbal: understanding simple sentences and words

Spatial: solving spatial problems, such as geometry

Holistic: combining parts that make up a whole

between the two hemispheres. Each hemisphere is connected to half of the body in a crisscrossed fashion.

The left hemisphere controls the movements of the right side of the body. For most people, the left side of the brain is where speech is located. The left side also is specialized for mathematical ability, calculation, and logic.

The right hemisphere controls the left side of the body. (Thus a stroke that causes damage to the right hemisphere will result in numbness or paralysis on the left side of the body.) The right hemisphere is more adept at visual and spatial relations. Putting together a puzzle requires spatial ability. Perceptual tasks seem to be more suited for the right hemisphere. The right side is better at recognizing patterns. Thus, music and art are better understood by the right hemisphere. Creativity and intuition are also found in the right hemisphere (see Figure 6.7) (Levy, 1985).

Split-Brain Operations   In a normal brain, the two hemispheres communicate through the corpus callosum. Whatever occurs on one side is communicated to the other side. Some people have epileptic seizures so severe that as a last resort, they have their brain hemispheres separated. This lessens the number and intensity of the seizures. As a result, the person has a split brain. The person has two brains that operate independently of each other. Since the corpus callosum is severed, there no longer is any communication between the hemispheres.

Many psychologists became interested in differences between the cerebral hemispheres when "split brain" operations were tried on epileptics like Harriet Lees. For most of her life Lees's seizures were mild and could be controlled with drugs. However, at age 25 they began to get worse, and by 30 Lees was having as many as a dozen violent seizures a day. An epileptic seizure involves massive uncontrolled electrical activity that begins in either hemisphere and spreads to the other. To enable Lees to live a normal life, she and the doctors decided to sever the corpus callosum so that seizures could not spread.

PSYCHOLOGY *Online*

Student Web Activity
Visit the *Understanding Psychology* Web site at psychology.glencoe.com and click on **Chapter 6— Student Web Activities** for an activity about biology and behavior.

Roger Wolcott Sperry

1913–1994

"In other words, each hemisphere [of the brain] seems to have its own separate and private sensations; its own perceptions; its own concepts; and its own impulses to act. . . . Following surgery, each hemisphere also has thereafter its own separate chain of memories that are rendered inaccessible to the recall processes of the other."

Roger Sperry first became well-known in the area of developmental neurobiology. He devised experiments that helped establish the means by which nerve cells become "wired up" in particular ways in the central nervous system.

Sperry is probably best known for his pioneering split-brain research. In the 1950s and 1960s, Sperry devised a number of experiments to test the functions of each hemisphere of the brain. He argued that two separate hemispheres of consciousness could exist under one skull. Sperry pioneered the behavioral investigation of "split-brain" animals and humans. His experiments and techniques laid the groundwork for constructing a map of mental functions. In 1981 he became corecipient of the Nobel Prize for Physiology and Medicine for his investigation of brain functions.

Not only did the operation reduce the severity of seizures, but it also resulted in fewer seizures (Kalat, 1992). Psychologists were even more interested in the potential side effects of this operation. Despite the fact that patients who have had this operation now had "two separate brains," they seemed remarkably normal. Researchers went on to develop a number of techniques to try to detect subtle effects of the operation.

If a person whose brain has been split holds a ball in the right hand, he would be able to say it is a ball. Place the ball in the left hand and he would not be able to say what it is. The information is sent to the right hemisphere. Because the speech center is in the left hemisphere, information cannot be sent across the corpus callosum.

Another experiment with split-brain patients involves studying tactile stimulation, or touch. In this experiment, objects, block letters, or even block letters spelling a word are held in a designated hand but are blocked from the split-brain patient's view. Researchers either present a word or a word describing an object on a screen to either visual field or relay it verbally. The patient's task is to find the object, block letter, or blocked word corresponding to the word they are shown or told. When words are presented for the right hemisphere to see, patients cannot say the word, but they can identify the object with their left hand touching it behind the screen.

To explore emotional reactions in split-brained individuals, researchers designed a test to incorporate emotional stimuli with objects in view. In one of these experiments, a picture of a nude person was flashed to either hemisphere. When researchers flashed the picture to the left hemisphere, the patient laughed and described what she saw. When the same was done to the right hemisphere, the patient saw nothing, but her face became flush and she began to grin.

Research on split-brain patients has presented evidence that each hemisphere of the brain is unique with specialized functions and skills. Individuals who have had split-brain operations remained practically unchanged in intelligence, personality, and emotions.

HOW PSYCHOLOGISTS STUDY THE BRAIN

Mapping the brain's fissures and inner recesses has supplied scientists with fascinating information about the role of the brain in behavior. Psychologists who do this kind of research are called physiological psychologists, or psychobiologists. Among the methods they use to explore the brain are recording, stimulating, lesioning, and imaging.

Recording

Electrodes are wires that can be inserted into the brain to record electrical activity in the brain. By inserting electrodes in the brain, it is possible to detect the minute electrical changes that occur when neurons fire. The wires are connected to electronic equipment that amplifies the tiny voltages produced by the firing neurons. Even single neurons can be monitored.

The electrical activity of whole areas of the brain can be recorded with an **electroencephalograph (EEG).** Wires from the EEG machine are attached to the scalp so that millions upon millions of neurons can be monitored at the same time (see Figure 6.8). Psychologists have observed that the overall electrical activity of the brain rises and falls rhythmically and that the pattern of the rhythm depends on whether a person is awake, drowsy, or asleep (as illustrated in Chapter 7). These rhythms, or brain waves, occur because the neurons in the brain tend to increase or decrease their amount of activity in unison.

Stimulation

Electrodes may be used to set off the firing of neurons as well as to record it. Brain surgeon Wilder Penfield stimulated the brains of his patients during surgery to determine what functions the various parts of the brain perform. In this way he could localize the malfunctioning part for which surgery was required, for example, for epilepsy. When Penfield applied a tiny electric current to points on the temporal lobe of the brain,

Quick Lab

Can you determine whether the left or right hemisphere of the brain is dominant?

The left hemisphere controls the movements of the right side of the body. This side of the brain is adept at language-related skills, mathematical ability, and logic. The right hemisphere controls the movements of the left side of the body. It is also the side that is more adept for creativity, intuition, and creative expressions such as art and music. Can you tell which side is dominant in people you know?

Procedure
1. Think about two of your friends or family members.
2. Compare them in terms of the areas that they seem to be most adept at—mathematics, logical thinking, musical ability, art, or speech.
3. Record your observations in a two-column chart.

Analysis
1. Based on your observations, which hemisphere seems to be dominant in each individual?

See the Skills Handbook, page 622, for an explanation of designing an experiment.

electroencephalograph (EEG): a machine used to record the electrical activity of large portions of the brain

Figure 6.8   An EEG Machine

Scientists use an electroencephalograph (EEG) machine to measure brain waves. *What have psychologists observed about the electrical activity of the brain?*

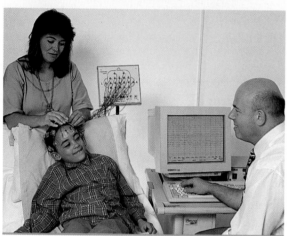

he could trigger whole memory sequences. During surgery, one woman heard a familiar song so clearly that she thought a record was being played in the operating room (Penfield & Rasmussen, 1950).

Stimulation techniques have aroused great medical interest. They have been used with terminal cancer patients to relieve them of intolerable pain without using drugs. A current delivered through electrodes implanted in certain areas of the brain may provide a sudden temporary relief (Delgado, 1969). Furthermore, some psychiatrists have experimented with similar methods to control violent emotional behavior in otherwise uncontrollable patients.

Lesions

Scientists sometimes create lesions by cutting or destroying part of an animal's brain. If the animal behaves differently after the operation, they assume that the destroyed brain area is involved with that type of behavior. For example, in one classic lesion study, two researchers removed a certain area of the temporal lobe from rhesus monkeys. Normally, these animals are fearful, aggressive, and vicious, but after the operation, they became less fearful and at the same time less violent (Klüver & Bucy, 1937). The implication was that this area of the brain controlled aggression. The relations revealed by this type of research are far more subtle and complex than people first believed.

Accidents

Psychologists can learn from the tragedies when some people suffer accidents. These accidents may involve the brain. Psychologists try to draw a connection between the damaged parts of the brain and a person's behavior. One such case involved an unusual accident in 1848. Phineas Gage was a respected railroad foreman who demonstrated restraint, good judgment, and the ability to work well with other men. His crew of men was about to explode some dynamite to clear a path for the railroad rails. As Gage filled a narrow hole with dynamite and tamped it down, it suddenly exploded. The tamping iron had caused a spark that ignited the dynamite. The tamping iron, which weighed over 13 pounds and was over 3 feet in length, shot into the air! It entered Gage's head right below the left eye, and it exited through the top of the skull.

Gage survived the accident, but his personality changed greatly. He became short-tempered, was difficult to be around, and often said inappropriate things. Gage lived for several years after the accident. In 1994 psychologists (Damasio & Damasio) examined Gage's skull using the newest methods available. They reported that the tamping iron had caused damage to parts of the frontal cortex. They found that damage to the frontal lobes prevents censoring of thoughts and ideas.

Another unusual case took place in the nineteenth century. Dr. Paul Broca had a young patient who could only respond with hand gestures and the word "tan." Broca theorized that a part of the brain on the left side was destroyed, limiting the young man's communication processes. Many years later, researchers examined the young man's brain using modern methods. They discovered that Dr. Broca's theory was correct. The left side of the cortex, which is involved with the production of speech, was damaged. This area of the cortex is now known as Broca's area.

Phineas Gage's skull

Images

Dr. Paul Broca uncovered the connection between brain and speech. Researchers proved Dr. Broca's theory using PET scans. Today psychologists and medical researchers are using this and other sophisticated techniques, including CAT scans and MRI scans.

In the 1970s, **computerized axial tomography (CAT)** scans were used to pinpoint injuries and other problems in brain deterioration. During a CAT scan, a moving ring passes X-ray beams around and through a subject's head. Radiation is absorbed in different amounts depending on the density of the brain tissue. Computers measure the amount of radiation absorbed and transform this information into a three-dimensional view of the brain.

The **positron emission tomography (PET)** scan can capture a picture of the brain as different parts are being used. It involves injecting a slightly radioactive solution into the blood and then measuring the amount of radiation absorbed by blood cells. Active neurons absorb more radioactive solution than nonactive ones (see Figure 6.9). Researchers use the PET scan to see which areas are being activated while performing a task (Raichle, 1994). PET scans show activity in different areas of the brain when a person is thinking, speaking, and looking at objects. The scan changes when one is talking and when one is looking at a piece of art. These pictures change as the activity changes.

Another device, **magnetic resonance imaging**, or **MRI**, enables researchers to study both activity and brain structures (see Figure 6.10). It

computerized axial tomography (CAT): an imaging technique used to study the brain to pinpoint injuries and brain deterioration

positron emission tomography (PET): an imaging technique used to see which brain areas are being activated while performing tasks

magnetic resonance imaging (MRI): an imaging technique used to study brain structure and activity

Hearing words

Seeing words

Reading words

Generating verbs

Figure 6.9	**Brain Activity on a PET Scan**

A computer transforms the different levels of absorption by neurons of radioactive solution into colors. Red and yellow indicate maximum activity of neurons, while blue and green indicate minimal activity. *Why would psychologists use a PET scan?*

Figure 6.10   An MRI

Magnetic resonance imaging (MRI) studies the activities of the brain. *Why does an MRI of the brain give a more thorough picture than a CAT or PET scan would give?*

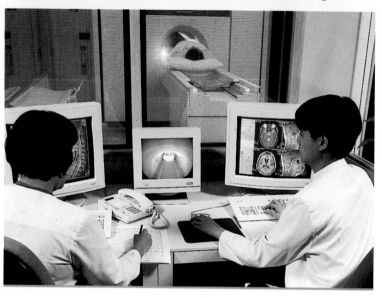

combines the features of both CAT and PET scans. It involves passing nonharmful radio frequencies through the brain. A computer measures how these signals interact with brain cells and translates these signals into a detailed image of the brain. Researchers use MRIs to study the structure of the brain as well as to identify tumors or types of brain damage.

Researchers use a new technique of imaging, functional magnetic resonance imaging (fMRI), to directly observe both the functions of different structures of the brain and which structures participate in specific functions. The fMRI provides high resolution reports of neural activity based on signals that are determined by blood oxygen level. The fMRI actually detects an increase in blood flow to the active structure of the brain. So, unlike the MRI, the fMRI does not require passing radio frequencies through the brain. With this new method of imaging, researchers have confirmed their hypotheses concerning the functions of areas such as the visual cortex, the motor cortex, and Broca's area of speech and language-related activities.

SECTION 2 Assessment

1. **Review the Vocabulary** List and describe the main functions of the lobes of the human brain.

2. **Visualize the Main Idea** In a diagram similar to the one below, list the parts of the brain.

Parts of the Human Brain

3. **Recall Information** What are the functions of the thalamus and hypothalamus?

4. **Think Critically** If a person suffers a traumatic head injury and then begins behaving differently, can we assume that brain damage is the reason for the personality change? Why or why not?

5. **Application Activity** A woman severely injured the right hemisphere of her brain. Create a scenario in which you describe two body functions that might be affected by the woman's injury.

Case Studies

One Person . . . Two Brains?

Period of Study: 1967

Introduction: Victoria had experienced intense epileptic seizures since she was six years old. Doctors placed Victoria on medication that prevented seizures for a period of time. However, after many years, the seizures returned with greater intensity. Weary and disgusted from living her life with the uncontrollable and agonizing seizures, Victoria decided it was time to seek a new treatment.

Doctors suggested and Victoria opted for a split-brain operation—an innovative procedure that has proved successful in treating patients with seizures. This operation involved opening the patient's skull and separating the two brain hemispheres by cutting the corpus callosum. Split-brain operations disrupt the major pathway between the brain hemispheres but leave each hemisphere functioning almost completely independently. The procedure prevents the spread of seizures from one hemisphere to the other. This reduces the chance of having a seizure or shortens the seizure if one does occur.

Upon completion of Victoria's split-brain operation, the time came to test her various brain functions that now involved nonconnected, independent hemispheres.

Hypothesis: Researchers wanted to explore the degree to which the two halves of the brain could communicate and function on their own after the operation.

HE•ART

ART   HE

Severed corpus callosum

Method: Researchers asked Victoria to stare at a black dot between the letters HE and ART. The information from each side of the black dot will be interpreted by the opposite hemisphere in Victoria's split brain. Victoria's right hemisphere will see HE and her left will only see ART (see diagram).

When Victoria was asked what she had seen, she reported to have seen the word ART. The word ART was projected to her left hemisphere, which contains the ability for speech. She did indeed see the word HE; however, the right hemisphere could not make Victoria say what she had seen. With her left hand, though, Victoria could point to a picture of a man, or HE. This indicated that her right hemisphere could understand the meaning of HE.

Results: Four months after Victoria's split-brain operation, she was alert and could easily remember and speak of past and present events in her life. Her reading, writing, and reasoning abilities were all intact. She could easily carry out everyday functions such as dressing, eating, and walking. Although the effects of her operation became apparent under special testing, they were not apparent in everyday life. Victoria, now free of her once-feared seizures, could live her life seizure-free, split-brained but unchanged.

Analyzing the Case Study

1. Why did Victoria choose to have a split-brain operation? What did the operation involve?

2. What questions did researchers set out to answer after Victoria's operation?

3. Critical Thinking   What problems do you think Victoria might encounter in everyday life?

The Endocrine System

■ Main Idea
The endocrine system controls and excites growth and affects emotions and behavior in people.

■ Vocabulary
- endocrine system
- hormones
- pituitary gland

■ Objectives
- Describe the endocrine system.
- Identify hormones and their function in the endocrine system.

Exploring Psychology

Running With the Bulls

And then the gun goes off. I run up the cobblestone street. People are jogging at a moderate pace. There's no tremendous push for speed. . . . The second gun goes off—now people pick up the pace: the bulls have been released. . . . There's a sudden burst of speed, energy, panic, of bodies, and the bulls are in the ring. I high tail it to the perimeter, having heard too many tales of bulls going mad in the ring. . . . I caught up with Von and Don. I was just about to ask Don a question when I saw a bull charging Von. He stood frozen for a second, and at the last second jumped sideways in a crescent shape, as the bull missed him and tried to put his shoulder into Von. We ran up to him and he was five shades of white. . . .

—from "I Run With the Bulls" by Mike Silva, 1995

Every year in Pamplona, Spain, many people experience what some consider the ultimate "adrenaline rush." Fighting bulls and steers run through the town every morning of a nine-day fiesta. Hundreds of revelers literally run with the bulls. The bull-racing ritual is inhumane (more than 50 bulls are killed each day), and participants risk death if they should get gored by a bull. Why do people do it?

Many do it for the "rush." The rush comes from a hormone secreted by the endocrine system called adrenaline or epinephrine. The adrenal hormone declares an emergency situation to the body, requiring the body to become very active.

THE ENDOCRINE GLANDS

The nervous system is one of two communication systems for sending information to and from the brain. The second is the **endocrine system.** The endocrine system sends chemical messages, called hormones. The **hormones** are produced in the endocrine glands and are distributed by the blood and other body fluids. (The names and locations of these glands are shown in Figure 6.11.) Hormones circulate throughout the bloodstream but are properly received only at a specific site: the particular organ of the body that they influence. The endocrine glands are also called ductless glands because they release hormones directly into the bloodstream. In contrast, the duct glands release their contents through small holes, or ducts, onto the surface of the body or into the inside of the digestive system. Examples of duct glands are sweat glands, tear glands, and salivary glands.

Hormones have various effects on your behavior. They affect the growth of bodily structures such as muscles and bones—so they affect what you can do physically. Hormones affect your metabolic processes; that is, they can affect how much energy you have to perform actions. Some hormonal effects take place before you are born. Essentially all the physical differences between boys and girls are caused by a hormone called testosterone. Certain other hormones are secreted during stressful situations to prepare the body for action. Hormones also act in the brain, though, to directly influence your moods and drives.

Pituitary Gland

Under the direction of the hypothalamus in the brain, the **pituitary gland** acts as the "master gland." The pituitary gland, located near the midbrain, secretes a large number of hormones, many of which control the output of hormones by other endocrine glands. The hypothalamus monitors the amount of hormones in the blood and sends out messages to correct imbalances.

What do these hormone messages tell the body to do? They carry messages to organs involved in regulating and storing nutrients so that despite changes in conditions outside the body, cell metabolism can continue on an even course. They also control growth and reproduction, including ovulation and lactation (milk production) in females.

Thyroid Gland

The *thyroid gland* produces the hormone thyroxine. Thyroxine stimulates certain chemical reactions that are important for all tissues of the body. Too little thyroxine makes people feel lazy and lethargic—a

PSYCHOLOGY and You

Do You Do This?

Human ethology is the study of human behavior as it naturally occurs. Basketball fans know that Michael Jordan stuck out his tongue when he attempted a difficult shot. Similarly, it has been found that expert billiard players stick out their tongues more often when making hard shots than when attempting relatively easy shots. According to ethologists, a tongue display acts as a nonverbal sign that interaction is not desired. For humans, the tongue displays seem to indicate that the person does not want to be interrupted because of the need to concentrate in a difficult situation.

endocrine system: a chemical communication system, using hormones, by which messages are sent through the bloodstream

hormones: chemical substances that carry messages through the body in blood

pituitary gland: the center of control of the endocrine system that secretes a large number of hormones

Reading Check
What is the function of the pituitary gland? The thyroid gland?

Figure 6.11   The Endocrine System

Hypothalamus
controls the
pituitary gland

Pineal gland
may affect sleep cycle;
inhibits reproductive functions

Pituitary gland
regulates growth
and water and
salt metabolism

Thymus gland
involved in
immunity

Thyroid gland
controls the
metabolic rate

Adrenal cortex
regulates carbo-
hydrate and salt
metabolism

Adrenal medulla
prepares the body
for action

Pancreas
regulates sugar
metabolism

Ovaries (female)
affects physical and
sexual development

Testes (male)
affects physical and
sexual development

The endocrine system, which consists
of ductless glands and the hormones
they produce, works closely with the
nervous system in regulating body
functions. *What is the function of
the adrenal glands?*

condition known as hypothyroidism. Too much thyroxine may cause people to lose weight and sleep and to be overactive—a condition known as hyperthyroidism.

Adrenal Glands

The *adrenal glands* become active when a person is angry or frightened. They release epinephrine and norepinephrine (also called adrenaline and noradrenaline) into the bloodstream. These secretions cause the heartbeat and breathing to increase. They can heighten emotions, such as fear and anxiety. These secretions and other changes help a person generate the extra energy he or she needs to handle a difficult situation.

The adrenal glands also secrete cortical steroids. Cortical steroids help muscles develop and cause the liver to release stored sugar when the body requires extra energy for emergencies.

Sex Glands

There are two types of sex glands—*testes* in males and *ovaries* in females. Testes produce sperm and the male sex hormone *testosterone*. Low levels of testosterone are also found in females. Ovaries produce eggs and the female hormones *estrogen* and *progesterone*, although low levels of these hormones are also found in males.

Testosterone is important in the physical development of males, especially in the prenatal period and in adolescence. In the prenatal period, testosterone helps decide the sex of a fetus. In adolescence, testosterone is important for the growth of muscle and bone along with the growth of male sex characteristics.

Estrogen and progesterone are important in the development of female sex characteristics. These hormones also regulate the reproductive cycle of females. The levels of estrogen and progesterone vary throughout the menstrual cycle. These variances can cause premenstrual syndrome (PMS) in some women. PMS includes symptoms such as fatigue, irritability, and depression.

HORMONES VS. NEUROTRANSMITTERS

Both hormones and neurotransmitters work to affect the nervous system. In fact, the same chemical (such as norepinephrine) can be used as both a hormone and a neurotransmitter. So what is the difference between a hormone and a neurotransmitter?

When a chemical is used as a neurotransmitter, it is released right beside the cell that it is to excite or inhibit. When a chemical is used as a hormone, it is released into the blood, which diffuses it throughout the body. For example, norepinephrine is a hormone when it is secreted into the blood by the adrenal glands. Norepinephrine is a neurotransmitter, though, when it is released by the sympathetic motor neurons of the peripheral nervous system.

Hormones and neurotransmitters appear to have had a common origin (Snyder, 1985). As early multicellular organisms evolved, the system of communication among cells coordinated their actions so that all the cells of the organism could act as a unit. As organisms grew more complex, this communication system began to split into two communication systems. One system—the nervous system—developed to send rapid and specific messages, while the other system—involving the circulatory system—formed to send slow and widespread communication. In this second system, the chemical messengers evolved into hormones. Whereas neural messages can be measured in thousandths of a second, hormonal messages may take minutes to reach their destination.

Figure 6.12   An Adrenaline Rush

In the event of a life-threatening or highly stressful situation, the adrenal glands produce adrenaline to give people the necessary energy to cope. *How does adrenaline affect emotions in people?*

SECTION 3 Assessment

1. **Review the Vocabulary**   What are three ways that the endocrine system affects behavior?

2. **Visualize the Main Idea**   In a chart similar to the one at right, identify the hormones produced by the glands and the functions of those hormones.

3. **Recall Information**   How does the endocrine system differ from the nervous system?

Glands of the Endocrine System	
Gland	Hormone(s) released

4. **Think Critically**   Explain what psychologists might learn about behavior by studying sex hormones.

5. **Application Activity**   Describe a medical situation in which a psychologist would examine the thyroid gland. Describe the situation from the perspective of a patient.

Heredity and Environment

Reader's Guide

■ Main Idea
Heredity is the transmission of characteristics from parents to children. Environment is the world around you. Heredity and environment affect your body and behavior.

■ Vocabulary
- heredity
- identical twins
- genes
- fraternal twins

■ Objectives
- Give examples of the effects of heredity and environment on behavior.
- Summarize research on the effects of heredity and environment on behavior.

EXPLORING PSYCHOLOGY

Nature or Nurture?

Two monozygotic [derived from the same egg] twin girls were separated at birth and placed in homes far apart. About four years later, researchers interviewed the adoptive parents of each girl. The parents of Shauna said, "She is a terrible eater—won't cooperate, stubborn, strong-willed. I can't get her to eat *anything* unless I put cinnamon on it." The parents of Ellen said, "Ellen is a lovely child—cooperative and outgoing." The researcher probed, asking, "How are her eating habits?" The response was: "Fantastic—she eats anything I put before her, as long as I put cinnamon on it!"

—from *Nature's Thumbprint: The New Genetics of Personality* by P.B. Neubauer and A. Neubauer, 1990

How much do genetic factors contribute to our behavior? How much do environmental factors? These questions have haunted psychologists for years. Some psychologists believe that genetics is like a flower, and the environment is like rain, soil, or fertilizer. Genes establish what you could be, and the environment defines the final product.

HEREDITY AND ENVIRONMENT

People often argue about whether human behavior is instinctive (due to heredity) or learned (due to environment). **Heredity** is the genetic transmission of characteristics from parents to their offspring. Do people learn to be good athletes, or are they born that way? Do people learn to

heredity: the genetic transmission of characteristics from parents to their offspring do well in school, or are they born good at it? The reason for the intensity of the argument may be that many people assume that something learned can probably be changed, whereas something inborn will be difficult or impossible to change. The issue is not that simple, however. Inherited factors and environmental conditions always act together in complicated ways. Asking whether heredity or environment is responsible for something turns out to be like asking, "What makes a cake rise, baking powder or heat?" Obviously, an interaction of the two is responsible.

A Question of Nature vs. Nurture

The argument over the nature-nurture question has been going on for centuries. Nature refers to the characteristics that a person inherits—his or her biological makeup. Nurture refers to environmental factors, such as family, culture, education, and individual experiences. Sir Francis Galton became one of the first to preach the importance of nature in the modern era. In 1869 he published *Hereditary Genius,* a book in which he analyzed the families of over 1,000 eminent politicians, religious leaders, artists, and scholars. He found that success ran in families and concluded that heredity was the cause.

Many psychologists, however, have emphasized the importance of the environment. The tone was set by John Watson, the founder of behaviorism, who wrote in 1930: "Give me a dozen healthy infants, well-formed, and my own specified world to bring them up in and I'll guarantee to take any one at random and train him to become any type of specialist I might select—a doctor, lawyer, artist, merchant-chief, and, yes, even beggarman and thief, regardless of his talents, penchants, tendencies, abilities, vocations, and race of his ancestors" (Watson, 1930).

Genes and Behavior Genes are the basic units of heredity. They are reproduced and passed along from parent to child. All the effects that genes have on behavior occur through their role in building and modifying the physical structures of the body. Those structures must interact with their environment to produce behavior. For example, if your parents are musicians, you may have inherited a gene that influences your musical ability by contributing to brain development that analyzes sounds well.

Twin Studies

One way to find out whether a trait is inherited is to study twins. **Identical twins** develop from a single fertilized egg (thus, they are called monozygotic) and share the same **genes.** Genes are the basic building blocks of heredity (see Figure 6.13).

Reading Check
What is heredity and how does it affect your behavior?

identical twins: twins who come from one fertilized egg; twins having the same heredity

genes: the basic building blocks of heredity

Figure 6.13	**DNA and Genes**

The molecules of DNA make up chromosomes that contain the codes for our biological makeup. *What are genes?*

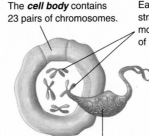

The *cell body* contains 23 pairs of chromosomes.

Each *chromosome* is made of a long strand of DNA. On each pair of chromosomes are *genes,* which are pieces of DNA that contain specific instructions.

A strand of *DNA* is stretched out to show that it looks like a twisted ladder with "chemical" rungs.

"Chemical rungs" carry instructions (genes) for development of millions of parts for your brain and body.

Source: Plotnick, 1999.

Figure 6.14   Identical Twins

Because identical twins share the same genes and most often the same environment, studying them is one way to find out whether a trait is inherited or learned. *What do psychologists mean by the "nature-nurture question"?*

fraternal twins: twins who come from two different eggs fertilized by two different sperm

Fraternal twins develop from two fertilized eggs (thus, dizygotic), and their genes are not more similar than those of brothers or sisters.

Twins growing up in the same house share the same general environment, but identical twins also share the same genes. So, if identical twins who grow up together prove to be more alike on a specific trait than fraternal twins do, it probably means that genes are important for that trait.

Psychologists at the University of Minnesota have been studying identical twins who were separated at birth and reared in different environments (Holden, 1980). One of the researchers, Thomas Bouchard, reports that despite very different social, cultural, and economic backgrounds, the twins shared many common behaviors. For example, in one set of twins (both named Jim), both had done well in math and poorly in spelling while in school, both worked as deputy sheriffs, vacationed in Florida, gave identical names to their children and pets, bit their fingernails, had identical smoking and drinking patterns, and liked mechanical drawing and carpentry. These similarities and others suggest that heredity may contribute to behaviors that we normally associate with experience.

Many researchers now believe that many of the differences among people can be explained by considering heredity as well as experience. Contrary to popular belief, the influence of genes on behavior does not mean that nothing can be done to change the behavior. Although it is true that it is difficult and may be undesirable to change the genetic code that may direct behavior, it is possible to alter the environment in which the genes operate.

SECTION 4   Assessment

1. **Review the Vocabulary**   Explain the difference between fraternal twins and identical twins.

2. **Visualize the Main Idea**   In a diagram like the one below, explain how proponents of each view argue the nature-nurture debate.

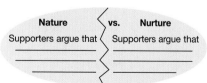

Nature	vs.	Nurture
Supporters argue that		Supporters argue that

3. **Recall Information**   What role do the genes play in influencing someone's behavior?

4. **Think Critically**   Sue and Tracy are identical twins. Sue is good at drawing. Tracy is a starter on the basketball team. Explain what may cause differences in these twins.

5. **Application Activity**   Describe a characteristic that you have. Explain whether you think this characteristic is hereditary or environmental.

Summary and Vocabulary

Some psychologists (psychobiologists) study how our behavior and psychological processes are connected to our biological processes. Our bodies and minds work together to create who we are.

Section 1 — The Nervous System: The Basic Structure

Main Idea: Learning about the nervous system helps us know how messages that are sent to the brain cause behavior.

- The nervous system is divided into two parts: the central nervous system and the peripheral nervous system.
- Messages to and from the brain travel along the nerves.
- Nerve cells called neurons have three basic parts: the cell body, dendrites, and the axon.
- The somatic nervous system controls the body's voluntary activities, and the autonomic nervous system controls the body's involuntary activities.

Section 2 — Studying the Brain

Main Idea: There are many parts in the human brain that work together to coordinate movement and stimulate thinking and emotions, resulting in behavior.

- The brain is made of three parts: the hindbrain, the midbrain, and the forebrain.
- The cortex of the brain is divided into the left and the right hemispheres; the left hemisphere controls the movements of the right side of the body, and the right hemisphere controls the movements of the left side of the body.
- Psychologists use recording, stimulation, lesions, and imaging to study the brain.

Section 3 — The Endocrine System

Main Idea: The endocrine system controls and excites growth and affects emotions and behavior in people.

- The endocrine system, in addition to the nervous system, is a communication system for sending information to and from the brain.
- The endocrine system sends chemical messages, called hormones.

Section 4 — Heredity and Environment

Main Idea: Heredity is the transmission of characteristics from parents to children. Environment is the world around you. Heredity and environment affect your body and behavior.

- Heredity is the genetic transmission of characteristics from parents to their offspring.
- Genes are the basic units of heredity; they are reproduced and passed along from parents to child.
- All the effects that genes have on behavior occur through their role in building and modifying the physical structures of the body.

Chapter Vocabulary

central nervous system (CNS) (p. 156)

spinal cord (p. 156)

peripheral nervous system (PNS) (p. 156)

neurons (p. 157)

synapse (p. 157)

neurotransmitters (p. 158)

somatic nervous system (SNS) (p. 158)

autonomic nervous system (ANS) (p. 158)

hindbrain (p. 160)

midbrain (p. 161)

forebrain (p. 161)

lobes (p. 162)

electroencephalograph (EEG) (p. 165)

computerized axial tomography (CAT) (p. 167)

positron emission tomography (PET) (p. 167)

magnetic resonance imaging (MRI) (p. 167)

endocrine system (p. 171)

hormones (p. 171)

pituitary gland (p. 171)

heredity (p. 174)

identical twins (p. 175)

genes (p. 175)

fraternal twins (p. 176)

CHAPTER 6 Assessment

PSYCHOLOGY Online

Self-Check Quiz
Visit the *Understanding Psychology* Web site at psychology.glencoe.com and click on **Chapter 6—Self-Check Quizzes** to prepare for the Chapter Test.

Reviewing Vocabulary

Choose the letter of the correct term or concept below to complete the sentence.

a. neurotransmitters
b. somatic nervous system
c. autonomic nervous system
d. hormones
e. forebrain
f. hindbrain
g. pituitary gland
h. synapse
i. identical twins
j. fraternal twins

1. The part of the nervous system that controls voluntary activities is the _____.
2. _____ develop from two fertilized eggs, and their genes are not more similar than those of brothers or sisters.
3. The space between neurons is called the _____.
4. The _____ is the part of the brain that integrates sensory information.
5. As a neuron transmits its message to another neuron across the synapse, it releases chemicals called _____.
6. _____ develop from a single fertilized egg and share the same genes.
7. Located at the rear base of the skull, the _____ is involved in the basic processes of life.
8. The _____ acts as the "master gland" of the body, controlling the output of hormones by other endocrine glands.
9. _____ are produced by endocrine glands and are distributed by the blood and other body fluids.
10. The part of the nervous system that controls activities such as heartbeat is the _____.

Recalling Facts

1. Explain how messages travel to and from the brain through the nervous system.
2. Using a chart similar to the one below, describe the main function of each of the four lobes of the cerebral cortex.

Lobe	Main Function
Occipital	
Parietal	
Temporal	
Frontal	

3. Describe four methods used to study the brain.
4. How are the messages of the endocrine system transmitted throughout the body?
5. One way to find out whether a trait is inherited is to compare the behavior of identical and fraternal twins. Explain how this works.

Critical Thinking

1. **Analyzing Concepts** How would people's lives be different if the nervous system were not made of the somatic and the autonomic nervous systems? What if people had only a somatic nervous system?
2. **Synthesizing Information** Suppose a person suffers a stroke that causes damage to the frontal lobes. What aspects of the person's behavior would you expect to see change?
3. **Making Inferences** Provide an example of how the physiological reaction created by adrenaline is helpful in emergency situations.
4. **Applying Concepts** Do you think it is important for parents who wish to adopt a child to find out about the genetic makeup of the child? Why do you think so?
5. **Evaluating Information** Which aspects of your personality, your way of acting, and your appearance seem obviously the result of heredity? Which seem to be more related to your environmental upbringing? Which characteristics are definitely the result of an interaction between heredity and environment?

CHAPTER 6

Assessment

Psychology Projects

1. **The Nervous System: The Basic Structure**
Working with two or three classmates, prepare a video that can be used to teach younger children how the brain and the nervous system work. You might consider making the video humorous to more easily gain the attention of younger children. Arrange to have children in lower grades view the video. Evaluate its effectiveness.

2. **Studying the Brain**   Contact a hospital to find out more about the uses of CAT scans, PET scans, and MRIs. Find out under what circumstances each of the techniques would be used. Report your findings in a written report.

3. **The Endocrine System**   Find out about problems that occur as a result of malfunctioning of parts of the endocrine system. Find out how such problems are treated and report your findings in an oral report.

Technology Activity

Scientists have recently gained greater insight into brain and neuron development in infants and young children. Search the Internet for information about this topic and about the implications the information has for parents and other caregivers. Summarize your findings in a brief report.

Psychology Journal

Much of what we know about the brain and its functioning has come from studies and experiments performed on animals. Animal rights groups protest the use of animals in experiments, citing the inhumane treatment of animals used in laboratory experiments. In your journal write an editorial explaining the reasons for your support of or opposition to using animals for psychological research.

Building Skills

Interpreting a Graph   Researchers have found that the brains of patients with Alzheimer's disease have a large number of destroyed neurons in the part of the brain that is crucial for making memories permanent. These patients have also exhibited a loss of the neurotransmitter acetylcholine, resulting in memory difficulties. Review the graph and then answer the questions that follow.

1. According to the graph, how many people in the United States suffer from Alzheimer's disease?

2. How would you describe the projected number of cases of Alzheimer's by the year 2050?

3. What impact might the researchers' findings and the information in the graph have on the direction researchers might take to find a cure for the disease?

Practice and **assess** key social studies skills with **Glencoe Skillbuilder Interactive Workbook CD-ROM, Level 2.**

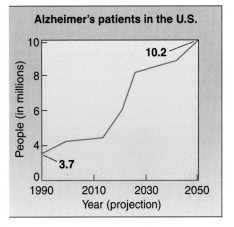

Alzheimer's patients in the U.S.

See the Skills Handbook, page 628, for an explanation of interpreting graphs.

TIME *REPORTS*

Glimpses of the Mind

**What is consciousness?
Memory? Emotion?
Science unravels the
best-kept secrets of the
human brain**

By **MICHAEL D. LEMONICK**

TO ALL OUTWARD APPEARANCES, Elliot is a perfectly normal middle-aged businessman. Despite an operation a decade ago for removal of a benign brain tumor the size of a small orange, he remains intelligent and seemingly rational, with a wry sense of humor. Yet his behavior makes it clear that there is something very wrong. After years of rock-solid competence, Elliot now has trouble keeping appointments and making decisions. He has squandered much of his life savings on a series of bad investments. And, strangest of all, the very fact that his behavior is self-destructive doesn't seem to bother him—and he keeps on making the same mistakes.

Patient "X" is much more clearly ill. She has suffered a major stroke; her entire left side is paralyzed. It's obvious to everyone that she's severely impaired—everyone, that is, except her. Ask her how she feels, and she responds, "Just fine." Point out her lifeless left arm, and she seems baffled. She can be convinced, through persistent effort, that the arm doesn't work. But a few minutes later, she has forgotten all about it.

Bill Noonan hasn't suffered any obvious physical damage to his brain.

Yet for more than two decades after his return from Vietnam, he has re-experienced the most terrifying event of his life several times a week as a waking dream. "It was a night ambush," he remembers. "The first seven guys to my right were machine-gunned down. My gas mask was shot right off my hip. That was my first fire fight." Bill knew his flashbacks weren't real—but they seemed so real that it made no difference. "I didn't know what was happening," he says. "The biggest fear I had was that I was crazy."

The victims of mental disease or brain damage are fascinating, not simply as exhibits in a neurological sideshow but also as stark demonstrations of how fragile reality can be. While the victims of mental disorders are certainly conscious and aware, their worlds are profoundly different from those of most of us. What can it possibly feel like, we wonder, to live without emotion, to be crippled without realizing it, to re-experience an event from the distant past complete with the fears that originally surrounded it?

As neurologists, psychologists and biologists have zeroed in more and more precisely on the physical causes of mental disorders, they have found themselves addressing a much deeper mystery, a set of interrelated conundrums probably as old as humanity: What, precisely, is the mind, the elusive entity where intelligence, decision making, perception, awareness and sense of self reside? Where is it located? How does it work? Does it arise from purely physical processes—

pulses of electricity zapping from brain cell to brain cell, helped along their way by myriad complex chemicals? Or is it something beyond the merely physical—something ethereal that might be close to the spiritual concept of the soul?

Great thinkers have had no shortage of ideas on the subject. Plato was convinced that the mind must be located inside the head, because the head is shaped more or less like a sphere, his idea of the highest geometrical form. Aristotle insisted that the mind was in the heart. His reasoning: warmth implies vitality; the blood is warm; the heart pumps the blood. By the Middle Ages, though, pretty much everyone agreed that the mind arose from the brain—but still had no clear idea how it arose. Finally, in the 17th century, the French philosopher René Descartes declared that the mind, while it might live in the brain, was a nonmaterial thing, entirely separate from the physical tissues found inside the head. Furthermore, said Descartes in one of history's most memorable sound bites, *"Cogito, ergo sum"* (I think, therefore I am). His point: consciousness is the only sure evidence that we actually exist.

Until just a few years ago, unraveling the relationship of mind and brain was beyond the realm of observation and experimentation. But science has finally begun to catch up with philosophy. Using sensitive electrodes inserted deep into the gray matter of test animals, researchers have watched vision as it percolates inward from the eye's retina to the inner brain. Powerful technologies such as magnetic resonance imaging (MRI) and positron-emission tomography (PET) have also provided a window on the human brain, letting scientists watch a thought taking place, see the red glow of fear erupting from the structure known as the amygdala, or note the telltale firing of neurons as a long-buried memory is reconstructed. "What's so exciting," says Patricia Churchland, a professor at the University of California at San Diego, "is that the philosophical questions

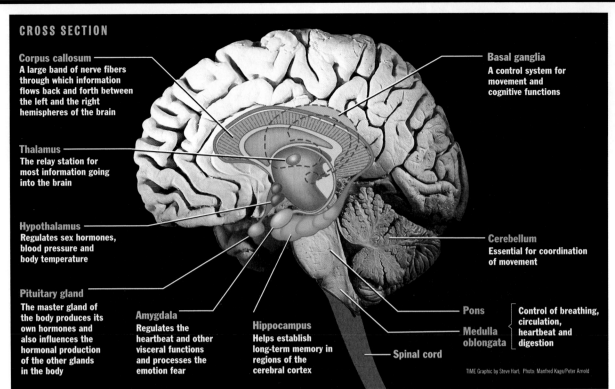

CROSS SECTION

Corpus callosum
A large band of nerve fibers through which information flows back and forth between the left and the right hemispheres of the brain

Thalamus
The relay station for most information going into the brain

Hypothalamus
Regulates sex hormones, blood pressure and body temperature

Pituitary gland
The master gland of the body produces its own hormones and also influences the hormonal production of the other glands in the body

Amygdala
Regulates the heartbeat and other visceral functions and processes the emotion fear

Hippocampus
Helps establish long-term memory in regions of the cerebral cortex

Basal ganglia
A control system for movement and cognitive functions

Cerebellum
Essential for coordination of movement

Pons

Medulla oblongata

Control of breathing, circulation, heartbeat and digestion

Spinal cord

TIME Graphic by Steve Hart; Photo: Manfred Kage/Peter Arnold

raised by the Greeks are coming within the province of science."

In response to this enormous opportunity—not just to clarify the mysteries of consciousness but also to understand and treat such devastating mind malfunctions as Alzheimer's disease, depression, drug addiction, schizophrenia and traumatic brain damage—research projects have multiplied dramatically. The brain is a hot topic, and while a complete understanding of its inner workings will be a long time coming, the surge of interest in things cerebral has already produced tantalizing results. Descartes was right in one sense: the mind is not a physical object, and while it exists within the brain, it has no particular location. The destruction of any given part of the brain can severely alter the mind in one way or another but not destroy it.

However, Descartes was profoundly wrong, it appears, in his assertion that mind and body are wholly independent. The mind, argues University of Iowa neurologist Antonio Damasio in his book *Descartes' Error*, is created by the

body—specifically by the brain. Utterly contrary to common sense, though, and to the evidence gathered from our own introspection, consciousness may be nothing more than a passing by-product of more mundane, wholly physical processes—much as a rainbow is the result of the interplay of light and raindrops. Input from the senses clearly plays a part; so do body chemicals whose ebb and flow we experience as feelings and emotions. Memory, too, is involved, along with language—the way humans translate concepts into symbolic form.

Physical trauma can distort memory, presumably by destroying all or part of one of our memory-processing structures. But other sorts of shock—strong emotion, for example—can do

the same. Virtually everyone who was over the age of 10 when J.F.K. was shot or when *Challenger* exploded remembers precisely where he or she was when the news arrived. While the intellectual memory of emotions is routed through the hippocampus, a different, gut-level sort of memory can be involuntarily revived with terrible clarity by abnormal activity in the amygdala. "It's been an eye opener to me that individuals we study who were traumatized 25 years ago still show abnormal brain function," says Dennis Charney, head of psychiatry at the VA hospital in West Haven, Connecticut. "Severe stress can change the way your brain functions biologically." ■

—For the complete text of this article and related articles from **TIME**, please visit www.time.com/teach

ANALYZING THE ARTICLE

1. How do we know we exist, according to Descartes?
2. **CRITICAL THINKING** How does physical trauma affect us? How can you explain Bill Noonan's flashbacks from the Vietnam War?

Altered States of Consciousness

PSYCHOLOGY JOURNAL

What is the purpose of sleep? Do you think it would be possible or desirable to perfect a way to eliminate the need for sleep or dreams? Write a one-page essay in your journal answering these questions. ■

PSYCHOLOGY Online

Chapter Overview
Visit the *Understanding Psychology* Web site at psychology.glencoe.com and click on **Chapter 7—Chapter Overviews** to preview the chapter.

Sleep and Dreams

Reader's Guide

■ Main Idea
Sleep—an essential state of consciousness—involves stages and periods of dreaming.

■ Vocabulary
- consciousness
- REM sleep
- circadian rhythm
- insomnia
- sleep apnea
- narcolepsy
- nightmares
- night terrors
- sleepwalking

■ Objectives
- Describe the research related to sleep and dreams.
- List and discuss sleep disorders.

EXPLORING PSYCHOLOGY

Losing Sleep

In 1959 New York disk jockey Peter Tripp stayed awake for 200 hours to raise money for charity. . . . After about 50 hours, he started having mild hallucinations, seeing cobwebs in his shoes when there were none there and thinking that specks of dirt were bugs; by 100 hours, he became delirious and saw a doctor's tweed suit as a tangle of furry worms; at 120 he needed a stimulant to keep him awake. After 150 hours, he was disoriented, not knowing who or where he was, and he became paranoid—he backed against a wall, letting no one pass behind him; by 200 hours, his hallucinations had taken a sinister turn, and he thought a doctor trying to examine him was an undertaker come to bury him.

—from *The Human Mind Explained* edited by Susan A. Greenfield, 1996

How important is sleep to humans? Sleep is vital to mental health. Peter Tripp found out that if a person is deprived of sleep, he or she will have psychological symptoms (although not all people have symptoms as extreme as Tripp's). What is sleep? Most people think of sleep as a state of unconsciousness, punctuated by brief periods of dreaming. This is only partially correct. Sleep is a state of *altered* consciousness, characterized by certain patterns of brain activity.

What is consciousness? **Consciousness** is a state of awareness. When we discuss *altered* states of consciousness, we mean that people can have different levels of awareness. Consciousness can range from

consciousness: a state of awareness, including a person's feelings, sensations, ideas, and perceptions alertness to nonalertness (see Figure 7.1). People who are fully aware with their attention focused on something are conscious of that "something." A person who is not completely aware is in a different level of consciousness—an altered state of consciousness. Sleep illustrates an altered state of consciousness.

Although sleep is a major part of human and animal behavior, it has been extremely difficult to study until recently. A researcher cannot ask a sleeping person to report on the experience without first waking the person. The study of sleep was aided by the development of the electroencephalograph (EEG), a device that records the electrical activity of the brain.

WHY DO WE SLEEP?

We are not sure why people sleep. Sleep is characterized by unresponsiveness to the environment and limited physical mobility. Some people believe that sleep is restorative; it allows people to "charge up their batteries." These people believe that sleep is a time when the brain recovers from exhaustion and stress. Other people believe it is a type of primitive hibernation: we sleep to conserve energy. Some suggest that sleep is an adaptive process; that is, in earlier times sleep kept humans out of harm's way at night when humans would have been most vulnerable. Still other researchers believe we sleep to clear our minds of useless information. As a variation of this theory, some people believe we sleep to dream.

STAGES OF SLEEP

As you begin to fall asleep, your body temperature declines, your pulse rate drops, and your breathing grows slow and even. Gradually, your eyes close and your brain briefly emits alpha waves, which are associated with the absence of concentrated thought and with relaxation (see Figure 7.2). Your body may twitch, your eyes roll, and brief visual images flash across your mind (although your eyelids are shut) as you enter Stage I sleep, the lightest level of sleep.

| Figure 7.1 | Freud's Levels of Consciousness |

Sigmund Freud identified three levels of consciousness. In his approach to consciousness, he claimed that preconscious ideas are not in your awareness now, but you are able to recall them. Unconscious ideas are hidden. *When would you use information from the preconscious level?*

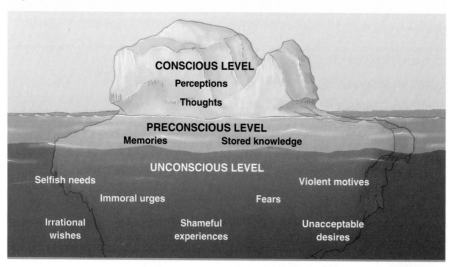

Early Stages

In Stage I sleep, your pulse slows a bit more and your muscles relax, but your breathing becomes uneven and your brain waves grow irregular. If you were awakened during this stage, you would report that you were "just drifting." This phase lasts for about 10 minutes and is marked by the presence of theta waves, which are lower in amplitude and frequency than alpha waves. At this point, your brain waves occasionally shift from low-amplitude, high-frequency waves to high-amplitude, low-frequency waves—a pattern that indicates you have entered Stage II sleep. Your eyes roll slowly from side to side. Some 30 minutes later, you drift down into a deeper level of Stage III sleep, and large-amplitude delta waves begin to sweep your brain every second or so.

Figure 7.2 **Patterns of Sleep**

The top diagram shows the passage of a sleeper through the various stages of sleep over a seven-hour period. The bottom diagram shows the patterns of electrical activity (EEGs) in the brain that correspond to the various stages of sleep. The EEG pattern shown for being awake is one that occurs when a person is resting quietly with eyes closed. *How often during a night's sleep does a person reach Stage IV?*

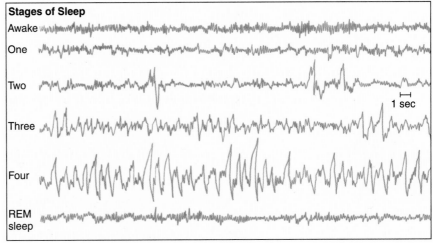

Later Stages

Stage IV is the deepest sleep of all, and it is difficult to waken a sleeper in this stage. Large, regular delta waves—occurring more than 50 percent of the time—indicate you are in a state of deep sleep. If you are awakened by a loud noise or sudden movement, you may feel disoriented. Talking out loud, sleepwalking, and bed-wetting—all of which may occur in this stage—leave no trace on the memory. Deep sleep is important to your physical and psychological well-being. Perhaps this is why people who are able to sleep only a few hours at a time descend rapidly into Stage IV and remain there for most of their nap.

On average a person spends 75 percent of sleep time in Stages I through IV. At this point, something curious happens. Although your muscles are even more relaxed than before, your eyes begin to move

REM sleep: a stage of sleep characterized by rapid eye movements, a high level of brain activity, a deep relaxation of the muscles, and dreaming

rapidly. You have entered a more active type of sleep characterized by rapid eye movement. This is called **REM sleep.** Your pulse rate and breathing become irregular, and the levels of adrenal and sexual hormones in your blood rise—as if you were in the middle of an intensely emotional or physically demanding activity. Often, your face or fingers twitch and the large muscles in your arms and legs are paralyzed. Your brain sends out waves that closely resemble those of a person who is fully awake. For this reason, REM sleep is called active sleep. Stages I through IV are sometimes referred to as NREM (non-REM) or quiet sleep because of the absence of rapid eye movement, which is accompanied by the slower pattern of brain waves. It is during REM sleep that almost all dreaming normally takes place.

REM sleep lasts from about 15 (early at night) to 45 (late at night) minutes, after which you retrace the descent to Stage IV. You go through this cycle every 90 minutes or so. Each time the period of Stage IV sleep decreases and the length of REM sleep increases—until you eventually wake up. At no point does your brain become inactive. REM sleep seems to serve psychological functions such as building efficient learning and memory processes.

Reading Check
What is Stage IV sleep?

HOW MUCH SLEEP?

Humans spend approximately one-third of their lives in sleep. The amount of sleep a person needs to function effectively varies considerably from individual to individual and from time to time within a person's life. Newborns spend an average of 16 hours a day sleeping, almost half of it in REM sleep. Sixteen-year-olds may spend as much as 10 to 11 hours asleep each night. Students in graduate school average 8 hours a night.

Men and women who are 70 years old or older may need only 5 hours of sleep. Adults average about 25 percent of their time in REM sleep and 75 percent in NREM sleep. Although the amount of sleep a person needs may vary, it does appear that everyone sleeps and that both types of sleep are important to normal functioning.

Have you ever noticed that there are certain times of the day when you are more alert or more tired? People seem to have an internal biological clock that regulates the sleep-wakefulness cycle. Blood pressure, heart rate, appetite, secretion of hormones and digestive enzymes, sensory sharpness, and elimination processes all follow circadian rhythms (Hrushesky, 1994). A **circadian rhythm** is a biological clock that is genetically programmed to regulate physiological responses within a time period of 24 or 25 hours. Circadian rhythms operate even when normal day and night cues are removed. For example, we usually standardize our sleep patterns according to the light of day and dark of night; yet experimenters who have lived for months at a time in the depths of a cave have still maintained a rhythm to their behaviors. Without environmental cues, people maintained their circadian rhythms on about a 24- to 25-hour cycle. Researchers have recently determined

circadian rhythm: the rhythm of activity and inactivity lasting approximately one day that humans have a circadian cycle of approximately 24.18 hours (Czeisler et al., 1999).

Circadian rhythms do not control your sleep cycles; the environment and the 24-hour day control our cycles. Thus, when you miss sleep, this disruption becomes very apparent. Some travelers experience jet lag. This occurs when their internal circadian rhythms do not match the external clock time. For example, when you travel from New York to Moscow, your body is on a different time clock when you reach Moscow. You may feel tired and disoriented. What do you do to cure jet lag? It usually takes about one day for each hour of time change to reset your circadian clock.

SLEEP DISORDERS

Sleep is an active state essential for mental and physical restoration. Sometimes, though, we may have problems falling asleep or have problems during sleep. These sleep disorders may interfere with the quality of life and personal health, as well as endanger public safety because of their role in industrial or traffic accidents.

Insomnia

Everyone has had a sleepless night at one time or another—a night where nothing you do brings the calm, soothing peace you want. Some people have sleep problems like this all the time, and they rarely get more than an hour or two of uninterrupted sleep a night. **Insomnia**— a prolonged and usually abnormal inability to obtain adequate sleep—can have many causes and takes many forms. Some people cannot sleep at night because of anxiety or depression. Overuse of alcohol or drugs can also cause insomnia.

insomnia: the failure to get enough sleep at night in order to feel rested the next day

Sleep Apnea

The sleep disorder **sleep apnea** causes frequent interruptions of breathing during sleep. One of the most common symptoms is a specific kind of snoring that may occur hundreds of times during the night. Each snoring episode lasts 10 to 15 seconds and ends suddenly, often with a physical movement of the entire body. A blockage of the breathing passages actually causes the snoring; during this time the victim is in fact choking—the flow of air to the lungs stops. The episode ends when low levels of oxygen or high levels of carbon dioxide in the blood trigger breathing reflexes.

sleep apnea: a sleep disorder in which a person has trouble breathing while asleep

Sleep apnea affects about 1 in 100 Americans, occurring most often among older people. People suffering from this disorder may feel listless, sleepy, and irritable during the day. Whereas insomnia is caused by mental stress, sleep apnea is usually caused by a physical problem that blocks the airway, such as enlarged tonsils, repeated infections in the throat or middle ear, or obesity. These conditions may cause the muscles at the base of the tongue to relax and sag repeatedly.

Narcolepsy

narcolepsy: a condition characterized by suddenly falling
asleep or feeling very sleepy
during the day

Another disorder, **narcolepsy,** is characterized by a permanent and overwhelming feeling of sleepiness and fatigue. Other symptoms include unusual sleep and dream patterns, such as dreamlike hallucinations or a feeling of temporary paralysis. People with narcolepsy may have sleep attacks throughout the day. The sleep attacks are accompanied by brief periods of REM sleep. Victims of narcolepsy may have difficulties in the area of work, leisure, and interpersonal relations and are prone to accidents.

Nightmares and Night Terrors

nightmares: unpleasant
dreams

night terrors: sleep disruptions that occur during Stage IV
of sleep, involving screaming,
panic, or confusion

Frightening dreams—**nightmares**—occur during the dream phase of REM sleep. A nightmare may frighten the sleeper, who will usually wake up with a vivid memory of a movielike dream. On the other hand, **night terrors** occur during Stage IV sleep (usually within an hour after going to bed). A night terror may last anywhere from five to twenty minutes and involve screaming, sweating, confusion, and a rapid heart rate. The subject may suddenly awake from sleep or have a persistent fear that occurs at night. Subjects usually have no memory of night terrors.

Sleepwalking and Sleep Talking

sleepwalking: walking or
carrying out behaviors while
asleep

A disorder in which a person is partly, but not completely, awake during the night is **sleepwalking.** That person may walk or do other things without any memory of doing so. Sleepwalking is a disorder associated with children, although some adults may sleepwalk. Most children who sleepwalk do not have emotional problems and will outgrow it. This disorder has been linked to stress, fatigue, and the use of sedative medicines. Sleepwalking may also be inherited. It is usually harmless; however, it may become dangerous if sleepwalkers fall or otherwise injure themselves—their movements are often clumsy. It is not dangerous to wake sleepwalkers.

Sleep talking is a common sleep disruption. Most people talk in their sleep more than they realize because they do not remember talking during sleep. Sleep talking can occur in either REM or NREM sleep. It can be a single word or a longer speech. Sometimes sleep talkers pause between sentences or phrases as if they are carrying on a conversation with someone else. You can even engage a sleep talker in a conversation sometimes. Like sleepwalking, sleep talking is harmless.

DREAMS

We call the mental activity that takes place during sleep dreaming. Everybody dreams, although most people are able to recall only a few, if any, of their dreams. (However, in cultures in which dreams are highly valued and talked about frequently, people remember their dreams almost every morning.) Sleep researchers sometimes make a point of waking study participants at regular intervals during the night to ask them about their dreams. The first few dreams are usually composed of vague thoughts left over from the day's activities. A participant may report that she was watching television, for example. As the night wears on, dreams become longer and more vivid and dramatic, especially dreams that take place during REM sleep. Because the amounts of time spent in REM sleep increase during the night, the last dream is likely to be the longest and the one people remember when they wake up. People, however, can rarely recall more than the last 15 minutes of a dream when they are awakened (Dement & Wolpert, 1958). Researchers have found that after people have been deprived of REM sleep, they subsequently increase the amount of time they spend in REM sleep. Thus, it appears that a certain amount of dreaming each night is necessary (Dement, 1976).

The Content of Dreams

When people are awakened randomly during REM sleep and asked what they had just been dreaming, the reports generally are commonplace, even dull (Hall & Van de Castle, 1966). The dreams we remember and talk about "are more coherent, sexier, and generally more interesting" than those collected in systematic research (Webb, 1975).

Often we incorporate our everyday activities into our dreams. Researchers who have recorded the contents of thousands of dreams have found that most—even the late-night REM adventures—occur in such commonplace settings as living rooms, cars, and streets. Most dreams involve either strenuous recreational activities or passive events such as sitting and watching. A large percentage of the emotions experienced in dreams are negative or unpleasant—anxiety, anger, sadness, and so on. Contrary to popular belief, dreams do not occur in a split second; they correspond to a realistic time scale.

Some dreams are negative enough to be considered nightmares. Nightmares often have such a frightening quality that we awaken in the middle of them. The sense of dread in nightmares may be related to the intensity of brain activity and to the stimulation of those parts of the brain responsible for emotional reactions. The emotional reaction of dread may then influence the content of the dream.

Dream Interpretation

Dream interpretations have been discovered dating back to 5000 B.C. Sigmund Freud believed that no matter how simple or mundane, dreams may contain clues to thoughts the dreamer is afraid to acknowledge in his or her waking hours.

The Inuit people of North America, like Freud, believe that dreams contain hidden meanings. They believe that when dreaming, people enter the

Figure 7.3   The Dream

Some researchers believe that when we sleep, electrical bursts occur that hit portions of the brain, firing off various memory circuits. The result? Dreams. Artist Jacob Lawrence created *Dreams No. 2* in 1965. *What are other explanations for dreaming?*

More About...

Freud on Dreams

Sigmund Freud was the first psychologist to study dreams thoroughly. He hypothesized that dreams express impulses and thoughts, often in highly symbolic form, that are unacceptable at the conscious level. Freud used the term *manifest content* to refer to the story line, images, and other perceptual aspects of dreams. Freud defined *latent content* as the hidden meaning of dreams that comes from the dreamer's unconscious wishes (Freud, 1965).

spiritual world where they interact with those who have passed away. These departed souls help the living reflect on some current or future event (Plotnick, 1999).

Some social scientists, however, are skeptical of dream interpretations. Nathaniel Kleitman, one of the pioneers who discovered REM sleep, wrote in 1960: "Dreaming may serve no function whatsoever." According to this view, the experience of a dream is simply an unimportant by-product of stimulating certain brain cells during sleep. Others argue that the common experience of feeling paralyzed in a dream simply means that brain cells that inhibit muscle activity were randomly stimulated (McCarley, 1978). One dream researcher advocates a problem-solving theory about dreaming (Cartwright, 1993). This theory proposes that dreaming allows people a chance to review and address some of the problems they faced during the day. One theorist, Francis Crick, believes that dreams are the brain's way of "unlearning" or removing certain unneeded memories. In other words, dreams are a form of mental housecleaning. This mental housecleaning may be necessary because it is not useful to remember every single detail of your life.

Daydreams Daydreaming requires a low level of awareness and involves fantasizing or dreaming while we are awake. Usually we daydream when we are in situations that require little attention or when we are bored. Daydreaming serves useful purposes such as reminding us of or preparing us for important things in our future. Daydreaming may also improve our creativity by generating thought processes. Some psychologists believe that daydreaming allows us to control our emotions.

SECTION 1 Assessment

1. **Review the Vocabulary** Describe the symptoms of insomnia, sleep apnea, narcolepsy, nightmares, night terrors, and sleepwalking.

2. **Visualize the Main Idea** Use a flowchart similar to the one below to list and describe the five stages of sleep.

3. **Recall Information** What is the difference between REM and NREM sleep? Which type lasts longer during a night's sleep?

4. **Think Critically** Why is sleep characterized as an *altered* state of consciousness? Why do you think we sleep?

5. **Application Activity** Create a "Daydream Diary." For one week keep a record of when, where, and why your daydreams occur. What are the psychological purposes of your daydreams?

Hypnosis, Biofeedback, and Meditation

Reader's Guide

■ Main Idea

Hypnosis, biofeedback, and meditation are altered states of consciousness that can occur when we are awake.

■ Vocabulary

- hypnosis
- posthypnotic suggestion
- biofeedback
- meditation

■ Objectives

- Determine how hypnosis relates to consciousness.
- Describe research into such techniques as biofeedback and meditation.

EXPLORING PSYCHOLOGY

Not Feeling the Pain

Victor Rausch entered a hypnotic trance by focusing on Chopin's *Lush Nocturne in E-flat,* as it was played in the movie *The Eddy Duchin Story.* Rausch visualized scenes from the movie and wrapped his mind in appealing thoughts. Rausch's blood pressure and pulse rate remained steady for 75 minutes. During this 75 minutes Rausch was undergoing a gallbladder operation! He had refused the anesthetic, and during the surgery, he swears he felt no pain—just a little tugging. He even talked and joked with the surgical team during the procedure. After the surgery, he stood up and walked down the hall, riding the elevator to his hospital room.

—**from** "The Healing Power of Hypnosis" **by** Jean Callahan, 1997

Surgery without anesthesia may sound like a trick, but such operations have been performed by hypnotizing the patient. Although hypnosis still conjures up images of a circus magician saying, "You are getting sleepy, very sleepy . . . ," researchers are learning more about this mind-body connection. Doctors and therapists use hypnosis to help people quit smoking, lose weight, manage stress, overcome phobias, and diminish pain.

WHAT IS HYPNOSIS?

So what exactly is hypnosis? **Hypnosis** is a form of altered consciousness in which people become highly suggestible to changes in behavior and thought. By allowing the hypnotist to guide and direct them,

hypnosis: a state of consciousness resulting from a narrowed focus of attention and characterized by heightened suggestibility

Franz Anton Mesmer
1734–1815

"Truth is nothing but a path traced between errors."

Franz Anton Mesmer missed the narrow path of truth; he missed the signs that his science was faulty. Mesmer, however, became the first person to practice hypnosis. Mesmer believed that the human body is filled with a magnetic fluid that can become misaligned, causing illness. Realignment would restore health. Mesmer treated medical problems by placing his patients in a tub filled with water and iron fillings protruding from which were larger iron rods. Mesmer would then pass a magnet back and forth across the patient's body to redirect the flow of the blood, nerve activity, and fluids. Some of his patients reported dramatic results.

Later, Mesmer got rid of the magnet and used his own hand, claiming that he himself was the magnet. He called the force he discharged *animal magnetism.* Before Mesmer treated his patients, he told them to expect certain reactions, and his patients responded as anticipated. After his death, his followers called this healing technique "mesmerism" or "hypnotism." Although Mesmer was denounced as a fraud, and Mesmer's magnetic fluid never existed, he paved the way for studies relating to the readiness of some subjects to obey hypnotic suggestions and enter an altered state of consciousness.

people can be made conscious of things they are usually unaware of and unaware of things they usually notice. (Participants may recall in vivid detail incidents they had forgotten or feel no pain when pricked with a needle.) It happens in this way: At all times, certain sensations and thoughts are filtered out of our awareness. For example, as you read this sentence, you were probably not aware of the position of your feet until I called attention to that. By mentioning the position of your feet, your attention shifted to your feet—an area of your body that seconds before was outside your consciousness. Hypnosis shifts our perceptions in the same way.

Hypnosis does not put the participant to sleep, as many people believe. A hypnotic trance is quite different from sleep. In fact, participants become highly receptive and responsive to certain internal and external stimuli. They are able to focus their attention on one tiny aspect of reality and ignore all other inputs. The hypnotist induces a trance by slowly persuading a participant to relax and to lose interest in external distractions. Whether this takes a few minutes or much longer depends on the purpose of the hypnosis, the method of induction, and the participant's past experiences with hypnosis.

In an environment of trust, a participant with a rich imagination can become very susceptible to the hypnotist's suggestions. Psychologists who use hypnosis stress that the relationship between the hypnotist and participant involves cooperation, not domination. The participant is not under the hypnotist's "power" and cannot be forced to do things against his or her will. Rather, the person is simply cooperating with the hypnotist. *Together* they try to solve a problem or to learn more about how the participant's mind works. Anyone can resist hypnosis by simply refusing to open his or her mind to the hypnotist, and people under hypnosis cannot be induced to do things they would not do when "awake" unless they want to.

Theories of Hypnosis

Psychologists do not agree about the nature of hypnosis. Some, like Theodore Barber (1965), argue that hypnosis is not a special state of consciousness but simply the result of suggestibility. If people are just given instructions and told to try their hardest, they will be able to do anything that hypnotized people can do.

Others, like Ernest Hilgard (1986), believe that there is something special about the hypnotic state. People who are hypnotized are very suggestible; they go along with the hypnotist and do not initiate activities themselves; and they can more easily imagine and remember things. Hilgard believes that consciousness includes many different aspects that may become separated, or dissociated, during hypnosis. This view is called the neodissociation theory, which includes a "hidden observer"—a portion of the personality that watches and reports what happens to the hypnotized person.

Another explanation of hypnosis is based on the importance of suggestibility in the hypnotic induction. According to some theorists (Sarbin & Coe, 1972, 1979), hypnotized people behave as they do because they have accepted the role of a hypnotized subject. We expect that hypnotized individuals will forget certain things when told or will recall forgotten material, and we play the role.

Whether hypnosis is a special state of consciousness or not, it does reveal that people often have potential abilities that they do not use. Continued study may help us understand where these abilities come from and how to use them better.

Uses of Hypnosis

Although people have often seen hypnosis as a part of an entertainment act, it has serious uses in medical and therapeutic settings.

Hypnotists can suggest things for their participants to remember or forget when the trance is over. This is known as **posthypnotic suggestion.** For example, the hypnotist can suppress memory by suggesting that after the person is awakened, she will be unable to hear the word "psychology." When she comes out of the trance, the participant

Reading Check
What type of relationship is needed between a hypnotist and participant?

posthypnotic suggestion: a suggestion made during hypnosis that influences the participant's behavior afterward

PSYCHOLOGY and You — Hypnosis and Athletics

Olympic athletes use self-hypnosis to achieve peak performance. Many coaches and trainers realize the power of mental rehearsal before competition begins. Although self-hypnosis cannot turn an average soccer player into a world-class athlete, it can help you achieve your personal best. By visualizing a top performance, you can convince your mind that achievement of that performance is possible. Here is how:

1. Relax. (If you have prepared physically for the upcoming challenge, relax and think about it.)
2. Set your short-term, specific, and achievable goals. (What is your objective?)
3. Concentrate, eliminate distractions, and visualize a peak performance.
4. Design a plan of action and mentally rehearse it by visualizing yourself performing to perfection.

Quick Lab

Can you hypnotize yourself?

Sometimes just thinking of an action can result in producing that action—if you can imagine that action clearly enough.

Procedure

1. Stretch your arms in front of you, making sure the palms are facing each other at the same height and about two inches apart.

2. Close your eyes. Imagine that your right arm is getting heavier and heavier, while your left arm is getting lighter and lighter.

3. To help yourself, imagine that your right hand is holding a strap wrapped around several heavy books, while your left hand is holding a string tied to a helium balloon.

Analysis

1. After about a minute, open your eyes and see how far your hands have actually moved. Are they one or two inches or several inches apart?

2. Using what you have learned about hypnosis, explain the results in a brief report.

See the Skills Handbook, page 622, for an explanation of designing an experiment.

biofeedback: the process of learning to control bodily states with the help of specialized machines

may report that some people around her are speaking strangely. They seem to leave out some words occasionally, especially when they are talking about topics involving the taboo word "psychology." The participant is not aware that part of her consciousness has been instructed to block out that word. Memory can also be aided or enhanced through posthypnotic suggestion. Posthypnotic suggestion has been found to be particularly helpful in changing unwanted behaviors, such as smoking or overeating.

Hypnosis is sometimes used to reduce pain. *Hypnotic analgesia* refers to a reduction of pain reported by patients after they had undergone hypnosis. In these situations, the hypnotist works with the patient to reduce his or her anxiety and encourage relaxation. Therefore, a patient's perception of pain is reduced.

Therapists use hypnosis to help clients reveal their problems or gain insight into their lives. For example, hypnotherapists use hypnosis to allow their patients to think of their problems in a new way. Hypnosis, though, is not for all patients. Some fear the loss of control associated with hypnosis. Therapists often combine hypnosis with other therapies to help patients work through their problems.

BIOFEEDBACK

A technique in which a person learns to control his or her internal physiological processes with the help of feedback is **biofeedback.** For example, you can be hooked up to a biofeedback machine so that a light goes on every time your heart rate goes over 80. You could then learn to keep your heart rate below 80 by trying to keep the light off.

Biofeedback has been used to teach people to control a wide variety of physiological responses, including brain waves (EEG), heart rate, blood pressure, skin temperature, and sweat-gland activity (Hassett, 1978a). The basic principle of biofeedback is simple: feedback makes learning possible.

Biofeedback involves using machines to tell people about very subtle, moment-to-moment changes in the body. People can then experiment with different thoughts and feelings while they watch how each affects their bodies. In time, people can learn to change their physiological processes.

Some of the best-documented biofeedback cures involve special training in muscular control. Tension headaches often seem to result from constriction of the frontalis muscle in the forehead. Thomas Budzynski and others (1973) used biofeedback to teach people to relax this specific muscle. The practice went on for several weeks, while other people were given similar treatments without biofeedback. Only the biofeedback group improved significantly. Biofeedback used without drugs seems to help many people.

MEDITATION

When a person focuses his or her attention on an image or thought with the goal of clearing the mind and producing relaxation, or an "inner peace," that person is practicing **meditation.** Meditation has been practiced in various parts of the world for thousands of years.

There are three major approaches to meditation. *Transcendental meditation* involves the mental repetition of a mantra, usually a Sanskrit sound. The participant sits with eyes closed and meditates for 15 to 20 minutes twice a day. *Mindfulness meditation* was developed from a Buddhist tradition. This form of meditation focuses on the present moment. For example, the participant may move his or her focus through the body from the tips of the toes to the top of the head, while paying particular attention to areas that cause pain. *Breath meditation* is a concentration on one's respiration—the process of inhaling and exhaling.

Researchers generally agree that most people can benefit from the sort of systematic relaxation that meditation provides. It has been found that meditation can help people lower their blood pressure, heart rates, and respiration rates. The issue is not clear-cut, however. Only people who benefit from meditation continue to use it. Thus, the reported benefits may come from a biased, self-selected sample of successful practitioners. Others have reported data that suggest that while meditating, some people may actually be sleeping. If so, the reported benefits of meditation may result simply from relaxation.

meditation: the focusing of attention to clear one's mind and produce relaxation

A mandala is used to focus one's attention during meditation.

---

1. **Review the Vocabulary** Explain how people can alter their consciousness by using meditation.

2. **Visualize the Main Idea** Using a diagram similar to the one below, list some explanations of hypnosis.

Explanations of Hypnosis		
1.	2.	3.

3. **Recall Information** What types of medical conditions could be helped through biofeedback?

4. **Think Critically** Do you think that hypnotized people will do anything that they otherwise would not do? Explain.

5. **Application Activity** Try this meditation technique: (1) Take a few moments and form your lips into a half smile; (2) Hold this half smile for at least 10 minutes as you go about your ordinary activities. Did you notice a shift in how you acted and responded to others? Did others respond to you differently? Record and analyze your experiences.

Case Studies

A Breath of Fresh Air

Period of Study: Late 1970s to early 1980s

Introduction: Approximately 13 million people in the United States suffer from a chronic respiratory condition characterized by hypersensitivity, inflammation, and obstruction or narrowing of the airways. This condition is commonly known as asthma. An asthmatic person develops swollen airways lined with thick mucus. This causes the surrounding muscles to constrict, making it extremely difficult to breathe and sometimes leading to a life-threatening event. The occurrence of these symptoms is known as an asthmatic episode.

The causes of asthma are generally the results of allergic reactions, stress, endocrine changes, genetic makeup, and/or psychological traits. Those afflicted with asthma suffer from both gasping and irritating interruptions of their daily routine. Asthmatic individuals who choose to participate in aerobic sports of any kind must constantly monitor their breathing patterns. They must always be prepared to manage an oncoming episode.

For the past decade, medication in the form of an oral inhaler was the common way to treat an asthmatic episode. Researchers, however, are currently investigating a possible connection between halting an asthmatic episode and the use of biofeedback.

Hypothesis: Through the use of biofeedback, or gaining conscious control over an unconscious event, an asthma sufferer can gain control and relieve the tightening of the muscles that constrict airways.

Method: Recent studies have attempted to find the relationship between changes in muscular tension and breathing patterns in both asthmatic and nonasthmatic individuals. Researchers instructed participants to use deep breathing exercises while hooked up to biofeedback monitors. This allowed the participants to learn to control their heart rates during breathing cycles. The goal of this experiment was to control the muscle reflex that constricts airways during an asthmatic episode. Other types of biofeedback experiments were performed as well. No biofeedback machine was used for these experiments; instead, an important biofeedback "monitor"—a mirror—was used. The participant would perform the same type of breathing exercises in front of the mirror, thus monitoring muscle tension.

Results: Initial observation showed that the performance of these types of exercises might decrease asthma symptoms. Participants took lower dosages of medication, sometimes eliminating the medication entirely. Emergency room visits by participants involving asthmatic episodes decreased significantly. Overall, the benefits of biofeedback techniques used to control asthma are apparent. A number of questions regarding biofeedback techniques and asthma, however, remain unanswered. One such question involves researching long-term effects of these techniques. Because this research is relatively new, such questions may not be answered for years to come. These studies, though, may be the foundation for future therapies such as biofeedback to control migraine headaches, speech disorders, and blood pressure.

Analyzing the Case Study

1. What causes asthma?

2. Describe how participants monitored their physiological processes in the experiments.

3. **Critical Thinking** How did participants use biofeedback in the experiments? Why was it successful?

Drugs and Consciousness

Reader's Guide

■ **Main Idea**

Psychoactive drugs interact with the central nervous system to alter consciousness.

■ **Vocabulary**

• psychoactive drugs
• marijuana
• hallucinations
• hallucinogens
• LSD

■ **Objectives**

• Describe the effects drugs have on consciousness.
• Define drug abuse.

EXPLORING PSYCHOLOGY

A Letter to Parents

Marijuana is the illegal drug most often used in this country. Since 1991, lifetime marijuana use has doubled among 8th- and 10th-grade students, and increased by a third among high school seniors. Our research shows that accompanying this upward pattern of use is a significant erosion in antidrug perceptions and knowledge among young people today. As the number of young people who use marijuana has increased, the number who view the drug as harmful has decreased. Among high school seniors surveyed in 1997, current marijuana use has increased by about 72 percent since 1991. The proportion of those seniors who believe regular use of marijuana is harmful has dropped by about 26 percent since 1991.

—**from** "Marijuana: Facts Parents Need to Know" **by the National Institute on Drug Abuse, 1998**

Marijuana use today starts at a young age, and potent forms of the drug are available. The National Institute on Drug Abuse (NIDA) warned parents in the letter above that marijuana is a serious threat—which they must talk to their children about. Marijuana is an example of a psychoactive drug. **Psychoactive drugs** interact with the central nervous system to alter a person's mood, perception, and behavior. These drugs range from stimulants like the caffeine in coffee and in cola drinks to depressants like alcohol to powerful hallucinogens like marijuana and LSD (see Figure 7.4).

psychoactive drugs: chemicals that affect the nervous system and result in altered consciousness

HOW DRUGS WORK

Like hormones, drugs are carried by the blood and taken up in target tissues in various parts of the body. Unlike hormones, though, drugs are taken into the body from the outside. People introduce drugs into their systems through routes that bring the drugs into contact with capillaries (the smallest blood vessels). From there, drugs are gradually absorbed into the blood. Then drug molecules act like neurotransmitters and hook onto the ends of nerve cells (neurons) and send out their own chemical messages. For example, alcohol molecules may tell a nerve cell not to fire. As more and more cells cease to fire, the alcohol user becomes slower and may eventually lose consciousness. LSD molecules may cause circuits in different areas of the brain to start firing together instead of separately, resulting in hallucinations.

MARIJUANA

marijuana: the dried leaves and flowers of Indian hemp *(cannabis sativa)* that produce an altered state of consciousness when smoked or ingested

Used as an intoxicant among Eastern cultures for centuries, **marijuana** is legally and morally acceptable in some societies, whereas alcohol is not. The sale and possession of marijuana is against the law in most states. Before 1960, marijuana use in the United States was common only

Figure 7.4	Some Psychoactive Drugs

Psychoactive drugs influence how we sense and perceive things and modify our moods, feelings, emotions, and thoughts. *What effects do depressants produce?*

Drug Category	Effects on Behavior
Depressants Alcohol	Relaxant; relieve inhibitions; impair memory and judgment
Tranquilizers Barbiturates, benzodiazepines (Valium, Xanax)	Relieve anxiety; relax muscles; induce sleep
Opiates Morphine, heroin	Decrease pain; decrease attention to real world; unpleasant withdrawal effects as drug's effect wears off
Stimulants Caffeine, amphetamines, cocaine	Increase energy, alertness
Mixed Stimulant-Depressants Nicotine	Stimulate brain activity, but most smokers say cigarettes relax them
Distortion of Experience Marijuana (THC)	Intensifies sensory experiences; distorts perception of time; can relieve glaucoma, nausea; sometimes impairs learning, memory
Hallucinogens LSD, mescaline	Cause hallucinations, sensory distortions, and occasionally panic

among members of certain subcultures. Marijuana use increased throughout the 1960s and most of the 1970s but then began to decline.

The active ingredient in marijuana is a complex molecule called tetrahydrocannabinol (THC), which occurs naturally in the common weed *cannabis sativa,* or Indian hemp. Marijuana is made by drying the plant; hashish is a gummy powder made from the resin exuded by the flowering tops of the female plant. Both marijuana and hashish are usually smoked, but they can also be cooked with food and eaten.

The effects of the drug vary somewhat from person to person and also seem to depend on the setting in which the drug is taken and the user's past experience. The effects can be both pleasant and unpleasant. In general, though, many marijuana users report most sensory experiences seem greatly augmented—music sounds fuller, colors look brighter, smells are stronger, foods have stronger flavors, and other experiences are more intense than usual. Users may feel elated, the world may seem somehow more meaningful, and even the most ordinary events may take on an extraordinary significance. Marijuana is not a physically addictive drug, but it may cause people to become psychologically addicted to the drug.

As many users of marijuana have discovered, the drug can instill or heighten a variety of unpleasant experiences. If a person is in a frightened, unhappy, or depressed mood to begin with, the chances are excellent that taking the drug will blow the negative feelings out of proportion so that the user's world, temporarily at least, becomes very upsetting. Cases have been reported in which marijuana appears to have helped bring on psychological disturbances in people who were already unstable before they used it.

Despite the obvious need for careful research on marijuana, the first well-controlled scientific studies of its effects did not appear until the late 1960s, scarcely anticipating its surging popularity later. Studies suggest that marijuana use is more damaging to the lungs than cigarette use. Although there is no direct evidence that marijuana use causes lung cancer, the tar and other chemicals in marijuana smoke are drawn deep into the lungs and held 20 to 40 seconds, adding to the drug's potential for hindering lung function (Ray & Ksir, 1993).

Marijuana also disrupts memory formation, making it difficult to carry out mental and physical tasks (Lictman, Dimen, & Martin, 1995; Pope & Yurgelun-Todd, 1996). Some researchers believe that long-term use of the drug can lead to dependence (Stephens, Roffman, & Simpson, 1994). Research also showed that adults using marijuana scored lower than equal-IQ nonusers on a twelfth-grade academic achievement test (Block & Ghoneim, 1993).

HALLUCINATIONS

Perceptions that have no direct external cause—seeing, hearing, smelling, tasting, or feeling things that do not exist—are **hallucinations.** Hypnosis, meditation, certain drugs, withdrawal from a drug to which

PSYCHOLOGY Online

Student Web Activity
Visit the *Understanding Psychology* Web site at psychology.glencoe.com and click on **Chapter 7— Student Web Activities** for an activity about altered states of consciousness.

✓ *Reading Check*
How does marijuana use change a person's consciousness?

hallucinations: perceptions that have no direct external cause one has become addicted, and psychological breakdown may produce hallucinations. Hallucinations can also occur under "normal" conditions. People hallucinate when they are dreaming and when they are deprived of the opportunity to sleep. Periods of high emotion, concentration, or fatigue may also produce false sensations and perceptions. For example, truck drivers on long hauls have been known to swerve suddenly to avoid stalled cars that do not exist. Even daydreams involve mild hallucinations.

Interestingly enough, it seems that hallucinations are very much alike from one person to the next. Soon after taking a drug that causes hallucinations, for example, people often see many geometric forms in a tunnel-like perspective. These forms float through the field of vision, combining with each other and duplicating themselves. While normal imagery is often in black and white, hallucinations are more likely to involve color.

One researcher (Seigel, 1977) traveled to Mexico's Sierra Madre to study the reactions of Huichol Native Americans who take peyote. He found that their hallucinations were much like those of American college students who took similar drugs. He believes that these reactions are similar because of the way such drugs affect the brain: portions of the brain that respond to incoming stimuli become disorganized, while the entire central nervous system is aroused.

hallucinogens: drugs that often produce hallucinations

LSD: a potent psychedelic drug that produces distortions of perception and thought

HALLUCINOGENS

So called because their main effect is to produce hallucinations, **hallucinogens** are found in plants that grow throughout the world. They have been used for their effects on consciousness since earliest human history (Schultes, 1976). These drugs are also called "psychedelic" because they create a loss of contact with reality. They can change a false body image and cause loss of self, dreamlike fantasies, and hallucinations.

The best-known, most extensively studied, and most potent hallucinogen is **LSD** (lysergic acid diethylamide). In fact, it is one of the most powerful drugs known. LSD is a synthetic substance. A dose of a few millionths of a gram has a noticeable effect; an average dose of 100 to 300 micrograms produces a "trip" that lasts from 6 to 14 hours. To control such small doses, LSD is often dissolved into strips of paper or sugar cubes.

During an LSD trip, a person can experience any number of mood states, often quite intense and rapidly changing. The person's expectations, mood, beliefs, and the circumstances under which he or she takes LSD can affect the experience, sometimes making it terrifying. Perceptual hallucinations are very common with LSD. Users may experience hallucinatory progressions in which simple geometric forms evolve into surrealistic impossibilities. The user may encounter such distortions that familiar objects become almost unrecognizable. A wall, for example, may seem to pulsate or breathe. One's

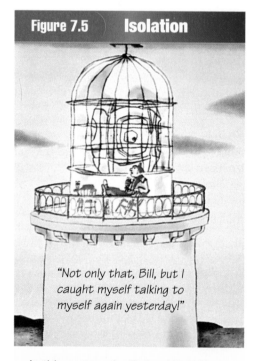

Figure 7.5   Isolation

"Not only that, Bill, but I caught myself talking to myself again yesterday!"

In this cartoon by Roland B. Wilson, the lighthouse keeper has apparently become a little disturbed psychologically by his isolated life. His unconscious has produced a hallucinatory companion. *What causes hallucinations?*

senses, too, seem to intermingle; sounds may be "seen" and visual stimuli may be "heard." A person may experience a dissociation of the self into one being who observes and another who feels. Distortions of time, either an acceleration or a slowing down, are also common. A single stimulus may become the focus of attention for hours, perceived as ever changing or newly beautiful and fascinating.

As measured by the ability to perform simple tasks, LSD impairs thinking, even though users may feel they are thinking more clearly and logically than ever before. Panic reactions are the most common of LSD's unpleasant side effects. Those who experience panic and later describe it often say that they felt trapped in the experience of panic and were afraid that they would never get out or that they would go mad. Use of LSD peaked in the 1960s. The likelihood of *flashback* experiences, even months after taking LSD, and public fears of chromosome damage—not confirmed by subsequent research—probably led to LSD's declining popularity (Ray & Ksir, 1993).

Figure 7.6   Just Say No

Many advertisements and programs aimed at kids, such as this one, warn of the dangers involved with drug use. *What is the general treatment for those who abuse drugs?*

OPIATES

Opiates, usually called narcotics, include opium, morphine, and heroin. Opiates produce analgesia, or pain reduction; euphoria, which is sometimes described as a pleasurable state somewhere between wake and sleep; and constipation. Regular use of opiates can lead to physical addiction. An overdose of opiates results in a loss of control of breathing—the user then dies from respiratory failure.

ALCOHOL

The most widely used and abused mind-altering substance in the United States is alcohol. The consumption of alcohol is encouraged by advertisements and by social expectations and traditions. The immediate effect of alcohol is a general loosening of inhibitions. Despite its seeming stimulating effect, alcohol is actually a depressant that serves to inhibit the brain's normal functions. When people drink, they often act without the social restraint or self-control they normally apply to their behavior.

The effects of alcohol consumption depend on the amount and frequency of drinking. As the amount consumed increases within a specific time, the drinker's ability to function diminishes. The person experiences slurred speech, blurred vision, and an impairment in judgment and memory. Permanent damage to the brain and liver and a change in personality can result from prolonged heavy use of alcohol.

Several studies suggested that not all of the early effects of drinking are the result of the alcohol alone; some are social effects. People expect to feel a certain way when they drink. In one study, men who were led to believe they were drinking alcohol when they were, in fact, drinking tonic water became more aggressive. They also felt more sexually aroused and were less anxious in social situations (Marlatt & Rohsenow, 1981).

DRUG ABUSE AND TREATMENT

Almost all of us have taken a psychoactive drug at some time—it may have been caffeine in a soda or a cup of tea. So at what point do we cross the line into drug abuse? Drug abusers are people who regularly use illegal drugs or excessively use legal drugs.

People abuse drugs for many reasons, such as to avoid boredom, to fit in with peers, to gain more self-confidence, to forget about problems, to relax, or simply to feel good. All of these reasons involve changing how people feel.

Why should people not abuse drugs? There are many risks associated with drug abuse, including danger of death or injury by overdose or accident, damage to health, legal consequences, and destructive behavior. The greatest risk associated with the abuse of psychoactive drugs, though, is loss of control. Drug abuse can turn into addiction—an overwhelming and compulsive desire to obtain and use drugs. Treatment for drug abuse usually involves the following steps:

1. The drug abuser must admit that he or she has a problem.

2. The drug abuser must enter a treatment program and/or get therapy.

3. The drug abuser must remain drug free. Many drug addicts are encouraged to join support groups to help them fight off the temptation of returning to drugs. Many drug addicts suffer a relapse; that is, they return to using drugs. Support groups can be a powerful force in preventing that occurrence.

SECTION 3 | Assessment

1. **Review the Vocabulary** How do psychoactive drugs affect consciousness? Describe the effects of marijuana and LSD.

2. **Visualize the Main Idea** Using a cause-and-effect diagram similar to the one below, describe the effects of three drugs on consciousness.

Cause	→	Effects
_____		_____
_____		_____

3. **Recall Information** When does drug use become drug abuse? Why do people abuse drugs?

4. **Think Critically** Do people use psychoactive drugs to increase or decrease their level of awareness? Explain.

5. **Application Activity** Design an antidrug advertisement for a billboard or magazine. Keep in mind the reasons people choose to abuse drugs when creating your ad.

Everything you think and feel is part of your conscious experience. An altered state of consciousness involves a change in mental processes, not just a quantitative shift (such as feeling more or less alert).

Section 1 Sleep and Dreams

Main Idea: Sleep—an essential state of consciousness—involves stages and periods of dreaming.

- Some researchers believe that sleep is restorative. Others believe sleep is a type of hibernation, necessary to conserve energy. Still others believe sleep clears the mind of useless information.
- There are several stages of sleep—from Stage I, the lightest level of sleep, to Stage IV, the deepest level of sleep. REM sleep is an active type of sleep characterized by rapid eye movement.
- Sometimes people have problems falling asleep or during sleep. Sleep disorders include insomnia, sleep apnea, narcolepsy, nightmares, night terrors, and sleepwalking.
- The mental activity that takes place during sleep is called dreaming.

Section 2 Hypnosis, Biofeedback, and Meditation

Main Idea: Hypnosis, biofeedback, and meditation are altered states of consciousness that can occur when we are awake.

- Hypnosis is a form of altered consciousness in which people become highly suggestible to changes in behavior and thought.
- Biofeedback has been used to teach people to control a wide variety of physiological responses.
- Studies have suggested that the regular practice of meditation is physically relaxing and can also lead to changes in behavior.

Section 3 Drugs and Consciousness

Main Idea: Psychoactive drugs interact with the central nervous system to alter consciousness.

- The effects of marijuana, a psychoactive drug, vary from person to person.
- Hallucinogens, whose main effect is to produce hallucinations, have been used for their effects on consciousness since earliest human history.
- LSD, a synthetic substance, is the most potent and most extensively studied hallucinogen.
- Alcohol is a depressant that serves to inhibit the brain's normal functions.
- Drug abusers are people who regularly use illegal drugs or excessively use legal drugs.

Chapter Vocabulary

consciousness (p. 183)

REM sleep (p. 186)

circadian rhythm (p. 186)

insomnia (p. 187)

sleep apnea (p. 187)

narcolepsy (p. 188)

nightmares (p. 188)

night terrors (p. 188)

sleepwalking (p. 188)

hypnosis (p. 191)

posthypnotic suggestion (p. 193)

biofeedback (p. 194)

meditation (p. 195)

psychoactive drugs (p. 197)

marijuana (p. 198)

hallucinations (p. 199)

hallucinogens (p. 200)

LSD (p. 200)

Self-Check Quiz
Visit the *Understanding Psychology* Web site at
psychology.glencoe.com and click on **Chapter 7—
Self-Check Quizzes** to prepare for the Chapter Test.

Reviewing Vocabulary

Choose the letter of the correct term or concept below to complete the sentence.

a. consciousness
b. insomnia
c. sleep apnea
d. narcolepsy
e. hypnosis
f. biofeedback
g. meditation
h. psychoactive drug
i. hallucinations
j. hallucinogens

1. _____ is a form of altered consciousness in which people become highly suggestible.

2. Marijuana is an example of a(n) _____, a drug that interacts with the central nervous system to alter a person's mood, perception, and behavior.

3. A prolonged and usually abnormal inability to obtain adequate sleep is called _____.

4. A person who focuses his or her attention on an image or thought with the goal of clearing the mind and producing relaxation is practicing _____.

5. A person's state of awareness is _____.

6. Substances such as LSD are called _____ because their main effect is to produce hallucinations.

7. A technique in which a person learns to control his or her internal physiological processes with the help of special machines is called _____.

8. A permanent and overwhelming feeling of sleepiness and fatigue is called _____.

9. _____ are perceptions that have no direct external cause.

10. _____ is a sleep disorder caused by a physical problem and results in frequent interruptions of breathing during sleep.

Recalling Facts

1. What percentage of sleep time do adults usually spend in REM sleep?

2. Using a chart similar to the one below, identify and describe six sleep disorders.

Sleep Disorder	Characteristics

3. Explain the phenomenon of posthypnotic suggestion.

4. List some health problems that biofeedback can potentially help.

5. What is the most widely used and abused mind-altering substance in the United States? How does it affect the user?

Critical Thinking

1. **Analyzing Concepts** Choose a behavior that you perform automatically and pay close attention to how you perform it. How does consciously thinking about the behavior affect your performance of it?

2. **Demonstrating Reasoned Judgment** Social scientists have varying ideas about the purpose and meaning of dreams. Review the various theories of social scientists presented in this chapter. Whose theory do you agree with the most? Why?

3. **Making Inferences** Do you think you could be hypnotized? Why or why not?

4. **Synthesizing Information** Have you ever hallucinated a sight or sound—perhaps when you were very tired or upset? What did you experience? Why do you suppose you created this particular hallucination?

5. **Making Comparisons** Look through magazines to find advertisements for alcoholic beverages. How do the ways that the advertisements portray drinking alcohol compare to the realities of drinking alcohol?

CHAPTER 7 Assessment

Psychology Projects

1. **Sleep and Dreams** Interview members of your family and friends to find out how many hours a night they sleep. Note their responses; then, as a class, record the results in a bar graph. What kinds of sleep patterns—in terms of age and gender—do you observe? Present your findings to the class in an oral report.

2. **Meditation** Meditation is an important part of some religions, such as Buddhism and Hinduism. Find out about the purpose of meditation in these religions and present your findings in a written report.

3. **Drugs and Consciousness** Research places in your community where a drug abuser can go for help. Locate the address, phone number, and the types of services offered in each place. Compile your findings in an informational pamphlet.

4. **Hypnosis** Contact a hypnotherapist and a stage hypnotist. Ask both: Is hypnosis an altered state of consciousness? What is the difference between a person's usual waking state and a hypnotic state? Do participants voluntarily agree to the hypnotist's suggestions? What applications of

hypnosis do you recommend to people? Ask other questions to compare their views and uses of hypnosis. Report your findings to the class.

Technology Activity

Search the Internet to find out about various meditation techniques. Enter the term *meditation* to obtain a list of sites that actually provide techniques you can use to meditate. Try one or two of the techniques and report on their effectiveness to the class.

Psychology Journal

Many psychologists have theorized that by interpreting the content of our dreams, we can better understand our unconscious desires. Other social scientists have maintained a more commonplace view of dreams. Write a two-page essay in your journal that presents a case for both viewpoints. You may want to look for recent magazine articles on dreams. If possible, use a recent dream that you remember as an example to support one of the viewpoints.

Building Skills

Analyzing a Chart Review the chart below, then answer the questions that follow.

Year	Total	School	Home	Party
Percentage of 12th Graders Who Reported Using Alcohol in the Past 12 Months, 1976 to 1996				
	Total			
1976	82.6	12.1	53.0	72.3
1978	86.7	12.2	55.8	76.1
1980	86.5	13.4	57.0	75.3
1982	85.6	10.1	54.6	74.9
1984	82.5	11.3	51.6	71.9
1986	84.2	10.9	49.8	72.4
1988	85.2	10.2	52.1	73.8
1990	79.0	6.6	42.9	68.3
1992	76.8	6.7	40.0	66.0
1994	74.3	7.8	39.9	63.3
1996	71.3	8.1	37.8	60.8

Note: "School" was not defined for the questionnaire respondent. Population sizes are not available.
Source: University of Michigan, Survey Research Center, Institute for Social Research, Monitoring the Future Study, 1976 to 1996.

Practice and assess key social studies skills with **Glencoe Skillbuilder Interactive Workbook CD-ROM, Level 2.**

1. According to the table, where does most drinking by high school seniors take place? Why do you think this is so?

2. In what year was alcohol use at its highest among high school seniors?

3. In what year was alcohol use at its lowest among high school seniors?

4. How has the number of seniors who used alcohol changed between 1976 and 1996? What factors might account for this fact?

See the Skills Handbook, page 628, for an explanation of interpreting charts.

Sensation and Perception

PSYCHOLOGY JOURNAL

Think about an occasion in which you were in a crowded and noisy setting. Did you find yourself listening to or picking up part of another conversation? Write an explanation for this occurrence in your journal. ■

PSYCHOLOGY
Online

Chapter Overview
Visit the *Understanding Psychology*
Web site at psychology.glencoe.com
and click on **Chapter 8—Chapter
Overviews** to preview the chapter.

Sensation

Reader's Guide

■ Main Idea
Sensations allow humans to understand reality. Sensations occur anytime a stimulus activates a receptor.

■ Vocabulary
- sensation
- perception
- psychophysics
- absolute threshold
- difference threshold
- Weber's law
- signal-detection theory

■ Objectives
- Describe the field of study known as psychophysics.
- Define and discuss threshold, Weber's law, and signal detection.

EXPLORING PSYCHOLOGY

Discovering a New World

Helen Keller had been blind and deaf since she was two years old. For the next four years, Helen was "wild and unruly." Then when she was six, Anne Sullivan, a teacher, entered her life. Using the sense of touch as the link between their two worlds, Anne tried again and again, by spelling words into Helen's hand, to make Helen grasp the connection between words and the things they stood for. The breakthrough came one day as Anne spelled the word *water* into Helen's hand as water from a spout poured over it. "I stood still, my whole attention fixed upon the motions of her fingers," Helen remembered. "Suddenly I felt . . . a thrill of returning thought; and somehow the mystery of language was revealed to me."

—adapted from *ABC's of the Human Mind,* Reader's Digest, 1990

From that day forward, Helen "saw" the world in a new way. She discovered new ways to experience her world. "Occasionally, if I am very fortunate, I place my hand gently on a small tree and feel the happy quiver of a bird in full song." Helen had entered a world of sensations after she began organizing the stimuli in her world. Try it yourself.

In the next few seconds, something peculiar will start hap pening to the material youa rereading. Iti soft ennotre alized howcom plext hepro- ces sof rea ding is.

sensation: what occurs when a stimulus activates a receptor

perception: the organization of sensory information into meaningful experiences

psychophysics: the study of the relationships between sensory experiences and the physical stimuli that cause them

As you can see, your success in gathering information from your environment, interpreting this information, and acting on it depends considerably on its being organized in ways you expect. In this chapter you will learn more about sensation and perception, both of which are necessary to gather and interpret information in our surroundings.

WHAT IS SENSATION?

The world is filled with physical changes—an alarm clock sounds; the flip of a switch fills a room with light; you stumble against a door; steam from a hot shower billows out into the bathroom, changing the temperature and clouding the mirror. Any aspect of or change in the environment to which an organism responds is called a *stimulus*. An alarm, an electric light, and an aching muscle are all stimuli for human beings.

A stimulus can be measured in many physical ways, including its size, duration, intensity, or wavelength. A **sensation** occurs anytime a stimulus activates one of your receptors. The sense organs detect physical changes in energy such as heat, light, sound, and physical pressure. The skin notes changes in heat and pressure, the eyes note changes in light, and the ears note changes in sound. Other sensory systems note the location and position of your body.

A sensation may be combined with other sensations and your past experience to yield a perception. A **perception** is the organization of sensory information into meaningful experiences (see Figure 8.1).

Psychologists are interested in the relationship between physical stimuli and sensory experiences. In vision, for example, the perception of color corresponds to the wavelength of the light, whereas brightness corresponds to the intensity of this stimulus.

What is the relationship between color and wavelength? How does changing a light's intensity affect your perception of its brightness? The psychological study of such questions is called **psychophysics.** The goal of psychophysics is to understand how stimuli from the world (such as frequency and intensity) affect the sensory experiences (such as pitch and loudness) produced by them.

THRESHOLD

In order to establish laws about how people sense the external world, psychologists first try to determine how much of a stimulus is necessary for a person to sense it at all. How much energy is required for someone to hear a sound or to see a light? How much of a scent must be in the room before one can smell it?

Figure 8.1　Fraser's Spiral

Fraser's spiral illustrates the difference between sensation and perception. Our perception of this figure is that of a spiral, but it is actually an illusion. Trace a circle carefully. Your finger will always come back to its starting point. *How do we use sensation and perception together to understand our world?*

How much pressure must be applied to the skin before a person will feel it?

To answer such questions, a psychologist might set up the following experiment. First, a person (the participant) is placed in a dark room and is instructed to look at the wall. He is asked to say "I see it" when he is able to detect a light. The psychologist then uses an extremely precise machine that can project a low-intensity beam of light against the wall.

The experimenter turns on the machine to its lowest light projection. The participant says nothing. The experimenter increases the light until finally the participant responds, "I see it." Then the experimenter begins another test in the opposite direction. He starts with a visible but faint light and decreases its intensity until the light seems to disappear. Many trials are completed and averaged. This procedure detects the **absolute threshold**—the weakest amount of a stimulus required to produce a sensation. It is usually accepted that the absolute threshold is the level that produces a positive response of detection 50 percent of the time.

Profiles In Psychology

Gustav Theodor Fechner

1801–1887

"Imagine that you look at the sky through a tinted glass and pick out a cloud that is just noticeably different from the sky background. Now you use a much darker glass; the cloud does not vanish but is still just barely visible—because although the absolute levels of intensity are much lower through the darker glass, the ratio of intensities between cloud and sky has not changed."

Gustav Theodor Fechner started out as a young professor trying to demonstrate that every person, animal, and plant in the universe is composed of both matter and soul. He failed. At one point, in the midst of a depression, he painted his room black and remained in it day and night, seeing no one. When he finally emerged from his isolation, he walked through a garden, and the flowers looked brighter than he had ever seen them before.

On the morning of October 22, 1850, as Fechner lay in bed, a thought occurred to him. He arrived at the conclusion that a systemic relationship between bodily and mental experience could be demonstrated if a person were asked to report changes in sensations as a physical stimulus was varied. While testing these ideas, Fechner created the area of psychology known as psychophysics. Fechner's methods of sensory measurement inspired experimental research on the subject and revolutionized experimental psychology.

The absolute thresholds for the five senses in humans are the following: in vision—seeing a candle flame 30 miles away on a clear night; for hearing—hearing a watch ticking 20 feet away; for taste—tasting 1 teaspoon of sugar dissolved in 2 gallons of water; for smell—smelling 1 drop of perfume in a 3-room house; for touch—feeling a bee's wing falling a distance of 1 centimeter onto your cheek.

absolute threshold: the weakest amount of a stimulus that a person can detect half the time

Figure 8.2 | The Human Senses

This chart lists the fundamental features that make up the human sensory system. *What is our vestibular sense?*

Sense	Stimulus	Sense Organ	Receptor	Sensation
Sight	Light waves	Eye	Rods and cones of retina	Colors, patterns, textures, motion, depth in space
Hearing	Sound waves	Ear	Hair cells located in inner ear	Noises, tones
Skin sensations	External contact	Skin	Nerve endings in skin	Touch, pain, warmth, cold
Smell	Volatile substances	Nose	Hair cells of olfactory membrane	Odors (musky, flowery, burnt, minty)
Taste	Soluble substances	Tongue	Taste buds of tongue	Flavors (sweet, sour, salty, bitter)
Vestibular sense	Mechanical and gravitational forces	Inner ear	Hair cells of semicircular canals and vestibule	Spatial movement, gravitational pull
Kinesthesis	Body movement	Muscles, tendons, and joints	Nerve fibers in muscles, tendons, and joints	Movement and position of body parts

While these thresholds may seem impressive, we respond to very little of the sensory world. We cannot see X rays or microwaves. Dogs can hear a dog whistle, while we cannot. Humans hear only 20 percent of what a dolphin can hear. Some animals, such as bats and dolphins, have a superior sense of hearing. Some animals, such as hawks, have extremely sharp vision; others, such as bloodhounds, possess a superior sense of smell. Humans use a somewhat limited sense of the physical world known as reality.

SENSORY DIFFERENCES AND RATIOS

difference threshold: the smallest change in a physical stimulus that can be detected between two stimuli

Another type of threshold is the **difference threshold.** The difference threshold refers to the minimum amount of difference a person can detect between two stimuli. To return to our example of the person tested in a dark room, a psychologist would test for the difference threshold by gradually increasing the intensity of a visible light beam until the person says, "Yes, this is brighter than the light I just saw." With this technique, it is possible to identify the smallest increase in light intensity that is noticeable to the human eye.

A related concept is the *just noticeable difference,* or *JND.* This refers to the smallest increase or decrease in the intensity of a stimulus that a person is able to detect. Psychologists have found that a particular sensory experience depends more on *changes* in the stimulus than on the absolute size or amount of the stimulus. For example, if you put a 3-pound package of food into an empty backpack, the perceived weight will be greatly increased. If you add the same amount to a backpack with a 100-pound weight in it, however, your perception of the weight will hardly increase at all. This is because the perception of the added weight reflects a proportional change—and 3 pounds does not provide much change in a 100-pound load.

This idea is known as **Weber's law:** the larger or stronger a stimulus, the larger the change required for a person to notice that anything has happened to it. By experimenting in this way with variations in sounds, temperatures, pressures, colors, tastes, and smells, psychologists are learning more about how each sense responds to stimulation. Some senses produce huge increases in sensation in response to small increases in energy. For instance, the pain of an electric shock can be increased more than eight times by doubling the voltage. On the other hand, the intensity of a light must be increased many times to double its brightness.

People who can detect minute changes in sensation are called experts. For example, such experts who can detect small differences work as food tasters, wine tasters, smell experts, perfume experts, and so on.

Quick Lab

Can you detect changes in stimuli?
What would it take for you to notice a difference in the weight of your backpack?

Procedure
1. Fill your backpack with materials so that it weighs 10 pounds and put it on your back.
2. Arrange a series of objects that differ in weight from very light (a piece of paper) to medium (a paperback book) to heavy (a 2-pound weight).
3. Ask a friend to insert the items into your backpack one at a time, in no particular order. Be sure you cannot see which object is being placed in the pack.

Analysis
1. After each object is placed in the pack, report on the perceived difference in weight.
2. Record the point at which you notice the difference in the weight of the pack.
3. Use the concept of difference threshold to explain your results.

See the Skills Handbook, **page 622,** for an explanation of designing an experiment.

SENSORY ADAPTATION

Psychologists have focused on people's responses to changes in stimuli because they have found that the senses are tuned to change. Senses are most responsive to increases and decreases, and to new events rather than to ongoing, unchanging stimulation. We are able to respond to changes in our environment because our senses have an ability to adapt, or adjust themselves, to a constant level of stimulation. They get used to a new level and respond only to changes away from it (see Figure 8.3).

A good example of this sensory adaptation is the increase in visual sensitivity that you experience after a short time in a darkened movie theater. At first you see only blackness, but after a while your eyes adapt to the new level, and you can see seats, faces, and so forth. Adaptation occurs for the other senses as well. Receptors in your skin adapt to the cold water when you go for a swim; disagreeable odors in a lab seem to disappear after a while; street noises cease to bother you after you have lived in a city for a time. Without sensory adaptation, you would feel the

Weber's law: the principle that the larger or stronger a stimulus, the larger the change required for an observer to notice a difference

Reading Check
According to Weber's law, how much must a strong stimulus change for a person to notice the change?

constant pressure of the clothes on your body, and other stimuli would seem to be bombarding all your senses at the same time.

Sensory adaptation allows us to notice differences in sensations and react to the challenges of different or changing stimuli. This principle is helpful when performing many activities, such as the work of police, security guards, and home inspectors. These people may notice minute changes and act appropriately.

SIGNAL-DETECTION THEORY

signal-detection theory: the study of people's tendencies to make correct judgments in detecting the presence of stimuli

There is no sharp boundary between stimuli that you can perceive and stimuli you cannot perceive. The **signal-detection theory** studies the relations between motivation, sensitivity, and decision making in detecting the presence or absence of a stimulus (Green & Swets, 1966). Detection thresholds involve recognizing some stimulus against a background of competing stimuli. A radar operator must be able to detect an airplane on a radar screen even when the plane's blip is faint and difficult to distinguish from blips caused by flocks of birds or bad weather, which can produce images that are like visual "noise." The radar operator's judgment will be influenced by many factors, and different operators appear to have different sensitivities to blips. Moreover, a specific individual's apparent sensitivity seems to fluctuate, depending on the situation. For example, a radar operator may be able to ignore other stimuli as long as she is motivated to keep focused; just as you may be motivated to complete your reading assignment no matter what distractions you encounter.

In studying the difficulties faced by radar operators, psychologists have reformulated the concept of absolute threshold to take into account the many factors that affect detection of minimal stimuli. As a result, signal-detection theory abandons the idea that there is a single true absolute threshold for a stimulus. Instead, it is based on the notion that the stimulus, here called a signal, must be detected in the presence of competing stimuli, which can interfere with detection of the signal.

Psychologists have identified two different types of processing stimuli, or signals. *Preattentive*

 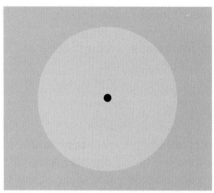

Figure 8.3	The Disappearing Circle

Sensation depends on change and contrast in the environment. Hold your hand over one eye and stare at the dot in the middle of the circle on the right. You should have no trouble maintaining the image of the circle. If you do the same with the circle on the left, however, the image will fade. The gradual change from light to dark does not provide enough contrast to keep the visual receptors in your eye firing at a steady rate. The circle reappears only if you close and reopen your eye or you shift your gaze to the X. **What is the purpose of sensory adaptation?**

Figure 8.4 **The Stroop Effect**

Red **Blue** Yellow Green

Orange Blue Red Yellow

Green Orange **Blue** Red

Red **Green Blue** Orange

a   b

Try to name the colors of the boxes in *a*. Then try to name the colors of the words in *b*. You probably proceeded slower when naming the colors in *b*. *Why was it more difficult to name the colors in b?*

process is a method for extracting information automatically and simultaneously when presented with stimuli. *Attentive process* is a procedure that considers only one part of the stimuli presented at a time. For example, when looking at Figure 8.4 *(b)*, the Stroop interference effect, preattentive, or automatic, processing acts as an interference. The tendency is to read the word instead of saying the color of the ink. Apparently people find it almost impossible not to read color names that appear before their eyes, because the name interferes with the response of naming the ink color when the two are different. In summary, we notice some things automatically in spite of distracting information. However, it requires more careful attention to notice other, less distinct items. This difference, though, is one of degree—all tasks require attention, but some require more attention than others.

SECTION 1 Assessment

1. **Review the Vocabulary** What is the difference between sensation and perception?

2. **Visualize the Main Idea** Complete the chart below by listing the five senses and their absolute thresholds.

Sense	Absolute Threshold
Sight	

3. **Recall Information** How does the signal-detection theory explain how you

may be able to study while others are watching television in the same room?

4. **Think Critically** Why do you think we do not respond to all stimuli present in our environment?

5. **Application Activity** Determine an absolute threshold by placing a watch or clock in an empty room. Move across the room to a point where you do not hear the ticking. Approach the clock one step at a time and mark the spot at which you first hear ticking. Repeat this experiment 10 times. What are your conclusions? Write a brief analysis.

The Senses

■ Main Idea

The sense organs—the eyes, ears, tongue, nose, skin, and others—are the receptors of sensations.

■ Vocabulary

- pupil
- lens
- retina
- optic nerve
- binocular fusion
- retinal disparity
- auditory nerve
- vestibular system
- olfactory nerve
- kinesthesis

■ Objectives

- Describe the nature and functioning of the sense organs.
- Identify the skin and body senses and explain how they work.

EXPLORING PSYCHOLOGY

Seeing in the Dark

Sit yourself in total darkness, a space so dark you cannot see your hand before your face. Now hold your hand before your face and move it from side to side. You see your hand in motion.

—from *A Second Way of Knowing: The Riddle of Human Perception* by Edmund Blair Bolles, 1991

Why did you see your hand moving even though it was totally dark while doing the experiment above? You have just experienced kinesthesis—one of the senses. Although people are thought to have five senses, there are actually more. In addition to vision, hearing, taste, smell, and touch, there are several skin senses and two "internal" senses: *vestibular* and *kinesthetic*.

Each type of sensory receptor takes some sort of external stimulus—light, chemical molecules, sound waves, and pressure—and converts it into a chemical-electrical message that can be understood by the brain. So far, we know most about these processes in vision and hearing. The other senses have received less attention and are more mysterious in their functioning.

VISION

Vision is the most studied of all the senses, reflecting the high importance we place on our sense of sight. Vision provides us with a great deal of information about our environment and the objects in it—the sizes, shapes, and locations of things, and their textures, colors, and distances.

How does vision occur? Light enters the eye through the **pupil** (see Figure 8.5) and reaches the **lens,** a flexible structure that focuses light on the **retina.** The retina contains two types of light-sensitive receptor cells, or photoreceptors: *rods* and *cones.* These cells are responsible for changing light energy into neuronal impulses, which then travel over the **optic nerve** to the brain, where it is routed to the occipital lobe.

Cones require more light than rods before they begin to respond, and cones work best in daylight. Since rods are sensitive to much lower levels of light than cones, they are particularly useful in night vision. There are many more rods (75 to 150 million) than there are cones (6 to 7 million), but only cones are sensitive to color. Rods and cones can be compared to black-and-white and color film. Color film takes more light and thus works best in daylight, like our cones. Sensitive black-and-white film works not only in bright light but also in shadows, dim light, and other poor lighting conditions, just like our rods.

pupil: the opening in the iris that regulates the amount of light entering the eye

lens: a flexible, transparent structure in the eye that changes its shape to focus light on the retina

retina: the innermost coating of the back of the eye, containing the light-sensitive receptor cells

optic nerve: the nerve that carries impulses from the retina to the brain

Figure 8.5   The Human Eye

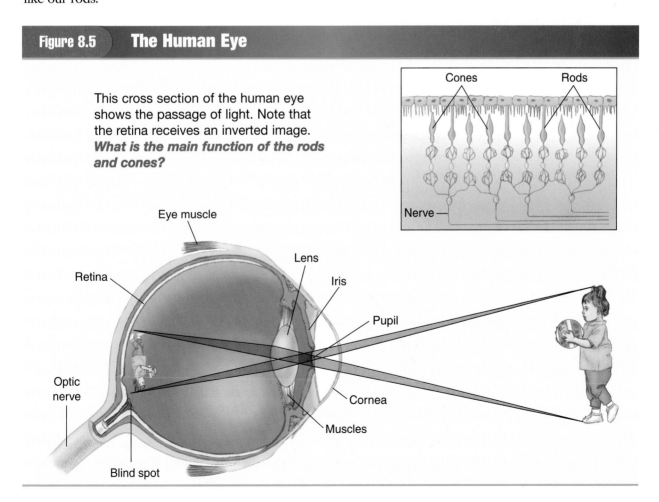

This cross section of the human eye shows the passage of light. Note that the retina receives an inverted image. *What is the main function of the rods and cones?*

Cones   Rods

Nerve

Eye muscle

Lens

Retina

Iris

Pupil

Optic nerve

Cornea

Muscles

Blind spot

Your Blind Spot

The point where the optic nerve leaves the eye is the blind spot (see Figure 8.5). When light hits that point, the eye registers nothing because this area lacks photoreceptors—neurons that are sensitive to light. Find your blind spot by holding the diagram below about an arm's length away from your eyes.

Make sure the cross is on the right. Close your right eye and look directly at the cross with your left eye. Notice that you can also see the dot. Focus on the cross, but be aware of the dot as you slowly bring the diagram toward your face. The dot will disappear and then reappear as you bring the diagram toward your face. Now close your left eye and look directly at the dot with your right eye. This time the cross will disappear and reappear as you bring the diagram slowly toward your face. What has happened? When you hold the diagram so that the light from the dot falls on the blind spot, you cannot see the dot. This is your blind spot.

Light

Light is a form of electromagnetic radiation. Other forms of electromagnetic radiation include radio waves, microwaves, infrared radiation, ultraviolet rays, X rays, and gamma rays. All of these are known collectively as the electromagnetic spectrum (see Figure 8.6).

The colors we see are actually different wavelengths of light. The rainbow of colors that we see in visible light represents only a small portion of the electromagnetic spectrum. Have you ever seen sunlight pass through a piece of cut glass or a prism? If you have, you probably saw a rainbow of colors. We see color only after the waves of light hit objects and bounce back to us at different speeds, or frequencies. The speed of light waves depends on the texture and solidity of the surfaces it hits. For example, a pea looks green because it reflects green light and absorbs all the other colors.

Color Deficiency

When some or all of a person's cones do not function properly, he or she is said to be color-deficient. There are several kinds of color deficiency, and most color-deficient people do see *some* colors (see Figure 8.7). For example, some people have trouble distinguishing between red and green. Fewer people have no trouble with red and green but cannot distinguish between yellow and blue. A very few people are totally color-deficient. They depend on their rods, so to them the world looks something like black-and-white television programs—nothing but blacks, whites, and shades of gray.

Color deficiency affects about 8 percent of American men and less than 1 percent of American women. It is a hereditary condition. This gene is carried in the genes of women whose vision is usually normal. These women pass the genes on to their sons, who are born color-deficient.

binocular fusion: the process of combining the images received from the two eyes into a single, fused image

Binocular Fusion

Because we have two eyes, located about 2.5 inches (6.4 cm) apart, the visual system receives two images. Instead of seeing double, however, we see a single image, probably a composite of the views of two eyes. The combination of the two images into one is called **binocular fusion.**

retinal disparity: the differences between the images stimulating each eye

Not only does the visual system receive two images but there is also a difference between the images on the retinas. This difference is called **retinal disparity.** You can easily observe retinal disparity by bringing an

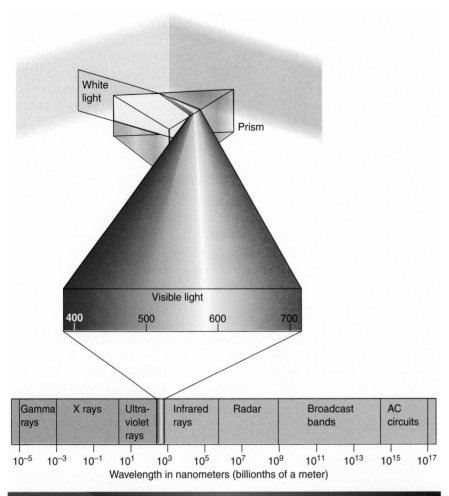

Figure 8.6 **The Electromagnetic Spectrum**

White
light

Prism

Visible light

400   500   600   700

| Gamma rays | X rays | Ultra-violet rays | Infrared rays | Radar | Broadcast bands | AC circuits |

10^{-5} 10^{-3} 10^{-1} 10^{1} 10^{3} 10^{5} 10^{7} 10^{9} 10^{11} 10^{13} 10^{15} 10^{17}
Wavelength in nanometers (billionths of a meter)

Light is the visible portion of the electromagnetic spectrum. When the wavelengths in white light are separated, the visual effect is an array of colors because different wavelengths are seen as different colors. *Why are we able to see the wavelengths of the visible spectrum?*

object, such as an eraser, close to your eyes. Without moving it, look at the eraser first with one eye, then with the other. You will see a difference in the two images because of the different viewpoint each eye has. When you open both eyes, you will no longer see the difference but will instead see the object as solid and three-dimensional, if you have good binocular vision.

Retinal disparity is essential to your sense of depth perception. The brain interprets a large retinal disparity (a large difference between what the right eye and what the left eye are seeing) to mean that an object is nearby. The brain interprets a small retinal disparity (not much difference between the images the left and right eyes receive) to mean a distant object.

PSYCHOLOGY *Online*

Student Web Activity
Visit the *Understanding Psychology* Web site at psychology.glencoe.com and click on **Chapter 8— Student Web Activities** for an activity on sensation and perception.

Figure 8.7 | **Testing for Color Deficiency**

Can you see numerals in the dot patterns that make up this figure? Those with normal vision will see a number, while those with red-green deficiency will see only random patches of color. *What is the cause of color deficiency?*

auditory nerve: the nerve that carries impulses from the inner ear to the brain, resulting in the sensation of sound

Nearsightedness and Farsightedness   Some of us are born with perfectly shaped eyeballs. These people have almost perfect vision. If your eyeball is a little too long, however, you are nearsighted. Objects are focused at a point slightly in front of the retina so that you can see objects that are near, but distant objects seem blurry. If your eyeball is too short, you are farsighted. Objects are focused at a point slightly behind the retina so that you can see distant objects clearly, but near objects appear blurry.

HEARING

Hearing depends on vibrations of the air, called sound waves. Sound waves from the air pass through various bones (see Figure 8.10) until they reach the inner ear, which contains tiny hairlike cells that move back and forth (much like a field of wheat waving in the wind). These hair cells change sound vibrations into neuronal signals that travel through the **auditory nerve** to the brain.

Loudness of sound is determined by the amplitude, or height, of sound waves. The higher the amplitude, the louder the sound. This strength, or sound-pressure energy, is measured in *decibels*. The sounds humans hear range upward from 0 decibels, the softest sound the human ear can detect, to about 140 decibels, which is roughly as loud as a jet plane taking off. Any sound over 110 decibels can damage hearing as can persistent sounds as low as 80 decibels. Any sound that is painful when you first hear it *will* damage your hearing if you hear it often enough. Figure 8.9 lists the decibel levels of some common sounds.

Pitch depends on sound-wave frequency, or the rate of the vibration of the medium through which the sound wave is transmitted. Low frequencies produce deep bass sounds, and high frequencies produce shrill squeaks. If you hear a sound composed of a combination of different frequencies, you can hear the separate pitches even though they occur simultaneously. For example, if you strike two keys of a piano at the same time, your ear can detect two distinct pitches.

Figure 8.8 | **A Changing Flag**

Stare steadily at the lowest right-hand star for about 45 seconds. Then stare at a blank piece of paper. You should see a negative afterimage of this figure. This occurs because the receptors for green, black, and yellow become fatigued or neuronal firing rates shift, allowing the complementary colors of each to predominate when you stare at the white paper. *What happens when you shift your glance to a blank wall some distance away? Why?*

Sources of sounds can be located when your ears work together. When a noise occurs on your right, for example, the sound wave comes to both ears, but it reaches your right ear a fraction of a second before it reaches the left. It is also slightly louder in the right ear. These differences tell you from which direction it is coming.

The Pathway of Sound

The ear is designed to capture sound waves (see Figure 8.10). The outer ear receives sound waves, and the earflap directs the sounds down a short tube called the auditory canal. The vibration of air (the sound wave) causes air in the auditory canal to vibrate, which in turn causes the eardrum to vibrate.

The middle ear is an air-filled cavity. Its main structures are three tiny bones—the hammer, anvil, and stirrup. These bones are linked to the eardrum at one end and to the cochlea at the other end. When sound waves cause the eardrum to vibrate, these bones vibrate and push against the cochlea.

The cochlea makes up the inner ear. The cochlea is a bony tube that contains fluids and neurons. The pressure against the cochlea makes the liquid inside the cochlea move. Tiny hairs inside the cochlea pick up the motion. These hairs are attached to sensory cells. The sensory cells turn the sound vibrations into neuronal impulses. The auditory nerve carries these impulses to the brain. This auditory input goes to the hearing areas of the cerebral cortex of the brain.

Deafness

There are two types of deafness. Conduction deafness occurs when anything hinders physical motion through the outer or middle ear or when the bones of the middle ear become rigid and cannot carry sounds inward. People with conduction deafness can usually be helped with a conventional hearing aid. A hearing aid picks up sound waves, changes them into vibrations, and sends them to the inner ear. Sensorineural deafness occurs from damage to the cochlea, the hair cells, or the auditory neurons. People with complete sensorineural deafness cannot be helped with a conventional hearing aid, but may be helped with a special hearing aid called a cochlear implant. A cochlear implant is a miniature electronic device that is surgically implanted into the cochlea. The device changes sound waves into electrical signals. These signals are fed into the auditory nerve, which carries them to the brain. The brain then processes the sensory input.

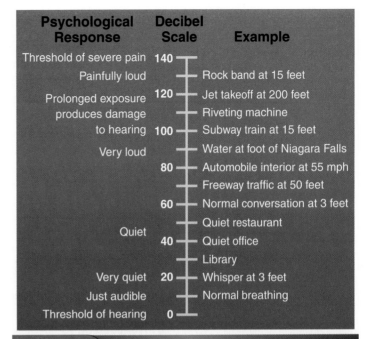

Psychological Response	Decibel Scale	Example
Threshold of severe pain	140	
Painfully loud		Rock band at 15 feet
Prolonged exposure produces damage to hearing	120	Jet takeoff at 200 feet
		Riveting machine
	100	Subway train at 15 feet
Very loud		Water at foot of Niagara Falls
	80	Automobile interior at 55 mph
		Freeway traffic at 50 feet
	60	Normal conversation at 3 feet
		Quiet restaurant
Quiet	40	Quiet office
		Library
Very quiet	20	Whisper at 3 feet
Just audible		Normal breathing
Threshold of hearing	0	

Figure 8.9   Decibel Levels

The loudness of a sound (its amplitude) is measured in decibels. Each increase of 10 decibels makes a sound 10 times louder. A normal conversation at 3 feet measures about 60 decibels, which is 10,000 times louder than a whisper of 20 decibels. Sound becomes painful at 130 decibels. *What is the measurement in decibels of a subway train?*

Reading Check
How does sound occur?

BALANCE

vestibular system: three semicircular canals that provide the sense of balance, located in the inner ear and connected to the brain by a nerve

The body's sense of balance is regulated by the **vestibular system** inside the inner ear. Its prominent feature is the three *semicircular canals*. Hair cells project into the fluid within each of the canals. When you turn your head, these canals also move. Inertia causes the fluid within at least one canal to be slow moving, which bends receptor hair cells projecting into the fluid.

The stimuli for vestibular responses include movements such as spinning, falling, and tilting the body or head. Overstimulation of the vestibular sense by such movements can result in dizziness and "motion sickness," as you probably have experienced by going on amusement-park rides. Although you are seldom directly aware of your sense of balance, without it you would be unable to stand or walk without stumbling or falling.

SMELL AND TASTE

olfactory nerve: the nerve that carries smell impulses from the nose to the brain

Smell and taste are known as the chemical senses because their receptors are sensitive to chemical molecules rather than to light energy or sound waves. For you to smell something, the appropriate molecules must come into contact with the smell receptors in your nose. These molecules enter your nose in vapors that reach a special membrane in the upper part of the nasal passages on which the smell receptors are located. These receptors send messages about smells through the **olfactory nerve** to the brain. For you to taste something, appropriate chemicals must stimulate receptors in the taste buds on your tongue. Taste information is relayed to the brain along with data about the texture and temperature of the substance you have put in your mouth (see Figure 8.11).

Studies show that four primary sensory experiences—sour, salty, bitter, and sweet—make up taste (Beebe-Center, 1949). The combining of taste, smell, and tactile sensations is known as *flavor*. Recent research suggests that a person can taste all flavors anywhere on the tongue, but the areas identified in Figure 8.11 are the most sensitive to specific

Figure 8.10   The Human Ear

The earflap funnels sound waves down the ear canal to the eardrum. The bones of the middle ear pick up the vibrations and transmit them to the inner ear. *What is the function of the cochlea?*

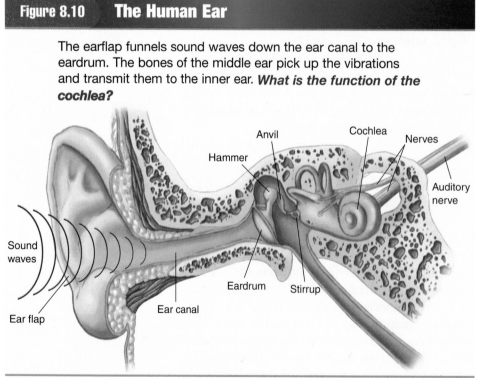

tastes. There are people who have greater taste sensibilities than others. Supertasters have two to three times more taste buds than normal, resulting in increased sensitivity to sweet, bitter, sour, and salty.

Much of what is referred to as taste is actually produced by the sense of smell. As people age, their sense of taste does not seem to decline. When older people complain that food does not taste as good as it once did, the reason usually is a loss of smell rather than a failing sense of taste (Bartoshuk, 1989). You have undoubtedly noticed that when your nose is blocked by a cold, foods usually taste bland.

Sensations of warmth, cold, and pressure also affect taste. Try to imagine eating cold chicken soup or drinking a hot soda. Now imagine the textural differences between a spoonful of pudding and a crunchy chocolate bar, and you will see how the texture and temperature of food influence taste.

The chemical senses seem to play a relatively unimportant role in human life when compared to their functions in lower animals. Insects, for example, often depend on smell to communicate with one another, especially in mating. In humans, smell and taste have become more a matter of pleasure rather than of survival.

THE SKIN SENSES

Receptors in the skin are responsible for providing the brain with at least four kinds of information about the environment: pressure, warmth, cold, and pain. Sensitivity to pressure varies from place to place in the skin. Some spots, such as your fingertips, are densely populated with receptors and are, therefore, highly sensitive. Other spots, such as the middle of your back or the back of your calf, contain relatively few receptors. Pressure sensations can serve as protection. For example, feeling the light pressure of an insect landing on your arm warns you of the danger of being stung.

Some skin receptors (such as neurons) are particularly sensitive to hot or cold stimuli. To create a hot or cold sensation, a stimulus must have a temperature greater or less than the temperature of the skin. If you plunge your arm into a sink of warm water on a hot day, you will experience little or no sensation of its heat. If you put your arm in the same water on a cold day, however, the water will feel quite warm.

Many kinds of stimuli—scratches, punctures, severe pressure, heat, and cold—can produce pain. What they have in common is real or potential injury to bodily tissues. Pain makes it possible for you to prevent damage to your body—it is an emergency system that demands immediate action.

Perceptions of Pain

Whereas other senses rely primarily on a single stimulus, pain results from many different stimuli. For example, pain can be caused by intense pressure, bright lights, loud noises, intense heat, and so on. There are two types of pain sensations—the sharp, localized pain you may feel immediately after an injury and the dull, generalized pain you may feel later.

Have you ever stubbed your toe and then rubbed it to reduce the pain? According to the *gate control theory of pain*, we can lessen some pains by shifting our attention away from the pain impulses or by sending other

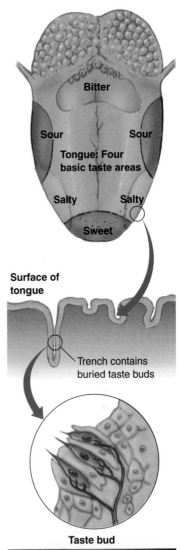

Surface of tongue

Trench contains buried taste buds

Taste bud

Figure 8.11 **The Human Tongue**

When you chew, chemicals of the food mix with saliva and run down into trenches in your tongue. Once there, taste buds react to chemicals dissolved in saliva. *How do the senses of taste and smell work together?*

PSYCHOLOGY and You

Orange Juice and Toothpaste

Have you ever brushed your teeth and then had orange juice for breakfast? How did the orange juice taste? Usually the orange juice will taste bitter. Our taste buds have membranes that contain fatlike phospholipids, while toothpastes contain a detergent that breaks down fat and grease. So the toothpaste first assaults the membranes with its detergents, leaving them raw. Then chemicals in the toothpaste, such as formaldehyde, chalk, and saccharin, cause a sour taste when they mix with the citric and ascorbic acids of orange juice. Try eating artichokes, then drinking water. What does the water taste like?

signals to compete with the pain signals. This creates a sort of competition between nonpain and pain impulses. This bottleneck, or gate, limits the number of impulses that can be transmitted. Thus, by increasing nonpainful impulses (rubbing your toe), you decrease the pain impulses, and the sensation of pain is dulled.

The gate control theory of pain could explain how athletes are able to complete a game even though they have injured themselves. Although a soccer player may know that she has bruised her side, she may not feel the pain fully until the game is over and she has calmed down.

THE BODY SENSES

kinesthesis: the sense of movement and body position

The sense of movement and body position is **kinesthesis.** It cooperates with the vestibular and visual senses to maintain posture and balance. The sensation of kinesthesis comes from receptors in and near the muscles, tendons, and joints. When any movement occurs, these receptors immediately send messages to the brain. Without kinesthetic sensations, your movements would be jerky and uncoordinated. You could not walk without looking at your feet and complex physical activities, such as conducting surgery, piano playing, and acrobatics, would be impossible.

SECTION 2 | Assessment

1. **Review the Vocabulary** What are the five basic senses? Describe two additional senses that humans have.

2. **Visualize the Main Idea** Use a flowchart similar to the one below to describe the pathway of sound.

The Pathway of Sound

[ ] → [ ] → [ ] → [ ]

3. **Recall Information** What is the electromagnetic spectrum and why do we see only a portion of it?

4. **Think Critically** Why can we see steadily and read street signs even though we may be walking or running?

5. **Application Activity** Take a friend to a brightly lit area and then to a dimly lit area and notice how the size of his or her pupils change. How can you explain this?

Perception

■ **Main Idea**

The way we interpret sensations and organize them into meaningful experiences is called perception.

■ **Vocabulary**

• Gestalt
• subliminal messages
• motion parallax
• constancy
• illusions
• extrasensory perception (ESP)

■ **Objectives**

• Outline the principles involved in perception.
• Describe how we learn to perceive and what illusions are.

EXPLORING PSYCHOLOGY

Trying to Catch a Fly

The frog's bug detector shows the rigidity of reflexive behavior. If you sever the frog's optic nerve, it will grow back together, and the bug detector will still work fine. If you sever the optic nerve and then rotate the frog's eye 180 degrees, the nerve will still heal and reestablish all the old connections; however, this time the results will not be so good. The bug detector does not know that everything has been rotated, so it miscomputes a bug's location. If the bug is high, the frog shoots its tongue low. If the bug is to the right, the tongue goes to the left. The frog never learns to compensate for the changed situation.

—from *A Second Way of Knowing: The Riddle of Human Perception* by Edmund Blair Bolles, 1991

The purpose of the excerpt above is to demonstrate to you how useful your powers of perception are. Perception goes beyond reflexive behavior and allows us to confront changes in our environment. Perceptual thinking is essential for us to adapt to change.

People do not usually experience a mass of colors, noises, temperatures, and pressures. Rather, we see cars and buildings, hear voices and music, and feel pencils, desks, and physical contact. We do not merely have sensory experiences; we perceive objects. The brain receives information from the senses and organizes and interprets it into meaningful experiences—unconsciously. This process is called perception.

PRINCIPLES OF PERCEPTUAL ORGANIZATION

Gestalt: the experience that comes from organizing bits and pieces of information into meaningful wholes

Through the process of perception, the brain is always trying to make sense out of the confusion of stimuli that bombards the senses. The brain makes sense of the world by creating "wholes" out of bits and pieces of information in the environment. Each "whole" that is organized by the brain is called a **Gestalt.** Here, the whole is greater than the sum of the parts. (*Gestalt* is a German word meaning "pattern" or "configuration.")

Gestalt psychologists have tried to identify the principles the brain uses in constructing perceptions (Koffka, 1963). Some of the principles they have discovered are demonstrated in Figure 8.12. For example, people tend to see dots in patterns and groups. Principles that people use in organizing such patterns are *proximity, continuity, similarity, simplicity,* and *closure.* If the elements of the pattern are close to one another or are similar in appearance, they tend to be perceived as belonging to one another.

The Gestalt principles of organization help explain how we group our sensations and fill in gaps to make sense of our world. In music, for instance, you tend to group notes on the basis of their closeness, or proximity, to one another in time—you hear melodies, not single notes. Similarity and continuity are also important. They allow you to follow the

---

Figure 8.12	**Gestalt Principles**

Humans see patterns and groupings in their environment rather than disorganized arrays of bits and pieces. *Why do we use the principles of organization illustrated here?*

Proximity
When we see a number of similar objects, we tend to perceive them as groups or sets of those that are close to each other.

•• •• •• •• •• •• ••
[ab cd ef gh ij kl mn]

Similarity
When similar and dissimilar objects are mingled, we see the similar objects as groups.

○○○●●○○●●○○●●○○●●○○●●

Closure
When we see a familiar pattern or shape with some missing parts, we fill in the gaps.

We see a star instead of five Vs.

Continuity
We tend to see continuous patterns, not disrupted ones.

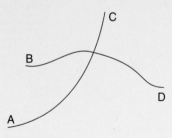

Two curves or two pointed shapes?

Simplicity
We see the simplest shapes possible.

---

sound of a particular voice or instrument even when many other sounds are occurring. Closure aids us in perceiving an object even though there may be gaps in what our senses pick up. The rule of simplicity states that we tend to perceive complex figures as divided into several simpler figures.

FIGURE-GROUND PERCEPTION

One form of perceptual organization is the division of experience into figure and ground (see Figure 8.13). Figure-ground perception is the ability to discriminate properly between a figure and its background. When you look at a three-dimensional object against the sky, you have no trouble distinguishing between the object and its background. Objects become the figure and stand out from the background. It is when something is two-dimensional, as in Figure 8.13, that you may have trouble telling the figure from the ground. Nevertheless, such figure-ground perceptions give clues as to the nature of perception. That we can perceive a single pattern in more than one way demonstrates that we are not passive receivers of stimuli.

Figure and ground are important in hearing as well as in vision. When you follow one person's voice at a noisy meeting, that voice is a figure and all other sounds become ground. Similarly, when you listen to a piece of music, a familiar theme may "leap out" at you: the melody becomes the figure, and the rest of the music merely background.

PERCEPTUAL INFERENCE

Often we have perceptions that are not based entirely on current sensory information. When you hear barking as you approach your house, you assume it is your dog—not a cat or a rhinoceros or even another dog. When you take a seat in a dark theater, you assume it is solid and will hold your weight even though you cannot see what supports the seat. When you are driving in a car and see in the distance that the road climbs up a steep hill then disappears over the top, you assume the road will continue over and down the hill, not come to an abrupt halt.

This phenomenon of filling in the gaps in what our senses tell us is known as *perceptual inference* (Gregory, 1970). Perceptual inference

Did You Know?

Hearing Colors All of her life, a woman, finally diagnosed with synesthesia, had seen colors when she heard words or letters. She always saw yellow with hints of green when she heard the word "king," for instance. *Synesthesia* is the mingling or swapping of sensory information in which stimulating one sense triggers conscious experience in another sense. People with synesthesia may experience spoken words as tastes or shapes, colors as smells, and touches as sounds. The condition occurs in about 1 in 25,000 people and may result from "crossed wires" in the sensory areas of the brain.

Figure 8.13   What Is It?

What did you see the first time you looked at this illustration—a vase or two profiles? People invariably organize their experience into figure and ground. *What does the fact that we perceive a single pattern more than one way demonstrate?*

This drawing seems to defy basic geometric laws.

subliminal messages: brief auditory or visual messages that are presented below the absolute threshold

Figure 8.14	Pop-Out Features

Reality is a jumble of sensations and details. The letter *P* probably pops out to you. The Qs may also pop out, but not as much as the *P*. You may not have noticed the *O*, though. *Why does the* P *pop out?*

QQQQQQQQ
QQQQQPQQ
QQOQQQQQ
QQQQQQQQ

is largely automatic and unconscious. We need only a few cues to inform us that a noise is our dog barking or that a seat is solid. Why? Because we have encountered these stimuli and objects in the past and know what to expect from them in the present. Perceptual inference, thus, often depends on experience. On the other hand, we are probably born with some of our ability to make perceptual inferences.

LEARNING TO PERCEIVE

In large part, perceiving is something that people *learn* to do. For example, infants under one month will smile at a nodding object the size of a human face, whether or not it has eyes, a nose, or other human features. At about 20 weeks, however, a blank oval will not make most infants smile, but a drawing of a face or a mask will. The infant has learned to distinguish something that looks like a person from other objects. Infants 28 weeks and older are more likely to smile at a female than a male face. By 30 weeks, most infants smile more readily when they see a familiar face than when they see someone they do not know. It takes, however, 7 or 8 months for infants to learn to recognize different people (Ahrens, 1954).

Experiments with human beings have also shown that active involvement in one's environment is important for accurate perception. People who have been blind from birth and who have had their sight restored by an operation have visual sensations, but initially they cannot tell the difference between a square and a circle or see that a red cube is like a blue cube (Valvo, 1971). In fact, some had difficulty making such simple distinctions six months after their vision was restored.

Learning to perceive is influenced by our needs, beliefs, and expectations. When we want something, we are more likely to see it. Psychologists (Wispe & Drambarean, 1953) have demonstrated that hungry people are faster at identifying food-related words when words are flashed quickly in front of them. What we identify as truth may be twisted and reconstructed to fit our own belief systems. Previous experiences influence what we see (Lachman, 1996). For example, if you have always perceived all elderly women as honest, you might not even question the elderly woman at the next table when your wallet disappears in a restaurant, even if she is the most obvious suspect. This is called a perceptual set. This set prepares you to see what you want to see.

Subliminal Perception

In his 1957 book *The Hidden Persuaders,* Vance Packard divulged that advertisers were using a revolutionary breakthrough in marketing techniques: subliminal advertising. The word "subliminal" comes from the Latin: *sub* ("below") and *limen* ("threshold"). This concept used **subliminal messages**, which are brief auditory or visual messages presented below the absolute threshold so that there is less than a 50 percent chance that they will be perceived.

One advertiser, James Vicary, claimed that the words "Eat Popcorn" and "Drink Coke" had been flashed on a movie screen in a New Jersey theater on alternate nights for six weeks. Although the flashes were so brief (1/3000 of a second, once every five seconds) that none of the moviegoers even seemed to notice them, Vicary claimed that the sales of popcorn had risen 58 percent and Coke sales rose 18 percent.

The public response to this announcement was long, loud, and hysterical. Congressional representatives called for FCC regulations, while several state legislatures passed laws banning subliminal ads. Meanwhile, more test results began to appear. Vicary demonstrated subliminal advertising to members of Congress and the FCC and downplayed the power of these "hidden persuaders." Later, the Canadian Broadcasting Corporation flashed the words "Telephone now" 352 times during a half-hour show. Only one viewer felt the urge to call.

The idea for subliminal ads was a natural outgrowth of a long series of controversial studies on *subliminal perception*—the ability to notice stimuli that affect only the unconscious mind. Most of these earlier studies involved presenting verbal or visual material at intensities that were considered too low for people to perceive. A more critical look at the studies, however, revealed several flaws in the way they were designed and carried out. For example, no attempt was made to assess or control factors other than the subliminal message that might have influenced the purchase of Coke or popcorn. The temperature in the theater or the length of the movie might have contributed to the increase in sales. Unfortunately, the study was not presented in enough detail to be evaluated by scientists.

Even if it is possible for people to perceive information at very low levels of intensity, there is no clear evidence that these weak, often limited messages would be more powerful in influencing people than would conscious messages. Nevertheless, many people believe that subliminal advertising is powerful.

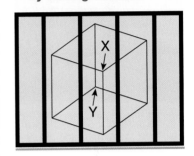

| Figure 8.15 | The Necker Cube |

The Necker cube is an ambiguous figure. You can will yourself to see it as if you were looking down on it, with corner X closest to you, or as if you were looking up at it, with corner Y closest to you. *How might you make this cube less ambiguous by adding details?*

DEPTH PERCEPTION

Depth perception—the ability to recognize distances and three-dimensionality—develops in infancy. Psychologists have placed infants on large tables and found that they most likely will not crawl over the edge. Infants seem able to perceive that it is a long distance to the floor. (This does not mean, though, that infants should be left unattended.)

Monocular Depth Cues

People use many monocular depth cues to perceive distance and depth. *Monocular depth cues* are cues that can be used with a single eye. There are at least a half-dozen monocular cues external to us that we use. In the absence of any other cues, the size of an object—bigger is nearer—will be used. We use *relative height*—objects that appear farther away

Figure 8.16 **Monocular Cues**

As you look down a long stretch of highway, the parallel sides of the road seem to converge. The expansive desert appears furrowed up close and smooth in the distance. *How would you use the relative height cue to perceive the distance of the desert?*

motion parallax: the apparent movement of stationary objects relative to one another that occurs when the observer changes position

from another object are higher on your plane of view. *Interposition,* or the overlapping of images, causes us to view the object we can see in its entirety to be closer than one whose outline is interrupted by another object. *Light and shadows* yield information about an object's shape and size. Brightly lit objects appear closer, while objects in shadows appear farther away. *Texture-density gradient* means that the farther removed an object is, the less detail we can identify (see Figure 8.16).

Another cue is **motion parallax**—the apparent movement of objects that occurs when you move your head from side to side or when you walk around. You can demonstrate motion parallax by looking toward two objects in the same line of vision, one near you and the other some distance away. If you move your head back and forth, the near object will seem to move more than the far object. In this way, motion parallax gives you clues as to which objects are closer than others.

Another distance cue, *linear perspective,* is based on the fact that parallel lines converge when stretched into the distance (see Figure 8.16). For instance, when you look at a long stretch of road or railroad tracks, it appears that the sides of the road or the tracks converge on the horizon. A final related cue is *relative motion.* When you are riding in a car, for example, and look at distant mountains, the objects in a nearby field seem to be moving in the opposite direction to your movement. Yet, when you look at an animal in a nearby field, the mountains or land beyond the animal seem to be moving in the same direction you are.

Binocular Depth Cues

Binocular depth cues depend upon the movement of both eyes. For example, *convergence* is the process by which your eyes turn inward to look at nearby objects. Another cue is the information provided by retinal disparity, as discussed earlier in the chapter. Because each of your eyes occupies a different position, each eye receives a slightly different image. That difference is *retinal disparity.* The brain interprets a large retinal disparity to mean a close object and a small retinal disparity to mean a distant object.

✓ Reading Check
How do monocular and binocular depth cues differ?

CONSTANCY

When we have learned to perceive certain objects in our environment, we tend to see them in the same way, regardless of changing conditions. You probably judge the whiteness of the various portions of these pages to be fairly constant, even though you may have read the book under a wide range of lighting conditions. The light, angle of vision, distance, and, therefore, the image on the retina all change, but your perception of the object does not. Thus, despite changing physical conditions, people are able to perceive objects as the same by the processes of size, shape, brightness and color **constancy** (see Figure 8.17).

An example of size constancy will illustrate how we have an automatic system for perceiving an object as being the same size whether it is far or near. A friend walking toward you does not seem to change into a giant even though the images inside your eyes become larger and larger as she approaches. To you, her appearance stays the same size because even though the size of your visual image is increasing, you are perceiving an additional piece of information: distance is decreasing. The enlarging eye image and the distance information combine to produce a perception of an approaching object that stays the same size.

Distance information compensates for the enlarging eye image to produce size constancy. If information about distance is eliminated, your perception of the size of the object begins to correspond to the actual size of the eye image. For example, it is difficult for most people to estimate the size of an airplane in the sky because they have little experience judging such huge sizes and distances. Pilots, however, can determine whether a flying plane is large and far away or small and close because they are experienced in estimating the sizes and distances of planes.

An example of brightness and color constancy is when you look out a window at night and see that the trees, grass, or parked cars do not appear to be the same color or brightness as they are during the daytime. You already know, though, that the grass is green, for instance. You perceive this quality (of color and brightness) even under conditions of different illumination.

constancy: the tendency to perceive certain objects in the same way regardless of changing angle, distance, or lighting

illusions: perceptions that misrepresent physical stimuli

ILLUSIONS

Illusions are incorrect perceptions. Illusions can be useful in teaching us about how our sensation and perceptual systems work. Illusions are created when perceptual cues are distorted so that our brains cannot correctly interpret space, size, and depth cues. For example, look at the lines in Figure 8.18. Which lines in

Figure 8.17) Shape Constancy

We perceive the opening door as being rectangular in shape, although our view of the shape of it changes as it opens. *Why are perceptual constancies important to our understanding of the world?*

Figure 8.18   **Lines of Different Lengths?**

The Müller-Lyer illusion (a) and the Ponzo illusion (b) are depicted here. The lines between the arrowheads in (a) are exactly the same length, as are the heavy black lines in (b). Some psychologists believe that the reason the lines in (a) seem of different lengths is because they are interpreted as offering different cues to their distance from the viewer. The lines in (b) may appear to be different in length because the brain interprets this diagram as though it is from a scene such as that in (c). *Why does the brain interpret scenes in certain ways?*

each set are longer? Measure the lengths of the pairs of lines with a ruler, then look again. Do the lines *look* as long now that you *know* they are the same? For most people, the answer is no.

A possible explanation of this type of illusion is that even though the patterns are two-dimensional, your brain treats them as three-dimensional. These illusions have features that usually indicate distance in three-dimensional space. The top line in Figure 8.18a, for example, can be thought of as the far corner of a room; the bottom line is like the near corner of the building. In Figure 8.18b and Figure 8.18c, the converging lines create the illusion of distance so that the lower bar looks nearer and shorter than the upper bar. This "perceptual compensation" seems to be unconscious and automatic.

Figure 8.19 shows two individuals in a room. Their sizes look dramatically different because you perceive the room as rectangular. In fact, the ceiling and walls are slanted so that the back wall is both shorter and closer on the right than on the left. Yet even when you know how this illusion was achieved, you still accept the peculiar difference in the sizes of the two people because the windows, walls, and ceiling appear rectangular. Your experience with rectangular rooms overrides your knowledge of how this trick is done.

EXTRASENSORY PERCEPTION

extrasensory perception (ESP): an ability to gain information by some means other than the ordinary senses

We are fascinated by things that cannot be seen, easily explained, or often even verified, such as flying saucers, atoms, genes, and extrasensory perception. **Extrasensory perception (ESP)**—receiving information about the world through channels other than the normal senses—is a hotly debated topic. There are four types of ESP: (1) clairvoyance is perceiving objects or information without sensory input; (2) telepathy involves reading someone else's mind or transferring one's thoughts; (3) psychokinesis involves moving objects through purely mental effort;

and (4) precognition is the ability to foretell events. Since the 1960s, James Randi, known as "The Amazing Randi," has campaigned against people who claim they have ESP. He has exposed many of these people as frauds.

Many people are convinced that ESP exists because of an intense personal experience that can never be scientifically validated. For instance, we all have some fears before traveling, and we imagine the worst: our plane will crash, our train will be derailed, or we will have an automobile accident. These events almost never happen, and we easily forget about our frightening premonitions. If the improbable should actually take place, however, our premonitions turn into compelling evidence for the existence of precognition. Such coincidences sometimes become widely publicized evidence supporting paranormal phenomena, and we may quickly forget all the occasions when our premonitions were completely wrong. If we are truly interested in validating the existence of ESP, though, we must keep track of the frequency of its failures as well as its successes.

Scientists have been investigating ESP since the 1900s. (Probably the most famous parapsychologist is J.B. Rhine.) Many scientists do not accept the results of experiments supporting ESP because the findings are highly unstable. One of the basic principles of scientific research is that one scientist should be able to replicate another scientist's results. Not only do different ESP experiments yield contradictory findings but also the same individual seems to show ESP on one day but not on the next. Perhaps the most telling argument against ESP is that when strict controls are used in an ESP experiment, there is little likelihood of demonstrating ESP. This is, of course, exactly contrary to what one normally expects when trying to demonstrate a phenomenon under strictly controlled conditions.

Figure 8.19   A Strange Room

The room, constructed by Adelbert Ames, changes depth cues to distort our perception. *What makes this illusion work?*

SECTION 3 Assessment

1. **Review the Vocabulary**   Describe the Gestalt principles of organization. How do these principles help us organize reality?

2. **Visualize the Main Idea**   Use a graphic organizer similar to the one below to list and briefly describe monocular depth cues.

Monocular Depth Cues

3. **Recall Information**   What are the binocular depth cues? How do they help us judge reality?

4. **Think Critically**   How do illusions demonstrate the difference between sensations and perceptions?

5. **Application Activity**   Consider the following question: You have suddenly lost all perceptual constancies—what specific problems do you encounter? Create a scene—in the form of a play, narrative, or newspaper article—that illustrates a problem you might encounter.

Seeing Is Believing

Period of Study: Late 1950s and early 1960s

Introduction: In the late 1950s and early 1960s, an anthropologist, C.M. Turnbull, traveled to the Ituri Forest in the present-day country of the Democratic Republic of the Congo (formerly Zaire) to study the life and culture of the BaMbuti Pygmies. Turnbull traveled from one village to another. A 22-year-old man named Kenge from a local Pygmy village accompanied and assisted him. Kenge had spent all of his life living in the dense forests surrounding his village. He was accustomed to seeing only the images contained within the forests.

Hypothesis: Because Kenge had been isolated by the forests all of his life, the sight of new images would appear complex and confusing. The thick forests blocked the local villagers' view of distant objects such as animals, mountains, and the sun and moon on the horizon. Because Kenge had never seen these things, his perceptual development (in this case, *size constancy*, or the ability to perceive a familiar object as being the same size regardless of its distance from you) was limited. He understood only what he could see directly in front of him. The information collected from Turnbull's experience with Kenge raised the question of whether perceptual understanding is a learned ability or biological mechanism: a question of nature versus nurture.

Method: The discovery of Kenge's perceptual limitations took place when Turnbull and Kenge came to a clearing on the eastern edge of the Ituri Forest. At that point Kenge and Turnbull enjoyed a clear view of the Ruwenzori Mountains. Confused by the sight of the mountains, Kenge asked Turnbull if the mountains were hills or clouds. Turnbull explained that they were hills but much larger than any Kenge had seen before. Kenge agreed to ride with Turnbull to the mountains for further inspection. A passing thunderstorm obstructed the travelers' view and did not clear until the two reached the mountains. When Kenge peered up at the enormous mountain range, he was amazed.

As Turnbull and Kenge turned to leave, Kenge noticed a wide open plain on which stood a herd of buffalo. Kenge wanted to know what type of "insects" the buffalo were. Turnbull explained that the animals were not insects but buffalo. When the two arrived close to the herd of buffalo, Kenge now knew that the "insects" were buffalo all along, but he still could not understand why they had appeared to be so small.

Results: Turnbull's accounts support the idea that human perception develops (at least in the case of size constancy) as we use the environment around us, or by nurture. However, some research with infants supports the nature side of perception. For example, individuals who were blind at birth and later gained their sight were able to perceive figure-ground relationships. Are we born with certain perceptual abilities and not others, or is perception something we learn? In Kenge's case, perceptual ability was a learned phenomenon. Certain perceptual skills may be necessary for our survival. In Kenge's case, he did not need to perceive size constancy to survive in the dense jungle.

Analyzing the Case Study

1. Why did some images seem confusing to Kenge?

2. According to Turnbull, how do we learn size constancy?

3. **Critical Thinking** Do you think that Kenge could adjust to life in your city or town? Explain the difficulties he might encounter.

People take in information through their senses. Through their senses they perceive the world around them.

Section 1 Sensation

Main Idea: Sensations allow humans to understand reality. Sensations occur anytime a stimulus activates a receptor.

■ The absolute threshold is the weakest amount of a stimulus required to produce a sensation; the difference threshold is the minimum amount of distinction a person can detect between two stimuli.
■ Senses are most responsive to increases and decreases, rather than to ongoing stimulation.
■ Sensory adaptation allows people to notice differences in sensations and react to the challenges of different or changing stimuli.

Section 2 The Senses

Main Idea: The sense organs—the eyes, ears, tongue, nose, skin, and others—are the receptors of sensations.

■ Vision provides people with a great deal of information about the environment and the objects in it.
■ Hearing depends on vibrations of the air, called sound waves.
■ The body's sense of balance is regulated by the vestibular system inside the inner ear.
■ Smell and taste are known as the chemical senses because their receptors are sensitive to chemical molecules.
■ Receptors in the skin are responsible for providing the brain with information about pressure, warmth, cold, and pain.
■ Kinesthesis cooperates with the vestibular and visual senses to maintain our sense of movement and body position.

Section 3 Perception

Main Idea: The way we interpret sensations and organize them into meaningful experiences is called perception.

■ The Gestalt principles of organization help explain how we group our sensations and fill in gaps to make sense of our world.
■ Figure-ground perception is the ability to discriminate properly between figure and ground.
■ Perceptual inference is the phenomenon of filling in the gaps in what our senses tell us.
■ Learning to perceive is influenced by our needs, beliefs, and expectations.
■ People use monocular depth cues and binocular depth cues to perceive distance and depth.
■ Incorrect perceptions, created when perceptual cues are distorted, are called illusions.

Chapter Vocabulary

sensation (p. 208)
perception (p. 208)
psychophysics (p. 208)
absolute threshold (p. 209)
difference threshold (p. 210)
Weber's law (p. 211)
signal-detection theory (p. 212)
pupil (p. 215)
lens (p. 215)
retina (p. 215)
optic nerve (p. 215)
binocular fusion (p. 216)
retinal disparity (p. 216)
auditory nerve (p. 218)
vestibular system (p. 220)
olfactory nerve (p. 220)
kinesthesis (p. 222)
Gestalt (p. 224)
subliminal messages (p. 226)
motion parallax (p. 228)
constancy (p. 229)
illusions (p. 229)
extrasensory perception (ESP) (p. 230)

Self-Check Quiz
Visit the *Understanding Psychology* Web site at
psychology.glencoe.com and click on **Chapter 8—
Self-Check Quizzes** to prepare for the Chapter Test.

Reviewing Vocabulary

Choose the letter of the correct term or concept below to complete the sentence.

a. sensation   **f.** perception
b. psychophysics   **g.** vestibular system
c. absolute threshold   **h.** kinesthesis
d. difference threshold **i.** subliminal messages
e. binocular fusion   **j.** illusions

1. The organization of sensory information into meaningful experiences is _____ .

2. The psychological study of questions such as the relationship between color and wavelength is called _____.

3. The minimum amount of difference a person can detect between two stimuli is the _____.

4. _____ are incorrect perceptions.

5. _____ is the sense of movement and body position.

6. The combination of two images into one is _____ .

7. A(n) _____ happens when a stimulus activates a receptor.

8. Advertisers sometimes use _____, which are brief auditory or visual messages presented below the absolute threshold so that there is less than a 50 percent chance that they will be perceived.

9. The weakest amount of stimuli required to produce a sensation is called the _____.

10. A body's sense of balance is regulated by the _____ inside the inner ear.

Recalling Facts

1. Using a graphic organizer similar to the one below, define stimulus and give at least four examples of stimuli.

2. What is the psychological principle that explains why you are more likely to notice when a single lightbulb burns out in a room with three lamps than when a single lightbulb burns out in a sports arena?

3. What is our vestibular system? Why do we need it?

4. List four kinds of information we receive from our skin.

5. Define figure-ground perception and provide an example of it.

Critical Thinking

1. **Synthesizing Information** Which of the senses do you consider most important to you? Why do you think so?

2. **Making Inferences** How might being color-deficient affect your daily life? Choosing certain careers?

3. **Analyzing Concepts** What is the difference between vestibular sense and kinesthesis? In what situations are both senses needed?

4. **Analyzing Concepts** What sensation do you experience when you close your eyes and gently press on one of your eyeballs at the outer edge? How can you explain the visual experience in the absence of light rays?

5. **Evaluating Information** One of the objections to the use of subliminal advertising techniques is that they could be used to manipulate or influence large numbers of people without their knowing it. Do you think this is an important objection? Why or why not?

Assessment

Psychology Projects

1. The Senses Peel a fresh potato and an apple. Have a friend close his eyes and smell a fresh onion while he takes a bite of each one. Can he tell which food is which without his sense of smell? Try this experiment with various people, using different foods that have similar textures. Report your findings in a chart. Explain the relationship between the sense of taste and smell.

2. Perception Watch a movie with your parents or grandparents. As soon as the film is over, ask each person to write a paragraph describing the last scene in the movie. Read each paragraph aloud. What was everyone's perception of the scene? How could you explain any differences?

3. Sensation Sensory adaptation refers to the ability of the senses to adjust themselves to a constant level of stimulation. Create a simple experiment to test for sensory adaptation. Ask a classmate to demonstrate the experiment.

Technology Activity

Search the Internet for information and examples of optical illusions. Present examples to your class and explain how the illusions were created.

Psychology Journal

1. Reread your journal entry about hearing another conversation in a crowded setting. Is your explanation still valid? If necessary, how would you change it?

2. Think about what it would be like if our senses did not have the limits they do. What visual problems might we have? What would we hear if our sense of hearing had a different range? Write answers to these questions in your journal.

Building Skills

Interpreting a Graph Review the graph, and then answer the questions that follow.

1. What three body parts are the least sensitive to touch?

2. Why are certain parts of the body more sensitive to touch than others?

3. How does the information in the graph help explain why people reading in Braille use their fingertips?

Practice and assess key social studies skills with **Glencoe Skillbuilder Interactive Workbook CD-ROM, Level 2.**

See the Skills Handbook, page 628, for an explanation of interpreting graphs.

Skin Sensitivity

READINGS IN PSYCHOLOGY

How do we recognize an object we are seeing? The experience of Virgil, a 55-year-old man who regained his sight after being blind, raises questions about seeing and perception. Oliver Sacks, a physician, is known for writing case histories of neurological experiences. This account appeared in *The New Yorker* on May 10, 1993.

Reader's Dictionary

acute: severe

indolence: laziness or sloth

retina: the sensory membrane that lines the eye and functions as the instrument of vision

cataract: a clouding of the lens of the eye

incessant: continuing without interruption

coherence: being unified or understandable

agnostic: loss of ability to recognize familiar objects

To See and Not See

BY OLIVER SACKS

Virgil (nearly all the names in this account have been changed, and some identifying details have been disguised) was born on a small farm in Kentucky soon after the outbreak of the Second World War. He seemed normal enough as a baby, but (his mother thought) had poor eyesight even as a toddler, sometimes bumping into things, seemed not to see them. At the age of three, he became gravely ill with a triple illness—a meningitis or meningoencephalitis (inflammation of the brain and its membranes), polio, and cat-scratch fever. During this acute illness, he had convulsions, became virtually blind, paralyzed in the legs, partly paralyzed in his breathing, and, after ten days, fell into a coma.

He remained in a coma for two weeks. When he emerged from it, he seemed, according to his mother, "a different person" and "sort of dull inside"; he showed a curious indolence, nonchalance, passivity, seemed nothing at all like the spunky, mischievous boy he had been.

The strength in his legs came back over the next year, and his chest grew stronger, though never, perhaps, entirely normal. His vision also recovered significantly—but his retinas were now gravely damaged. Whether the retinal damage was caused wholly by his acute illness or perhaps partly by a congenital retinal degeneration was never clear.

In Virgil's sixth year, cataracts began to develop in both eyes, and it was evident that he was becoming functionally blind. That same year, he was sent to a school for the blind, and there he eventually learned to read Braille and to become adept with the use of a cane. . . .

Virgil graduated from the school, and when he was twenty, decided to leave Kentucky, to seek training, work, and a life of his own in a city in Oklahoma. He trained as a massage therapist, and soon found employment at a Y.M.C.A. He was obviously good at his job, and highly esteemed, and the Y was happy to keep him on its permanent staff and to provide a small house for him across the road, where he lived with a friend, also employed at the Y. Virgil had many clients—it is fascinating to hear the tactile detail with which he can describe them—and seemed to take a real pleasure and pride in his job. . . . Life was limited, but stable in its way.

Then, in 1991, he met Amy. . . . [Amy] saw Virgil stuck (as she perceived it) in a vegetative, dull life. . . . Restoring his sight [through surgery], she must have felt, would, like marriage, stir him from his indolent bachelor existence and provide them both with a new life. . . . Virgil himself showed no preference in the matter; he seemed happy to go along with whatever they decided.

Finally, in mid-September, the day of the surgery came. Virgil's right eye had its cataract removed, and a new lens implant was inserted; then the eye was bandaged, as is customary, for twenty-four hours of recovery. The following day, the bandage was removed, and Virgil's eye was finally exposed, without cover, to the world. The moment of truth had come.

Or had it? The truth of the matter (as I pieced it together later), if less "miraculous" than Amy's journal suggested, was infinitely stranger. The dramatic moment stayed vacant, grew longer, sagged. No cry ("I can see!") burst from Virgil's lips. He seemed to be staring blankly, bewildered, without focusing, at the surgeon, who stood before him, still holding the bandages. Only when the surgeon spoke—saying "Well?"— did a look of recognition cross Virgil's face.

Virgil told me later that in this first moment he had no idea what he was seeing. There was light, there was movement, there was color, all mixed up, all meaningless, a blur. Then out of the blur came a voice that said, "Well?" Then, and only then, he said, did he finally realize that this chaos of light and shadow was a face—and, indeed, the face of his surgeon. . . .

The rest of us, born sighted, can scarcely imagine such confusion. For we, born with a full complement of senses, and correlating these, one with the other, create a sight world from the start, a world of visual objects and concepts and meanings. When we open our eyes each morning, it is upon a world we have spent a lifetime *learning* to see. We are not given the world: we make our world through incessant experience,

categorization, memory, reconnection. But when Virgil opened his eye, after being blind for forty-five years—having had little more than an infant's visual experience, and this long forgotten—there were no visual memories to support a perception, there was no world of experience and meaning awaiting him. He saw, but what he saw had no coherence. His retina and optic nerve were active, transmitting impulses, but his brain could make no sense of them; he was, as neurologists say, agnostic.

Everyone, Virgil included, expected something simpler. A man opens his eyes, light enters, and falls on the retina: he sees. It is as simple as that, we imagine. And the surgeon's own experience, like that of most ophthalmologists, had been with the removal of cataracts from patients who had almost always lost their sight late in life—and such patients do indeed, if the surgery is successful, have a virtually immediate recovery of normal vision, for they have in no sense lost their ability to see. And so, though there had been a careful surgical discussion of the operation and of possible postsurgical complications, there was little discussion or preparation for the neurological and psychological difficulties that Virgil might encounter. . . .

On the day he returned home after the bandages were removed, his house and its contents were unintelligible to him, and he had to be led up the garden path, led through the house, led into each room, and introduced to each chair.

Analyzing the Reading

1. How did Virgil become blind?
2. Why didn't Virgil realize what he was seeing after his sight was regained?
3. **Critical Thinking** What psychological difficulties do you think Virgil encountered after regaining his sight?

UNIT 4

Learning and Cognitive Processes

Contents

A soccer player shoots for the goal. ▶

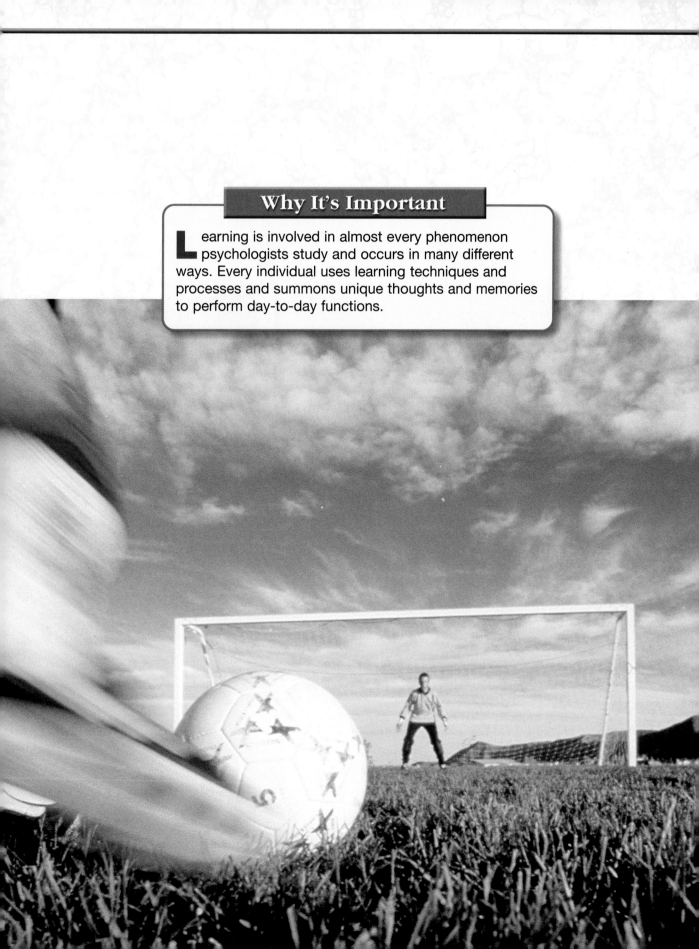

Why It's Important

Learning is involved in almost every phenomenon psychologists study and occurs in many different ways. Every individual uses learning techniques and processes and summons unique thoughts and memories to perform day-to-day functions.

Learning: Principles and Applications

PSYCHOLOGY JOURNAL

Recall a situation in which you taught another person a skill or how to do a task. Write a brief account about it in your journal. Make sure to include a description of the strategy you used in teaching. ■

PSYCHOLOGY Online

Chapter Overview
Visit the *Understanding Psychology* Web site at psychology.glencoe.com and click on **Chapter 9—Chapter Overviews** to preview the chapter.

Classical Conditioning

Reader's Guide

■ Main Idea
People acquire certain behaviors through classical conditioning, a learning procedure in which associations are made between an unconditioned stimulus and a neutral stimulus.

■ Vocabulary
- classical conditioning
- neutral stimulus
- unconditioned stimulus (UCS)
- unconditioned response (UCR)
- conditioned stimulus (CS)
- conditioned response (CR)
- generalization
- discrimination
- extinction

■ Objectives
- Describe the principles of classical conditioning.
- Outline the techniques of classical conditioning.

EXPLORING PSYCHOLOGY

Which Pen Would You Choose?

The researchers placed the participants in a room. In this room the participants first viewed purple pens. As the participants sat staring at the purple pens, pleasant music played in the background. Then the music stopped, and the purple pens were taken away. Suddenly green pens appeared. As the participants sat staring at the green pens, they heard unpleasant music in the background. Later, the researchers offered the pens to the participants. The participants could pick a purple or green pen. The participants overwhelmingly chose purple pens. Why?

—adapted from *The Story of Psychology* by Morton Hunt, 1993

W hy did the participants choose purple pens over green in the experiment above? This experiment took place in 1982 and was based on a principle that is widely used today in television commercials. Pairing a product with pleasant sensations motivates consumers to make a choice without an awareness of why they made that choice.

The Russian physiologist Ivan Pavlov called what was taking place in similar situations *conditioning*. In **classical conditioning,** a person's or animal's old response becomes attached to a new stimulus. This is one example of learning. What is learning? *Learning* can be defined as a relatively permanent change in behavior that results from experience.

classical conditioning: a learning procedure in which associations are made between a natural stimulus and a learned, neutral stimulus

Pavlov's discovery of this type of learning—the principle of classical conditioning—was accidental. Around the turn of the century, Pavlov had been studying the process of digestion. Pavlov wanted to understand how a dog's stomach prepares to digest food when something is placed in its mouth. Then he noticed that the mere sight or smell of food was enough to start a hungry dog salivating. Pavlov became fascinated with how the dog anticipated the food and how salivation occurred before the food was presented, and he decided to investigate.

CLASSICAL CONDITIONING

neutral stimulus: a stimulus that does not initially elicit a response

Pavlov began his experiments by ringing a tuning fork and then immediately placing some meat powder on the dog's tongue. He chose the tuning fork because it was a **neutral stimulus**—that is, one that had nothing to do with the response to meat (salivation) prior to conditioning. After only a few times, the dog started salivating as soon as it heard the sound, even if the food was not placed in its mouth (see Figure 9.1). Pavlov went on to demonstrate that a neutral stimulus (here, tuning fork or bell's ring) will cause a formerly unrelated response if it is presented regularly just before the stimulus (here, food) that normally brings about that response (here, salivation).

unconditioned stimulus (UCS): an event that elicits a certain predictable response without previous training

unconditioned response (UCR): an organism's automatic (or natural) reaction to a stimulus

Pavlov used the term *unconditioned* to refer to stimuli and to the automatic, involuntary responses they caused. Such responses include blushing, shivering, being startled, or salivating. In the experiment, food was the **unconditioned stimulus (UCS)**—an event that leads to a certain, predictable response without previous training. Food normally causes salivation. A dog does not have to be taught to salivate when it smells meat. The salivation is an **unconditioned response (UCR)**—a reaction that occurs naturally and automatically when the unconditioned stimulus is presented, in other words, a reflex.

conditioned stimulus (CS): a once-neutral event that elicits a given response after a period of training in which it has been paired with an unconditioned stimulus

conditioned response (CR): the learned reaction to a conditioned stimulus

Under normal conditions, the sound of a tuning fork would not cause salivation. The dog had to be taught, or conditioned, to associate this sound with food. An ordinarily neutral event that, after training, leads to a response such as salivation is termed a **conditioned stimulus (CS).** The salivation it causes is a **conditioned response (CR).** A conditioned response is learned. A wide variety of events may serve as conditioned stimuli for salivation—the sight of food, an experimenter entering the room, the sound of a tone, or a flash of light. A number of different reflex responses that occur automatically following an unconditioned stimulus (UCS) can be conditioned to occur whenever the correct conditioned stimulus (CS) occurs.

GENERAL PRINCIPLES OF CLASSICAL CONDITIONING

Classical conditioning helps animals and humans adapt to the environment. It also helps humans and animals avoid danger. Psychologists have investigated why and in what circumstances classical conditioning occurs, leading to a greater understanding of the principles of classical conditioning.

Figure 9.1 | Classical Conditioning Experiment

Pavlov's students used this apparatus. The tube leading from the dog's mouth deposited saliva to the kymograph. *What were Pavlov's students trying to prove with this experiment?*

Before Conditioning

Neutral stimulus → No response or orienting response

Some stimuli are neutral (neutral stimulus). The dog shows no response to the bell's ring.

During Conditioning

Bell (CS)
Salivation (UCR)
Food (UCS)

The bell (CS) and meat (UCS) are presented together.

After Conditioning

Bell (CS) → Salivation (CR)

The bell was neutral before, but now can trigger salivation.

Before Conditioning

Food (UCS) → Salivation (UCR)

Some stimuli are already meaningful (unconditioned stimulus); for example, food causes the dog to salivate.

Fistula (tube) is implanted to collect saliva.

Harness holds dog in place.

Kymograph records dog's response to stimulus.

Stimulus (food)

Acquisition

Acquisition of a classically conditioned response generally occurs gradually. With each pairing of the conditioned stimulus (CS) and the unconditioned stimulus (UCS), the conditioned response (CR)—or learned response—is strengthened. In Pavlov's experiment, the more frequently the tuning fork was paired with the food, the more often the tone brought about salivation—the conditioned response.

The timing of the association between the conditioned stimulus (the tone) and the unconditioned stimulus (food) also influences learning. Pavlov tried several different conditioning procedures in which he varied the time between presenting the conditioned stimulus and the unconditioned stimulus. He found that classical conditioning was most reliable and effective when the conditioned stimulus was presented just before the unconditioned stimulus. He found that presenting the conditioned stimulus (CS) about half a second before the unconditioned stimulus (UCS) would yield the strongest associations between the tuning fork and the meat.

generalization: responding similarly to a range of similar stimuli

discrimination: the ability to respond differently to similar but distinct stimuli

Generalization and Discrimination

In the same set of experiments, Pavlov also explored the processes of *generalization* and *discrimination*. **Generalization** occurs when an animal responds to a second stimulus similar to the original CS, without prior training with the second stimulus. When Pavlov conditioned a dog to salivate at the sight of a circle (the CS), he found that the dog would salivate when it saw an oval as well. The dog had generalized its response to include a similar stimulus. Pavlov was later able to do the opposite, to teach the dog to respond only to the circle by always pairing meat powder with the circle but never pairing it with the oval. He thus taught the dog **discrimination**—the ability to respond differently to different stimuli.

Generalization and discrimination are complementary processes and are part of your everyday life. Both may occur spontaneously in some situations, and both can be taught in others. For example, assume a friend has come to associate the sound of a dentist's drill (CS) with a fearful reaction (CR). After several exposures to a dentist's drill, your friend may find that he or she has generalized this uncomfortable feeling to the sound of other, nondental drills. Later, your friend may learn to discriminate between the sound of a dentist's drill and other drills.

Figure 9.2   Pavlov's Research

The name of Pavlov is well-known in the field of psychology because of his pioneering research. *In this cartoonist's depiction, what is the neutral stimulus? The CR?*

THE FAR SIDE   By GARY LARSON

© 1993 FarWorks, Inc. All Rights Reserved

Unbeknownst to most students of psychology, Pavlov's first experiment was to ring a bell and cause his dog to attack Freud's cat.

Extinction and Spontaneous Recovery

A classically conditioned response, like any other behavior, is subject to change. Pavlov discovered that if he stopped presenting food after the sound of the tuning fork, the sound gradually lost its effect on the dog. After he repeatedly struck the tuning fork without giving food, the dog no longer associated the sound with the arrival of food—the sound of the tuning fork no longer caused the salivation response. Pavlov called this effect **extinction** because the CR had gradually died out.

Even though a classically conditioned response may be extinguished, this does not mean that the CR has been completely unlearned. If a rest period is given following extinction, the CR may reappear when the CS is presented again but not followed by a UCS. This *spontaneous recovery* does not bring the CR back to original strength, how-

Profiles In Psychology

Ivan Petrovich Pavlov

1849–1936

"While you are experimenting, do not remain content with the surface of things. Don't become a mere recorder of facts, but try to penetrate the mystery of their origin."

Born in central Russia, Pavlov abandoned his family's hopes that he would become a priest, in favor of scientific pursuits. After receiving his doctorate degree from the University of St. Petersburg in 1897, he began performing his own research into digestion and blood circulation. The work that made Pavlov famous actually began as a study in digestion. Pavlov discovered that salivation and the action of the stomach were closely linked to reflexes in the autonomic nervous system. By studying conditioned reflexes, it became possible to examine human behavior objectively, instead of resorting to subjective methods.

Pavlov distrusted the new science of psychiatry. He did think, though, that conditioned reflexes could explain the behavior of psychotic people. He believed that those who withdrew from the world may associate all stimuli with possible injury or threat.

ever. Pavlov's dogs produced much less saliva during spontaneous recovery than they did at the end of their original conditioning. Alternating lengthy rest periods and the tone without food caused more rapid loss of salivation each time and less recovery the next time the CS was presented.

A good example of extinction and spontaneous recovery can occur if you are involved in a car accident. Following the accident it may at first be difficult to drive again. You might even find it difficult to open the door and get into the car. As you approach the car, your hands begin to shake and your knees get shaky as well. Your heartbeat even increases as you get nearer. After a few days, opening the door and getting into the car does not bother you as much. Several months go by and the fears of the car and the accident have been extinguished. One day, several months later, as you begin to approach the car, your heart begins to race and your knees and hands begin to shake. You have had a spontaneous recovery of the fear reaction.

extinction: the gradual disappearance of a conditioned response when the conditioned stimulus is repeatedly presented without the unconditioned stimulus

CLASSICAL CONDITIONING AND HUMAN BEHAVIOR

John B. Watson and Rosalie Rayner (1920) used conditioning on a human infant in the case of Little Albert (see Case Studies, page 249). Watson questioned the role that conditioning played in the development of emotional responses in children. He and Rayner attempted to condition an 11-month-old infant named Albert to fear laboratory rats. At first Albert happily played with the rats. When the experimenters struck a steel bar with a hammer to produce a loud sound, Albert began to display a fear response. Eventually Albert showed fear each time he saw the rat even though the loud sound was not repeated. Although this demonstration is now viewed as unethical (because the researchers taught Little Albert to fear things which he previously had no fear of), it provided evidence that emotional responses can be classically conditioned in humans. In this case the UCS is the loud noise, the UCR is fear, the CS is the rat, and the CR is fear.

Using the principle of classical conditioning, O. Hobart Mowrer and his wife Mollie (1938) discovered a practical solution to the problem of bed-wetting. One reason bed-wetting occurs is that children do not wake up during the night when they have a full bladder. The Mowrers developed a device known as the *bell and pad*. It consists of two metallic sheets perforated with small holes and attached by wires to a battery-run alarm. The thin, metal sheets—wrapped in insulation or padding—are placed under the child's bedsheets. When the sleeping child moistens the sheet with the first drops of urine, the circuit closes, causing the alarm to go off and wake the child. The child can then use the bathroom.

The alarm is the unconditioned stimulus that produces the unconditioned response of waking up. The sensation of a full bladder is the conditioned stimulus that, before conditioning, did not produce wakefulness. After several pairings of the full bladder (CS) and the alarm (UCS), the child is able to awaken to the sensation of a full bladder without the help of the alarm. This technique has proven to be a very effective way of treating bed-wetting problems.

Did You Know?

Classical Conditioning Have you ever noticed how movie directors use music in their movies? Did you ever hear a song and then think about either the movie it was from or the person you were with when you saw the movie? If so, you experienced classical conditioning. The music had become a "signal" that triggers memories and emotions. A conditioned emotion, such as fear, is a very difficult response to extinguish. It may trigger physical, cognitive, and emotional reactions.

Taste Aversions

Reading Check
How do people develop taste aversions?

Suppose you go to a fancy restaurant. You decide to try an expensive appetizer you have never had—for instance, snails. Then suppose that, after dinner, you go to a concert and become violently ill. You will probably develop a taste aversion—you will never be able to look at another snail without becoming at least a little nauseated.

Your nausea reaction to snails is another example of classical conditioning. What makes this type of conditioning interesting to learning theorists is that when people or other animals become ill, they seem to decide, "It must have been something I ate," even if they have not eaten

Figure 9.3 **Examples of Common Conditioned Responses**

If you have pets and feed them canned food, what happens when you use the electric can opener? The animals may come running even when you are opening a can of peas. *Why do you feel distress at the mere sight of flashing police lights?*

UCS	CS	UCR	CR
Drill	Dentist/ sound of drill	Tension	Tension
Catchy jingle or slogan	Product (soda pop)	Favorable feeling	Favorable feeling
Speeding ticket	Flashing police car lights	Distress	Distress

for several hours. It is unlikely that the concert hall in which you were sick will become the conditioned stimulus, nor will other stimuli from the restaurant—the wallpaper pattern or the type of china used. What is more, psychologists can even predict which part of your meal will be the CS—you will probably blame a new food. Thus, if you get sick after a meal of salad, steak, and snails, you will probably learn to hate snails, even if they are really not the cause of your illness.

John Garcia and R.A. Koelling (1966) first demonstrated this phenomenon with rats. The animals were placed in a cage with a tube containing flavored water. Whenever a rat took a drink, lights flashed and clicks sounded. Then, some of the rats were given an electric shock after they drank. All these rats showed traditional classical conditioning—the lights and the sounds became conditioned stimuli, and the rats tried to avoid them in order to avoid a shock. The other rats were not shocked but were injected with a drug that made them sick after they drank and the lights and sounds occurred. These rats developed an aversion not to the lights or the sounds but only to the taste of the flavored water.

This special relationship between food and illness was used in a study that made coyotes avoid sheep by giving them a drug to make them sick when they ate sheep (Gustavson et al., 1974). This application is important because sheep farmers in the western United States would like to eliminate the coyotes that threaten their flocks, while naturalists are opposed to killing the coyotes. The psychologists realized that coyotes could be trained to eat other kinds of meat and thus learn to coexist peacefully with sheep.

In summary, classical conditioning helps animals and humans predict what is going to happen. It provides information that may be helpful to their survival. Learning associated with classical conditioning may aid animals in finding food or help humans avoid pain or injury. For example, parents may "condition" an infant to avoid a danger such as electrical outlets by shouting "NO!" and startling the infant each time he approaches an outlet. The infant fears the shouts of the parents, and eventually the infant may fear the outlet even when the parents do not shout.

PSYCHOLOGY Online

Student Web Activity
Visit the *Understanding Psychology* Web site at psychology.glencoe.com and click on **Chapter 9—Student Web Activities** for an activity about learning.

Figure 9.4 Classical Conditioning vs. Operant Conditioning

Classical conditioning and operant conditioning both involve the establishment of relationships between two events. Classical conditioning and operant conditioning, though, use very different procedures to reach their goals. *What role does the learner's environment play in each type of conditioning?*

Classical Conditioning	Operant Conditioning
1. Always a specific stimulus (UCS) that elicits the desired response	1. No stimulus; learner must first respond appropriately, then behavior is reinforced
2. UCS does not depend upon learner's response	2. Reinforcement depends upon learner's behavior
3. Learner responds to its environment	3. Learner actively operates on its environment

Classical conditioning is an example of a behaviorist theory. *Behaviorism* is the attempt to understand behavior in terms of relationships between observable stimuli and observable responses. *Behaviorists* are psychologists who study only those behaviors that they can observe and measure. Behaviorists are not concerned with unobservable mental processes. They emphasize actions instead of thoughts. We will discuss another behaviorist learning theory—operant conditioning—in the next section. Whereas classical conditioning is a process by which a stimulus that previously did not elicit a response comes to elicit a response after it is paired with a stimulus that naturally elicits a response, operant conditioning is a process by which the consequences of a response increase or decrease the likelihood that the response will occur again (see Figure 9.4).

SECTION 1 Assessment

1. **Review the Vocabulary** What is the difference between a neutral stimulus and an unconditioned stimulus?

2. **Visualize the Main Idea** In a graphic organizer similar to the one below, list and describe the general principles of classical conditioning.

3. **Recall Information** How are generalization and discrimination related to classical conditioning?

4. **Think Critically** Under what conditions might a conditioned response become extinct?

5. **Application Activity** You have a friend who inhales noisily when standing next to you and then puffs air into your eye. You find that you now blink when you hear your friend inhale. Identify and decribe the neutral stimulus, the UCS, UCR, CS, and CR in your behavior.

The Case of
Little Albert

Period of Study: Winter, 1919–1920

Introduction: John B. Watson and Rosalie Rayner showed how conditioning could be used on a human infant. The study led to ethical questions on research with humans. Despite that, Watson was able to conclude that there are only a few instinctive reflexes in humans, among them, sucking, reaching, and grasping. In addition, infants have three innate emotional responses to certain stimuli: fear at hearing a loud sound or at suddenly being dropped; rage when arm or head movements are forcibly restrained; and love when stroked, rocked, gently patted, and the like.

Hypothesis: Most human behaviors and emotional reactions are built up of conditioned responses. (When an emotionally exciting object stimulates the subject simultaneously with an object not emotionally exciting, the latter object may in time arouse the same emotional reaction as the former object.)

Method: Watson and Rayner presented Albert (a well-adjusted 9-month-old) with many objects, including a rat, blocks, a rabbit, a dog, a monkey, masks with and without hair, cotton, wool, and burning newspapers. Albert showed no fear of any of these objects—they were all neutral stimuli for the fear response.

Watson and Rayner decided that, when Albert was 11 months old, they would attempt to condition him to fear rats. They began by placing a furry white rat in front of him. Albert would reach out to touch it, and each time he did, one of Watson's assistants would strike a metal bar with a hammer behind Albert. The first time the metal bar was struck, Albert fell forward and buried his head in a pillow. The next time he reached for the rat and the bar

was struck, Albert began to whimper. The noise, the unconditioned stimulus, brought about a naturally unconditioned response, fear. After only a few such pairings, the rat became a *conditioned stimulus* that elicited a *conditioned response,* fear.

Five days after Watson and Rayner conditioned Albert to fear rats, they presented him with blocks, a rabbit, a rat, and a dog, each alone. They also showed him a number of other stimuli, including a Santa Claus mask. Albert reacted fearfully to all but the blocks. His conditioned fear response generalized to include the rabbit and all of the white furry objects he was shown, but not to the blocks.

Results: One of the most frequent criticisms of the experiment was that Watson and Rayner taught a well-adjusted child to be fearful. Apparently, the researchers knew at least one month ahead of time that Albert would be leaving the study, and yet they made no attempt to extinguish his conditioned fears (Harris, 1979). Psychologists today are unable to repeat the Little Albert study because of the ethical standards of the APA (see Chapter 2).

One of Watson's students, Mary Cover Jones (1924, 1974), developed an extinction procedure called counterconditioning to reduce people's existing fears. Peter was a boy who was extremely fearful of rabbits. Jones helped Peter eliminate his fear by pairing the feared object (the rabbit) with pleasant experiences such as eating ice cream or receiving special attention.

Analyzing the Case Study

1. Did the results of Watson and Rayner's experiment support their hypothesis? Explain.

2. How did Albert's response become generalized?

3. Critical Thinking   How were the principles of classical conditioning used to reduce Peter's fear of rabbits?

Operant Conditioning

Reader's Guide

■ Main Idea
Operant conditioning occurs when the consequences that follow a behavior increase or decrease the likelihood of that behavior occurring again.

■ Vocabulary
- operant conditioning
- reinforcement
- primary reinforcer
- secondary reinforcer
- fixed-ratio schedule
- variable-ratio schedule
- fixed-interval schedule
- variable-interval schedule
- shaping
- response chain
- aversive control
- negative reinforcement
- escape conditioning
- avoidance conditioning

■ Objectives
- Outline the principles of operant conditioning.
- Describe applications of operant conditioning.

Exploring Psychology

Saved by a Theory
The therapists noted that the depressed woman did not eat; she was in critical danger of dying of starvation. What should they do? The woman did seem to enjoy visitors at the hospital and the TV set, radio, books and magazines, and flowers in her room. The therapists moved her into a room devoid of all these comforts, and put a light meal in front of her; if she ate anything at all, one of the comforts was temporarily restored. The therapists gradually withheld the rewards unless she continued to eat more. Her eating improved, she gained weight. Within months she was released from the hospital. A follow-up consultation with her 18 months later found her leading a normal life.

—from *The Story of Psychology* by Morton Hunt, 1993

---

operant conditioning: learning in which a certain action is reinforced or punished, resulting in corresponding increases or decreases in occurrence

Suppose your dog is wandering around the neighborhood, sniffing trees, checking garbage cans, looking for a squirrel to chase. A kind neighbor sees the dog and tosses a bone out the kitchen door to it. The next day, the dog is likely to stop at the same door on its rounds, if not go to it directly. Your neighbor produces another bone, and another the next day. Your dog becomes a regular visitor.

Both stories are examples of **operant conditioning**—that is, learning from the consequences of behavior. The term *operant* is used because the subject (the depressed woman and the wandering dog in our examples) operates on or causes some change in the environment. This produces a result that influences whether the subject will operate or respond in the same way in the future. Depending on the effect of the operant behaviors, the learner will repeat or eliminate these behaviors—to get rewards or avoid punishment.

How does operant conditioning differ from classical conditioning? One difference lies in how the experimenter conducts the experiment. In classical conditioning, the experimenter presents the CS and UCS independent of the participant's behavior. Reactions to the CS are then observed. In operant conditioning, the participant must engage in a behavior in order for the programmed outcome to occur. In other words, operant conditioning is the study of how voluntary behavior is affected by its consequences (see Figure 9.5).

REINFORCEMENT

Burrhus Frederic (B.F.) Skinner has been the psychologist most closely associated with operant conditioning. He believed that most behavior is influenced by a person's history of rewards and punishments. Skinner trained rats to respond to lights and sounds in a special enclosure called a Skinner box (see Figure 9.6). To conduct this experiment, a rat is placed inside the box. The rat must learn how to solve the problem of how to get food to appear in the cup. (This can be done by pressing a bar on the cage wall.) The rat first explores the box. When the rat moves toward the bar, the experimenter drops food into the cup. The food is important to the hungry rat. After the rat begins to approach the cup for food consistently, the experimenter begins to drop food into the cup only if the rat presses the bar. Eventually, when the rat is hungry it will press the bar to get food.

The food that appears in the cup is a reinforcer in this experiment. **Reinforcement** can be defined as a stimulus or event that increases the likelihood that behavior will be repeated. Whether or not a particular stimulus is a reinforcement depends on the effect the stimulus has on the learner. Examples of reinforcers that people usually respond to are social approval, money, and extra privileges.

Suppose you want to teach a dog to shake hands. One way would be to give the animal a treat every time it lifts its paw up to you. The treat is called a *positive reinforcer*. In this example, the dog will eventually learn to shake hands to get a reward.

Your dog will stop shaking hands when you forget to reward it for the trick. Extinction will occur because the reinforcement is withheld, but

✓ **Reading Check**
How is operant conditioning different from classical conditioning?

reinforcement: stimulus or event that follows a response and increases the likelihood that the response will be repeated

Figure 9.5	**Operant Conditioning**

Behavior

Positive reinforcer	Negative reinforcer

Changed behavior

We do not just react to our environment, we behave in ways that seem designed to *produce* certain environmental changes. For example, I flip the light switch to illuminate a room. I say, "Please, pass the salt," to get the salt shaker. *According to the diagram, what must happen for behavior to change?*

Figure 9.6   A Skinner Box

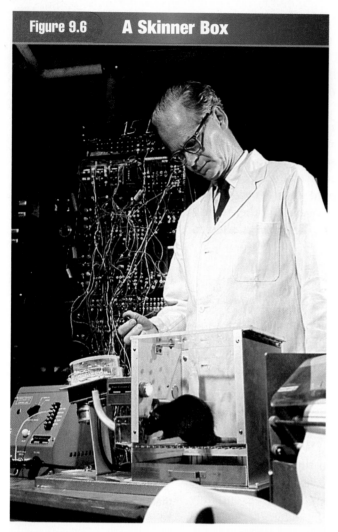

The Skinner box is a basic apparatus used to test theories of operant conditioning. When the rat presses the bar located on the side of the box, food is delivered to the cup. *How does the rat display that learning has occurred?*

it will take a period of time. (Remember, in classical conditioning, extinction is the disappearance of a conditioned response when an unconditioned stimulus no longer follows a conditioned stimulus.) In fact, for a while after you stop rewarding the dog, it will probably become impatient, bark, and paw even more insistently than it did before, until it "gives up" on shaking hands. Eventually the dog will try to shake hands again, indicating that spontaneous recovery has occurred.

Whereas positive reinforcement occurs when something the animal wants (a treat for the dog) is *added* after an action, negative reinforcement occurs when something unpleasant is *taken away* if the animal performs an action.

Primary and Secondary Reinforcers

Reinforcers come in many varieties. Some reinforcers are primary and some are secondary. A **primary reinforcer** is one that satisfies a biological need such as hunger, thirst, or sleep. A **secondary reinforcer** is one that has been paired with a primary reinforcer and through classical conditioning has acquired value and reinforcement. With conditioning, almost any stimulus can acquire value and become a secondary reinforcer.

One experimenter (Wolfe, 1936) demonstrated this with chimpanzees. Poker chips have no value for chimps—they are not edible and they are not very much fun to play with. This experimenter, however, used operant and classical conditioning to teach chimps to value poker chips as much as humans value money. He provided the animals with a "Chimp-O-Mat" that dispensed peanuts or bananas, which are primary reinforcers. To obtain food, the chimps had to pull down on a heavily weighted bar to obtain poker chips, then insert the chips in a slot in the machine. With repetition, the poker chips became conditioned reinforcers. Their value was evident from the fact that the chimpanzees would work for them, save them, and sometimes try to steal them from one another.

Money is the best example of a secondary reinforcer in human society. You have learned that getting money is associated with buying food or material things. Other examples of secondary reinforcers would include praise, status, and prestige. All of these items are associated with a primary reinforcer and have acquired value, so they reinforce certain types of behavior when used.

primary reinforcer: stimulus that is naturally rewarding, such as food or water

secondary reinforcer: stimulus such as money that becomes reinforcing through its link with a primary reinforcer

SCHEDULES OF REINFORCEMENT

One important factor in operant conditioning is the timing and frequency of reinforcement. Behavior that is reinforced every time it occurs is said to be on a *continuous schedule* of reinforcement. You might suppose that behavior would best be maintained by reinforcing every response. However, when positive reinforcement occurs only intermittently or on a *partial schedule,* the responses are generally more stable and last longer once they are learned. A person or animal that is continuously reinforced for a behavior tends to maintain that behavior only when the reinforcement is given. If the reinforcement stops, the behavior quickly undergoes extinction. For example, a rat learns to press a bar most rapidly when it receives food each time it does so. When the rat stops receiving food each time it presses the bar, however, it quickly stops its bar-pressing. Behaviors that are acquired on partial schedules of reinforcement are established more slowly but are more persistent. For example, a rat that is only sometimes rewarded with food for pressing a bar will continue to press even though no food appears. Rats and humans that are reinforced on partial schedules of reinforcement cannot predict when the next reinforcement will occur, so they have learned to be persistent.

Skinner discovered the strength of partial reinforcement when his apparatus kept breaking down. Skinner found that the rats kept responding even though they were reinforced randomly. In fact, the rats responded with even greater endurance.

Although intermittent reinforcement may be arranged in a number of ways, four basic methods, or schedules, have been studied in the laboratory (see Figure 9.7). Schedules of partial reinforcement may be based either on the *number* of correct responses that the animal makes between reinforcements (*ratio* schedule) or on the *amount of time* that elapses before reinforcement is given (*interval* schedule). In either case, reinforcement may appear on a *fixed,* or predictable, schedule or on a *variable,* or unpredictable, schedule. The four basic schedules result from the combination of these four possibilities. People and animals respond differently to each type.

- In a **fixed-ratio schedule,** reinforcement depends on a specified quantity of responses, such as rewarding every fourth response. The student who receives a good grade after completing a specified amount of work and the typist who is paid by the number of pages

Quick Lab

What reinforcement schedules operate in your classroom?

Do you think that students would do schoolwork if there were no grading system? What reinforcements would operate if grades were abolished?

Procedure
1. Identify the types of reinforcers that operate in your classroom.
2. Make a chart that lists the type of reinforcer (primary, secondary, positive, negative) and the classroom behavior it usually elicits.
3. Devise a system for your classroom that could replace the existing reinforcers with new ones (and achieve the same results).

Analysis
1. Describe how the new reinforcers operate.
2. Indicate what responses the new reinforcers are supposed to elicit.

See the Skills Handbook, page 622, for an explanation of designing an experiment.

fixed-ratio schedule: schedule of reinforcement in which a specific number of correct responses is required before reinforcement can be obtained completed are on fixed-ratio schedules. People tend to work hard on fixed-ratio schedules. Another example would be dentists who get paid $75 for *each* cavity repaired or filled.

variable-ratio schedule: schedule of reinforcement in which an unpredictable number of responses are required before reinforcement can be obtained

- A **variable-ratio schedule** does not require that a fixed or set number of responses be made for each reinforcement, as in the fixed-ratio schedule. Rather, the number of responses needed for a reinforcement changes from one time to the next. Slot machines are a good example of a variable-ratio schedule. They are set to pay off after a varying number of attempts at pulling the handle. Generally, animals on variable-ratio schedules of reinforcement tend to work or respond at a steady, high rate. Since the reinforcement is unpredictable, there is typically no pause after a reward because it is possible that a reward will occur on the very next response. Door-to-door salespeople and individuals who do telephone surveys are also operating on variable-ratio schedules since they never know how many doorbells they will have to ring or how many calls they will have to make before they make a sale or find someone who will answer the survey.

fixed-interval schedule: schedule of reinforcement in which a specific amount of time must elapse before a response will elicit reinforcement

- On a **fixed-interval schedule,** the first correct response after a specified amount of time is reinforced. The time interval is always the same. Once animals gain experience with a fixed-interval reinforcement schedule, they adjust their response rates. Since no reinforcement occurs for a period of time no matter what their behavior, they learn to stop responding immediately after reinforcement is given and then begin to respond again toward the end of the interval. The result is regular, recurring periods of inactivity followed by short bursts of responding. Your teachers, for example, often give quizzes or tests on a fixed-interval schedule. It is likely that you will study feverishly the day before a test but study much less immediately afterwards.

	Ratio	Interval
Fixed schedules	**Fixed Ratio** (reinforcement after a fixed number of responses) • being paid for every 10 pizzas made • being allowed no more than five fouls in a basketball game	**Fixed Interval** (reinforcement of first response after a fixed amount of time has passed) • cramming for an exam • picking up your check from your part-time job
Variable schedules	**Variable Ratio** (reinforcement after varying number of responses) • playing a slot machine • sales commissions	**Variable Interval** (reinforcement of first response after varying amounts of time) • surprise (pop) quizzes in class • dialing a friend on the phone and getting a busy signal

Figure 9.7   Partial Schedules of Reinforcement

B.F. Skinner pointed out many examples of how schedules of reinforcement maintain and control different behaviors. The different schedules produce different response rates. *How does a fixed-ratio schedule differ from a fixed-variable schedule of reinforcement?*

- On a **variable-interval schedule**, the time at which the reinforcement is given changes. If you are trying to call a friend, but the line is busy, what do you do? You keep trying. The reinforcer will be gained the first time you dial after your friend has hung up, but you do not know when that is going to occur. The usual response rate on a variable-interval schedule is slow, but steady—slower than on any other schedule of partial reinforcement. In fact, your eagerness to reach your friend probably will determine roughly how often you try the phone again . . . and again.

In summary, ratio schedules are based on numbers of responses, while interval schedules are based on time. Responses are more resistant to extinction when reinforced on a variable rather than on a fixed schedule. To be most effective, however, the reinforcement must be consistent for the same type of behavior, although it may not occur each time the behavior does. The complexity of our behavior means that most reinforcers in human relationships are on a variable schedule. How people will react cannot always be predicted.

SHAPING AND CHAINING

Operant conditioning is not limited to simple behaviors. When you acquire a skill such as knitting, photography, playing basketball, or talking persuasively, you learn more than just a single new stimulus-response relationship. You learn a large number of them, and you learn how to put them together into a large, smooth-flowing unit.

Shaping is a process in which reinforcement is used to sculpt new responses out of old ones. An experimenter can use this method to teach a rat to do something it has never done before and would never do if left to itself. He or she can shape it, for example, to raise a miniature flag. The rat is physically capable of standing on its hind legs and using its mouth to pull a miniature flag-raising cord, but at present it does not do so. The rat probably will not perform this unusual action by accident, so the experimenter begins by rewarding the rat for any action similar to the wanted responses, using reinforcement to produce closer and closer approximations of the desired behavior.

Imagine the rat roaming around on a table with the flag apparatus in the middle. The rat inspects everything and finally sniffs at the flagpole. The experimenter immediately reinforces this response by giving the rat a food pellet. Now the rat frequently sniffs the flagpole, hoping to get another pellet, but the experimenter waits until the rat lifts a paw before he gives it another reward. This process continues with the experimenter reinforcing close responses and then waiting for even closer ones. Eventually, the experimenter has the rat on its hind legs nibbling at the cord. Suddenly the rat seizes the cord in its teeth and yanks it.

Figure 9.8   Clicker Training

Clicker training is a form of shaping. The trainer waits for the dog to sit on its own. The instant its rear goes down, the trainer hits the clicker (an audio signal) and the dog gets the treat. The clicker acts as an acoustical marker to tell the dog "that's what I'm reinforcing." *How might you use shaping to teach a dog to shake?*

variable-interval schedule: schedule of reinforcement in which changing amounts of time must elapse before a response will obtain reinforcement

shaping: technique in which the desired behavior is "molded" by first rewarding any act similar to that behavior and then requiring closer approximations to the desired behavior before giving the reward

Immediately the rat is rewarded, and it begins pulling rapidly on the cord. A new response has been shaped. Shaping has been used to teach animals tricks. For example, if a television character points her finger to the ground and her dog immediately lays down, we need to remember that shaping was involved in the dog's behavior. If shaping is done properly, almost any animal can learn some unusual tricks.

Combining Responses: Chaining

In order to learn a skill, a person must be able to put various new responses together. Responses that follow one another in a sequence are combined into **response chains.** Each response produces the signal for the next one.

In learning, chains of responses are organized into larger *response patterns*. For example, the complex skill of swimming has three major chains that are combined to make up the whole swimming pattern—an arm-stroking chain, a breathing chain, and a leg-kicking chain (see Figure 9.9). After much practice, you no longer have to think about the different steps involved. The behavior takes on a rhythm of its own: the chains of responses flow naturally as soon as you dive into the water.

It is often necessary to learn simple responses before mastering the complex pattern. If you cannot hit a nail with a hammer, you certainly cannot build a house. Therefore, before a person can learn to perform a particular skill, he or she must learn all the lower skills that make the larger skill possible.

AVERSIVE CONTROL

Reinforcement refers to anything that increases the frequency of an immediately preceding behavior. Aversive, or unpleasant, consequences influence much of our everyday behavior. **Aversive control** refers to this type of conditioning or learning. There are two ways in which unpleasant events can affect our behavior—as negative reinforcers or as punishers.

Negative Reinforcement

In **negative reinforcement**, a painful or unpleasant stimulus is removed. The removal of unpleasant consequences increases the frequency of a behavior. It may help you to understand negative reinforcement if you remember that it *follows* and *negates*, or takes away, an aversive stimulus. B.F. Skinner provided this example:

response chain: learned reactions that follow one another in sequence, each reaction producing the signal for the next

aversive control: process of influencing behavior by means of unpleasant stimuli

negative reinforcement: increasing the strength of a given response by removing or preventing a painful stimulus when the response occurs

Figure 9.9   Swimming—A Response Chain

To learn to swim, you must first learn the arm stroke, then how to breathe properly, and finally how to kick your legs. *What similar response chains can you describe that you would have to develop to learn other skills?*

If walking with a stone in your shoe causes you to limp, removing the stone (negating it) allows you to walk without pain. Other examples of negative reinforcers are fear and experiencing disapproval of unwelcome behavior.

Two uses of negative reinforcement that psychologists have studied in detail are *escape conditioning* and *avoidance conditioning*. In **escape conditioning,** a person's behavior causes an unpleasant event to stop. Consider the case of a child who hates liver and is served it for dinner. She whines about the food and gags while eating it. At this point, her father removes the liver. The gagging and whining behavior has been thus negatively reinforced, and the child is likely to gag and whine in the future when given an unpleasant meal. This kind of learning is called escape conditioning because the behavior of the child allowed her to escape the liver meal.

In **avoidance conditioning,** the person's behavior has the effect of preventing an unpleasant situation from happening. In our example, if the child's past whining and gagging behavior had stopped the father from even serving liver, we would identify the situation as avoidance conditioning; the child avoided the unpleasant consequences because of past behavior. The reinforcer here is the reduction of the child's disgust—not having to eat liver.

escape conditioning: training of an organism to remove or terminate an unpleasant stimulus

avoidance conditioning: training of an organism to withdraw from an unpleasant stimulus before it starts

Punishment

The most obvious form of aversive control is punishment. In punishment, an unpleasant consequence occurs and decreases the frequency of the behavior that produced it. Negative reinforcement and punishment operate in opposite ways. In negative reinforcement, escape or avoidance behavior is *repeated* and increases in frequency. In punishment, behavior that is punished decreases or is *not repeated*. If you want to stop a dog from pawing at you when it wants attention, you should loudly say, "NO!" and reprimand it when it paws at you. Such actions are called *punishers* (see Figure 9.10).

As with reinforcers, the events or actions that serve as punishers depend on their effect on the learner. For example, if a young child in a large family seeks extra attention from her parents, that child may misbehave. In response the parents punish the child by reprimanding her. The reprimands are meant to be punishers. The reprimands, however, may actually serve as reinforcers for a child who wants attention. Perhaps sending her to her room every time she misbehaved would have been an appropriate punisher; this unpleasant stimulus would have discouraged her from repeating the behavior.

Disadvantages of Punishment

Psychologists have found several disadvantages in using aversive stimuli (punishment) to change behavior. For one thing, aversive stimuli can produce unwanted side effects such as rage, aggression, and fear. Then, instead of having to change only one problem behavior, there may be two

Figure 9.10 **Aversive Stimuli**

Punishment occurs when an unpleasant consequence following a behavior decreases the chances that the behavior will recur. *How might Calvin's tumbles act as punishers?*

or more. For example, children whose parents rely on spanking to control disobedience may also have to deal with the problem of their children's increased aggressiveness toward other children.

A second problem with punishment is that people learn to avoid the person delivering the aversive consequences. Children learn to stay away from parents or teachers who often punish them. One consequence of this is that such parents and teachers have less opportunity to correct the children's inappropriate behavior. Also, punishment is likely to merely suppress rather than eliminate such behaviors. The punished behavior is likely to occur at some other time or in some other place.

Punishment alone does not teach appropriate and acceptable behavior. Without positive coaching and modeling, the child may never learn the correct behavior, nor does the child understand what the parents think is the acceptable behavior in any situation.

SECTION 2 | Assessment

1. **Review the Vocabulary** Explain how the four schedules of partial reinforcement work.

2. **Visualize the Main Idea** In a chart similar to the one below, list four types of reinforcers and give an example of each.

Types of Reinforcers	Example

3. **Recall Information** What is the difference between escape conditioning and avoidance conditioning?

4. **Think Critically** What are aversive stimuli? Do you think that caretakers should use aversive stimuli to discipline children? Why or why not?

5. **Application Activity** Using principles of operant conditioning, design a plan to teach a puppy a new trick.

Social Learning

Reader's Guide

■ Main Idea
Social learning, consisting of cognitive learning and modeling, involves how people make decisions and act upon the information available to them.

■ Vocabulary
- social learning
- cognitive learning
- cognitive map
- latent learning
- learned helplessness
- modeling
- behavior modification
- token economy

■ Objectives
- Cite the principles involved in cognitive learning and modeling.
- Identify the principles of learning used in behavior modification.

EXPLORING PSYCHOLOGY

Would You Treat Bobo This Way?

Children were told to play while in another part of the room an adult "model" aggressively "played" with a 5-foot inflated Bobo doll. The model laid the Bobo doll on its side, sat on it, and punched it repeatedly in the nose. The model then raised the Bobo doll, picked up a mallet and struck the doll on the head, then kicked the doll around the room. Following this experience, the youngsters were brought to a room that contained many attractive toys and the Bobo doll. The children exhibited a good deal of aggressive behavior toward the Bobo doll—behavior resembling that of the adult model.

—adapted from "Transmission of Aggression Through Imitation of Aggressive Models" by Albert Bandura, Dorothea Ross, and Sheila A. Ross, published in *Journal of Abnormal and Social Psychology,* 1961

Why did the children display such aggressive behavior? Albert Bandura performed the study above in 1961 to demonstrate that the children learned aggressive behaviors simply by watching a model perform these behaviors. The study illustrated the third type of learning, called **social learning.** Social learning theorists view learning as purposeful—going beyond mechanical responses to stimuli or reinforcement. The two types of social learning are cognitive learning and modeling.

social learning: form of learning in which the organism observes and imitates the behavior of others

"THEN, AS YOU CAN SEE, WE GIVE THEM SOME MULTIPLE CHOICE TESTS."

Figure 9.11   Mazes and Maps

This cartoonist exaggerates the cognitive learning capabilities of rats. *In what ways do humans use information obtained from latent learning in daily life?*

cognitive learning: form of altering behavior that involves mental processes and may result from observation or imitation

cognitive map: a mental picture of spatial relationships or relationships between events

latent learning: learning that is not demonstrated by an immediate, observable change in behavior

COGNITIVE LEARNING

Cognitive learning focuses on how information is obtained, processed, and organized. Such learning is concerned with the *mental* processes involved in learning. Latent learning and learned helplessness are examples of cognitive learning.

Latent Learning and Cognitive Maps

In the 1930s, Edward Tolman argued that learning involved more than mechanical responses to stimuli; it involved mental processes. Tolman would place a rat in a maze and allow it to explore the maze without giving the rat any reinforcement, such as food. Then he would place food at the end of the maze and record which path the rat took to reach the food. The rat quickly learned to take the shortest route to the food. Next, Tolman blocked the shortest path to the food. The rat then followed the next shortest path to the food. Tolman believed that the rat had developed a **cognitive map** of the maze. A cognitive map is a mental picture of a place, such as the maze. The rats had developed a cognitive map of the maze when allowed to explore the maze on their own.

Tolman called the type of learning demonstrated by the rat **latent learning.** Latent learning is not demonstrated by an immediately observable change in behavior at the time of the learning. Although the learning typically occurs in the absence of a reinforcer, it may not be demonstrated until a reinforcer appears. For example, have you ever had to locate a building or street in a section of your city or town that you were unfamiliar with? You may have been through that section of town before and remembered details such as an unusual sign or large parking lot. Remembering these details may have helped you find the building or street you were looking for. You had learned some details without intending to do so.

Learned Helplessness

Psychologists have shown that general learning strategies can affect a person's relationship to the environment. For example, if a person has numerous experiences in which his or her actions have no effect, he or she may learn a general strategy of helplessness or laziness.

In the first stage of one study (Hiroto, 1974), one group of college students were able to turn off an unpleasant loud noise, while another group had no control over the noise. Later, all were placed in a situation in which they merely had to move a lever to stop a similar noise. Only the ones who had control over the noise in the first place learned to turn it off. The others did not even try!

It is not hard to see how these results can apply to everyday situations. In order to be able to try hard and to be full of energy, people must learn that their actions *do* make a difference. If rewards come without effort, a person never learns to work (learned laziness). If pain comes no matter how hard one tries, a person gives up. This occurrence is called **learned helplessness.**

Martin Seligman believes that learned helplessness is one major cause of depression. He reasons that when people are unable to control events in their lives, they generally respond in one of the following ways. They may be less motivated to act and thus stop trying. They may experience a lowered sense of self-esteem and think negatively about themselves. They may also feel depressed (see Figure 9.12).

Seligman identified three important elements of learned helplessness: *stability, globality,* and *internality.* Stability refers to the person's belief that the state of helplessness results from a permanent characteristic. For example, a student who fails a math test can decide that the problem is either temporary ("I did poorly on this math test because I was sick") or *stable* ("I never have done well on math tests and never will"). Similarly, the person can decide that the problem is either specific ("I'm no good at math tests") or *global* ("I'm just dumb"). Both stability and globality focus on the student—on *internal* reasons for failure. The student could have decided that the problem was external ("This was a bad math test") instead of internal. People who attribute an undesirable outcome to their own inadequacies will probably experience depression along with guilt and self-blame.

learned helplessness: condition in which repeated attempts to control a situation fail, resulting in the belief that the situation is uncontrollable

---

Figure 9.12   Learned Helplessness

Examples of How Learned Helplessness Develops

- Parents punish children constantly for any and all offenses.
- You are overly critical of all your friend's actions.
- A student is placed in an advanced math course without proper preparation (taking and passing the basic math course first).

Common Factors of Learned Helplessness Situations

| Subjects believe they have no control over their own environment. | Success seems a matter of luck rather than skill. |

What happens when it is impossible for a learner to have an effect on the environment? What happens when a learner is punished and cannot escape the punishment? The learner may give up trying to learn. *How can learned helplessness cause depression?*

More About...

TV and Violence

Before you turn 18 years old, you probably will have witnessed 18,000 simulated murders on TV. What effect does this have on you? Since the 1960s more than 3,000 studies have investigated the link between television violence and real violence.

A study released in 1996 (Mediascope National Television Violence Study [NTVS]) found that by watching violence on television, viewers risk the following results: (1) They learn to behave violently. (2) They become more desensitized to violence. (3) They become more fearful of being attacked.

The study also found the following:

- Perpetrators go unpunished in 73 percent of all violent scenes.

- 47 percent of violent scenes show no harm to victims, while 58 percent show no pain.

- 25 percent of violent scenes on TV involve handguns.

- Only 4 percent of violent programs emphasize a nonviolent theme.

- Less than 3 percent of violent scenes feature close-ups, while only 15 percent show blood.

modeling: learning by imitating others; copying behavior

Reading Check

How does observational learning differ from disinhibition?

MODELING

The second type of social learning is **modeling.** When you go to a concert for the first time, you may be very hesitant about where to go, when to enter (especially if you are late), when to clap, how to get a better seat after the first intermission, and so on. So you observe others, follow them, and soon you are an "old hand." This illustrates a third type of learning—observation and imitation.

The general term for this kind of learning is *modeling.* It includes three different types of effects. In the simplest case—the first type of modeling—the behavior of others simply increases the chances that we will do the same thing. We clap when others do, look up at a building if everyone else is looking there, and copy the styles and verbal expressions of our peers. No learning occurs in this case, in the sense of acquiring new responses. We simply perform old responses that we otherwise might not be using at the time.

The second type of modeling is usually called *observational learning,* or imitation. In this sort of learning an observer watches someone perform a behavior and is later able to reproduce it closely, though the observer was unable to do this before observing the model. An example is watching someone else do an unfamiliar dance step and afterward being able to do the dance step yourself.

Have you ever noticed that some children seem to behave in a manner similar to their parents? Albert Bandura suggested that we watch models perform and then imitate the models' behavior. Bandura and his colleagues demonstrated observational learning by using a Bobo doll (see Exploring Psychology on page 259). The experimenters found that children were more likely to act aggressively after they had observed aggressive behavior.

Individual differences in personality may help to explain why people act differently when shown the same movie containing violent material. The American Psychological Association (APA) Commission on Violence and Youth (1993) reported that personal qualities do play a role. One child may learn that violence is right and another child may view violence as pitiful. Others have found that more aggressive children seek out violent television and are also more affected by it.

A third type of modeling involves *disinhibition.* When an observer watches someone else engage in a threatening activity without being punished, the observer may find it easier to engage in that behavior later. For example, someone with a snake phobia may watch another person handling snakes. Such observation may help alleviate the phobia. This procedure is used in clinical work as we will see in the chapter on therapies (Chapter 17).

Figure 9.13   The Imitation of Others

Social learning theorists argue that much learning results from observing the behavior of others and from imagining the consequences of our own behavior. *What behaviors might this child be learning?*

Inflated doll similar to Bobo doll

BEHAVIOR MODIFICATION

The term *behavior modification* often appears in magazine articles describing research on changing people's behavior through drugs, "mind control," or even brain surgery. In fact, it is none of these things. **Behavior modification** refers to the systematic application of learning principles (classical conditioning, operant conditioning, and social learning) to change people's actions and feelings. When you give your little brother a quarter to leave you alone, that is very much like behavior modification. Behavior modification involves a series of well-defined steps to change behavior. The success of each step is carefully evaluated to find the best solution for a given situation.

The behavior modifier usually begins by defining a problem in concrete terms. For example, Johnnie's mother might complain that her son is messy. If she used behavior modification to reform the child, she would first have to define "messy" in objective terms. For example, he does not make his bed in the morning, he drops his coat on the couch when he comes inside, and so on. She would not worry about where his bad habits come from. Rather, she would work out a system of rewards and punishments aimed at getting Johnnie to make his bed, hang up his coat, and do other straightening-up tasks.

Modeling, operant conditioning, and classical conditioning principles have been used in behavior modification. Classical conditioning principles are particularly useful in helping people to overcome fears, and we shall discuss them when we consider the problem of treating psychological disorders (Chapter 17). Modeling is often used to teach desired behaviors. In addition, as you will see in the following examples, operant conditioning principles have also been applied to everyday problems.

behavior modification: systematic application of learning principles to change people's actions and feelings

Computer-Assisted Instruction

Some instructors teach their students by a conversational method very similar to what computer-assisted instruction (CAI) is using today. CAI is a refinement of the concept of programmed instruction that was

PSYCHOLOGY and You

How You Form Bad Habits

Do you procrastinate? For example, have you ever found yourself cramming for an important test the night before? Operant conditioning probably played a role in your bad habit of procrastination. You selected immediate positive reinforcement and delayed punishment. That is, you opted to spend your time doing something else, such as watching TV, instead of studying.

Procrastination provided the *immediate* reinforcement of giving you more leisure time. The punishment, lower grades or lack of sleep the day before the test, was *delayed*. Many bad habits are formed when people follow this pattern of immediate reinforcement and delayed punishment.

token economy: conditioning in which desirable behavior is reinforced with valueless objects, which can be accumulated and exchanged for valued rewards

introduced by S.L. Pressey (1933) and refined by B.F. Skinner in the 1950s.

The essential concept of programmed instruction is based on operant conditioning. The material to be learned is broken down into simpler units called "frames." Each time the student shows that she or he has learned the information in a frame, the student is given positive reinforcement in the form of new information, choices, or point rewards similar to those used in video games. Each question, or "prompt," builds on information already mastered. The computer retains (as does the student) exactly what the learner understands on the basis of the student's answers to questions.

Several principles of learning are at work in CAI. The student is learning complex material through a response chain. She or he is reinforced constantly. Knowledge is being shaped in a systematic and predictable way. The student is able to have a dialogue with the instructor on every point, which is impossible for a class of students in a conventional setting.

Token Economies

Psychologists tried an experiment with a group of extremely troubled boys in Washington, D.C. In fact, the boys had been labeled "uneducable" and placed in the National Training School. The experimenters used what is known as a **token economy** to motivate the boys. The youngsters received points—or secondary reinforcers—for good grades on tests. They could "cash in" these points for such rewards as snacks, lounge privileges, or items in a mail-order catalog. Within a few months, a majority of the students showed a significant increase in IQ scores (an average gain of twelve-and-a-half points). The boys continued to improve in the months that followed, showing that they were, indeed, educable (Cohen & Filipczak, 1971).

In token economies, people are systematically paid to act appropriately. In the real world, behaviorists argue, the rewards are just as real; they are simply less systematic. In overcrowded mental hospitals, for example, the only way some patients can get attention is by "acting crazy." Most staff members

Figure 9.14   How Social Learning Works

Social learning theorists argue that much learning results from observing the behavior of others and from imagining the consequences of our own behavior. *What role does the environment play in social learning?*

simply do not have time to bother with people who are not causing trouble. Since attention from the staff is reinforcing for these patients, in effect, people are rewarded for undesirable behavior. By systematically rewarding only desirable behavior, token economies have been set up in prisons, mental hospitals, halfway houses, and classrooms.

Self-Control

One of the most important features in behavior modification is an emphasis on asking people to set up personal systems of rewards and punishments to shape their own thoughts and actions—this is a self-control program. As in any application of behavior modification, the first step in self-control is to define the problem. People who smoke too much would be encouraged to actually count how many cigarettes they smoked every hour of the day and note what kinds of situations led them to smoke. (After a meal? When talking to friends? Driving to work?) Similarly, people who have a very poor opinion of themselves would have to define the problem more concretely. They might begin by counting the number of self-deprecating remarks they make and thoughts they have. Researchers have found that just keeping track of behavior in this way often leads a person to start changing it.

The next step may be to set up a behavioral contract. A behavioral contract simply involves choosing a reinforcer (buying a new shirt, watching a favorite TV program) and making it depend on some less desirable but necessary act such as getting to work on time or washing the kitchen floor. One soda lover who had trouble studying decided

Figure 9.15   Improving Study Habits

Studying effectively is an active process. By using successive approximations (reading one more page each time you sit down to study) and positive reinforcements (rewarding yourself for productive studying), you can improve your study habits. The SQ4R and PQ4R methods are active methods of studying. *How can you improve your own study habits?*

SQ4R Method	PQ4R Method
Survey the chapter. Read the headings. Read any summaries. Your goal is to get a general understanding of the chapter.	**Preview** the chapter by surveying general topics to be studied.
Question the material. Formulate questions about the material as if you were the instructor writing the test.	**Question** yourself by transforming heads into questions.
Read carefully and try to answer the questions you formulated. If you become distracted or tired, stop reading. Pick it up later.	**Read** the section or chapter carefully while trying to answer the questions you created.
Write down the answers to your questions. Sum up the information in your own words.	**Reflect** on the text as you are reading to try and understand it, think of examples, and relate to information about the topic that you already know.
Recite to yourself what you have read. Recall main headings and ideas. Be sure to put the material into your own words. Answer questions aloud.	**Recite** the information by answering your own questions aloud.
Review the material. Summarize the main points in the chapter. Answer the questions you have formulated.	**Review** the material by recalling and summarizing main points.

that she would allow herself a soda only after she studied for half an hour. Her soda addiction remained strong, but her study time increased dramatically under this system.

Improving Your Study Habits

One psychologist designed a program to help students improve their study habits. A group of student volunteers were told to set a time when they would go to a small room in the library they had not used before. They were then to work only as long as they remained interested. As soon as they found themselves fidgeting, daydreaming, or becoming bored, they were to read one more page before they left.

The next day they were asked to repeat the same procedure, adding a second page to the amount they read between the time they decided to leave and the time they actually left the library. The third day they added a third page, and so on. Students who followed this procedure found that in time they were able to study more efficiently and for longer periods.

Why did this procedure work? Requiring students to leave as soon as they felt distracted helped to reduce the negative emotions associated with studying. Studying in a new place removed the conditioned aversive stimulus. Thus, aversive responses were not conditioned to the subject matter or the room, as they are when students force themselves to work. The procedure also made use of successive approximations. The students began by reading just one more page after they became bored and only gradually increased the assignment. In conclusion, it is important to note that classical and operant conditioning and social learning do not operate independently in our lives. All three forms of learning interact in a complex way to determine what and how we learn.

SECTION 3 | **Assessment**

1. **Review the Vocabulary** How is a token economy an example of behavior modification?

2. **Visualize the Main Idea** In a diagram similar to the one below, identify three important elements of learned helplessness.

Learned Helplessness

3. **Recall Information** How can you improve your study habits through conditioning?

4. **Think Critically** What principles of modeling should parents consider when rewarding and punishing their children? Provide reasons for your answer.

5. **Application Activity** Devise a plan of behavior modification (such as teaching your dog not to bark indoors or stopping your friend from cracking her knuckles) by applying learning principles.

Summary and Vocabulary

Learning is a relatively permanent change in behavior that results from experience. Not all behaviors we learn are acquired in the same way. Psychologists have studied three basic types of learning: classical conditioning, operant conditioning, and social learning.

Section 1 — Classical Conditioning

Main Idea: People acquire certain behaviors through classical conditioning, a learning procedure in which associations are made between an unconditioned stimulus and a neutral stimulus.

- Ivan Pavlov discovered the principle of classical conditioning.
- The four elements involved in classical conditioning are UCS, UCR, CS, and CR.
- Generalization and discrimination are complementary processes in which the participant responds to similar stimuli in the same manner or has the ability to respond differently to dissimilar stimuli.
- A CR will sometimes reappear spontaneously after extinction in a process called spontaneous recovery.
- Classical conditioning may be used to affect human behavior, such as taste aversions and fears.

Section 2 — Operant Conditioning

Main Idea: Operant conditioning occurs when the consequences that follow a behavior increase or decrease the likelihood of that behavior occurring again.

- Operant conditioning, as explained by B.F. Skinner, means that human behavior is influenced by one's history of rewards and punishments.
- Reinforcers (positive and negative, and primary and secondary) are stimuli that increase the likelihood that certain behaviors will be repeated.
- Behavior is reinforced according to continuous or partial reinforcement schedules that are based on numbers of responses or times of responses.
- Reinforcing responses that are increasingly similar to the desired behavior is a process called shaping.
- Punishments are stimuli that decrease the likelihood that certain behaviors will be repeated.

Section 3 — Social Learning

Main Idea: Social learning, consisting of cognitive learning and modeling, involves how people make decisions and act upon the information available to them.

- Latent learning is not demonstrated by an immediately observable change in behavior at the time of learning.
- If people have numerous experiences in which their actions have no effect, they may learn a general strategy of learned helplessness.
- Modeling is a type of learning that occurs as the result of observation and imitation.
- Behavior modification uses learning principles to change people's actions or feelings.

Chapter Vocabulary

classical conditioning (p. 241)

neutral stimulus (p. 242)

unconditioned stimulus (UCS) (p. 242)

unconditioned response (UCR) (p. 242)

conditioned stimulus (CS) (p. 242)

conditioned response (CR) (p. 242)

generalization (p. 244)

discrimination (p. 244)

extinction (p. 245)

operant conditioning (p. 250)

reinforcement (p. 251)

primary reinforcer (p. 252)

secondary reinforcer (p. 252)

fixed-ratio schedule (p. 253)

variable-ratio schedule (p. 254)

fixed-interval schedule (p. 254)

variable-interval schedule (p. 255)

shaping (p. 255)

response chain (p. 256)

aversive control (p. 256)

negative reinforcement (p. 256)

escape conditioning (p. 257)

avoidance conditioning (p. 257)

social learning (p. 259)

cognitive learning (p. 260)

cognitive map (p. 260)

latent learning (p. 260)

learned helplessness (p. 261)

modeling (p. 262)

behavior modification (p. 263)

token economy (p. 264)

Self-Check Quiz
Visit the *Understanding Psychology* Web site at
psychology.glencoe.com and click on **Chapter 9—
Self-Check Quizzes** to prepare for the Chapter Test.

Reviewing Vocabulary

Choose the letter of the correct term or concept below to complete the sentence.

a. extinction   **f.** secondary
b. behavior modification   **g.** token economy
c. unconditioned stimulus   **h.** modeling
d. generalization   **i.** operant conditioning
e. schedules   **j.** escape conditioning

1. A stimulus that elicits a predictable response without training is called a(n) _____.
2. Money is an example of a(n) _____ reinforcer.
3. _____ is a type of learning based on the consequences of actions.
4. In conditioning, _____ results from the repeated performance of a response without reinforcement.
5. _____ is the process of removing an aversive stimulus after it has started.
6. In a(n) _____, people are rewarded for behaving in an appropriate manner with value-less objects.
7. _____ refers to the systematic application of learning principles to change people's actions and feelings.
8. When children imitate the behavior of their parents, they are practicing a form of learning called _____.
9. The tendency for a stimulus similar to the original conditioned stimulus to elicit a response similar to the conditioned response is called _____.
10. The various ways that reinforcers occur after a behavior has been elicited are referred to as _____.

Recalling Facts

1. What are the differences between classical and operant conditioning?
2. How do taste aversions develop?
3. What are the four partial schedules of reinforcement, and how do they differ?
4. Create three diagrams like the one below on your paper—one each for classical conditioning, operant conditioning, and social learning. Fill in each with the definition, how it works, and an example of that type of learning.

5. Name and describe the three different types of modeling.

Critical Thinking

1. **Identifying Alternatives** Which of the schedules of reinforcement do your instructors generally use in conducting their classes? How would your classes be different if they used the other schedules?
2. **Applying Concepts** Businesses often make use of conditioning techniques in their commercials. Think of specific examples of such advertising. Describe how the principles of conditioning are used in those advertisements.
3. **Synthesizing Information** How might a therapist help cigarette smokers quit smoking using classical conditioning techniques? Using operant conditioning techniques? Using social learning techniques?
4. **Evaluating Information** Is punishment an effective tool of learning? Describe the advantages or disadvantages of using punishment to teach a child a behavior.
5. **Predicting Consequences** Do you think that it is effective to study films of videos to learn how to swing a golf club? Explain.

Assessment

Psychology Projects

1. **Classical Conditioning** Select some particular task that you find difficult or unpleasant. Whenever you begin to work at this task, play one of your favorite tapes or CDs. Do this for two weeks and then analyze your reactions. Have your feelings toward the music become associated with the task? Do you find it easier to work and complete the task? Write a report that explains your findings in light of what you know about conditioning techniques.

2. **Operant Conditioning** Go to a public place where you can watch parents and children interacting. Watch a parent-child interaction long enough to identify an aversive stimulus the parent or child may be using to control behavior. What particular behavior of the child is the parent attempting to change? What particular behavior of the parent is the child attempting to change? Are they successful? Collect your observations and conclusions in a report.

Technology Activity

Use the Internet to locate the Web site of a self-help or support group at which self-control and other self-improvement techniques are taught. You should look for the following stages/techniques: definition of the problem, establishment of behavioral contracts, and application of reinforcers in a program of successive approximations. Evaluate the site and summarize your findings in a brief report.

Psychology Journal

Reread the journal entry in which you described your attempts to teach a skill or task. Did you use classical conditioning, operant conditioning, or social learning techniques? Make a new entry, describing and identifying your learning techniques. Explain why your teaching strategy was successful or unsuccessful.

Building Skills

Interpreting a Chart Review the chart of O. Hobart Mowrer's experiment to stop bed-wetting below. Then answer the questions that follow.

Practice and **assess** key social studies skills with **Glencoe Skillbuilder Interactive Workbook CD-ROM, Level 2.**

Mowrer's Experiment	Stimulus	Response
Before Conditioning	Full Bladder (neutral stimulus) Alarm (UCS)	Does not produce wakening Awakening (UCR)
During Conditioning	Full Bladder (CS) paired with Alarm (UCS)	Awakening (UCR)
After Conditioning	Full Bladder (CS)	Awakening (CR)

1. What happened in this situation? What things were paired to lead to awakening?

2. Explain how the CS, UCS, CR, and UCR relate to the end result (awakening).

3. Which type of learning is displayed in this chart?

See the Skills Handbook, page 628, for an explanation of interpreting charts.

TIME
REPORTS

Fertile Minds

From birth, a baby's brain cells proliferate wildly, making connections that may shape a lifetime of experience. The first three years are critical

By J. MADELEINE NASH

R AT-A-TAT-TAT. RAT-A-TAT-TAT. If scientists could eavesdrop on the brain of a human embryo 10, maybe 12 weeks after conception, they would hear an astonishing racket. Inside the womb, long before the earliest dreamy images flicker through the cortex, nerve cells in the developing brain crackle with purposeful activity. Like teenagers with telephones, cells in one neighborhood of the brain are calling friends in another, and these cells are calling their friends, and they keep calling one another over and over again, "almost," says neurobiologist Carla Shatz of the University of California, Berkeley, "as if they were autodialing."

But these neurons—as the long, wiry cells that carry electrical messages through the nervous system and the brain are called—are not transmitting signals in scattershot fashion. That would produce a featureless static, the sort of noise picked up by a radio tuned between stations. On the contrary, evidence is growing that the staccato bursts of electricity that form those distinctive rat-a-tat-tats arise from coordinated waves of neural

Wiring Vision

WHAT'S GOING ON Babies can see at birth, but not in fine-grained detail. They have not yet acquired the knack of focusing both eyes on a single object or developed more sophisticated visual skills like depth perception. They also lack hand-eye coordination.
WINDOW OF LEARNING Unless it is exercised early on, the visual system will not develop.

activity, and that those pulsing waves, like currents shifting sand on the ocean floor, actually change the shape of the brain, carving mental circuits into patterns that over time will enable the newborn infant to perceive a father's voice, a mother's touch, a shiny mobile twirling over the crib.

The finding that the electrical activity of brain cells changes the physical structure of the brain is breathtaking. For the rhythmic firing of neurons is no longer assumed to be a by-product of building the brain but essential to the process, and it begins well before birth. The brain begins working long before it is finished. And the same processes that wire the brain before birth also drive the explosion of learning that occurs immediately afterward.

At birth, a baby's brain contains 100 billion neurons. Also in place are a trillion glial cells which form a kind of honeycomb that protects and nourishes the neurons. But while the brain contains virtually all the nerve cells it will ever have, the pattern of wiring between them has yet to stabilize. Up to this point, says Shatz, "what the brain has done is lay out circuits that are its best guess about what's required for vision, for language, for whatever." And now it is up to neural activity—no longer spontaneous, but driven by sensory experiences—to take this rough blueprint and refine it.

During the first years of life, the brain undergoes a series of extraordinary changes. Starting shortly after birth, a baby's brain produces trillions more connections between neurons than it can possibly use. Then the brain eliminates connections, or synapses, that are seldom or never used. The excess synapses in a child's brain undergo a pruning, starting around the age of 10 or earlier, leav-

FROM LEFT TO RIGHT: PENNY GENTIEU, JADE ALBERT, JADE ALBERT, PENNY GENTIEU

Wiring Feelings

WHAT'S GOING ON Among the first circuits the brain constructs are those that govern emotions. Around two months of age, the distress and contentment experienced by newborns start to evolve into more complex feelings: joy and sadness, pride and shame.
WINDOW OF LEARNING Emotions develop in increasingly complex layers.

ing behind a mind whose patterns of emotion and thought are unique.

Deprived of a stimulating environment, a child's brain suffers. Researchers at Baylor College of Medicine, for example, have found that children who don't play much or are rarely touched develop brains 20% to 30% smaller than normal for their age. Lab animals provide another parallel. Not only do young rats reared in toy-strewn cages exhibit more complex behavior than rats confined to sterile, uninteresting boxes, researchers at the University of Illinois have found, but the brains of these rats contain as many as 25% more synapses per neuron. Rich experiences, in other words, really do produce rich brains.

The new insights into brain development have profound implications for parents and policymakers. In an age when mothers and fathers are

Wiring Language

WHAT'S GOING ON Even before birth, an infant tunes into the melody of its mother's voice. Over the next six years, its brain will set up the circuitry to decipher and reproduce the lyrics. A six-month-old can recognize the vowel sounds that are building blocks of speech.
WINDOW OF LEARNING Language skills, sharpest early on, grow throughout life.

increasingly pressed for time, the results coming out of the labs are likely to increase concerns about leaving very young children in the care of others. For the data underscore the importance of hands-on parenting, of finding the time to cuddle a baby, talk with a toddler and provide infants with stimulating experiences.

The new insights have infused new passion into the political debate over early education and day care. There is an urgent need, say child-development experts, for preschool programs designed to boost the brain power of kids born into impoverished households. Without such programs, they warn, the current drive to curtail welfare costs by pushing mothers with infants and toddlers into the work force may backfire. "There is a time

scale to brain development, and the most important year is the first," notes Frank Newman, president of the Education Commission of the States. By three, a neglected child bears marks that are very difficult to erase.

But the new research offers hope as well. Scientists have found that the brain during the first years of life is so malleable that very young children who suffer strokes or injuries that wipe out an entire hemisphere can still mature into highly functional adults. Moreover, it is becoming clear that well-designed preschool programs can help many children overcome glaring deficits in their home environment. With appropriate therapy, say researchers, even serious disorders like dyslexia may be treatable. While inherited problems may place certain children at greater risk than others, says Dr. Harry Chugani, a neurologist at Wayne State University in Detroit, that is no excuse for ignoring the environment's power to remodel the brain. "We may not do much to

Wiring Movement

WHAT'S GOING ON At birth babies can move their limbs, but in a jerky, uncontrolled fashion. Over the next four years, the brain progressively refines the circuits for reaching, grabbing, sitting, crawling, walking and running.
WINDOW OF LEARNING Motor-skill development moves from gross to increasingly fine.

change what happens before birth, but we can change what happens after a baby is born," he observes.

Strong evidence that activity changes the brain began accumulating in the 1970s. But only recently have researchers had tools powerful enough to reveal the precise mechanisms by which those changes are brought about. Neural activity triggers a biochemical cascade that reaches all the way to the nucleus of cells and the coils of DNA that encode specific genes. In fact, two of the genes affected by neural activity in embryonic fruit flies, neurobiologist Corey Goodman and his colleagues at Berkeley reported, are identical to those that other studies have linked to learning and memory. How thrilling, exclaims Goodman, that the snippets of DNA that embryos use to build their brains are the same ones that will later allow adult organisms to process and store new information.

As researchers explore the once hidden links between brain activity and brain structure, they are beginning to construct a sturdy bridge over the chasm that previously separated genes from the environment. Experts now agree that a baby does not come into the world as a genetically preprogrammed automaton or a blank slate, but arrives as something much more interesting. For this reason the debate that engaged countless generations of philosophers—whether nature or nurture calls the shots—no longer interests most scientists. They are much too busy chronicling the ways in which genes and the environment interact. "It's not a competition," says Dr. Stanley Greenspan, a psychiatrist at George Washington University. "It's a dance." ■

—For the complete text of this article and related articles from TIME, please visit www.time.com/teach

ANALYZING THE ARTICLE

1. What "discovery" does this article detail?
2. **CRITICAL THINKING** Do you agree that your "uniqueness" was developed in the first three years of your life? Why or why not?

Memory and Thought

PSYCHOLOGY JOURNAL

Think back to your child-
hood and recall your earliest
memory. Describe this
memory in your journal. ■

PSYCHOLOGY
Online

Chapter Overview
Visit the *Understanding Psychology*
Web site at psychology.glencoe.com
and click on **Chapter 10—Chapter
Overviews** to preview the chapter.

Taking in and Storing Information

Reader's Guide

■ Main Idea
There are three processes involved in memory: encoding, storage, and retrieval.

■ Vocabulary
- memory
- encoding
- storage
- retrieval
- sensory memory
- short-term memory
- maintenance rehearsal
- chunking
- semantic memory
- episodic memory
- declarative memory
- procedural memory

■ Objectives
- Explain the three processes of memory.
- Describe the information-processing model of memory.

EXPLORING PSYCHOLOGY

A Life Without Memory

John Kingsley came to our attention in a shocking news story about an 83-year-old Alzheimer's patient who was found unattended in his wheelchair at a dog race track outside of Spokane, Washington. Attached to his chair was a note misidentifying him. John did not know who he was or how he got to the races. He could not help authorities find his family or his previous caregivers. John Kingsley, like many other patients during advanced stages of Alzheimer's disease, is alive, but without life. Without a memory of his past, or the ability to remember anything new, John's life is nothing but the existing moment.

—from *Psychology: Science, Behavior, and Life* by R.H. Ettinger, Robert L. Crooks, and Jean Stein, 1994

What would life without memory be like? Can you even imagine it? Consider all the material stored in your memory: your Social Security number, the capital of South Dakota, "The Star-Spangled Banner," your first love's phone number, the important generals of the Civil War, the starting lineup for the Boston Red Sox, your best friend in first grade, and so on. What kind of incredible filing system allows you to instantly recover a line from your favorite movie? How does all that information fit in your head?

THE PROCESSES OF MEMORY

memory: the storage and retrieval of what has been learned or experienced

The storage and retrieval of what has been learned or experienced is **memory.** What is the name of your favorite song? Who sings it? Who were your friends in eighth grade? To recall this information, you use three memory processes (see Figure 10.1).

encoding: the transforming of information so the nervous system can process it

The first memory process is **encoding**—the transforming of information so that the nervous system can process it. Basically you use your senses—hearing, sight, touch, taste, temperature, and others—to encode and establish a memory. You use *acoustic codes* when you try to remember something by saying it out loud, or to yourself, repeatedly. For example, in trying to remember the notes that make up the spaces in the treble clef of a musical measure, you would repeat the letters "F," "A," "C," and "E." When you attempt to keep a mental picture of the letters, you are using *visual codes.* Another way you might try to remember the notes is by using *semantic codes.* In this way, you try to remember the letters by making sense of them. For example, if you wanted to remember the letters "F," "A," "C," "E," you might remember the word "face." In this way, you have to remember only the word rather than the individual letters.

storage: the process by which information is maintained over a period of time

After information is encoded, it goes through the second memory process, **storage.** This is the process by which information is maintained over a period of time. How much information is stored depends on how much effort was put into encoding the information. Information can be stored for a few seconds or for much longer.

retrieval: the process of obtaining information that has been stored in memory

The third memory process, **retrieval,** occurs when information is brought to mind from storage. The ease in which information can be retrieved depends on how efficiently it was encoded and stored (as well as on other factors such as genetic background).

THREE STAGES OF MEMORY

Once the senses encode a memory in the brain, the brain must hold on to the input and store it for future reference. Psychologists distinguish three types of memory—sensory, short-term, and long-term—each of which has a different function and time span (see Figure 10.2).

Sensory Memory

sensory memory: very brief memory storage immediately following initial reception of a stimulus

In **sensory memory,** the senses of sight and hearing (among other senses) are

Figure 10.1 — **The Processes of Memory**

Memory involves three processes. *What does the first process of memory involve?*

Encoding
(recording information)

Storage
(saving information)

Retrieval
(calling up stored information)

loading from/
drive a

able to hold an input for a fraction of a second before it disappears. For example, when you watch a motion picture, you do not notice the gaps between frames. The actions seem smooth because each frame is held in sensory storage until the next frame arrives.

George Sperling (1960) demonstrated this phenomenon in an ingenious experiment. He used a tachistoscope (a device that presents a picture for a very brief time) to present a group of letters and numbers to people for a twentieth of a second. Previous studies had shown that if you present a stimulus like this,

7	1	V	F
X	L	5	3
B	7	W	4

people will usually be able to tell you four or five of the items. Sperling believed that people took a mental photograph of the letters and were able to read back only a few before the picture faded. Psychologists refer to this visual sensory memory as *iconic memory*. (Iconic memories are those that hold visual information for about a quarter of a second or more.)

Sperling then told the participants in his experiment that after he flashed the letters on the tachistoscope screen, he would present a tone. Upon hearing a high tone, the participants were to tell him the top row; a medium tone, the middle row; and a low tone, the bottom row. Once people learned this system, they were indeed able to remember about 75 percent of any one row. Thus, he proved that the participant retains a brief image of the whole picture so that he or she can still read off the items in the correct row after the picture has left the screen. Psychologists refer to auditory sensory memory as *echoic memory*. (Echoic memory is a type of sensory memory that holds auditory information for 1 or 2 seconds.)

Sensory memory serves three functions. It prevents you from being overwhelmed. Every second of every day, you are bombarded with various incoming stimuli. If you had to pay attention to all of these stimuli—what you are immediately seeing, hearing, smelling, feeling, and so on—you might easily feel overwhelmed. Since the information in sensory memory is short-lived, anything that you do not pay attention to vanishes in seconds. Sensory memory also gives you some decision time. The information in sensory memory is there for only a few seconds—just long enough for you to decide whether this information is worth paying attention to. Information that you choose to pay attention to is automatically transferred

Figure 10.2 Stages of Memory

Psychologists often compare human memory to a computer; however, unlike a computer, people can never fill their long-term memories so full that there is no room left for storage. *How do the capacities of sensory memory and short-term memory differ?*

	Sensory memory	Short-term memory	Long-term memory
Capacity	Virtually everything you see or hear at one instant	About 7 items in healthy adults	Vast; uncountable
Duration	Fraction of a second	About 20 seconds if not rehearsed	Perhaps a lifetime
Example	You see something for an instant, and then someone asks you to recall one detail	You look up a telephone number and remember it long enough to dial it	You remember the house where you lived when you were 7 years old

Reading Check
What is the difference between iconic and echoic memory?

to short-term memory. Finally, sensory memory allows for continuity and stability in your world. For instance, iconic memory makes images in your world smooth and continuous, whereas echoic memory lets you play back auditory information, giving you time to recognize sounds as words. The information held momentarily by the senses has not yet been narrowed down or analyzed. It is short-lived, temporary, and fragile. However, by the time information gets to the next stage—short-term memory—it has been analyzed, identified, and simplified so that it can be conveniently stored and handled for a longer time.

Short-Term Memory

short-term memory: memory that is limited in capacity to about seven items and in duration by the subject's active rehearsal

maintenance rehearsal: a system for remembering involving repeating information to oneself without attempting to find meaning in it

The things you have in your conscious mind at any one moment are being held in **short-term memory.** Short-term memory does not necessarily involve paying close attention. You have probably had the experience of listening to someone only partially and then having that person accuse you of not paying attention. You deny it, and to prove your innocence, you repeat, word for word, the last words he or she said. You can do this because you are holding the words in short-term memory.

Maintenance Rehearsal   To keep information in short-term memory for more than a few seconds, you usually have to repeat the information to yourself, in your mind or out loud. This is what psychologists mean by **maintenance rehearsal.** When you look up a telephone number, for example, you can remember the seven digits long enough to dial them if you repeat them several times. If you are distracted or make a mistake in dialing, the chances are you will have to look up the number again. It has been lost from short-term memory. By using maintenance rehearsal (repeating the telephone number over and over again), you can keep the information longer in short-term memory.

Psychologists have measured short-term memory by seeing how long a participant can retain a piece of information without rehearsal. The experimenter shows the participant three letters, such as CPQ, replaced by three numerals, such as 798, one second later. To prevent rehearsal, the participant has been instructed to start counting backward by threes and reporting the result in time with a metronome striking once per second. (A *metronome* is an instrument designed to mark exact time by a regularly repeated tick.) If the participant performs this task for only a short time, she or he will usually remember the letters. If kept from rehearsing for 18 seconds, however, recall will be no better than a random guess; the information is forgotten. Short-term memory lasts a bit less than 20 seconds without rehearsal.

Chunking   Short-term memory is limited not only in its duration but also in its capacity. It can hold only about seven unrelated items. Suppose, for

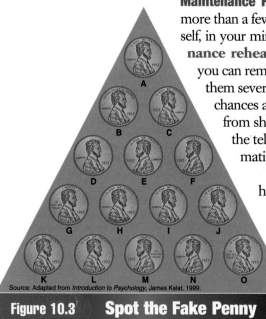

Source: Adapted from *Introduction to Psychology*, James Kalat, 1999.

Figure 10.3   Spot the Fake Penny

Which is the genuine penny among the fakes? (Ask your teacher for the correct answer.) Even though you live in the United States and probably see hundreds of pennies a week, it is difficult to identify the real one. Mere repetition, such as seeing something over and over again, does not guarantee a strong memory. *What could you do to remember exactly how a penny looks?*

Figure 10.4   Using Short-Term Memory

Glance quickly at the left figure in this pair, then look away. How many dots did you see? Now do the same with the right figure. You were probably surer and more accurate in your answer for the right figure. **Why is this so?**

example, someone quickly reels off a series of numbers to you. You will be able to keep only about seven or eight of them in your immediate memory. Beyond that number, confusion about the numbers will set in. The same limit is there if the unrelated items are a random set of words. We may not notice this limit to our capacity because we usually do not have to store so many unrelated items in our immediate memory. Either the items are related (as when we listen to someone speak), or they are rehearsed and placed in long-term memory.

The most interesting aspect of this limit, discovered by George Miller (1956), is that it involves about seven items (plus or minus two items) of any kind. Each item may consist of a collection of many other items, but if they are all packaged into one "chunk," then there is still only one item. Thus we can remember about seven unrelated sets of initials, such as COMSAT, DDT, SST, or the initials of our favorite radio stations, even though we could not remember all the letters separately. This is referred to as **chunking,** because we have connected, or "chunked," them together previously so that DDT is one item, not three.

One of the tricks of memorizing a lot of information quickly is to chunk together the items as fast as they come in. If we connect items in groups, we have fewer to remember. For example, we remember new phone numbers in two or three chunks (555-6794 or 555-67-94) rather than as a string of seven digits (5-5-5-6-7-9-4). As Figure 10.4 illustrates, we use chunking to remember visual as well as verbal inputs.

Even with chunking, storage in short-term memory is only temporary. Information is available, generally, for less than 20 seconds and no more than 30 seconds assuming no rehearsal has occurred. After that, it is part of the long-term memory. Short-term memory contains information that is "of possible interest." Information worth holding on to must be rehearsed—with intent to learn—to transfer it to long-term memory. Rehearsal without out intent to learn yields no transfer.

The Primacy-Recency Effect   The *primacy-recency effect* refers to the fact that we are better able to recall information presented at the beginning and end of a list. For example, read the grocery list at right.

Immediately after reading this list, write down as many of the items as you can remember. Which items did you remember? Most likely you

chunking: the process of grouping items to make them easier to remember

PSYCHOLOGY Online

Student Web Activity
Visit the *Understanding Psychology* Web site at psychology.glencoe.com and click on **Chapter 10— Student Web Activities** for an activity about memory.

milk
cheese
butter
eggs
flour
apples
grapes
shampoo
bread
ground beef
cereal
catsup
green beans
jam

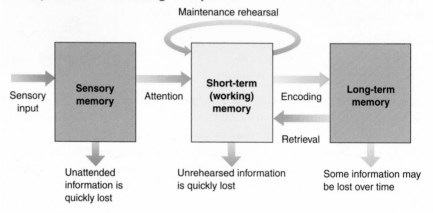

Figure 10.5   Three Systems of Memory

The moment you pay attention to information in sensory memory, that information enters short-term memory. Then that information remains in short-term memory for a few seconds. If you rehearse that information, it stays; if you do not, it disappears. *When does the process of encoding take place?*

Maintenance rehearsal

Sensory input → **Sensory memory** → Attention → **Short-term (working) memory** → Encoding → **Long-term memory**

Retrieval

Unattended information is quickly lost

Unrehearsed information is quickly lost

Some information may be lost over time

remembered the first four or five items in the list because you had more time to rehearse them. This is the primacy effect. You may have also recalled the last four or five items in the list because they were still accessible in short-term memory. This is the recency effect. However, you may have forgotten the middle items in the list. When trying to remember the middle items in a list, such as this one, your attention is split between trying to remember previous items and trying to rehearse new ones.

Working Memory Short-term memory is also called *working memory.* Working memory serves as a system for processing and working with current information. Working memory includes both short-term memory (events that just occurred) and information stored in long-term memory, now recalled for current information.

Long-Term Memory

Long-term memory refers to the storage of information over extended periods of time. Information is not stored like a piece of paper in a filing cabinet; it is stored according to categories or features. You reconstruct what you must recall when you need it. When you say a friend has a good memory, you probably mean he or she can recall a wide variety of information accurately. The capacity of long-term memory appears to be limitless. Long-term memory contains representations of countless facts, experiences, and sensations. You may not have thought of your childhood home for years, but you can probably still visualize it.

Long-term memory involves all the processes we have been describing. Suppose you go to see a play. As the actors say their lines, the sounds flow through your sensory storage. These words accumulate in short-term memory and form meaningful phrases and sentences.

Learning to perform activities requiring skills, such as in-line skating, is part of procedural memory.

You attend to the action and changing scenery in much the same way. Together, they form chunks in your memory. An hour or two later, you will have forgotten all but the most striking lines, but you have stored the meaning of the lines and actions in long-term memory. The next day, you may be able to give a scene-by-scene description of the play. Throughout this process, the least important information is dropped and only the essentials are retained (see Figure 10.5). A month or two later, without much rehearsal, you may remember only a brief outline of the plot and perhaps a few particularly impressive moments. In time you may not remember anything about the play. Other, more recently stored items block access to earlier memories or may even replace them. Yet if you see the play again, you will probably recognize the lines of the play and anticipate the actions. Although it has become less accessible, elements of the play are still stored in long-term memory.

Did You Know?

Prospagnosia Memory problems can sometimes take a surprising twist. One example is the peculiar condition known as *prospagnosia*, in which the patient is unable to recognize familiar faces—even his or her own face. People who have this condition can still perceive other aspects of faces, however, such as whether a person's expression is happy or sad. This memory problem usually results from a stroke or head injury.

Types of Long-Term Memory For almost a century, the study of memory focused on how long information was stored for usage. Then a Canadian psychologist, Endel Tulving (1972), proposed that we have two types of memory. **Semantic memory** is our knowledge of language, including its rules, words, and meanings. We share that knowledge with other speakers of our language. **Episodic memory** is our memory of our own life—such as when you woke up this morning. Stored here are things where time of occurrence is important.

L.R. Squire (1987) proposed a related model of memory. **Declarative memory** involves both episodic and semantic memory. This is information you call forth consciously and use as you need it. **Procedural memory** does not require conscious recollection to have past learning or experiences impact our performance. One form of procedural memory involves *skills*, learned as we mature—including both complex skills such as swimming or driving a car and simple skills such as tying a tie. As we gain a skill, we gradually lose the ability to describe what we are doing. Other types of procedural memory, such as fear of bugs, include habits and things learned through classical conditioning.

semantic memory: knowledge of language, including its rules, words, and meanings

episodic memory: memory of one's life, including time of occurrence

declarative memory: memory of knowledge that can be called forth consciously as needed

procedural memory: memory of learned skills that does not require conscious recollection

MEMORY AND THE BRAIN

What happens in the brain when something is stored in long-term memory? This question is highly controversial. Although psychologists agree that some physiological changes occur in the brain, they are only beginning to identify how and where memories are stored.

What physiological changes occur when we learn something? Some psychologists theorize a change in the neuronal structure of nerves occurs. Others contend that learning is based on molecular or chemical changes in the brain. The evidence is more and more clear that both sides are correct.

Figure 10.6   **Memory Centers in the Brain**

Researchers have identified the parts of the brain that are involved in memory. *What parts of the brain are involved in remembering the date of a special event?*

Cortex: Short-Term Memory
Our ability to remember words, facts, and events (declarative memory) in short-term memory depends on activity in the cortex.

Cortex: Long-Term Memory
Our ability to remember words, facts, and events (declarative memory) from the past depends on activity in the cortex.

Thalamus: Information Processing
Our ability to process sensory information, crucial to creating memories, depends on the thalamus.

Amygdala: Emotional Associations
Our ability to associate memories with emotions depends, to a large degree, on the amygdala.

Hippocampus: Long-Term Memory
Our ability to transfer words, facts, and events (declarative memory) from short-term into long-term memory depends on activity in the hippocampus.

Source: Adapted from *Introduction to Psychology*, Rod Plotnick, 1996.

What changes occur depend on the level at which you are examining the changes that learning creates.

Where does learning occur? There is growing evidence that formation of procedural memories involves activity in an area of the brain called the striatum, deep in the front part of our cortex (see Figure 10.6). Declarative memories result from activity in the hippocampus and the amygdala (Mishkin, Saunders, & Murray, 1984).

It is not clear yet how individual nerve cells—called neurons—establish connections with one another when learning occurs. It is clear that a very complex chemical process precedes the formation of new connections between neurons. Some have credited increases in calcium. Others talk of decreased potassium flow. Processes as diverse as increased protein synthesis, heightened levels of glucose, and other biochemical processes are involved (Kalat, 1992). Exactly how it all fits together remains an active area of research.

SECTION 1   Assessment

1. **Review the Vocabulary** List and describe the processes of memory.

2. **Visualize the Main Idea** In a diagram similar to the one below, list the different stages of memory and write an example of each.

Stages of Memory

3. **Recall Information** What is the purpose of maintenance rehearsal? How does the process work?

4. **Think Critically** In what ways is your memory like a computer? In what ways is it different? Explain your responses.

5. **Application Activity** Create a skit that illustrates how you would perform activities such as swimming or bicycle riding if you did not have procedural memory. Share your skit.

The Case of H.M.

Period of Study: 1953

Introduction: In 1953 a man, known by the initials H.M., underwent major surgery in an effort to cease or minimize the occurrence of epileptic seizures. The doctors chose to remove the hippocampus. Knowledge regarding the function of the hippocampus, however, was limited at that time.

The surgery proved quite effective in decreasing the frequency and severity of the seizures. In fact, preliminary tests showed that H.M.'s IQ had risen slightly because he now could better concentrate on tasks. As time passed, doctors detected an unforeseen and devastating result of the surgery—H.M. had lost the ability to store new long-term memories. Although he could remember events that occurred before the operation, H.M. could no longer retain information about events occurring after the surgery. Amazingly, he could still read, carry on conversations, and solve problems. He could recall information he learned five to ten minutes beforehand, but H.M.'s brain could not transfer that short-term information into long-term memory.

Hypothesis: The case of H.M. sparked many theories about the functions of the hippocampus region of the brain. One theory proposed that the transfer of short-term memory into long-term memory was fixed in the hippocampus region. H.M.'s memories before the operation remained mostly intact, but after the operation, there was no hippocampus region to which to transfer new memories—new information had nowhere to go and so could not be recalled at a later time.

Method: Doctors tested H.M. by presenting him with information, distracting him momentarily, and then asking him to recall the information first discussed. H.M. was unable to learn sequences of digits beyond the usual short-term memory span of seven digits. Likewise, H.M. could not recognize the photographs of people shown and described to him just a short time earlier.

Interestingly, H.M. demonstrated that he could learn difficult motor skills such as solving puzzles. Although H.M. clearly demonstrated skill in completing these activities, he reported never to have learned the activities. This implied that H.M. could learn new motor abilities even though he could not retain new long-term memories.

Results: The most apparent source of H.M.'s problem was a disruption in transferring short-term memory to long-term memory. This indicated that the hippocampus region is not involved with storing long-term memory, because recollection of pre-surgery events was intact. Thus, the hippocampus region of the brain *may be* the component involved in this memory transferring process but *definitely is* a pathway through which this information travels.

H.M. lived the rest of his life with the frustration of not remembering the current year, his age, or where he lived. He was placed in the care of a nursing home and had to be accompanied by someone everywhere he wanted to go. He needed constant reminders of what he was doing. He could not remember anything following the year 1953—the year of his surgery. Sadly, H.M. was literally "frozen in time."

Analyzing the Case Study

1. What type of surgery did H.M. have? Why?

2. What problems did H.M. encounter following the surgery? Why?

3. Critical Thinking If a virus suddenly destroyed your hippocampus, what effect would it have on your performance in school?

Retrieving Information

■ Main Idea

Stored memory can be retrieved by recognition, recall, and relearning.

■ Vocabulary

- recognition
- recall
- reconstructive memory
- confabulation
- schemas
- eidetic memory
- decay
- interference
- elaborate rehearsal
- mnemonic devices

■ Objectives

- Identify several memory retrieval processes.
- Explain the processes involved in forgetting.

EXPLORING PSYCHOLOGY

What a Memory!

Rajan Mahadevan stood before the packed house of the International Congress on Yoga and Meditation. He recited, from memory, the first 30,000 digits of pi, which is often rounded off to two decimal points, or 3.14. He did not err until the 31,812th digit. This feat took 3 hours and 44 minutes and earned him a place in the *Guinness Book of World Records*. . . .

Rajan can repeat a string of 60 numbers after a single hearing, while most of us can repeat an average of about seven random numbers. Rajan is one of only a half-dozen people in the world known to have such gargantuan memory powers.

Despite Rajan's unbelievable ability to memorize numbers, he seems to be worse than average at recalling faces, and he constantly forgets where he put his keys.

—adapted from *Introduction to Psychology* by Rod Plotnik, 1996

The example above illustrates the brain's tremendous capacity for storing and retrieving information. Stored information is useless unless it can be retrieved from memory. Once you have forgotten to send a card for your mother's birthday, for example, it is not very consoling to prove that you have the date filed away in your brain. We have all experienced the acute embarrassment of being unable to remember a close friend's name. There are few things in life more frustrating than having a word "on the tip of your tongue" and not being able to remember it.

The problem of memory is to store many thousands of items in such a way that you can find the one you need when you need it. The solution to retrieval is organization. Because human memory is extraordinarily efficient, it must be extremely well organized. Psychologists do not yet know how it is organized, but they are studying the processes of retrieval for clues.

RECOGNITION

Human memory is organized in such a way as to make recognition quite easy—people can say with great accuracy whether or not something is familiar to them. If someone asked you the name of your first-grade teacher, for example, you might not remember it. Chances are, however, that you would recognize the name if you heard it. Similarly, a multiple choice test may bring out knowledge that a student might not be able to show on an essay test. The ability to recognize suggests that much more information is stored in memory than one might think.

The process of **recognition** provides insight into how information is stored in memory. We can recognize the sound of a particular musical instrument (say, a piano) no matter what tune is being played on it. We can also recognize a tune no matter what instrument is playing it. This pattern of recognition indicates that a single item of information may be "indexed" under several "headings" so that it can be reached in a number of ways. A person's features, for instance, may be linked to a large number of categories. The more categories an item is filed in, the more easily it can be retrieved.

PSYCHOLOGY and You — Remembering Classmates

Few of us will ever forget our high school days, but how many of us will remember the names and faces of our high school classmates 10, 20, 30, and even 40 years after graduation? According to one study, apparently more of us will than you might think.

To find out just how long our long-term memory is, researchers showed nearly 400 high school graduates, ranging in age from 17 to 74, pictures from their high school yearbooks. Here are some of the surprising results:

- Thirty-five years after graduation, people could identify the faces of 9 out of 10 of their classmates. The size of the high school made no difference in their response.

- Fifteen years after graduation, participants could recall 90 percent of their classmates' names.

- Name recall began to fade to between 70 and 80 percent by the time people reached their late 30s.

- Women generally had better memories for names and faces than men.

Researchers explain these amazing results by looking at the way we collect this information in the first place. Our storehouse of names and faces is built over our four-year high school career, and continual repetition helps cement this knowledge in our memories for decades (Bahrick, Bahrick, & Wittinger, 1974; Kolata, 1993).

recognition: memory retrieval in which a person identifies an object, idea, or situation as one he or she has or has not experienced before

RECALL

More remarkable than the ability to recognize information is the ability to recall it. **Recall** is the active reconstruction of information. Just think about the amount of recall involved in a simple conversation. Each person uses hundreds of words involving all kinds of information, even though each word and bit of information must be retrieved separately from the storehouse of memory.

recall: memory retrieval in which a person reconstructs previously learned material

More About...

Eyewitness Testimony

One situation in which recognition is extremely important is in the courtroom. It is very convincing to a judge or jury when an eyewitness points to someone in the room and says, "He's the one who did it."

Elizabeth Loftus (1974) has shown that even after it had been proven that the eyesight of a witness was too poor for her to have seen a robber's face from where she stood at the scene of a robbery, the jury was still swayed by her testimony. Lawyers cite many cases of people falsely accused by eyewitnesses whose testimonies later proved to be inaccurate.

A person's memory of an event can be distorted in the process of remembering it. Shocking events, such as those involving violence, can disrupt our ability to form a strong memory. Without a strong, clear memory of the event, the eyewitness is more likely to incorporate misinformation into the recall. Jurors should remember that the eye is not a camera and recall is not videotape.

reconstructive memory: memory that has been simplified, enriched, or distorted, depending on an individual's experiences and attitudes

confabulation: the act of filling in memory gaps

schemas: conceptual frameworks a person uses to make sense of the world

eidetic memory: the ability to remember with great accuracy visual information on the basis of short-term exposure

Recall involves more than searching for and finding pieces of information, however. It involves a person's knowledge, attitudes, and expectations. The brain is not like a video recorder that plays back episodes intact. Remembering is an active process guided by our experience, knowledge, and cues we receive from the environment. Our recall seems to result from **reconstructive memory.** Our memories may be simplified, enriched, or distorted, depending on our experiences and attitudes. One type of mistake is called **confabulation,** which is when a person "remembers" information that was never stored in memory. If our reconstruction of an event is incomplete, we fill in the gaps by making up what is missing. Sometimes we may be wrong.

Occasionally our memories are reconstructed in terms of our **schemas.** These are conceptual frameworks we use to make sense of the world. They are sets of expectations about something that is based on our past experiences. Elizabeth Loftus and J.C. Palmer (1974) conducted a classic study on the roles that schemas play in memory reconstruction. Participants in this study watched a film of a two-car accident. They were then asked to fill out a questionnaire about the accident. One of the questions had four different versions. Some participants were asked, "About how fast were the two cars going when they *contacted* each other?" In the other versions of the questions, the words *hit, bumped,* or *smashed* were substituted for the word *contacted.* Participants given the question with the word *contacted* recalled a speed of 32 mph. Those given the word *hit* recalled a speed of 34 mph, those given the word *bumped* recalled 38 mph, and those given the word *smashed* recalled speeds of 41 mph. Therefore, the schemas people used—whether the cars contacted, hit, bumped, or smashed—affected the way they reconstructed the crash.

About 5 percent of all children do not seem to reconstruct memories actively. They have an **eidetic memory**—a form of "photographic memory"—an ability shared by few adults. Children with eidetic memory can recall very specific details from a picture, a page, or a scene briefly viewed. Photographic memory can occur in adults. It is extremely rare and involves the ability to form sharp visual images after examining a picture or page for a short time and then recalling the entire image later.

State-Dependent Learning

Have you ever become upset at someone and while doing so remembered many past instances of when you were upset at the same person? This is an example of state-dependent learning. *State-dependent learning* occurs when you recall information easily when you are in the same physiological or emotional state or setting as you were when you originally encoded the information. This is why some people advise you to study for a test in the same classroom or setting in which you will take the test. Being in a certain physiological or emotional state serves as a cue to help you easily recall stored information.

RELEARNING

While recognition and recall are measures of declarative memory, relearning is a measure of both declarative and procedural memory. Suppose you learned a poem as a child but have not rehearsed it in years. If you can relearn the poem with fewer recitations than someone with ability similar to yours, you are benefiting from your childhood learning.

FORGETTING

Everyone experiences a failure of memory from time to time. You are sure you have seen that person before but cannot quite place her. You have the word on the tip of your tongue, but . . . When information that once entered long-term memory is unable to be retrieved, it is said to be forgotten. Forgetting may involve decay, interference, or repression.

Some inputs may fade away, or **decay,** over time. Items quickly decay in sensory storage and short-term memory, as indicated earlier. It is not certain, however, whether long-term memories can ever decay. We know that a blow to the head or electrical stimulation of certain parts of the

Profiles In Psychology

Elizabeth Loftus

1944–

"One of the things that we know about memory for very upsetting experiences, traumatic experiences, is that the memory does not work like a videotape recorder."

The work of Elizabeth Loftus has been in the forefront of a raging debate over memory. Loftus has spent much of her life gathering evidence that memory is extremely fragile and not always accurate. She has shown that eyewitness testimony is often unreliable and that false memories can be triggered merely by suggestion. The manner in which a person builds memories can be altered by information acquired after the original experience.

Her work is controversial because it raises doubts about the validity of repressed memories of repeated trauma—such as that of childhood abuse. Loftus has testified in more than 200 trials, including the case of George Franklin. Franklin was sent to jail in 1990 for first-degree murder after his daughter Eileen "remembered," 20 years later, that her father had killed her friend in 1969. Eileen had recounted the details of the murder to the police in amazing detail. Eileen's memory of the event, though, changed—matching media descriptions of it. Loftus noted that memory changes over time, and as more time passes, our memories become more distorted. Loftus believes that there exists a very real possibility that Eileen unconsciously created the memory as a result of guilt, anger, fear, and desperation connected to the childhood abuse she suffered at the hands of her father.

decay: fading away of memory over time

"WHEN YOU'RE YOUNG, IT COMES NATURALLY, BUT WHEN YOU GET A LITTLE OLDER, YOU HAVE TO RELY ON MNEMONICS."

Figure 10.7   Memory Failure

You may experience memory failure because of decay, interference, or repression. *What is decay?*

interference: blockage of a memory by previous or subsequent memories

brain can cause loss of memory. The memories lost, however, are the most recent ones; older memories seem to remain. The fact that apparently forgotten information can be recovered through meditation, hypnosis, or brain stimulation suggests that at least some memories never decay. Rather, interference or repression causes people to lose track of them.

Interference refers to a memory being blocked or erased by previous or subsequent memories. This blocking is of two kinds: proactive and retroactive. In *proactive interference* an earlier memory blocks you from remembering related new information. In *retroactive interference* a later memory or new information blocks you from remembering information learned earlier. Suppose you move to a new home. You now have to remember a new address and phone number. At first you may have trouble remembering them because the memory of your old address and phone number gets in the way (proactive interference). Later, you know the new information but have trouble remembering the old data (retroactive interference). It is important to note that proactive interference does not lead to retroactive interference; the two are separate concepts.

It may be that interference actually does erase some memories permanently. In other cases the old data have not been lost. The information is in your memory somewhere, if only you could find it. According to Sigmund Freud, sometimes blocking is no accident. A person may subconsciously block memories of an embarrassing or frightening experience. This kind of forgetting is called *repression*. The material still exists in the person's memory, but it has been made inaccessible because it is so disturbing.

Amnesia

Some people also forget information due to amnesia. *Amnesia* is a loss of memory that may occur after a blow to the head or as a result of brain damage. Amnesia may also be the result of drug use or severe psychological stress.

Infant amnesia is the relative lack of early declarative memories. For example, why is it that we do not seem to remember much from when we were 2 or 3 years old? Although some children do form lasting memories, most memories from early childhood seem to fade away.

Psychologists have proposed several theories to explain infant amnesia. Freud thought that infant

Did You Know?

Flashbulb Memories   Ask your parents or grandparents where they were when they found out that John F. Kennedy had been assassinated, and they will most likely vividly remember the details. This ability is referred to as "flashbulb memory." These types of memories usually involve events that are very shocking, emotional, or have serious consequences. Scientists have concluded that flashbulb memories involve special kinds of encoding that occur when events are extreme and/or personal.

memories are repressed because of the emotional traumas of infancy. Others believe that because infants do not yet understand language, their memories are nonverbal, whereas later memories are verbal (once language is learned). Still others claim that the hippocampus may not be mature enough in infancy to spark memories or that infants have not yet developed a sense of "self" to experience memories.

IMPROVING MEMORY

Techniques for improving memory are based on efficient organization of the things you learn and on chunking information into easily handled packages.

Meaningfulness and Association

As we discussed earlier, using repetition, or maintenance rehearsal, can help you remember for a short period of time. In this method, words are merely repeated with no attempt to find meaning. A more efficient way of remembering new information involves **elaborate rehearsal.** In this method, you relate the new information to what you already know. The more meaningful something is, the easier it will be to remember. For example, you would be more likely to remember the six letters DFIRNE if they were arranged to form the word FRIEND.

Similarly, you remember things more vividly if you associate them with things already stored in memory or with a strong emotional experience. The more categories a memory is indexed under, the more accessible it is. If an input is analyzed and indexed under many categories, each association can serve as a trigger for the memory. If you associate the new information with strong sensory experiences and a variety of other memories, any of these stimuli can trigger the memory. The more senses and experiences you use when trying to memorize something, the more likely it is that you will be able to retrieve it—a key to improving memory.

For similar reasons, a good way to protect a memory from interference is to overlearn it—to keep on rehearsing it even after you think you know it well. Another way to prevent interference while learning new material is to avoid studying similar material together. Instead of studying history right after political science, study biology in between. Still another method is to space out your learning. Trying to absorb large amounts of information at one sitting results in a great deal of interference. It is far more effective to study a little at a time.

In addition, how you originally learn or remember something influences how readily you recall that information later. If a bit of information is associated with a highly emotional event or if you learned this bit of

Quick Lab

Can you improve your memory?
At one time or another we have all had to memorize items—a list of facts, telephone numbers, or a dialogue in a play. Are there ways to improve these memorization tasks?

Procedure
1. Give several friends and classmates the following list of numbers to memorize: 6, 9, 8, 11, 10, 13, 12, 15, 14, 17, 16, etc.
2. Tell some people to simply memorize the number sequence.
3. Tell others that there is an organizational principle behind the number sequence (which they are to discover) and to memorize the numbers with the aid of this principle. (The principle here is "plus 3, minus 1.")

Analysis
1. Which group was better at remembering the number sequence? Why do you think this is so? Write a brief analysis.

See the Skills Handbook, page 622, for an explanation of designing an experiment.

elaborate rehearsal: the linking of new information to material that is already known

PSYCHOLOGY and You

On the Tip of Your Tongue

Have you ever tried to remember something but could not quite do so, saying, "I know it; it's on the tip of my tongue"? What you experienced is called the tip-of-the-tongue phenomenon. Later, in a different situation, the information you were looking for earlier comes to you. Why does this happen? In certain cases, maybe you encoded the information in your memory with insufficient retrieval cues and just cannot find an association to retrieve the memory. In other cases, the information may be blocked through interference. When you think about other things, the information pops back into your memory.

mnemonic devices:
techniques for using associations to memorize and retrieve information

Reading Check
What are some common mnemonic devices?

information in absence of interference, you will more easily recall that information because of the strength of that memory.

Mnemonic Devices

Techniques for using associations to memorize information are called **mnemonic devices.** The ancient Greeks memorized speeches by mentally walking around their homes or neighborhoods and "placing" each line of a speech in a different spot—called the Method of Loci. Once they made the associations, they could recall the speech by mentally retracing their steps and "picking up" each line. The rhyme we use to recall the number of days in each month ("Thirty days has September") is a mnemonic device. In the phrase "Every Good Boy Does Fine," the first letters of the words are the same as the names of the musical notes on the lines of a staff (E, G, B, D, and F).

Another useful mnemonic device is to form mental pictures. Suppose you have trouble remembering the authors and titles of books or which artists belong to which schools of painting. To plant the fact in your mind that John Updike wrote *Rabbit, Run,* you might picture a RABBIT RUNning UP a DIKE. To remember that Picasso was a Cubist, picture someone attacking a giant CUBE with a PICKAX, which sounds like Picasso (Lorayne & Lucas, 1974). Mnemonic devices are not magical. Indeed, they involve extra work—making up words, stories, and so on. The very effort of trying to do this, however, may help you remember things.

SECTION 2 | Assessment

1. **Review the Vocabulary** What is the difference between proactive and retroactive interference? Between maintenance and elaborate rehearsal?

2. **Visualize the Main Idea** In a graphic organizer similar to the one below, explain the three processes of memory retrieval.

3. **Recall Information** What is state-dependent learning? How does it relate to studying and taking exams?

4. **Think Critically** What types of test questions do you prefer: those that require recall, such as essay questions, or those that require recognition, such as multiple choice questions? Why?

5. **Application Activity** Provide an example of a mnemonic device that helped you learn or remember something.

Summary and Vocabulary

Memory is a complex mental process that allows us to recognize friends and family as well as to do things such as drive, speak a language, and play an instrument. Psychologists have sought to understand memory and to find ways to improve it.

Section 1   Taking in and Storing Information

Main Idea: There are three processes involved in memory: encoding, storage, and retrieval.

- During encoding, you use your senses to encode and establish a memory.
- Storage is the process by which information is maintained over a period of time.
- Retrieval occurs when information is brought to mind from storage.
- There are three types of memory—sensory, short-term, and long-term—each of which has a different purpose and time span.
- Although psychologists agree that some physiological changes occur in the brain when something is stored in long-term memory, they are only beginning to identify how and where memories are stored.

Section 2   Retrieving Information

Main Idea: Stored memory can be retrieved by recognition, recall, and relearning.

- Human memory is organized in such a way as to make recognition quite easy.
- Recall involves a person's knowledge, attitudes, and expectations.
- Recall seems to be the result of reconstructive memory.
- People's memories are sometimes reconstructed in terms of their schemas.
- State-dependent learning occurs when you recall information easily when you are in the same physiological or emotional state as you were when you originally encoded the information.
- Forgetting can be the result of decay, interference, or repression.
- Memory can be improved through meaningfulness, association, lack of interference, and degree of original learning.

Chapter Vocabulary

memory (p. 274)
encoding (p. 274)
storage (p. 274)
retrieval (p. 274)
sensory memory (p. 274)
short-term memory (p. 276)
maintenance rehearsal (p. 276)
chunking (p. 277)
semantic memory (p. 279)
episodic memory (p. 279)
declarative memory (p. 279)
procedural memory (p. 279)
recognition (p. 283)
recall (p. 283)
reconstructive memory (p. 284)
confabulation (p. 284)
schemas (p. 284)
eidetic memory (p. 284)
decay (p. 285)
interference (p. 286)
elaborate rehearsal (p. 287)
mnemonic devices (p. 288)

Self-Check Quiz
Visit the *Understanding Psychology* Web site at
psychology.glencoe.com and click on **Chapter 10—Self-Check Quizzes** to prepare for the Chapter Test.

Reviewing Vocabulary

Choose the letter of the correct term or concept below to complete the sentence.

a. memory   **f.** recall

b. storage   **g.** confabulation

c. short-term memory   **h.** schemas

d. episodic memory   **i.** eidetic memory

e. procedural memory   **j.** elaborate rehearsal

1. _____ is the second memory process during which information is maintained over a period of time.

2. When you relate new information to what you already know you are practicing _____.

3. _____ is a mistake in memory during which a person "remembers" information that was never stored in memory.

4. The skills you develop when you learn how to swim become part of your _____.

5. The active reconstruction of information is called _____.

6. _____ are conceptual frameworks we use to make sense of the world.

7. _____ is the storage and retrieval of what has been learned or experienced.

8. The things you have in your conscious mind at any one moment are held in your _____.

9. When you remember what you did on your vacation, you are experiencing _____.

10. A small percentage of children have a(n) _____, or "photographic memory."

Recalling Facts

1. Using a graphic organizer similar to the one below, identify and describe the codes used to encode a memory.

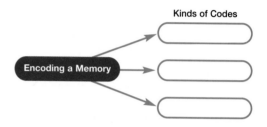

Kinds of Codes

Encoding a Memory

2. List two strategies for expanding the limits of short-term memory.

3. Describe the primacy-recency effect.

4. What are the two types of interference that block memory?

5. Describe five methods you can use to improve your memory.

Critical Thinking

1. **Evaluating Information**   Explain what methods you use to memorize items such as lists or phone numbers. Which method do you find most effective? Why?

2. **Analyzing Information**   How would having a photographic memory make your life different?

3. **Synthesizing Information**   Try to remember what you did on your last birthday. As you probe your memory, verbalize the mental steps you are going through. What processes do you use to remember?

4. **Making Inferences**   As a juror, what concerns might you have when hearing eyewitness testimony? Why?

5. **Applying Concepts**   Why is it important for teachers to make learning meaningful to their students?

CHAPTER 10 Assessment

Psychology Projects

1. **Taking in and Storing Information**   Research the latest findings about the workings of the brain in terms of memory. Share your findings in a written report. You might include diagrams in your report.

2. **Retrieving Information**   Research the use of repressed memories in recent child abuse cases. Find out the results of the cases and how effective the repressed-memory defense worked.

3. **Approaches to Memory**   Use this textbook and other sources to research several psychological, approaches to memory, such as psychoanalytic, behavioral, humanistic, or cognitive. Summarize your findings in a chart.

4. **Recall**   Pick several events that should produce flashbulb memories. Interview 10 people about their memories of the events, and identify similarities and differences in their remembrances.

Technology Activity

Search the Internet for Web sites that provide information to help you improve your memory. Several sites provide tips and techniques to help you remember a variety of facts, such as mathematical formulas. Explore and evaluate these sites, try out several tips for yourself, and then report your findings to the class.

Psychology Journal

Reread the journal entry you wrote about your earliest memory. Write an analysis explaining why you think this is your first memory and why it continues to stay in your mind. Explain whether any confabulation might be involved in this memory. Were other people involved? Is their recall of the memory consistent with the way you remember it? Explain.

Building Skills

Interpreting a Graph   The graph below shows the results of an experiment in which the ability to remember names and faces of classmates by high school graduates was tested. In a recognition test, participants were asked to match yearbook pictures of classmates with their names. In a recall test, participants were shown yearbook pictures and asked to simply recall the names. Review the graph below, then answer the questions that follow.

Recognition and Recall Test

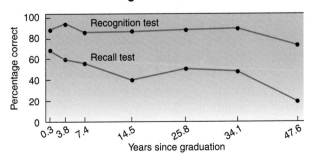

Source: Bahrick, Bahrick, & Wittinger, 1974.

 Practice and **assess** key social studies skills with **Glencoe Skillbuilder Interactive Workbook CD-ROM, Level 2.**

1. Which group was most able to recall the names of their classmates?

2. What percentage of participants recalled the names of their classmates 34 years after graduation? 47 years after graduation?

3. How did retrieving information using recall change over a period of 50 years?

4. What effect does time have on retrieving information when recall is used? When recognition is used?

5. When you remember past events and people, how accurate do you think your memory is? Explain.

See the Skills Handbook, page 628, for an explanation of interpreting graphs.

In 1953, doctors performed brain surgery on a man named Henry, also known as H.M. The doctors hoped to alleviate Henry's severe epileptic seizures by removing his hippocampus, where they believed the seizures originated. Although the surgery relieved Henry's seizures, he suffered severe memory problems. For years after the operation he cited the year as 1953 and could not encode new long-term memories, even though his existing long-term memories remained intact. Philip F. Hilts chronicled Henry's story in *Memory's Ghost*, published in 1995.

Reader's Dictionary

M.I.T.: Massachusetts Institute of Technology

hippocampus: a curved structure within the temporal lobe of the brain involved in transforming many kinds of short-term memories into permanent storage

MEMORY'S GHOST

BY PHILIP F. HILTS

We were out in the sun once, Henry in his wheelchair and I beside him, waiting for the taxi to take us for his brain scan. It was the usual changeable, disturbing weather of a Boston spring, but just now, it was bright and warm. "Great day!" I said. "And sunny!" As I said it, a shadow crossed the walk, and the sun dived into a cloud. Henry laughed. "Well, just as soon as you say it, it isn't!"

Across the street was a construction site. We watched at length; the crane—it must have been ten stories tall—swung out over the deep hole and back up to its bank, a huge bucket of gray muck gliding down. "I bet they are glad they don't have to haul

that all the way up," said Henry. I glanced up the street for the taxi, and quickly Henry's gaze followed. He wasn't sure why we were looking there, and he studied me. My head was turning back to the construction, and Henry's gaze settled there again, too. He watches and listens for clues, for the implications of a question, for hints at what the subject is, how he should feel, and how he should answer. How else could he be more than like a dog, waiting expectantly at the door? I imagine him walking, always a little uncertain, but compelled to press ahead while around him is a blank fog. "And I moved forward," said poet W.S. Merwin, "because you must live forward, which is away from whatever it was that you had, though you think when you have it that it will stay with you forever."

I recall one of my visits to Henry. As he talked with Dr. Corkin, who had come to get him for tests, I observed in silence. When she approached, he looked up, blank at first. I could almost put words to passing expressions on his face: Ah, a face that seems familiar. To talk to me? Yes—she takes up my eyes.

"How are you, Henry?"

He groped a little, feeling just behind him for something. "Fine, I guess," he said, and smiled a little. Again he watched, expectantly.

"Do you know what we're going to do today?"

I felt him turn metaphorically to search for an answer. Then he shrugged. "I don't remember."

But then she handed him his walker. He can grasp it, flip out the legs, set it just ahead of himself, and lean up into it.

"Why do you use a walker, Henry, do you know?"

A brief look into the fog. Nothing there. He looked down. "Well, it's my legs," he said. He quickly realized the humor in this too-obvious reply, and grinned.

Down the hall, he turned left, heading for the experiment room. How did his body know to go that way? Part of his brain has learned, though the other has not. The one that is supposed to keep track of what has been learned is missing.

At the plain gray table in the experiment room, Dr. Corkin asked, "Do you know where you are, Henry?"

Again, he looked out into a fog. But here! There is something! "Well, at M.I.T.!" He beamed; he gathered a scrap for his questioners; he always likes to please. It has taken decades of travel to M.I.T. and frequent talk of the place for him to know that if he's being tested, this must be M.I.T.

Finally, as we stood out in the sun, the taxi arrived to take us across the Charles River. We bundled the awkward wheelchair in the trunk, him in the back seat, and we took the taxi over to Brigham and Women's Hospital where the magnetic resonance scanner awaited him. It is more than a device, it is the size of a room, and it is not pressed against the patient like an X-ray scope, but surrounds the patient as he is inserted *within* the machine.

Henry was a bit dubious about this, especially as he had to remove all metal objects from his person. That meant his belt, and he was shy removing it in front of the women researchers in the room. He was more chagrined after he removed it and everyone could see that there was a paper clip holding his trousers together.

I sat in the room with him, while everyone else retreated to another room, behind a large observation window. They spoke to Henry by microphone, trying to reassure him by tone of voice while they were in fact being distant and cold. And that noise! It was like being in a closet with a jackhammer operating in slow motion.

From all this crudeness issued, on the other end of the computing systems and wires, an elegant, flickering color image. A live image of his brain, slice by slice, as the imager moved backward through his brain taking images one plane at a time. When the imager reached Henry's temporal lobes and the place where his middle brain should be, the researcher at the panel let out a low gasp. "Oh! That's beautiful!" he said. Used to peering at subtle shading differences denoting massive tumors, he was now confronted with a huge black hole in the center of the brain, the first thing of its kind he had ever seen.

The series of images lead to measurements, recalculations, new guesses. There is, Dr. Corkin has discovered, a little more of the hippocampus present than was thought. But the other bits of middle brain linked to it, the parahippocampal gyrus, the entorhinal cortex, and the perirhinal cortex are all destroyed: they must be an important part of the "hippocampal" system of memory consolidation.

The pictures from within the dome of Henry's skull are a bit startling. Of course, we could have guessed what they might look like. But it is not the same to guess as to see the lovely textured images of the brain and then the black, ragged edges where tissue has been sucked out.

Analyzing the Reading

1. What types of things does Henry seem unable to recall?
2. Why does the researcher seem excited by Henry's brain scan?
3. **Critical Thinking** Why does the author compare Henry to a dog?

Thinking and Language

PSYCHOLOGY JOURNAL

In your journal, answer the following question: If you increase the size of your vocabulary, will you think better? Use past experiences to explain your answer. ■

PSYCHOLOGY Online

Chapter Overview
Visit the *Understanding Psychology* Web site at psychology.glencoe.com and click on **Chapter 11—Chapter Overviews** to preview the chapter.

Thinking and Problem Solving

Reader's Guide

■ Main Idea
Thinking involves changing and reorganizing the information stored in memory to create new or transformed information, such as creative problem-solving strategies.

■ Vocabulary
- thinking
- image
- symbol
- concept
- prototype
- rule
- metacognition
- algorithm
- heuristic
- mental set
- functional fixedness
- creativity
- flexibility
- recombination
- insight

■ Objectives
- Identify the units of thought and the kinds of thinking.
- Explain strategies for and obstacles to problem solving.

EXPLORING PSYCHOLOGY

A Radical Assumption

Historians often refer to "the Copernican revolution" as a milestone in the history of science. Copernicus was a careful and creative scientist who eventually solved a problem that others before him had failed to solve: how to account for the movement of the planets in the heavens. . . . Copernicus finally created a theory that nicely predicted the movements of the planets. To do so, however, he had to make a radical assumption. Prior to Copernicus, everyone had taken it for granted that the sun and the other planets revolve around the Earth, and indeed, it looks that way to the naked eye. Copernicus argued that, if one made this assumption, it would be impossible to predict with accuracy the movement of the planets. His theory began with an alternate assumption, namely, that the Earth and the other planets in our solar system revolve around the sun.

—from *The Ideal Problem Solver* by John D. Bransford and Barry S. Stein, 1984

Going beyond memory, how do we think? How do we solve problems? How do we create ideas? How did Copernicus come up with his idea? If storage and retrieval were the only processes we used to handle information, human beings would be little more than glorified cameras and VCRs. Yet we are capable of doing things with information that make the most complex computers seem simple by comparison. These processes—thinking and problem solving—are most impressive when they show originality or creativity.

THINKING

thinking: changing and reorganizing the information stored in memory to create new information

You may view **thinking** as changing and reorganizing the information stored in memory to create new or transformed information. By thinking, humans are able to put together any combination of words from memory and create sentences never devised before—such as this one.

Units of Thought

The processes of thought depend on several devices or units of thought: images, symbols, concepts, prototypes, and rules. The most primitive unit of thought is an **image,** a mental representation of a specific event or object. The representation is not usually an exact copy; rather, it contains only the highlights of the original. For example, if an adult tries to visualize a grandmother who died when he was seven, he would probably remember only a few details—perhaps the color of her hair or a piece of jewelry that she wore.

image: a mental representation of an event or object

Imaging is an effective way to think about concepts. In 1971 two researchers (Shepard & Metzler) presented participants with 1,600 pairs of geometric images (see Figure 11.1). The researchers then asked the participants to determine if the objects in each pair were identical or different. The researchers discovered that the participants completed the task by rotating an image of one of the objects in their minds until they could see both patterns from the same perspective.

symbol: an abstract unit of thought that represents an object or quality

A more abstract unit of thought is a **symbol,** a sound or design that represents an object or quality. The most common symbols in thinking are words: almost every word is a symbol that stands for something other than itself. An image represents a specific sight or sound, but a symbol may have a number of meanings. That symbols differ from the things they represent enables us to think about things that are not present, to consider the past and future, and to imagine things and situations that never will be or were. Numbers, letters, punctuation marks, and icons are all familiar symbols of ideas that have no concrete existence.

concept: a label for a class of objects or events that share common attributes

When a symbol is used as a label for a class of objects or events with certain common attributes—or for the attributes themselves—it is called a **concept.** "Animals," "music," "liquid," and "beautiful people" are examples of concepts based on the common attributes of the objects and experiences belonging to each category. Thus the concept "animal" separates a group of organisms from such things as automobiles, carrots, and Roquefort cheese. Concepts enable us to chunk large amounts of information. We do not have to treat every new piece of information as unique, since we already know something about the class of objects or experiences to which the new item belongs.

prototype: a representative example of a concept

When we think of a concept, we often think of a representative example of it. When you think of a vehicle, for example, you might picture a car or a truck. This representation is called a **prototype.** The prototype you picture may not be an example that you have actually experienced. Most often it simply is an example that has most of the characteristics of the particular concept.

A more complex unit of thought is a **rule,** a statement of a relation between concepts. The following are examples of rules: a person cannot be in two places at the same time; mass remains constant despite changes in appearance.

Images, symbols, concepts, prototypes, and rules are the building blocks of mental activity. They provide an economical and efficient way for people to represent reality, to manipulate and reorganize it, and to devise new ways of acting. For example, a person can think about pursuing several different careers, weigh their pros and cons, and decide which to pursue without having to try every one of them.

Kinds of Thinking

People think in several ways. *Directed thinking* is a systematic and logical attempt to reach a specific goal, such as the solution to a problem. This kind of thinking, also called *convergent thinking,* depends heavily on symbols, concepts, and rules. Another type, called *nondirected thinking* (or *divergent thinking*), consists of a free flow of thoughts with no particular plan and depends more on images (see Figure 11.2).

Nondirected thinking is usually rich with imagery and feelings such as daydreams, fantasies, and reveries. People often engage in nondirected thought when they are relaxing or escaping from boredom or worry. This kind of thinking may provide unexpected insights into one's goals and beliefs. Scientists and artists say that some of their best ideas emerge from drifting thoughts that occur when they have set aside a problem for the moment.

In contrast, directed thinking is deliberate and purposeful. It is through directed thinking that we solve problems; formulate and follow rules; and set, work toward, and achieve goals.

A third type of thinking is **metacognition,** or thinking about thinking. When you tackle an algebra problem and cannot solve it, thinking about your strategy may cause you to change to another strategy.

PROBLEM SOLVING

One of the main functions of directed thinking is to solve problems—to bridge the gap mentally between a present situation and a desired goal. The gap may be between hunger and food, a column of figures and a

Figure 11.1   Using Imagery

Rotate pairs of images of the patterns below in your mind to make them match. Do the drawings in each pair represent the same object, or are they different objects? (Check with your teacher to find out which pairs match.) *How do we use images when we are thinking about something?*

a

b

c

Reading Check
What is the difference between a symbol and a concept? An image and a prototype?

rule: a statement of relation between concepts

metacognition: the awareness of one's own cognitive process

Figure 11.2   Directed vs. Nondirected Thinking

An old money-lender offered to cancel a merchant's debt and keep him from going to prison if the merchant would give the money-lender his lovely daughter. Horrified yet desperate, the merchant and his daughter agreed to let Providence decide. The money-lender said he would put a black pebble and a white pebble in a bag and the girl would draw one. The white pebble would cancel the debt and leave her free. The black one would make her the money-lender's, although the debt would be canceled. If she refused to pick, her father would go to prison. From the pebble-strewn path they were standing on, the money-lender picked two pebbles and quickly put them in the bag, but the girl saw he had picked up two black ones. What would you have done if you were the girl?

This problem was devised by psychologist Edward De Bono, who believes that conventional directed thinking is insufficient for solving new and unusual problems. His approach to problem solving requires use of nondirected thinking to generate new ways of looking at the problem situation. (The answer to this problem is provided in Figure 11.7.) *When are people most likely to engage in nondirected thinking?*

total, a lack of money and bills to pay, or cancer and a cure. In all these examples, getting from the problem to the solution requires some directed thinking.

Strategies

Problem solving depends on the use of strategies, or specific methods for approaching problems. One strategy is to break down a complex problem into a number of smaller, more easily solved subgoals. *Subgoals* are intermediate steps toward a solution. For example, it is the end of the semester and your life is falling apart. You do not even have time to tie your shoelaces. You solve the problem by breaking it down into small pieces: studying for a science exam, finishing that overdue paper, canceling your dinner date, scheduling regular study breaks to maintain what is left of your sanity, and so forth.

For some problems, you may work backward from the goal you have set. Mystery writers often use this method: They decide how to end the story ("who did it") and then devise a plot leading to this conclusion.

Another problem may require you to examine various ways of reaching a desired goal. Suppose a woman needs to be in Chicago by 11 A.M. on July 7 for a business conference. She checks train departures and arrivals, airline schedules, and car-rental companies. The only train to Chicago that morning arrives at 5 A.M. (too early), and the first plane arrives at 11:30 A.M. (too late). So she decides to rent a car and drive.

PSYCHOLOGY *Online*

Student Web Activity
Visit the *Understanding Psychology* Web site at psychology.glencoe.com and click on **Chapter 11—Student Web Activities** for an activity on thinking and problem solving.

To determine which strategy to use, most of us analyze the problem to see if it resembles a situation we have experienced in the past. A strategy that worked in the past is likely to work again. We tend to do things the way we have done them before, and often, we shy away from new situations that call for new strategies. The more unusual the problem, the more difficult it is to devise a strategy for dealing with it.

Algorithms An **algorithm** is a fixed set of procedures that, if followed correctly, will lead to a solution. Mathematical and scientific formulas are algorithms. For example, to find the product of 345 and 23, we multiply the numbers according to the rules of multiplication to get a correct answer of 7,935. To play chess or checkers, we follow algorithms, or a fixed set of rules.

algorithm: a step-by-step procedure for solving a problem

Heuristics While algorithms can be useful in finding solutions, they are a time-consuming method. People often use shortcuts to solve problems, and these shortcuts are called heuristics. **Heuristics** are rules of thumb that simplify a problem, allowing one to solve problems quickly and easily (see Figure 11.3). For example, when watching the Wheel of Fortune game show, you might use what you already know about prefixes, suffixes, and roots of words to fill in the missing letters of a word or phrase. If a friend comes to you with a problem, your advice might include what has worked for you in the past.

heuristic: a rule-of-thumb problem-solving strategy

mental set: a habitual strategy or pattern of problem solving

Although heuristics allow us to make quick decisions, they can result in bad decisions because we make the decisions using shortcuts and sometimes ignore pertinent information.

Obstacles to Problem Solving

There are times when certain useful strategies become cemented into the problem-solving process. When a particular strategy becomes a habit, it is called a **mental set**—you are "set" to treat problems in a certain way. For example, a chess player may always attempt to control the four center squares of the chessboard. Whenever her opponent attacks, she responds by looking for ways to

Figure 11.3 Types of Heuristics

Heuristics are mental shortcuts. Although they are not rules that always provide the correct answers, they are strategies that experience has taught us to apply. *What is the availability heuristic?*

1. **Availability Heuristic:** We rely on information that is more prominent or easily recalled and overlook information that is available but less prominent.
   Example: In the news, we see people winning the lottery all the time and overestimate our chances at winning it also.
2. **Representativeness Heuristic:** We tend to assume that if an item is similar to members of a particular category, it is probably a member of that category, too.
   Example: I have flipped a coin 10 times and it has landed on tails every time. The odds are it will land on heads this time. (The odds are still 50–50.)
3. **Anchoring Heuristic:** We make decisions based on certain ideas, or standards, that are important to us.
   Example: In my family, everyone gets up by 8:00 A.M. every day, including weekends. I believe that only lazy people sleep past 8:00 A.M. (I formed a judgment about other people based on a standard in my family.)

Figure 11.4 | Connecting the Dots

Connect all nine dots shown by drawing four straight lines without lifting your pencil from the paper or retracing any lines. (The answer appears in Figure 11.7.) *How does following a mental set sometimes interfere with problem solving?*

functional fixedness: the inability to imagine new functions for familiar objects

creativity: the capacity to use information and/or abilities in a new and original way

regain control of those four squares. She has a "set" for this strategy. If this set helps her win, fine. Sometimes, however, a set interferes with problem solving, and then it is called rigidity. You probably know the old riddle "What is black, white, and read all over? A newspaper." When you say the riddle, the word "read" sounds like "red," which is why some people cannot guess the answer. "Read" is heard as part of the black and white set—it is interpreted as being a color. If you asked, "What is read by people every day and is black and white?" the correct answer would be obvious—and boring.

One form of set that can interfere with problem solving is **functional fixedness**—the inability to imagine new functions for familiar objects. In experiments on functional fixedness, people are asked to solve a problem that requires them to use a familiar object in an unfamiliar way (Duncker, 1945). Because they are set to use the object in the usual way, people tend to pay attention only to the features of the object that relate to its everyday use (see Figures 11.4 and 11.5). They respond in a rigid way.

Another type of rigidity occurs when a person makes a wrong assumption about a problem. In Figure 11.6, for example, the problem is to arrange the six matches into four equilateral triangles. Most people have trouble solving this puzzle because they falsely assume that they must stay within a two-dimensional figure.

People trying to solve the kind of problem described in the *Psychology and You* feature experience a third kind of rigidity. Most people look for direct methods of solving problems and do not see solutions that require several intermediate steps.

Rigidity can be overcome if the person realizes that his or her strategy is not working and looks for other ways to approach the problem. The more familiar the situation, the more difficult this will be. Rigidity is less likely to occur with unusual problems. Many individuals are trained, through formal education, to think of only one way to do things. Rigidity can be overcome by thinking about—or being taught to think about—and analyzing situations from many perspectives.

Figure 11.5 | Overcoming Functional Fixedness

Given the materials pictured here, how would you go about mounting a candle vertically on a wooden wall in such a way that it can be lit? (The solution is presented in Figure 11.7.) *How might functional fixedness make it difficult to solve this problem?*

CREATIVITY

The ability to use information in such a way that the result is somehow new, original, and meaningful is **creativity.** All problem solving requires some creativity. Certain ways of solving problems, however, are simply more brilliant or beautiful or efficient than others. Psychologists do not know exactly why some people are able to think more creatively than others, although they have identified some of the characteristics of creative thinking—including flexibility and the ability to recombine elements to achieve insight.

Flexibility

The ability to overcome rigidity is **flexibility.** Psychologists have devised a number of ingenious tests to measure flexibility. In one test, psychologists ask people how many uses they can imagine for a single object, such as a brick or a paper clip. The more uses a person can devise, the more flexible he or she is said to be. Whether such tests actually measure creativity is debatable. Nevertheless, it is obvious that inflexible, rigid thinking leads to unoriginal solutions or no solutions at all.

Recombination

When the elements of a problem are familiar but the required solution is not, it may be achieved by **recombination,** a new mental arrangement of the elements. In football and basketball, for example, there are no new moves—only recombinations of old ones. Such recombination seems to be a vital part of creativity. Many creative people say that no truly great poem, no original invention, has ever been produced by someone who has not spent years studying his or her subject. The creative person is able to take the information that he or she and others have compiled and put it together in a totally new way. The brilliant philosopher and mathematician Sir Isaac Newton, who discovered the laws of motion, once said, "If I have seen further, it is by standing on the shoulders of giants." In other words, he was able to recombine the discoveries of the great scientists who had preceded him to uncover new and more far-reaching truths.

Insight

The sudden emergence of a solution by recombination of elements is called **insight.** Insight usually occurs when problems have proved resistant to all problem-solving efforts and strategies. The scientist or artist reaches a point of high frustration and temporarily abandons the task. Yet the recombination process seems to continue on an unconscious level. When the person is absorbed in some other activity, the answer seems to appear out of nowhere. This sudden insight has appropriately been called the "aha" experience.

Certain animals appear to experience this same cycle of frustration, temporary diversion (during which time the problem "incubates"), and then sudden insight. For example, Wolfgang Köhler (1976) placed a chimpanzee in a cage where a cluster of bananas was hung out of its reach. Also in the cage were several wooden boxes. At first the chimpanzee tried various unsuccessful ways of getting at the fruit. Finally it sat down, apparently giving up, and simply stared straight ahead for a while. Then suddenly it jumped up, piled three boxes on top of one another, climbed to the top of the pile, and grabbed the bananas.

Figure 11.6 Overcoming Wrong Assumptions

Arrange these six matches so that they form four equilateral triangles. (The solution appears in Figure 11.7.) *What are two characteristics of creative thinking?*

flexibility: the ability to overcome rigidity

recombination: mentally rearranging the elements of a problem to arrive at an original solution

insight: the sudden realization of the solution to a problem

PSYCHOLOGY and You

Solve This Problem

How would you go about solving this problem? A man and his two sons want to get across a river. The boat they have available can hold a maximum of only 200 pounds. The father weighs 200 pounds and the sons weigh 100 pounds each. How can all three people cross the river? (You'll find the answer in Figure 11.7.)

| Figure 11.7 | Answers to Pages 298, 300, and 301 |

*W*hen the girl put her hand into the bag to draw out the fateful pebble, she fumbled and dropped it, where it was immediately lost among the others. "Oh," she said, "well, you can tell which one I picked by looking at the one that's left." The girl's lateral thinking saved her father and herself.

page 298

page 300

page 300

page 301

"F" represents "Father," and each "S" represents a "Son."

page 301

SECTION 1 Assessment

1. **Review the Vocabulary** Describe two obstacles to problem solving.

2. **Visualize the Main Idea** In a diagram similar to the one below, describe the characteristics of creative thinking.

Characteristics of Creative Thinking

3. **Recall Information** What is the difference between convergent and nondirected thinking? Give specific examples.

4. **Think Critically** If you were a teacher, would you allow students to solve math problems using different approaches if they reached the same answer? Why?

5. **Application Activity** Focus on a favorite board game. Provide a written description of problem-solving techniques you would use to win the game. Ask classmates to use and evaluate the techniques.

Checkmate

Period of Study: 1997

Introduction: On May 11, 1997, a rematch took place in the contemplative game of chess. The champion of the previous match, which had taken place a year earlier, was Garry Kasparov, a former scientist. Many consider Kasparov to be the best chess player to have ever lived. Kasparov's opponent was "Big Blue," a computer.

Hypothesis: The idea of "human versus machine" fascinated experts in a wide range of scientific studies. Most of them had the highest confidence in Kasparov's chances to defeat the computer for the second time. Psychologists believed that a computer pre-programmed with information of any kind would prove no match for the thought capacity and perceptions of the human mind. Even though Big Blue was designed to play the game of chess with perfection, a nonfeeling and nonthinking machine could not defeat the ability of the human mind to think abstractly. A machine could also not match the human mind's feelings of determination and desire.

Method: As we know, computers are not thinkers—they can only do what they are programmed to do. Big Blue, however, has amazing capacities. It can consider 300 million possible chess moves per second. With each of these 300 million possibilities, Big Blue is programmed to assess the situation these moves will put it in. The human brain can evaluate only a very small fraction of moves compared to what Big Blue can do. The Big Blue defeated by Kasparov the previous year was a "younger" version of the 1997 model. A victory for Big Blue could mean computers would not have to operate like a human brain to surpass it.

For his rematch with Big Blue, Kasparov planned to copy his strategy from last year. This would involve using the early match (in a series of matches) to inspect the mighty computer for weaknesses and then to exploit those weaknesses.

Results: Big Blue, the computer, defeated Kasparov. Experts explained that Kasparov's defeat was the result of comparing Big Blue too much to the version he had played against the year before. The new and improved Big Blue seemed to use moves that were very "human-like." For every seemingly well-conceived move Kasparov made, the computer countered in devastating ways.

The time-consuming chess game robbed Kasparov of much of his concentration, whereas Big Blue displayed no fatigue, frustration, or other human weaknesses. Now that psychologists know a human's mental capacity can be outmatched by a computer's programming, what assumptions can they make? Can a machine really prove to be more intelligent than the person who creates it? Do the physical limitations or the emotions of humans prevent us from using our full brain capacity? These questions and others like them may not be answered for years to come. This situation is new, and further testing in this area is needed to accurately assess the issues.

Analyzing the Case Study

1. Why was Kasparov favored to win the rematch?

2. What advantages did each opponent bring to the contest?

3. Critical Thinking Why were psychologists interested in the rematch between these two opponents?

Reader's Guide

■ **Main Idea**

Language and thought are closely related. Language requires the learning of a set of complex rules and symbols, yet most people have little difficulty learning their native language.

■ **Vocabulary**

- language
- phoneme
- morpheme
- syntax
- semantics

■ **Objectives**

- Explain the structure of language.
- Describe how children develop language.

EXPLORING PSYCHOLOGY

What Language Do You Understand?

Listen to someone speaking a language you do not know. You hear an unsung song, ever changing, rising and falling, occasionally illuminated by flashes of feeling. The sounds themselves are little more than vocal noises. If there are words, you cannot disentangle them; if there is a message, you cannot understand it. Interest evaporates. You might as well stare at a brick wall.

Now listen to a good friend. It is the same kind of vocalization, but you cannot hear it in the same way. The noises are there, but they are totally transparent. Your mind passes right through the sounds, through the words, through the sentences, and into the mind of your friend. Your experience is totally different.

—from *The Science of Words* by George A. Miller, 1991

O f all the things we do, nothing seems as complex and as important as understanding and speaking a language. We must learn thousands of words and countless rules of grammar to make sense of those words to communicate and share ideas.

THE STRUCTURE OF LANGUAGE

language: the communication of ideas through symbols and sounds that are arranged according to rules

Do you ever talk to yourself? Some people talk to themselves when they are thinking or solving a problem. When we are talking or thinking, we are using language. What is language? **Language** is a system of communication that involves using rules to make and combine symbols in ways that produce meaningful words and sentences. Language permits us to communicate facts and ideas. It allows us to tell each other not only about the present but also the future and the past. We can solve problems and make decisions every day largely because of what we learn from experience and from each other. This learning is transmitted through language. Language consists of four rules, or parts: phonemes, morphemes, syntax, and semantics.

Phonemes

The smallest units of sound in the human language, such as consonants and vowels, are **phonemes.** Phonemes can be a single letter, such as *t,* or a combination of letters, such as *sh* (see Figure 11.8).

We can produce about 100 different recognizable sounds, but not all sounds are used in all languages. For instance, the English language uses about 43 sounds while some languages use as few as 15 sounds and others use as many as 85 sounds.

phoneme: an individual sound that is a basic structural element of language

Morphemes

A **morpheme** is a unit of meaning (see Figure 11.8). It is made up of one or more phonemes. Morphemes can be a word, a letter (*s*), a prefix (*un* in *uncertain*), or a suffix (*ly* in *slowly*). For example, the words *book, love,* and *reason* are single morphemes, while *loves, relearn,* and *walked* have two morphemes *(love* and *s, re* and *learn, walk* and *ed).*

morpheme: the smallest unit of meaning in a given language

Syntax

A set of rules for combining words, phrases, and sentences to express thoughts that can be understood by others is **syntax.** For example, the following sentence does not make sense to you: *Boy small bike small rode.* In English we follow certain grammatical rules, such as placing adjectives in front of nouns. If you applied the rules of grammar to the sentence above, it would read: *The small boy rode a small bike.* Every language has these rules, although rules differ from language to language.

syntax: language rules that govern how words can be combined to form meaningful phrases and sentences

semantics: the study of meaning in language

Semantics

Understanding the meaning of words or phrases when they appear in certain sentences or context is **semantics.** The same word can have different meanings. Consider the following sentences. *A mind is a terrible thing to waste. Do you mind if I sit next to you?* The word "mind" is understood differently in the sentences. How did you know what

Figure 11.8   Phonemes and Morphemes

The word *fearlessness* has nine phonemes and three morphemes. *What is the difference between phonemes and morphemes?*

Phonemes (units of sound):

FEARLESSNESS

Morphemes (units of meaning):

Noam Chomsky

1928–

"[A] human being is a biological organism like any other. It's a biological organism with a very unique intellectual capacity that we are only barely beginning to understand. I think our intellectual capacities are very highly structured."

Avram Noam Chomsky created the idea of *transformational grammar.* Transformational grammar is a system for describing the rules that determine all the sentences that can possibly be formed in any language. Chomsky claims that each of us is born with brain structures that make it relatively easy to learn the rules of language. Chomsky called those innate brain structures the *language-acquisition device,* or *LAD.* The LAD includes inborn mechanisms that guide a person's learning of the unique rules of his or her native language.

the word "mind" meant in each sentence? From your knowledge of semantics, you knew that in the first sentence "mind" was a noun, while in the second sentence it was a verb. You know what different words mean depending on the context.

LANGUAGE DEVELOPMENT

For many years a debate over exactly how children learn language raged. B.F. Skinner believed that children learned language as a result of operant conditioning. When children utter sounds that are similar to adult speech patterns, their behavior is reinforced through smiles and extra attention; therefore, children repeat those sounds. Eventually children learn to produce speech. Critics state that children understand language before they speak—and before they receive any reinforcement. Also, chidren learn the rules of language before they receive any feedback on speaking correctly.

Some psychologists propose that children learn language through observation, exploration, and imitation. These social learning advocates point out that children use language to get attention, ask for help, or to gain other forms of social contact. Parents can stimulate language acquisition by responding to and encouraging language development. These psychologists argue that both innate and environmental factors play a part in how a child learns language.

Although Noam Chomsky believed that reinforcement and imitation do contribute to language development, he did not believe that all the complex rules of language could be learned that way. Chomsky (1957) proposed that infants possess an innate capacity for language; that is, children inherit a mental program that enables them to learn grammar.

HOW LANGUAGE DEVELOPS

If Chomsky is right, then we would expect that all children go through similar stages of language development, no matter what culture or language group they belong to. Infants, in fact, do go through four stages of language development.

Beginning at birth, infants can cry and produce other sounds indicating distress. Around 2 months of age, infants begin to *coo*. Cooing refers to long, drawn-out sounds such as *oooh* or *eeeh*. At around 4 months of age, infants reach the first stage of language development and begin to *babble*. Babbling includes sounds found in all languages, such as *dadada* and *bababa*. When babbling, infants learn to control their vocal cords and to make, change, repeat, and imitate the sounds of their parents. At around 9 months of age, infants refine their babbling to increasingly include sounds that are part of their native language. Whereas in children who can hear, babbling is oral, deaf children babble by using hand signals. They repeat the same hand signals over and over again.

At around 12 months of age, infants begin to utter single words. They use these words to describe familiar objects and people, such as *da-da* or *doggie*. At this stage, children use single words to describe longer thoughts. For example, a child may say "da" to mean "Where is my father?" or "I want my father."

Toward the end of their second year, children place two words together to express an idea. Children may say "Milk gone" to indicate that the milk has spilled or "Me play" to mean "I want to play." This stage indicates that the child is beginning to learn the rules of grammar. The child's vocabulary has expanded to about 50 to 100 words and continues to expand rapidly.

At around age 4, children begin to form sentences. These sentences generally consist of several words that express ideas. The first sentences a child utters, though, follow a pattern called *telegraphic speech*. Telegraphic speech is a pattern of speaking in which the child leaves out articles (the), prepositions (with), and parts of verbs. For example, a child may say "I go to park" to mean "I am going to the park."

Bilingualism

Bilingualism is the ability to speak and understand two languages. How do bilingual people, though, keep the two languages separate? They do not. Try this experiment. Say the ink color of the following words aloud.

> YELLOW GREEN RED BLUE VERDE AZUL AMARILLO ROJO

If you speak only English, you probably had a little trouble with the first four and had less trouble with the last four. If you speak Spanish, though, you knew that *verde, azul, amarillo,* and *rojo* are the Spanish words for *green, blue, yellow,* and *red*. You had difficulty with all the items.

Although it takes children longer to master two languages rather than just one, bilingual people can express their thoughts in a wide variety of ways. Bilingual children also learn early that there are different ways of expressing the same idea.

Reading Check
What is the nature versus nurture debate concerning the development of language?

DO ANIMALS LEARN LANGUAGE?

Animals communicate with one another. We have all seen dogs bark or growl at each other. Do animals, though, learn language? Language involves more than just communicating—it involves rules of grammar. It involves combining words or phrases into meaningful sentences. Although animals do not possess the ability to use grammatical rules, they have been taught to communicate with humans. (Refer to Chapter 3 for an in-depth discussion.)

GENDER AND CULTURAL DIFFERENCES

People use language to communicate their culture and express their ideas. Do people who speak different languages actually think differently from one another? Benjamin Whorf (1956) argued that language affects our basic perceptions of the physical world. Whorf used the term *linguistic relativity* to refer to the idea that a person's language influences his or her thoughts. For instance, consider the word "snow." Whorf estimated that the Inuit have many words for snow because their survival depends upon traveling and living in snow. According to Whorf's theory, these different terms for snow help the Inuit see the different types of snow as different. On the other hand, Whorf claimed that Americans have one word for snow. Critics have pointed out, though, that Americans actually do have many words for snow (flurry, blizzard, powder). Whorf's theory of linguistic relativity still claims supporters, although it is difficult to separate culture from language when studying the use of language and the perceptions it influences.

Does the English language express a particular value system? Some people argue that certain words in language create gender stereotypes. For example, a chairman may be a man or a woman. The use of pronouns also affects our thinking. Nurses, secretaries, and schoolteachers are often referred to as *she,* while doctors, engineers, and presidents are often referred to as *he.* Many organizations have instituted guidelines for the use of nonsexist language.

SECTION 2

Assessment

1. **Review the Vocabulary** How many phonemes are in the word "thoughtfully"? How many morphemes?

2. **Visualize the Main Idea** Using a flowchart similar to the one below, list the stages of language development.

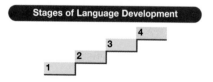
Stages of Language Development

3. **Recall Information** How might we express gender values in our use of language?

4. **Think Critically** You have taught your pet parrot to speak perfect English and understand several commands. Have you taught it language? Explain.

5. **Application Activity** In ordinary English, there is no resemblance between the written appearance of a word and the idea for which it stands. Write the following words in such a way that the word illustrates the idea: war, empty, fly, kick, Mommy.

Summary and Vocabulary

Solving problems, creating ideas, and expressing our ideas through language are some of the most important skills that we acquire in our lives.

Section 1 Thinking and Problem Solving

Main Idea: Thinking involves changing and reorganizing the information stored in memory to create new or transformed information, such as creative problem-solving strategies.

- The processes of thought depend on several devices or units of thought: images, symbols, concepts, prototypes, and rules.
- There are several kinds of thinking: directed, or convergent thinking, and nondirected, or divergent thinking, and metacognition.
- Problem solving depends upon the use of strategies or specific methods for approaching problems.
- People use algorithms, or fixed sets of procedures, and heuristics, or mental shortcuts, to solve problems.
- At times certain useful strategies become so cemented into the problem-solving process that they actually interfere with problem solving. When a particular strategy becomes a habit, it is called a mental set.
- Functional fixedness, or the inability to imagine new functions for familiar objects, can interfere with problem solving.
- Some characteristics of creative thinking include flexibility and the ability to recombine elements to achieve insight.

Chapter Vocabulary

thinking (p. 296)
image (p. 296)
symbol (p. 296)
concept (p. 296)
prototype (p. 296)
rule (p. 297)
metacognition (p. 297)
algorithm (p. 299)
heuristic (p. 299)
mental set (p. 299)
functional fixedness (p. 300)
creativity (p. 300)
flexibility (p. 301)
recombination (p. 301)
insight (p. 301)
language (p. 304)
phoneme (p. 305)
morpheme (p. 305)
syntax (p. 305)
semantics (p. 305)

Section 2 Language

Main Idea: Language and thought are closely related. Language requires the learning of a set of complex rules and symbols, yet most people have little difficulty learning their native language.

- Language consists of four parts: phonemes, morphemes, syntax, and semantics.
- According to B.F. Skinner, children learn language as a result of operant conditioning.
- Noam Chomsky proposed that children inherit a mental program that enables them to learn grammar.
- Infants go through four stages of language development—babbling at around 4 months of age, uttering single words at around 12 months of age, placing words together to express ideas at around 2 years of age, and forming sentences at around 4 years of age.
- People use language to communicate their culture and express their ideas.

Self-Check Quiz
Visit the *Understanding Psychology* Web site at
psychology.glencoe.com and click on **Chapter 11—Self-Check Quizzes** to prepare for the Chapter Test.

Reviewing Vocabulary

Choose the letter of the correct term or concept below to complete the sentence.

a. prototype **f.** syntax
b. algorithm **g.** semantics
c. functional fixedness **h.** mental set
d. insight **i.** thinking
e. phonemes **j.** metacognition

1. A(n) _____ is a fixed set of procedures that, if followed correctly, will lead to a solution.
2. _____ indicates the meaning of words or phrases when they appear in certain sentences or contexts.
3. Changing or reorganizing the information stored in memory to create new or transformed information is _____.
4. A person experiences _____ when he or she comes upon a solution to a problem by creating a new mental arrangement of the elements of the problem.
5. The strategy of problem solving that you use over and over again is your _____.
6. _____ is a set of rules for combining words, phrases, and sentences to express thoughts that can be understood by others.
7. Thinking about thinking is called _____.
8. When you think of a car as an example of a vehicle, you are thinking of a(n) _____.
9. The smallest units of sound in the human language are called _____.
10. The inability to imagine new functions for familiar objects is called _____.

Recalling Facts

1. Define the five units of thought. Then list the five units of thought in order of increasing complexity.
2. What is creativity? What are the three characteristics of creative thinking? Give an example of one of the three characteristics.
3. Using a graphic organizer similar to the one below, identify and explain the structures of language.

4. What are three strategies people often use to solve problems? Explain how you have used one of these strategies to solve a problem.
5. How did B.F. Skinner and Noam Chomsky differ in their ideas about how children learn language?

Critical Thinking

1. **Applying Concepts** Do you think using algorithms rather than heuristics is always the best way to solve problems? Why or why not?
2. **Making Inferences** What kind of thinking—directed or nondirected—do you think is required for creativity? Why do you think so?
3. **Analyzing Concepts** Based on what you have learned about language development, do you think all students in elementary school should be taught a foreign language? Why or why not?
4. **Synthesizing Information** According to the theory of linguistic relativity, a person's language influences his or her thoughts. Do you believe that bilingual people have more complex thought processes than people who speak only one language? Explain your answer.
5. **Demonstrating Reasoned Judgment** What theory of language development do you agree with the most? Why?

CHAPTER 11 Assessment

Psychology Projects

1. **Problem Solving** Suppose you wanted to put together a jigsaw puzzle. What are the problem-solving strategies you might use? Which one do you think would work best? Present your strategies in an illustrated "how-to" pamphlet for others to refer to.

2. **Language** Listen to the speech of a child between the ages of 2 and 4. Pay special attention to the child's language skills. Then write a report explaining what parts of language structure the child is exhibiting.

3. **Thinking** Ask 15 to 20 people to give you directions to a specific location, such as the school gym. Notice how they describe the directions (by using only words, creating a map, or using their hands). After they have finished, ask them to describe the mental imagery they used. In a brief report, summarize your findings.

Technology Activity

The Internet has several sites designed for parents of preschool children. Locate some of these sites to find out what suggestions parents can obtain to improve language development in their young children. Report and evaluate the suggestions in light of the information about language development you have learned in this chapter.

Psychology Journal

Consider how language shapes your thinking and how language and thought are integrated processes. Recall an episode in your life in which you used language (your communication skills) to solve an important problem. Describe the event and analyze why you were equipped to resolve this particular issue.

Building Skills

Interpreting a Graph Many factors contribute to a child's language development. Review the graph, then answer the questions that follow.

1. What does the graph illustrate?

2. What conclusion can you draw about the relationship of the number of words that a parent says to a child and the size of the child's vocabulary?

3. What theory of language development does the information in this graph best support?

 Practice and **assess** key social studies skills with **Glencoe Skillbuilder Interactive Workbook CD-ROM, Level 2.**

 See the Skills Handbook, page 628, for an explanation of interpreting graphs.

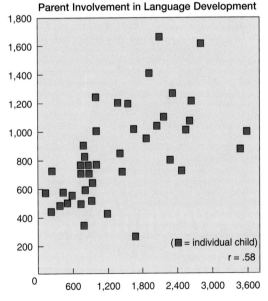

The number of words in the child's recorded vocabulary at age 3

Parent Involvement in Language Development

(■ = individual child)

r = .58

The average number of words said per hour by the parent to the child before the child was 3 years old

Source: Robert S. Feldman, *Understanding Psychology*, 1999.

Motivation and Emotion

PSYCHOLOGY JOURNAL

Think about the present-day concerns and future aspirations that are most important to you. List 6 to 10 of them in any order in your journal. ■

PSYCHOLOGY Online

Chapter Overview
Visit the *Understanding Psychology* Web site at psychology.glencoe.com and click on **Chapter 12—Chapter Overviews** to preview the chapter.

Theories of Motivation

Reader's Guide

■ Main Idea
Psychologists explain motivation and why we experience it in different ways through instinct, drive-reduction, incentive, and cognitive theories of motivation.

■ Vocabulary
- motivation
- instincts
- need
- drive
- homeostasis
- incentive
- extrinsic motivation
- intrinsic motivation

■ Objectives
- Describe four theories of motivation.
- Discuss the difference between intrinsic and extrinsic motivation.

EXPLORING PSYCHOLOGY

Don't Look Back

Willie Davis, the great defensive end at Green Bay . . . had given [another player] a kind of mental tip that he used to motivate himself. He had used it ever since a game the Packers lost against the Eagles back in the 1960s. As he left the field at the end of the game, Davis had turned around, the stands emptying, and he realized that he was leaving something on the field—namely, regrets that he had not given the extra effort, the extra push . . . and that he was going to have to live with that regret for the rest of his life because there was no way that he could recapture that moment. He made up his mind then that he would never again look back at a football field or even a day's effort at what he was doing with any sense of regret.

—from *The X Factor: A Quest for Excellence* by George Plimpton, 1995

Why did Davis play football so intensely? Why do people try to climb Mount Everest or cross the Atlantic in a balloon? Why do some people spend every waking moment memorizing batting averages, while others do not know the difference between the New York Yankees and the Toledo Mud Hens? As the song asks, why do fools fall in love?

motivation: an internal state that activates behavior and directs it toward a goal

Although all psychology is concerned with what people do and how they do it, research on motivation and emotion focuses on the underlying why of behavior. **Motivation** includes the various psychological and physiological factors that cause us to act a certain way at a certain time.

We see Kristin studying all weekend while the rest of us hang out, and since we know she wants to go to law school, we conclude that she is "motivated" by her desire to get good grades. We see Mikko working after classes at a job he does not like, and since we know he wants to buy a car, we conclude that he is "motivated" to earn money for the car. Movies often have motives or emotions as their central theme. On the street, you hear words like "anger," "fear," "pain," "starving," and hundreds of others describing motives and emotions. Conceptions of motivation in psychology are in many ways similar to those expressed in everyday language. Because motivation cannot be observed directly, psychologists, like the rest of us, infer motivation from goal-directed behavior. Behavior is usually energized by many motives that may originate from outside of us or inside of us.

Psychologists explain motivation and why we experience it in different ways. We will discuss instinct, drive-reduction, incentive, and cognitive theories of motivation.

INSTINCT THEORY

instincts: innate tendencies that determine behavior

In the 1900s, psychologist William McDougall (1908) proposed that humans were motivated by a variety of instincts. **Instincts** are natural or inherited tendencies of an organism to make a specific response to certain environmental stimuli without involving reason. Instincts occur in almost the same way among all members of a species. For example, salmon respond to instinctive urges to swim thousands of miles through ocean waters and up rivers to reach the exact spot in a gravel bed where they were spawned years earlier. Psychologist William James (1890) proposed that humans have instincts such as cleanliness, curiosity, parental love, sociability, and sympathy.

Eventually, though, psychologists realized a flaw in the instinct theory. Instincts do not explain behavior; they simply label behavior. Although some psychologists still study instinctual behaviors (now called fixed action patterns), they have focused on other theories to explain motivation.

DRIVE-REDUCTION THEORY

need: biological or psychological requirement of an organism

Something that *motivates* us moves us to action. That "something" that motivates us starts with a **need** and leads to a drive. A need results from a lack of something desirable or useful. We have both physiological and psychological needs. We need oxygen and food to survive (physiological needs). We may also need self-esteem or social approval (psychological needs). We do not necessarily need to fulfill psychological needs to survive; we often learn them.

A need produces a drive. A **drive** is an internal condition that can change over time and orients an individual toward a specific goal or goals. We have different drives with different goals. For example, hunger drives us to eat, curiosity drives us to find something out, and fatigue drives us to rest.

Drive-reduction theory emerged from the work of experimental psychologist Clark Hull (1943) who traced motivation back to basic physiological needs. According to Hull, when an organism is deprived of something it needs or wants (such as food or water), it becomes tense and agitated. To relieve this tension, it engages in more or less random activity. Thus biological needs *drive* an organism to act, and the organism strives to maintain homeostasis. **Homeostasis** is the tendency of the body to return to or maintain a balanced state.

If a behavior reduces the drive, the organism will begin to acquire a habit. That is, when the drive is again felt, the organism will first try the same response again. Habits channel drives in certain directions. In short, drive-reduction theory states that physiological needs drive an organism to act in either random or habitual ways until its needs are satisfied (until the organism returns to a preset optimal state).

Hull suggested that all human motives—from the desire to acquire property to striving for excellence and seeking affection or amusement— are extensions of basic biological needs. For example, people develop the need for social approval because as infants they were fed and cared for by a smiling mother or father. Gradually, through conditioning and generalization, the need for approval becomes important in itself. So, according to Hull, approval becomes a learned drive.

The results of subsequent experiments suggested, however, that Hull had overlooked some of the more important factors in human—and animal—motivation. According to drive-reduction theory, infants become attached to their mothers because mothers usually relieve such drives as hunger and thirst. Harry Harlow (among others) doubted that this was the only or even the main source of an infant's love for its mother. Harlow took baby monkeys away from their mothers and put them alone in cages with two surrogate "mothers" made mostly of wire (see Figure 12.1). One of the wire mothers was equipped with a bottle. If the drive-reduction theory was correct, the monkeys would become attached to this figure because it was their only source of food. The other wire mother was covered with soft cloth but could not provide food and relief from hunger. In test after test, the baby monkeys preferred to cling to the cloth mother, particularly when strange, frightening objects were put into their cages (Harlow & Zimmerman, 1959).

Some drive theorists overlooked the fact that some experiences (such as hugging something or someone soft) are inherently pleasurable.

Figure 12.1   Harlow's Monkeys

The monkeys in Harlow's study spent most of their time with the cloth mother even though they fed from the wire mother. *What did this experiment indicate?*

drive: a state of tension produced by a need that motivates an organism toward a goal

homeostasis: the tendency of all organisms to correct imbalances and deviations from their normal state

Reading Check
What is the difference between a need and a drive?

How do advertisements "motivate" people to buy products?

Advertisers use a variety of techniques to appeal to consumers. Do any of these techniques appeal to human motivations?

Procedure
1. Find examples of various advertisements in magazines.
2. Record the kinds of items being advertised.
3. Focus on the way the advertisers promote the items.

Analysis
1. Describe how the advertisers appeal to consumers to buy the product.
2. Apply the method used to advertise the product to one of the theories of motivation discussed in the chapter.
3. How do the advertisements appeal to human motives? Present your analysis in a written report.

See the Skills Handbook, page 622, for an explanation of designing an experiment.

incentive: an external stimulus, reinforcer, or reward that motivates behavior

extrinsic motivation: engaging in activities that either reduce biological needs or help us obtain external incentives

intrinsic motivation: engaging in activities because they are personally rewarding or because they fulfill our beliefs and expectations

Although these experiences do not seem to reduce biological drives, they serve as incentives or goals for behavior. Also, sometimes we engage in activities that increase the tension we experience. For example, although you do not need or want extra anxieties, you may enjoy riding roller coasters or watching scary movies. These activities momentarily increase your anxiety and disrupt your homeostasis.

Many psychologists conclude that there could be no general theory of motivation of the type Hull suggested. There are many types of behavior that cannot be explained through deprivation.

INCENTIVE THEORY

The drive-reduction theory of motivation emphasizes the internal states of the organism; however, the incentive theory stresses the role of the environment in motivating behavior. Whereas a drive is something inside of us that causes us to act, our actions are directed toward a goal, or incentive. An **incentive** is the object we seek or the result we are trying to achieve through our motivated behavior. Incentives are also known as reinforcers, goals, and rewards. While drives push us to reduce needs, incentives pull us to obtain them. For example, hunger may cause us to walk to the cafeteria, but the incentive for our action is the sandwich we intend to eat. Sometimes our drive (hunger) is so strong that we do not care if the incentive (sandwich) is weak. For example, if we are really hungry, we may eat a sandwich from the cafeteria even though we know that the cafeteria's sandwiches are not that tasty. However, if our drive (hunger) is weak, our incentive must be strong. For instance, you may be slightly hungry but really like peanut butter sandwiches, so you will eat one.

In this case, people are motivated to obtain positive incentives and to avoid negative incentives. For example, you may go to the refrigerator when you are hungry or ask your teacher a question to help you solve a math problem. The cognitive expectations of humans also guide their behavior.

COGNITIVE THEORY

Cognitive psychologists seek to explain motivation by looking at forces inside and outside of us that energize us to move. They propose that we act in particular ways at particular times as a result of extrinsic and intrinsic motivations. **Extrinsic motivation** refers to engaging in activities to reduce biological needs or obtain incentives or external rewards. **Intrinsic motivation** refers to engaging in activities because those activities are personally rewarding or because engaging in them fulfills our beliefs or expectations. For example, if you spend hours and hours playing basketball because you wish to excel at the sport, you are following intrinsic motivation. If you spend hours playing basketball because your parents want you to excel at the sport, you are following extrinsic motivation. However, if you play basketball just for the fun of it, you are following intrinsic motivation.

In many instances, you engage in an activity because of both extrinsic and intrinsic motivations. For example, you may go out to dinner with your friends because you need to satisfy your hunger (an extrinsic motivation) and because you enjoy the taste of the restaurant's food and wish to socialize with your friends (intrinsic motivations). If you are motivated by both intrinsic and extrinsic motivations, do you perform more effectively or persistently at a task? Psychologists have proposed the *overjustification effect*—when people are given more extrinsic motivation than necessary to perform a task, their intrinsic motivation declines. Say, for example, you enjoy reading books. According to the overjustification effect, if someone started paying you to read books, you would enjoy reading books less. You might ask yourself, "Why am I doing this?" and answer, "It's not because I enjoy reading books; it's because I'm getting paid to do it." If you would stop getting paid to read books, you might lose interest in the task. Like many psychological theories, the overjustification effect applies to some situations and not others.

Figure 12.2   Incentive to Win

The incentive theory explains that we engage in certain behaviors because we are motivated by positive incentives such as praise or recognition. *How are incentives different from drives?*

SECTION 1   Assessment

1. **Review the Vocabulary**   What is the difference between extrinsic and intrinsic motivation?

2. **Visualize the Main Idea**   Compare and contrast two theories of motivation by using a diagram similar to the one below.

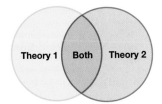

3. **Recall Information**   Give an example of a fixed action pattern. Why are fixed action patterns unable to explain motivation adequately?

4. **Think Critically**   Which theory of motivation might best explain why you work (or do not work) to get good grades? Explain.

5. **Application Activity**   When you are motivated, you do three things: you are energized to engage in an activity, you focus your energies toward reaching a goal, and you have differing intensities of feelings about achieving your goal. Use the criteria above to describe two activities or behaviors you engaged in today.

Case Studies

A Balance for Living

Period of Study: 1940

Introduction: When you are driving a car for a long time, eventually the gas tank will need refueling. Many cars are built today with computer systems that can tell when many other things need our attention, such as changing the oil or simply closing a door that did not shut completely. It is important that we respond to these signals. The same can be said for human beings who require maintenance for "operating properly" as well.

Like modern cars, humans also have a "built-in" computer. This computer is the human brain. The human body must keep in balance all of the particles and liquids that help maintain our organ systems and, together, keep us alive and well every day. This collective action is known as *homeostasis*. Homeostasis refers to a person's behavior and the corresponding actual physical need. For example, when a person is hungry, he eats. When he has completed a strenuous physical activity and becomes thirsty, he drinks.

In 1940 a one-year-old boy referred to as D.W. developed an odd craving for salt. His favorite foods included any items in which a major ingredient was salt. These foods included salted crackers, pretzels, and potato chips. Also, to the shock of his parents, D.W. would pour salt from the shaker directly into his mouth. When his parents denied him access to these salted edibles, D.W. would cry and throw tantrums until his parents gave in. As he developed a vocabulary, one of D.W.'s first words was indeed "salt."

Hypothesis: At this time, doctors were not aware of any physiological need for a person, especially at this young age, to consume as much salt as D.W. demanded. The only possible explanation was that the young child just liked the taste of salt. The case of D.W. would eventually result in a number of both physiological and psychological hypotheses.

Method: D.W.'s parents placed him in a hospital setting where he could be checked by doctors because they believed there was more to this unusual situation than just a child's pleasure in tasting salt. The doctors planned to begin general physiological testing to check for chemical deficiencies, disease, or even mental disabilities. During this time—about two days—D.W. became excessively aggravated and enraged. His hospital diet did not include the sufficient amount of salt that D.W. had craved his whole life. Unfortunately, D.W. died only a short time after he entered the hospital and before the scheduled tests could be completed.

Results: An autopsy on D.W. revealed that his adrenal glands did not adequately supply his body with the amount of salt it needed. Although he was very young, D.W.'s body relayed to his brain that he needed to consume more salt to balance out his body systems. It is safe to believe that a child at that age could not understand what salt is or how it operates within the human body, yet somehow young D.W. knew that he did indeed need to have salt and he knew where to get it. This example very much proves the important role homeostasis plays within the human body and the effect it has on the mind and behavior of a person to try to maintain its balance.

Analyzing the Case Study

1. What is homeostasis? How does it affect behavior?
2. Why did D.W. crave salt?
3. **Critical Thinking** Recall a time when you experienced your body's own homeostasis in action. Describe the episode. How did you know what you needed?

Biological and Social Motives

Reader's Guide

■ Main Idea
Much of life is spent trying to satisfy biological and social needs. Biological needs are physiological requirements that we must fulfill to survive, whereas social needs are those that are learned through experience.

■ Vocabulary
- lateral hypothalamus (LH)
- ventromedial hypothalamus (VMH)
- fundamental needs
- psychological needs
- self-actualization needs

■ Objectives
- Describe the biological and social needs of humans.
- Explain Maslow's hierarchy of needs.

EXPLORING PSYCHOLOGY

Why Do We Eat?
Many psychologists have noticed that rats often begin to eat and drink after being handled. For example, if you remove a number of rats from their cages, weigh them, and then return them to their cages, you will soon hear the crunching sound of food pellets being eaten. Two psychologists (Antelmen & Szechtman, 1975) reasoned that the handling, a form of mild stress, activated mechanisms involved in eating. So they devised a way of administering stress to the rats—pinching the rats' tails gently with a pair of padded pliers. The technique did indeed induce eating. Normal animals that were pinched twice a day gained more weight than non-pinched rats.

—adapted from *Psychology: The Science of Behavior* by Neil R. Carlson, 1984

Eating, as demonstrated above, serves both biological and psychological (social) needs. People spend much of their lives trying to satisfy biological and social needs. We choose what, how much, and when to eat because of both biological and social factors. Why is it, though, that some people seem more motivated than others when it comes to achieving something, such as a win in basketball or success at a job? Social needs, such as achievement, also influence our lives.

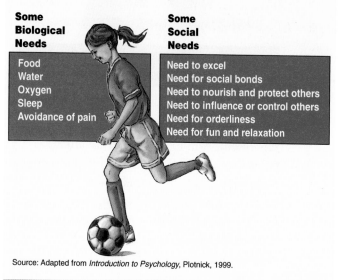

Figure 12.3   Some Biological and Social Needs

Whereas biological needs are physiological requirements critical to our survival, we acquire social needs through experience and learning. *Which needs do you think we try to satisfy first?*

Some Biological Needs

Food
Water
Oxygen
Sleep
Avoidance of pain

Some Social Needs

Need to excel
Need for social bonds
Need to nourish and protect others
Need to influence or control others
Need for orderliness
Need for fun and relaxation

Source: Adapted from *Introduction to Psychology*, Plotnick, 1999.

BIOLOGICAL MOTIVES

Some behavior is determined by the internal, or physiological, state of the organism. Like other animals, human beings have certain survival needs. Our biological needs are critical to our survival and physical well-being (see Figure 12.3). The nervous system is constructed in such a way that dramatic variations in blood sugar, water, oxygen, salt, or essential vitamins lead to changes in behavior designed to return the body to a condition of chemical balance. The first part of this section discusses the role of such physiological factors in motivating behavior.

All organisms, including humans, have built-in regulating systems that work like thermostats to maintain such internal processes as body temperature, the level of sugar in the blood, and the production of hormones. When the level of thyroxine in the bloodstream is low, the pituitary gland secretes a thyroid-stimulating hormone, causing the thyroid gland to secrete more thyroxine. When the thyroxine level is high, the pituitary gland stops producing this hormone. Similarly, when your body temperature drops below a certain point, you start to shiver, certain blood vessels constrict, and you put on more clothes. All these activities reduce heat loss and bring body temperature back to the correct level. If your body heat rises above a certain point, you start to sweat, certain blood vessels dilate, and you remove some clothes. These processes cool you.

The tendency of all organisms to correct imbalances and deviations from their normal state is known as *homeostasis*. Several of the drives that motivate behavior are homeostatic—hunger, for example.

Hunger

What motivates you to seek food? Often you eat because the sight and smell of, say, pizza tempts you into a restaurant. Other times you eat out of habit because you always have lunch at 12:30 or to be sociable because a friend invites you out for a snack. Yet suppose you are working frantically to finish a term paper. You do not have any food, so you ignore the fact that it is dinnertime and you keep working. At some point your body will start to demand food. You may feel an aching sensation in your stomach. What produces this sensation? What makes you feel hungry?

Your body requires food to grow, to repair itself, and to store reserves. To what is it responding? If the portion of the hypothalamus called the **lateral hypothalamus (LH)** is stimulated with electrodes, a laboratory animal will begin eating, even if it has just finished a large meal. Conversely, if the LH is removed surgically, an animal will stop eating

lateral hypothalamus (LH): the part of the hypothalamus that produces hunger signals and eventually die of starvation if it is not fed artificially. Thus the LH provides the "go" signals: it tells you to eat.

If a different portion of the hypothalamus called the **ventromedial hypothalamus (VMH)** is stimulated, an animal will slow down or stop eating altogether, even if it has been kept from food for a long period. If the VMH is removed, however, the animal will eat everything in sight until it becomes so obese it can hardly move (see Figure 12.4). This indicates that the VMH provides the "stop" signals: it tells you when you have had enough food. In addition, the hypothalamus responds to temperature—the LH signal is more active in cold temperatures, while the VMH signal is more active in warm temperatures.

Other factors also influence your hunger. The *glucostatic theory* suggests that the hypothalamus monitors the amount of glucose, or ready energy, available in the blood. As the level of blood glucose entering cells drops, the LH fires to stimulate you to start eating. At the same time, the pancreas releases *insulin* to convert the incoming calories into energy—whether to be consumed by active cells or converted into stored energy in the form of fat for use later (Woods, 1991). After your meal—as your blood glucose level drops—the pancreas secretes *glucagon,* which helps convert the stored energy back into useful energy. Some believe that glucostatic receptors in the liver play a role in stimulating the LH.

Another factor affecting eating is the *set-point*—the weight around which your day-to-day weight tends to fluctuate. Although your daily calorie intake and expenditure of energy vary, your body maintains a very stable weight over the long run.

The hypothalamus "interprets" at least three kinds of information: the amount of glucose entering the cells of your body, your set-point, and your body temperature. These determine whether or not the hypothalamus will contribute to causing you to eat.

Hunger—Other Factors Besides the biological motives, other factors may be at work when you feel hungry or eat. These factors are sometimes called *psychosocial hunger factors*. These are external cues that can affect eating as well, such as where, when, and what we eat. Cues such as smell and the appearance of food can affect eating behavior. When other people are eating, we tend to eat more. You may also choose not to eat because of social pressures, such as trying to look like the thin models in magazines. Sometimes when we are bored or stressed, we also eat more. You may eat popcorn when watching a movie because this is what you always do, or you may eat just because it is lunchtime.

Psychosocial factors have a huge impact on our eating habits and sometimes contribute to eating disorders, such as binge eating, eating when depressed, or not eating enough.

ventromedial hypothalamus (VMH): the part of the hypothalamus that can cause one to stop eating

Figure 12.4 **When to Stop Eating**

This obese rat has a damaged ventromedial hypothalamus and so overate until it weighed 1,080 grams—about eight times what a normal rat at that age weighs. *How does the hypothalamus help determine whether you will eat or not?*

Obesity

There is a growing body of evidence that a person's weight is controlled by biological factors. There appears to be a genetic component that may predispose some people to obesity (Jackson et al., 1997; Montague et al., 1997). An obese person is 30 percent or more above his or her ideal body weight. An *overweight* person is 20 percent over his or her ideal body weight. Currently, about one-third of Americans are obese (Gura, 1997) (see Figure 12.5).

Stanley Schachter (1971) and his colleagues at Columbia University conducted a number of ingenious studies that show that obese people respond to external cues—they eat not because they are hungry, but because they see something good to eat or their watches tell them it is time to eat.

To prove this, Schachter first set up a staged taste test in which people were asked to rate five kinds of crackers. The goal was to see how many crackers normal-weight and overweight people would eat. Each person, instructed to skip lunch, arrived hungry. Some were told that the taste test required a full stomach, and they were given as many roast beef sandwiches as they wanted. The rest stayed hungry. Schachter predicted that normal-weight people eat because they are hungry, while obese people eat whether they are hungry or not. This was true. People of normal weight ate more crackers than overweight people did when both groups were hungry and fewer crackers after they had eaten the roast beef.

In another study, Schachter put out a bowl of almonds that people could eat while they sat in a waiting room. Overweight people ate the nuts only when they did not have to take the shells off. Thus, again they ate simply because the food was there. People of normal weight were equally likely to try a few nuts whether they were shelled or not.

In summary, Schachter argued that overweight people respond to external cues (for example, the smell of cookies hot from the oven), while normal-weight people respond to internal cues, such as the stomach signals of hunger. His work shows that, for people, even physiological needs like hunger are influenced by complex factors.

Other factors are also important. Anxiety and depression are not causes of overeating. These conditions occur just as frequently among people of normal weight as among those who are overweight (Wadden & Stunkard, 1987). Exercise leads to weight loss

Reading Check
What did Schachter conclude about the differences between overweight and normal-weight people?

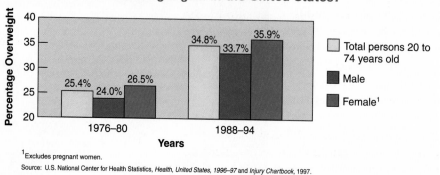

Figure 12.5   Percentage of Overweight Americans

Overweight people face double the risk for heart disease, stroke, high blood pressure, clogged arteries, adult onset diabetes, and early death. *What is the trend in weight gain in the United States?*

[1] Excludes pregnant women.

Source: U.S. National Center for Health Statistics, *Health, United States, 1996–97* and *Injury Chartbook, 1997.*

unless you start eating more as your exercise increases. Obviously, then, another cause of weight gain is too little exercise in proportion to the amount of food you eat.

SOCIAL MOTIVES

Many psychologists have concentrated their research on social motives rather than on the unlearned, biological motives we have been discussing. Social motives are learned from our interactions with other people.

Measuring the Need for Achievement

The achievement motive concerns the desire to set challenging goals and to persist in trying to reach those goals despite obstacles, frustrations, and setbacks. One reason the achievement motive has been so well researched is that David McClelland became interested in finding some quantitative way of measuring social motives

PSYCHOLOGY and You — Genetics and Weight

Besides our individual set-points—the weight that our bodies strive to maintain throughout our lives—other genetic, or inherited, factors affect our weights. We inherit a certain number of fat cells. Fat cells multiply when people become obese and shrink when people cut out fat and lose weight. However, if you have inherited a large number of fat cells, you have the ability to store more fat and, therefore, may be fatter than average.

We also inherit different rates of metabolism. Your metabolism involves how efficiently your body breaks down food into energy and how quickly your body burns off calories. You may eat the same number of calories as your friend, but if you have a lower metabolic rate than your friend, you burn less fuel (calories) and are more likely to store excess food as fat. (Exercise can raise your metabolic rate.)

Recently, researchers have found weight-regulating genes that play a role in metabolism. One gene increases neuropeptide Y, a brain chemical that leads to increased eating (Gura, 1997). Another gene increases a person's metabolism (Warden, 1997).

(McClelland et al., 1953). His main tool for measuring achievement motivation was the Thematic Apperception Test (TAT). This test consists of a series of pictures. Participants are told to make up a story that describes what is happening in each picture. (Tests of this sort are called projective tests, and we will describe them in detail in Chapter 13.) At this point, it is only important to know that there are no right or wrong answers. Since the test questions are ambiguous, the answers must be created from the participant's own beliefs, motives, and attitudes. Each story is "coded" for certain kinds of themes. These themes are scored according to their relevance to various types of needs, such as achievement, that is, setting goals, competing, and overcoming obstacles.

Based on these tests, McClelland developed a scoring system for the TAT. For example, a story would be scored high in achievement imagery if the main character was concerned with standards of excellence and a high level of performance, with unique accomplishments (such as inventions and awards), or with the pursuit of a long-term career or goal. Coding has been refined to the point where trained coders agree about 90 percent of the time.

Participants register a high need for achievement if they display persistence on tasks or the ability to perform better on tasks, set challenging but realistic goals, compete with others to win, and are attracted to challenging tasks or careers.

Student Web Activity
Visit the *Understanding Psychology* Web site at psychology.glencoe.com and click on **Chapter 12—Student Web Activities** for an activity on motivation.

People who scored high and low in achievement on the TAT were compared in a variety of situations. McClelland followed up the careers of some students at Wesleyan University who had been tested with the TAT in 1947. He wanted to see which students had chosen entrepreneurial work—that is, work in which they had to initiate projects on their own. He found that 11 years after graduation, 83 percent of the entrepreneurs (business managers, insurance salespeople, real estate investors, consultants, and so on) had scored high in achievement, but only 21 percent of the nonentrepreneurs had scored that high (McClelland, 1965).

McClelland did not believe we should all train ourselves as high achievers. In fact, he said that such people are not always the most interesting and they are usually not artistically sensitive (McClelland & Harris, 1971). They would also be less likely to value intimacy in a relationship. Studies have shown that high achievers prefer to be associated with experts who will help them achieve, instead of with more friendly people.

Critics have claimed that using McClelland's TAT is not a reliable method of testing the need for achievement. They assert that TAT stories are difficult to score because a person's thoughts and feelings cannot be objectively analyzed.

Fear of Failure   While some people are motivated by a need for achievement, others may be motivated by a fear of failure. A person displays a fear of failure, for example, when he stops taking guitar lessons because improvement seems too difficult or decides not to try out for the baseball team because she probably cannot make it anyway. How does the fear of failure differ from the need for achievement? People display fear of failure when they choose easy or nonchallenging tasks in which failure is unlikely or difficult. For example, let us say that you have your choice of three puzzles to solve. The first puzzle is extremely easy, and you know that you can solve it. The second puzzle is more difficult, and you are not sure how well you will do. The third puzzle is extremely difficult, and you are certain it is impossible to solve. Most people, especially people with a strong need for achievement, would choose the difficult but not impossible puzzle. People who choose the extremely easy puzzle, however, display a fear of failure. The fear of failure may motivate a student to study only enough to just pass an exam but not enough to get a good grade.

People who are motivated by the fear of failure often find excuses to explain their poor performances. They do this to maintain a good self-image. For example, a sprinter may explain her slow time in the race as a result of missed sleep. If you receive a poor grade on a test, you may claim that the test was biased. Although creating these types of excuses helps us maintain good feelings about ourselves, it may also prevent us from taking responsibility for our own actions.

Fear of Success   Matina Horner (1970, 1972) asked 89 men to write a story beginning with the line, "After first term finals, John finds himself at the top of his medical school class." Substituting the name Anne for John in the opening line, she also asked 90 women to write a story. Ninety percent of the men wrote success stories. However, more than 65 percent of the women predicted doom for Anne.

On the basis of this study, Horner identified another dimension of achievement motivation—the *motive to avoid success*. Some people (like the females in Horner's study) are (or were) raised with the idea that being successful in all but a few careers is odd and unlikely. Thus, a woman who is a success in medicine, law, and other traditionally male occupations must be a failure as a woman. It might have been acceptable for Anne to pass her exams, but the fact that she did better than all the men in her class made the female participants anxious.

Horner discovered that bright women, who had a very real chance of achieving in their chosen fields, exhibited a stronger fear of success than did women who were average or slightly above average. Expecting success made them more likely to avoid it, despite the obvious advantages of a rewarding career. This seemed to confirm Horner's belief that success involves deep conflicts for some people.

Other researchers then set out to verify Horner's findings. They quickly found that the picture was more complicated than Horner's study suggested. For one thing, it is very difficult to define success. Being a mother might be quite satisfying for one woman but a sign of failure for someone who would have preferred a career outside the home. Also, it is often difficult to tell whether a person who does not try something is more afraid of success or failure.

In the late 1960s, when Horner's study was conducted, medical school was still dominated by males. Likewise, nursing school was dominated by females. What if females write about males and vice versa? What if females or males write about males' success in a female-dominated occupation? Then we find both men and women write stories reflecting Horner's "fear of success" (Cherry & Deaux, 1978). Later, researchers analyzed 64 studies bearing on the issue that Horner had raised. Measured on a mean rate, 45 percent of the men expressed a fear of success, while 49 percent of the women did—a small difference (Paludi, 1984). So, fear of success is found in both men and women.

Other Theories J.W. Atkinson developed an *expectancy-value* theory to explain goal-directed behavior. *Expectancy* is your estimated likelihood of success, and *value* is simply what the goal is worth to you.

Others have argued instead for a *competency* theory. Too easy a task or too difficult a task means we do not learn anything about how competent we are. So, to prove and improve our competency, we choose moderately difficult tasks where both successes and failures may be instructive (Schneider, 1984).

For example, in one experiment in a ring-toss game, children could choose to stand 1 to 15 feet

Reading Check
What is the motive to avoid success?

Level of Arousal

Source: Plotnick, 1999.

Figure 12.6 **Your Performance**

The Yerkes-Dodson law says that your performance on a task is an interaction between the level of physiological arousal and the difficulty of the task. So on difficult tasks, you do better if your arousal level is low. *According to the Yerkes-Dodson law, what level of arousal would help you do well on an exam?*

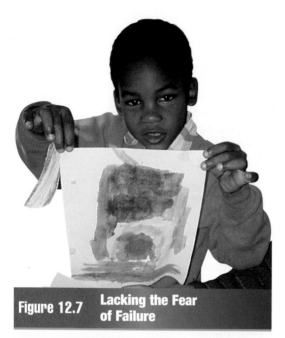

Figure 12.7

Figure 12.7 **Lacking the Fear of Failure**

Preschool children are very optimistic about their own abilities. They show great joy after successfully completing a task but rarely get discouraged by their failures. *Why do people who are motivated by the fear of failure not perform as well as people who are motivated by the need for achievement?*

fundamental needs: biological drives that must be satisfied to maintain life

psychological needs: the urge to belong and to give and receive love, and the urge to acquire esteem

self-actualization needs: the pursuit of knowledge and beauty or whatever else is required for the realization of one's unique potential

away from the stake onto which they tried to toss rings as a group watched. Those with a high need for achievement were up to 10 times more likely to choose an intermediate distance from the stakes than to choose ridiculously easy or impossibly difficult distances (McClelland, 1958).

Maslow's Hierarchy of Needs

Abraham Maslow, one of the pioneers of humanistic psychology, believed that *all* human beings need to feel competent, to win approval and recognition, and to sense that they have achieved something. He placed achievement motivation in the context of a hierarchy of needs all people share (see Figure 12.8). Maslow proposed that after we satisfy needs at the bottom of the triangle, we advance up to the next level and seek to satisfy the needs at that level. If we are at a higher level and our basic needs (on a lower level) are not satisfied, we may come back down the hierarchy.

Maslow's scheme incorporates all the factors we have discussed so far in this chapter and goes a step further. He begins with biological drives, including the need for physical safety and security. He asserted that people have to satisfy these **fundamental needs** to live. If people are hungry, most of their activities will be motivated by the drive to acquire food, and their functioning on a higher level will be hindered.

The second level in Maslow's hierarchy consists of **psychological needs:** the need to belong and to give and receive love, and the need to acquire esteem through competence and achievement. Maslow suggested that these needs function in much the same way that biological needs do and that they can be filled only by an outside source. A lack of love or esteem makes people anxious and tense. There is a driven quality to their behavior. They may engage in random, desperate, and sometimes maladaptive activities to ease their tensions.

Self-actualization needs are at the top of Maslow's hierarchy. These may include the pursuit of knowledge and beauty or whatever else is required for the realization of one's unique potential. Maslow believed that although relatively few people reach this level, we all have these needs. To be creative in the way we conduct our lives and use our talents, we must first satisfy our fundamental and psychological needs. The satisfaction of these needs motivates us to seek self-actualization. Maslow thus added to motivation theory the idea that some needs take precedence over others and the suggestion that achieving one level of satisfaction releases new needs and motivations.

Other research does not support Maslow's conclusion that one need must be satisfied before another can be (Liebert & Spiegler, 1994). Christopher Columbus, for example, may have achieved self-actualization, but he certainly put his (and many others') need for safety at risk in opting to seek a new route to China. Would we not conclude that his need for esteem was dominant in his search? Also, some people do not seem interested in fulfilling higher needs, such as achievement, although their lower, biological needs or safety needs have been met.

These researchers are suggesting that perhaps Maslow identified types of needs that may operate in all of us, but there is no guarantee that the needs must be satisfied in order. Any one need may dominate at a particular time, even as the organism is seeking to respond to others among his or her dominant needs. A need may be dominant in any of us at a particular moment, without necessarily meaning the other needs are not present and influencing our behavior at some level.

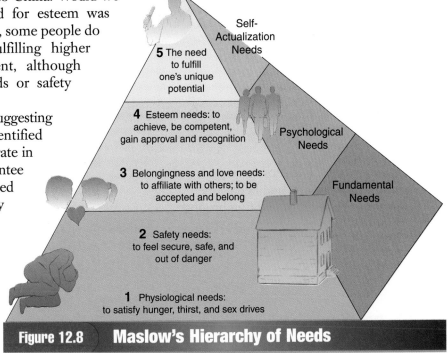

5 The need to fulfill one's unique potential — Self-Actualization Needs

4 Esteem needs: to achieve, be competent, gain approval and recognition

3 Belongingness and love needs: to affiliate with others; to be accepted and belong

2 Safety needs: to feel secure, safe, and out of danger

1 Physiological needs: to satisfy hunger, thirst, and sex drives

Psychological Needs

Fundamental Needs

Figure 12.8   Maslow's Hierarchy of Needs

According to Maslow, only after satisfying the lower level of needs is a person free to progress to the ultimate need of self-actualization. *Into what category in the hierarchy do biological needs fall?*

SECTION 2 Assessment

1. **Review the Vocabulary** Describe how fundamental, psychological, and self-actualization needs differ.

2. **Visualize the Main Idea** Use an organizer similar to the one below to list four motives associated with hunger.

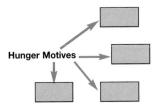

Hunger Motives

3. **Recall Information** What is the difference between the expectancy-value theory and the competency theory?

4. **Think Critically** What strategies would you offer to a friend who wanted to increase his or her need for achievement level? Explain why.

5. **Application Activity** Review Maslow's hierarchy of needs and analyze your life according to Maslow's scheme. Which groups of needs are frequently met? How do your needs—both fulfilled and unfulfilled—affect your thoughts and behaviors?

Reader's Guide

■ Main Idea
All emotions consist of three parts—the physical, cognitive, and behavioral aspects. Theories of emotion propose that emotions result from physical changes and/or mental processes.

■ Vocabulary
• emotion

■ Objectives
• Give examples of the physiological theories of emotion.
• Explain the cognitive theorists' approach to the study of emotion.

EXPLORING PSYCHOLOGY

Victory!

The United States and China were locked in a scoreless tie. . . . The game—the Women's World Cup final—had come down to a single penalty kick. [Brandi] Chastain approached the ball and barely hesitated before drilling her shot perfectly into the upper right corner of the net. As frenzied fans in Pasadena, Calif.'s Rose Bowl roared, she whipped off her shirt and waved it at the crowd before being buried in celebration by a pile of her teammates. "I didn't hear any noise. I didn't look at the [Chinese goalkeeper]," she said of her shot. "As soon as the whistle blew, I just stepped up and hit it. I just kind of lost my mind."

—from *Newsweek*, July 19, 1999

W hat drove Brandi Chastain to perfect her soccer game? Why did she try so hard? How did she feel when she scored the winning goal? Was she tired, thirsty, excited, nervous, or happy? It is difficult to draw a clear line between motives and emotions. When a person needs food, the stomach contracts, the level of sugar in the blood drops, neural and endocrine systems are thrown slightly off balance, and taste buds become more sensitive. When a person is frightened, heart and breathing rates quicken, energy level rises, the senses mobilize, and blood rushes away from the stomach into the brain, heart, and other muscles. Of course, a poet might diagnose a pounding heart, loss of appetite, and heightened awareness of the moonlight and scented breezes as love. Why, if all three involve identifiable physiological changes, do we call hunger a biological drive, and fear and love emotions?

It depends on whether we are describing the source of our behavior or the feelings associated with our behavior. When we want to emphasize the needs, desires, and mental calculations that lead to goal-directed behavior, we use the word "drive" or "motivation." When we want to stress the feelings associated with these decisions and activities, we use the word "emotion" or "affect."

Clearly, the two are intertwined. We frequently explain our motives in terms of emotions. Why did you walk out of the meeting? I was angry. Why do you go to so many parties? I enjoy meeting new people and love to dance. Why did you lend your notes to someone you do not particularly like? I felt guilty about talking behind his back.

As these examples demonstrate, emotions push and pull us in different directions. Sometimes emotions function like biological drives: Our feelings energize us and make us pursue a goal. Which goal we pursue may be determined by our social learning experiences. Other times we do things because we think they will make us feel good: Anticipated emotions are the incentive for our actions. Finally, emotions help us make decisions and communicate what is going on inside of us. As a result, others respond to our emotions and treat us accordingly.

Many psychologists talk about our *emotional intelligence*. This is the ability to perceive, imagine, and understand emotions and to use that information in decision making. We often need to make complicated decisions at work, in school, and with family and friends. The wrong decision can get us in trouble. Our emotional intelligence helps us gauge the situation and determine an appropriate action. For example, suppose you were talking with friends and wanted to tell a joke. Will your friends enjoy the joke, or will they think it is offensive? Judging the emotions involved in this social situation is a sign of your emotional intelligence.

emotion: a set of complex reactions to stimuli involving subjective feelings, physiological arousal, and observable behavior

EXPRESSING EMOTIONS

An **emotion** is a subjective feeling provoked by real or imagined objects or events that have high significance to the individual. Emotions result from four occurrences: (1) you must interpret some stimulus;

Figure 12.9 — The Range of Emotions

Emotions are subjective feelings, so psychologists cannot agree on how many emotions exist or the exact impact of a specific emotion. *How can you explain "avoidance behavior" and "approach behavior" indicated in this chart?*

Terror Hatred Rage Surprise Excitement Ecstasy Passion

Disgust Fear Contempt Anger Enthusiasm Rhapsody Love Joy

Shame Distaste Timidity Hostility Interest Like Happiness

Dislike

Shyness Boredom Contentment Desire

Depression Want

Guilt

Sadness

Level of Arousal

AVOIDANCE BEHAVIOR **APPROACH BEHAVIOR**

Negative Emotion Positive Emotion

Source: Kissin, 1986.

Did You Know?

Emotions and Decisions During surgery to remove a brain tumor, "Elliot" suffered damage to his prefrontal cortex (Damasio, 1994). After the surgery, Elliot reported feeling almost no emotions. He described his brain surgery and the following deterioration of his life with calm detachment. Along with the loss of emotions, though, Elliot lost his ability to make decisions. When given information, he could discuss probable outcomes of each decision he might make, but he could not actually make the decision. If he forced himself to make a decision, he soon abandoned his decision. As a result, Elliot could not maintain normal relationships with friends. This points to the fact that our emotions play a large role in our decision making.

(2) you have a subjective feeling, such as fear or happiness; (3) you experience physiological responses, such as an increased heart rate; and (4) you display an observable behavior, such as smiling or crying (Plotnick, 1999).

All emotions have three parts: the physical, the behavioral, and the cognitive parts. The physical aspect has to do with how the emotion affects the physical arousal of an individual. This level of arousal directs the body how to respond to the experienced emotion. The behavioral part is the outward expression of the emotion such as body language, hand gestures, and the tone of a person's voice. The cognitive aspect concerns how we think or interpret a situation, which affects our emotions. For example, if someone says hello, we interpret that person as being friendly, hostile, or mocking, which in turn affects our emotional response.

In *The Expression of the Emotions in Man and Animals* (1872), Charles Darwin argued that all people express certain basic feelings in the same ways. Without knowing a person's language, you can tell whether he or she is amused or infuriated just by looking at that person's face (see Figure 12.10). One group of researchers (Ekman, Friesen, & Ellsworth, 1972) selected a group of photographs they thought depicted surprise, anger, sadness, and happiness. They then showed the photographs to people from five different cultures and asked them to say what they believed the person in each photograph was feeling. The overwhelming majority of the participants identified the emotions as the researchers expected they would. Was this simply because they had met Americans—or at least seen American television shows and movies—and so learned how to "read" our facial expressions? Apparently not. A second study was conducted in a remote part of New Guinea, with people who had relatively little contact with outsiders and virtually no exposure to mass media. They, too, were able to identify the emotions being expressed.

These studies imply that certain basic facial expressions are *innate*—that is, part of our biological inheritance. Observations of children who were born without sight and hearing lend support to this view. These youngsters could not have learned how to communicate feelings by observing other people. Still, they laugh like other children when they are happy, pout and frown to express

Figure 12.10 Facial Feedback

There are many specific inherited facial expressions that signal specific feelings or emotional states. *Which emotions are expressed in these photos? Explain your answers.*

resentment, and clench their fists and teeth in anger (Goodenough, 1932).

Psychologist Carroll Izard and his colleagues (Trotter, 1983) developed a coding system for assessing emotional states in people. By noticing changes in different parts of the face, such as the eyebrows, eyes, and mouth, they have been able to identify 10 different emotional states. For example, anger is indicated when a person's eyebrows are sharply lowered and drawn together, and the eyes narrowed or squinted (see Figure 12.11). Another psychologist (Russell, 1994) studied the impact of emotions on facial structures in 11 cross-cultural studies. He concluded that there are universally recognized facial expressions of emotions.

Learning is an important factor in emotional expression. James Averill (1983) believes that many of our everyday emotional reactions are the result of social expectations and consequences. He believes

Profiles In Psychology

Paul Ekman

1934–

"The face is the primary site for the display of emotions. Together with the voice, it may tell the listener how the speaker feels about what is being said . . ."

Paul Ekman claims that human faces express emotion in a universal way. That is, we all smile when we are happy and scowl when we are angry. Ekman did not always believe this, though. He once thought that facial expressions were learned and differed depending on our culture. Then Ekman traveled to Papua New Guinea and studied the Fores—an isolated group. He found that they grinned when they were happy and scowled when angry, just like we do.

Since then Ekman has developed the Facial Action Coding System (FACS), which organizes facial expressions into 46 separate movements, such as blinking, raising our brows, and pursing our lips. Ekman and other researchers used FACS to identify the facial characteristics of seven emotions: anger, fear, contempt, disgust, sadness, surprise, and happiness. Ekman claims that few of us (10 to 20 percent) can actually hide our true emotions. Despite our efforts, for example, to hide our disgust, some facial movements give us away.

that emotions are responses of the whole person and that we cannot separate an individual's physical or biological experience of emotions from that person's thoughts or actions associated with those emotions. We learn to express and experience emotions in the company of other people, and we learn that emotions can serve different social functions. Parents, for example, modify their children's emotions by responding angrily to some outbursts, by being sympathetic to others, and on occasion by ignoring their youngsters. In this way, children are taught which emotions are considered appropriate in different situations.

Learning explains the differences we find among cultures once we go beyond such basic expressions as laughing or crying. Children will imitate the expressions used by their parents or caregivers. Thus, emotions are universal, but the expression of them is limited by learning how to

Figure
12.11

Threatening
Elements

When people from various cultures were asked to identify the threatening shapes in each pair, they consistently selected the triangular and diagonal elements. *Which elements would you use to make a scary mask? Why?*

express them. Children are taught—either directly or indirectly—which emotions are appropriate in certain circumstances. Children learn how to express these emotions at the appropriate times. In effect, children are learning an emotional culture. What these findings suggest is that all of us are born with the capacity for emotion and with certain basic forms of expression, but when, where, and how we express different feelings depend in large part on learning.

Analyzing facial expressions helps us to describe emotions, but it does not tell us where emotions come from. Some psychologists believe emotions derive from physical changes, while others believe that emotions result from mental processes.

Physiological Theories

Trying to figure out the cognitive, behavioral, and physical parts of emotions has led to several theories of emotions. In *Principles of Psychology*, a classic work published in 1890, William James attempted to summarize the best available literature on human behavior, motivations, and feelings. When it came to drawing up a catalog of human emotions, James gave up; he felt there were too many subtle variations. Yet he was struck by the fact that nearly every description of emotions he read emphasized bodily changes. We associate feelings with sudden increases or decreases in energy, muscle tension and relaxation, and sensations in the pits of our stomachs.

The James-Lange Theory   After much thought, James concluded that we use the word "emotion" to describe our visceral or "gut" reactions to the things that take place around us. In other words, James (1890) believed that emotions are the perception of certain internal bodily changes.

> My theory . . . is that *the bodily changes follow directly the perception of the exciting fact, and that our feeling of the same changes as they occur IS the emotion.* Commonsense says, we lose our fortune, are sorry and weep; we meet a bear, are frightened and run; we are insulted by a rival, are angry and strike. . . . [T]he more rational statement is that we feel sorry because we cry, angry because we strike, afraid because we tremble. . . . Without the bodily states following on the perception, the latter would be . . . pale, colorless, destitute of emotional warmth.

Whereas other psychologists had assumed that emotions trigger bodily changes, James argued that bodily reactions form the basis of labeling and experiencing emotions. Because Carl Lange came to the same conclusion at about the same time, this position is known as the *James-Lange theory* (Lange & James, 1922). Carroll Izard's (1972) theory of emotions bears a striking resemblance to the James-Lange theory. He believed that our conscious experience of emotion results from the sensory feedback we receive from the muscles in our faces (see More About Facial Feedback Theory). You can check this out by noticing the difference in your emotional experience when you smile for two minutes as opposed to when you frown for two minutes. According to Izard's view, if you continue to frown, you will experience an unpleasant emotion. Thus, we react to our physiological state and label it as sadness.

Critics of the James-Lange theory claim that different emotions such as anger, sadness, or fear are not necessarily associated with different physiological reactions. For example, anger and fear may cause the same bodily reactions. Therefore, James had it backwards—you do not run from trouble and then feel fear; you feel fear first and then run. Critics also allege that some complex emotions such as jealousy or love require much interpretation and thought on our part. The James-Lange theory leaves out the influence of our own cognitive influences on emotions. Although physiological changes do not cause emotions, they may increase the intensity of the emotions that we feel. For instance, when we feel anger and our hearts race, that anger may be heightened by the way our body reacts to it.

The Cannon-Bard Theory In 1929 Walter B. Cannon published a summary of the evidence against the James-Lange theory. Cannon argued that the thalamus (part of the lower brain) is the seat of emotion—an idea Philip Bard (1934) expanded and refined. According to the *Cannon-Bard theory*, certain experiences activate the thalamus, and the thalamus sends messages to the cortex and to the other body organs. This theory states that the brain sends two reactions—arousal and experience of emotion. But one does not cause the other. Thus, when we use the word "emotion," we are referring to the *simultaneous* burst of activity in the brain and "gut" reactions. In Cannon's words, "The peculiar quality of emotion is added to simple sensation when the thalamic processes are aroused" (1929). Later, more sophisticated experiments showed that the thalamus is not involved in emotional experience, but the hypothalamus is.

Cannon also emphasized the importance of physiological arousal in many different emotions. He was the first to describe the "fight-or-flight" reaction of the sympathetic nervous system that prepares us for an emergency. Some of the signs of physiological arousal are measured in one of the most famous applications of psychological knowledge: lie detection.

Cognitive Theories

Cognitive theorists believe that bodily changes and thinking *work together* to produce emotions. Physiological arousal is only half of the story. What you feel depends on how you interpret your symptoms. This, in turn, depends on labeling the physical arousal with an emotion to interpret our internal state.

The Schachter-Singer Experiment Stanley Schachter and Jerome Singer designed an experiment to explore this theory (1962). They told all their

Facial Feedback Theory

The facial feedback theory says that your brain interprets feedback from the movement of your facial muscles as different emotions (Ekman, 1984). For example, you see a dark shadow in the corner of your bedroom at night. You react by raising your eyebrows and widening your eyes. Your brain interprets these facial expressions as those associated with fear, and you feel fear.

Critics of this theory claim that although your facial expressions may influence your emotions, they do not cause your emotions. People whose facial muscles are paralyzed can experience emotions even though their facial muscles do not move (McIntosh, 1996). You can influence your mood, though, with your expressions. For instance, have you ever noticed that if you just smile, you feel a little happier?

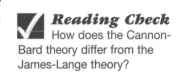

Reading Check
How does the Cannon-Bard theory differ from the James-Lange theory?

Lie Detection

Throughout time, people have tried to find a way to detect when others are lying. The polygraph is an instrument that records the arousal of the sympathetic nervous system, including blood pressure, heart rate, and breathing rate. The polygraph works under the assumption that people feel nervous when they lie, so their physiological reactions will give them away. How effective are polygraphs? Many innocent people become nervous when questioned and so appear to be lying.

The Guilty-Knowledge test, though, is a modified version of the polygraph test. The questioner asks more accurate questions—questions that could be threatening only to someone who knows the unpublicized facts of the crime. For example, instead of asking, "Did you rob the gas station?" the person is asked, "Was the gas station robbed at 6:00 P.M.? At midnight? With a gun? With a knife?" People who display heightened arousal in response to the correct answers are presumed guilty. This test identifies guilty people more accurately.

Reading Check
According to Schachter, what role does the environment play in the emotions you experience?

participants they were testing the effects of vitamin C on eyesight. In reality, most received an adrenaline injection. The informed group was told that the "vitamin" injection would make their hearts race and their bodies tremble (which was true). The misinformed group was told that the injection would make them numb. An uninformed group was not told anything about how their bodies would react to the shot. A control group received a neutral injection that did not produce any symptoms. Like the third group, these participants were not given any information about possible side effects.

After the injection, each participant was taken to a reception room to wait for the "vision test." There they found another person who was actually part of the experiment. The participants thought the accomplice had had the same injection as theirs. With some participants, the accomplice acted wild and crazy—dancing around, laughing, making paper airplanes with the questionnaire they had been asked to fill out. Other participants had to fill out a long and offensive questionnaire. The accomplice for this group acted more and more angry as the participants filled out the questionnaire.

Participants from the first group, who had been told how the injection would affect them, watched the accomplice with mild amusement. So did participants who had received the neutral injection. However, those from the second and third groups, who either had an incorrect idea or no idea about the side effects, joined in with the accomplice. If he was euphoric, so were they; if he was angry, they became angry.

What does this experiment demonstrate? Internal components of emotion (such as those adrenaline produces) affect a person differently, depending on his or her interpretation or perception of the social situation. When people cannot explain their physical reactions, they take cues from their environment. The accomplice provided cues. Yet when people knew that their hearts were beating faster because of the shot, they did not feel particularly happy or angry. The experiment also shows that internal changes are important—otherwise the participants from the neutral group would have acted in the same way as those from the misinformed groups. Perception and arousal *interact* to create emotions.

Critics of this theory point out that you do not need to first experience physiological arousal to feel an emotion. Sometimes you feel an emotion first, and then your body reacts. For example, you may let your brother use your computer. When you go to use your computer and see that all of your files have been destroyed, you get angry, and then your body reacts with anger. Critics also say that you use processes other than environmental cues to interpret your emotions. Your thoughts play a large role in appraising your emotions.

Opponent-Process Theory Physiological processes clearly are controlled by homeostatic mechanisms that keep the body within certain narrow limits. Emotions, such as being in love, are just as disabling to normal activity. Why would the body not develop a homeostatic mechanism to control the effects of extreme emotions? The body has sympathetic and parasympathetic systems. The sympathetic system energizes the body for activity, while the parasympathetic system calms and relaxes the body. The opponent-process theory states that these two systems act in concert to regulate and manipulate our emotions.

Psychologists Richard Solomon and John Corbit (1974) proposed the opponent-process theory—a homeostatic theory of emotional reactions based on classical conditioning. They proposed that the removal of a stimulus that excites one emotion causes a swing to an opposite emotion. If the external, emotion-arousing event is State A, the internal force is labeled State B (see Figure 12.13).

Suppose you meet someone on the first day of school, and from the start, you like each other. The two of you stun your English teacher with sharp questions and quick answers when challenged. Later, you share a wonderful lunch—both of you love the same four-topping pizza. An afternoon in the park was glorious, and doing homework assignments together is fun and easy. Then, later that day, your friend tells you that his or her family is moving to the coast—gone forever. You are annoyed . . . but let us face it, the next day you are back out looking for another special person (because little classical conditioning has occurred). The opponent-process theory would indicate that with this person you were subjected to State A, which aroused your emotions, but no State B had developed.

Now let us put a different slant on the ending. Your friend did not move away. You marry and enjoy a loving relationship and a long, healthy life together. One morning, however, your spouse dies. Your years together had produced a strong countering State B, which occurred anytime you were in the presence of your beloved. It kept your emotions near neutral and allowed you to get on with your daily activities. Yet now

Figure 12.12 Theories of Emotion

These theories of emotion differ depending on the relationship of physiological change and cognitive interpretation of emotion. *What causes the emotion in each theory?*

James-Lange Theory

↓ You experience physiological changes.

↓ Your brain interprets the physiological changes.

↓ You feel a specific emotion.

↓ You demonstrate observable behavior.

Facial Feedback Theory

↓ The muscles in your face move to form an expression.

↓ Your brain interprets the muscle movement.

↓ You feel an emotion.

↓ You demonstrate observable behavior.

Cannon-Bard Theory

↓ Your experience activates the hypothalamus.

↓ The hypothalamus sends messages to the cerebral cortex and body organs simultaneously.

↓ You feel an emotion and your body reacts at the same time.

Schachter-Singer Experiment

↓ You experience physiological arousal.

↓ You interpret (cognitively) environmental cues.

↓ You feel an emotion.

↓ You demonstrate observable behavior.

Figure 12.13 Fear and Relief

According to the opponent-process theory, when the stimulus for one emotion is removed, you feel the opposite emotion. *According to this theory, what happens when the experience is repeated many times?*

that your spouse is gone, you are left with only the incredibly depressing effects of the remaining classically conditioned State B. Have you ever had the misfortune of watching one of your grandparents lose the partner to whom he or she was deeply devoted?

The significance of this theory is that if the State A event is a terrifying one—such as your first parachute jump—it still predicts what will happen. Novice parachutists are terrified coming out of a plane but are briefly but wildly delighted when they return to the ground—they are subject to State A. An experienced jumper knows that how he or she packs the chute is crucial, how they coordinate during the fall is important, and it is important that they know how to land. The jump is eventually only a bit stressful—thanks to State B. They usually jump for the long-term satisfaction that is generated—again, thanks to the aftereffects of State B—once the jump itself is completed.

In fact, other emotion researchers believe that emotion may play an important role in our survival as human beings and in our ability to achieve goals, precisely because it spurs us to action. Emotions and physical changes are intertwined. It will probably be many years before we understand all the complex ways in which the two interact in human behavior.

SECTION 3 Assessment

1. **Review the Vocabulary** What are the three parts of an emotion?

2. **Visualize the Main Idea** Use a flowchart similar to the one below to describe how the opponent-process theory works.

The Opponent-Process Theory

3. **Recall Information** What does it mean when psychologists say that certain facial expressions are *innate?*

4. **Think Critically** You are awakened by a loud noise in the middle of the night. You feel frightened and you start to tremble. According to the James-Lange theory, which came first—the fright or the trembling? According to Schachter and Singer's theory, which came first?

5. **Application Activity** Create a "self-test" to evaluate the presence and intensity of an emotion. For example, if you are testing for anger, you may create a checklist that includes the following: People tell you that you need to calm down. You feel tense much of the time. Give the self-test to several people and rate their responses.

Summary and Vocabulary

The study of motivation and emotion focuses on the underlying why of behavior. Motivation refers to the physical and mental factors that cause us to act in a specific way at a specific time. Emotion involves our subjective feelings, physical arousal, and external expressions in response to situations and events.

Section 1 | Theories of Motivation

Main Idea:
Psychologists explain motivation and why we experience it in different ways through instinct, drive-reduction, incentive, and cognitive theories of motivation.

- The instinct theory of motivation stressed that humans were motivated by a variety of instincts.
- The drive-reduction theory is based on the idea that all human motives are extensions of basic biological needs.
- The incentive theory stresses the role of the environment in motivating behavior.
- The cognitive theory proposes that motivation is influenced by forces both inside and outside individuals that energize them to move.

Section 2 | Biological and Social Motives

Main Idea: Much of life is spent trying to satisfy biological and social needs. Biological needs are physiological requirements that we must fulfill to survive, whereas social needs are those that are learned through experience.

- Biological motives often involve the organisms' need to correct imbalances and deviations from their normal state.
- The hypothalamus interprets three kinds of information—the amount of glucose entering a body's cells, an individual's set-point, and body temperature—to determine whether an individual will eat or not.
- Social motives are learned from people's interactions with other people.
- The achievement motive concerns the desire to set challenging goals and to persist in trying to reach those goals despite obstacles, frustrations, and setbacks.

Section 3 | Emotions

Main Idea: All emotions consist of three parts—the physical, cognitive, and behavioral aspects. Theories of emotion propose that emotions result from physical changes and/or mental processes.

- An emotion is a subjective feeling provoked by real or imagined objects or events that have high significance to the individual.
- All emotions have three parts: the physical, the behavioral, and the cognitive parts.
- Some psychologists believe emotions derive from physical changes, while others believe that emotions result from mental processes.

Chapter Vocabulary

motivation (p. 314)

instincts (p. 314)

need (p. 314)

drive (p. 315)

homeostasis (p. 315)

incentive (p. 316)

extrinsic motivation (p. 316)

intrinsic motivation (p. 316)

lateral hypothalamus (LH) (p. 320)

ventromedial hypothalamus (VMH) (p. 321)

fundamental needs (p. 326)

psychological needs (p. 326)

self-actualization needs (p. 326)

emotion (p. 329)

Self-Check Quiz
Visit the *Understanding Psychology* Web site at
psychology.glencoe.com and click on **Chapter 12—
Self-Check Quizzes** to prepare for the Chapter Test.

Reviewing Vocabulary

Choose the letter of the correct term or concept
below to complete the sentence.

a. motivation
b. need
c. drive
d. incentive
e. lateral hypothalamus (LH)

f. ventromedial hypothalamus (VMH)
g. fundamental needs
h. psychological needs
i. self-actualization needs
j. emotion

1. An internal condition that orients an individual
toward a specific goal is a(n) _____.
2. A(n) _____ is a subjective feeling provoked by real or imagined objects or events that
have high significance to the individual.
3. The need to belong and to give and receive love
are part of an individual's _____.
4. The _____ is the part of the brain that
sends signals to tell you to eat.
5. The result an individual is trying to achieve
through his or her motivated behavior is a(n)
_____, also known as a reinforcer.
6. According to Maslow, needs such as the pursuit
of knowledge and beauty are part of an individual's _____.
7. The _____ is the part of the brain that
sends signals to tell you when you have had
enough food.
8. _____ includes the various psychological
and physiological factors that cause people to
act a certain way at a certain time.
9. According to Maslow, _____ are the first
level of needs that people have to satisfy.
10. A lack of something desirable or useful is a(n)
_____.

Recalling Facts

1. Which theory of motivation suggests that all
human motives are extensions of basic biological needs?
2. Explain the difference between extrinsic motivation and intrinsic motivation.
3. How does McClelland measure a person's need
for achievement?
4. Describe the five levels of needs in Maslow's
hierarchy.
5. Using diagrams similar to the ones below, identify the basic principles in the James-Lange theory and the Cannon-Bard theory of emotions.

Critical Thinking

1. **Evaluating Information** Try going without
bread in your meals for several days a week. Do
you find that you are beginning to think about
bread more often? Are you becoming more
aware of advertisements for bread? Compare
your experience with the description of drive-
reduction behavior in this chapter.
2. **Making Inferences** Which theory of motivation would best explain why some people
engage in high-risk activities, such as sky-diving
or mountain climbing?
3. **Demonstrating Reasoned Judgment** Cognitive
psychologists believe that people behave in particular ways because of extrinsic motivation or
intrinsic motivation. Which of the two do you
think is the stronger motivator? Why do you
think so?
4. **Synthesizing Information** What factors might
account for overeating at holiday dinners, such
as Thanksgiving?
5. **Applying Concepts** Using what you have
learned about emotions in the chapter, respond
to the following statement: Men feel fewer emotions than women.

Assessment

Psychology Projects

1. **Theories of Motivation**   Choose one of the following theories of motivation: the drive-reduction theory, the incentive theory, or the cognitive theory. Review each theory's explanation of motivation. Then work with a partner to create a skit that illustrates the basic premises of the theory you chose.

2. **Emotions**   With a partner or as a group, select 10 emotions to express. Then play a variation of charades, with one person attempting to convey each of these emotions by facial expression alone. What emotions are harder to convey than others? Are there consistent differences in interpretation between individuals? How important do you think context (the social situation in which the facial expression occurs) is in perceiving other people's emotions? Summarize your group interaction.

Technology Activity

Use the Internet to find the latest research about motivation. Summarize your findings in a short paper, comparing the latest research results with the theories discussed in the chapter.

Psychology Journal

Analyze the list of concerns and aspirations you wrote in your journal. Evaluate these items in terms of Maslow's hierarchy of needs. In other words, classify the items in terms of fundamental needs, psychological needs, and self-actualization needs. In your journal, write a rationale for classifying the individual items as you did.

Building Skills

Interpreting a Chart   In an experiment run by Paul Ekman, actors were hired to assume specific facial expressions that mirrored emotions. One group was told which facial muscles to contract, but they were not told to feel or express any particular emotion. Another group was asked to think of emotional experiences in their lives that produced the six emotions listed. The researchers then measured several physiological responses of both groups. Review the information in the chart, then answer the questions that follow.

Changes in Heart Rate and Skin Temperature for Six Emotions

Specific Emotion	Change in Heart Rate (beats/min.)	Changes in Skin Temperature (degrees C)
Anger	+8.0	+.16
Fear	+8.0	−.01
Distress	+6.5	+.01
Joy	+2.0	+.03
Surprise	+1.8	−.01
Disgust	−0.3	−.03

Source: Ekman, Levenson, & Friesen, 1983.

1. What emotions did the study address? What physiological changes were measured?

2. Which emotion seemed to have the greatest effect on physiology? The least effect?

3. Why do you think that certain emotions cause greater physiological changes than other emotions?

See the Skills Handbook, page 628, for an explanation of interpreting charts.

Practice and **assess** key social studies skills with **Glencoe Skillbuilder Interactive Workbook CD-ROM, Level 2.**

UNIT
5

Personality and Individuality

Contents

A range of ▶
personalities

Why It's Important

Throughout time people have proposed different theories to explain the development of human personality. In the seventeenth century, Thomas Hobbes argued that all humans are inherently selfish. In the eighteenth century, Jean-Jacques Rousseau claimed that humans are basically good. Which is it? What makes us who we are?

Psychological Testing

PSYCHOLOGY JOURNAL

Suppose you were asked to select the best person to be your teacher from among a group of applicants. How would you go about making the selection? Write your answer in your journal. ■

PSYCHOLOGY Online

Chapter Overview
Visit the *Understanding Psychology* Web site at psychology.glencoe.com and click on **Chapter 13—Chapter Overviews** to preview the chapter.

Characteristics of Psychological Tests

Reader's Guide

■ Main Idea
To be useful, tests have to exhibit reliability, validity, and standardization.

■ Vocabulary
- reliability
- validity
- percentile system
- norms

■ Objectives
- Identify three ways of measuring reliability.
- Explain test standardization and how test validity is assessed.

EXPLORING PSYCHOLOGY

Not Fair!

I vividly remember my first genuine IQ test. I was 17 at the time. The youth director at my church was in graduate school, working on an advanced degree in psychology, and as part of a course in intelligence testing, he was required to administer an IQ test to several subjects. I was one of his selected "volunteers," although I was also a friend. I remember wondering later about whether or not he had given me an unfair advantage on the test. He often responded to my asking for clarification by going into great detail while explaining a particular kind of question. I wondered if my score would be comparable to that of another person who was tested by someone who was not so generous about clarifying items.

—from *Psychology: Science, Behavior, and Life* by Robert L. Crooks and Jean Stein, 1988

All tests have one characteristic that makes them both fascinating and remarkably practical: they try to make it possible to find out a great deal about a person in a short time. Tests can be somewhat useful with the following: in predicting how well a person might do in a particular career; in assessing an individual's desires, interests, and attitudes; and in revealing psychological problems. One virtue of standardized tests is that they can provide comparable data about many individuals. Tests can show how an individual compares to others. Further, psychologists can use some tests to help people understand things about themselves more clearly. Using tests to predict behavior, though, is controversial. It is important to keep in mind what the test is measuring.

One of the great dangers of testing is that we tend to forget that tests are merely tools for measuring and predicting human behavior. We start to think of test results (for example, an IQ) as an end in itself. The justification for using a test to make decisions about a person's future depends on whether a decision based on test scores would be fairer and more accurate than one based on other criteria. The fairness and usefulness of a test depend on several factors: its reliability, its validity, and standardization.

TEST RELIABILITY

reliability: the ability of a test to give the same results under similar conditions

The term **reliability** refers to a test's consistency—its ability to yield the same result under a variety of different circumstances. There are three basic ways of determining a test's reliability. First, if a person retakes the test or takes a similar test within a short time after the first testing, does he or she receive approximately the same score? If, for example, you take a mechanical aptitude test three times in the space of six months and score 65 in January, a perfect score of 90 in March, and 70 in June, then the test is unreliable because it does not produce a measurement that is stable over time. The scores vary too much. This is assessing the measure's *test-retest* reliability (see Figure 13.2).

The second measure of reliability is whether the test yields the same results when scored at different times by different people. If both your teacher and another teacher critique an essay test that you have taken, and one gives you a B while the other gives you a D, then you have reason to complain about the test's reliability. The score you receive depends more on the grader than on you. This is called *inter-scorer* reliability. If the same teacher grades papers at different times, he or she may score the same essay differently. This is *scorer* reliability. On a reliable test, your score would be the same no matter who graded it and when it was graded.

One final way of determining a test's reliability is to find out whether, if you divide the test in half and score each half separately, the two scores are approximately the same. This is called *split-half* reliability. If a test is supposed to measure one quality in a person—for example, reading comprehension or administrative ability—it should not have some sections on which the person scores high and others on which he or she scores low.

Figure 13.1 **Taking Psychological Tests**

Americans rely heavily on psychological testing because such tests promise to reveal a great deal about a person in a very short time. *How can you judge the fairness and usefulness of a test?*

In checking tests for reliability, psychologists try to prevent variables from influencing a person's score. All kinds of irrelevant matters can interfere with a test. No test can screen out all interferences, but a highly reliable test can eliminate a good part of them.

TEST VALIDITY

A test may be reliable but still not valid. **Validity** is the ability of a test to measure what it is intended to measure (see Figure 13.3). For example, a test that consists primarily of vocabulary lists will not measure ability for engineering. A history test will not measure general learning ability. A test you take in physical education class may not measure your knowledge of grammar, or a history test that asks questions that were not covered in class does not measure what you learned in class.

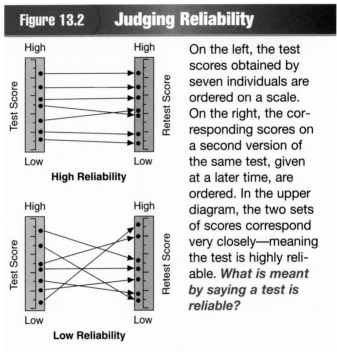

Figure 13.2 | Judging Reliability

High Reliability

Low Reliability

On the left, the test scores obtained by seven individuals are ordered on a scale. On the right, the corresponding scores on a second version of the same test, given at a later time, are ordered. In the upper diagram, the two sets of scores correspond very closely—meaning the test is highly reliable. *What is meant by saying a test is reliable?*

validity: the ability of a test to measure what it is intended to measure

Determining the validity of a test is more complex than assessing its reliability. One of the chief methods for measuring validity is to find out how well a test *predicts* performance—its *predictive* validity. For example, a group of psychologists designs a test to measure management ability. They ask questions about management systems, attitudes toward employees, and other relevant information. Will the people who score high on this test really make good managers?

Suppose the test makers decide that a good way to check the validity of the test is to find out how much a manager's staff improves in productivity in one year. If the staffs of those managers who scored high on the test produce more than the staffs of those managers who scored low on the test, the test may be considered valid. Corporations may then adopt it as one tool to use in deciding whom to hire as managers, assuming the test is also valid in their situation.

What if managers who are good at raising productivity are poor at decision making? It may be that this test measures talent for improving productivity, not general management ability. This is the kind of difficulty psychologists encounter in trying to assess the validity of a test. As the example shows, nothing can be said about a test's validity unless the purpose of the test is absolutely clear.

STANDARDIZATION

Tests must be *standardized*. Standardization refers to two things. First, standardized tests must be administered and scored the same way every time. Test administrators are trained to follow the same procedures and

Figure 13.3   **Judging Validity**

The lower diagram might represent the comparison of scores on the "head size" test of intelligence on the left with school grades on the right. (The "head size" test is simply measuring the size of a student's head.) The upper diagram might represent the result of comparing the Stanford-Binet Intelligence Scale scores with school grades. *What defines a valid test?*

to ask the same questions the same way. If test administrators give instructions in an inconsistent manner or provide hints, errors in assessing the test taker would result. Second, standardization refers to establishing the norm, or average score, made by a large group of people.

Establishing Norms

Once a test result is obtained, the examiner must translate the score into something useful. Suppose a child answers 32 of 50 questions on a vocabulary test correctly. What does this score mean? If the test is reliable and valid, it means that the child can be expected to understand a certain percentage of the words in a book at the reading level being tested. In other words, the score predicts how the child will perform at a given level.

Yet a "raw" score does not tell us where the child stands in relation to other children at his or her age and grade level. If most children answered 45 or more questions correctly, 32 is a low score. If most answered only 20 questions correctly, however, 32 is a very high score.

When psychologists design a test to be used in a variety of settings, they usually set up a scale for comparison by establishing norms. This is usually done by transforming raw test scores into a **percentile system,** which resembles what is called "grading on the curve." In the percentile system, the scores actually achieved on the test are placed in order, ranging from the highest to the lowest. Each score is then compared with this list and assigned a percentile according to the percentage of scores that fall at or below this point. For example, if half the children in the above example scored 32 or below, then a score of 32 is at the 50th percentile. If 32 were the top score, it would be at the 100th percentile. In the example given in Figure 13.4, a score of 32 puts the child in the 75th percentile, because only 25 percent of the children scored higher than she did.

The test is given to a large representative sample of the group to be measured—for example, sixth graders or army privates or engineers. Percentiles are then established on the basis of the scores achieved by this standardization group. These percentiles are called the test's **norms.** Most of the intelligence, aptitude, and personality tests you will encounter have been provided with norms in this way. Your percentile on an aptitude test such as the Scholastic Assessment Test (SAT), for example, reflects your standing among people of your age and grade who have taken these exams.

percentile system: ranking of test scores that indicates the ratio of scores lower and higher than a given score

✔ *Reading Check*
Why must raw scores be transformed into percentiles?

norms: standard of comparison for test results developed by giving the test to large, well-defined groups of people

You should remember, however, that norms are not really standards—even though a norm group is sometimes misleadingly referred to as a "standardization group." Norms refer only to what has been found to be average for a particular group. If John can read at the 50th percentile level, that does not mean that he has met some absolute standard for ability to read. It means only that he reads better than half the population and worse than the other half in his particular group.

In summary, when you take a test and obtain your score, you should consider the following questions in evaluating the results. (1) Do you think that if you took the same test again, you would receive a similar score? (2) Does your performance on this test reflect your normal performance in the subject? (3) If you were to compare your score with those of your classmates, would it reflect your general standing within that group?

Figure 13.4   Establishing Percentiles

The range of possible raw scores on a test is shown in relation to an idealized curve that indicates the proportion of people who achieved each score. The vertical lines indicate percentiles, or proportions of the curve below certain points. Thus, the line indicated as the 1st percentile is the line below which only 1 percent of the curve lies. *How do psychologists establish a scale for comparing test results?*

<table>
</table>

SECTION 1   Assessment

1. **Review the Vocabulary** What is meant when we ask about the reliability or validity of a test?

2. **Visualize the Main Idea** Using a diagram similar to the one below, identify three measures of a test's reliability.

3. **Recall Information** What does it mean if a test is standardized? Why do we standardize tests?

4. **Think Critically** Do you think an intelligence test would be a valid test for measuring a person's knowledge of a foreign language? Explain.

5. **Application Activity** Ask a teacher for an anonymous listing of all the scores on a recent test. Using the information in this section, establish the percentiles for the test scores.

Chapter 13 / Psychological Testing   **347**

Intelligence Testing

Reader's Guide

■ Main Idea
Several IQ tests are used to measure intelligence, although there are many views about what constitutes intelligence.

■ Vocabulary
- intelligence
- two-factor theory
- triarchic theory
- emotional intelligence
- intelligence quotient (IQ)
- heritability
- cultural bias

■ Objectives
- Explain the various views of intelligence.
- Identify two kinds of IQ tests.

EXPLORING PSYCHOLOGY

Is This Intelligence?

It is typical for members of the Trukese, a small tribe in the South Pacific, to sail a hundred miles in open ocean waters. Although their destination may be just a small dot of land less than a mile wide, the Trukese are able to sail unerringly toward it without the aid of compass, chronometer, sextant, or any of the other sailing tools that are indispensable to modern western navigation. They are able to sail accurately, even when prevailing winds do not allow a direct approach. . . .

How are the Trukese able to navigate so effectively? If you ask them, they could not explain it.

—from *Understanding Psychology* by **Robert S. Feldman, 1993**

Trukese intelligence

rukese navigation abilities point out the difficulty in coming to grips with what is meant by intelligence. Some might say that the inability of the Trukese to explain their sailing techniques is a sign of unintelligent behavior. It is hard to accuse the Trukese of being unintelligent, though. They sail successfully through the open ocean waters every day.

VIEWS OF INTELLIGENCE

Psychologists do not agree on the meaning of the word *intelligence*. Most believe that **intelligence** is the ability to acquire new ideas and new behavior and to adapt to new situations. Others believe that intelligence is what allows you to do well on intelligence tests and in school. The concept, however, continues to be difficult to pin down. Over the years, psychologists have presented several different views of intelligence.

Two-Factor Theory of Intelligence

British psychologist Charles Spearman proposed his **two-factor theory** of intelligence in 1904. According to Spearman's theory, two factors contribute to a person's intelligence. The first factor, g, represents a person's general intelligence. This involves a person's ability to perform complex mental work, such as problem solving. A second factor, s, represents a person's specific mental abilities, such as verbal or math skills. Spearman believed that every individual had a certain level of general intelligence.

Critics argue that g does not measure many other kinds of mental abilities such as motor, musical, or creative abilities. These critics argue that intelligence cannot be reduced to just g and expressed by a single IQ score.

Figure 13.5	Thurstone's Seven Primary Mental Abilities
Theory	**Main Ideas**
Verbal comprehension	The ability to understand the meaning of words, concepts, and ideas.
Numerical ability	The ability to use numbers quickly to compute answers to problems.
Spatial relations	The ability to visualize and manipulate patterns and forms in space.
Perceptual speed	The ability to grasp perceptual details quickly and accurately and to determine similarities and differences between stimuli.
Word fluency	The ability to use words quickly and fluently in performing such tasks as rhyming, solving anagrams, and doing crossword puzzles.
Memory	The ability to recall information such as lists of words, mathematical formulas, definitions, etc.
Inductive reasoning	The ability to derive general rules and principles from presented information.

Thurstone's theory of intelligence did not include the idea of a general intelligence. *How does Thurstone's theory compare to Gardner's theory?*

Thurstone's Theory of Intelligence

A major opponent of Spearman's theory was L.L. Thurstone (1938). After testing a large number of people on more than 50 different ability tests, Thurstone concluded that there was no evidence for the general intelligence that Spearman had identified. Instead, Thurstone proposed that intelligence is composed of seven primary mental abilities (see Figure 13.5). He believed that a person's intelligence needed to be a measurement of all seven mental abilities and not just a measurement of one factor.

Gardner's Theory of Multiple Intelligences

Psychologist Howard Gardner (1983) rejected the traditional idea of intelligence as primarily the ability to think logically. He believes this view is inadequate because it omits many other important skills. Gardner argues for a broader perspective that includes eight types of intelligence (see Figure 13.6). Seven types of intelligence are: (1) verbal ability;

intelligence: the ability to acquire new ideas and new behavior, and to adapt to new situations

two-factor theory: proposes that two factors contribute to an individual's intelligence

Reading Check
How did Thurstone's definition of intelligence differ from Spearman's?

Howard Gardner

1943–

"I'm sure there are lots of different intelligences. I'm sure an educational approach that pays attention to this is going to be more effective than one that denies it."

Many parents and teachers have embraced Howard Gardner's idea of multiple intelligences. Critics, though, doubt that the multiple intelligences theory should be implemented in the classroom. Critics argue that although Gardner's theory has helped teachers appreciate the many talents of students, the theory is weak. The danger lies in wasting precious school time.

How do teachers implement Gardner's theory? The most common method is to use it to teach by attacking a concept from many different angles. For example, to teach kids about the oceans, teachers have them write about cleaning a fish, draw a sea creature, role-play a sea creature, use diagrams to compare and contrast ships, and so forth (Collins, 1998).

Again, critics argue that although a teacher may tap into a child's strongest intelligence by using various instructional approaches, that child must still rely on verbal and math skills to succeed in higher education and a career. Gardner's theory has yet to be stringently tested. Gardner himself claims, "We are not yet certain of the goodness of the idea of multiple intelligences."

(2) logical-mathematical reasoning skills; (3) spatial ability, or the ability to find your way around an environment and to form mental images of it; (4) musical ability, or the ability to create and perceive pitch and rhythm patterns; (5) body-kinesthetic ability, or skill at fine motor movements required for tasks such as gem cutting, surgery, and athletics; (6) interpersonal skills, involving understanding the feelings of others; and (7) intrapersonal skills, or knowledge of oneself. Recently Gardner added an eighth intelligence—naturalist intelligence. Naturalist intelligence is a person's ability to identify and classify patterns in nature. (Gardner is also considering a ninth intelligence, "existential intelligence." This intelligence concerns the experience of existence.)

Gardner's research on the results of brain disease convinced him that humans possess these eight different and often unrelated intellectual capacities or "intelligences." Moreover, he argues that the biological organization of the brain affects one's strength in each of the eight areas.

Critics of Gardner's theory argue that some of what Gardner called "intelligence" are really skills. For instance, someone with exceptional musical abilities or body-kinesthetic abilities is really just talented. These critics claim that intelligence and talent are two different things.

Sternberg's Theory of Intelligence

triarchic theory: proposes that intelligence can be divided into three ways of processing information

Robert Sternberg (1985) proposed a **triarchic theory,** or three-part theory, of intelligence. Sternberg proposed that intelligence can be divided into three ways of processing information. The first way is using *analytical* thinking skills, or the ability to solve problems. These kinds of skills are the

Figure 13.6   Gardner's Multiple Intelligences

Gardner proposed that each person has numerous and unrelated intelligences. He points out that a person can be outstanding in some intelligences and not in others. *What is the difference between interpersonal and intrapersonal intelligence?*

Intelligence	Description	Example
Body-Kinesthetic	ability to control movement, balance, agility, grace	sense of how one's body should act and react in a physically demanding situation
Interpersonal	ability to interact and understand others and to interpret their behavior	skill at gauging others' moods and motivations
Intrapersonal	ability to understand and sense our "self"	skill at using self-esteem, self-enhancement, and strength of character to solve internal problems
Linguistic/Verbal	ability to utilize language	skill at learning and using multiple languages
Logical-Mathematical	ability to mentally process logical problems and equations	skill at answering multiple choice questions
Musical	ability to perform and compose music	skills at performing and comprehending music
Naturalist	ability to identify and classify patterns in nature; how we relate to our surroundings	skill at distinguishing differences between large numbers of similar objects
Spatial	ability to comprehend shapes and images in three dimensions	skill at putting puzzles together or molding sculptures

ones that are traditionally measured on intelligence tests. The second way is applying *creative* thinking to solving problems and the ability to deal with new situations. The third is using *practical* thinking skills to help adjust to and cope with one's environment. Sternberg's ideas stress the point that traditional intelligence tests do not measure and assess intelligences found in everyday life. Like Gardner's theory, though, Sternberg's theory makes it difficult to actually measure intelligence, at least with traditional types of measurements.

Emotional Intelligence

Another type of "intelligence" has been raised in the popular press and television. It is called **emotional intelligence** and is related to Gardner's concepts of interpersonal and intrapersonal intelligences. Emotional intelligence has four major aspects (Mayer & Salovey, 1997):

emotional intelligence: includes four major aspects of interpersonal and intrapersonal intelligences

- The ability to perceive and express emotions accurately and appropriately
- The ability to use emotions while thinking
- The ability to understand emotions and use the knowledge effectively
- The ability to regulate one's emotions to promote personal growth

This view of intelligence has intrigued many psychologists. Major proponents of this view have linked emotional intelligence to success in the workplace. Some psychologists, however, argue that emotional intelligence is simply a measurement of extroversion. More research needs to be done to confirm this theory of intelligence (see TIME Reports, p. 372).

THE DEVELOPMENT OF INTELLIGENCE TESTS

Among the most widely used and widely disputed tests in the United States and Canada today are those that are designed to measure "intelligence" and yield an "IQ" score. Alfred Binet, a French psychologist, worked with Theodore Simon to develop a useful intelligence test. In 1904 Binet was asked by the Paris school authorities to devise a means of picking out "slow learners" so they could be placed in special classes from which they might better profit. Binet was unable to define intelligence, but he believed it was complex. He thought it was reflected in the things children do—making common-sense judgments, telling the meanings of words, and solving problems and puzzles. Binet assumed that whatever intelligence was, it increased with age. That is, older children had more intelligence than younger children. Therefore, in selecting items for his test, he included only items on which older children did better than younger children.

By asking the same questions of many children, Binet determined the average age at which a particular question could be answered. For example, he discovered that certain questions could be answered by most 12-year-olds but not by most 11-year-olds. If a child of 11—or even 9—could answer these questions, he or she was said to have a mental age of 12. If a child of 12 could answer the 9-year-old-level questions but not the questions for 10-year-olds and 11-year-olds, he or she was said to have a mental age of 9. Thus a slow learner was one who had a mental age that was less than his or her chronological age.

The Stanford-Binet Intelligence Scale

Binet's intelligence test has been revised many times since he developed it. The Binet test currently used in the United States is a revision created at Stanford University—the Stanford-Binet Intelligence Scale (Terman & Merrill, 1973). The Stanford-Binet, like the original test, groups test items by age level. To stimulate and maintain the child's interest, several tasks are included, ranging from defining words to drawing pictures and explaining events in daily life. Children are tested one at a time. The examiner must carry out standardized instructions—at the same time putting the child at ease, getting him to pay attention, and encouraging him to try as hard as he can (see Figure 13.7).

The **IQ**, or **intelligence quotient**, was originally computed by dividing a child's mental age (the average age of those who also received the same score as that child) by chronological (actual) age and multiplying by 100.

$$ IQ = \frac{\text{Mental Age}}{\text{Chronological Age}} \times 100 $$

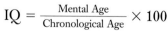

Student Web Activity
Visit the *Understanding Psychology* Web site at psychology.glencoe.com and click on **Chapter 13— Student Web Activities** for an activity on intelligence testing.

intelligence quotient (IQ): standardized measure of intelligence based on a scale in which 100 is average

So an 8-year-old child who scored at the mental age of 8 would have an IQ of 100. Although the basic principles behind the calculation of IQ remain, scores are figured in a slightly different manner today. Researchers assign a score of 100 to the average performance at any given age. Then, IQ values are assigned to all the other test scores for this age group. If you have an IQ of 100, for example, this means that 50 percent of the test takers who are your age performed worse than you. In addition, test scores for several abilities are now reported instead of one general score, but the test is no longer widely used (Vernon, 1987). Instead, the Otis-Lennon Ability Test is often used. This test seeks to measure the cognitive abilities that relate a student's ability to learn and succeed in school. It does this by assessing a student's verbal and nonverbal reasoning abilities.

The Wechsler Tests

Three frequently used intelligence tests are the revised versions of the Wechsler-Adult Intelligence Scale, now called WAIS-R (Wechsler, 1981) for adults; the Wechsler Intelligence Scale for Children, now called WISC-III (Wechsler, 1981) for children 6 to 16 years old; and the Wechsler Preschool and Primary Scales of Intelligences (WPPSI-R) for children 4 to 6½ years old.

In addition to yielding one overall score, the Wechsler tests yield percentile scores in several areas—vocabulary, information, arithmetic, picture arrangement, and so on (see Figure 13.8). These ratings are used to compute separate IQ scores for verbal and performance abilities. This type of scoring provides a more detailed picture of the individual's strengths and weaknesses than a single score does.

THE USES AND MEANING OF IQ SCORES

In general, the norms for intelligence tests are established in such a way that most people score near 100 (see Figure 13.9). This means that about 95 percent of people score between 70 and 130. Only a little more than 2 percent score at or above 130. These people are in at least the 97th percentile. Those who score below 70 have traditionally been classified as mentally handicapped. More specific categories include: mildly handicapped, but educable (55–69); moderately handicapped, but trainable (40–54); severely handicapped (25–39); and profoundly handicapped (below 25).

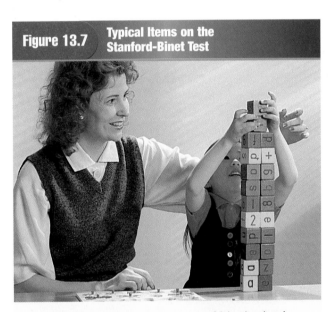

Figure 13.7 Typical Items on the Stanford-Binet Test

An examiner has built a tower of blocks (top) and has told the child, "You make one like this." *Why is "age" important in administering and scoring the Stanford-Binet test?*

Age	Sample Test Item
4	"Why do people live in houses?" "Birds fly in the air; fish swim in the ____."
8	"What should you do if you find a lost puppy?" "Stephanie can't write today because she twisted her ankle. What is wrong with that?"
12	"What does *regret* mean?" "Here is a picture. Can you tell me what is wrong with it?"

Figure 13.8 | Sample Items on the Wechsler Tests

These test items are similar to those included in the various Wechsler intelligence scales. *How do the Wechsler tests compare to the Stanford-Binet Intelligence test?*

VERBAL SCALE	EXAMPLE
Information	What day of the year is Independence Day?
Arithmetic	If eggs cost $.60 a dozen, what does one egg cost?
Vocabulary	Tell me the meaning of *scoff*.
Similarities	In what way are hats and shoes alike?
Digit Span	Listen carefully, and when I am through, say the numbers right after me. 7 5 1 8 2 9

PERFORMANCE SCALE	EXAMPLE
Picture Completion	What part is missing from this picture?

Picture Arrangement   Arrange the panels to make a meaningful story.

Block Design   Put the blocks together to make this picture.

What do these scores mean? What do the tests measure? IQ scores seem to be most useful when related to school achievement: they are quite accurate in predicting which people will do well in schools, colleges, and universities. Critics of IQ testing do not question this predictive ability. They do wonder, however, whether such tests actually measure "intelligence." As stated earlier, most psychologists agree that intelligence is the ability to acquire new ideas and new behavior and to adapt to new situations. Is success in school or the ability to take a test a real indication of such ability? Generally, IQ tests measure the ability to solve certain types of problems. Yet they do not directly measure the ability to pose those problems or to question the validity of problems set forth by others (Hoffman, 1962). This is only part of the reason why IQ testing is so controversial.

CONTROVERSY OVER IQ TESTING

Much of the debate about IQ testing centers around the following issues: do genetic differences or environmental inequalities cause two people to receive different scores on intelligence tests? The question of cultural bias in intelligence tests has also been controversial.

Nature vs. Nurture

A technique researchers use to help determine whether genetics or environment affects scores on intelligence tests is studying the results of testing of people with varying degrees of genetic relationship. In regard to intelligence, researchers have found a high degree of **heritability**—

PSYCHOLOGY and You Your IQ

Can we say that you do well in school because you have a high IQ? Consider this: a baseball player has a low batting average. A fan explains that the player does not get a lot of hits because he has a low batting average. Is this statement true? No, that baseball player has a low batting average because he does not get a lot of hits. In the same way, we cannot say that a student does poorly in school because he has a low IQ score. IQ tests measure the same skills that schoolwork requires. An IQ score measures performance—it does not explain it.

heritability: the degree to which a characteristic is related to genetic, inherited factors

Figure 13.9	**Distribution of IQ Scores**

This normal curve displays intelligence as measured by IQ tests. The average IQ score is 100. *About how many people score at least 145 on IQ tests?*

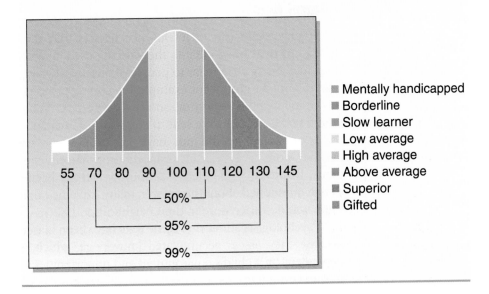

- Mentally handicapped
- Borderline
- Slow learner
- Low average
- High average
- Above average
- Superior
- Gifted

a measure of the degree to which a characteristic is related to genetic, inherited factors. They found that as genetic relationship increases—say, from parent and child to identical twins—the similarity of IQ also increases.

The best way to study the effect of nature and nurture is to study identical twins who have been separated at birth and raised in different homes or environments. Since 1979, Dr. Tom Bouchard has studied more than 100 sets of twins who were raised apart from one another. Bouchard concluded that IQ is affected by genetic factors. He believes that 70 percent of the variance in IQ can be attributed to heredity. However, not everyone agrees. Others (Plomin et al., 1994) found the hereditary estimate to be only 52 percent.

Regarding environment, studies show that brothers and/or sisters raised in the same environment are more likely to have similar IQs than siblings raised apart. Environment, therefore, does impact IQs.

Some researchers study the effects of the environment on IQ factors by focusing on preschool programs, such as Head Start, which expose economically disadvantaged youths to enriching experiences. Some studies show that quality preschool programs help raise IQs initially, but the increase begins to fade after some years. Participating children, however, are less likely to be in special education classes, less likely to be held back, and more likely to graduate from high school than are children without such preschool experiences (Zigler, Styfco, & Gilman, 1993). Each year of school missed may drop a person's IQ as much as 5 points (Ceci, 1991). The richness of the home environment, the quality of food, and the number of brothers and sisters in the family all affect IQ.

Both heredity and environment have an impact on intelligence. Advances in behavioral genetics research continue to refine results on the contributions that heredity and experience have on IQ. It remains clear that these two factors are both contributing and interact in their effects.

Cultural Bias

A major criticism of intelligence tests is that they have a **cultural bias**—that is, the wording used in questions may be more familiar to people of one social group than to another group. For example, the correct response to the following question on an intelligence test "What would you do if you were sent to buy a loaf of bread and the grocer said he did not have any more?" is "try another store." A significant proportion of minority students, however, responded that they would go home. When questioned about the answer, many explained that there was no other store in their neighborhood.

Psychologists admit that some tests have been biased because they assess accumulated knowledge, which is dependent on a child's environment and opportunities in that environment. As a consequence, efforts have been

cultural bias: an aspect of an intelligence test in which the wording used in questions may be more familiar to people of one social group than to another group

Family Size and IQ

The classic study of family size and IQ was conducted in the Netherlands. It was based on the military examinations of more than 386,000 Dutch people. Researchers found that the brightest children came from the smallest families and had few, if any, brothers and sisters when they were born. Thus, the first-born child in a family of two was usually brighter than the last child in a family of 10. The differences in IQ, however, from one birth-order position to another average only about one-quarter point.

The effects of family size on intelligence may be explained by what a houseful of children does to the home environment. It increases the amount of time a child spends with other children and decreases the amount of parental attention he or she receives. When this happens and children have limited contact with adults, development of intelligence has been known to suffer (Zajonc & Markus, 1976).

made to make the tests less biased (see Figure 13.10). However, it is unlikely that a test will ever be developed that will be completely free of cultural bias. All tests are based on the assumptions of a particular culture.

Figure 13.10) The Dove Counterbalance Intelligence Test

In the 1960s, psychologist Adrian Dove developed the Counterbalance Intelligence Test to stress that cultural background can influence performance on an intelligence test. *What characteristics would a test without cultural bias have?*

1. "T-Bone Walker" got famous for playing what?
   a. Trombone
   b. Piano
   c. "T-Flute"
   d. Guitar
   e. "Hambone"

2. Who did "Stagger Lee" kill (in the famous blues legend)?
   a. His mother
   b. Frankie
   c. Johnny
   d. His girlfriend
   e. Billy

3. If you throw the dice and "7" is showing on top, what is facing down?
   a. "seven"
   b. "snake eyes"
   c. "boxcars"
   d. "little Joes"
   e. "eleven"

4. "You've got to get up early in the morning if you want to _____."
   a. catch the worms
   b. be healthy, wealthy, and wise
   c. try to fool me
   d. fare well
   e. be the first one on the street

5. Many people say that "Juneteenth" (June 19) should be made a legal holiday because this was the day when _____.
   a. the slaves were freed in the USA
   b. the slaves were freed in Texas
   c. the slaves were freed in Jamaica
   d. the slaves were freed in California
   e. Martin Luther King was born
   f. Booker T. Washington died

SECTION 2 | Assessment

1. **Review the Vocabulary** What are the two-factor and triarchic theories of intelligence?

2. **Visualize the Main Idea** Using a chart similar to the one below, describe how the two major tests of intelligence are scored.

Name of Test	How Scored
Stanford-Binet	
Wechsler tests	

3. **Recall Information** What are Gardner's eight types of intelligence?

4. **Think Critically** Which has the greatest effect on intelligence—nature or nurture? Explain.

5. **Application Activity** Develop a list of criteria that you think are essential in determining intelligence. Compare your list with your classmates' lists and together create a class list.

Case Studies

WAIS-R:
Is It Reliable?

Period of Study: Withheld

Introduction: What happens when the results of psychological testing cross over into another field? This situation takes place numerous times within the judicial system. It is common for psychologists to be called in on a court case to assess the competency and ability of certain individuals to play key roles in a court case. Psychologists, in most of these cases, use tests measuring intelligence levels. The judicial system correlates intelligence level with the ability of an individual to take part in a legal proceeding. In these instances, the validity of the tests used is assumed. However, the important element is reliability. Psychological tests can be administered to an individual to gain certain results. If these results are not consistent with a repeat testing, the original results are meaningless.

In a trial involving the alleged statutory rape of a 22-year-old woman, psychological testing played a vital role in the outcome. Even though the victim was of legal age, prosecutors filed charges of force or threatening of force to commit a sexual act, stating that the alleged victim was incapable of giving meaningful consent because of a mental disability. Prosecutors called in a psychologist to perform testing on the victim using the Wechsler-Adult Intelligence Scale-Revised test, or WAIS-R. This specific intelligence test is highly useful for measuring conditions of mental handicap in individuals.

The results of the first test indicated the woman had an IQ below 70, demonstrating significant, but not clear, signs of possible mental handicap. The defense attorney demanded a repeat test be performed.

Hypothesis: The prosecuting team expected the test results to prove the reliability of the respected WAIS-R. They knew the test clearly measured what it is supposed to measure; thus, they wanted to see consistent results. The defending team, however, wanted to see inconsistencies in the test scores of the 22-year-old woman in the hopes the defendant would be set free. Because the WAIS-R holds much prestige within the psychological field, it seemed most likely that results would resemble that of the first test.

Method: The psychologist who administered the WAIS-R informed the court that the odds were against a substantial rise in the IQ of the woman. The psychologist, however, also informed the court that pressure and stress surrounding the trial could have played a major impact on how the woman scored on the first test. With this second scenario weighing heavily on the minds of the prosecution, the psychologist presented the woman with the WAIS-R once again.

Results: On the second WAIS-R test, the woman scored only one point higher than her score the first time. The psychological test proved reliable.

As mentioned, the factors of validity and reliability are highly valuable in studying and testing psychological hypotheses. These two concepts proved equally important in deciding the fate of a man accused in a court of law. The concept of reliability paved the way for a man to be found guilty of rape and sentenced to 15 years in prison.

Analyzing the Case Study
1. Why was the WAIS-R used in this instance?
2. Why did the defense on this case want the alleged victim to retake the test?
3. **Critical Thinking** What might significantly different results on the WAIS-R have meant in this case?

Measuring Achievement, Abilities, and Interests

■ Main Idea
Psychologists have developed tests to assess special abilities and experiences.

■ Vocabulary
- aptitude test
- achievement test
- interest test

■ Objectives
- Identify the most widely used aptitude tests, achievement tests, and interest tests.
- Explain the application of aptitude tests, achievement tests, and interest tests.

EXPLORING PSYCHOLOGY

What Are Your Interests?

Breathless, Vin dashed into the chemistry lab, "Sorry I'm late, Mrs. Baker," he told his instructor. "I was helping Mr. Eads plant marigolds around the flagpole."

Mrs. Baker sighed patiently. "I'm glad to give you extra help, Vin, but try to be on time."

"Sorry," Vin repeated. "I guess I have more fun in a garden than I do in chem lab."

Mrs. Baker smiled in surprise. "You like to garden? A garden *is* a chemistry lab."

Now Vin looked surprised. "It is?"

"Sure," Mrs. Baker replied. "Making food from sunlight, drawing nutrients from soil—these are chemical processes. . . ."

—from *Shaping Your Future* by Eddye Eubanks, Connie R. Sasse, and Linda R. Glosson, 2000

Vin views digging in the garden as fun, not work. What subject fascinates you? What career should you choose? What are your interests and aptitudes? Which subject most motivates you to learn more? Intelligence tests are designed to measure a person's overall ability to solve problems that involve symbols such as words, numbers, and pictures. Psychologists have developed other tests to assess special abilities and experiences. These include aptitude tests, achievement tests, and interest tests.

Figure 13.11　The GATB

Samples of items from the GATB testing verbal skills, mathematical skills, and manual skills are shown here. *What is the purpose of an aptitude test?*

1. Which two words have the same meaning?
   (a) open　　(b) happy
   (c) glad　　(d) green

2. Which two words have the opposite meaning?
   (a) old　　(b) dry
   (c) cold　　(d) young

3. A man works 8 hours a day, 40 hours a week. He earns $1.40 an hour. How much does he earn each week?
   (a) $40.00　　(b) $50.60
   (c) $44.60　　(d) $56.00

4. At the left is a drawing of a flat piece of metal. Which object at the right can be made from this piece of metal?

a　b　c　d

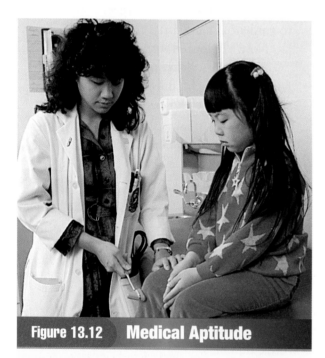

Figure 13.12　Medical Aptitude

The Law School Admissions Test (LSAT) and the Medical College Admissions Test (MCAT) help predict how well a student will do in law school and medical school. *How do tests like the SAT, LSAT, and MCAT also measure achievement?*

APTITUDE TESTS

Aptitude tests attempt to discover a person's talents and to predict how well he or she will be able to learn a new skill. They are assessed primarily in terms of their *predictive validity.* Two such tests are the Differential Aptitude Test (DATE) and the General Aptitude Test Battery (GATB). The GATB is the most widely used of these tests (see Figure 13.11). Actually, the GATB comprises nine different tests, ranging from vocabulary to manual dexterity. Test results are used to determine whether a person shows promise for each of a large number of occupations. In addition to the GATB, there are aptitude tests in music, language, art, mathematics, and other special fields.

The SAT and the American College Test (ACT) are general aptitude tests. These tests were designed to predict a student's success in college. The best predictor of how a student will do in college is how he or she did in high school. However, grading standards differ among high schools. So, combined with high school grades, the SAT is a fairly good predictor of student success in college.

ACHIEVEMENT TESTS

Whereas aptitude tests are designed to predict how well a person will be able to learn a new skill, **achievement tests** are designed to measure how much a person has already learned in a particular area. Such tests not only enable an instructor to assess a student's knowledge, but they also help students assess their progress for themselves. They are validated in terms of their *content validity,* or how well they measure students' mastery of a set of knowledge.

The distinction between achievement and aptitude tests has become somewhat blurred. What psychologists had thought were tests of aptitude—defined as *innate* ability or talent—turned out to measure experience as well, so that in part they were achievement tests. On the other hand, achievement tests often turned out to be the best predictors of many kinds of occupational abilities, so that they were in some sense aptitude tests. Because of this overlap, the distinction between the two types of tests rests more on purpose and validation than on content. If a test is used to predict future ability, it is considered an aptitude test; if it is used to assess what a person already knows, it is an achievement test.

Computers are often used to administer achievement tests. One computer-based method is called "adaptive testing" or "tailored testing" (Weiss & Vale, 1987). To understand adaptive testing, recall that in a standard test everyone gets the same questions in the same order. With an adaptive test, however, the order of questions is changed by the computer as it adapts the test to the individual's performance.

If you are taking the test and answer several problems correctly, the computer will begin to challenge you with harder problems. If you miss a question, the computer will follow it with an easier problem, and so on. The purpose of this testing method is to measure your ability by finding the difficulty level where you correctly answer most, but not all, of the problems (70 percent, for example). Adaptive testing is more accurate than standard testing, especially when test takers are either very high or very low in ability.

INTEREST TESTS

The instruments for measuring interests are fundamentally different from the instruments for measuring abilities. Answers to questions on an intelligence test indicate whether a person can, in fact, do certain kinds of thinking and solve certain kinds of problems. There are right and wrong answers. The answers to questions on an interest or a personality test, however, are not scored as right or wrong. The question in this type of testing is not "How much can you do?" or "How much do you know?" but "What are you like?"

The essential purpose of an **interest test** is to determine a person's preferences, attitudes, and interests. Most interest tests compare the test taker's responses to the responses given by people in clearly defined groups, such as professions or occupations. The more a person's interest patterns correspond to those of people in a particular occupation, the more likely that person is to enjoy and succeed in that profession.

For example, when constructing the widely used Campbell Interest and Skill Survey (Campbell, 1992), psychologists compared the responses of people who are successfully employed in different occupations to the responses of "people in general." Suppose most engineers said they liked the idea of becoming astronomers but would not be interested in a

Quick Lab

Do interest tests help determine a career?
Interest tests are used as a predictor of how likely an individual taking the test will enjoy and succeed in the profession.

Procedure
1. Choose a profession that you might be interested in pursuing and find information about its requirements and responsibilities.
2. Develop a series of questions that would address and point to a person's interest in the particular profession.
3. Administer the test to a few classmates.

Analysis
1. Determine whether the responses indicate an interest in the profession you chose.
2. After you make your determination, ask each individual who took the test if a career in the profession you chose is something he or she might enjoy.
3. Evaluate your test in terms of its predictive value.

See the Skills Handbook, page 622, for an explanation of designing an experiment.

aptitude test: estimates the probability that a person will be successful in learning a specific new skill

achievement test: measures how much a person has learned in a given subject or area

interest test: measures a person's preferences, attitudes, and interests in certain activities

✔ Reading Check
Why is the SAT considered an aptitude test?

Figure 13.13　The KPR

Shown are items from the Kuder Preference Record (KPR). The individual taking the test chooses from among three possible activities the one he or she would most like to do and the one he or she would least like to do. *What is the Kuder Preference Record designed to measure?*

	Most		Least
G. Read a love story	○	G.	○
H. Read a mystery	○	H.	○
I. Read science fiction	○	I.	○
J. Visit an art gallery	○	J.	○
K. Browse in a library	○	K.	○
L. Visit a museum	○	L.	○
M. Collect autographs	○	M.	○
N. Collect coins	○	N.	○
O. Collect butterflies	○	O.	○
P. Watch television	○	P.	○
Q. Go for a walk	○	Q.	○
R. Listen to music	○	R.	○

coaching job, whereas "people in general" were evenly divided on these (and other) questions. A person who responded as the engineers did would rank high on the scale of interest in engineering. The Kuder Preference Record, part of which is shown in Figure 13.13, is based on the same principle.

The purpose of these measures is to help people find the career that is right for them. It is important to note that although interest tests can be of great value to people who are undecided about the career path they should take, tests provide only one source of information on career choice. A student's abilities along with interests should be taken into account. A person should not make an important decision, such as that of career, on the basis of a single test.

SECTION 3　Assessment

1. **Review the Vocabulary**　Write a short paragraph explaining what aptitude, achievement, and interest tests are designed to measure.

2. **Visualize the Main Idea**　Using a diagram similar to the one below, identify why an individual might take an aptitude, achievement, or interest test.

Why would someone take this test?

Aptitude test	
Achievement test	
Interest test	

3. **Recall Information**　What is the content validity of a test? What is the predictive validity of a test?

4. **Think Critically**　Do you think a person should base his or her career choice on the results of an interest test? Why? Explain your reasons.

5. **Application Activity**　Choose a favorite sport or hobby. Devise a short aptitude test that you think would help predict how well an individual would be able to learn the skills needed for the sport or hobby you chose.

SECTION 4 Personality Testing

Reader's Guide

■ Main Idea
Personality tests are used to assess personality characteristics and to identify problems.

■ Vocabulary
- personality test
- objective test
- projective test

■ Objectives
- Identify the most widely used personality tests.
- Describe the use of personality tests.

EXPLORING PSYCHOLOGY

Why Do You Have Your Personality?

What makes people different from one another? The ancient Greeks thought the answer had something to do with the four basic body fluids or humors: blood, phlegm, black bile, and yellow bile. According to the Greek physician Hippocrates (460–371 B.C.), there were four possible personality types. *Sanguine* individuals had an abundance of blood: they tended to be cheerful, optimistic, and active. *Phlegmatic* people were listless, sluggish, and tired because they had too much phlegm. Sad, brooding *melancholic* temperaments resulted from too much black bile, and *choleric* (easy to anger) personalities resulted from an excess of yellow bile.

—from *Psychology: Science, Behavior, and Life* by R.H. Ettinger, Robert L. Crooks, and Jean Stein, 1994

Hippocrates' adjectives survive today in the words we use to describe personality types. The explanations for what causes personality differences, though, have changed dramatically. Psychologists and psychiatrists use **personality tests** to assess personality characteristics and to identify problems and psychological disorders, as well as to predict how a person might behave in the future. Some of these tests are objective tests, while others are projective tests.

personality test: assesses personality characteristics and identifies problems

OBJECTIVE PERSONALITY TESTS

objective test: a forced-choice test (in which a person must select one of several answers) designed to study personality characteristics

Some of the most widely used tests in personality testing are based on simple pencil-and-paper responses. **Objective tests** are forced-choice tests; that is, a person must select one of a small number of possible responses.

The MMPI

One of the most widely used tests for general personality assessment is the Minnesota Multiphasic Personality Inventory (MMPI). (The MMPI was revised, updated, and published in 1990. The new version is called MMPI-2.) Like other personality tests, the MMPI-2 has no right or wrong answers. The test consists of 567 statements to which a person can respond *true, false,* or *cannot say.* Some examples of test statements are: I like tall women; I wake up tired most mornings; I am envied by most people; and I often feel a tingling in my fingers.

The items on the MMPI reveal habits, fears, delusions, sexual attitudes, and symptoms of psychological disorders. Psychologists originally developed the test to help diagnose psychiatric disorders. Although the statements that relate to a given characteristic (such as depression) are scattered throughout the test, the answers to them can be pulled out and organized into a single depression scale. There are 10 such clinical scales to the MMPI (Graham, 1990) (see Figure 13.14). In scoring the MMPI, a psychologist looks for patterns of responses, not a high or low score on one or all of the scales. This is because the items on the test do not, by themselves, identify personality types.

In creating the original MMPI, the test makers did not try to think up statements that would identify depression, anxiety, and so forth. Rather, they invented a wide range of statements about all sorts of topics and gave the test to groups of people already known to be well adjusted, depressed, anxious, and so on. They also retained for the test those questions that discriminated among these groups—questions, for example, that people suffering from depression almost always answered differently from other groups (Hathaway & McKinley, 1940). As a result, many of the items on the test may cause critics to question the test's validity. For example, if you answer *false* to "I attend religious services frequently," you will score one point on the depression scale. This and other items like it were included simply because more depressed people than nondepressed people answer *false* to this item.

One of the ways in which the MMPI identifies individuals who give inaccurate responses is that an untrue response to one statement may be caught by the rephrasing of the same question at a later point.

Did You Know?

The Validity of Horoscopes How can astrologers and horoscopes accurately describe you and your life? Horoscope writers and astrologers actually describe your personality traits in such a way that they apply to almost everyone. They use what is called the *Barnum principle.* Named after circus owner P.T. Barnum, it is a method of naming general traits, not specific traits. Horoscopes, though, lack validity—an essential factor in any good personality test. Because horoscopes are aimed at applying to everyone, they do not measure what they are supposed to measure—individual personality traits, so they lack validity (Plotnick, 1999).

Figure 13.14 MMPI Scales

The MMPI is a true-false self-questionnaire that is designed to assess major patterns of personality and emotional disorders. Clinical scales identify the specific areas whose content includes references to a specific disorder. Validity scales assess whether the test taker was lying or faking answers. *Why is the MMPI considered an objective test?*

Clinical Scales

Hs–Hypochondriasis	High score indicates that the test taker expresses stress in physical terms
D–Depression	High score indicates depression and hopelessness
Hy–Conversion Hysteria	High score indicates that the test taker expresses emotion without insight
Pd–Psychopathic Deviate	High score indicates that test taker is maladaptive and fights authority
Mf–Masculinity-Feminity	High score indicates that test taker rejects gender roles
Pa–Paranoia	High score indicates that test taker has tendency to misinterpret others' motives
Pt–Psychasthenia	High score indicates test taker worries obsessively
Sc–Schizophrenia	High score indicates a situational problem, not necessarily schizophrenia
Ma–Hypomania	High score indicates that test taker has too much energy and is unable to get anything done
Si–Social Introversion	High score indicates that test taker is withdrawn

Validity Scales

?–Question	Corresponds with the number of items left unanswered
L–Lie	Some individuals fail to truthfully mark items and describe someone whom they envision as having a perfect personality
F–Infrequency	Some individuals are unwilling to cooperate with the test instructions and mark items in a random manner; others exaggerate their difficulties to get special attention
K–Correction	Some individuals deny certain characteristics about themselves and their families and so slant their answers to hide something

The subject of thousands of studies, the MMPI has been one of the most frequently used psychological tests (Lubin, Larsen, & Matarazzo, 1984). The MMPI-2 includes revisions aimed at modernizing the language, removing sexist terms or phrases, and adding items reflecting current issues such as Type A personalities, alcohol abuse, drug abuse, eating disorders, and suicide. The test can also differentiate common demeanors such as extroversion-introversion and assertiveness. Most psychologists believe that scores on the MMPI should be supplemented and confirmed with interviews and observation for proper diagnosis. The test is best for diagnosing extreme cases of psychological disorders.

The CPI

Similar to the MMPI is the California Psychological Inventory (CPI), developed to assess the "normal person." Even though it uses some of the same questions, it does not have any of the questions that reveal psychiatric illnesses (Gough, 1987). It measures traits such as responsibility, self-control, and tolerance. The CPI is used to predict things like adjustment to stress, leadership, and job success. Although it is known to be *fairly* valid and reliable, the CPI can prove faulty for an individual. The test results may point out that the individual has a problem when that individual really does not have a problem. Like all personality tests, the CPI is useful for general screening and in locating individuals who may need help. If an individual's scores indicate that a problem exists, though, the test should be followed by one-on-one discussion with a counselor or psychologist for further investigation.

The Myers-Briggs Test

Another popular personality test is the Myers-Briggs test. The test focuses on how a person takes in information and makes decisions, and the person's basic day-to-day lifestyle. This test characterizes personality on four different scales: extrovert vs. introvert, intuitive vs. sensing, feeling vs. thinking, and judging vs. perceptive.

For example, an extrovert prefers engaging in activities involving other people, whereas an introvert enjoys solitude. Sensing or intuition refers to the contrast between using senses primarily in a practical way ("I have to see it to believe it") or sensing something without knowing exactly why. In the thinking and feeling contrast, thinking is more logical, whereas feeling involves using a personal, values-oriented way of responding to events and people. Finally, in the judgment vs. perceptive contrast, those who prefer judgment tend to have a more organized and structured manner, while those who prefer using perceptive abilities are more flexible.

The creators of the Myers-Briggs test believe that each person's personality is a combination of these characteristics. Your personality type influences your communication style, how you carry out personal relationships, your work style, as well as other lifestyle choices. The purpose of the test is to offer test takers an evaluation of their personalities so that they may better understand how they relate to others and how others relate to them. With this knowledge, the creators of the test hope to help people live more productive, rewarding lives. Businesses may use this test to make better decisions about whom to hire and promote. Students can use this test to optimize the match between their learning style and the teaching style of their instructor.

PROJECTIVE PERSONALITY TESTS

Unlike objective tests, **projective tests** encourage test takers to respond freely, giving their own interpretations of various test stimuli. These tests are open-ended examinations that invite people to tell stories about pictures, diagrams, or objects. The idea is that because the test material has no established meaning, the story a person tells must say something

Reading Check
What is the purpose of the MMPI?

projective test: an unstructured test in which a person is asked to respond freely, giving his or her own interpretation of various ambiguous stimuli

Figure 13.15	Taking the Rorschach Test

In interpreting a person's responses to the ink blots on the Rorschach test, as much attention may be paid to the style of the responses as to their content. *What are projective tests?*

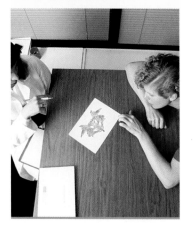

about his or her needs, wishes, fears, and other aspects of personality. In other words, the test taker will project his or her unconscious feelings onto the test items.

The Rorschach Inkblot Test

Perhaps the best-known and most widely discussed projective measure is the Rorschach inkblot test, developed by Swiss psychiatrist Hermann Rorschach in 1921. Rorschach created 10 cards with inkblot designs and a system for interpreting responses (see Figure 13.15). After 10 years of researching responses to thousands of ink blots, he chose 10 specific ones that elicited emotional responses in people. Five of the blots are entirely black and gray; two have red splotches; and three cards have a mixture of different colors.

To administer the test, a psychologist hands the ink blots one by one to the test taker, asking the person to say what he or she sees. The person might say that a certain area represents an airplane or an animal's head. The psychologist then asks certain general questions in an attempt to discover what aspects of the ink blot determined the person's response. There are no right or wrong answers. The psychologist may keep a record of everything the test taker does, such as what he says he sees, where and how he holds the cards, the length of time he pauses before answering, and so on.

The theory underlying the test is that anything that someone does or says will reveal an aspect of that person's personality. There are several systems for scoring Rorschach responses. Some are very specific; for example, according to one system, a person who mentions human movement more often than color in the ink blots is probably introverted, while an extrovert will mention color more than movement. Other systems are far more intuitive—for example, noting whether the test taker is open or hostile. Many researchers have criticized the Rorschach, charging that the scoring systems are neither reliable nor valid and that the results often depend on the psychologist's expectations. The test, though, continues to be used by therapists as an introduction to therapy.

The TAT

The second most widely used projective measure was developed by Henry Murray (1943). The Thematic Apperception Test (TAT) consists of a series of 20 cards containing pictures of vague but suggestive situations (see Figure 13.16). The individual is asked to tell a story about the picture, indicating how the situation shown on the card developed, what the characters are thinking and feeling, and how it will end. The TAT is used to urge clients to speak freely about their problems (see Chapter 12 for more on the TAT).

As with the Rorschach, there are many different scoring systems for the TAT. The interpreter usually focuses on the themes that emerge from the story and the needs of the main characters: Are they aggressive? Do they seem to have needs for achievement, love, or sex? Are they being attacked or criticized by another person, or are they receiving affection and comfort? The responses are used to assess the motivation and personality characteristics of the individuals taking the test. The test can also be used to assess personality problems of individuals.

Figure 13.16 Taking the TAT

A person taking the TAT might be shown a picture similar to this and asked to make up a story about what the woman is thinking. *What does the TAT assess?*

Figure 13.17 Approaches to Reducing Test Anxiety

Many people worry about taking tests—any kind of tests. When someone comes to a psychologist complaining of test anxiety, the psychologist may approach the problem differently, depending on his or her theoretical orientation. *How would a behaviorist attempt to reduce testing anxiety?*

Approach	Solution
Biological (focus on physiological arousal, i.e. sweaty palms)	Reduce anxiety through stress-reducing activities
Cognitive (focus on thinking/excessive worrying)	Channel worry into studying
Behavioral (focus on actual behaviors)	Increase study time by selecting a good place to study, rewarding yourself for studying, keeping a record of your study time, establishing priorities, specifying time for specific tasks
Psychoanalytic (focus on personality problems that underlie bad study habits)	Work to change personality characteristics, such as procrastination
Humanistic (focus on conscious beliefs and perceptions)	Teachers work with students so that students develop feelings of competence and reach their full potential
Sociocultural (focus on influence of culture and ethnicity)	Students from different cultures have different values and resources; work to understand differences and similarities

Source: Adapted from Plotnick, 1999.

It is important to note that the personality tests, as well as aptitude, achievement, interest, and intelligence tests, are just one tool that a psychologist can use to evaluate a person's psychological state. A conscientious psychologist should pair testing with other evidence gained through interviews and observation before drawing any conclusions or making any diagnoses.

SECTION 4 Assessment

1. **Review the Vocabulary** What is the difference between objective and projective tests?

2. **Visualize the Main Idea** Using a chart similar to the one below, identify the characteristics of the Rorschach inkblot test and the Thematic Apperception Test (TAT).

Name of Test	Characteristics
Rorschach test	
Thematic Apperception Test	

3. **Recall Information** How does the CPI differ from the MMPI? How does the CPI differ from the Myers-Briggs test?

4. **Think Critically** What are the advantages and disadvantages of using objective personality tests versus projective personality tests?

5. **Application Activity** Choose two personality traits. Develop several test questions that you think would assess these traits. Discuss and evaluate your questions with your classmates.

Tests evaluate academic performance and measure mental abilities or personality characteristics. The usefulness of a test depends upon how well it is constructed and the extent to which scores are related to actual performance.

Section 1 Characteristics of Psychological Tests

Main Idea: To be useful, tests have to exhibit reliability, validity, and standardization.

- There are three basic ways of determining a test's reliability—test-retest, scorer or inter-scorer, and split-half reliability.
- One of the chief methods for measuring validity is to find out how well a test predicts performance.
- Tests must be standardized—they must be administered and scored the same way every time, and they must have established norms.

Section 2 Intelligence Testing

Main Idea: Several IQ tests are used to measure intelligence, although there are many views about what constitutes intelligence.

- Charles Spearman proposed that two factors contributed to a person's intelligence.
- L.L. Thurstone proposed that intelligence is composed of seven primary mental abilities.
- Howard Gardner proposed that there are eight types of intelligence.
- Two major intelligence tests are the Stanford-Binet and the Wechsler tests.
- Much of the debate about IQ testing centers around whether genetic differences or environmental inequalities affect performance on intelligence tests.

Section 3 Measuring Achievement, Abilities, and Interests

Main Idea: Psychologists have developed tests to assess special abilities and experiences.

- Aptitude tests attempt to discover a person's talents and to predict how well he or she will be able to learn a new skill.
- Achievement tests are designed to measure how much a person has already learned in a particular area.
- Interest tests are used to determine a person's preferences, attitudes, and interests.

Section 4 Personality Testing

Main Idea: Personality tests are used to assess personality characteristics and to identify problems.

- Personality tests can be objective or projective.
- One of the most widely used objective personality tests is the Minnesota Multiphasic Personality Inventory (MMPI).
- The two major projective personality tests are the Rorschach inkblot test and the Thematic Apperception Test (TAT).

Chapter Vocabulary

reliability (p. 344)

validity (p. 345)

percentile system (p. 346)

norms (p. 346)

intelligence (p. 348)

two-factor theory (p. 349)

triarchic theory (p. 350)

emotional intelligence (p. 351)

intelligence quotient (IQ) (p. 352)

heritability (p. 355)

cultural bias (p. 356)

aptitude test (p. 360)

achievement test (p. 360)

interest test (p. 361)

personality test (p. 363)

objective test (p. 364)

projective test (p. 366)

Self-Check Quiz
Visit the *Understanding Psychology* Web site at
psychology.glencoe.com and click on **Chapter 13—
Self-Check Quizzes** to prepare for the Chapter Test.

Reviewing Vocabulary

Choose the letter of the correct term or concept
below to complete the sentence.

a. validity
b. reliability
c. norms
d. intelligence
e. triarchic theory

f. emotional intelligence
g. heritability
h. cultural bias
i. objective
j. projective

1. A test's _____ are the percentiles established on the basis of the scores achieved by a standardization group.

2. The ability of a test to measure what it is intended to measure is its _____.

3. Researchers have found a great degree of _____, a measure of the degree to which a characteristic is related to genetic factors.

4. The _____ of intelligence proposes that intelligence can be divided into three ways of processing information.

5. In a(n) _____ test, a person is asked to give his or her own interpretations of various test stimuli.

6. _____ occurs when the wording used in questions may be more familiar to people of one cultural group than to another.

7. The ability of a test to yield the same result under a variety of different circumstances is its _____.

8. A person's _____ is related to concepts of interpersonal and intrapersonal intelligences.

9. _____ is the ability to acquire new ideas and new behavior and to adapt to new situations.

10. In a(n) _____ test, a person must select one of a small number of possible responses.

Recalling Facts

1. What is the validity of a test? How is the validity of a test determined?

2. Explain what norms are. How are norms established?

3. Using a chart similar to the one below, explain the following views of intelligence: Thurstone's, Gardner's, and Sternberg's.

Theory	View of Intelligence
L.L. Thurstone	
Howard Gardner	
Robert Sternberg	

4. Explain the difference between an aptitude test and an achievement test. Give an example of each type of test.

5. What are the two basic types of personality tests? What are some of the differences between the types? Give an example of each test.

Critical Thinking

1. **Demonstrating Reasoned Judgment** Which theory of intelligence discussed in the chapter do you agree with the most? Give reasons for your choice.

2. **Synthesizing Information** If you were asked to rate people on an intelligence scale of your own making, what criteria would you use and how would you make your decision? What roles would memory, creativity, and emotional maturity play in your scale?

3. **Evaluating Information** Only a few tests have been used to predict how happy people will be with their lives or how successful they will be in their careers. Explain why you think this may be the case.

4. **Making Inferences** How accurate do you think the scoring for projective tests is? Can the scoring for these kinds of tests be standardized? Explain.

5. **Applying Concepts** Do you think personality tests should be used by employers to make decisions about hiring employees? Explain.

Psychology Projects

1. **Characteristics of Psychological Tests** Ask one of your academic teachers if you can spend some time after class talking about how he or she makes up a test. How does the teacher decide the number and type of questions? Does the teacher consider the validity or reliability of the test? How is the test scored? Report your findings in a written report.

2. **Intelligence Testing** Research various intelligence tests. Determine the criteria used to measure intelligence. Report your findings in a chart.

3. **Achievement and Personality Tests** In recent years, controversies have surrounded the use of achievement tests and personality tests. Research newspapers and magazines to find articles that explain these controversies. Summarize them in a short paper. Include your opinion of the arguments involved.

4. **Personality Testing** Contact the human resources department of a business in your community. Find out what criteria the company uses for hiring employees. Specifically, find out if the company uses personality tests or interviews to help in the hiring and what kinds of tests are used. Report your findings in a presentation.

Technology Activity

In recent years, take-at-home computerized IQ tests have become increasingly popular. Search the Internet to find examples of these kinds of tests. Also, find out about intelligence tests offered on CD-ROMs that parents can administer to their children. Evaluate the pros and cons of using these kinds of intelligence tests.

Psychology Journal

Reread your journal entry about selecting the best teaching prospect from among a group of applicants. Devise a test to use in your assessment. Consider and list in your journal the behaviors you most want to evaluate in the applicants.

Building Skills

Identifying Cause-and-Effect Relationships Review the cartoon below, then answer the questions that follow.

THE FAR SIDE   By GARY LARSON

© 1982 FarWorks Inc. All Rights Reserved

"Freeze!. . .Okay, now. . .Whose the brains of this outfit?"

1. Which person shown in the cartoon is the "brains of this outfit"?
2. How does this cartoonist illustrate the characters' intellects?
3. What "view" of intelligence might this cartoon illustrate? Explain your answer.

See the Skills Handbook, page 624, for an explanation of identifying cause-and-effect relationships.

Practice and **assess** key social studies skills with **Glencoe Skillbuilder Interactive Workbook CD-ROM, Level 2.**

TIME REPORTS

The EQ Factor

New research suggests that emotions, not IQ, may be the true measure of human intelligence

By NANCY GIBBS

I T TURNS OUT THAT A SCIENTIST CAN see the future by watching four-year-olds interact with a marshmallow. The researcher invites the children, one by one, into a plain room and begins the gentle torment. You can have this marshmallow right now, he says. But if you wait while I run an errand, you can have two marshmallows when I get back. And then he leaves.

Some children grab for the treat the minute he's out the door. Some last a few minutes before they give in. But others are determined to wait. They cover their eyes; they put their heads down; they sing to themselves; they try to play games or even fall asleep. When the researcher returns, he gives these children their hard-earned marshmallows. And then, science waits for them to grow up.

By the time the children reach high school, something remarkable has happened. A survey of the children's parents and teachers found that those who as four-year-olds had the fortitude to hold out for the second marshmallow generally grew up to be better adjusted, more popular, adventurous, confident and dependable teenagers. The children who gave in to temptation early on were more likely to be lonely, easily frustrated and stubborn. They buckled under stress and shied away from challenges. And when some of the students in the two groups took the Scholastic Aptitude Test, the kids who had held out longer scored an average of 210 points higher.

When we think of brilliance we see Einstein, deep-eyed, woolly haired, a thinking machine with skin and mismatched socks. High achievers, we imagine, were wired for greatness from birth. But then you have to wonder why, over time, natural talent seems to ignite in some people and dim in others. This is where the marshmallows come in. It seems that the ability to delay gratification is a master skill, a triumph of the reasoning brain over the impulsive one. It is a sign, in short, of emotional intelligence. And it doesn't show up on an IQ test.

For most of this century, scientists have worshipped the hardware of the brain and the software of the mind; the messy powers of the heart were left to the poets. But cognitive theory could simply not explain the questions we wonder about most: why some people just seem to have a gift for living well; why the smartest kid in the class will probably not end up the richest; why we like some people virtually on sight and distrust others; why some people remain buoyant in the face of troubles that would sink a less resilient soul. What qualities of the mind or spirit, in short, determine who succeeds?

The phrase "emotional intelligence" was coined by Yale psychologist Peter Salovey and the University of New Hampshire's John Mayer five years ago to describe qualities like understanding one's own feelings, empathy for the feelings of others and "the regulation of emotion in a way that enhances living." Their notion, handily shortened to EQ, is the subject of a new book, *Emotional Intelligence*. Author Daniel Goleman has brought together a decade's worth of behavioral research into how the mind processes feelings. His goal, he announces on the cover, is to redefine what it means to be smart. His thesis: when it comes to predicting people's success, brainpower as measured by IQ and standardized achievement tests may actually matter less than the qualities of mind once thought of as "character" before the word began to sound quaint.

"You don't want to take an average of your emotional skill," argues Harvard psychology professor Jerome Kagan, a pioneer in child-development research. "That's what's wrong with the concept of intelligence for

SEYMOUR CHWAST/PUSHPIN GROUP INC.

mental skills too. Some people handle anger well but can't handle fear. Some people can't take joy. So each emotion has to be viewed differently."

EQ is not the opposite of IQ. Some people are blessed with a lot of both, some with little of either. What researchers have been trying to understand is how they complement each other; how one's ability to handle stress, for instance, affects the ability to concentrate and put intelligence to use. Among the ingredients for success, researchers now generally agree that IQ counts for about 20%; the rest depends on everything from class to luck to the neural pathways that have developed in the brain over millions of years of human evolution.

It is actually the neuroscientists and evolutionists who do the best job of explaining the reasons behind the most unreasonable behavior. In the past decade or so, scientists have learned enough about the brain to make judgments about where emotion comes from and why we need it. Primitive emotional responses held the keys to survival: fear drives the blood into the large muscles, making it easier to run; surprise triggers the eyebrows to rise, allowing the eyes to gather more information about an unexpected event. Disgust wrinkles up the face and closes the nostrils to keep out foul smells.

Emotional life grows out of an area of the brain called the limbic system, specifically the amygdala, whence come delight and disgust and fear and anger. Millions of years ago, the neocortex was added on, enabling humans to plan, learn and remember. Lust grows from the limbic system; love, from the neocortex. Animals like reptiles that have no neocortex cannot experience anything like maternal love; this is why baby snakes have to hide to avoid being eaten by their parents. Humans, with their capacity for love, will protect their offspring, allowing the brains of the young time to develop. The more connections between the limbic system and the neocortex, the more emotional responses are possible.

Without these emotional reflexes, rarely conscious but often terribly powerful, we would scarcely be able to function. "Most decisions we make have a vast number of possible outcomes, and any attempt to analyze all of them would never end," says University of Iowa neurologist Antonio Damasio, author of *Descartes' Error: Emotion, Reason and the Human Brain.* "I'd ask you to lunch tomorrow, and when the appointed time arrived, you'd still be thinking about whether you should come." What tips the balance, Damasio contends, is our unconscious assigning of emotional values to some of those choices. Whether we experience a somatic response—a gut feeling of dread or a giddy sense of elation—emotions are helping to limit the field in any choice we have to make. If the prospect of lunch with a neurologist is unnerving or distasteful, Damasio suggests, the invitee will conveniently remember a previous engagement.

When Damasio worked with patients in whom the connection between emotional brain and neocortex had been severed because of damage to the brain, he discovered how central that hidden pathway is to how we live our lives. People who had lost that linkage were just as smart, but their lives often fell apart nonetheless. They could not make decisions because they didn't know how they felt about their choices. They couldn't react to warnings or anger in other people. If they made a mistake, like a bad investment, they felt no regret or shame and so were bound to repeat it.

How much happier would we be, how much more successful as individuals and civil as a society, if we were more alert to the importance of emotional intelligence and more adept at teaching it? From kindergartens to business schools to corporations across the country, people are taking seriously the idea that a little more time spent on the "touchy-feely" skills so often derided may in fact pay rich dividends.

The problem may be that there is an ingredient missing. Emotional skills are morally neutral. Just as a genius could use his intellect either to cure cancer or engineer a deadly virus, someone with great empathic insight could use it to inspire colleagues or exploit them. Without a moral compass to guide peo-

ple in how to employ their gifts, emotional intelligence can be used for good or evil. Columbia University psychologist Walter Mischel, who invented the marshmallow test, observes that the knack for delaying gratification that makes a child one marshmallow richer can help him become a better citizen or—just as easily—an even more brilliant criminal. Given the passionate arguments that are raging over moral instruction in this country, it is no wonder Goleman chose to focus more on neutral emotional skills than on the values that should govern their use. That's another book—and another debate. ■

—For the complete text of this article and related articles from TIME, please visit www.time.com/teach

ANALYZING THE ARTICLE

1. What is the purpose of the marshmallow test? How does it demonstrate EQ?
2. **CRITICAL THINKING** Is EQ the same as morality? How are they related? Do you think you can teach EQ to children?

PSYCHOLOGY JOURNAL

Think of a person you have had a chance to observe in a variety of social settings. Write an entry in your journal describing that person's characteristic way of interacting with people. How do others respond to this person? ■

PSYCHOLOGY
Online

Chapter Overview
Visit the *Understanding Psychology* Web site at psychology.glencoe.com and click on **Chapter 14—Chapter Overviews** to preview the chapter.

Purposes of Personality Theories

Reader's Guide

■ Main Idea
Personality theories provide a way of organizing the many characteristics that people have.

■ Vocabulary
• personality

■ Objectives
• Describe the major purposes of personality theories.
• List the major schools of personality theory.

EXPLORING PSYCHOLOGY

It's in the Personality

Shelly and Deirdre both failed their semester examinations in psychology, but they reacted in very different ways. When Shelly saw her grade, she felt sick to her stomach and had to fight back tears. She rushed home, and shut herself up in her room to lie in bed, stare at the ceiling, and feel inadequate. Deirdre, on the other hand, was all bluster. She ran to the cafeteria to join her friends and make loud jokes about the stupid questions on the test.

—from *Understanding Psychology*, Glencoe/ McGraw-Hill, 1995

W hy did Shelly and Deirdre act so differently in similar situations? There is "something inside" people that makes them think, feel, and act differently, and that "something inside" is what we mean by *personality*. When psychologists talk about aspects of personality, most agree that **personality** consists of the consistent, enduring, and unique characteristics of a person.

personality: the consistent, enduring, and unique characteristics of a person

PURPOSES OF THEORIES

The first purpose of personality theories is to provide a way of organizing the many characteristics you know about yourself and other people. You know people may be outgoing or shy, bossy or meek, quick-tempered or calm, witty or dull, fun-loving or gloomy, industrious or lazy. These words describe general ways of behaving that characterize an individual. Personality theorists try to determine whether certain traits go together, why a person has some traits and not others, and why a person might exhibit different traits in different situations. There is a good deal of disagreement among theorists as to which traits are significant. Nevertheless, all theorists look to discover patterns in the ways people behave.

A second purpose of any personality theory is to explain the differences among individuals. In so doing, theorists probe beneath the surface. Some theorists might explain different behaviors in terms of motives. Others might try to find out how motives were established in the first place. Still other theorists might seek less obvious causes for individual differences, arguing, for example, that the roots of these differences could be traced back to childhood conflicts.

A third goal of personality theory is to explore how people conduct their lives. It is no accident that most personality theorists began as psychotherapists. In working with people who had difficulty coping with everyday problems, psychotherapists inevitably developed ideas about what it takes to live a relatively happy, untroubled life. Personality theorists try to explain why problems arise and why they are more difficult for some people to manage than for others.

In addition, the fourth purpose of personality theory is to determine how life can be improved. It seems obvious that some people are dissatisfied with themselves, their parents, their husbands or wives and children, or their home lives. People resign themselves to unrewarding jobs, and there is a widespread feeling that much is wrong with society and the world. Almost everyone recognizes that we need to grow and change, individually and collectively. But what are the proper goals of growth and change? How can we cope with the inevitable conflicts of life?

Personality psychologists attempt to answer these questions with systematic theories about human behavior. These theories are used to guide research, and research, as we saw in Chapter 2, can test parts of a theory to determine whether they are right or wrong. Thus, formal personality theories try to make ideas about why people act in certain ways more scientific by stating them precisely and then testing them.

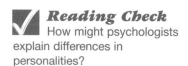

Reading Check
How might psychologists explain differences in personalities?

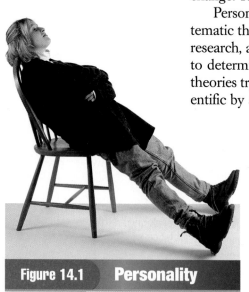

Figure 14.1   Personality

Psychologists who study personality explore whatever it is that makes one person think, feel, and act differently from another. *What are the purposes of personality theories?*

MAJOR SCHOOLS OF PERSONALITY THEORY

Psychology is a young discipline, and the development and testing of personality theories are still gaining sophistication. There are now many conflicting theories of personality, each with positive and negative aspects. Discussing both sides of various theories helps invigorate the discussion about personality.

In this chapter, we will describe major schools of thought among personality theorists. Psychoanalytic theories, developed by Sigmund Freud and his followers, emphasize the importance of motives hidden in the unconscious. B.F. Skinner and the behaviorists study the way rewards and punishments shape our actions. Social learning theories examine the impact of observational learning on personality. Cognitive

Figure 14.2 **Characteristics of Personality**

In psychology, personality refers to the essential characteristics of a person. Cathy Guisewite, a cartoonist, has given personality characteristics to an animal—a dog. *What factors do you think are influencing the personality of the dog in this cartoon?*

theorists focus on how our thoughts, perceptions, and feelings shape our personalities. Humanistic theorists, like Abraham Maslow and Carl Rogers, stress one's human potential growth, such as creativity and spontaneity. Finally, trait theorists, like Gordon Allport and Hans Eysenck, emphasize the importance of understanding basic personality characteristics such as friendliness and aggression.

Each of the theories we will discuss has a different image of human nature. What they have in common is a concern with understanding the differences among people.

SECTION 1 Assessment

1. **Review the Vocabulary** Write your own definition of *personality*. How does your definition compare to the textbook's definition?

2. **Visualize the Main Idea** Use a graphic organizer similar to the one below to list the purposes of personality theories.

Purposes of Personality Theories

3. **Recall Information** What are the major schools of personality, and how do they differ?

4. **Think Critically** Do you think that you choose your own behaviors freely, or do you believe that your current behaviors are determined by previous behaviors and events? Explain.

5. **Application Activity** Work with another student and take turns recalling some early memories. Jot down those memories, and discuss the following question: Do these early memories relate to your present personality?

SECTION **2** Psychoanalytic Theories

Reader's Guide

■ Main Idea
Freud's psychoanalytic theory proposes that personality is made up of three components: the id, ego, and superego.

■ Vocabulary
- unconscious
- id
- ego
- superego
- defense mechanisms
- collective unconscious
- archetype
- inferiority complex

■ Objectives
- Explain Sigmund Freud's structural concepts of personality.
- Describe Carl Jung's theory of personality.

EXPLORING PSYCHOLOGY

Just a Slip

One of my colleagues was lecturing on the importance of regular health care. She said, "It is important to visit a veterinarian for regular checkups." According to Freud, mistakes like substituting *veterinarian* for *physician* are not accidental but rather "intentional" ways of expressing unconscious desires.

As it turns out, my colleague, who is in very good health, was having serious doubts about her relationship with a person who happened to be a veterinarian.

—from *Introduction to Psychology* by **Rod Plotnik**, 1996

S lips in speaking are common. People usually laugh at them, even if they are meaningful; sometimes, however, they are disturbing. Everyone has made a remark that hurt a friend and has later asked himself, "Why did I say that? I didn't mean it." Yet, when he thinks about it, he may realize that he was angry at his friend and wanted to "get back" at him.

SIGMUND FREUD AND THE UNCONSCIOUS

It was Sigmund Freud who first suggested that the little slips that people make, the things they mishear, and the odd misunderstandings they have are not really mistakes at all. Freud believed there was something behind these mistakes, even though people claimed they were just accidental and quickly corrected themselves. Similarly, when he listened to people describe their dreams, he believed the dreams had some unconscious meaning, even though the people who dreamed them did not know what they meant.

Freud was a neurologist who practiced in Vienna in the early 1900s. Since he specialized in nervous disorders, a great many people talked to him about their private lives, conflicts, fears, and desires. He concluded that some of the most powerful influences on human personality are things we are not conscious of.

Freud was the first modern psychologist to suggest that every personality has a large **unconscious,** or unaware, component. For Freud, experiences include feelings and thoughts as well as actual events. Freud believed that many of our experiences, particularly the painful episodes of childhood, are not forgotten but are stored in the unconscious. Although we may not consciously recall these experiences, they continue to influence our behavior. For example, a child who never fully pleases her demanding mother or father may feel unhappy much of the time and will doubt her abilities to succeed and to be loved. As an adult, the person may suffer from feelings of unworthiness and low self-esteem, despite her very real abilities. Freud believed that unconscious motives and the feelings people experience as children have an enormous impact on adult personality and behavior.

PSYCHOLOGY Online

Student Web Activity
Visit the *Understanding Psychology* Web site at psychology.glencoe.com and click on **Chapter 14— Student Web Activities** for an activity on theories of personality.

unconscious: the part of the mind that contains material of which we are unaware but that strongly influences conscious processes and behaviors

THE ID, EGO, AND SUPEREGO

Freud explained human personality by saying that it was a kind of energy system, like a steam engine or an electric dynamo. The energy in personality comes from two kinds of powerful instincts—the life instinct and the death instinct. Freud theorized that all of life moves toward death and that the desire for a final end shows up in human personality as destructiveness and aggression. It is important to remember, however, that *life* instincts were more important in Freud's theory and he saw them primarily as erotic or pleasure-seeking urges. By 1923, Freud had described what became known as the structural concepts of the personality: id, ego, and superego (see Figure 14.3). Freud introduced them simply as a model of how the mind works. In other words, the id, ego, and superego do not refer to actual portions of the brain; instead, they explain how the mind functions and how the instinctual energies are regulated.

In Freud's theory, the **id** is the reservoir or container of the instinctual and biological urges. At birth, all your energy is invested in the id, responding unconsciously to inborn instinctive urges for food and water. The id

id: the part of the unconscious personality that contains our needs, drives, instincts, and repressed material

Figure 14.3   Freud's Model

The ego tries to balance the demands of the id and the superego against each other and the realities of the world. These interactions and conflicts are represented by arrows in the figure. *Which of these components is the source of guilt feelings?*

is the lustful, impulsive, fun, or drive-ridden part of the unconscious. The demand of Sesame Street's Cookie Monster—"Me want cookie!"—is pure id. It operates in terms of the *pleasure principle,* seeking immediate gratification of desires, regardless of the consequences. Doing something that may hurt someone's feelings, lying, and having fun are examples of the id.

ego: the part of the personality that is in touch with reality and strives to meet the demands of the id and the superego in socially acceptable ways

The personality process that is mostly conscious is called the **ego.** Gradually forming during the second and third years of life and driven by psychic energy borrowed from the id, the ego is the rational, thoughtful personality process that operates in terms of the *reality principle.* If, for example, a person is hungry, the id might drive her to seek immediate satisfaction by dreaming of food or by eating all the available food at once instead of keeping some of it for a later time. The ego would recognize that the body needs real food and that it will continue to need food in the future. It would use the id's energy to preserve some of the food available now and to look for ways of finding more.

superego: the part of the personality that is the source of conscience and inhibits the socially undesirable impulses of the id

Suppose you thought of stealing the desired food from someone else. The part of the personality that would stop you is called the **superego.** The id is concerned with what the person *wants* to do, the ego is concerned with planning what she *can* do, and the superego is concerned with what she *should* do. It is the moral part of the personality—the source of conscience and of high ideals—that operates in terms of a *moral principle.* The superego can also create conflicts and problems. It is sometimes overly harsh, like a very strict parent. The superego, then, is also the source of guilt feelings, which come from mild as well as serious deviations from what it defines as "right"— better known as the conscience.

The id and the superego frequently come into conflict with each other. Because neither is concerned with reality, they may both come into conflict with the outside world as well. Freud saw the ego as the part of the person that must satisfy the demands of the id without offending the superego. If the id is not satisfied, the person feels an intolerable tension of longing or anger or desire. If the superego is not obeyed, the person feels guilty and inferior. If outside reality is ignored, the person suffers such outcomes as starvation or dislike by other people.

DEFENSE MECHANISMS

defense mechanisms: certain specific means by which the ego unconsciously protects itself against unpleasant impulses or circumstances

The ego's job is so difficult that unconsciously all people resort to psychological defenses. Rather than face intense frustration, conflict, or feelings of unworthiness, people deceive themselves into believing nothing is wrong. If the demands of the id and the ego cannot be resolved, it may be necessary to distort reality. Freud called these techniques **defense mechanisms** because they defend the ego from experiencing anxiety about failing in its tasks (see Figure 14.5). Freud believed that these defense mechanisms stem mainly from the unconscious part of the ego. They ordinarily become conscious to the individual only during a form of psychotherapy called psychoanalysis—and then only with great difficulty.

To some degree, defense mechanisms are necessary for psychological well-being. They relieve intolerable confusion and stress, help people weather intense emotional crises, and give individuals time to work out problems they might not be able to solve if they allowed themselves to feel all the pressures at work within them. However, if a person resorts to defense mechanisms all of the time, he will avoid facing and solving his problems realistically. A few of the defense mechanisms Freud identified are discussed below.

Rationalization

If you explained your poor performance on your last math test by saying, "The test questions were bad; they didn't make sense," rather than admitting that you did not study for the test, you practiced *rationalization*. Rationalization involves making up acceptable excuses for behaviors that cause us to feel anxious.

Repression

When a person has painful memories and unacceptable thoughts and motives that cause the ego too much anxiety, she may push those thoughts or urges out of consciousness down into the unconscious. This process is called *repression*. The person simply "forgets" the thing that disturbs her or pushes it out of awareness without ever realizing it. For example, a grown woman whose father is meddling in her life may have the impulse to say, "I hate you, Dad." The woman may feel so anxious and afraid about having such an impulse that she unconsciously will come to believe that what she feels is not hatred. She replaces the feeling with apathy. She says, "I don't hate you. I have no special feelings at all about you." Nevertheless, the feelings of anger and hostility remain in the unconscious and may show themselves in cutting remarks or sarcastic jokes, slips of the tongue, or dreams.

Denial

You are in *denial* if you refuse to accept the reality of something that makes you anxious. For example, it is a stormy and frightening night, and the local television and radio announcers are advising citizens to take cover and observe the tornado warnings in effect. David does not believe that his town will get hit (he is in denial) and is severely injured after failing to heed the warnings.

Projection

Another way the ego avoids anxiety is to believe that impulses coming from within are really coming from other people. For example, a boy who is extremely jealous of his girlfriend but does not

Figure 14.4	Freudian Slip

"Freudian slips" are mistakes or slips of the tongue that we make in everyday speech. Freud believed that these "slips" reflect our unconscious thoughts or wishes. *What is the Freudian slip that this turkey makes?*

Figure 14.5 **Defense Mechanisms**

Projection refers to a person seeing attributes of his own personality in others. Repression is shown by a woman who is not only restraining a monstrous impulse but also trying to conceal from herself that she is doing so. The displacement of a widow's love for her lost husband onto her pets is another defense mechanism. *In what ways are defense mechanisms helpful?*

Projection: a person believes that impulses really coming from within himself are coming from other people. (He is jealous of his girlfriend but claims that she's the one who is jealous.)

Displacement: a widow transfers her love for her late husband to her cats.

Repression: a person pushes painful memories or anxiety out of her consciousness; a person "forgets" what is disturbing her.

want to admit to himself that he is threatened by her independence may claim, "I'm not jealous—she's the one who's always asking where I've been, who that girl was I was talking to. She's the one who's jealous." This mechanism is called *projection* because inner feelings are thrown, or projected, outside the self and assigned to others. If a person thinks, for example, that others dislike him when in reality he dislikes himself, he is said to be projecting. This is a common mechanism, which you may have used yourself from time to time.

Reaction Formation

Reaction formation involves replacing an unacceptable feeling or urge with an opposite one. For example, a divorced father may resent having his child for the weekend. Unconsciously, he believes it is terribly wrong for a father to react that way, so he showers the child with expressions of love, toys, and exciting trips. A woman who finds her powerful ambitions unacceptable may play the role of a weak, helpless, passive female who wants nothing more than to please the men in her life—unconsciously covering up her true feelings. Have you ever put on a front and acted strong and confident when you were really scared?

Regression

Regression means going back to an earlier and less mature pattern of behavior. When a person is under severe pressure, he may start acting in ways that helped him in the past. For example, he may throw a temper tantrum, make faces, cry loudly, or revert to eating and sleeping all the time the way he did as a small child. If you have ever been tempted to stick out your lower lip and pout when you know that you should really accept that you cannot have your own way, you have experienced regression.

Displacement

Displacement occurs when you cannot take out your anger on the source of your frustrations, so you displace it or take it out on an unrelated person. For example, if you wanted to hit your father but were afraid to, you might hit your little brother instead. Your poor brother gets slapped around partly because he reminds you of your father and partly because he is not as likely to hit back.

Sublimation

Sublimation refers to redirecting a forbidden desire into a socially acceptable desire. For example, you may be so frustrated by your friend's arrogant attitude that you work extra hard at soccer practice, pushing yourself to your physical limits. You have channeled your aggressive feelings into physical activities.

EVALUATING FREUD'S CONTRIBUTION

The recognition of the tremendous forces that exist in human personality and the difficulty of controlling and handling them were Freud's great contributions to understanding human life. After Freud, it became easier to understand why human life contains so much conflict. It is a matter, Freud thought, of a savage individual coming to terms with the rules of society. The id is the savage part, and the superego is the representative of society. In a healthy person, the ego (the "I") is strong enough to handle the struggle (Hall, 1954).

Freud was also the first psychologist to claim that infancy and childhood are critical times for forming a person's basic character structure. In his theory of psychosexual development, Freud reasoned that a child goes through five stages of development—oral, anal, phallic, latency, and genital. Conflicts arise in each of

More About...

Birth Order

Are you either the oldest child in the family or the youngest? Does this affect your personality? Frank Sulloway (1996) studied birth-order effects on personalities, coming up with the following characteristics:

- Firstborns are interested in preserving the status quo; later-borns are more open to new experiences and ideas.

- Firstborns are usually more responsible, achievement-oriented, and organized than those born later.

- Later-borns are usually more agreeable than firstborns.

- Firstborns are more jealous and fearful than later-borns.

- Firstborns have more assertive and dominant personalities but may not be as sociable as later-borns.

It is important to note that Sulloway's research focused on middle- to upper-class people in Western cultures and therefore may not apply to other cultures. Sulloway's research also is generalized, meaning it may not apply to every individual or every family.

the stages. Freud claimed that a child's personality largely developed in the first five years, during which the child went through the stages of development. That child's personality became the result of how the child dealt with the conflicts that arose in each stage of development. Freud believed that personality was well formed by the time the child entered school and that subsequent growth consisted of elaborating this basic structure. Freud was the first person to demonstrate how the personality is developed in a person. (See Chapter 3 for a discussion of Freud's stages of development.)

Freud became the first person to propose a unified theory to understand and explain human behavior. No theory that has followed has been more complete, more complex, or more controversial. Some psychologists treat Freud's writings as a sacred text—if Freud said it, it must be so. At the other extreme, many have accused Freud of being unscientific—of proposing a theory that is too complex ever to be proved true or false. Freud's theories continue to be debated. His theories continue to provide people with thoughts and challenging ideas.

IN FREUD'S FOOTSTEPS

Freud's revolutionary ideas attracted many followers who disagreed with him, and a number of these psychoanalysts developed important theories of their own.

Carl Jung

collective unconscious: the part of the mind that contains inherited instincts, urges, and memories common to all people

archetype: an inherited idea, based on the experiences of one's ancestors, which shapes one's perception of the world

At one time, Carl Jung (1875–1961) was Freud's closest associate. When Freud and Jung started to argue about psychoanalytic theory, though, their personal relationship became strained. They stopped speaking to each other entirely, a mere seven years after they met.

Jung disagreed with Freud on two major points. First, he took a more positive view of human nature, believing that people try to develop their potential as well as handle their instinctual urges. Second, he distinguished between the personal unconscious, which was similar to Freud's idea of the unconscious, and the **collective unconscious,** which is a storehouse of instincts, urges, and memories of the entire human species throughout history. He called these inherited, universal ideas **archetypes.** The same archetypes are present in every person. They reflect the common experiences of humanity regarding mothers, fathers, nature, war, and so on (see Figure 14.7).

Jung went on to identify the archetypes by studying dreams and visions, paintings, poetry, folk stories, myths, and religions. He found that the same themes—the archetypes—appear again and again. He found that many cultures share certain myths, dreams, religious beliefs, and symbols separated by time. For example, the story of Jack and the Beanstalk is essentially the same as the story of

Figure 14.6   Carl Jung

Carl G. Jung was one of the most mystical and metaphysical of the pioneer theorists. *What is the collective unconscious?*

David and Goliath. Both tell how a small, weak, good person triumphs over a big, strong, bad person. Jung believed such stories are common and easy to understand because the situations they describe have occurred over and over again in human history and have been stored as archetypes in the unconscious of every human being (Jung, 1963). Jung argued that these archetypes influence our thoughts and feelings and help us build the foundation of our personalities. For example, one archetype is our sense of self. Our sense of self gives us direction and provides a sense of completeness. We use the concepts in our personal unconscious and collective unconscious to develop our personalities. We fit our personalities to these concepts. In the process of fitting our personalities to these beliefs, we may hide our real feelings and our real personalities, though.

Alfred Adler

Like Jung, Alfred Adler (1870–1937) was an associate of Freud who left his teacher in the early part of the twentieth century to develop his own approach to personality theory. Adler believed that the driving force in people's lives is a desire to overcome their feelings of inferiority. Classic examples are Demosthenes, who overcame a speech impediment by practicing speaking with pebbles in his mouth and became the greatest orator of ancient Greece; Napoleon, a short man who conquered Europe in the early 1800s; and Glenn Cunningham, an Olympic runner who, as a child, lost his toes in a fire and had to plead with doctors who wanted to amputate his legs because they thought he would never be able to use them again.

Everyone struggles with inferiority, said Adler. He describes a person who continually tries to compensate for his weakness and avoid feelings of inadequacy as having an **inferiority complex.** Children first feel inferior because they are so little and so dependent on adults. Gradually they learn to do the things that older people can do. The satisfaction that comes from such simple acts as walking or learning to use a spoon sets up a pattern of overcoming inadequacies, a pattern that persists throughout life. Adler called these patterns *lifestyles.*

Adler believed that the way parents treat their children influences the styles of life they choose. Overpampering, in which the parents attempt to satisfy the child's every whim, tends to produce a self-centered person who has little regard for others and who expects everyone else to do what he or she wants. On the other hand, the child who is neglected by his or her parents may seek revenge by becoming an angry, hostile person. Both the pampered and the neglected child tend to grow into adults who lack confidence in their ability to meet the demands of life. Ideally, said Adler, a child should learn self-reliance and courage from the father and generosity and a feeling for others from the mother (Adler, 1959). Adler believed that all humans are motivated by social urges and that each person is a social being with a unique personality.

Figure 14.7   Archetypes

According to Jung's theory, Luke Skywalker can be considered an archetype of a hero and of goodness. *What are archetypes?*

inferiority complex: a pattern of avoiding feelings of inadequacy rather than trying to overcome their source

Figure 14.8   **Finding Individual Fulfillment**

According to Adler, each person creates a plan—a lifestyle—for achieving superiority. The lifestyle of this Buddhist monk differs from that of Bill Gates. Each may have a different path to fulfillment. *How does Adler's theory differ from Freud's?*

Other Theorists

Although Jung and Adler were the first figures to break with Freud, many others followed. Erich Fromm's (1900–1980) theory centered around the need to belong and the loneliness freedom brings. Karen Horney (1885–1952) stressed the importance of basic anxiety, which a child feels because she is helpless, and basic hostility, a resentment of one's parents that generally accompanies this anxiety. She also disagreed with Freud on several basic beliefs. Horney believed that if a child is raised in an atmosphere of love and security, that child could avoid Freud's psychosexual parent-child conflict.

Erik Erikson (1902–1994) accepted Freud's basic theory, but he outlined eight psychosocial stages (described in Chapter 3) that every person goes through from birth to old age and which describe the importance of interacting with other people. These and other neo-Freudians have helped keep psychoanalytic theory alive and debated (Friman et al., 1993).

SECTION 2   Assessment

1. **Review the Vocabulary** Explain how the id, ego, and superego work together in a person.

2. **Visualize the Main Idea** Using a diagram similar to the one below, describe the basic views of personality of the following psychoanalysts: Carl Jung, Alfred Adler, and Sigmund Freud.

Psychoanalyst	Views of Personality

3. **Recall Information** What is the difference between personal unconscious and collective unconscious? How does the unconscious affect our personalities?

4. **Think Critically** What part of a personality—id, ego, or superego—do you think is the most important part of a personality? Why?

5. **Application Activity** Create a cartoon that illustrates the use of one of the defense mechanisms discussed in this section.

Learning Theories

Reader's Guide

■ Main Idea
Behaviorists are interested in how aspects of personality are learned.

■ Vocabulary
- behaviorism
- contingencies of reinforcement

■ Objectives
- Describe Skinner's concept of personality.
- Explain Bandura's social cognitive theory of personality.

EXPLORING PSYCHOLOGY

Responding to Oppression

There is such a thing as the freedom of exhaustion. Some people are so worn down by the yoke of oppression that they give up. A few years ago in the slum areas of Atlanta, a Negro guitarist used to sing almost daily: "Ben down so long that down don't bother me." This is the type of negative freedom and resignation that often engulfs the life of the oppressed.

But this is not the way out. To accept passively an unjust system is to cooperate with that system; thereby the oppressed become as evil as the oppressor. . . .

—from *Stride Toward Freedom: The Montgomery Story* by **Martin Luther King, Jr., 1963**

In the excerpt above, Martin Luther King, Jr., described the behavior of some African Americans in the 1950s. King, a leader in the struggle for civil rights, observed this behavior and looked to the environment to see what was causing it. King recognized that an oppressive system maintained these behaviors. Like King, behaviorists look to the environment to see what is reinforcing behavior.

American psychology has long been dominated by the study of human and animal learning. John Watson believed that the proper subject matter of psychology ought to be observable behavior. He believed that if it could not be seen, then it could not be studied. His beliefs led to the study of behavior and what is called **behaviorism.** Behaviorists believe that as individuals differ in their learning experiences, they acquire different behaviors and, hence, different personalities.

behaviorism: belief that the proper subject matter of psychology is objectively observable behavior—and nothing else

Figure 14.9   B.F. Skinner's Box

Skinner devised a box (the "Skinner box") to test the observable behavior of rats. *According to Skinner, what motivates behavior?*

"IF WE DIDN'T DO SO WELL IN THE EASY BOX, THEY WOULDN'T HAVE GIVEN US THIS COMPLICATED BOX."

contingencies of reinforcement: the occurrence of a reward or punishment following a particular behavior

Reading Check
How do behaviorists study personality?

B.F. SKINNER: BEHAVIORISM

Although his behaviorism was not proposed as a theory of personality, B.F. Skinner had a major impact on personality theory. Skinner saw no need for a general concept of personality structure. He focused instead on precisely what causes a person to act in a specific way. It is a very pragmatic approach, one that is less concerned with understanding behavior than with predicting it and controlling it. He was interested in how aspects of one's personality are learned. (See Chapter 9 for more discussion of behaviorism.)

Consider the case of Ruben, a college sophomore who has been rather depressed lately. Sigmund Freud would likely seek the roots of Ruben's unhappiness in events in his childhood. Skinner's approach is more direct. First, Skinner would reject the vague label "depressed." Instead he would ask exactly how Ruben behaves. The answer may be that Ruben spends most of the day in his room, cuts all his classes, rarely smiles or laughs, and makes little effort to talk to anyone.

Skinner would try to understand the **contingencies of reinforcement.** What conditions are reinforcing these behaviors? What rewards does Ruben receive for never leaving his room? One hypothesis is that Ruben's girlfriend Brandi has unintentionally reinforced this behavior by spending a lot of time with him, trying to cheer him up. Perhaps she did not pay much attention to Ruben before he was depressed. Note that Skinner's approach immediately suggests a hypothesis that can be proved true or false. If paying attention to Ruben encourages his depression, then ignoring him should decrease the likelihood of this behavior. Brandi, therefore, might try ignoring Ruben for a few days. If he then starts leaving his room—which she should reinforce—she has discovered the contingencies of reinforcement that govern Ruben's behavior. If he does not leave his room, she will know that the hypothesis is wrong, and she can try something else. Perhaps Ruben is glued to the television in his room all day and has become a game-show addict. Take away the television, and you will find out whether that is the reinforcer.

At first, behaviorism may seem to imply that Ruben is somehow faking his depression so that he can watch "Wheel of Fortune" or see more of his girlfriend. Skinner does not make this assumption. Ruben may be entirely unaware of the rewards that are shaping his behavior. In any case, Ruben's feelings are beside the point. What matters is not what is going on inside Ruben's head but how he is behaving. The point is to specify his behavior and then find out what causes it.

Skinner's approach has become very popular among psychologists, partly because it is so pragmatic and action-oriented. Followers of Skinner have applied the techniques to a wide range of behaviors, from teaching pigeons to play table tennis to teaching severely mentally handicapped people to dress themselves and take part in simple activities once believed beyond their abilities. Therapies have also been devised to help people with specific behavioral problems, such as phobias and obsessive-compulsive behavior.

Other human behavior, too, can be changed using rewards and punishments. The success of behaviorists with most people has been limited, however, partly because our reinforcers are so complex. To behaviorists, behavior is a combination of behaviors that have been reinforced, or "learned." To change behavior, you change the reinforcer.

ALBERT BANDURA: SOCIAL COGNITIVE THEORY

PSYCHOLOGY and You

What Is Your Locus of Control?

Julian Rotter wrote the first book describing the social cognitive approach to personality. Rotter argued that a person's behavior depends not only on objective, situational factors but also on that person's subjective beliefs. Our *locus of control* refers to our beliefs about how much control we have over certain situations. If you believe that you do have control over situations, you have an *internal* locus of control. If you think that your fate is guided by forces beyond your control, you have an *external* locus of control. People with an internal locus of control are, on average, less anxious and more content with life than those with an external locus of control.

To find a person's locus of control, a psychologist might ask the person if he believes the following are true:

1. In the long run, people get what they deserve.

2. Most tests are fair if a student is prepared.

3. Many times, tests are so unfair that studying is wasted energy.

4. It is better to make decisions and take action than to trust fate.

Skinner emphasized reinforcement in his description of how personalities develop. Albert Bandura and his colleague Richard Walters (1963), however, argued that personality is acquired not only by direct reinforcement of behavior but also by observational learning, or imitation. In *observational learning,* a person acquires a new behavior by watching the actions of another person. For example, to teach a child how to hit a baseball with a bat, you could hand the child the bat and ball and reinforce him every time he used the bat and ball correctly. However, you would probably demonstrate the correct way to hold the bat and swing at the ball instead because this way the child would acquire the behavior more quickly. Bandura and Walters believed that much of a young child's individual behavior and personality is acquired by exposure to specific everyday models.

In Bandura's view, people are capable of directing their own behavior by their choice of models. In part, when your parents object to the company you keep, they are trying to change the models you use. The most effective models are those who are the most similar to and most admired by the observer. Thus, you are more likely to learn new behaviors from your friends than from your parents' friends.

Figure 14.10 Bandura's Social Cognitive Theory

According to Bandura's theory, a person's personality is shaped by an interaction among three forces—cognitive factors, behaviors, and environmental factors. *What are the cognitive factors?*

1. Cognitive-Personal Factors:
our beliefs, expectations, values, intentions, social roles, as well as our emotional makeup and biological and genetic influences

2. Behaviors:
our personal actions

3. Environmental Factors:
our social, political, and cultural influences and our personal learning experiences

Personality Development

Bandura has made significant contributions to the development of behavioral theories of personality. His social cognitive theory (1986) recognizes the interaction—called *reciprocal determinism*—that occurs among the observing individual, the behavior of that individual, and the environment in which the behavior occurs (see Figure 14.10). One important concept that governs our behavior is our view of our ability to succeed, which Bandura called *self-efficacy*. You decide whether to go on a date by assessing the environment—the weather, your parents' current state of mind, your potential date's recent behaviors—the effects of your own past behavior, and your long-term past successes and failures. This leads to the development of an expectancy of success. As the behavior unfolds, you also develop *outcome expectations*. As long as they remain positive, you will keep trying.

Whereas psychoanalytic theories emphasize the influence of childhood experiences, irrational thoughts, and unconscious forces, the advantage of learning theories of personality is that they focus on behavior—a concept that can be tested and measured. However, critics argue that the learning theories do not explain personality nor do they give enough attention to the influence of genetic factors, emotional influences, and childhood experiences on personality.

SECTION 3 Assessment

1. **Review the Vocabulary** According to behaviorism, what is the proper subject matter of psychology? How does this relate to the study of personality?

2. **Visualize the Main Idea** Using a diagram similar to the one below, compare and contrast the behaviorist and social cognitive theories of behavior.

Behaviorist — Similarities — Social Cognitive

3. **Recall Information** Why do you think people have different personalities? What is the purpose of having different personalities?

4. **Think Critically** How would behaviorists and social learning theorists explain a person's persistence in becoming an accomplished tennis player?

5. **Application Activity** Choose a behavior of a younger sibling or of a friend whom you would like to see change. Suggest a way to do so, using reinforcers to change the particular behavior.

Humanistic and Cognitive Theories

Reader's Guide

■ **Main Idea**

Humanistic and cognitive theories of personality stress the positive aspects of human nature.

■ **Vocabulary**

- humanistic psychology
- self-actualization
- self
- positive regard
- conditions of worth
- unconditional positive regard
- fully functioning

■ **Objectives**

- Explain Maslow's idea of self-actualization.
- Describe Carl Rogers's view of human behavior.

EXPLORING PSYCHOLOGY

Changing a Nation

Jackie Robinson had to be bigger than life. He had to be bigger than the Brooklyn teammates who got up a petition to keep him off the ball club, bigger than the pitchers who threw at him or the base runners who dug their spikes into his shin, bigger than the bench jockeys who hollered for him to carry their bags and shine their shoes, bigger than the so-called fans who mocked him with mops on their heads and wrote him death threats. . . . Somehow, though, Jackie had the strength to suppress his instincts, to sacrifice his pride for his people's. It was an incredible act of selflessness that brought the races closer together than ever before and shaped the dreams of an entire generation.

—from "Jackie Robinson" by Henry Aaron in *TIME* magazine, June 14, 1999

In 1947 life in America was one of segregation. There were separate schools for African Americans and whites, separate restaurants, separate hotels, separate drinking fountains, and even separate baseball leagues—that is, until Jackie Robinson began playing for the Brooklyn Dodgers. Robinson played the game passionately and, despite colossal obstacles, changed the face of baseball. His experience shows the impact that believing in one's own abilities can have on personal success. The idea that individuals' perceptions of themselves can become their reality is part of the humanistic and cognitive theories of personality.

HUMANISTIC PSYCHOLOGY

humanistic psychology: an approach that stresses the uniqueness of the individual

Humanistic psychology may be viewed as a rebellion against the rather negative, pessimistic view of human nature that dominated personality theory in the early 1900s. Psychoanalysts emphasized the struggle to control primitive, instinctual urges on the one hand and to come to terms with the demands of the superego, or conscience, on the other. The behaviorists, too, saw human behavior in mechanistic terms: our actions are shaped by rewards and punishments. Humanistic psychologists object to both approaches on the grounds that they demean human beings—Freud by emphasizing irrational and destructive instincts, Skinner by emphasizing only external causes of behavior. In contrast, the humanists stress our ability to create and live by personal standards and perceptions.

self-actualization: the humanist term for realizing one's unique potential

Humanistic psychology is founded on the belief that all human beings strive for **self-actualization**—that is, the realization of our potentialities as unique human beings. Self-actualization involves an openness to a wide range of experiences, an awareness of and respect for one's own and other people's uniqueness, accepting the responsibilities of freedom and commitment, a desire to become more and more authentic or true to oneself, and an ability to grow.

Figure 14.11   An American First

Jackie Robinson became the first African American to play in major league baseball and became a hero to millions. Here he steals home. *How does Robinson's life reflect the humanist ideal of self-actualization?*

ABRAHAM MASLOW: GROWTH AND SELF-ACTUALIZATION

Abraham Maslow (1908–1970) became one of the guiding spirits of the humanistic movement in psychology. He deliberately set out to create what he called "a third force in psychology" as an alternative to psychoanalysis and behaviorism. Maslow tried to base his theory of personality on studies of healthy, creative, self-actualizing people who fully utilize their talents and potential rather than on studies of disturbed individuals.

When Maslow decided to study the most productive individuals he could find—in history as well as in his social and professional circles—he broke new ground. Psychotherapists developed the theories of personality discussed earlier after years of working with people who could not cope with everyday frustrations and conflicts. In contrast, Maslow was curious about people who not only coped with everyday problems effectively but who also created exceptional lives for themselves, people like Abraham Lincoln, Albert Einstein, and Eleanor Roosevelt.

Maslow found that although these people sometimes had great emotional difficulties, they adjusted in ways that allowed them to become highly productive. Maslow also found that self-actualized individuals share a number of traits (see Figure 14.12). First, they perceive reality accurately, unlike most people who, because of prejudices and wishful thinking, perceive it rather inaccurately. Self-actualized people also accept themselves, other people, and their environments more readily than most people do. Without realizing it, most of us project our hopes and fears onto the world around us. We deny our own shortcomings and try to rationalize or change things we do not like about ourselves. Self-actualizing individuals accept themselves as they are.

Figure 14.12   Characteristics of Self-Actualized People

Maslow proposed the concept of a "self-actualized personality," which is a better-than-normal personality with high productivity and enjoyment of life. *Do you think any person can develop a self-actualized personality, regardless of his or her social or economic status? Explain.*

They are realistically oriented.

They accept themselves, other people, and the natural world for what they are.

They have a great deal of spontaneity.

They are problem-centered rather than self-centered.

They have an air of detachment and a need for privacy.

They are autonomous and independent.

Their appreciation of people and things is fresh rather than stereotyped.

Most of them have had profound mystical or spiritual experiences, although not necessarily religious in character.

They identify with humanity.

Their intimate relationships with a few specially loved people tend to be profound and deeply emotional rather than superficial.

Their values and attitudes are democratic.

They do not confuse means with ends.

Their sense of humor is philosophical rather than hostile.

They have a great fund of creativeness.

They resist conformity to the culture.

They transcend the environment rather than just coping with it.

Source: Abraham Maslow, *Motivation and Personality*, New York: Harper & Row, 1970.

Because they are secure in themselves, self-actualized individuals are more problem-centered than self-centered. They are able to focus on tasks in a way that people concerned about maintaining and protecting their self-image cannot. They are more likely to base decisions on ethical principles rather than on calculations of the possible costs or benefits to themselves. They have a strong sense of identity with other human beings, and they have a strong sense of humor but laugh with people, not at them.

Maslow also found that self-actualized people are exceptionally spontaneous. They do not try to be anything other than themselves, and they know themselves well enough to maintain their integrity in the face of opposition, unpopularity, and rejection. They are autonomous. They value privacy and frequently seek out solitude. This is not to say that they are detached or aloof; rather than trying to be popular, they focus on deep, loving relationships with the few people to whom they are truly close.

Finally, the people Maslow studied had a rare ability to appreciate even the simplest things. They approached their lives with a sense of discovery that made each day a new day. They rarely felt bored or uninterested. Given to moments of intense joy and satisfaction, or "peak experiences," they enjoyed life itself. Maslow believed this to be both a cause and an effect of their creativity and originality (Maslow, 1970).

Maslow believed that to become self-actualized, a person must first satisfy his or her basic, primary needs—for food and shelter, physical safety, love and belonging, and self-esteem. Of course, to some extent the ability to satisfy these needs is often beyond our control. Still, no amount of wealth, talent, or beauty can totally shield someone from frustration and disappointment. All people have to adjust to maintain themselves and to grow.

Many psychologists have criticized Maslow's work. His claim that human nature is "good," for example, has been called an intrusion of subjective values into what should be a neutral science. The levels of specific needs, such as physical contact comfort, discussed in Chapter 12, have not been defined (Feist, 1985). His study of self-actualizing people has been criticized because the sample was chosen on the basis of Maslow's own subjective criteria. How can one identify self-actualized people without knowing the characteristics of such people? But then, if one knows these characteristics to begin with, what sense does it make to list them as if they were the results of an empirical study?

Figure 14.13 **Proclaiming Your Self-Worth**

You can progress toward self-actualization after you have developed a sense of self-esteem, or self-worth. *What traits associated with Maslow's definition of a self-actualized person does Charlie Brown display?*

CARL ROGERS: SELF THEORY

Carl Rogers (1902–1987) called the people he counseled "clients," not "patients." The word "patient" implies illness, a negative label that Rogers rejected. As a therapist, Rogers was primarily concerned with the path to self-actualization, or "full functioning," as he called it. Rogers believed that many people suffer from a conflict between what they value in themselves and what they believe other people value in them. There are two sides or parts to every person. Rogers believed that each person is constantly struggling to become more and more complete and perfect. Anything that furthers this end is good—the person wants to become everything he or she can possibly be. Different people have different potentialities, but every person wants to realize these potentialities, to make them real, whatever they are. Whatever you can do, you want to do—and do as well as possible. This optimism about human nature is the essence of humanism.

Profiles In Psychology

Carl Rogers
1902–1987

"[T]he client knows what hurts, what directions to go, what problems are crucial, what experiences have been buried."

Carl Rogers is best known for his role in the development of counseling. Rogers believed that therapy should focus on present problems—psychologists should not dwell on the past and the causes of present problems. Rogers believed that people are basically good and can solve their own problems once they realize that they can.

Rogers started out by rejecting two principles. He first began studying to become a minister, but then he started to doubt that the religious approach was the most effective way of helping people. Then, while training to become a psychoanalyst, Rogers realized that psychoanalysts focused on gaining insight into the causes of a patient's problems. Rogers rejected this approach, finally creating his client-centered approach. Rogers used his approach to help clients better understand their subjective experiences and then work to change their own subjective views of themselves, the world, and other people.

Rogers was also a teacher. He advocated one-on-one approaches to teaching. He saw the role of the teacher as one who creates an environment for engagement; that is, the teacher inspires an exploratory atmosphere in which students seek answers to problems.

Each individual also has what Rogers called a **self.** The self is essentially your image of who you are and what you value—in yourself, in other people, in life in general. The self is something you acquire gradually over the years by observing how other people react to you. You want approval or **positive regard.** You ask yourself, "How does she see me?" If the answer is "She loves me. She likes what I am and what I do," then you begin to develop positive regard for yourself.

Yet often this does not happen. In other words, she places conditions on her love: *If* you do what she wants, she likes you. Young and impressionable, you accept these verdicts and incorporate **conditions of worth**

self: one's experience or image of oneself, developed through interaction with others

positive regard: viewing oneself in a positive light due to positive feedback received from interaction with others

conditions of worth: the conditions a person must meet in order to regard himself or herself positively into yourself. You begin to see yourself as good and worthy only if you act in certain ways. You have learned from your parents and from other people who are significant to you that unless you meet certain conditions, you will not be loved.

Reading Check
What is the "self" as Rogers defines it?

Rogers's work as a therapist convinced him that people cope with conditions of worth by rejecting or denying parts of their person that do not fit their self-concept. For example, if your mother grew cold and distant whenever you became angry, you learned to deny yourself the right to express or perhaps even feel anger. Being angry "isn't you." In effect, you are cutting off a part of your whole being; you are allowing yourself to experience and express only part of what you are.

The greater the gap between the self and the person, the more limited and defensive a person becomes. Rogers believed the cure for this situation—and the way to prevent it from ever developing—is **unconditional positive regard.** If significant others (parents, friends, a mate) convey the feeling that they value you for what you are in your entirety, you will gradually learn to grant yourself the same unconditional positive regard. The need to limit yourself declines or never develops in the first place. You will be able to accept your person and become open to *all* your feelings, thoughts, and experiences—and hence to other people. This is what Rogers meant by **fully functioning.** The person and the self are one. The individual is free to develop all of his or her potentialities. Like Maslow and other humanistic psychologists, Rogers believed that self-regard and regard for others go together and that the human potential for good and self-fulfillment outweighs the potential for evil and despair (Rogers, 1951, 1961, 1980).

unconditional positive regard: the perception that individuals' significant others value them for what they are, which leads the individuals to grant themselves the same regard

fully functioning: an individual whose person and self coincide

Humanistic approaches to personality emphasize that life is a conscious experience—that is, we freely choose how we spend our lives. Our conscious experience, though, is private and subjective. Critics argue that the humanistic theories cannot be tested. These theories describe behavior rather than explain it. Humanists themselves argue that each individual is unique, and therefore their theories cannot predict behavior.

COGNITIVE THEORY

Cognitive theory is based on analysis of our own perceptions, thoughts, and feelings. George Kelly (1905–1967) based his theory simply on an analysis of our perception of ourselves and our environment. In Kelly's view, our personality consists of our thoughts about ourselves.

The fundamental idea of Kelly's *personal construct theory* of personality is that our "processes are psychologically channelized by the ways in which (each of us) anticipates events" (Kelly, 1958). He was concerned with

More About...

Culture and Personality

As you read this chapter, you should realize that the personality theories presented here do not apply to all humans. The observations on which these theories are based center primarily on studies of people in North America and Western Europe. Those studied, then, represent only a minority of the humans on Earth. People in non-Western cultures may look at themselves differently. For instance, such a person may not view herself as a separate entity from her family or community. Concepts such as internal locus of control, self-efficacy, and optimism may have different meanings depending on one's culture. In one study of Asian Americans, for example, those who expressed pessimism about their abilities performed better at solving problems than those who expressed optimism (Chang, 1996). In studies of Caucasian Americans, just the opposite results occurred—an optimistic belief in one's abilities correlates positively with problem solving.

individual people and their cognitive behavior. He emphasized psychological processes within each of us, noting that these processes are channeled. By that he meant that there is organization to how we behave, governed by a network of potential but limited responses. The emphasis is on the individual and his or her plans—including biases, errors, mistakes, and false conclusions. The primary feature of these personally constructed ideas about the world and how to behave in it is the individual's anticipations—or predictions—about his or her world. All of this is focused on governing the individual's behavior in real events. In effect, our ideas of ourselves, of others, and of our world shape our behavior and our personalities.

Kelly went on to develop ideas involving our individuality in how we develop our personal constructs. Our personal constructs are basically our schemas—our mental representations of people, events, and concepts. These constructs, or schemas, influence what we pay attention to, how we interpret events and people, and how we respond to events and people. Our constructs may bias our thoughts or distort our perceptions. Kelly took an optimistic view of humans. In his theory, we are masters rather than victims of our destiny. Our personal constructs tend to be stable, but we are able to change them in light of new evidence. All in all, Kelly's is a very flexible model of human behavior.

Figure 14.14 I'm OK—You're OK

Rogers proposed that people should relate to one another with unconditional positive regard. *What is unconditional positive regard?*

SECTION 4 Assessment

1. **Review the Vocabulary** What is self-actualization? How does one achieve it?

2. **Visualize the Main Idea** Using a diagram similar to the one below, illustrate the steps an individual needs to take to be fully functioning, according to Rogers's theory.

3. **Recall Information** How do conditions of worth influence your personality, according to Rogers?

4. **Think Critically** Do you think unconditional positive regard is important for healthy personality development? Why or why not?

5. **Application Activity** Think of a close friend, family member, or one of your heroes. Using the information in Figure 14.12, evaluate which traits of self-actualized individuals he or she shares.

Trait Theories

Reader's Guide

■ Main Idea
Trait theorists believe that character traits account for consistency of behavior in different situations.

■ Vocabulary
- trait
- cardinal trait
- factor analysis
- surface trait
- source trait
- extrovert
- introvert

■ Objectives
- Explain the main features of trait personality.
- Describe Allport's, Cattell's, and Eysenck's theories of personality.

EXPLORING PSYCHOLOGY

Characteristics of Personality

"Tell me about Nelson," said Johnetta.

"Oh, he's just terrific. He's the friendliest guy I know—goes out of his way to be nice to everyone. He hardly ever gets mad. He's just so even-tempered, no matter what's happening. And he's really smart, too. About the only thing I don't like is that he's always in such a hurry to get things done. He seems to have boundless energy, much more than I have."

"He sounds great to me, especially in comparison to Rico," replied Johnetta. "He is so self-centered and arrogant it drives me crazy. I sometimes wonder why I ever started going out with him."

—from *Understanding Psychology* by Robert S. Feldman, 1999

---

trait: a tendency to react to a situation in a way that remains stable over time

Terms such as *nice, smart,* and *arrogant* refer to personality traits. Some theorists have argued that studying such traits in detail is the best approach to solving the puzzle of human behavior.

A **trait** is "any relatively enduring way in which one individual differs from another" (Guilford, 1959). A trait, then, is a predisposition to respond in a certain way in many different kinds of situations—in a dentist's office, at a party, or in a classroom. More than any other personality theorists, trait theorists emphasize and try to explain the consistency of a normal, healthy individual's behavior in different situations.

WHAT IS THE TRAIT THEORY OF PERSONALITY?

Trait theorists generally make two basic assumptions about these underlying sources of consistency. First, every trait applies to all people. For example, everyone can be classified as more or less dependent. Second, these descriptions can be quantified. We might, for example, establish a scale on which an extremely dependent person scores 1, while a very independent person scores 10.

Thus, every trait can be used to describe people. Aggressiveness, for example, is measured on a continuum: a few people are extremely aggressive or extremely unaggressive, and most of us fall somewhere in the middle. We understand people by specifying their traits, and we use traits to predict people's future behavior.

Trait theorists go beyond this kind of common-sense analysis, however, to try to discover the underlying sources of the consistency of human behavior. What is the best way to describe the common features of someone's behavior? Is he friendly, or socially aggressive, or interested in people, or sure of himself, or something else? What is the underlying trait that best explains his behavior?

Most (but not all) trait theorists believe that a few basic traits are central for all people. An underlying trait of self-confidence, for example, might be used to explain more superficial characteristics like social aggressiveness and dependency. If this were true, it would mean that a person would be dependent because he or she lacked self-confidence. Psychologists who accept this approach set out on their theoretical search for basic traits with very few assumptions.

This is very different from the starting point of other personality theorists we have considered. Freud, for example, began with a well-defined theory of instincts. When he observed that some people were stingy, he set out to explain this in terms of his theory. Trait theorists would not start by trying to understand stinginess. Rather, they would try to determine whether stinginess was a trait. That is, they would try to find out whether people who were stingy in one type of situation were also stingy in others. Then they might ask whether stinginess is a sign of a more basic trait like possessiveness: Is the stingy person also very possessive in relationships? Thus, the first and foremost question for the trait theorists is: What behaviors go together?

"That's Mr. Brock. He didn't have a happy New Year, a happy Valentine's Day, a happy St. Patrick's Day, a happy Easter, a happy Father's Day, a happy Halloween, a happy Thanksgiving, or a merry Christmas. He <u>did</u> have, however, a safe and sane Fourth of July."

Figure 14.15   Personality Traits

This cartoon highlights personality traits. Often we describe a person's personality in terms of traits. *Which personality traits does this cartoon emphasize?*

> ✓ **Reading Check**
> How does trait theory differ from psychoanalytic theories of personality?

GORDON ALLPORT: IDENTIFYING TRAITS

Gordon W. Allport (1897–1967) was an influential psychologist in his day. A trait, Allport said, makes a wide variety of situations "functionally equivalent"; that is, a person's traits will be consistent in different situations. Allport, along with H.S. Odbert, probed an English dictionary, searching for words that described personality traits. They found almost 18,000 such words. They then narrowed the list by grouping synonyms and keeping just one word for each cluster of synonyms. Finally, they found the opposites of each word and eliminated them. For example, if they found *honesty* and *dishonesty,* they eliminated *dishonesty* because it is the opposite of *honesty.* Allport defined common traits as those that apply to everyone and individual traits as those that apply more to a specific person.

cardinal trait: a trait that is so pervasive that the person is almost identified with the trait

Allport described three kinds of individual traits. A **cardinal trait** is one that is so pervasive that the person is almost identified with that trait. An example would be Scrooge, who is identified as stingy and cold-hearted in Charles Dickens's tale *A Christmas Carol. Secondary traits* are not very important to Allport and describe transient or less consistent traits, such as food and music preferences. A *central trait* is one that best describes a person, such as shy, loyal, friendly, or generous.

An example of an individual trait is found in Allport's book *letters from Jenny* (1965), which consists of hundreds of letters that a woman whom Allport calls Jenny Masterson wrote to a friend (see Readings in Psychology, p. 408). Jenny reveals herself in these letters, which she wrote between the ages of 58 and 70, as a complex and fiercely independent woman. In his preface to the book, Allport wrote:

> [The] fascination of the Letters lies in their challenge to the reader (whether psychologist or layman) to "explain" Jenny—if he can. Why does an intelligent lady behave so persistently in a self-defeating manner?

Allport's own attempt to understand Jenny began with a search for the underlying traits that would explain the consistency of her behavior.

Figure 14.16 Cattell's Sixteen Source Traits

Cattell used his sixteen source traits to develop a personality questionnaire, which was used to measure the traits in an individual. Each trait is listed as a pair of opposites on a continuum. *What did Cattell believe measuring the source traits could predict?*

Reserved	Outgoing
Less intelligent	More intelligent
Affected by feelings	Emotionally stable
Submissive	Dominant
Serious	Happy-go-lucky
Expedient	Conscientious
Timid	Venturesome
Tough-minded	Sensitive
Trusting	Suspicious
Practical	Imaginative
Forthright	Shrewd
Self-assured	Apprehensive
Conservative	Experimenting
Group-dependent	Self-sufficient
Uncontrolled	Controlled
Relaxed	Tense

RAYMOND CATTELL: SIXTEEN TRAIT THEORY

More recent theorists have concentrated on what Allport called *common traits,* which they try to quantify in a precise, scientific manner. Their primary tool in this task has been a sophisticated mathematical technique called **factor analysis,** which describes the extent to which different personality variables are related.

Using Allport's list of traits, Raymond Cattell (1905–) proposed that characteristics that can be observed in certain situations make up 46 traits, called **surface traits,** of observable behavior. These traits make up behavior that is based on people's perceptions of personality. Using further factor analyses, Cattell found that certain surface traits seem to occur in clusters. Cattell further researched what these clusters had in common. This analysis resulted in 16 **source traits**—traits that he considered to be at the core of personality (see Figure 14.16). Cattell believed that by measuring these traits, psychologists could predict people's behavior in certain situations.

HANS EYSENCK: DIMENSIONS OF PERSONALITY

Using factor analysis of personality data, Hans Eysenck (1916–), an English psychologist, concluded that there are two basic dimensions of personality (see Figure 14.17). The first dimension, *stability versus instability,* refers to the degree to which people have control over their feelings. At the emotionally stable end of the personality spectrum is a person who is easygoing, relaxed, well-adjusted, and even-tempered. At the anxiety-dominated end of the spectrum is the moody, anxious, and restless person.

Eysenck's second dimension was actually identified years earlier by Carl Jung as *extroversion versus introversion.* **Extroverts** are sociable, outgoing, active, lively people. They enjoy parties and seek excitement. On the other end of the dimension are **introverts,** who are more thoughtful, reserved, passive, unsociable, and quiet.

Years after he identified the first two dimensions, Eysenck added a third, *psychoticism.* At one end of this dimension are self-centered, hostile, and aggressive people, who act without much thought. Individuals at the other end of this dimension have what Freud might label high superego. They tend to be socially sensitive, high on caring and empathy, and easy people with whom to work (Eysenck, 1970, 1990).

THE ROBUST FIVE

Over the years, trait theorists have devised a number of ways to measure personality. Each involves a different number of traits or factors. Trait psychologists have shown that five traits appear repeatedly in

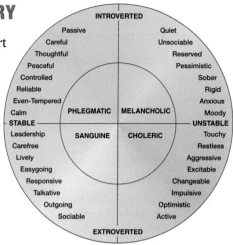

Figure 14.17   Eysenck's Personality Table

Eysenck hypothesized that introverted people share a number of traits, while extroverted people share the opposite traits. Eysenck's theory is similar to Galen's ancient theory for four temperaments (see the Case Study on page 23). *What traits would an extroverted and stable (sanguine) person exhibit?*

factor analysis: a complex statistical technique used to identify the underlying reasons variables are correlated

surface trait: a characteristic that can be observed in certain situations

source trait: a characteristic that can be considered to be at the core of personality

extrovert: an outgoing, active person who directs his or her energies and interests toward other people and things

introvert: a reserved, withdrawn person who is preoccupied with his or her inner thoughts and feelings

Do we see ourselves as others see us?

Some personality theorists talk about extroversion versus introversion as being a basic part of personality. Do people exhibit these traits in all situations? Are these traits easily identified?

Procedure

1. Choose five people (family members, friends, or acquaintances) and observe their behavior in several situations.

2. Record your observations by classifying each person as extroverted, introverted, or a combination of both.

3. Ask the five people whether they would consider themselves extroverted or introverted, and then record their responses.

Analysis

1. What do your results tell you about extroversion and introversion as personality traits? Are people extroverted or introverted in all situations all the time?

2. What do your results tell you about people's own perceptions of their personality versus the perceptions of others? What might account for any differences?

See the Skills Handbook, page 622, for an explanation of designing an experiment.

different research studies. Often called the "five robust factors," or "the big five," they are:

- *Extroversion,* which is associated with warmth, talkativeness, and being energetic. The opposite of this dimension is introversion, meaning being quiet or reserved.

- *Agreeableness,* which involves being sympathetic to others, kind, and trusting; the opposite is cruel and nontrusting.

- *Conscientiousness,* which identifies individuals who are dutiful, dedicated to completing tasks, organized, and responsible.

- *Openness to experience,* which describes people who are open-minded and willing to try intellectual experiences, new ideas, or creative experiences.

- *Emotional stability,* which identifies individuals who experience things relatively easily and without getting upset. The opposite is neuroticism—a tendency to experience unpleasant emotions a great deal of the time. (John, 1990; Costa, McCrae, & Dye, 1991)

Think of each big-five trait as a continuum. Each trait has many related traits. For example, conscientiousness at one end includes being responsible and dependable. On the other end, though, it involves being impulsive or careless.

Trait theorists assume that traits are relatively fixed, or unchanging. The advantage of trait theories is that by identifying a person's personality traits, that person's behavior can be predicted. However, critics argue that trait theories describe personality rather than explain it. Trait theorists cannot explain or predict behaviors across different situations. For example, a person may be quiet and reserved in class but outgoing and wild at a party. Why? Critics of trait theories propose that personality is an interaction between a person's traits and the effects of being in a particular situation. For example, whereas most theories of personality consider the person as an individual, some psychologists regard personality as a function of a person's social environment. One of the first of these thinkers was Harry Stack Sullivan (1892–1949).

Sullivan's ideas have been organized into a two-dimensional model. One dimension is power, which ranges from dominance at one end of the scale to submissiveness at the other. The second dimension is friendliness, which ranges from friendliness to hostility. Most behaviors can be described as a combination of these two dimensions. For example, "helpfulness" is a combination of dominance and friendliness, while "trust" is a combination of submissiveness and friendliness.

Figure 14.18   Theories of Personality

Theories of personality are used to organize personality characteristics, explain differences among individuals, explore how people conduct their lives, and determine how life can be improved. *Which theory do you think best describes your personality? Explain.*

Theory	Main Ideas
Behaviorist Theories	focus on the way rewards and punishment shape our actions
Social Learning Theories	cognitive-personal factors, our behaviors, and environmental factors interact to shape our personalities
Psychoanalytic Theories	emphasize the importance of early childhood experiences, repressed thoughts, and conflict between conscious and unconscious forces
Cognitive Theories	our analysis of our own perceptions, thoughts, and feelings shape our personalities
Humanistic Theories	emphasize our capacity for personal growth, development of our full potential, and freedom to make choices
Trait Theories	focus on identifying, measuring, and classifying similarities and differences in personality characteristics or traits

Researchers also noticed that a person's actions tend to elicit specific responses from other people. A behavior and its most likely response are said to be complementary. For example, most people will respond to a request for help (trusting) by offering advice (helping), regardless of how "helpful" they are as individuals. Thus, many behaviors result not simply from a person's personality but also from that person's social environment.

SECTION 5   Assessment

1. **Review the Vocabulary** What is the difference between cardinal and central traits? Between surface and source traits?

2. **Visualize the Main Idea** Using a diagram similar to the one below, list the traits that make up each of Eysenck's three dimensions of personality.

Eysenck's Dimensions of Personality

3. **Recall Information** What is the importance of common traits in Cattell's theory? What are Cattell's source traits?

4. **Think Critically** Do the five factors of personality in the "big five" describe you? If not, what other characteristics would you want to add?

5. **Application Activity** Choose a character in a movie or television show you have recently seen. Describe the character in terms of the personality dimensions proposed by one of the trait theorists discussed in this section.

Case Studies

Personality Disorder

Period of Study: 1967

Introduction: An actor and radio disc jockey, Dan was highly successful in his professional roles, which required an entertaining and extremely outspoken personality. Although Dan had to maintain these personality traits at work, sometimes traces of those traits leaked out into his private life. In one situation while Dan and a friend dined at a restaurant, Dan explicitly and loudly complained about the condition of the food. In actuality, according to Dan's friend, the food was fine—there was no valid reason for Dan's public display.

Dan's friend, psychologist Elton McNeil, described Dan's reactions as inappropriate. When McNeil asked Dan why he had acted that way, Dan said he did it because "he wanted to show how gutless the rest of the world is." Dan then said acting like that separates the classy people from the ordinary and that the next time he eats at that restaurant, he will be treated well. Concerned by his friend's statements, McNeil asked Dan if he felt guilty at all about treating his fellow human beings that way. Dan's answer was "Who cares?"

Hypothesis: For those of us who are familiar with actors and radio disc jockeys, we know that their jobs require straightforward and sometimes confrontational behavior. An excess of these traits, though, can prove to be too much for healthy functioning in life.

Method: McNeil encouraged his friend to take part in some sort of counseling or therapy. Dan agreed. During a therapy session, Dan disclosed:

I can remember the first time in my life when I began to suspect I was a little different from most people. When I was in high school my best friend got leukemia

and died and I went to his funeral. Everybody else was crying and feeling sorry for themselves and as they were praying to get him into heaven, I suddenly realized that I wasn't feeling anything at all. He was a nice guy but what the hell. That night I thought about it some more and found that I wouldn't miss my mother and father if they died and that I wasn't too nuts about my brothers and sisters for that matter. I figured there wasn't anybody I really cared for but, then, I didn't need any of them anyway so I rolled over and went to sleep.
(Davison & Neale, 1996)

Results: This description detailing the absence of emotion clearly indicated the possibility of a personality disorder. The *Diagnostic and Statistical Manual of Mental Disorders, Fourth Edition (DSM-IV)* defines a personality disorder as an enduring pattern of inner experience and behavior that differs significantly from the individual's culture, is extensive and inflexible, has an onset in adolescence or early adulthood, is stable over time, and leads to distress or impairment. An individual with a personality disorder is often capable of functioning normally in society, including holding a job, maintaining some personal relationships, and, on some occasions, showing signs of emotions. This is what makes discovering a personality disorder so difficult.

Dan's unusual behavior may have gone unnoticed for so long because his occupations required a person to behave a certain way. Unfortunately, it is not always easy to actually know if a person is acting out a role or displaying his or her own personality traits. In Dan's case, his role was his personality.

Analyzing the Case Study

1. Why did McNeil encourage Dan to enter therapy?

2. Why do psychologists consider Dan's behavior a disorder rather than just a personality type?

3. **Critical Thinking** Does everyone's personality change depending on the role they are playing (for instance, as student, friend, son, or daughter)? Explain.

Summary and Vocabulary

Psychologists have proposed various theories of personality. The theories attempt to help explain similarities and to provide reasons for differences in personality.

Section 1 Purposes of Personality Theories

Main Idea: Personality theories provide a way of organizing the many characteristics that people have.

- Personality theorists try to determine whether certain traits go together, why a person has some traits and not others, and why a person might exhibit different traits in different situations.

Section 2 Psychoanalytic Theories

Main Idea: Freud's psychoanalytic theory proposes that personality is made up of three components: the id, ego, and superego.

- Sigmund Freud believed that every personality has an unconscious component and that childhood experiences, even if not consciously recalled, continue to influence people's behaviors.
- The id, ego, and superego explain how the mind functions and how instinctual energies are regulated.

Section 3 Learning Theories

Main Idea: Behaviorists are interested in how aspects of personality are learned.

- Behaviorists believe that as individuals differ in their learning experiences, they acquire different behaviors and different personalities.
- Albert Bandura believed that personality is acquired not only by reinforcement but also by observational learning.

Section 4 Humanistic and Cognitive Theories

Main Idea: Humanistic and cognitive theories of personality stress the positive aspects of human nature.

- Humanistic psychology is founded on the belief that all human beings strive for self-actualization.
- Carl Rogers believed that many people suffer from a conflict between what they value in themselves and what they believe other people value in them.

Section 5 Trait Theories

Main Idea: Trait theorists believe that character traits account for consistency of behavior in different situations.

- Trait theorists believe we understand people by specifying their traits, and we use traits to predict people's future behavior.
- Gordon W. Allport defined common traits as those that apply to everyone and individual traits as those that apply more to a specific person.

Chapter Vocabulary

personality (p. 375)

unconscious (p. 379)

id (p. 379)

ego (p. 380)

superego (p. 380)

defense mechanisms (p. 380)

collective unconscious (p. 384)

archetype (p. 384)

inferiority complex (p. 385)

behaviorism (p. 387)

contingencies of reinforcement (p. 388)

humanistic psychology (p. 392)

self-actualization (p. 392)

self (p. 395)

positive regard (p. 395)

conditions of worth (p. 395)

unconditional positive regard (p. 396)

fully functioning (p. 396)

trait (p. 398)

cardinal trait (p. 400)

factor analysis (p. 401)

surface trait (p. 401)

source trait (p. 401)

extrovert (p. 401)

introvert (p. 401)

Self-Check Quiz
Visit the *Understanding Psychology* Web site at psychology.glencoe.com and click on **Chapter 14—Self-Check Quizzes** to prepare for the Chapter Test.

Reviewing Vocabulary

Choose the letter of the correct term or concept below to complete the sentence.

a. personality
b. contingencies of reinforcement
c. trait
d. defense mechanism
e. inferiority complex
f. self-actualization
g. positive regard
h. conditions of worth
i. extrovert
j. introvert

1. People who continuously try to compensate for their weakness and avoid feelings of inadequacy have a(n) _____.

2. A(n)_____ is a person who is reserved, passive, and unsociable.

3. A(n)_____ is a tendency to react the same way to different situations.

4. According to Carl Rogers, people require _____, or approval, from other people in order to acquire a self.

5. Conditions that maintain certain behaviors are called _____.

6. _____ consists of the consistent, enduring, and unique characteristics of a person.

7. When a person deceives herself into thinking nothing is wrong instead of facing intense conflict, she is using a(n)_____.

8. A(n)_____ is a person who is outgoing and lively.

9. According to humanistic psychologists, all people strive for _____, or the realization of their potentialities as unique human beings.

10. _____ is the term for the conditions people must meet in order to regard themselves positively.

Recalling Facts

1. Using a graphic organizer similar to the one below, list the "robust five" factors of personality.

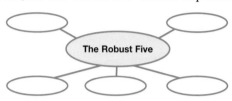

The Robust Five

2. How did Bandura and Walters believe personality is acquired?

3. What technique might you be using if you think a teacher is angry at you because he or she gave a difficult test, when in reality the teacher actually is not angry?

4. According to Rogers, what situation creates a gap between the person and the self?

5. What are the two basic assumptions behind trait theories?

Critical Thinking

1. **Synthesizing Information** Imagine that you have a friend who is failing several subjects in school, does little homework, and fails to study for tests. Based on your knowledge of personality theories, how would Skinner explain your friend's behavior? How would Bandura explain the behavior?

2. **Making Inferences** What would life be like if people had only an id, an ego, or a superego?

3. **Analyzing Concepts** Look and listen for "Freudian slips." Write them down and try to determine the reasons for each slip.

4. **Applying Concepts** List the qualities and traits that you think comprise the "self-actualized" person.

5. **Demonstrating Reasoned Judgment** Some opponents of the humanistic theory of personality have criticized it for promoting the "me first" approach to living. They believe that the theory encourages selfishness. Do you agree with these critics? Why or why not?

Assessment

Psychology Projects

1. **Purposes of Personality Theories** Create a collage that depicts your personality, using pictures and words from magazines and newspapers. Display your collage in class and explain which theory discussed best describes your personality.

2. **Psychoanalytic Theories** Archetypes are evident in many myths and fairy tales. Choose a myth or fairy tale and identify the archetypes in it and the common experiences of humanity that these archetypes reflect.

3. **Trait Theories** Select a newspaper or news magazine article that describes the activities or accomplishments of a person—for example, a popular sports figure, politician, or businessperson. Then select one of the trait theories of personality to describe the person's behavior and outlook on life. You may have to go beyond the material in the article to make a convincing argument for the theory you have selected. Present your description in a report.

Technology Activity

There are various personality tests available on the Internet. Locate the Web sites of these tests. Report on the aspects of personality that these tests address and evaluate how well they do so. Share the Web addresses you found with the class.

Psychology Journal

1. Analyze the entry in your journal you wrote at the beginning of the study of this chapter. Now write another entry answering these questions: Does the person change behavior depending on the setting? Explain your observations using a behavioral model of personality. What would you say are important reinforcers for this person?

2. In your journal, describe the theory of personality that is most appealing to you. Which seems to make the most sense? Why?

Building Skills

Identifying Cause-and-Effect Relationships Review the cartoon, then answer the questions that follow.

1. What does "Robert's facade" refer to?
2. What aspect of Freud's psychoanalytic theory of personality is reflected in the cartoon?
3. How might a behaviorist explain Robert's behavior?
4. How might a trait theorist describe Robert's behavior?
5. How might a humanistic psychologist, such as Carl Rogers, explain Robert's behavior?

"We have to go now. Robert's façade is beginning to crumble."

Practice and **assess** key social studies skills with **Glencoe Skillbuilder Interactive Workbook CD-ROM, Level 2.**

See the Skills Handbook, page 624, for an explanation of identifying cause-and-effect relationships.

Psychologist Gordon Allport presents the letters of Jenny Gove Masterson (and others) as an intense case study of personality. Jenny's letters trace a life of frustration and defeat. Between the ages of 58 and 70, Jenny wrote a series of 301 letters to Glenn and Isabel, two young friends. The letters dramatically illustrate her relationship with her son Ross. Jenny tells of her interests, hates, fears, and conflicts. These letters have led many psychologists and students to seek to explain Jenny's behavior and her personality.

 ## Reader's Dictionary

philanderer: one who has many love affairs
enigma: a mystery

EDITED AND INTERPRETED BY
GORDON W. ALLPORT

Friday, April 19/29

Dear Glenn:

I'm afraid that I am quite a nuisance in shoving my affairs on Isabel and you, but when you remember the compact we made that time I was in Chicago, and all your care over me since, you will pardon. You are my only confidant.

My motive in telling you all this is not to gossip, or backbite, but because I know that when *I* drop out Ross will lie to you and make it appear that things were quite different with us. . . .

The chances are that Ross and I are again near the parting of the ways. He has never cared anything at all for me since he adopted, and was adopted by,

the old philanderer. It is as well for him to try his luck again in matrimony—he can then take his other wife to visit his "Beloved Mother" his "B.M." as he did the first one, and they can all be happy together.

I have truly a noble son—an honor to his College, his friends, his family. And all for what? Can it be possible all this is merely for the sake of co-habiting with a woman who sells her body to the highest bidder?

Oh! If he would only settle down for 2 or 3 years and get a footing in business and not always belong to the "floating" population. He is not so very old yet altho' he has squandered 10 precious years. What in the world is the matter, Glenn dear?

I am not a charming person—not beautiful—not clever, but what of that? I carried him in my body for 9 mos. was good to him for many years (you know that) altho' he says I wasn't—that it was all *selfishness* on my part—but even granting all that to be so—I am still *his* Mother. Oh! what is it that's so wrong?

Be patient with me—I try you sadly—but I'm *alone,* and it's awful to be in the dark, and be alone.

I sincerely hope you are all well.

Jenny

P.S. *Do not* write to Ross about me. You would mean all right, of course, but Ross would be very angry, and resent it dreadfully. He says you don't "live"—don't know what "life" is—sometimes I think he is a little "off" and might kill me—he resents your having helped me, and my gratitude to Isabel and you.

Excerpts from a letter written by Ross to Glenn:

April 21, 1929

Your last letter was the one about Mother. I appreciate your interest and your desire to help me that I might help her. And yet, in a word, your letter merely emphasized my own feeling of frustration and futility. I'm afraid there is little one can do, or that I can do, to be a comfort and service of any real or lasting pleasure.

Mother has entrenched herself behind truths, half-truths, and utter fabrications concerning my limitations as the ideal son, and there is no dislodging her. No amount of even demonstrating my presence will change her constant reiteration that I am entirely bad and have cast her off in her old age. . . . Day and night, Mother recites her own good deeds to her family, her friends, her husband, her son, and how each in turn failed to pay her back. . . .

Dear Mr. Editor:

It is now twenty-seven years since Jenny Masterson died. You have asked me to re-read her Letters addressed to Glenn and myself, and in this perspective to make comments and interpretations concerning her tortured life.

Her Letters bring back many memories, but even in the perspective of years I cannot pretend to discover the key to her nature. Our relationship to her was essentially "neutral." We took pains not to become too deeply involved, but we always answered her communications and tried to help her in emergencies.

Her behavior, like the Letters, was intense, dramatic, and sometimes "hard to take." But to us her nature posed a challenge to understanding. What made her so intense, so vivid, so difficult? Even now her communications arouse in me a sense of the enigma of her personality as well as sympathy for her predicament. . . .

So we know that early in her life Jenny showed some of the factors evident in the Letters: her aloneness, her intense individuality and dramatization, her temper and tendency to quarrel. She was a puzzle to her family, and socially a problem long before we knew her. But to me the enigma is *how* she came to be such a problem to herself as well as to others. . . .

This self-defeating formula was with her from early years. At the age of 70 she is "the same only more so." . . .

Analyzing the Reading

1. What personality traits does Jenny display?
2. How does Ross view his mother?
3. **Critical Thinking** Isabel writes that Jenny's personality did not change as she aged, but became more difficult. Do you think that it is possible for a person to change his or her personality? Explain.

Adjustment and Breakdown

Contents

Theater masks ▶

Why It's Important

How are you supposed to live successfully day to day? One way to do so is by adjusting to the society in which you live. Whether you live in the city or country, you must adapt to your environment and the challenges it presents. Psychologists who study adjustment—the process of adapting to and actively shaping one's environment—try to understand why some people handle the experiences of life while others fail.

Stress and Health

PSYCHOLOGY JOURNAL

What are the major sources of stress in school? Can you pinpoint specific occasions, times, and events when many students feel stressed? Answer these questions in your journal. ■

PSYCHOLOGY
Online

Chapter Overview
Visit the *Understanding Psychology* Web site at psychology.glencoe.com and click on **Chapter 15—Chapter Overviews** to preview the chapter.

Sources of Stress

Reader's Guide

■ **Main Idea**

Stress results from our perceptions of demands placed upon us and our evaluations of situations we encounter.

■ **Vocabulary**
- stress
- stressor
- stress reaction
- distress
- eustress
- conflict situation

■ **Objectives**
- Define stress.
- Identify various sources of stress.

EXPLORING PSYCHOLOGY

Mental Tension

Brandon, an ambitious high school junior, fails his final exam in French; he is terrified that his chances of getting into college have been ruined, and a day or two later he develops an unsightly rash. Juanita, Brandon's classmate, learns that her parents cannot afford to pay her tuition for her first year of college; her friends wonder why she has suddenly become so bad-tempered. Angela gets her first leading role in a high school play; while running to call her boyfriend, she realizes that she cannot remember his phone number.

—from *Understanding Psychology,* Glencoe/McGraw-Hill, 1995

Brandon, Juanita, and Angela may all suffer from the effects of stress. What exactly is stress? There are many definitions, and even researchers in the field use the term in several ways. To some psychologists, stress is an *event* that produces tension or worry. Others describe it as a person's physical or psychological *response* to such an event. Still other researchers regard stress as a person's *perception* of the event. A slight variation on these ideas is the definition that will be used in this chapter. **Stress** is the anxious or threatening feeling resulting from our appraisal of a situation and our perception of demands placed upon us.

stress: a person's perception of his or her inability to cope with a certain tense event or situation

COMPONENTS OF STRESS

stressor: a stress-producing event or situation

To refer to the stress-producing event or situation, we shall use the term **stressor.** It is important to note that an event that is a stressor for one person may not be for another. For example, traveling in an airplane may be a stressor for someone who has never flown but not for a flight attendant. Stress, then, will be used to refer to a person's reactions—whether perceptual, cognitive, physical, or emotional—to a stressor. To discuss the body's observable response to a stressor, we shall use the term **stress reaction.**

stress reaction: the body's response to a stressor

Many people think of stress only as a condition to be avoided. Canadian researcher Hans Selye, however, distinguished between two types of stress. Negative stress, or **distress,** stems from acute anxiety or pressure and can take a harsh toll on the mind and body. Positive stress, or **eustress,** results from the strivings and challenges that are the spice of life (Selye & Cherry, 1978; Selye, 1982).

distress: stress that stems from acute anxiety or pressure

eustress: positive stress, which results from motivating strivings and challenges

Stress is a normal—even essential—part of life that goes hand in hand with working toward any goal or facing any challenge. In fact, as athletes gearing up for a game or students cramming for an exam can testify, stress can spur us on to greater effectiveness and achievement in some situations. In addition, whether we like it or not, we cannot escape stress; "complete freedom from stress," notes one psychologist (Selye, 1974), "is death." We can, however, learn to cope with stress so that it makes our lives interesting without overwhelming us.

conflict situation: when a person must choose between two or more options that tend to result from opposing motives

There is another component of stress. Richard Lazarus (1993) believes that how a person perceives and evaluates an event makes a difference. This is called the cognitive model of stress. People analyze and then evaluate a situation before it is labeled as "stressful." For example, maybe you have accidentally cut your finger and did not realize it at the time. Only when you looked at the cut did you evaluate the situation as "dangerous."

Figure 15.1   Suffering From Stress

Most of us have experienced a headache, upset stomach, muscle tension, or sleeplessness as a result of feeling stressed. *What causes stress?*

CONFLICT SITUATIONS

In our daily lives, we often have to evaluate situations and then make difficult decisions between two or more options—for example, going to a movie with friends or staying home to study for tomorrow's exam. These alternatives tend to result from conflicting motives—say, the desire to socialize versus the desire to do well in school—and they are major sources of stress. These choices are **conflict situations** (Miller, 1944), and they fall into four broad categories (see Figure 15.2).

In an *approach-approach conflict,* the individual must choose between *two attractive alternatives.* For example, a high school senior has been accepted at two excellent colleges, and she must decide which

Figure 15.2   Types of Conflict Situations

Conflict situations cause stress because you must give up something you want to get or face something you wish to avoid. *How is the double approach-avoidance conflict different from the approach-avoidance conflict?*

Approach-Approach	Avoidance-Avoidance	Approach-Avoidance	Double Approach-Avoidance
You must choose between two attractive options.	You must choose between two disagreeable options.	You find yourself in a situation that has both enjoyable and disagreeable consequences.	You must choose between multiple options, each of which has pleasurable and disagreeable aspects.
Do I want to go to the concert or ballgame on Saturday?	Should I stay up all night studying for my physics or math final?	Should I ask him to go to the party with me? (He may say yes, or he may say no.)	Should I stay home and wait for my girlfriend to call me, or should I just go out with my friends and maybe miss the call?

one to attend. Such a conflict is generally easy to resolve. The student in this situation will find some reason to attend one college rather than the other—perhaps better climate or more courses in her intended major field. An approach-approach conflict is a "conflict" in name only. It does not produce a great deal of stress, because both choices are satisfying.

An *avoidance-avoidance conflict* occurs when an individual confronts *two unattractive alternatives*. Consider the case of a college graduate unable to find a job after many months of searching. She is finally offered a position that has no future and does not pay well. Should she accept it, or should she continue to look for something better? Either course of action will be frustrating, and there is usually a high level of indecision and stress. The young woman in this example may decide that one option is "the lesser of two evils," or she may try to escape the decision, for instance, by registering with a temporary-employment agency until she gets the "right" job.

An individual who wants to do something but has fears or doubts or is repulsed by it at the same time is experiencing an *approach-avoidance conflict*. For example, a man wants to ask for a raise, but he is afraid he will be fired if he does. In cases like this, the degree of stress depends on the intensity of the desire or of the perceived threat. Resolution of this type of conflict often is very difficult and depends generally on the person's finding added reasons to choose one alternative over the other. The man in this example may learn that his boss thinks his work has been excellent; therefore, he feels there is little risk of being fired if he asks for more money.

Probably the most common conflict situation is a *double approach-avoidance conflict* in which the individual must choose between *two or more alternatives, each of which has attractive and unattractive aspects*. To use a simple illustration, a young woman working in Chicago cannot decide whether to spend her vacation in Paris or at her parents' home in North Carolina. She has never been to Paris, but the airfare and hotel bills will be more than she can really afford. Visiting her parents will be inexpensive and relaxing but not very exciting. As in an approach-avoidance conflict, the degree of stress generated depends on the intensity of the attractions and repulsions.

Appraising a Situation

Why is it that some people view a situation, such as looking for a parking space, as stressful while others do not? The level of stress you feel depends on how you appraise the situation. *Primary appraisal* refers to our immediate evaluation of a situation. For instance, can we meet the demands of this situation? Does this situation present us with more challenges than we think we can handle? There are three ways you can appraise a situation—as irrelevant, positive, or negative. For example, if your teacher suddenly announces a pop quiz, you may feel okay about the situation. You think you know the material, and your teacher does not give difficult quizzes. You may look forward to pop quizzes and feel positive about the situation because you know the material on the quiz and are assured of a good grade. You may also evaluate the situation as a negative one—you have not looked at your notes in days. In this last example, you feel stressed.

A *secondary appraisal* involves deciding how to deal with a potentially stressful situation. At this point an individual appraises the situation and then decides on a coping strategy. We will discuss coping strategies in Section 3.

Reading Check
What is the difference between a primary and secondary appraisal?

ENVIRONMENTAL STRESSORS

Environmental conditions such as noise may cause stress on the job, and these factors can have similar effects on the public at large. In fact, surveys have shown that Americans regard noise as one of the foremost irritants in their lives. Noise is particularly aggravating when it is loud, irregular, or uncontrollable. Constant exposure to unpleasant noise levels can lead to hearing loss and can interfere with learning. One study found that there was an association between high levels of noise and elevated blood pressure among children attending school near Los Angeles International Airport (Cohen et al., 1973). People exposed to excessive noise at work have reported more headaches, nausea, and moodiness than others (Cohen et al., 1991).

It was long assumed that crowding was an environmental stressor. Indeed, most people dislike certain high-density situations and can feel stress when other people get too close. Studies on crowding have found a relationship between high-rise apartments with many crowded people and aggression. Crowding itself,

Did You Know?

Personal Space The subway system in Tokyo hires people to push more people onto the subways during rush hours. It is an accepted part of Japanese culture to be able to function effectively within a small "personal space." People of Middle Eastern derivation tend to have markedly small personal spaces compared to Americans. As a result, they stand much closer in a conversation than is comfortable for most citizens of the United States or Canada.

Figure 15.3 The Social Readjustment Rating Scale

Rank	Life Event	Mean Value	Rank	Life Event	Mean Value
1	Death of spouse	100	23	Son or daughter leaving home	29
2	Divorce	73	24	Trouble with in-laws	29
3	Marital separation	65	25	Outstanding personal achievement	28
4	Jail term	63			
5	Death of close family member	63	26	Spouse begin or stop work	26
6	Personal injury or illness	53	27	Begin or end school	26
7	Marriage	50	28	Change in living conditions	25
8	Fired at work	47	29	Revision of personal habits	24
9	Marital reconciliation	45	30	Trouble with boss	23
10	Retirement	45	31	Change in work hours or conditions	20
11	Change in health of family member	44	32	Change in residence	20
12	Pregnancy	40	33	Change in schools	20
13	Sex difficulties	39	34	Change in recreation	19
14	Gain of new family member	39	35	Change in church activities	19
15	Business readjustment	39	36	Change in social activities	18
16	Change in financial state	38	37	Mortgage or loans less than $10,000	17
17	Death of close friend	37			
18	Change to different line of work	36	38	Change in sleeping habits	16
19	Change in number of arguments with spouse	35	39	Change in number of family get-togethers	15
20	Mortgage over $10,000	31	40	Change in eating habits	15
21	Foreclosure of mortgage or loan	30	41	Vacation	13
			42	Christmas	12
22	Change in responsibilities at work	29	43	Minor violations of the law	11

Reprinted with permission from T.H. Holmes and R.H. Rahe, "The Social Readjustment Rating Scale," *Journal of Psychosomatic Research*, 1967, Table 3, p. 216. © 1967, Pergamon Press Ltd.

The SRRS lists 43 items that require individuals to make the most changes in their lives. Each number (mean value) refers to the expected impact that event would have on one's life. To obtain your score, add the numbers associated with each event you experienced in the past year. The total number reflects how much life change you have experienced. *Which of the life events have the greatest impact on an individual?*

however, is not the problem. The problems occur not when you are crowded but when you *feel* crowded (Taylor, 1991).

Jonathan Freedman (1975) has concluded that the effects of crowding depend on the situation. If the situation is pleasant, crowding makes people feel better; if the situation is unpleasant, crowding makes them feel worse. In other words, being packed together *intensifies* people's reactions, but it does not *create* them.

Life Changes and Stress

Major life changes—marriage, serious illness, a new job, moving away, and a death in the family—are important sources of stress. Common to most of these events is the separation of an individual from familiar friends,

What stresses teenagers?

The SRRS lists events considered stressful for adults. Assume your job is to develop a similar scale for teenagers only. In what ways would your scale be different?

Procedure

1. First, develop a list of life events that you deem stressful to teenagers and rank them from 1 to 20, with 1 being the most stressful. Assign each event a value based on how much adjustment the event required.

2. Provide a copy of your list to several friends and ask them to circle the events that they have experienced in the past year.

3. Ask each person to indicate any illnesses they have had in the past year.

Analysis

1. For each person, add up the values for the events they have circled. Note the illnesses they recorded.

2. Does your rating scale show any relationship between stressful events that teenagers face and illnesses they experience? Explain.

See the Skills Handbook, page 622, for an explanation of designing an experiment.

relations, or colleagues. Even marriage—a positive change—may involve breaking free from many longstanding ties.

Many stress researchers have concentrated on these life changes to determine how much stress they are likely to cause. Two of the foremost life-change researchers are Thomas H. Holmes and Richard H. Rahe (1967), who developed a scale to measure the effects of 43 common events, ranging from the death of a spouse to going on a vacation. Holmes and Rahe asked a cross section of the population to rate each of these events on a scale of 1 to 100, with marriage assigned a value of 50, on the basis of how much adjustment the event required. The figures they obtained form the basis of their Social Readjustment Rating Scale (SRRS), which is shown in Figure 15.3. Please note that the SRRS was created in 1967 and was based on the stress in men's lives (Holmes and Rahe's participants were male). Updated studies include female participants.

It is important to note that one life change can trigger others, thus greatly increasing the level of stress. Marriage, for example, may be accompanied by a change in financial status, a change in living conditions, and a change in residence.

Rahe (1975) administered this scale to thousands of naval officers and enlisted men and found that the higher a man's score, the more likely he was to become ill. Men with scores below 150 tended to remain healthy, while about 70 percent of those with scores over 300 became sick. There are problems, however. Some of the items on the SRRS may result from illness, rather than cause it (Brett et al., 1990). Some of the items, such as marriage, are joyful events that are not related to illness (Taylor, 1991). Several studies suggest there is only a small relationship between stressful life events and illness (Brett et al., 1990). The scale also fails to measure stress caused by ongoing situations such as racism and poverty.

Hassles

In addition to the impact that major stressful events such as a divorce or a death in the family can have, psychologists have studied the effects that relatively minor, day-to-day stressors have on health. These more common stressors are called *hassles*. Examples of hassles include losing your car keys, being caught in a crowded elevator with a smoker, or being late for work or school because you were stuck in traffic (see Figure 15.4). Research has found a connection between hassles and health problems. It may be that hassles gradually weaken the body's defense system, making it harder to fight off potential health problems.

It has also been suggested that small, positive events—called *uplifts*—can protect against stress. Uplifts are things that make a person feel good, such as winning a tough chess match, going out to lunch with a friend, or doing well on an exam. Some psychologists claim that uplifts can have the opposite effect of hassles—they can reduce stress and protect a person's health.

Every one of us faces many daily hassles: traffic, arguments, car trouble, and so on. Could it be that the primary effects of stress are the accumulation of little things that just constantly seem to hassle us (Weinberger, Hiner, & Tierney, 1987)? Seventy-five married couples recorded their everyday hassles, and it turned out that those with more hassles had significantly more health problems such as sore throats and headaches, which they experienced later (DeLongis, Folkman, & Lazarus, 1988).

Figure 15.4 Some Daily Hassles

We face frustrations every day—these are the daily hassles of life. *How can we combat the effects of hassles?*

- Household duties (cleaning, cooking, shopping)
- Concerns about health
- Time pressures (not enough time to get something done)
- Environmental hassles (noise, pollution, crime)
- Financial hassles (paying bills, saving for the future)
- Worries about your job
- Concerns about your future
- Inner hassles (feelings of low self-esteem or loneliness)

Source: Lazarus et al., 1985.

SECTION 1 Assessment

1. **Review the Vocabulary** What is the difference between eustress and distress? Should stress always be avoided? Explain.

2. **Visualize the Main Idea** Use a chart similar to the one below to list examples of the different conflict situations.

Conflict Situation	Example
Approach-approach conflict	

3. **Recall Information** Why are life changes sources of stress? What are other sources of stress?

4. **Think Critically** Many people have criticized the SRRS. Can you think of a better way to measure stress? Explain.

5. **Application Activity** Select a day and keep a log of your daily hassles and uplifts. At the end of the day analyze your general mood—were you in a bad or good mood? Did your hassles outnumber your uplifts? Briefly outline a strategy by which you pay more attention to uplifts and brighten your mood.

Reader's Guide

■ **Main Idea**

People react differently to life's stressors. These reactions may be beneficial or harmful.

■ **Vocabulary**

• anxiety
• anger
• fear
• social support

■ **Objectives**

• Give examples of the psychological, physical, and behavioral reactions to stress.
• Identify stages of the stress reaction.

EXPLORING PSYCHOLOGY

Beating the Odds

As a child, Joel Block couldn't reconcile who he knew he was with how he was perceived by his teachers.

"Every week, tests were given," he says. "The students were seated for the rest of the week according to their grades. I vied with another boy for the most weeks in The Dummy Row at the back. I remember vividly when he spit across the room at the 100 percent papers posted on the wall. The teacher yelled at him. He threw a chair in her direction and walked out. He never came back, so I held the record for the longest stay in The Dummy Row."

—from *Resilency: How to Bounce Back* by Tessa Albert Warschaw and Dee Barlow, 1995

A person who encounters a stressor that is intense or prolonged will react to it. There is a wide variety of stress reactions, and their effects range from beneficial to harmful. Joel encountered stress throughout his educational career. Faced with sitting in "The Dummy Row" and not performing well on exams, Joel probably reacted in various ways—acting out, pouting, and feeling bad. Eventually (in college) Joel discovered he had a natural aptitude for psychology. He became a straight-A student and earned a Ph.D. in psychology. His reactions to stress may have changed from negative to positive ones.

Many of the physiological responses to stress are inborn methods that probably evolved to cope with stress effectively. In addition, many responses to stress are automatic. Just as the body reacts to a cut by producing new tissue, it has methods to heal the wounds of stress—crying, for example.

Coping mechanisms that worked for our remote ancestors are not necessarily successful in our modern technological society. Human beings are often slow to give up anything that is well established. We are more likely to depend solely on these ancient stress responses than to make conscious attempts to modify them or adopt others that we now know are more appropriate to our modern lifestyle.

The ways in which different people react to stress vary considerably; each person's response is the product of many factors. Stress reactions may be physical, psychological, or behavioral, but these categories are not clear-cut. The human body is a *holistic* (integrated) organism, and our physical well-being affects how we think and behave. For example, poor mental health can trigger physical illness and so on.

FIGHT-OR-FLIGHT RESPONSE

Regardless of the stressor, the body reacts with immediate arousal. The adrenal glands are stimulated to produce: (a) hormones that increase the amount of blood sugar for extra energy; and (b) adrenaline, which causes rapid heartbeat and breathing and enables the body to use energy more quickly. These responses are designed to prepare a person for self-defense and are often called the *fight-or-flight response*. Wild animals experience the fight-or-flight response in reaction to attacks (see Figure 15.5). This response is needed for survival. Although you do not need to fight wild animals, the fight-or-flight response prepares you to face potentially dangerous situations in the same way. However, if stress persists for a long time, the body's resources are used up. The person becomes exhausted and, in extreme cases, dies.

GENERAL ADAPTATION SYNDROME

Hans Selye (1956, 1976) identified three stages in the body's stress reaction: alarm, resistance, and exhaustion. Selye called this the *general adaptation syndrome*. In the *alarm* stage, the body mobilizes its fight-or-flight defenses: heartbeat and breathing quicken, muscles tense, the pupils dilate, and hormones that sustain these reactions are secreted. The person becomes exceptionally alert and sensitive to stimuli in the environment and tries to keep a firm grip on his or her emotions. For example, a hiker who confronts a rattlesnake on a mountain trail freezes in his tracks, is suddenly aware of every sound around him, and tries not to panic. If the alarm reaction is insufficient to deal with the stressor, the person may develop symptoms such as anxiety.

In the *resistance* stage, the person often finds means to cope with the stressor and to ward off, superficially at least, adverse reactions. Thus an airline passenger who recovers from the shock and frustration of losing her luggage may tell

Figure 15.5	Fight-or-Flight Reaction

When an animal senses possible danger, great sources of energy are directed to its muscles and brain, and its body prepares for action. You react the same way. *How is stress necessary for survival?*

Figure 15.6   Stressful Situations

Our reactions to various events depend on our personalities and on the severity of the event itself. The family facing the destruction of their home, the high school senior waiting for her college admissions interview, and the man coping with a terminal illness are all experiencing various levels of stress. *What happens during the resistance stage of stress?*

ADMISSIONS OFFICE WAITING ROOM

herself to keep calm when reporting its disappearance to airline officials, calling her insurance company, and so on. At this stage, the person may suffer psychosomatic symptoms, which result from strain that he or she pretends is nonexistent. (Psychosomatic symptoms are real, physical symptoms that are caused by stress or tension.)

If exposure to the stressor continues, the individual reaches the stage of *exhaustion*. At this point, the adrenal and other glands involved in the fight-or-flight response have been taxed to their limit and become unable to secrete hormones. The individual reaches the breaking point. He or she becomes exhausted and disoriented and may develop delusions—of persecution, for example—in an effort to retain some type of coping strategy. The problem is that the very responses that were good for immediate resistance to stress—such as reducing digestion and boosting blood pressure—are detrimental in the long run. Think about the importance of control over environmental stressors in keeping stress at bay discussed earlier. Some investigators have found that assembly-line workers in repetitive jobs over which they exercise very little control are likely to show the effects of stress. It is not surprising that the corporate executives running the company—who can control their own destiny to some degree—are less likely to show such stress (Karasek & Theorell, 1990).

EMOTIONAL AND COGNITIVE RESPONSES

anxiety: a vague, generalized apprehension or feeling of danger

anger: the irate reaction likely to result from frustration

fear: the usual reaction when a stressor involves real or imagined danger

Short-term psychological stress reactions may be either emotional or cognitive. The most common response to a sudden and powerful stressor is **anxiety**, which is a feeling of an imminent but unclear threat. An employee whose boss passes by in the hall without saying hello may develop anxiety about her future on the job. **Anger** is likely to result from frustration. A student who does not make the lacrosse team may fly into a rage when he puts his favorite CD in the player and it skips. **Fear** is usually the reaction when a stressor involves real danger—a fire, for example. Fear directs the individual to withdraw or flee, but in severe cases he or she may panic and be unable to act. Common examples of short-term emotional stress reactions are overreacting to minor irritations, getting no joy from daily pleasures, and doubting one's own abilities, while feeling tense, short-tempered, and more anxious.

Cognitive reactions include difficulty in concentrating or thinking clearly, recurring thoughts, and poor decision making. A student who must give an oral presentation may worry about it but find himself unable to prepare for it. Another student wants to surprise her father with the news that she has been admitted to her first-choice college, but she cannot recall where his office is. Another type of cognitive stress reaction is unjustified suspicion or distrust of others.

Continued frustration can lead to burnout. People feel *burned out* when they feel they are incapable of doing their job well and they are physically worn out and emotionally exhausted from giving too much time or energy to a project while not receiving sufficient gratification. Pro-

Profiles In Psychology

Deepak Chopra

1949–

"By quieting the mind which then quiets the body and the less turbulent the body is, the more the self-repair, healing mechanisms get amplified."

Dr. Deepak Chopra is a major figure in the trend of holistic healing. *Holistic healing* refers to the idea that a person's mind and body are not independent matters—they function together as a unit. Instead of prescribing drugs to heal patients, Chopra believes that healing is a process that involves integrating the mind and the body.

A writer of both fiction and nonfiction, Chopra argues that what we think and feel can actually change our biology. He believes that by finding an inner peace and by relieving the stress of living, we can become healthy in mind and body.

Chopra blends Western medicine with the techniques of an ancient health care called Ayurveda. The basic idea behind Ayurveda is that a person's physical health is achieved through the integration of body, mind, and spirit. Chopra is a popular writer and adviser because he helps many people get past the hassles of daily existence and find pleasure in life.

longed stress, such as burnout, in combination with other factors, affects mental health. It does not necessarily cause mental illness, but it may contribute to the severity of mental illness. There is an increased likelihood of developing a psychological disorder following a major life change, for example. Among those who attempt suicide and those with depression or anxiety-based disorders, there seems to be quite a definite link between stress and subsequent symptoms.

In Chapter 16, we will discuss a psychological disorder called *posttraumatic stress disorder*. This is a condition in which a person who has experienced a traumatic event feels severe and long-lasting aftereffects. This disorder is common among the following: veterans of military combat; survivors of natural disasters, such as floods or tornadoes; and victims of human aggression, such as rape and assault, and unnatural catastrophes, such as a plane crash (see Figure 15.7). The event that triggers the disorder overwhelms a person's normal sense of reality and ability to cope. The high stress levels associated with this disorder could result in a range of psychosomatic symptoms, such as insomnia, high blood pressure, and stomach problems.

BEHAVIORAL REACTIONS

There are many short-term behavioral changes that result from stress. A person may develop nervous habits (trembling or pacing, for example), gulp meals, smoke or drink more, take drugs, or feel tired for no reason. That person may develop a shaky voice, tremors, or strained expressions. There may be changes in his or her posture. He or she may temporarily lose interest in eating, grooming, bathing, and so on. Aggression toward family members is another way to deal with stress.

Some behavioral reactions are positive, however. In a tornado, for example, some people will risk their lives to help others. Such stressors often create attitudes of cooperation that override individual differences and disagreements.

Escape is another behavioral stress reaction, and it is often the best way to deal with frustration. For example, a woman who is on a bus that is caught in snarled traffic may get off and walk to her destination.

Figure 15.7   How Will This Affect Them?

In August 1999, a terrible earthquake struck the industrial heartland of Turkey. Many survivors may suffer from the effects of post-traumatic stress disorder. *What is post-traumatic stress disorder, and whom does it affect?*

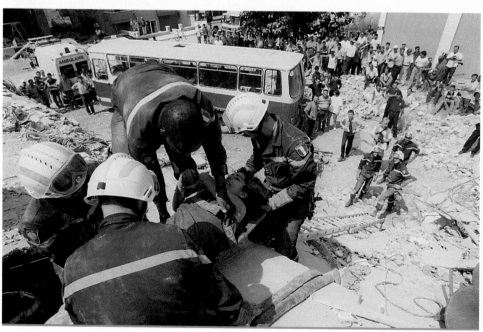

Figure 15.8   The Fight-or-Flight Response

Our fight-or-flight response is triggered by potentially dangerous or stressful situations, such as a scare in the middle of the night or giving a speech in public. As soon as you feel threatened, your body prepares itself for action. *Why do our pupils dilate during the fight-or-flight reaction? Why do our muscles tense?*

> **1.** You appraise a situation as physically or psychologically threatening.

> **2.** Your thoughts activate the hypothalamus (in the brain). The hypothalamus stimulates the pituitary gland to secrete ACTH (adrenocorticotropic hormone)—a stress-fighting hormone. The hypothalamus also activates the sympathetic division of the autonomic nervous system.

> **3.** The sympathetic nervous system stimulates a variety of physical responses to prepare the body for the stressful situation—this is the fight-or-flight response. (The parasympathetic nervous system later returns the body to its normal state.)

Fight-or-Flight Response

- heart rate increases
- blood pressure increases
- respiration becomes rapid and shallow
- liver releases stores of glycogen (blood sugar)
- digestive system shuts down and blood reroutes to muscles
- pupils dilate
- hair stands up on end
- excitatory hormones secreted (epinephrine and norepinephrine)
- muscles tense

While many people can endure great amounts of stress without marked behavioral responses, others may be seriously affected. Severe stress can be significant to the development of escapist personality styles—alcoholism, drug addiction, chronic unemployment, and attempted suicide, for example. Stress has also been noted as a contributing cause of aggressive personalities, delinquency, and criminal behavior.

PHYSICAL REACTIONS

Why do the daily hassles of life and major life changes sometimes make people ill? Your thoughts and emotions can produce physiological changes in your body. For example, some people develop *psychosomatic symptoms* as a result of stress. As mentioned earlier, psychosomatic symptoms are real, physical symptoms that are caused by stress or tension. They can include headaches, stomachaches, and muscle pains.

The physiological fight-or-flight response—accelerated heart rate and so on—is the body's immediate reaction to stress. This response is geared to prepare human beings to fight or run from an enemy such as a

Figure 15.9 **Attacking Pathogens**

An immune system cell attacks a foreign invader—a bacteria cell. When the immune system is not suppressed by stress, for instance, it destroys pathogens that enter the body. *What effect does the fight-or-flight response have on your immune system?*

savage animal or band of warriors, and it was probably useful earlier in human history. We cannot deal with most modern stressors—a financial problem, for instance—in this manner, and physical responses to stress are now generally inappropriate. In fact, prolonged physical arousal can cause health problems, including difficulty in breathing, insomnia, migraine headaches, urinary and bowel irregularities, muscle aches, sweating, and dryness of mouth.

Stress is certainly a contributing cause of illness. We have already discussed the study by Rahe (1975) that linked low scores on the Holmes-Rahe scale to reports of good health for the following year, while high scores were linked with becoming sick in the following year.

Emotional stress clearly is related to such illnesses as peptic ulcers, hypertension, certain kinds of arthritis, asthma, and heart disease. Those who work in high-stress occupations may pay a high price. Air-traffic controllers, for example, spend their days juggling the lives of hundreds of people on air routes where a minor error can mean mass death. They are said to suffer from the highest incidence of peptic ulcers of any professional group (Cobb & Rose, 1973). Similarly, a student may come down with the flu on the day before an important exam, or a director may have an asthma attack on the opening night of a play.

Stress can be at least partly responsible for almost *any* disease, as shown by the scope of illness associated with high Holmes-Rahe scores. Stress can contribute to disease in several ways. Sometimes it can be the direct cause of illness. A migraine headache, for example, is usually a physical reaction to stress. Stress may also contribute indirectly to illness. It reduces our resistance to infectious disease by tampering with the immune defense system (O'Leary, 1990). The *immune system* is your body's natural defense system against infection.

Have you ever caught a cold right in the middle of final exams week? Why did this happen? When you experience stressful situations for a long period of time, it decreases your immune system's ability to cope. Your body is constantly exposed to millions of pathogens (disease-causing bacteria or viruses). When these pathogens enter your body, they attack your body cells and use these cells to grow and multiply. The end result is an infection. Most of the time your body manages to stay free of infection because of the immune system. However, recall the third stage of Selye's general adaptation syndrome—exhaustion. When your body is continually involved in the fight-or-flight response, it reaches the breaking point. You become exhausted, and the immune system is suppressed. Your body becomes more susceptible to the diseases and infections caused by the pathogens, which are continually assaulting your body.

FACTORS INFLUENCING REACTIONS TO STRESS

People's reactions to stress vary considerably. These reactions help people meet challenges in life, but they may also determine the amount of stress one feels.

Personality Differences

In some cases, an individual's personality may make him or her more vulnerable to stress. Some psychologists have suggested that people who exhibit a behavior pattern they call "Type A" are very likely to have coronary artery disease, often followed by heart attacks, in their thirties and forties. Those who do not have this pattern (Type B people) almost never have heart attacks before the age of 70 (Friedman & Rosenman, 1974).

Whereas Type B people are generally relaxed, patient, and do not easily become angry, the Type A person's body is in a chronic state of stress with an almost constant flow of adrenaline into the bloodstream. This adrenaline apparently interacts with cholesterol or other chemical agents to block the coronary arteries that lead to the heart. It may be that high levels of adrenaline prevent the normal chemical breakdown of cholesterol in the blood.

Reading Check
What is a Type A personality?

Type A people are always prepared for fight or flight. They have a great deal of "free-floating" hostility—that is, anger that has no real object or focus. They are extremely irritable, and one of the things that irritates Type A people most is delay of any kind. They become impatient waiting in line, always move and eat rapidly, often try to do two or three things at once (such as reading while eating), and feel guilty when they are not doing *something*. They are also extremely competitive. In short, Type A people are always struggling—with time, other people, or both. Note that this describes an extreme version of the Type A personality. Most people respond to the world with Type A behavior at times, but they are not in a constant state of stress. (It is important to note that psychologists disagree about both the definition of Type A personality and its relation to heart disease.)

Another personality trait that can affect the strength of a stress reaction is emotional expressiveness. Some research suggests that people who neither express nor admit to strong feelings of despair,

Road Rage

Have you witnessed it—rage on roads, streets, and highways? Road rage is the inability to handle frustrations on the road, and it involves a desire to retaliate and punish another driver. Road rage is, in effect, a driver's stress. It is an aggressive style of driving that results from hostile emotions and lack of self-control. Road rage is a national epidemic. Between 1990 and 1996, at least 218 people were killed as a result of road rage, and another 12,610 were injured (AAA Foundation for Traffic Safety, 1997).

What should you do to avoid road rage? Here is some advice:

- Do not retaliate against another driver.
- Before you react to another driver, consider if this episode is worth risking your life.
- Be polite and courteous, even when others are not.
- If you are harassed by another driver and being followed, go to the nearest police station.
- Slow down and relax.
- Allow enough travel time.
- Remember that although you cannot control the behavior of other drivers, you can control your own behavior. Be calm and drive safely.

depression, and anger are more likely to develop cancer than those who can give vent to their emotions. Some investigators have proposed a cancer-prone behavior pattern. People who deny their negative emotions tend to express feelings less freely, show a high tendency toward social conformity, and have a greater risk of getting cancer (Baltrusch, Stangel, & Titze, 1991). Negative life events such as those measured by the Holmes and Rahe scale do seem to be related to an increased likelihood of cancer in later life (Forsen, 1991).

Perceived Control Over Stressors

The accepted view today is that physical disorders are more likely when we do not have control over stressors. Most evidence to support this theory comes from experiments on animals. J.M. Weiss (1972), for example, gave two groups of rats identical electric shocks. In one group, a rat could avoid the shock by touching its nose to a panel, while the other group had no control over the shocks. The group that could regulate the shocks developed far fewer ulcers than those that could not.

Subsequent experiments showed that feedback is also an important factor. Animals that responded to avoid shock and then heard a tone to signal that they had done the "right" thing suffered fewer ulcers than those that responded to avoid the shock but were given no feedback.

Weiss (1971) found that lack of feedback could harm human beings as well. His research showed that people develop ulcers when they have to make large numbers of responses but receive no feedback about their effectiveness.

So, in general, people prefer to have predictable stress over unpredictable stress. For example, when you know that a teacher has certain preferences in grading essay questions, it makes writing the paper a little easier. If you do not have any idea how the teacher plans to grade the essay, the writing is much harder. In one study (Matthews et al., 1989), psychologists exposed people to predictable and unpredictable noise, concluding that people may prefer predictable noise because it allows us to prepare and thus cope better. Our physical and psychological well-being is profoundly influenced by the degree to which we feel a sense of control over our lives (Rodin & Salovey, 1989).

Social Support

Much research has pointed to the importance of social support in helping people work to decrease the effects of stressful situations. Social support can buffer an individual from the effects of stress. Sidney Cobb (1976) has defined **social support** as information that leads someone to believe that he or she is cared for, loved,

social support: information that leads someone to believe that he or she is cared for, loved, respected, and part of a network of communication and mutual obligation

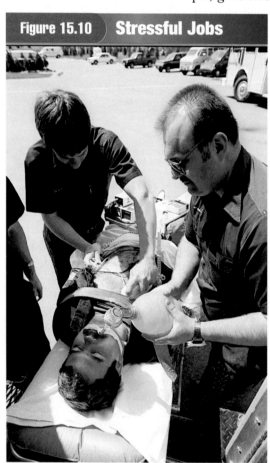

Figure 15.10 Stressful Jobs

Some work such as air traffic control, construction, and rescue operations involve stress because of the job itself. People in these fields must deal with stress over which they have no control. *How does your perceived control over stressors affect your stress levels?*

respected, and part of a network of communication and mutual obligation. He has found that social support can reduce both the likelihood and the severity of stress-related diseases—a finding often replicated (Cohen, 1988). Social support benefits have been documented for cancer, crowding, military combat, natural disasters, and AIDS.

Social groups seem to offer at least four kinds of support. First, *emotional* support involves concerned listening, which forms a basis for offering affection and concern and bolstering the stressed person's self-confidence. Second, *appraisal* support is interactive. The listener feeds back information and probing questions to the stressed person as an aid in sorting out and understanding the sources of the stress. A third kind, *informational* support, emerges from appraisal support. Here the stressed person responds to what he or she has learned and evaluates the manner in which he or she is dealing with stressors. Finally, *instrumental* support represents active, positive support in the form of direct help such as money or living quarters. Yet there is evidence that some friends, despite the best intentions, may be more of a strain than a help in a crisis (Rook, 1990).

Some sources of social support can be especially helpful. Studies of male blue-collar workers have reported that social support from wives and supervisors counteracted the health consequences of stress more effectively than did support from coworkers, friends, or relatives.

More About...

Gender Differences and Stress

Who has higher stress levels—men or women? Women in the United States are more likely than men to live in poverty, to experience discrimination, and to be sexually or physically abused. Also, some psychologists argue that the traditional roles of women—as primary caretakers and wives—place them in positions in which anxiety and depression are more likely. For example, mothers are often made to feel responsible for events that they have little control over, such as the illness of a child or accidents in the home. Taking a job outside the home often reduces psychological stress for women. Studies show that as more and more women take jobs outside the home, the stress and anxiety experienced by the different genders is becoming equalized (Kessler & McRae, 1981).

SECTION 2 Assessment

1. **Review the Vocabulary** How does social support reduce stress?

General Adaptation Syndrome

2. **Visualize the Main Idea** Use a graphic organizer similar to the one above to describe the stages of the general adaptation syndrome.

3. **Recall Information** What is the fight-or-flight response? Why is it necessary for animals? For humans?

4. **Think Critically** Would you feel more stressed about a scheduled exam or a pop quiz? Why?

5. Application Activity Measure a friend's heart rate. Then have the person think of a terrifying situation. Did the heart rate increase? Choose another person and measure his or her heart rate. Have the person think of a peaceful, calming situation. Did the heart rate decrease? Summarize your findings.

Coping With Stress

Reader's Guide

■ Main Idea
People deal with stress by employing defensive and active coping strategies.

■ Vocabulary
- cognitive appraisal
- denial
- intellectualization
- progressive relaxation
- meditation
- biofeedback

■ Objectives
- Explain defensive strategies of coping with stress.
- Describe active strategies of coping with stress.

EXPLORING PSYCHOLOGY

How Do You View Life?

There were two women who had rose gardens. One would awaken every morning, look out into the garden and groan: "Oh, there are so many weeds in my garden. It is going to take me forever to get rid of them!"

The other woman calmly put on her gardening gloves and hummed to herself as she methodically removed the weeds surrounding her roses.

"Oh, my beautiful roses," she said. "How lovely you look and smell!"

—from *Natural Stress-Busters for the Whole Family* by Lynn Allison, 1993

Stress, like those weeds in the women's rose gardens, can spring up and choke you—if you let it. Stress can smother your enjoyment of life and make you miserable. If you focus on the positive, however— the delightful blooming roses—the weeds need not be a source of stress but instead may be merely obstacles to overcome. Coping with stress is an attempt to gain control over a part of one's life. It is an attempt to master, control, reduce, and tolerate the stressors in one's life. People cope with stress in many ways. There is not just one way that is best for all people in all situations. People also have individualized coping styles. People know what works best for them. They have come to rely on what has worked in the past. What is your way of handling difficult situations?

Coping strategies may not always be healthy ways to adapt. Sometimes when we are under stress, we act in ways that are not in our best interests. There are methods that people use that hurt or harm others. These are known as maladaptive ways of coping.

PSYCHOLOGICAL COPING STRATEGIES

Our interpretation or evaluation of an event—a process psychologists call **cognitive appraisal**—helps determine its stress impact. For example, suppose you have a huge exam scheduled for next week. The way you appraise—or evaluate—the situation will determine the level of stress you feel. If you appraise the situation as a challenge that you can meet, you have positive feelings and your stress level is reduced. If you think of the situation as a threat, however, your negative feelings will increase your stress level. Drugs can affect cognitive appraisal. For example, drinking may help convince a man who has been fired that his troubles are not serious or that he will enjoy unemployment or that getting drunk is the best solution for the time being.

cognitive appraisal: the interpretation of an event that helps determine its stress impact

Defensive Coping Strategies

We can also try to influence our cognitive appraisals by means of defensive coping strategies, and stress reactions are more likely to occur when these strategies fail. Common defense mechanisms are **denial,** in which a person decides that the event is not really a stressor, and **intellectualization,** in which the person watches the situation from an emotionally detached standpoint.

denial: a coping mechanism in which a person decides that the event is not really a stressor

intellectualization: a coping mechanism in which the person analyzes a situation from an emotionally detached viewpoint

Figure 15.11	Types of Coping Strategies

The two major ways that people deal with stress are by either focusing on it and trying to reduce it or ignoring the stress completely. *Which of the strategies listed here involve an active attempt to reduce stress?*

Coping strategy	Example
Active coping	I take additional action to try to get rid of the problem.
Planning	I come up with a strategy about what to do.
Suppression of competing activities	I put aside other activities to concentrate on this.
Restraint coping	I force myself to wait for the right time to do something.
Seeking social support	I talk to someone about how I feel.
Positive reinterpretation and growth	I look for the good in what is happening.
Acceptance	I learn to live with it.
Turning to religion	I seek God's help.
Venting of emotions	I get upset and let my emotions out.
Denial	I refuse to believe that it has happened.
Behavioral disengagement	I give up the attempt to get what I want.
Mental disengagement	I turn to work or other substitute activities to take my mind off things.
Alcohol-drug disengagement	I drink alcohol or take drugs to think about it less.

Student Web Activity
Visit the *Understanding Psychology* Web site at psychology.glencoe.com and click on **Chapter 15—Student Web Activities** for an activity about stress.

Both denial and intellectualization can prevent physical reactions to stress. In one study (Lazarus et al., 1965), three groups of participants viewed a film that showed gruesome accidents at a sawmill. One group was told that the injuries were not real but were staged by the actors (denial). A second group was advised that they were seeing an educational film about the importance of safety measures (intellectualization). The third group was told nothing. The levels of physical reaction were lower in the first two groups than in the third. Thus, if a person does not evaluate an event or situation as stressful, a stress reaction will not occur. Yet that is really failing to deal with what could be a legitimate stressor (Holahan & Moos, 1985).

Active Coping Strategies

By appraising a situation as a challenge and not a threat, we can adopt an active coping strategy for dealing with stress. Active coping strategies involve changing our environment or modifying a situation to remove stressors or reduce the level of stress.

Hardiness   Some people acquire personality traits that are, in effect, active coping strategies. *Hardiness* refers to the personality traits of control, commitment, and challenge that help us reduce the stress we feel. Control involves feeling that we have the ability to affect the outcome of the situation. Commitment refers to establishing and pursuing our goals, while challenge means that we actively confront and solve problems instead of feeling threatened and powerless by them. For instance, you may demonstrate hardiness if, when confronted with the assignment of giving a speech in public, you approach the assignment as a positive experience (challenge), believe that you can prepare and give a good speech (control), and prepare for and practice your speech (commitment).

Controlling Stressful Situations   There are several ways in which we can control our exposure to stressful events and thereby reduce levels of stress. As noted earlier, escape or withdrawal, when possible, can be an effective coping strategy. A young woman who is not enjoying herself at a party, for example, can leave. When avoiding an event is not practical, controlling its timing may be helpful; you can try to space out stress-producing events. A couple who is planning to have a baby in the summer, for instance, may postpone looking for a new house.

Problem Solving   Sometimes neither avoiding nor spacing events is possible. A high school senior may face a deadline for a college application and an important exam on the same day. In cases like this, problem solving or confronting the matter head-on can be the best way to cope. Regarding frustrations or conflicts as problems to be solved means the situation becomes a positive challenge rather than a negative setback. Problem solving involves a rational analysis of the situation that will lead to an appropriate decision. The student in our example may map out the remaining days and allocate specific times to work on the application and other times to study for the test. He may also decide that he can gain more time for these activities by skipping band practice or postponing a date. Problem solving is a very healthy strategy that tends to sharpen insights and attention to detail and develop flexibility.

Explanatory Style Martin Seligman (1991) describes two very different styles of thinking. The *optimist* typically puts the best face on any set of events. Following a loss, an optimistic quarterback will suggest, "What's done is done. Start thinking about next week!" The *pessimist* always sees the dark side. After becoming ill and missing the senior prom, the pessimist will say, "This always happens to me! I never get to . . ." Seligman studied baseball players, grouping them as optimists or pessimists from their quotes in the sports pages. He found that the pessimists were much more likely to die at a younger age.

Figure 15.12	**Irrational Assumptions That Can Cause Stress**
Irrational Assumptions	**Constructive Alternative**
1. Everyone must approve of what I do.	I should concentrate on my own self-respect.
2. I must do everything to perfection.	I am imperfect; I have limitations, and that's okay.
3. Things must be the way I want them to be.	There are some situations that I cannot control. It's better to concentrate on matters that I can control.
4. Unhappiness is inevitable.	Unhappiness is the result of how I look at things.
5. I need someone stronger than I am to rely on.	I must rely on myself and act independently when necessary.
6. The world should be fair and just.	Although I can try to be fair and just in my behavior, sometimes the world is not fair.
7. I should worry about dangerous and fearsome things.	I realize that I can face what I consider fearful and try to render it nondangerous.
8. There's always a perfect solution out there that I should find.	Life is filled with probability and chance. I can enjoy life even though sometimes no perfect solution to a problem exists.
9. I should not question authorities or social beliefs.	It's better to evaluate situations and beliefs for myself.
10. It's better to avoid difficult and stressful situations.	There is no "easy way out"; I need to face my problems and work on solutions.

Source: Ellis, 1986.

Some people hold self-defeating, irrational beliefs that cause stress and prevent them from adequately adjusting to life's challenges. *How might recognizing your irrational assumptions help you better cope with stress?*

progressive relaxation: lying down comfortably and tensing and releasing the tension in each major muscle group in turn

meditation: a focusing of attention with the goal of clearing one's mind and producing an "inner peace"

biofeedback: the process of learning to control bodily states with the help of machines that provide feedback

Relaxation   Many techniques of relaxation have been developed especially to cope with stress. More than half a century ago, Dr. Edmond Jacobson devised a method called **progressive relaxation** to reduce muscle tension. This involves lying down comfortably and tensing and then learning how to relax each major muscle group in turn. Jacobson later added exercises for mental relaxation in which a person conjures up images and then lets them go. This is known as **meditation** and is a relaxation technique that has been shown to counteract both physical and psychological responses to stress (see Chapter 7). Experienced meditators quickly reach an alpha-wave mental state related to that of Stage I sleep and are able to resume their activities feeling refreshed.

Biofeedback   As explained in Chapter 7, **biofeedback** is a technique for bringing specific body processes—blood pressure and muscle tension, for example—under a person's conscious control. The participant is hooked up to an electronic device that measures the process he or she wants to regulate and plays that process back in the form of either sounds or visual patterns. This feedback enables many, although not all, people to learn to control various bodily responses. Biofeedback has been used most successfully to train tense people to relax.

Humor   Stress management experts often advise clients to try to maintain a sense of humor during difficult situations. Laughing actually releases the tension of pent-up feelings and can help you keep a proper perspective of the situation. In fact, people often resort to humor in very stressful situations. For example, a person may break out in hysterical laughter during the trying times following the death of a loved one. This laughter helps the individual deal with the intense emotional pain of a loss.

Exercise   Physical exercise is another constructive way to reduce stress. It stimulates and provides

Figure 15.13   Stress: A Summary Model

Your evaluation of a situation interacts with the stressor and what you perceive to be the available resources to determine how you react to the stressor. You respond to stress on several levels. *What are the levels of possible reactions to stress? Give an example for each level.*

Source: Zimbardo and Gerrig, 1999.

an outlet for physical arousal, and it may burn off stress hormones. Continuous rhythmic exercise—running or swimming, for example—is not only effective against stress but also ideal for respiratory and cardiovascular fitness. David Holmes and colleagues have performed experiments that indicate aerobic exercise reduces cardiovascular response and arousal following both stressful life events and immediate stress (Roth & Holmes, 1987; Holmes & Roth, 1988).

Support Groups and Professional Help We have discussed the positive role that social support plays in reducing stress. There are groups that operate beyond ordinary personal networks to help people with specific stress-related problems—Alcoholics Anonymous, Weight Watchers, crisis intervention centers, and so on. Professionals such as psychologists, doctors, social workers, and ministers can also be consulted.

Training A situation can be stressful because we are unsure we can deal with it, and it may be new, unfamiliar, or dangerous. Training to prepare for such a situation can ease the stress. For instance, a person who is nervous about going to a friend's country club because she does not play tennis might take a few tennis lessons. Exposure to moderate stressors in a relatively safe but challenging environment allows a person to gain experience and confidence in coping.

Improving Interpersonal Skills Much of the stress we undergo results from interpersonal relations. Developing skills in dealing with others—family, friends, and coworkers—is thus one of the best ways to manage stress. There are several advantages to being able to interact well with others: increased self-confidence and self-esteem, less chance of loneliness or interpersonal conflict, and development of social support systems.

Reading Check
How can the use of humor reduce stress?

SECTION 3 Assessment

1. **Review the Vocabulary** How does your cognitive appraisal of an event determine your stress level?

2. **Visualize the Main Idea** Use a graphic organizer similar to the one below to list several active coping strategies for dealing with stress.

Active Coping Strategies

3. **Recall Information** How do people use denial and intellectualization to cope with stress?

4. **Think Critically** Why would writing about a stressful experience help you better cope with it?

5. **Application Activity** Think of a stressful situation that you have recently experienced. How did you cope with it? Describe and analyze your coping mechanism as a psychologist would in a brief report.

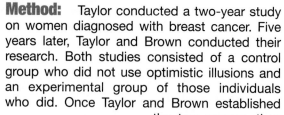

Case Studies

The Illusion of Stress

Period of Study: 1983, 1988

Introduction: In psychology, the term *illusions* is usually considered to be related to a psychosis, or a major psychological disorder in which a person's ability to think, respond emotionally, remember, communicate, or interpret reality is noticeably impaired. Although everyone experiences some perceptual illusions, the diagnosis for people experiencing bizarre illusions, hallucinations, or delusions is usually labeled a schizophrenic-type disorder. However, Shelley Taylor in 1983 and Taylor with Jonathon Brown in 1988 discovered that illusions might actually promote healthy living. These illusions are voluntary, unlike those associated with schizophrenia. Individuals use illusions to maintain optimistic, hopeful outlooks on situations that otherwise could cause an unhealthy amount of stress. Illusions such as these work for cancer sufferers, AIDS patients, individuals with physical injuries or mental disabilities, and people suffering from other serious illnesses.

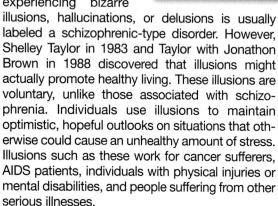

Hypothesis: Taylor described illusions as beliefs that were based on "an overly optimistic view of the facts or that had no factual basis at all" (1983). Her hypothesis stated that women suffering from breast cancer who had illusions, by her definition, would cope better with stress from disfiguring surgeries, painful treatments, and the possibilities of death than would the same women who did not have these illusions. The women who would have illusions would benefit from placing themselves in hopeful situations. In addition to studying women with breast cancer, Taylor and Brown researched the illusion hypothesis further by expanding the population studied in 1988.

Method: Taylor conducted a two-year study on women diagnosed with breast cancer. Five years later, Taylor and Brown conducted their research. Both studies consisted of a control group who did not use optimistic illusions and an experimental group of those individuals who did. Once Taylor and Brown established the two groups, they assessed the emotions the participants displayed concerning their conditions, expectations for the future, how they maintained social relationships during their illness, and other measures focusing on self-esteem.

Results: Taylor and Brown found that the participants who used illusions to maintain an optimistic view for the future were cheerful, had more friends, and were usually more persistent, creative, and productive than those without such positive illusions (Morris, 1996). The positive outlooks these people hold create confidence and the motivation to pursue their interests. Thus, according to Taylor and Brown's findings, the use of illusions can reduce the occurrence of stress in situations that may otherwise be extremely stressful.

Extreme caution, though, should be taken when a person uses illusions. As mentioned earlier, illusions are often associated with psychological disorders. Not everyone can separate reality from fantasy. Some people who may use illusions by Taylor's definition could become fixed in their fantasy and lose the capability of returning to the real world. The use of illusions to reduce or eliminate stress not only requires a vivid imagination but also a strong mind.

Analyzing the Case Study

1. How is the use of illusions related to stress?
2. How did Taylor and Brown test their hypothesis?
3. **Critical Thinking** When do you think the use of illusions crosses the line from healthy to unhealthy living?

■ Main Idea
For many people, college and work involve adjustment and stress.

■ Vocabulary
- autonomy
- developmental friendship
- resynthesis
- career
- comparable worth

■ Objectives
- Identify some of the issues related to adjustment to college life.
- Describe issues related to starting a first job.

EXPLORING PSYCHOLOGY

Are You Ready for Independence?

I thought when I was a senior [in high school] that I was really independent. You know what I mean: I kept my own schedule, had a job and car, decided when I needed to do homework or not. But you and Dad were always there to back me up. If I didn't know how to do something, I could walk into the kitchen and ask you. Now I have to figure everything out by myself. *That's* independence.

–from *Almost Grown: Launching Your Child From High School to College* by Patricia Pasick, 1998

The quotation above is what a first-year college student at Tufts University told his mother during parents' weekend. Families do not stay together forever. Children grow up and leave home to set up new households and start their own families. This period of life signifies a major life change for both teens and parents. This life change involves dealing with stress.

Growing up involves gaining a sense of **autonomy**—the ability to take care of oneself—and independence. Each person learns to make decisions, develop a value system, be responsible, and to care for himself or herself. Growing up is a process that starts long before an individual leaves home to live as a self-sufficient adult. Yet ultimately, it means separating from the family, both physically and emotionally.

autonomy: ability to take care of oneself and make one's own decisions

CHOOSING COLLEGE

For millions of young Americans, college is one of the first big steps toward this separation. As college students individuals are freer than they ever have been or may ever be again. This can be a personally liberating and stimulating experience, but it also requires adjustment. The emotional upheaval many first-year college students feel has been called "college shock."

Peter Madison (1969) spent nearly 10 years collecting data on how several hundred students adjusted to college. Each student provided a detailed life history and kept a weekly journal. Madison had classmates write descriptions of some of the students, and he tested and retested some at various points in their college careers. What were the results?

Madison found that many students approach college with high, and often unrealistic, aspirations. For example, Bridget wanted to be an astronomer. She liked the idea of being different, and she considered astronomy an elite and adventuresome field, but she did not know how many long, hard, unadventuresome hours she would have to spend studying mathematics to fulfill her dream. Keith planned to become a physician for what he described as "humanitarian" reasons. He had never thought about working in a hospital or watching people sicken and die, though.

These two students, like many others, based their goals on fantasy. They did not have the experience to make realistic choices or the maturity to evaluate their own motives and needs. Their experiences during the first semesters of college led them to change both their minds and their images of themselves.

Sources of Change

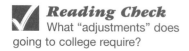

Reading Check
What "adjustments" does going to college require?

How does going to college stimulate change? First, college may challenge the identity a student has established in high school. A top high school student may go to a top college. Nearly everyone there is as bright and competitive as she is. Within a matter of weeks the student's identity as a star pupil has evaporated, and she may have to struggle to get average grades. Young people who excelled in sports, drama, or student politics may have similar experiences. The high school student-body president discovers two other high school presidents in his dormitory alone.

Second, whether students come from small towns or big cities, they are likely to encounter greater diversity in college than they ever have before—diversity in religious and ethnic backgrounds, family income levels, and attitudes. A student who develops a close relationship with another, then discovers that the person holds beliefs or engages in behavior he or she has always considered immoral, may be badly shaken. You are faced with a choice—abandon deeply held values or give up an important friendship. Madison (1969) calls close relationships between individuals who force each other to reexamine their basic assumptions **developmental friendships.** He found that developmental friendships in particular and student culture in general have more impact on college students than professors do.

developmental friendship:
friends force one another to reexamine their basic assumptions and perhaps adopt new ideas and beliefs

However, if instructors and assigned books clarify thoughts that have been brewing in a student's mind, they can make all the difference. This was true of Keith. Keith did extremely well in the courses required for a pre-med student, but he found he enjoyed his literature and philosophy classes far more. He began reading avidly. He felt as if each of the authors had deliberately set out to put all his self-doubts into words. In time Keith realized that his interest in medicine was superficial. He had decided to become a doctor because it was a respected profession that would give him status, security, and a good income—and would guarantee his parents' love. The self-image Keith had brought to college was completely changed.

Coping With Change   Madison found that students cope with the stress of going to college in several different ways. Some "tighten up" when their goals are threatened by internal or external change. They redouble their efforts to succeed in the field they have chosen and avoid people and situations that might bring their doubts to the surface. Troy, for example, stayed with a chemical-engineering program for three years, despite a growing interest in social science. By the time he realized that engineering was not the field for him, it was too late to change majors. He got the degree but left college with no idea where he was heading.

Others avoid confronting doubt by frittering away their time, going through the motions of attending college but detaching themselves emotionally. Some students manage to keep their options open until they have enough information and experience to make a choice. Madison calls this third method of coping **resynthesis**. For most students this involves a period of indecision, doubt, and anxiety. The student tries to combine the new and old, temporarily abandons the original goal, retreats, heads in another direction, retreats again—and finally reorganizes his or her feelings and efforts around an emerging identity.

Figure 15.14   **Experiencing Diversity**

Going to college means orienting oneself to different faces, personalities, and living habits. *How can experiencing different personalities and issues at college help a person develop his or her own identity?*

resynthesis: combining old ideas with new ones and reorganizing feelings in order to renew one's identity

WORKING

Graduating from college or high school involves thinking about and finding your first job and your career, but what is work? For one person work means loading 70,000 pounds on his five-axle truck, driving alone for several hours a day, perhaps for several days, with only a few stops for food and fuel, talk, relief, and sleep. While he is alone in the cab, tension is constant: it is hard to brake a truck suddenly while carrying thousands of pounds, so he must always think ahead. The work is wearing, yet he likes the odd hours and the independence.

For another person work means spending eight or nine hours a day at an advertising agency, dealing with clients and supervising commercial writers. She earns good money, spends a great deal of time talking with people and has plenty of opportunities to exercise her talents as a manager. All three are qualities she likes about her job. Yet she must also deal with deadlines and worry about whether millions of dollars' worth of ads will sell the products or not—and, subconsciously, whether it is worth the effort if they do.

Figure 15.15   Adjusting to Work

Entering the world of work can cause excitement, but it may also lead to disappointment. *How might submitting a report at work be different from submitting a report in class for a grade?*

For a third person work means training severely handicapped children to use their muscles to grasp a spoon, to gesture in sign language, and perhaps to take a few steps. The job is often depressing and frustrating, but there are also moments of intense personal satisfaction when a child makes progress. The point is that each person's work experience is different and each person reacts differently to a job as a result of his or her own personality.

Work Satisfaction and Dissatisfaction

Industrial/organizational psychologists explore what factors contribute to job satisfaction. This research is important because low job satisfaction is associated with high rates of employee absenteeism and turnover, which leads to lower productivity. Job satisfaction is simply the attitude a worker has toward his or her job.

Some workers may seek high salaries, pleasant working conditions, and low-pressure jobs, while others may be concerned only with finding personal fulfillment at work. Most workers, however, have both economic and personal goals. One study (Quinn et al., 1971) identified five major sources of work satisfaction.

1. *Resources:* The worker feels that he or she has enough available resources—help, supplies, and equipment—to do the job well.

2. *Financial reward:* The job pays well, offers good fringe benefits, and is secure.

3. *Challenge:* The job is interesting and enables the worker to use his or her special talents and abilities.

4. *Relations with coworkers:* The worker is on good terms professionally and socially with colleagues.

5. *Comfort:* Working conditions and related factors—hours, travel to and from the job, work environment, and so on—are attractive.

Changing Careers

career: a vocation in which a person works at least a few years

Some theorists predict that in the future, people will change their **career**—a vocation in which a person works at least a few years—several times in their lifetimes. People today live longer than ever before, and so they have a longer work life. It is not uncommon for a person to retire from one job at the age of 60 or 65, then embark on a new career as a real-estate agent, travel broker, writer, or consultant. Some employers have early-retirement programs that allow people at a relatively young age to leave jobs with partial pay. Alumni of these programs have been especially good candidates for "second wind" careers. Many women also split their careers by stepping out of the job market to raise children, then reentering the working world for a second full career.

As we have seen, people want work that is psychologically as well as financially rewarding. If a person is unhappy at a job, changing careers may provide the answer. "Job shopping," or trying out several careers, is most common among people who have recently entered the labor force and are still trying to get a feel for the work that suits them best. Across all ages, however, worker satisfaction is affected by the availability of *other* jobs. Research indicates that during periods when jobs are hard to find, workers tolerate more dissatisfaction with their present job (Carsten & Spector, 1987).

Does this mean you should forget about career training, since you probably will not stick with your first job? Not at all. You should acquire as many abilities and interests as you can—in and out of school. You should work to develop your interpersonal skills, and you should look at change as desirable and challenging. In these ways, more occupations will be open to you, and the better your chances of employment will be.

Comparable Worth

Consider the following two cases. Tonya is employed as a day-care supervisor for a state government. To qualify for this job, she needed three years of experience as well as college credit. In her job, she is responsible for not only the care and well-being of the children but also the supervision of several subordinates. Trent, also a state worker, is in charge of a storeroom and is responsible for supplying goods to various departments in his building as well as supervising several subordinates. To qualify for his job, Trent needed four years of experience. In terms of actual job demands, Trent's and Tonya's jobs might seem to be quite comparable. However, Trent is paid more than Tonya, despite Tonya's job requiring college credit.

In theory, jobs of comparable training, skill, and importance should be compensated at the same rate—this is **comparable worth.** In practice, however, the market value of many jobs traditionally held by females is considerably lower than that of comparable jobs traditionally held by males. Moreover, men and women are not evenly distributed among the various occupations (see Figure 15.16). Men have tended toward higher-paid occupations, while women have held lower-paid occupations. Overall, women face a considerable gap between their income and that received by men.

Many groups have been working to achieve equal pay for comparable work. The National Organization for Women has made the upgrading of traditionally female jobs one of its highest priorities. Labor unions have also

> **Did You Know?**
>
> **Enjoying Work** Most people enjoy their work more if it is complex rather than simple, varied rather than routine, and not closely supervised by someone else. Most workers enjoy making many choices throughout the workday.

Reading Check
What is comparable worth? Why is it important?

comparable worth: the concept that women and men should receive equal pay for jobs calling for comparable skill and responsibility

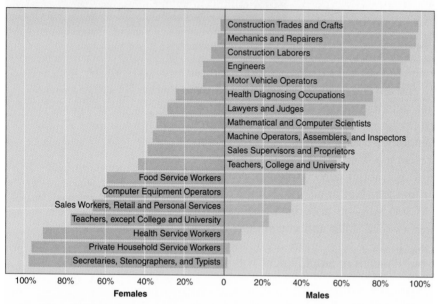

Figure 15.16   Distribution of Male and Female Jobs by Occupation

One of the reasons for differences in pay between the genders is that men and women are not evenly distributed among occupations. If men tend to cluster in higher-paid occupations and if women tend to cluster in lower-paid occupations the average pay of men and women will differ. *What is the occupation of most men? Of most women?*

Construction Trades and Crafts
Mechanics and Repairers
Construction Laborers
Engineers
Motor Vehicle Operators
Health Diagnosing Occupations
Lawyers and Judges
Mathematical and Computer Scientists
Machine Operators, Assemblers, and Inspectors
Sales Supervisors and Proprietors
Teachers, College and University
Food Service Workers
Computer Equipment Operators
Sales Workers, Retail and Personal Services
Teachers, except College and University
Health Service Workers
Private Household Service Workers
Secretaries, Stenographers, and Typists

100% 80% 60% 40% 20% 0 20% 40% 60% 80% 100%
Females   **Males**

Source: *Employment and Earnings,* 1997.

been addressing the issue of pay equity. Congress passed two major laws to prevent discrimination and income discrepancies between men and women. The Equal Pay Act of 1963 prohibits wage and salary discrimination for jobs that require equivalent skills and responsibilities. The Civil Rights Act of 1964 prohibits discrimination in all areas of employment on the basis of gender, race, color, religion, and national origin. It may seem surprising that such laws are necessary. For economic reasons, though, many employers are unwilling to raise salaries, especially if they are able to find workers who will accept the low wages that they do offer. It is up to the workers, therefore, to demand the wages to which they are entitled.

SECTION 4   Assessment

1. **Review the Vocabulary**   Explain how going to college involves autonomy.

2. **Visualize the Main Idea**   Use a diagram similar to the one below to identify five sources of work satisfaction.

Sources of Work Satisfaction

3. **Recall Information**   Why do developmental friendships have so much impact on a person?

4. **Think Critically**   How do you think job satisfaction and productivity are related? Does good worker performance occur as a result of high job satisfaction, or is high job satisfaction a result of good worker performance? Explain your answers.

5. **Application Activity**   Your future happiness in the world of work depends on four factors: what you are doing, where you are doing it, who you are doing it for/with, and why you are doing it. Using these four factors, create a list of possible jobs or careers that would suit you.

Summary and Vocabulary

Although all people experience stress at some point in their lives, how they react to it varies from individual to individual. People also use various techniques to cope with stress in their lives.

| Section 1 | Sources of Stress |

Main Idea: Stress results from our perceptions of demands placed upon us and our evaluations of situations we encounter.

- Stress is a normal part of life that goes hand in hand with working toward any goal or facing any challenge.
- Making difficult decisions between two or more options results in conflicting motives and is a major source of stress.
- Major life changes are important sources of stress.

| Section 2 | Reactions to Stress |

Main Idea: People react differently to life's stressors. These reactions may be beneficial or harmful.

- The body reacts to stress with the fight-or-flight response. This prepares the individual to either face potentially dangerous situations or escape them.
- The general adaptation syndrome identifies three stages in the body's stress reaction: alarm, resistance, and exhaustion.
- How people react to stress depends on their personality type, their perception of control over stressors, and the social support they receive.

| Section 3 | Coping With Stress |

Main Idea: People deal with stress by employing defensive and active coping strategies.

- A person's interpretation and evaluation of an event helps determine its stress impact.
- Common defense mechanisms used to cope with stress are denial and intellectualization.
- Active coping strategies involve changing the environment or modifying a situation to remove stressors or reduce the level of stress.

| Section 4 | Stress in Your Life |

Main Idea: For many people, college and work involve adjustment and stress.

- Attending college stimulates change in many students.
- Students find several ways of coping with the stress of going to college.
- Job satisfaction is simply the attitude a worker has toward his or her job.
- Overall, women face a considerable gap between their income and that received by men.

Chapter Vocabulary

stress (p. 413)

stressor (p. 414)

stress reaction (p. 414)

distress (p. 414)

eustress (p. 414)

conflict situation (p. 414)

anxiety (p. 422)

anger (p. 422)

fear (p. 422)

social support (p. 428)

cognitive appraisal (p. 431)

denial (p. 431)

intellectualization (p. 431)

progressive relaxation (p. 434)

meditation (p. 434)

biofeedback (p. 434)

autonomy (p. 437)

developmental friendship (p. 438)

resynthesis (p. 439)

career (p. 440)

comparable worth (p. 441)

PSYCHOLOGY Online

Self-Check Quiz
Visit the *Understanding Psychology* Web site at
psychology.glencoe.com and click on **Chapter 15—
Self-Check Quizzes** to prepare for the Chapter Test.

Reviewing Vocabulary

Choose the letter of the correct term or concept below to complete the sentence.

a. stressor
b. stress reaction
c. distress
d. eustress
e. anxiety
f. social support
g. cognitive appraisal
h. progressive relaxation
i. autonomy
j. comparable worth

1. _____ is a feeling of imminent but unclear threat.
2. People who are able to take care of themselves have gained a sense of _____.
3. Negative stress is called _____.
4. _____ is a technique used to reduce muscle tension.
5. A stress-producing event or situation is called the _____.
6. Information that leads an individual to believe that he or she is cared for, loved, and respected is called _____.
7. Positive stress is called _____.
8. The theory that jobs of comparable training, skill, and importance should be compensated at the same rate is called _____.
9. The body's observable response to a stress-producing event is called _____.
10. The process of interpreting and evaluating an event is called _____.

Recalling Facts

1. What is probably the most common conflict situation, and in what ways can this conflict be resolved?

2. Using a graphic organizer similar to the one below, identify and explain the four kinds of support that social groups offer for reducing stress.

Types of Support Offered by Social Groups

3. What are two relaxation techniques that can be used for coping with stress? How do they work?
4. List at least two of the new experiences and challenges that a student faces when entering college. How might these new experiences cause stress?
5. How can stress impact you physically? How does stress affect the immune system?

Critical Thinking

1. **Analyzing Concepts** As you have learned, some psychologists believe that stress is an event that produces worry. Others believe that stress is an individual's response to such an event. Still others believe stress is an individual's perception of the event. Which definition of stress do you agree with? Why?
2. **Synthesizing Information** Do you think all individuals are equally susceptible to stress-related illnesses? Are some people better able to cope with stress than others? What does this say about stress as a *cause* of illness? Explain.
3. **Evaluating Information** Two kinds of coping strategies include defensive coping strategies and active coping strategies. What is the difference between these coping strategies? Which of the two do you think is more effective in helping an individual cope with stress? Why do you think so?
4. **Making Inferences** Do you think increasing autonomy can create positive or negative feelings in a college student? Why do you think so?
5. **Demonstrating Reasoned Judgment** Which of the five major sources of job satisfaction do you think is the most essential? Why do you think so?

Psychology Projects

1. Sources of Stress Work with a partner to create a skit that illustrates each of the four conflict situations: approach-approach, avoidance-avoidance, approach-avoidance, and double approach-avoidance. Present your skit to the class and have your classmates identify the conflict situation you are demonstrating.

2. Reactions to Stress Find recent magazine articles about the latest research in the connection between stress and illness. Find out how stress contributes to the development of certain diseases. Report your findings in an oral report.

3. Coping With Stress Find out about various support groups and professional help available in your community (for illnesses, causes, etc.). You might look through your local phone book, contact a local hospital, or contact your local government offices for information. Identify the groups and help available and explain how they can help an individual cope with stress. Present your findings in an informational pamphlet.

Technology Activity

The Internet provides many sites regarding jobs and careers. Find several of these sites. What kinds of information do they provide? Do any of these sites offer advice for dealing with stress in the workplace or during a job hunt? Create a report with your findings. Include the addresses of the sites you found in your report.

Psychology Journal

Reread the journal entry you made at the beginning of the chapter. Next, consider these questions: Do students seem more stressed prior to tests or exams? Can you discover any common elements among these sources of stress? What might be done to alleviate stress in school? Would stress be reduced or eliminated if there were no grades? What if there were no tests? What would school be like without stress? Should stress in school be eliminated? Write your answers to these questions in your journal.

Building Skills

Interpreting a Graph Review the graph, then answer the questions that follow.

1. What are the three phases of the general adaptation syndrome?

2. In what phases might a person become most vulnerable to catching a cold? Why?

3. From the information contained in this graph, explain why some people with stressful occupations, for instance, develop serious illnesses.

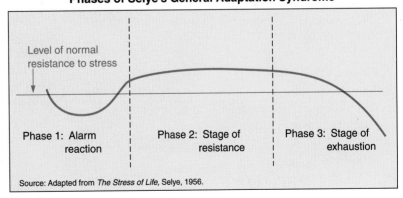

Phases of Selye's General Adaptation Syndrome

Level of normal resistance to stress

Phase 1: Alarm reaction

Phase 2: Stage of resistance

Phase 3: Stage of exhaustion

Source: Adapted from *The Stress of Life*, Selye, 1956.

Practice and **assess** key social studies skills with **Glencoe Skillbuilder Interactive Workbook CD-ROM, Level 2.**

See the Skills Handbook, page 628, for an explanation of interpreting graphs.

Psychological Disorders

PSYCHOLOGY JOURNAL

What is a phobia? Write its definition as well as the definition of the following terms in your journal: *acrophobia, xenophobia, agoraphobia.* Use a dictionary to help you with the assignment. ■

PSYCHOLOGY Online

Chapter Overview
Visit the *Understanding Psychology* Web site at psychology.glencoe.com and click on **Chapter 16—Chapter Overviews** to preview the chapter.

What Are Psychological Disorders?

Reader's Guide

■ Main Idea
Psychologists draw the line between normal and abnormal behavior by looking at deviance, adjustment, and psychological health.

■ Vocabulary
• DSM-IV

■ Objectives
• Define psychological disorder.
• Distinguish between the concepts of normality and abnormality.

EXPLORING PSYCHOLOGY

Normal or Not?

A man living in the Ozark Mountains has a vision in which God speaks to him. He begins preaching to his relatives and neighbors, and soon he has the whole town in a state of religious fervor. People say he has a "calling." His reputation as a prophet and healer spreads, and in time he is drawing large audiences everywhere he goes. However, when he ventures into St. Louis and attempts to hold a prayer meeting, blocking traffic on a main street at rush hour, he is arrested. He tells the policemen about his conversations with God, and they hurry him off to the nearest mental hospital.

—from *Understanding Psychology*, Glencoe/ McGraw-Hill, 1995

Who is right? The "prophet" or the police officers? It is often difficult to draw a line between normal and abnormal behavior. Behavior that some people consider normal seems abnormal to others. Many believe that having visions and hearing voices are important parts of a religious experience. Other people believe these are symptoms of a psychological disorder. The man in the example above was interviewed by psychiatrists, diagnosed as "paranoid schizophrenic," and hospitalized. Had he stayed home, people would have continued to see him as perfectly normal—even popular.

Figure 16.1   **Defining Behavior**

This person is obviously suffering, but is her behavior abnormal? The abnormality of her behavior would depend on whether other elements of a psychological disorder are present. *Why is adjustment an important way to distinguish normal behavior from abnormal behavior?*

DEFINING AND IDENTIFYING PSYCHOLOGICAL DISORDERS

In our example, the man was classified as mentally troubled because his behavior was so different from what other people felt was "normal." Yet the fact that a person is different does not necessarily mean that he or she is suffering from a mental illness. Indeed, going along with the crowd may at times be self-destructive. Most readers—and most psychologists—would agree that a teenager who uses cocaine because nearly everyone in his social circle does has problems.

How, then, do psychologists distinguish the normal from the abnormal? There are a number of ways to define abnormality, none of which is entirely satisfactory. We will look at the most popular ways of drawing the line between normal and abnormal in terms of deviance, adjustment, and psychological health. Then we will look at the application of these principles in legal definitions of abnormality. Finally, we will consider the criticism that in all these models people are arbitrarily labeled mentally ill.

Deviation From Normality

One approach to defining abnormality is to say that whatever most people do is normal. Abnormality, then, is any deviation from the average or from the majority. It is normal to bathe periodically, to express grief at the death of a loved one, and to wear warm clothes when going out in the cold, because most people do so. Because very few people take 10 showers a day, laugh when a loved one dies, or wear bathing suits in the snow, those who do so may be considered abnormal.

The deviance approach, however, as commonly used as it is, has serious limitations. If most people cheat on their income-tax returns, are honest taxpayers abnormal? If most people are noncreative, was Shakespeare abnormal? Different cultural norms must also be taken into consideration (see Figure 16.2). Because the majority is not always right or best, the deviance approach to defining abnormality is not by itself a useful standard.

Did You Know?

Hysteria Sometimes a lack of knowledge leads to nonsensical explanations for psychological phenomena. For example, the term *hysteria* comes from the Greek word for "uterus." The ancient Greeks diagnosed women with mental disorders by using a theory that the womb somehow moved around the body, occupying different positions. This "wandering of the uterus" theory led to characterizing any highly emotional behavior as "hysteria." In the Middle Ages, the "wandering uterus" theory explained demonic possession and led to witchcraft persecutions.

Adjustment

Another way to distinguish normal from abnormal people is to say that normal people are able to get along in the world—physically, emotionally, and socially. They can feed and clothe themselves, work, find friends, and live by the rules of society. By this definition, abnormal people are the ones who fail to *adjust*. They may be so unhappy that they refuse to eat or so lethargic that they cannot hold a job. They may experience so much anxiety in relationships with others that they end up avoiding people, living in a lonely world of their own. However, not all people with psychological disorders are violent, destructive, or isolated. Sometimes, a person's behavior may only seem normal. Also, behavior that is socially acceptable in one society may not be acceptable in another. The cultural context of a behavior must also be taken into consideration.

Psychological Health

The terms *mental illness* and *mental health* imply that psychological disturbance or abnormality is like a physical sickness—such as the flu or tuberculosis. Although many psychologists think that mental illness is different from physical illness, the idea remains that there is some ideal way for people to function psychologically, just as there is an ideal way for people to function physically. Some psychologists believe that the normal or healthy person would be one who is functioning ideally or who is at least striving toward ideal functioning. Personality theorists such as Carl Jung and Abraham Maslow (see Chapter 14) have tried to describe this striving process, which is often referred to as *self-actualization*. According to this line of thinking, to be normal or healthy involves full acceptance and expression of one's own individuality and humanness.

One problem with this approach to defining abnormality is that it is difficult to

Figure 16.2   Is This Normal?

What we consider normal and abnormal behavior depends on the context of the behavior. Here two men in Michoacan State, Mexico, display cultural dance masks. *Why must you consider the cultural context of a behavior when determining whether the behavior is abnormal?*

determine whether or not a person is doing a good job of actualizing himself or herself. How can you tell when a person is doing his or her best? What are the signs that he or she is losing the struggle? Answers to such questions often are arbitrary.

That definitions of abnormality are somewhat arbitrary has led some theorists to conclude that labeling a person as "mentally ill" simply because his or her behavior is odd is a mistake as well as cruel and irresponsible. The foremost spokesperson of this point of view is American psychologist Thomas Szasz (1962).

Szasz argued that most of the people whom we call mentally ill are not ill at all. They simply have "problems in living"—serious conflicts with the world around them. Yet instead of dealing with the patients' conflict as something that deserves attention and respect, psychiatrists simply label them as "sick" and shunt them off to hospitals. Society's norms remain unchallenged, and psychiatrists remain in a comfortable position of authority. The ones who lose are the patients, who by being labeled "abnormal" are deprived both of responsibility for their behavior and of their dignity as human beings. As a result, Szasz claimed, the patients' problems intensify. Szasz's position, however, is a minority stand. Most psychologists and psychiatrists would agree that a person who claims to be God or Napoleon is truly abnormal and disturbed.

The fact that it is difficult to define abnormality does not mean that such a thing does not exist. What it does mean is that we should be very cautious about judging a person to be "mentally ill" just because he or she acts in a way that we cannot understand. It should also be kept in mind that mild psychological disorders are common. It is only when a psychological problem becomes severe enough to disrupt everyday life that it is thought of as an "abnormality" or "illness."

More About...

The Insanity Defense

When John Hinckley was tried for shooting President Ronald Reagan in 1981, he was found "not guilty by reason of insanity." This raised public concerns about the legal definition of sanity.

In this case, "not guilty" did not mean that Hinckley did not commit the crime; it meant that he could not tell right from wrong or could not control his behavior because of a psychological disorder. Therefore, he could not be held criminally responsible for his behavior.

The terms sane and insane are legal terms. Psychological research has identified so many disorders of varying degrees that "insane" is too simplistic a definition for a person with a psychological disorder. In fact, many people with psychological disorders would test "sane" if they took current legal tests.

People found not guilty by reason of insanity are not simply released; they are confined for treatment in special hospitals. Studies show that people found not guilty by reason of insanity are held for at least as long as people found guilty and sent to prison for similar crimes (American Psychiatric Association, 1993). After the Hinckley insanity defense, many states created review boards to oversee the treatment provided to those who have been found not guilty by reason of insanity.

THE PROBLEM OF CLASSIFICATION

For years psychiatrists have been trying to devise a logical and useful method for classifying emotional disorders. This task is difficult, because psychological problems do not lend themselves to the same sort of categorizing that physical illnesses do. The causes and symptoms of psychological disturbances and breakdowns and the cures for those breakdowns are rarely obvious or clear-cut.

All of the major classification schemes have accepted the medical model—they assume that abnormal behavior can be described in the same manner as any physical illness. The physician diagnoses a specific disease when a person has certain symptoms.

In 1952 the American Psychiatric Association agreed upon a standard system for classifying abnormal symptoms, which it published in the *Diagnostic and Statistical Manual of Mental Disorders,* or DSM. This has been revised four times as the DSM-II (in 1968), the DSM-III (in 1980), and the DSM-III-Revised (1987). The most recent revision, the **DSM-IV,** was published in 1994.

A major change occurred in the shifts from DSM-II to DSM-IV. Before 1980, the two most commonly used diagnostic distinctions were *neurosis* and *psychosis.* Although these terms have been replaced by more specific ones, they still are used by many psychologists. However, the conditions originally identified under neurosis and psychosis have been expanded into more detailed categories, including anxiety disorders, somatoform disorders, dissociative disorders, mood disorders, and schizophrenia.

Profiles In Psychology

Abraham Maslow
1908–1970

"Human life will never be understood unless its highest aspirations are taken into account."

One of the founders of humanistic psychology, Abraham Maslow spent his life developing theories that shaped counseling, education, social work, theology, marketing, and management. Early in his career, Maslow upset behaviorists by contradicting their theories of motivation and personality. If you recall, behaviorists propose that individuals learn new behaviors by responding to environmental stimuli that reward or punish their behaviors. Maslow emphasized that each individual has freedom in directing his or her own future. Maslow believed that individuals could achieve personal growth and self-fulfillment.

Maslow developed a theory of motivation that describes an individual's hierarchy of needs. Individuals progress from filling basic, biological needs to the highest social needs of what Maslow called self-actualization—the fulfillment of one's greatest human potential. Individuals organize their lives around these needs, trying to fulfill the needs at each level. If needs are not fulfilled at any level, conflict results. Attention to these needs, then, is a method to resolve psychological conflict.

DSM-IV: New Ways to Categorize Mental Illness

Within each diagnostic category of the DSM-IV, the following descriptions are included:

DSM-IV: the fourth version of the American Psychiatric Association's *Diagnostic and Statistical Manual of Mental Disorders*

1. *essential features* of the disorder—characteristics that "define" the disorder;

2. *associated features*—additional features that are usually present;

3. information on *differential diagnosis*—that is, how to distinguish this disorder from other disorders with which it might be confused; and

4. *diagnostic criteria*—a list of symptoms, taken from the lists of essential and associated features, that must be present for the patient to be given this diagnostic label.

These more precise diagnostic criteria reduce the chances that the same patient will be classified as schizophrenic by one doctor and manic depressive by another. Because researchers often rely on diagnostic labels to study underlying factors that may cause disorders, it is particularly important for their work that patients with similar symptoms be classified in the same diagnostic category.

The DSM-IV also recognizes the complexity of classifying people on the basis of mental disorders. Often a person may exhibit more than one disorder or may be experiencing other stresses that complicate the diagnosis. In early classification systems, it was difficult to give a patient more than one label. The DSM-III-R and now the DSM-IV have overcome this

Figure 16.3   DSM-IV—Major Psychological Disorders of Axis I

Individual cases of psychological disorders are diagnosed on the five axes of the DSM-IV. Axis I classifies symptoms into categories. *What are impulse control disorders?*

Disorders usually first diagnosed in infancy, childhood, or adolescence	Includes disorders that arise before adolescence, including attention deficit disorders, mental retardation, and stuttering
Delirium, dementia, and other cognitive disorders	Includes disorders of perception, memory, and thought that stem from damage to the brain, such as Alzheimer's disease
Substance-related disorders	Includes maladaptive use of alcohol and drugs
Schizophrenia and other psychotic disorders	Characterizes types of schizophrenia and psychotic disorders by symptoms
Mood disorders	Includes disorders characterized by emotional disturbance, such as depression and bipolar disorder
Anxiety disorders	Includes disorders characterized by signs of anxiety, such as panic disorders and phobias
Somatoform disorders	Includes disorders characterized by somatic symptoms that resemble physical illnesses, such as conversion and hypochondriasis
Dissociative disorders	Includes disorders that are characterized by sudden and temporary changes in memory, consciousness, identity, and behavior, such as dissociative identity disorder
Sexual and gender-identity disorders	Includes gender-identity disorders, preferences for unusual acts to achieve sexual arousal, and sexual dysfunctions
Eating disorders	Includes disorders such as anorexia nervosa and bulimia nervosa
Sleep disorders	Includes disorders associated with sleep, such as insomnia and sleepwalking
Impulse control disorders	Includes disorders characterized by a tendency to act on impulses that others usually inhibit, such as to gamble excessively or steal

Source: DSM-IV, American Psychiatric Association, 1994.

Figure 16.4) **PET Scans**

The biological roots of abnormal behavior include genetic factors and occurrences that can lead to abnormal brain development. From left to right, these PET scans show a normal human brain, a brain tumor, and a brain aneurysm. *Which axis of the DSM-IV describes the medical conditions of psychological disorders?*

problem by using five major dimensions, or *axes,* to describe a person's mental functioning. Each axis reflects a different aspect of a patient's case.

Axis I is used to classify current symptoms into explicitly defined categories. These categories range from disorders that are usually first evident in infancy, childhood, or adolescence (such as conduct disorders) to substance-use disorders (such as alcoholism), to schizophrenia. Figure 16.3 shows a listing of major Axis I categories.

Axis II is used to describe developmental disorders and long-standing personality disorders or maladaptive traits such as compulsiveness, over-dependency, or aggressiveness. Axis II is also used to describe specific developmental disorders for children, adolescents, and, in some cases, adults. Examples of developmental problems that would be classified under Axis II are language disorders, reading or writing difficulties, mental retardation, autism, and speech problems.

It is possible for an individual to have a disorder on both Axis I and Axis II. For example, an adult may have a major depression noted on Axis I and a compulsive personality disorder noted on Axis II. A child may have a conduct disorder noted on Axis I and a developmental language disorder on Axis II. In other cases, a person may be seeking treatment primarily for a condition noted on Axis I or Axis II only. The use of both Axes I and II permits multiple diagnoses and allows the clinician flexibility in making provisional diagnoses when there is not enough information available on the patient to make a firm diagnosis.

Axis III is used to describe physical disorders or medical conditions that are potentially relevant to understanding or managing the person. In some cases, a physical disorder such as brain damage or a chemical imbalance may be causing the syndrome diagnosed on either Axis I or II.

> **Reading Check**
> How does the DSM-IV categorize psychological disorders?

Did You Know?

Neurosis vs. Psychosis Psychosis refers to a fundamental mental breakdown. It involves a severe loss of contact with reality. Neurosis affects only part of one's personality. It is characterized by a less distorted perception of reality than is psychosis. Neurosis causes no disturbance in the use of language; however, it may lead to various physical and psychological disturbances.

PSYCHOLOGY Online

Student Web Activity
Visit the *Understanding Psychology* Web site at psychology.glencoe.com and click on **Chapter 16— Student Web Activities** for an activity on psychological disorders.

Axis IV is a measurement of the current stress level at which the person is functioning. The rating of stressors (such as death of a spouse or loss of a job) is based on what the person has experienced within the past year. The prognosis may be better for a disorder that develops following a severe stressor than for one that develops after no stressor or a minimal stressor.

Axis V is used to describe the highest level of adaptive functioning present within the past year. Adaptive functioning refers to three major areas: social relations, occupational functioning, and the person's use of leisure time. *Social relations* refer to the quality of a person's relationships with family and friends. *Occupational functioning* involves functioning as a worker, student, or homemaker and the quality of the work accomplished. *Use of leisure time* includes recreational activities or hobbies and the degree of involvement and pleasure a person has in them.

This five-part diagnosis may be extremely helpful to researchers trying to discover connections among psychological disorders and other factors such as stress and physical illness. Although it is helpful, the DSM-IV "labels" a person, which may have negative influences on that person in the long run. As mentioned earlier, when the label of a mental disorder is applied to a person it can reduce that person's self-esteem. It also affects how others, including mental health professionals, regard that person. Experiments have demonstrated that labels affect how others view someone. In one experiment, grade-school boys behaved in a more critical manner toward other boys if they had been led to believe that those other boys had a psychological disorder, such as attention deficit disorder (Harris et al., 1992). It is important to note that many people develop a disorder listed in the DSM-IV at some point in their lifetimes. Of course, many of these incidences are temporary. In effect, many people who qualify for a disorder as diagnosed according to the DSM-IV are not very different from anyone else.

SECTION 1 Assessment

1. **Review the Vocabulary** What is the DSM-IV? How do psychologists use it?

2. **Visualize the Main Idea** Using a diagram similar to the one below, identify and describe three approaches psychologists use to identify psychological disorders.

Approaches

Identifying a Psychological Disorder

3. **Recall Information** What are the advantages and disadvantages of categorizing people by the DSM-IV?

4. **Think Critically** Many people may suffer from mild psychological disorders. When do you think it is necessary for them to seek help?

5. **Application Activity** Come up with your own definitions of normal and abnormal behavior. Explain how they differ from the descriptions in this section and why you defined them the way you did.

Anxiety Disorders

Reader's Guide

■ Main Idea

Anxiety disorders are marked by excessive fear, caution, and attempts to avoid anxiety.

■ Vocabulary

- anxiety
- phobia
- panic disorder
- post-traumatic stress disorder

■ Objectives

- Identify the behavioral patterns that psychologists label as anxiety disorders.
- Explain what causes anxiety disorders.

EXPLORING PSYCHOLOGY

Normal Anxiety or Not?

If you are walking down the street and a large dog runs at you barking, it's perfectly normal to be afraid. However, if you get anxious if a dog appears on the TV you're watching, that's a disorder. If a student gets up to give a speech in class and finds that his hands are trembling and his throat is dry, that's normal anxiety. If a student runs out of the room crying when called on to speak or faints while giving a speech, that isn't normal.

—from the files of Judith R. Levine, SUNY Farmingdale

A
nxiety is a general state of dread or uneasiness that a person feels in response to a real or imagined danger. People suffering from anxiety disorders feel anxiety but not just normal anxiety. They suffer from anxiety that is out of proportion to the situation provoking it. This intense anxiety may interfere with normal functioning in everyday life. Fifteen percent of adults have endured symptoms typical of anxiety disorders (Regier et al., 1988). These disorders share certain characteristics, including feelings of anxiety and personal inadequacy and an avoidance of dealing with problems. People with anxiety disorders often have unrealistic images of themselves. People who are deeply anxious seem unable to free themselves of recurring worries and fears. Their emotional problems may be expressed in constant worrying, sudden mood swings, or a variety of physical symptoms (for example, headaches, sweating, muscle tightness, weakness, and fatigue).

Anxious people often have difficulty forming stable and satisfying relationships. Even though their behavior may be self-defeating and ineffective in solving problems, those driven by anxiety often refuse to give up their behaviors in favor of more effective ways of dealing with anxiety. In the DSM-IV, the anxiety disorders discussed include generalized anxiety disorder, phobic disorder, panic disorder, obsessive-compulsive disorder, and post-traumatic stress disorder.

GENERALIZED ANXIETY DISORDER

Once in a while, everyone feels nervous for reasons he or she cannot explain, but a severely anxious person almost always feels this way. **Anxiety** is a generalized apprehension—a vague feeling that one is in danger. This anxiety potentially could blossom into full-fledged panic attacks, which may include choking sensations, chest pain, dizziness, trembling, and hot flashes. Unlike fear, which is a reaction to real and identifiable threats, anxiety is a reaction to vague or imagined dangers.

Some people experience a continuous, generalized anxiety. Fearing unknown and unforeseen circumstances, they are unable to make decisions or enjoy life. They may become so preoccupied with their internal problems that they neglect their social relationships. People who experience generalized anxiety often have trouble dealing with their family and friends and fulfilling their responsibilities, and this adds to their anxiety. They are trapped in a vicious cycle. The more they worry, the more difficulty they have; the more difficulty they have, the more they worry.

Often the experience of generalized anxiety is accompanied by physical symptoms such as muscular tension, an inability to relax, a furrowed brow, and a strained face. Poor appetite, indigestion, diarrhea, and frequent urination are also common. Because anxious people are in a constant state of apprehension, they may have difficulty sleeping or, once asleep, may wake up suddenly in the night. As a result, they may feel tired when they wake up in the morning.

Why are some people so anxious? Some theorists stress the role of learning in producing anxiety. If a man feels very anxious on a date, for example, even the thought of another date may make him nervous, so he learns to avoid having dates and therefore never has a chance to unlearn the anxiety. His anxiety may then generalize to other situations and become a worse problem.

Other research suggests that anxiety disorders may be partly inherited. Environmental factors, such as unpredictable traumatic experiences in childhood, may also predispose someone to developing an anxiety disorder. Such a disorder usually occurs following a major life change, such as getting a job or having a baby. The uncertainties of modern life also may help explain the high incidence of generalized anxiety.

PHOBIC DISORDER

When severe anxiety is focused on a particular object, animal, activity, or situation that seems out of proportion to the real dangers involved, it is called a phobic disorder, or **phobia.** Phobias

anxiety: a vague, generalized apprehension or feeling that one is in danger

phobia: an intense and irrational fear of a particular object or situation

Figure 16.5   Normal Anxiety

Many situations may cause temporary anxiety or tension. Anxiety becomes a problem only when it interferes with your ability to cope with everyday life. *What are some characteristics of people who suffer from anxiety disorders?*

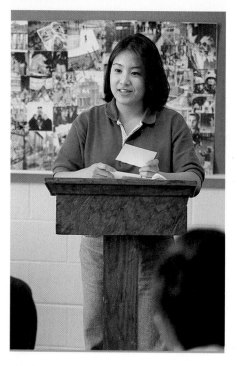

Figure 16.6 Phobias

Some people's lives are consumed by inappropriate fears. These fears interfere with normal, everyday life. These people are suffering from a phobia. *What is the fear of flying called?*

Acerophobia: fear of itching or the insects that cause itching
Acrophobia: fear of heights
Aerophobia: fear of flying
Agoraphobia: fear of open spaces
Atelophobia: fear of imperfection
Autophobia: fear of being alone
Catagelophobia: fear of being ridiculed
Claustrophobia: fear of closed spaces
Entomophobia: fear of insects
Felinophobia: fear of cats
Heliophobia: fear of the sun
Hemophobia: fear of blood
Hydrophobia: fear of water
Logizomechanophobia: fear of computers
Lygophobia: fear of darkness
Nosocomephobia: fear of hospitals
Verminophobia: fear of germs
Zoophobia: fear of animals

may be classified as specific phobias, social phobias, and agoraphobia. A *specific phobia* can focus on almost anything, including high places (acrophobia), enclosed spaces (claustrophobia), and darkness (nyctophobia) (see Figure 16.6). Victims of *social phobias* fear that they will embarrass themselves in a public place or a social setting. Perhaps the most common specific fear is of speaking in public, but others include eating in public, using public restrooms, meeting strangers, and going on a first date.

Phobic individuals develop elaborate plans to avoid the situations they fear. For example, people suffering from an extreme fear of being in a public place *(agoraphobia)* may stop going to movies or shopping in large, busy stores. Some reach the point where they will not leave their houses at all because that is the only place they feel safe.

Phobias range in intensity from mild to extremely severe. Most people deal with their phobias by avoiding the thing that frightens them. Thus the phobias are learned and maintained by the reinforcing effects of avoidance. One common form of treatment for phobias involves providing the phobic person with opportunities to experience the feared object under conditions in which he or she feels safe.

PANIC DISORDER

Another kind of anxiety disorder is **panic disorder.** (*Panic* is a feeling of sudden, helpless terror, such as the overwhelming fright one might experience when cornered by a predator.) During a panic attack, a victim

panic disorder: an anxiety disorder that manifests itself in the form of panic attacks

What fears are most common among teenagers?

Although most people do not experience severe phobias, many do experience mild fears. Find out what fears your classmates experience or have experienced.

Procedure

1. Prepare a list identifying some objects, animals, activities, or situations that are feared.

2. Distribute the list among your friends, classmates, and the adults you know.

3. Direct them to check the items on the list that identify a fear that they have; encourage them to write a fear they have that does not appear on the list.

4. Tally the responses.

Analysis

1. Record the results in a chart or graph, differentiating responses of the teenagers from those of the adults.

2. Determine the most common fears. What reasons can you provide for the similarities or the differences between the two groups?

See the Skills Handbook, page 622, for an explanation of designing an experiment.

Reading Check

What is a panic attack?

experiences sudden and unexplainable attacks of intense anxiety, leading the individual to feel a sense of inevitable doom or even the fear that he or she is about to die. Although symptoms of panic disorder differ from individual to individual, they may include a sense of smothering, choking, or difficulty breathing; faintness or dizziness; nausea; and chest pains. Although panic attacks sometimes last for an hour or more, they usually last just a few minutes.

Panic disorder may be inherited, in part. However, the panic victim usually experiences the first attack shortly after a stressful event. The disorder may also be the result of interpreting physiological arousal, such as an increased heart rate, as disastrous.

OBSESSIVE-COMPULSIVE DISORDER

A person suffering from acute anxiety may find himself thinking the same thoughts over and over. Such an uncontrollable pattern of thoughts is called *obsession*. A person also may repeatedly perform irrational actions, which is called a *compulsion*. The neurotic person may experience both these agonies together—a condition called *obsessive-compulsive disorder*.

A compulsive person may feel compelled to wash his hands 20 or 30 times a day or to avoid stepping on cracks in the sidewalk when he goes out. An obsessive person may be unable to rid herself of unpleasant thoughts about death or of a recurring impulse to make obscene remarks in public. The obsessive-compulsive may wash her hands continually *and* torment herself with thoughts of obscene behavior.

Everyone has obsessions and compulsions. Love might be described as an obsession, so might a hobby that occupies most of a person's spare time. Striving to do something "perfectly" is often considered to be a compulsion. If the person who is deeply engrossed in a hobby or who aims for perfection enjoys this intense absorption and can still function effectively, he or she usually is not considered disabled by anxiety. Psychologists consider it a problem only when such thoughts and activities interfere with what a person wants and needs to do. Someone who spends so much time double-checking every detail of her work that she can never finish a job is considered more anxious than conscientious.

Why do people develop obsessions and compulsions? Perhaps it is because they serve as diversions from a person's real fears and their origins and thus may reduce anxiety somewhat. In addition, compulsions provide a disturbed person with the evidence that she is doing something well, even if it is only avoiding the cracks on a sidewalk. Obsessive-compulsive disorder does run in families, so there may be a possible genetic basis. Although most people with obsessive-compulsive disorder realize that their thoughts and actions are irrational, they feel unable to stop them.

POST-TRAUMATIC STRESS DISORDER

Post-traumatic stress disorder is a condition in which a person who has experienced a traumatic event feels severe and long-lasting aftereffects. This disorder is common among veterans of military combat; survivors of natural disasters, such as floods or tornadoes; and victims of human aggression, such as rape and assault, and unnatural catastrophes, such as plane crashes. The event that triggers the disorder overwhelms a person's normal sense of reality and ability to cope. The disorder may begin immediately after the occurrence of the traumatic event or it may develop later. Typical symptoms include involuntary "flashbacks" or recurring nightmares during which the victim reexperiences the ordeal, often followed by insomnia and feelings of guilt. Post-traumatic stress disorder can be extremely long-lasting. Studies show that survivors of Nazi concentration camps and soldiers returning from war may display symptoms decades after the traumatic event. Not everyone who experiences a traumatic event, though, develops post-traumatic stress disorder. Often people who are exposed repeatedly or over a long period of time to distressing conditions are more likely to develop the disorder. Social support may protect a victim of trauma from the psychological aftereffects.

Figure 16.7   Trauma and Stress

Thousands of ethnic Albanians from Kosovo fled to escape the war in 1999. Here they clamor for food in a refugee camp. *How might war cause someone to develop post-traumatic stress disorder?*

post-traumatic stress disorder: disorder in which victims of traumatic events experience the original event in the form of dreams or flashbacks

---

Assessment

1. **Review the Vocabulary**   Explain how excessive anxiety may lead to phobias or panic disorders.

2. **Visualize the Main Idea**   Using a diagram similar to the one below, list five symptoms of generalized anxiety disorder.

3. **Recall Information**   What is anxiety? When is it normal? Abnormal?

4. **Think Critically**   How would you differentiate between someone who is simply a perfectionist and someone who is suffering from obsessive-compulsive disorder?

5. **Application Activity**   Interview a doctor or nurse who deals with war veterans (such as at your local vets center). Ask the professional to list the symptoms of post-traumatic stress disorder. Summarize your findings.

Somatoform and Dissociative Disorders

Reader's Guide

■ Main Idea
Dealing with anxiety and stress can lead to somatoform and dissociative disorders.

■ Vocabulary
- somatoform disorder
- conversion disorder
- dissociative disorder
- dissociative amnesia
- dissociative fugue
- dissociative identity disorder

■Objectives
- Identify the behavioral patterns that psychologists label as somatoform disorders.
- Describe the symptoms of dissociative disorders.

EXPLORING PSYCHOLOGY

Why Can't the Prince Walk?

There is an ancient Persian legend about a physician named Rhazes who was called into the palace for the purpose of diagnosing and treating a young prince. Apparently, the prince could not walk. After the usual examination of the day, Rhazes determined that there was nothing wrong with the prince's legs, at least not physically. With little more than a hunch, Rhazes set out to treat what may be the first recorded case of conversion. In doing so, he took a risk: Rhazes unexpectedly walked into the prince's bathroom brandishing a dagger and threatened to kill him. Upon seeing him, "the startled prince abruptly fled, leaving his clothes, his dignity, his symptom, and undoubtedly part of his self-esteem behind."

—from *The Neuroses* by H.P. Laughlin, 1967

The prince in the excerpt above suffered from a somatoform disorder. These disorders are characterized by physical symptoms brought about by psychological distress. Today psychologists treat somatoform disorders with a less drastic technique. Psychologists may challenge conversion patients, attempting to force them out of the symptoms. It is important to note that the prince did not consciously "fake" his symptoms to avoid pressure or work; it is likely that he honestly could not move his legs. Psychologists must take this into account when treating such disorders.

SOMATOFORM DISORDERS

Anxiety can create a wide variety of physical symptoms for which no physical cause is apparent. This phenomenon is known as a **somatoform disorder,** or hysteria. The term *hysteria* was more commonly used in Sigmund Freud's time to refer to unexplainable fainting, paralysis, or deafness. Today the term *somatoform disorder* is preferred. Two of the major types of somatoform disorders that psychologists identify are *conversion disorders* and *hypochondriasis.*

somatoform disorder: physical symptoms for which there is no apparent physical cause

Conversion Disorders

A **conversion disorder** is the conversion of emotional difficulties into the loss of a specific physiological function. While the loss of functioning is real, no actual physical damage is present. Many people occasionally experience mild conversion disorders, such as when someone is so frightened he or she cannot move, but a conversion disorder is not simply a brief loss of functioning due to fright. It persists.

conversion disorder: changing emotional difficulties into a loss of a specific voluntary body function

A conversion disorder results in a real and prolonged handicap—the person literally cannot hear or feel anything in his left hand or move his legs or exercise some other normal physical function. For example, a man might wake up one morning and find himself paralyzed from the waist down. The normal reaction to this would be panic. However, he might accept the loss of function with relative calm—called *la belle indifférence.* This calmness is one sign that a person is suffering from a psychological rather than a physiological problem. Most psychologists believe that people suffering from conversion disorders unconsciously invent physical symptoms to gain freedom from unbearable conflict. For example, a woman who lives in terror of blurting out things that she does not want to say may lose the power of speech. This "solves" the problem. Conversion disorders are comparatively rare.

Hypochondriasis

Conversion disorders must be distinguished from *hypochondriasis,* in which a person who is in good health becomes preoccupied with imaginary ailments. The hypochondriac spends a lot of time looking for signs of serious illness and often misinterprets minor aches, pains, bruises, or bumps as early signs of a fatal illness. Despite negative results in medical tests and physical

| Figure 16.8 | **Avoiding Happiness** |

Some people may accuse those suffering from hypochondriasis of faking their illness (and preventing their own happiness). These people, though, do not fake their symptoms; they unrealistically interpret normal aches and pains as symptoms of more serious illnesses. *How does hypochondriasis differ from a conversion disorder?*

evaluations, the hypochondriac typically continues to believe that a disease or malfunction exists. Hypochondriasis occurs mainly during young adulthood and is common equally in men and women. According to psychoanalytic theory, hypochondriasis, like conversion, occurs when an individual represses emotions and then expresses them symbolically in physical symptoms.

DISSOCIATIVE DISORDERS

dissociative disorder: a disorder in which a person experiences alterations in memory, identity, or consciousness

You have probably had the experience of being lost in a daydream and failing to notice your friend calling your name. This is a normal dissociative experience. A **dissociative disorder** involves a more significant breakdown in a person's normal conscious experience, such as a loss of memory or identity. These psychological phenomena fascinate many people, so we hear a good deal about amnesia and "multiple personalities." Actually, they are very rare.

dissociative amnesia: the inability to recall important personal events or information; is usually associated with stressful events

Memory loss that has no biological explanation, or **dissociative amnesia,** may be an attempt to escape from problems by blotting them out completely. Amnesiacs remember how to speak and usually retain a fund of general knowledge, but they may not know who they are, where they live and work, or who their family is. This amnesia should be distinguished from other losses of memory that result from physical brain damage, normal forgetting, or drug abuse. Dissociative amnesia most often results from a traumatic event, such as witnessing a terrible accident.

dissociative fugue: a dissociative disorder in which a person suddenly and unexpectedly travels away from home or work and is unable to recall the past

In **dissociative fugue,** another type of dissociative reaction, amnesia is coupled with active flight to a different environment. For example, a woman may suddenly disappear and "wake up" three days later in a restaurant 200 miles from home. She may actually establish a new identity—assume a new name, marry, take a job, and so forth—in a new place. She may repress all knowledge of a previous life. A fugue state may last for days or for decades. However long it lasts, the individual, when she comes out of it, will have no memory of what she has done in the interim. Fugue, then, is a sort of traveling amnesia, and it probably serves the same psychological function as dissociative amnesia: escape from unbearable conflict or anxiety.

dissociative identity disorder: a person exhibits two or more personality states, each with its own patterns of thinking and behaving

In **dissociative identity disorder** (previously known as multiple personality disorder), a third type of dissociative disorder, someone seems to have two or more distinct identities, each with its own way of thinking and behaving. These different personality states may take control at different times.

Eve White, a young woman who sought psychiatric treatment for severe headaches and blackouts, has become a famous example. Eve White was a conscientious, self-controlled, rather shy person. However, during one of her therapy sessions, her expression—and her personality—suddenly changed. Eve Black, as she now called herself, was childlike, fun-loving, and irresponsible—the opposite of the woman who originally walked into the psychiatrist's office. Eve Black was conscious of

Reading Check
How is dissociative amnesia different from dissociative fugue?

Eve White's existence but considered her a separate person. Eve White did not know about Eve Black, however, and neither was she conscious of Jane, a third personality that emerged during the course of therapy. (This case served as the basis for the book and film *The Three Faces of Eve.*) Some psychologists believe that this dividing up of the personality is the result of the individual's effort to escape from a part of herself that she fears. The "secret self" then emerges in the form of a separate personality. It is an extremely rare disorder.

Eve's real name is Chris Costner Sizemore, and she published a book many years later (Sizemore & Pittillo, 1977) explaining that Eve ultimately had 22 separate personalities. Her case is often confused with Sybil, a woman whose 16 personalities were also described in a book and a film. While cases like Eve and Sybil are fascinating, they are extremely rare and somewhat controversial.

People diagnosed with this disorder usually suffered severe physical, psychological, or sexual abuse during childhood. Individuals with dissociative disorders have learned to dissociate themselves from such stressful events by selectively forgetting them, thereby reducing the anxiety they feel.

Figure 16.9 **The Personalities of Eve**

Chris Sizemore (Eve) was able to overcome her disorder through therapy. She created this painting to symbolize the personalities present within her when she began therapy. *What causes dissociative identity disorder?*

SECTION 3 **Assessment**

1. **Review the Vocabulary** Define and describe three dissociative disorders. Explain how these disorders differ from one another.

2. **Visualize the Main Idea** Use a graphic organizer similar to the one below to list dissociative disorders.

   Dissociative Disorders

3. **Recall Information** What is the difference between a conversion disorder and hypochondriasis?

4. **Think Critically** Besides anxiety, how might you realize that you are suffering from a somatoform or dissociative disorder?

5. **Application Activity** As a class or in groups, arrange an appointment with a local nurse, physician, or counselor. Question this person regarding the most common psychological problems that young people face. Report your findings to the class.

Munchausen's Syndrome

Period of Study: 1994

Introduction: In 1994 a physician consulted psychiatrist Berney Goodman regarding the condition of a patient who seemingly had a rare bowel condition—the patient vomited every time she ate. Together they diagnosed the patient with bowel paralysis. Goodman himself wanted to examine the patient. From the start, the patient refused to cooperate with Goodman. Goodman discovered that the patient had low blood pressure. This, though, did not correspond with the diagnosis of bowel paralysis.

Hypothesis: Goodman suspected that the patient suffered from *Munchausen's Syndrome*. Those who suffer from the ailment have developed great sensitivity to emotional pain and will use any methods possible to avoid feeling it. These methods are quite extreme and often deadly. The sufferers often attempt to hospitalize themselves with self-defined or self-induced symptoms. Their ultimate goal is to have the physician take extraordinary measures to save their life.

Method: After further investigation, Goodman discovered that the patient was secretly taking diuretics to produce the symptoms associated with bowel paralysis. His suspicions had been correct. A Munchausen's patient might complain of a variety of symptoms. A physician, though, has trouble finding these symptoms when examining the patient. Patients have added sugar to samples of urine, suggesting the presence of diabetes. They have visited dermatologists with rashes, sores, and lesions with no medical explanation but used sandpaper, chemical irritants, or excessive heat to make these symptoms appear. Munchausen's patients have swallowed corrosive substances, eroding the lining of their stomachs and throats to produce vomiting.

Munchausen's patients are not limited to displaying physical symptoms—they also imitate psychiatric disorders. Overdosing on psychoactive drugs to induce delusions and hallucinations is common for them. Patients may use techniques of persuasion to try to influence the physician to perform thorough medical investigations.

Although Munchausen's patients can puzzle and deceive physicians, they have a tendency to hide their methods poorly. Syringes are left lying around, they do not conceal pills neatly, and they allow themselves to be observed during their symptom-causing routines. These scenarios result in most diagnoses.

Results: Describing "how" Munchausen's Syndrome sufferers behave is much easier than explaining "why." Some leads suggest that either all-caring or all-rejecting parental relationships are experienced and then re-created by the patient. They seem to invite their physicians into an all-nurturing relationship, and at other times they despise their physician and create an all-rejecting relationship.

The difficulty in discovering and diagnosing Munchausen's Syndrome led to the absence of a clear-cut definition by the DSM-IV. Because of this, it is extremely difficult to treat those who are affected.

Analyzing the Case Study

1. What is Munchausen's Syndrome?

2. What are some possible causes of Munchausen's Syndrome?

3. **Critical Thinking** Why might a physician or psychologist suspect that someone is suffering from Munchausen's Syndrome? What is the danger in misdiagnosing this disorder?

Schizophrenia and Mood Disorders

Reader's Guide

■ Main Idea

Schizophrenia involves disordered thoughts. Mood disorders involve disturbances in the experience and expressions of depression.

■ Vocabulary

- schizophrenia
- delusions
- hallucinations
- major depressive disorder
- bipolar disorder

■ Objectives

- Describe the disorder of schizophrenia.
- Describe several theories that try to explain mood disorders.

EXPLORING PSYCHOLOGY

Word Salad

A woman was delighted to receive a letter from her son abroad, but distraught when she read it: "Dear mother . . . I am writing on paper. The pen I am using is from a factory called Perry and Co. The factory is in England. The city of London is in England. I know this from my school days. Then I always liked geography. My last teacher in that subject was Professor August A. He was a man with black eyes. There are also blue and grey eyes and other sorts too. I have heard it said that snakes have green eyes. All people have eyes. There are some, too, who are blind."

—from *The Human Mind Explained*, edited by Susan A. Greenfield, 1996

The man who wrote this letter later was diagnosed with schizophrenia. Sufferers of schizophrenia often have difficulty using language to communicate. They seem to go from one phrase to another by random association. This confused language may result because schizophrenia affects the working memory, which is used to form sentences. A person with schizophrenia will not remember the beginning of a sentence and thus finishes it with nonsense. Schizophrenia is often misunderstood. Why?

We can understand depression, and most of us have experienced anxiety. In addition, we can appreciate how people with these problems strive to overcome them as best they can. An individual with schizophrenia, however, who withdraws from normal life and whose distorted perceptions and behavior reach an irrational, fantastic, fear-laden, unimaginable

schizophrenia: a group of disorders characterized by confused and disconnected thoughts, emotions, and perceptions

delusions: a false belief that a person maintains in the face of contrary evidence

hallucinations: perceptions that have no direct external cause

level, does so in ways that are difficult to understand. Yet, psychologists are making progress in furthering our understanding of schizophrenia—the most complex and severe psychological problem we encounter.

WHAT IS SCHIZOPHRENIA?

While the disorders discussed thus far are primarily problems of emotion, schizophrenia is a problem of cognition, but it also involves emotion, perception, and motor functions. Schizophrenia affects 1 in 100 people worldwide (British Columbia Schizophrenia Society, 1997), but the odds increase to 1 in 10 if schizophrenia is already in the family. What distinguishes this disorder from other types of psychological disturbance? **Schizophrenia** involves confused and disordered thoughts and perceptions. With schizophrenia, a person's thought processes are somewhat disturbed, and the person has lost contact with reality to a considerable extent. One expert has noted that someone with depression or severe anxiety problems dreams in an unreal way about life, while a person with schizophrenia lives life as an unreal dream. Schizophrenia is not a single problem; it has no single cause or cure. Rather, it is a collection of symptoms that indicates an individual has serious difficulty trying to meet the demands of life.

Suppose a psychiatrist is interviewing a patient who has just been admitted to a hospital. The individual demonstrates a wide assortment of symptoms. He is intensely excited, expresses extreme hostility toward members of his family, and at the same time claims that he loves them, showing conflicting feelings. One minute he is extremely aggressive, questioning the psychiatrist's motives and even threatening her. The next minute he withdraws and acts as if he does not hear anything she says. Then he begins talking again. "Naturally," he says, "I am growing my father's hair." Although all of the person's other behavior indicates psychological problems, this last statement would be the "diagnostic bell ringer." It reveals that the man is living in a private, disordered reality.

Many people with schizophrenia experience **delusions**—false beliefs maintained in the face of contrary evidence—and **hallucinations**—perceptions in the absence of corresponding sensation. For example, a person with schizophrenia may perceive a voice when, in fact, there is no sound present. A person with schizophrenia may show a number of other symptoms as well. One is *incoherence*, or a marked decline in thought processes. The language of someone with schizophrenia may be sped up; sometimes, it is described as "word salad"—lots of words thrown together. Another symptom is *disturbances of*

More About...

Schizophrenia and Autism

On the surface, schizophrenia and autism may appear to be the same condition. Sufferers of both conditions, for example, share the appearance of being detached from the real world and living in a different one. Psychologists, however, have concluded after long debate that autism and schizophrenia are different conditions.

Obvious to the parents in haunting ways soon after birth, *infantile autism* causes children to differ from normal children in three ways. First, children with autism do not respond to other people. If you pick up an autistic child, he or she is stiff or limp; the child will not cling to you as normal children will. Second, an autistic child is very slow in developing language and communication skills. By age 5 or 6, they may simply repeat what has been said, a condition called *echolalia*. Third, autistic children are very limited in their interests and behavior. They may abuse themselves or repeat a simple hand motion for hours without ceasing.

Explaining autism's cause has been difficult. Learning-based and psychoanalytic attempts have failed. The best guess is that genetics play no role (Smalley, 1991), but an inborn defect may interact with later environmental or biological events (Carson & Butcher, 1992) to produce autism.

affect, or emotions that are inappropriate for the circumstances. In addition, an individual with schizophrenia may display severe *deterioration in normal movement,* which may occur as slowed movement, nonmovement, or as highly agitated behavior. Another symptom is a marked *decline in previous levels of functioning;* for example, a sharp dropoff in productivity at work. Yet another symptom is *diverted attention,* perhaps brought about by cognitive flooding, as if the person is unable to focus his or her attention.

TYPES OF SCHIZOPHRENIA

Psychologists classify schizophrenia into several subtypes. One, the *paranoid type,* involves hallucinations and delusions, including *grandeur:* "I am the savior of my people;" or *persecution:* "Someone is always watching me" (see Figure 16.10). People with the *catatonic type* may remain motionless for long periods, exhibiting "waxy flexibility" in which limbs in unusual positions may take a long time to return to a resting, relaxed position—exactly as if melting a wax statue (see Figure 16.11). Symptoms of the *disorganized type* include incoherent language, inappropriate emotions, giggling for no apparent reason, generally disorganized motor behavior, and hallucinations and delusions. Another form of schizophrenia is the *remission type.* This diagnostic label is applied to anyone whose symptoms are completely gone or still exist but are not

Figure 16.10 **Paranoia**

A male patient diagnosed with schizophrenia with paranoid tendencies created this painting. It displays the symbolism of watchful eyes, grasping hands, and the self as subject matter. *How is the paranoid type of schizophrenia characterized?*

severe enough to have earned a diagnosis of schizophrenia in the first place. The expectation is that symptoms will return, so the schizophrenia is simply viewed as "in remission." It is sometimes difficult to differentiate between types of schizophrenia because some symptoms are shared by all types. The *undifferentiated type* encompasses the basic symptoms of schizophrenia, such as deterioration of daily functioning, hallucinations, delusions, inappropriate emotions, thought disorders, and so on.

Schizophrenia is a very complex condition, and treatment is long-term and usually requires hospitalization. Long-term institutionalization sometimes leads to a patient who is *burned out*—one who is unlikely to function normally in society. Schizophrenia may go into remission, in which the symptoms disappear and the person seems quite normal, but according to the DSM-IV, adjustment tends to deteriorate between successive episodes of

Did You Know?

Split Personality The term *schizophrenia* comes from Greek for "split personality." Schizophrenia does not refer to split personalities such as dissociative identity disorder, though. Schizophrenia involves a split between the intellectual and emotional parts of a single personality.

the reappearance of symptoms. Although recovery from schizophrenia is possible, no real cure for schizophrenia exists, and once an individual is diagnosed with schizophrenia, he or she may never escape from it.

CAUSES OF SCHIZOPHRENIA

What is the actual cause of schizophrenia? There are many theories, and just as certainly, there is disagreement. In all likelihood, the ultimate cause is an interaction of environmental, genetic, and biochemical factors.

Biological Influences

Genetics is almost certainly involved in causing schizophrenia. One psychologist (Gottesman, 1991) summarized the results of more than 35 studies conducted in Western Europe from 1920 to 1987. He found that there is a 1 percent likelihood that anyone in the general population will develop schizophrenia. These odds, however, increase to 10 percent if schizophrenia is already in the family. Yet, even among identical twins, if one twin develops schizophrenia, only 42 percent of the twin's siblings will develop it. This finding implies that other factors in addition to heredity also have a role (see Figure 16.12).

In trying to define the role of genetics more precisely, researchers have studied children born to schizophrenic mothers who are separated from their mothers at birth and raised in different homes. Using an *adoption study,* one study (Kety, 1983) found that 16 percent of 47 children of schizophrenic mothers developed schizophrenia; none of 50 control children whose natural mother did not have schizophrenia developed it, although they were also raised in foster homes. Even studies of children raised in natural families where both parents were later diagnosed as having schizophrenia reveal that as much as 28 percent of the children show no signs of schizophrenia. In summary, these studies show that psychologists cannot specify the exact contribution hereditary factors make to schizophrenia (Carson & Sanislow, 1992).

Biochemistry and Physiology

The proper working of the brain depends on the presence of right amounts of many different chemicals, from oxygen to proteins. Some psychologists believe that psychosis is due largely to chemical imbalances in the brain. According to some theories, some people are born with a nervous system that gets aroused very easily and takes a long time to return to normal. Such people might be particularly likely to get upset when they are stressed.

Figure 16.11 Catatonic Type

A person suffering from the catatonic type of schizophrenia can hold an unusual position for long periods of time. *Is schizophrenia curable?*

Figure 16.12 **The Genain Quadruplets**

In 1930 four identical girls were born. By high school, people had labeled the girls as somehow "different." By the time they were young adults, all four were diagnosed with schizophrenia. *From this case, what can psychologists infer about the causes of schizophrenia?*

Chemical problems may also be involved in schizophrenia. A number of researchers think that the basic problem in schizophrenia is that too much or too little of certain chemicals has "knocked out of kilter" the brain's mechanisms for processing information, perhaps interfering with normal synaptic transmission.

The *dopamine hypothesis* suggests that an excess of dopamine at selected synapses is related to a diagnosis of schizophrenia. One psychologist (Carlsson, 1988) notes that correlational studies are not enough to demonstrate a direct role for dopamine in schizophrenia. It seems likely that chemicals play a role, but it is hard to tell whether these chemicals are the cause of schizophrenia or the result of it. Symptoms of schizophrenia may even be caused by the fact that people with schizophrenia tend to live in hospitals, where they get little exercise, eat institutional food, and are usually given daily doses of tranquilizers. Living under such conditions, anyone might develop chemical imbalances and abnormal behavior.

The use of CAT and MRI scans (see Chapter 6) has led to the discovery that the brains of people with schizophrenia often show signs of deteriorated brain tissue (Pearlson et al., 1989). One consistent result is that women who at some time develop schizophrenia are likely to have difficult pregnancies and difficulties giving birth. Yet researchers are not sure what role these difficulties have in determining whether the children develop schizophrenia. This problem emphasizes that environment may play an important role in fostering the development of schizophrenia.

Family and Interactions

From Freud onward, it has been tempting to blame the family situation in childhood for problems that develop during adulthood. Paul Meehl (1962, 1989) suggests that bad experiences during childhood are not enough, in and of themselves, to lead to schizophrenia; being part of a *pathogenic,* or unhealthful, family may contribute to problems in the adult years.

Studies show that families of individuals who later develop schizophrenia are often on the verge of falling apart. Another frequent finding is that family members organize themselves around—or in spite of—the very unusual, demanding, or maladaptive behavior of one member of the family. Communication, too, often seems disorganized in the early family life of people who later develop schizophrenia.

In Summary   Which of these theories is correct? At this point, psychologists do not know. It may be that each is partially true. Perhaps people who inherit a tendency toward psychological disorders react more strongly to stressful situations than others would. The *diathesis-stress hypothesis* states that an individual may have inherited a predisposition toward schizophrenia. For schizophrenia to develop, however, that person must be exposed to an environment with certain stressors, such as bad family experiences, before the schizophrenia will develop. Explaining the causes of schizophrenia is perhaps the most complex research problem psychologists face.

MOOD DISORDERS

We all experience mood swings. Sometimes we are happy or elated, while at other times we feel dejected, miserable, or depressed. Yet even when we are discouraged, most of us still feel we can control our emotions and that these feelings will pass.

Occasional depression is a common experience. In some people, however, these moods are more intense and tend to last for longer periods. These individuals often get the sense that their depression will go on forever and that there is nothing they can do to change it. As a result, their emotions hamper their ability to function effectively. In extreme cases, a mood may cause individuals to lose touch with reality or seriously threaten their health or lives.

Major Depressive Disorder

major depressive disorder: severe form of depression that interferes with functioning, concentration, and mental and physical well-being

Individuals suffering from **major depressive disorder** spend at least two weeks feeling depressed, sad, anxious, fatigued, and agitated, experiencing a reduced ability to function and interact with others. The depression ranges from mild feelings of uneasiness, sadness, and apathy to intense suicidal despair. To be diagnosed as depression, these feelings cannot be attributed to bereavement (the loss of a loved one). This disorder is marked by at least four of the following symptoms: problems with eating, sleeping, thinking, concentrating, or decision making; lacking energy; thinking about suicide; and feeling worthless or guilty (American Psychiatric Association, 1994).

Bipolar Disorder

One type of mood disorder is **bipolar disorder,** in which individuals are excessively and inappropriately happy or unhappy. These reactions may take the form of high elation, hopeless depression, or an alternation between the two.

In the *manic phase,* a person experiences elation, extreme confusion, distractibility, and racing thoughts. Often the person has an exaggerated sense of self-esteem and engages in irresponsible behavior, such as shopping sprees or insulting remarks. As an example, consider the following behavior:

> On admission she slapped the nurse, addressed the house physician as God, made the sign of the cross, and laughed loudly when she was asked to don the hospital garb. This she promptly tore to shreds. . . . She sang at the top of her voice, screamed through the window, and leered at the patients promenading in the recreation yard. (Karnash, 1945)

This state is not as easy to detect as some others because the person is optimistic, seeming to be in touch with reality and blessed with an unending sense of optimism. During a manic episode, a person may behave as if he or she needs less sleep, and the activity level typically increases, as does the loudness and the frequency with which he or she speaks.

In the *depressive phase,* the individual is overcome by feelings of failure, sinfulness, worthlessness, and despair. In contrast to the optimism and high activity of a manic-type reaction, a depressive-type reaction is marked by lethargy, despair, and unresponsiveness. The behavior of someone who is depressed in a bipolar disorder is essentially the same as someone with a major depressive disorder (Perris, 1982), as in the following case:

> The patient lay in bed, immobile, with a dull, depressed expression on his face. His eyes were sunken and downcast. Even when spoken to, he would not raise his eyes to look at the speaker. Usually he did not respond at all to questions, but sometimes, after apparently great effort, he would mumble something about the "Scourge of God." (Morris, 1990)

In some cases, a patient will alternate between frantic action and motionless despair. Some people experience occasional episodes of a manic-type or depressive-type reaction, separated by long intervals of relatively normal behavior. Others exhibit almost no normal behavior, cycling instead from periods of manic-type reactions to equally intense depressive-type reactions. Some theorists have speculated that the manic periods serve as an attempt to ward off the underlying hopelessness of the depressive periods. Others believe that mania can be traced to the same biochemical disorder responsible for depression.

Figure 16.13 Down in the Dumps

This scene expresses the emptiness and bleakness that a depressed person feels. *When does depression become a psychological disorder?*

bipolar disorder: disorder in which an individual alternates between feelings of mania (euphoria) and depression

✔ *Reading Check*
What is the difference between a major depressive disorder and a bipolar disorder?

Figure 16.14 | Rates of Suicide

Suicide rates differ according to age and gender. *Which age group has the highest suicide rate? Which gender has the highest suicide rate?*

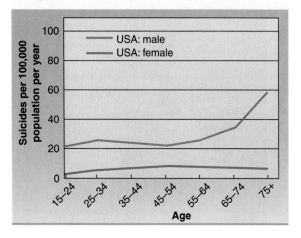

Seasonal Affective Disorder

Many of us may feel a tinge of sadness when looking at a mid-February landscape of dull grays and browns. However, there are people who develop a deep depression in the midst of winter. These people are victims of *seasonal affective disorder,* or *SAD.* Throughout the winter they struggle with depression; their spirits lift only with the coming of spring. (People may also suffer annual depressions during the summer.) People suffering from SAD tend to sleep and eat excessively during their depressed periods.

Researchers have proposed that the hormone melatonin may play a role. The less light available (in winter), the more melatonin is secreted by the brain's pineal gland. A higher level of melatonin in their blood levels may cause some people to suffer from SAD. Researchers do not know why higher levels of melatonin lead to SAD in some people and not in others. Many SAD sufferers can be treated by sitting under bright fluorescent lights during the evening or early morning hours.

Explaining Mood Disorders

Psychological factors underlying mood disorders include certain personality traits (such as self-esteem), amount of social support, and the ability to deal with stressful situations. The cognitive theories of Aaron Beck and Martin Seligman have often served as the basis for research on depression. Beck (1983) believes that depressed people draw illogical conclusions about themselves—they blame themselves for normal problems and consider every minor failure a catastrophe. As described in Chapter 9, Martin Seligman (1975) believes that depression is caused by a feeling of learned helplessness. The depressed person learns to believe that he has no control over events in his life and that it is useless even to try.

Psychologists developed theories to provide a physiological or biological explanation of depression. Researchers are currently searching for the neurotransmitters (such as serotonin and noradrenaline) that cause mood disorders. They are also looking at genetic factors and faulty brain structure and function as possible causes. Many causes of depression may result from an interaction of biological and psychological factors.

Suicide and Depression

Not all people who commit suicide are depressed, and not all depressed people attempt suicide. Many depressives, though, do think about suicide, and

More About...

Depression and Gender

After adolescence, women are about twice as likely as men to experience major depression. Why? One possibility is that hormonal changes occurring as a result of pregnancy lead to depression. In fact, some women go through postpartum depression shortly after giving birth. Some psychologists believe that the numbers are high for female depression simply because more women report their depression and seek help. Other psychologists believe that men may simply distract themselves when experiencing depression. For example, a man might go play basketball and not think about his feelings.

some of them translate these thoughts into action.

People may take their lives for any number of reasons. It may be to escape from physical or emotional pain—perhaps a terminal illness or the loneliness of old age. It might be an effort to end the torment of unacceptable feelings, to punish themselves for wrongs they think they have committed, or to punish others who have not perceived their needs (Mintz, 1968). In many cases we simply do not know why the suicide occurred.

Statistics show, however, that every year more than 32,000 Americans end their lives—about 1 every 16 minutes. More women than men attempt suicide, but more men than women succeed. Suicide is most common among the elderly but also ranks as the second most common cause of death among college students. Contrary to popular belief, people who threaten suicide or make an unsuccessful attempt usually *are* serious. Studies show that about 70 percent of people who kill themselves had threatened to do so within the three months preceding the suicide, and an unsuccessful attempt is often a trial run (American Foundation for Suicide Prevention, 1999).

PSYCHOLOGY and You — What Should You Do?

If you suspect someone you know is thinking about suicide, what should you do? Treat him (or her) like a normal human being. (Meanwhile, contact a professional psychologist or trusted teacher on how to guide your own behavior.) Do not assume that you will upset him—just talk to him. Do not be afraid to ask him about his thoughts (even suicidal ones). Listen to him—he might be relieved to have someone just listen. Urge him to get professional help. Most cities have suicide prevention hot lines.

SECTION 4 Assessment

1. **Review the Vocabulary** Define schizophrenia and list five symptoms of the disorder.

2. **Visualize the Main Idea** Use a graphic organizer similar to the one below to identify types of schizophrenia.

Types of Schizophrenia

3. **Recall Information** What is the diathesis-stress hypothesis? How does it explain the development of schizophrenia?

4. **Think Critically** Recall the last time you failed or did not do well at something. What kind of explanation did you offer for your failure? Was this explanation pessimistic or optimistic? Explain. How did your explanation affect your mood or feelings?

5. **Application Activity** Schizophrenia often is misunderstood. Conduct research to find three facts about schizophrenia or someone who has been diagnosed with schizophrenia and share this information with the class. As a class discuss and correct the false impressions about schizophrenia that you hold.

Personality Disorders and Drug Addiction

Reader's Guide

■ **Main Idea**
Personality disorders and drug addiction prohibit normal relationships and normal functioning.

■ **Vocabulary**
• personality disorders
• antisocial personality
• psychological dependence
• addiction
• tolerance
• withdrawal

■ **Objectives**
• Describe how personality disorders differ from other psychological disorders.
• Explain how drug abuse is a psychological problem.

EXPLORING PSYCHOLOGY

Aimless Crime

On October 7, 1976, Gary Gilmore was sentenced to death by a Utah court after a seemingly purposeless crime spree, and on January 16, 1977, he became the first person to be executed in the United States since 1966. . . . Gilmore had been released from prison only six months earlier, after serving time for armed robbery. . . . Gilmore himself described the next events: "I pulled up near a gas station. I told the service station guy to give me all of his money. I then took him to the bathroom and told him to kneel down and then I shot him in the head twice. The guy didn't give me any trouble but I just felt like I had to do it."

The very next morning, Gilmore left his car at another service station. . . . "I went in and told the guy to give me the money. . . . [T]hen I shot him. . . ."

—from *Abnormal Psychology* by David L. Rosenhan and Martin E.P. Seligman, 1984

ary Gilmore's crimes are an example of crime without understandable motives. During a psychiatric interview, Gilmore observed, "I don't remember any real emotional event in all my life. . . . When you're in the joint, you stay pretty even all the time. . . . I'm not really excitable you know. I don't get emotional" (Rosenhan & Seligman, 1984). For Gilmore, emotions and social rules did not constrain his behavior. This lack of constraint is a sign of a personality disorder, specifically an antisocial personality disorder.

PERSONALITY DISORDERS

Personality disorders are different from the problems we have been discussing. People with personality disorders generally do not suffer from acute anxiety nor do they behave in bizarre, incomprehensible ways. Psychologists consider these people "abnormal" because they seem unable to establish meaningful relationships with other people, to assume social responsibilities, or to adapt to their social environment. This diagnostic category includes a wide range of self-defeating personality patterns, from painfully shy, lonely types to vain, pushy show-offs (see Figure 16.15). In this section we focus on people with **antisocial personalities,** who in the past were referred to as sociopaths or psychopaths.

Antisocial Personality

Individuals with antisocial personalities exhibit a persistent disregard for and violation of others' rights. They treat people as objects—as things to be used for gratification and to be cast coldly aside when no longer wanted. Intolerant of everyday frustrations and unable to save or plan or wait, they live for the moment. Seeking thrills is their major occupation. If they should injure other people along the way or break social rules, they do not seem to feel any shame or guilt. Getting caught does not seem to rattle them, either. No matter how many times they are reprimanded, punished, or jailed, they never learn how to stay out of trouble. They simply do not profit from experience.

Many individuals with antisocial personalities can get away with destructive behavior because they are intelligent, entertaining, and able to feign emotions they do not feel. They win affection and confidence from

personality disorders: maladaptive or inflexible ways of dealing with others and one's environment

antisocial personality: a personality disorder characterized by irresponsibility, shallow emotions, and lack of conscience

Figure 16.15 > Types of Personality Disorders

An individual with a personality disorder displays an inflexible, long-standing, and maladaptive way of dealing with the environment and other people. *What are the characteristics of an individual with a paranoid personality disorder?*

Disorder	Characteristics
Antisocial	displays pattern of disregarding and violating the rights of others without feeling remorse
Dependent	displays pattern of submissiveness and excessive need to be taken care of
Histrionic	displays excessive emotions; excessively seeks attention
Obsessive-Compulsive	has an intense interest in being orderly, having control, and achieving perfection
Paranoid	distrusts others; perceives others as having evil motives
Schizotypal	feels intense discomfort in close relationships; has distorted thinking and eccentric behavior

others whom they then take advantage of. If caught, these individuals will either spin a fantastic lie or simply insist, with wide-eyed sincerity, that their intentions were utterly pure. Guilt and anxiety have no place in the antisocial personality.

An example is that of Hugh Johnson, a con man who was caught after defrauding people out of thousands of dollars in 64 separate swindles. Hugh stated the following when asked why he had victimized so many people: "He replied with some heat that he never took more from a person than the person could afford to lose, and further, that he was only reducing the likelihood that other more dangerous criminals would use force to achieve the same ends" (Nathan & Harris, 1975).

How do psychologists explain such a lack of ordinary human decency and shame? According to one theory, individuals with antisocial personalities have simply imitated their own antisocial parents. Other theories point to lack of discipline or inconsistent discipline or other problems during childhood. Finally, some researchers believe that these individuals have a "faulty nervous system." Psychologists are still investigating the relationship between genes and antisocial behavior. While most of us get very nervous when we do something that we have been punished for in the past, those with antisocial personalities never seem to learn to anticipate punishment and remain calm while committing antisocial acts.

Reading Check
How are personality disorders different from anxiety disorders?

DRUG ADDICTION

In American society, drug abuse has become a major psychological problem. Millions of Americans depend so heavily on drugs that they hurt themselves physically, socially, and psychologically. For these reasons, drug addiction and alcoholism are covered in the DSM-IV.

Abuse of drugs invariably involves **psychological dependence.** Users come to depend so much on the feeling of well-being they obtain from the drug that they feel compelled to continue using it. People can become psychologically dependent on a wide variety of drugs, including alcohol, caffeine, nicotine (in cigarettes), cocaine, marijuana, and amphetamines. When deprived of the drug, a psychologically dependent person becomes restless, irritable, and uneasy.

psychological dependence: use of a drug to such an extent that a person feels nervous and anxious without it

In addition to psychological dependence, drugs can lead to physiological **addiction.** A person is addicted when his system has become so used to the drug that the drugged state becomes the body's "normal" state. If the drug is not in the body, the person experiences extreme physical discomfort as he would if he were deprived of oxygen or water.

addiction: a pattern of drug abuse characterized by an overwhelming and compulsive desire to obtain and use the drug

Just as dependence causes a psychological need for the drug, addiction causes a physical need. Furthermore, once a person is addicted to a drug, he develops **tolerance;** that is, his body becomes so accustomed to the drug that he has to keep increasing his dosage to obtain the "high" that he achieved with his earlier doses. With certain sleeping pills, for example, a person can rapidly develop a tolerance for up to 16 times the original dose. Further, an addict must have his drug to

tolerance: physical adaptation to a drug so that a person needs an increased amount in order to produce the original effect retain what little physical and psychological balance he has left. If he does not get it, he is likely to go through the dreaded experience of withdrawal.

Withdrawal is a state of physical and psychological upset during which the body and the mind revolt against and finally get used to the absence of the drug. Withdrawal symptoms vary from person to person and from drug to drug. They range from a mild case of nausea and "the shakes" to hallucinations, convulsions, coma, and death.

withdrawal: the symptoms that occur after a person discontinues the use of a drug to which he or she has become addicted

Alcoholism

This country's most serious drug problem is alcoholism. In American society, consumption of alcohol often begins at an early age. Researchers estimate that 88 percent of all high school seniors have consumed alcohol at some time since entering adolescence and that 54 percent have consumed it within the past month (Johnston, Bachman, & O'Malley, 1992). More than half of the students entering high school have already tried alcohol; by the time of graduation, 92 percent have tried it. An estimated 35 percent report having consumed five or more drinks in a row within the previous two weeks, and 4 percent of graduating seniors are drinking alcohol daily (Payne, Hahn, & Pinger, 1991). Fifty percent or more of the deaths in automobile accidents each year can be traced to alcohol; in half of all murders, either the killer or the victim had been drinking. The cost in human suffering to the alcoholic and her family is impossible to measure.

In small doses, alcohol might be called a social wonder drug. The first psychological function that it slows down is our inhibitions. Two drinks can make a person relaxed, talkative, playful, even giggly. It is for this reason that many people consider alcohol a stimulant, when it is really a depressant.

As the number of drinks increases, the fun decreases. One by one, the person's psychological and physiological functions begin to shut down. Perceptions and sensations become distorted, and behavior may become obnoxious. The person begins to stumble and weave, speech becomes slurred, and reactions—to a stop sign, for example—become sluggish. If enough alcohol accumulates in the body, it leads to unconsciousness and, in some cases, coma and death. It all depends on how much and how rapidly alcohol enters the bloodstream—which, in turn, depend on a person's weight, body chemistry, how much he or she drinks and how quickly, and his or her past experience with drinking.

Alcohol can produce psychological dependence, tolerance, and addiction. One researcher (Jellinek, 1960) has outlined three stages of alcoholism. In the first stage, the individual discovers that alcohol reduces her tensions, gives her self-confidence, and reduces social pressures. Drinking makes her feel better. In the second stage, the beverage becomes a drug. The individual begins to drink so heavily that she feels she has to hide her habit. Thus she begins "sneaking" drinks. In this

Figure 16.16) Alcohol Abuse

About 100 million U.S. citizens drink alcohol, whereas 10 to 12 million Americans abuse alcohol. *When does alcohol use become a problem?*

Figure 16.17 | Effects of Alcohol Use

As a person consumes more and more alcohol, psychological and physiological functions begin to shut down, as shown in these handwriting samples. *How do you treat alcoholism?*

I can drive when I drink.
The party begins.

I can drive when I drink
2 drinks later.

I can drive when I drink.
4 drinks later.

I can drive when I drink
5 drinks later.

I can drive when I drink
7 drinks in all.

stage she may also begin to suffer from blackouts—she is unable to recall what happened during a drinking episode. In the final stage, she drinks compulsively, beginning in the morning. She becomes inefficient at work and tends to go on drinking sprees that may last for weeks. She is now an alcoholic, drinking continuously, eating infrequently, and feeling sick when deprived of her drug. Her health deteriorates rapidly.

Alcoholism may develop from both environmental and genetic factors. A person's risk of becoming an alcoholic is three to four times higher if a member of the family is an alcoholic. Children of alcoholic parents may also be raised in an atmosphere of distrust, overdependence, and stress, which contributes to the possible development of alcoholism.

The first step in treating the alcoholic is to help her through the violent withdrawal—called *delirium tremens*—typical of alcohol addiction and then to try to make her healthier. She may be given a variety of treatments, from drugs to psychotherapy. Alcoholics Anonymous (AA), an organization for alcoholics run by people who have had a drinking problem in the past, has been more successful than most organizations. Some alcoholics must turn to medical treatment. Some doctors prescribe *Antabuse* to alcoholics (Peachey & Naranjo, 1983). Antabuse, or disulfiram, is a chemical that blocks the conversion of acetaldehyde to acetic acid. (Ordinarily, the liver converts alcohol into acetaldehyde—a toxic substance—and then converts acetaldehyde into a harmless substance—acetic acid.) When alcoholics take a daily Antabuse pill, they become violently sick if they have a drink of alcohol. The threat of the violent sickness may become an effective prevention. There is, however, no certain cure for alcoholism. One problem is that our society tends to encourage social drinking and to tolerate the first stage of alcoholism.

SECTION 5 | Assessment

1. **Review the Vocabulary** How are addiction, tolerance, and withdrawal related to drug abuse?

2. **Visualize the Main Idea** Use an outline similar to the one below to list characteristics of an antisocial personality.

   I. Characteristics of an Antisocial Personality
      A. _____
      B. _____

3. **Recall Information** What are the three stages of alcoholism? How can alcohol lead to psychological dependence?

4. **Think Critically** How do personality disorders differ from other psychological disorders?

5. **Application Activity** Create a questionnaire for teens to help them determine when drinking alcohol becomes a problem.

Summary and Vocabulary

When people's psychological processes break down, they can no longer function on a daily basis.

Section 1 | What Are Psychological Disorders?

Main Idea: Psychologists draw the line between normal and abnormal behavior by looking at deviance, adjustment, and psychological health.

- One approach to defining abnormality is to say that whatever most people do is normal and any deviation from the majority is abnormal.
- Abnormality can be viewed as an inability to adjust to getting along in the world—physically, emotionally, and socially.
- Psychiatrists use the DSM-IV to help them classify psychological disorders.

Section 2 | Anxiety Disorders

Main Idea: Anxiety disorders are marked by excessive fear, caution, and attempts to avoid anxiety.

- Generalized anxiety is often accompanied by physical symptoms.
- Other anxiety disorders include phobic, obsessive-compulsive, post-traumatic stress, and panic disorders.

Section 3 | Somatoform and Dissociative Disorders

Main Idea: Dealing with anxiety and stress can lead to somatoform and dissociative disorders.

- Somatoform disorders are psychological problems in which symptoms are focused on the body.
- Dissociative disorders involve a breakdown in a person's normal conscious experience.

Section 4 | Schizophrenia and Mood Disorders

Main Idea: Schizophrenia involves disordered thoughts. Mood disorders involve disturbances in the experience and expressions of depression.

- Schizophrenia is a collection of symptoms relating to impairments in cognition, emotion, perception, and motor movement.
- Psychologists have classified several types of schizophrenia.
- Types of mood disorders are major depressive disorder, bipolar disorder, and seasonal affective disorder.

Section 5 | Personality Disorders and Drug Addiction

Main Idea: Personality disorders and drug addiction prohibit normal relationships and normal functioning.

- People with personality disorders seem unable to establish meaningful relationships with other people or to adapt to their social environment.
- Abuse of drugs often involves psychological dependence, addiction, tolerance, and sometimes withdrawal.

Chapter Vocabulary

DSM-IV (p. 451)

anxiety (p. 456)

phobia (p. 456)

panic disorder (p. 457)

post-traumatic stress disorder (p. 459)

somatoform disorder (p. 461)

conversion disorder (p. 461)

dissociative disorder (p. 462)

dissociative amnesia (p. 462)

dissociative fugue (p. 462)

dissociative identity disorder (p. 462)

schizophrenia (p. 466)

delusions (p. 466)

hallucinations (p. 466)

major depressive disorder (p. 470)

bipolar disorder (p. 471)

personality disorders (p. 475)

antisocial personality (p. 475)

psychological dependence (p. 476)

addiction (p. 476)

tolerance (p. 476)

withdrawal (p. 477)

CHAPTER 16 Assessment

Self-Check Quiz
Visit the *Understanding Psychology* Web site at psychology.glencoe.com and click on **Chapter 16— Self-Check Quizzes** to prepare for the Chapter Test.

Reviewing Vocabulary

Choose the letter of the correct term or concept below to complete the sentence.

a. DSM-IV
b. phobia
c. anxiety
d. post-traumatic stress disorder
e. somatoform disorder
f. bipolar disorder
g. delusions
h. hallucinations
i. antisocial personality
j. withdrawal

1. An extreme fear of crowds is an example of a(n) _____.

2. A mood disorder in which individuals are excessively and inappropriately happy or unhappy is called a(n) _____.

3. A person who experiences severe and long-lasting aftereffects of a traumatic event is suffering from _____.

4. The _____ is a standard system for classifying abnormal behavior.

5. During _____, an addicted person's body and mind revolt against and finally get used to the absence of a drug.

6. _____ are perceptions in the absence of corresponding sensations.

7. A psychological disorder in which there is no apparent physical cause for certain physical symptoms is known as a(n) _____.

8. People suffering from schizophrenia sometimes experience _____, or false beliefs maintained in the face of contrary evidence.

9. A person who is experiencing a generalized apprehension is suffering from _____.

10. People with a(n) _____ are generally irresponsible and immature.

Recalling Facts

1. In what way does the system psychologists currently use to classify abnormal behavior differ from the one that preceded it?

2. Describe the symptoms associated with anxiety. Give two explanations for the occurrence of anxiety.

3. What is a dissociative fugue? What psychological function might it serve? How does it differ from dissociative amnesia?

4. Use a diagram similar to the one below to list and explain three possible causes of schizophrenia.

Causes

Schizophrenia

5. How would you describe someone who is classified as having an antisocial personality disorder?

Critical Thinking

1. **Synthesizing Information** Develop your own definition of *psychological disorder*. Is your definition free of social values, or are values a necessary part of such a definition? Explain.

2. **Analyzing Information** Consider times you have experienced a general apprehension and try to list the particular settings or situations in which you are most likely to feel this way. How do you cope with your anxiety?

3. **Applying Concepts** Why do you think it can be difficult for people suffering from major depressive disorder to take action to overcome the disorder?

4. **Making Inferences** Why might using drugs to treat schizophrenia be more effective than psychotherapy?

5. **Synthesizing Information** Why do you think people who have been treated for alcohol or drug abuse run the risk of a relapse?

CHAPTER 16 Assessment

Psychology Projects

1. What Are Psychological Disorders? Find out how psychological disorders were viewed in the past. You might focus on the views of ancient Greeks and of Europeans during the Middle Ages. Find out what were thought to be the causes of certain psychological disorders and how people with these disorders were treated. Summarize your findings in a brief report.

2. Anxiety Disorders Research magazine articles about programs available to help people combat certain phobias. For example, you might find out about classes that airlines provide to help people overcome their fear of flying. Summarize the information you find in an "informational pamphlet."

3. Mood Disorders The artist Vincent van Gogh suffered from a mood disorder. Find out how his disorder affected his work. You might provide examples of paintings that were created when he was psychologically healthy and those that were created when he was suffering from the disorder. Create a biography of 1–5 pages that details your findings.

4. Personality Disorders and Drug Addiction Contact a drug rehabilitation center for information about drug treatment programs in your community. If possible, have a qualified person from the center address the class about the kinds of treatment programs available. You might prepare a list of questions in advance to ask the speaker.

Technology Activity
Locate Web sites on the Internet about some of the psychological disorders discussed in this chapter. Find out about the latest methods of diagnosing and treating these disorders. Present your findings in a written report.

Psychology Journal
Read the definitions of the three phobias that you wrote in your journal at the beginning of your study of Chapter 16. Choose one of these phobias and write a paragraph that describes how it can adversely affect an individual.

Building Skills

Interpreting a Graph Review the graph at right, then answer the questions that follow.

1. According to the graph, what is the most common anxiety disorder reported in the United States?
2. What percentage of the United States population reports any anxiety disorder?
3. Do you think that suffering from an anxiety disorder is a common or rare occurrence? Explain.

 See the Skills Handbook, page 628, for an explanation of interpreting graphs.

Reported Anxiety Disorders in the United States, 1999

25%	Any anxiety disorder
13%	Social phobia
11%	Specific phobia
5%	Generalized anxiety
5%	Agoraphobia
4%	Panic
3%	Obsessive-compulsive disorder

Source: Plotnick, *Introduction to Psychology,* 1999.

 Practice and **assess** key social studies skills with **Glencoe Skillbuilder Interactive Workbook CD-ROM, Level 2.**

TIME *REPORTS*

The Grief Brigade

When tragedy strikes, the counselors rush in. They offer support, but their methods are up for debate

By NADYA LABI

WHEN THE LORD OF THE under-world snatched away her beloved daughter, Demeter was inconsolable. She wandered the world and in her misery allowed the fields to lie barren. In modern parlance, she was "in trauma." Today the Greek goddess of agriculture might have talked about her loss, vented her frustration and worked through her grief. Certainly, she would not have been left alone with her sorrow.

Tragedy is immemorial, but we have grown less tolerant of its psychic consequences. In Littleton, Colo., where Hades visited in the guise of two teenage boys, counselors spent 1,500 hours talking to students in the first week after the April 20 shooting. "The trauma is astronomical throughout this community," says Steve Poos-Benson, pastor of a church near Columbine High School. "It has affected even those who casually drive by." Oklahoma City, riven by catastrophes twice in the past four years, has settled into painful routine. At the Community Counseling Center, counselors who helped after the 1995 bombing of the Alfred P. Murrah Federal Building were called on again following recent tornadoes. The American Red Cross, which has more than 80 counselors in the area, put its 2,000 mental-health officials on alert.

Where there is no consolation, there is now counseling. But is it necessarily helpful? The huge growth in such on-the-scene therapy has raised questions about the value of pouring out one's grief to the social workers, psychologists, psychiatrists and clergy who are invariably on hand at disasters to lend empathic support. If local resources feel the strain, the Red Cross, Salvation Army, National Organization for Victim Assistance and a host of other nonprofit organizations send in volunteers. During presidentially declared disasters, the Center for Mental Health Services contributes federal funds for counseling. It spent $10 million in 1998.

The notion of talking through trauma gained currency during World War II, when soldiers were "debriefed" on the beaches of Normandy. In the 1970s, Jeffrey Mitchell, then a paramedic and now president of the International Critical Incident Stress Foundation, developed one of the most popular debriefing models. Intended to be used in conjunction with other services, such as one-on-one counseling and on-scene support, Critical Incident Stress Debriefing is conducted in groups a couple of days after a disaster. Typical questions include "What were the first thoughts that raced through your mind at the time of the crisis?" and "What was the worst moment for you?"

After the Columbine High shooting, school psychologists employed a similar approach, not only with students from Columbine but with those at 12 nearby schools. "Debriefing is a therapeutic opportunity to get people to open up, ask questions and unburden the psychic pain they are carrying around," says Theodore Feinberg, a New York-based psychologist who flew to Littleton as part of a team sent by the National Association of School Psychologists.

But others wonder whether talk is truly the best remedy. British psy-

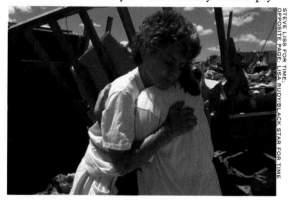

COMFORTING: A counselor hugs the survivor of a tornado amid the ruins of her home in Oklahoma.

STEVE LISS FOR TIME; OPPOSITE PAGE: LISA RUDY/BLACK STAR FOR TIME

chologist Simon Wessely reviewed half a dozen studies of debriefing last year and found that it had no effect. "People race into disaster areas, but there is no research that says people benefit from trauma counseling," according to Tana Dineen, a psychologist who wrote *Manufacturing Victims: What the Psychology Industry Is Doing to People.* "These counselors get people to talk about how upset they are, but they may be doing damage."

The trauma experts handle the immediate aftershocks of disaster. Once they leave, grief counselors take over, providing longer-term help for those who have suffered a loss. The discipline of grief counseling was virtually unknown three decades ago. Today there's a national organization—the Association for Death Education and Counseling—that certifies grief counselors.

Most grief counselors rely on the seminal teachings of J. William Worden, a Harvard psychologist who published *Grief Counseling and Grief Therapy: A Handbook for the Mental Health Practitioner* in 1982. Worden identified four basic tasks of mourning: 1) to accept the reality of the loss; 2) to experience emotions connected to that loss; 3) to adjust to life without the deceased; and 4) to relocate the deceased in one's mind so that progress is possible. Though Worden hoped to inform mental-health counselors about bereavement, he didn't anticipate that his theories would give rise to a veritable industry of professional grief counselors. "I don't know what I've spawned," he says ruefully.

One such counselor is Alan Wolfelt, founder of the Center for Loss and Life Transition in Colorado, who describes himself as "a person who creates safe places for people to mourn." He argues that as life expectancy has increased, Americans have lost the "art" of grieving. "Our culture is full of buck-up therapists who want to move people away from grief," he says. "But you have to feel it to heal it. You have to go through the wilderness."

That kind of sound bite appeals to a generation raised on *Oprah*, but some psychologists are skeptical. George Bonanno, assistant professor of psychology at the Catholic University of America, studied bereaved individuals over 25 months. He found that those who focused on their pain, either by talking about it or displaying it in their facial expressions, tended to have more trouble sleeping and maintaining everyday functions. In other words, there may be benefits to the discredited practice of keeping a stiff upper lip. ∎

—For the complete text of this article and related articles from TIME, please visit www.time.com/teach

How Can Young Survivors Cope?

By **MICHAEL D. LEMONICK**

Living through a bomb attack—the sudden deafening noise; the flying glass and masonry; the bloody, broken bodies and screams of the injured—is traumatic enough to throw most adults into profound shock. But if the grownups who survived the Oklahoma City explosion are numb in its aftermath, what could be going through the minds of the blast's smallest and most vulnerable victims, the children?

Although it is natural to assume that kids would be particularly devastated at seeing their safe world literally fall apart, research suggests that on average, children are no more adversely affected than adults are. That isn't to say there aren't severe emotional consequences. After the initial shock has worn off, children who have survived a shooting, explosion or natural disaster tend to be generally fearful, have trouble sleeping and have difficulty concentrating and carrying on their normal activities. Those who are especially sensitive to stress may suffer from posttraumatic stress disorder, in which the

MOURNING: A service for victims of the 1995 Oklahoma City bombing

mind keeps replaying the trauma with terrifying realism. Others will deny the experience entirely, treating the disaster as a story, often as something that happened to someone else. Many become edgy and almost hyperactive.

One important way to restore these children to emotional health, say the experts, is to reassure them that their once stable world, rocked by a sudden calamity, can right itself again. Children too young to express complex feelings verbally will ask for extra attention in other ways—by regressing to immature behavior, for example, or temporarily losing skills such as toilet training, or clinging to parents or other caretakers. Older children, say psychologists, should be encouraged to ventilate their thoughts and fears. And for kids of all ages, it's important to restore a sense of stability by returning as quickly as possible to a predictable routine. For most children, says Dr. Gaston Blom, a psychiatrist at Boston University Medical School, these measures can ease the anxiety of a traumatic event within a few months.

For very young children, the healing may be much quicker. In kids under 18 months old, some specialists contend, the central nervous system is still too undeveloped for memories to become firmly established. But other experts insist that memories are stored and may resurface when children are old enough to verbalize their trauma. In any case, says Dr. Blom, "we can only give them a stable, warm environment and hope that the nervous system by its immaturity will allow them some relief." ∎

ANALYZING THE ARTICLES

1. What is the purpose of trauma counseling?
2. How is the grief of children different from adults' grief?
3. **CRITICAL THINKING** Why is grief counseling controversial? Do you think that it's better to express grief or hold it in? Why?

Therapy and Change

PSYCHOLOGY
Online

Chapter Overview
Visit the *Understanding Psychology*
Web site at psychology.glencoe.com
and click on **Chapter 17—Chapter
Overviews** to preview the chapter.

PSYCHOLOGY JOURNAL

Recommend a treatment for
the following problems: compulsive overeating, inability to
finish work, severe depression.
Write your recommendations in
your journal. ■

What Is Psychotherapy?

Reader's Guide

■ Main Idea
Psychotherapy is a general term for the several approaches used by mental health professionals to treat psychological disorders.

■ Vocabulary
- psychotherapy
- eclectic approach
- placebo effect
- empathy
- group therapy

■ Objectives
- Explain the nature of psychotherapy.
- Describe the role of a therapist.

EXPLORING PSYCHOLOGY

When Should You Seek Help?

Her husband had brought her to the hospital because she had refused to eat for about three days, slept fitfully, and spent long hours staring off into space. She would speak to those around her, but only after more or less continuous coaxing. In very slow monotonous speech, she commented that she was talking to her dead sister who was wearing a white gown, but with a face eaten up by worms and with part of her eyesocket missing. This hallucination was intermixed with some discussion between the patient and God that seemed to center around a mixture of pleading with Him to do something about her sister and reprimanding Him for letting her get into that condition.

—from *Abnormal Behavior, Psychology's View* by F.B. McMahon, 1976

At certain times of transition and crisis in life, we may feel an urgent need to find someone trustworthy with whom to share our doubts and problems. A parent, relative, or close friend is often helpful in such times of need. Many psychological problems, however, are too bewildering and complex to be solved in this way. When people become dissatisfied or distraught with life and suspect that the reason lies within themselves, they are likely to seek help from someone with training and experience in such matters. These people seek *therapy,* which refers to treatment of behavioral, bodily, or psychological disorders. Mental health professionals who have been trained to deal with the psychological problems of others include psychologists, psychiatrists, and

psychotherapy: any treatment used by therapists to help troubled individuals overcome their problems

social workers. The special kind of help they provide is called psychotherapy. **Psychotherapy** involves three things: verbal interaction between a therapist and client; the development of a supportive and trusting relationship; and an analysis by the therapist of the client's problems, including suggestions for overcoming those problems.

THE NATURE OF PSYCHOTHERAPY

Psychotherapy literally means "healing of the soul," and in early times people often thought that psychological disturbances represented some sort of moral or religious problem. Troubled people were sometimes viewed as being inhabited by devils or demons, and treatment consisted of exorcism—the driving out of these demons by religious ceremonies or by physical punishment. Within the last 200 years, however, views of psychological disorders have changed. Psychological disorders slowly came to be thought of as diseases, and the term *mental illness* was applied to many psychological problems.

That psychological disturbance is seen as the symptom of a disease has helped reduce the stigma associated with such problems, and it has done much to convince society that troubled people need care and treatment. Nevertheless, many psychotherapists feel that the term *mental illness* has outlived its usefulness and that, in fact, it may now be doing more harm than good.

The trouble with letting a person think of himself as mentally ill is that he sees himself in a passive, helpless position. He sees his troubles as being caused by forces over which he has no control. By thinking of himself in this way, the person can avoid taking responsibility for his own situation and for helping himself change.

Functions of Psychotherapy

One of the functions of psychotherapy is to help people realize that they are responsible for their own problems and that, even more importantly, they are the only ones who can really solve these problems. This approach does not imply that people become disturbed on purpose or that no one should need outside help. People often adopt certain techniques for getting along in life that seem appropriate at the time but that lead to trouble in the long run. Such patterns can be difficult for the individual to see or change. The major task of the therapist, therefore, is to help people examine their way of living, to understand

Figure 17.1   Is This Treatment?

In earlier times, people with serious psychological disorders were labeled "mad" or "lunatics." "Treatment" consisted of torture, hanging, burning at the stake, or being sent to sea in "ships of fools" to be saved by fate. *How do you think society regards people with psychological disorders today?*

how their present way of living causes problems, and to start living in new, more beneficial ways. The therapist can be thought of as a guide who is hired by the individual to help him find the source of his problems and some possible solutions.

Main Kinds of Therapy

There are many different kinds of therapy, only a few of which will be described in this chapter: psychoanalysis, humanistic approaches to treatment, cognitive approaches to treatment, behavioral approaches to treatment, and biological approaches to treatment (see Figure 17.2). Each one is based on different theories about how human personality works, and each one is carried out in a different style. Some psychotherapists stick rigorously to one style and consider the others useless. Other psychotherapists use an **eclectic approach** to therapy, choosing methods from many different kinds of therapy and using the one that works best. Whatever the style or philosophy, all types of psychotherapy have certain characteristics in common.

Goals of Therapy

Profiles In Psychology

Dorothea Dix
1802–1887

"I proceed, Gentlemen, briefly to call your attention to the present state of Insane Persons confined within this Commonwealth, in cages, closets, stalls, pens! Chained, naked, beaten with rods, and lashed into obedience!"

Although at the early age of 14 Dorothea Dix established her own school for young children, she is best remembered as an activist for the rights of the mentally ill. In 1841 a member of the clergy asked Dix to teach a Sunday school class at a local prison in Massachusetts. When she arrived at the prison, Dix became horrified to see mentally ill patients locked up with prisoners in dark, unheated, and filthy rooms.

Dix set out on a crusade that would last a lifetime. She toured similar jails throughout several states, reporting to the public the appalling things she witnessed. She saw people chained up and sitting in filth. She found people confined and beaten in prisons whose worst crimes were having psychological disorders. She observed men, women, and children thrown together in jail cells.

At a time when women were thought incapable of speaking in public, Dix reported her findings to state legislatures. Her struggles resulted in the reform of prisons and the treatment of people with psychological disorders.

eclectic approach: method that combines various kinds of therapy or combinations of therapies

The primary goal of psychotherapy is to strengthen the patient's control over his or her life. People seeking psychotherapy want to gain control over their thoughts, feelings, and behaviors. Over the years, they have developed not only certain feelings about themselves but also behaviors that reinforce those feelings. Their behavior and feelings make it impossible for them to reach their goals.

Figure 17.2 **Types of Psychotherapies**

There are several types of therapies. The ones listed in this chart are commonly used methods. *Which method would probably be most effective for treating someone with an eating disorder?*

Therapy Method	Main Technique(s)	Main Goal	Means of Achieving Goal
Psychoanalysis	Free association, dream analysis, transference	Reduce anxiety and guilt over unconscious urges	Verbal processes
Humanistic Therapy	Active listening, acceptance, support	Help see and fulfill one's potential	Verbal processes
Cognitive Therapy	Rational-emotive therapy; Beck's cognitive therapy	Unite behaviors and thought	Mental training
Behavior Therapy	Counterconditioning, operant conditioning, systematic desensitization	Change one's unwanted or abnormal behaviors and acquire desirable behaviors	Behavioral training

placebo effect: the influence that a patient's hopes and expectations have on his or her improvement during therapy

One of the most important factors in effective treatment is the patient's belief or hope that he can change. The influence that a patient's hopes and expectations have on his improvement is often called the **placebo effect.** This name comes from giving medical patients placebos, harmless sugar pills, when they complain of ailments that do not seem to have any physiological basis. The patients take the tablets, and their symptoms disappear.

The placebo effect does not imply that problems can be solved simply by fooling the patient. It does demonstrate, however, the tremendous importance of the patient's attitude in finding a way to change. A patient who does not believe he can be helped probably cannot be. A patient who believes he can change and believes he has the power to change will find a way. Therapy goes beyond the placebo effect. It combines the patient's belief that he can change with hard work and professional guidance.

WHO ARE THERAPISTS?

In American society, there are many people who practice psychotherapy. Some, like clinical neuropsychologists, are trained in psychology and physiology; others, like counseling psychologists, have different forms of formal training. The various kinds of therapists and the training that each goes through before practicing psychotherapy are shown in Figure 17.3.

What Makes a Good Therapist?

Before going to a professional therapist, most people first turn to a friend or other nonprofessional for help and advice. Sometimes, this is exactly what's needed. Professional therapists, however, are likely to be more skillful in encouraging the person to examine uncomfortable feelings and problems.

There are three characteristics found in effective therapists. First, a therapist needs to be psychologically healthy. A therapist who is anxious, defensive, and withdrawn will not be able to see the patient's problems clearly. A second important characteristic is **empathy,** a capacity for warmth and understanding. Troubled people are usually fearful and confused about explaining their problems. The therapist needs to be able to give the patient confidence that he is capable of caring and understanding. Finally, a good therapist must be experienced in dealing with people and understanding their complexities. Only by having worked with many people can a therapist learn when to give support, when to insist that the patient stand on his own feet, and how to make sense of the things people say.

empathy: capacity for warmth and understanding

GROUP THERAPIES

In some forms of therapy, the patient is alone with the therapist. In **group therapy,** however, she is in the company of other patients. There are several advantages to this situation. A person in group therapy has a

group therapy: patients work together with the aid of a leader to resolve interpersonal problems

Figure 17.3	**Kinds of Therapists**

Clinical psychologists are therapists with a Ph.D. or a Psy.D., a Doctor of Psychology. They treat people with psychological disorders in hospitals and clinics.

Counseling psychologists generally have a master's or Ph.D. degree in counseling psychology. They usually work in educational institutions, where they are available for consultation about personal problems. They customarily refer clients with serious problems to clinical psychologists or psychiatrists.

Clinical Neuropsychologists have Ph.D. degrees. They have extensive education in neurophysiology regarding the mechanisms and operation of the brain. They typically work with patients who have a brain injury that is interfering with normal behavior. Such damage may result from drug use, accidents, or normal aging. Their primary role has been in assessing neurological damage; some are now involved in therapy.

Psychiatrists are medical doctors. They take postgraduate training in abnormal behavior. Because of their medical background, psychiatrists are the primary group licensed to prescribe medicines and the only group that can perform operations.

Psychoanalysts are usually medical doctors who have taken special training in the theory of personality and techniques of psychotherapy of Sigmund Freud, typically at a psychoanalytic institute. They must themselves be psychoanalyzed before they can practice.

Psychiatric social workers are people with a master's degree in social work. They counsel people with everyday problems.

Psychiatric nurses have a standard nursing license and advanced training in psychology. They dispense medicine and act as a contact person between counseling sessions.

Counselors have a master's degree from a counseling program. They dispense a great deal of advice. They may or may not have any training in psychology. Nevertheless, more troubled people turn to counselors than to professionals.

Several groups of people practice psychotherapy. Not all of them have professional training in psychology. *What is the difference between a counselor and a psychoanalyst?*

chance to see how other people are struggling with problems similar to her own, and she discovers what other people think of her. She, in turn, can express what she thinks of them, and in this exchange she discovers where she is mistaken in her views of herself and of other people and where she is correct (Drum, 1990). In group therapy she can also see other people with similar problems recovering, giving her the hope of recovery.

Reading Check
What are the advantages of group therapy?

Another advantage to group therapy is that one therapist can help a large number of people. Most group-therapy sessions are led by a trained therapist who makes suggestions, clarifies points, and keeps activities from getting out of hand. In this way, her training and experience are used to help as many as 20 people at once, although 8–10 is a more comfortable number. It is possible to use psychoanalytical, cognitive, and behavioral techniques in a group setting.

Family Therapy

Therapists often suggest, after talking to a patient, that the entire family unit should work at group therapy. This method is particularly useful because the members of the group are all people of great importance in one another's lives. In *family therapy,* it is possible to untangle the twisted web of relationships that has led one or more members of the family to experience emotional suffering.

Often family members are unhappy because they are mistreating or are being mistreated by other family members in ways no one understands or wants to talk about. The family therapist can point out what is happening from an objective viewpoint and can suggest ways of improving communication and fairness in the family. Not all group therapies are run by professionals, however. Some of the most successful examples are provided in nonprofessional organizations, such as self-help groups.

| Figure 17.4 | **Family Therapy** |

In a family-therapy session, the therapist observes the interactions in order to discern, describe, and treat the patterns that contribute to the disturbance of one or more of its members. *What does a skilled therapist provide in a family-therapy session?*

Self-Help Groups

An increasing number of *self-help groups* have emerged in recent years. These voluntary groups, composed of people who share a particular problem, are often conducted without the active involvement of a professional therapist.

During regularly scheduled meetings, members of the group come together to discuss their difficulties and to provide support and possible solutions.

Self-help groups have been formed to deal with problems ranging from alcoholism, overeating, and drug addiction to child abuse, widowhood, single parenting, adjusting to cancer, and gambling. The best-known self-help group is Alcoholics Anonymous (AA), which was founded in 1935. Far more people find treatment for their drinking problems through AA than in psychotherapy or treatment centers. Many self-help groups have based their organizations on the AA model in which individual members can call on other members for help and emotional support.

The purpose of Alcoholics Anonymous is "to carry the AA message to the sick alcoholic who wants it." According to AA, the only way for alcoholics to change is to admit publicly that they are powerless over alcohol and that their lives have become unmanageable. Alcoholics must come to believe that only some power greater than themselves can help them. Those who think they can battle out the problem alone will not be successful. There are also AA groups for family members for mutual support.

Members of AA usually meet at least once a week to discuss the meaning of this message, to talk about their experiences with alcohol, and to describe the new hope they have found with AA. Mutual encouragement, friendship, and an emphasis on personal responsibility are used to keep an individual sober.

AA logo

DOES PSYCHOTHERAPY WORK?

In 1952 Hans Eysenck published a review of five studies of the effectiveness of psychoanalytic treatment and 19 studies of the effectiveness of "eclectic" psychotherapy, treatment in which several different therapeutic approaches are combined. Eysenck concluded that psychotherapy was no more effective than no treatment at all. According to his interpretation of these 24 studies, only 44 percent of the psychoanalytic patients improved with treatment, while 64 percent of those given eclectic psychotherapy were "cured" or had improved.

Most startling, Eysenck argued that even this 64 percent improvement rate did not demonstrate the effectiveness of psychotherapy, since it has been reported that 72 percent of a group of hospitalized neurotics improved without treatment. If no treatment at all leads to as much improvement as psychotherapy, the obvious conclusion is that psychotherapy is not effective. Eysenck (1966) vigorously defended his controversial position, which generated a large number of additional reviews and a great many studies of the effectiveness of psychotherapy.

> ## Did You Know?
>
> **Conducting Therapy** There are four areas of concern that a therapist might discuss with the patient.
>
> 1) Identify the problem behavior based on the classification scheme for psychological disorders.
> 2) Propose some ideas about the history and cause of the problem.
> 3) Explain the details of what is included in the treatment program.
> 4) Make a time line for the course of treatment.

More About...

Therapy and HMOs

Recent economic trends have affected the length of time a person spends in psychotherapy. People who receive their health care through health maintenance organizations (HMOs) pay a fixed amount of money per month for health care. The HMO will then pay for only a certain amount of therapy per month. The HMO in effect minimizes the amount of services a person can obtain, so a person who requires extensive therapy may not be able to get it unless he pays for it on his own.

Allen Bergin (1971) wrote one of the most thoughtful and carefully reasoned reviews. Bergin's review leads one to question the validity of Eysenck's sweeping generalization that psychotherapy is no more effective than no treatment at all. Much of Bergin's argument is based on differences of opinion about how patients should be classified. Precise criteria for "improvement" are difficult to define and apply. Some people may experience "spontaneous remission," or the sudden disappearance of symptoms without therapy at all. However, such people may have received help from unacknowledged sources—family, friends, relatives, religious advisers, or family physicians. Additionally, if, as some researchers believe, the prime ingredient in therapy is the establishment of a close relationship, then "spontaneous remission" in people who have received continuing help from such sources is not spontaneous at all.

An analysis of nearly 400 studies on the effectiveness of psychotherapy, conducted by Mary Lee Smith and Gene V. Glass (1977), used elaborate statistical procedures to estimate the effects of psychotherapy. They found that therapy is generally more effective than no treatment and that on the average most forms of therapy have similar effects; that is, therapy may improve the quality of life for the patients. Will any therapy do for any client? Probably not. Smith and Glass were able to show that for some specific clients and situations, some forms of therapy would be expected to have a greater effect than others. Together, the psychologist and client may discuss the appropriate form of psychotherapy to achieve a cure.

SECTION 1 Assessment

1. **Review the Vocabulary** Cite and describe two examples of group therapy and how these types of therapy help patients.

2. **Visualize the Main Idea** In a diagram similar to the one below, list and describe the characteristics that make a good, effective therapist.

Characteristics of a Good Therapist

3. **Recall Information** What are the goals of therapy? What is the eclectic approach to therapy?

4. **Think Critically** When should a person seek psychotherapy? Explain your answer.

5. **Application Activity** You have a family member who is unsure of himself. He does not know what he wants to do with his future. He needs the help of a professional to get his personal life on track. Identify the kind of psychotherapy and the kind of therapist that might help your family member and explain your choices.

Psychoanalysis and Humanistic Therapy

Reader's Guide

■ Main Idea
Psychoanalysis is an analysis of the conscious and unconscious mind based on the theories of psychiatrist Sigmund Freud. Humanistic therapy helps people reach their full potential.

■ Vocabulary
- psychoanalysis
- insight
- free association
- resistance
- dream analysis
- transference
- humanistic therapy
- client-centered therapy
- nondirective therapy
- active listening
- unconditional positive regard

■ Objectives
- Describe psychoanalysis and its aims.
- Explain humanistic therapy and its goals.

EXPLORING PSYCHOLOGY

What Does This Dream Mean?

I was a child again, and riding my bicycle along the village street, but its wheels began to sink into sticky, muddy earth, so that I could barely move. Finally, however, the earth began to dry, and I found that I was able to cycle along quite easily once more.

—from *Parker's Complete Book of Dreams* by Julia and Derek Parker, 1995

The dream above was experienced by an elderly lady who was fighting a serious illness. Psychoanalysts might interpret the dream in the following manner: the earth symbolized the illness as well as the lady's concern that she might die. As a child, she had never been allowed to own a bicycle, so possessing one represented freedom. The bike symbolized something she badly wanted—good health. Psychoanalysts would then use this information—the dream interpretation—to help this lady understand the psychological dilemmas she faces.

WHAT IS PSYCHOANALYSIS?

psychoanalysis: therapy aimed at making patients aware of their unconscious motives so that they can gain control over their behavior

For a long time **psychoanalysis** was the only formalized psychotherapy practiced in Western society. It was this type of therapy that gave rise to the classic picture of a bearded Viennese doctor seated behind a patient who is lying on a couch.

Psychoanalysis is based on the theories of Sigmund Freud. According to Freud, psychological disturbances are due to anxiety about hidden conflicts among the unconscious components of one's personality. (Freud's theory of personality is described in Chapter 14.) One job of the psychoanalyst, therefore, is to help make the patients aware of the unconscious impulses, desires, and fears that are causing the anxiety. Psychoanalysts believe that if patients can understand their unconscious motives, they have taken the first step toward gaining control over their behavior and freeing themselves of their problems. Such understanding is

insight: the sudden realization of the solution to a problem

called **insight.**

Free Association

Psychoanalysis is a slow procedure. It may take years of 50-minute sessions several times a week before the patient is able to make fundamental changes in her life. Throughout this time, the analyst assists his patient in a thorough examination of the unconscious motives behind her behavior. This task begins with the analyst telling the patient to relax and talk about everything that comes into her mind. This method is called

free association: a method used to examine the unconscious; the patient is instructed to say whatever comes into his or her mind

free association. The patient may consider her passing thoughts too unimportant or too embarrassing to mention. The analyst suggests that she express everything—the thought that seems most inconsequential may, in fact, offer insight into the unconscious.

As the patient lies on the couch, she may describe her dreams, discuss private thoughts, or recall long-forgotten experiences. The psychoanalyst often says nothing for long periods of time. The psychoanalyst also occasionally makes remarks or asks questions that guide the patient, or he may suggest an unconscious motive or factor that explains something the patient has been talking about, but most of the work is done by the patient herself.

The patient is understandably reluctant to reveal painful feelings and to examine lifelong patterns that need to be changed, and as the analysis proceeds, she is likely to unconsciously try to hold back the flow of information. This phenomenon—in fact, any behavior that impedes the course of therapy—is called **resistance.** The patient may have agreed to

resistance: the reluctance of a patient either to reveal painful feelings or to examine long-standing behavior patterns

cooperate fully, yet she finds at times that her mind is blank, that she feels powerless and can no longer think of anything to say. At such times the analyst will simply point out what is happening and wait for the patient to continue. The analyst may also suggest another line of approach to the area of resistance. By analyzing the patient's resistances, both the therapist and the patient can understand how the patient deals with anxiety-provoking material.

Dream Analysis

Freud believed that dreams express unconscious thoughts and feelings. In a technique known as **dream analysis,** the psychoanalyst interprets the client's dreams to find out about unconscious thoughts and feelings.

Freud believed that dreams contain manifest and latent content. *Manifest content* refers to what you remember about your dream. For instance, you recall seeing your house fall apart, brick by brick, in last night's dream. *Latent content* refers to the hidden meanings represented symbolically in the dream that the therapist interprets from the manifest content. For example, a therapist might interpret a dream involving a deteriorating house to mean that you are upset about current health problems or are worried about your health.

Figure 17.5   What Do Our Dreams Mean?

While we sleep, our dreams probably do not follow logical thought patterns. Because of this, Freud considered dreams the purest form of free association. *What do therapists hope to learn from analyzing dreams?*

Transference

Sooner or later, the analyst begins to appear in the patient's associations and dreams. The patient may begin feeling toward the analyst the way she feels toward some other important figure in her life. This process is called **transference.**

If the patient can recognize what is happening, transference may allow her to experience her true feelings toward the important person. Often, instead of experiencing and understanding her feelings, the patient simply begins acting toward the therapist in the same way she used to act toward the important person, usually one of her parents.

The therapist does not allow the patient to resort to these tactics. Remaining impersonal and anonymous, the therapist always directs the patient back to herself. The therapist may ask, for example, "What do you see when you imagine my face?" The patient may reply that she sees the therapist as an angry, frowning, unpleasant figure. The therapist never takes this personally. Instead, he may calmly say, "What does this make you think of?" Gradually, it will become clear to both patient and therapist that the patient is reacting to the neutral therapist as though he were a threatening father, for example.

By understanding why she is engaging in transference, the patient becomes aware of her real feelings and motivations. She may begin to understand, for example, why she has trouble with her boss at work: she may be seeing her boss, her therapist—and indeed any man in a position of authority—in the same way that as a child she saw her father.

The purpose of psychoanalysis is to show the role of the unconscious and to provide insight for the client. This type of classical psyche (mind) analysis, however, is not for everyone. It requires an average of 600 sessions and years of meeting with a psychoanalyst. Psychoanalysis has

dream analysis: a technique used by psychoanalysts to interpret the content of patients' dreams

transference: the process, experienced by the patient, of feeling toward an analyst or therapist the way he or she feels or felt toward some other important figure in his or her life changed with patients, disorders, and the prevailing cultures. There are many versions available today of this classical psychoanalysis. For example, *short-term dynamic psychotherapy* is a shortened version of psychoanalysis. This type of therapy focuses on a client's problems. The therapist uses a direct and more active approach in identifying and resolving the problems. This approach to therapy, along with psychoanalysis, works well for clients who are able to gain insight into their behavior. People who lose touch with reality—for instance, a person suffering from schizophrenia—will probably not benefit from psychoanalysis, though.

"Of course you have strengths, dear. It's just that you don't communicate them."

Figure 17.6	Humanistic Approaches to Therapy

Humanistic therapies attempt to help clients make better use of their own abilities. *How does this cartoon reflect a humanistic approach?*

humanistic therapy: focuses on the value, dignity, and worth of each person; holds that healthy living is the result of realizing one's full potential

client-centered therapy: reflects the belief that the client and therapist are partners in therapy

Reading Check
Why did Rogers choose to refer to a patient as a "client"?

nondirective therapy: the free flow of images and ideas, with no particular direction

HUMANISTIC THERAPY

The goal of **humanistic therapy** is to help people fulfill their human potential. Humanistic psychology has given rise to several approaches to psychotherapy, known collectively as **client-centered therapy.** Humanistic psychologists stress the actualization of one's unique potentials through personal responsibility, freedom of choice, and authentic relationships.

Client-Centered Therapy

Client-centered therapy (also called person-centered therapy) is based on the theories of Carl Rogers (1951, 1977). This therapy depends on the person's own motivation toward growth and self-actualization. The use of the term "person" or "client" instead of "patient" gives one an insight into the reasoning behind Rogers's method. "Patient" may suggest inferiority, whereas "person" or "client" implies an equal relationship between the therapist and the individual seeking help. According to Rogers, this equal relationship reflects three therapeutic components: positive regard, empathy, and genuineness. Positive regard refers to the therapist's ability to demonstrate caring and respect for the client. Empathy is the ability to understand what the client is feeling. Genuineness refers to the therapist's ability to act toward the client in a real and nondefensive manner.

Client-centered therapists assume that people are basically good and that they are capable of handling their own lives. Psychological problems arise when the true self becomes lost and the individual comes to view himself according to the standards of others. One of the goals of therapy, therefore, is to help him recognize his own strength and confidence so that he can learn to be true to his own standards and ideas about how to live effectively.

Techniques of Client-Centered Therapy In the course of an interview, the client is encouraged to speak freely about matters that may be bothering him. He is told that what he talks about is up to him. This method is called **nondirective therapy** because the therapist does not direct it. The therapist listens and encourages conversation but tries to avoid giving opinions.

The therapist tries to echo back, as clearly as possible, the feelings the client has expressed. This communication technique is called **active listening.** The therapist may try to extract the main points from the client's hesitant or rambling explanations. Between them, the client and therapist form a clearer picture of how the client really feels about himself, his life, and the people around him.

Client-centered therapy is conducted in an atmosphere of emotional support that Rogers calls **unconditional positive regard.** The therapist never says what she thinks of the client or whether what the client has said is good or bad. Instead she shows the client that she will accept anything that is said without embarrassment, reservation, or anger. The therapist's main responsibility is creating a warm and accepting relationship between herself and her client. This acceptance makes it easier for the client to explore thoughts about himself and his experiences. He is able to abandon old values without fear of disapproval, and he can begin to see himself, his situation, and his relationships with others in a new light and with new confidence.

As he reduces his tensions and releases his emotions, the client feels that he is becoming a more complete person. He gains the courage to accept parts of his personality that he had formerly considered weak or bad, and by recognizing his self-worth, he can set up realistic goals and consider the steps necessary to reach them. The client's movement toward independence signals the end of the need for therapy—he can assume the final steps to independence on his own.

Although client-centered therapy has proved more effective than no treatment, it seems to be no more or less effective than other types of therapy. Client-centered therapy has helped, though, make therapists aware of the importance of developing good relations with their clients.

active listening: empathetic listening; a listener acknowledges, restates, and clarifies the speaker's thoughts and concerns

unconditional positive regard: a therapist's consistent expression of acceptance for the patient, no matter what the patient says and does

PSYCHOLOGY Online

Student Web Activity
Visit the *Understanding Psychology* Web site at psychology.glencoe.com and click on **Chapter 17— Student Web Activities** for an activity about psychotherapy.

SECTION 2 Assessment

1. **Review the Vocabulary** Cite and describe the techniques involved in client-centered therapy.

2. **Visualize the Main Idea** In a chart similar to the one below, list and describe the main processes involved in psychoanalysis.

Processes of Psychoanalysis
1
2
3
4

3. **Recall Information** What is the purpose of dream analysis? How do therapists use it?

4. **Think Critically** What are the main differences between psychoanalysis and humanistic therapy?

5. **Application Activity** Some therapists may view therapy as a process of teaching a client a philosophy of life. Do you think this therapy goal is appropriate? Does this goal assume the therapist has the *better* philosophy of life? Argue your point in an editorial-type essay.

The Case of *Rat Man*

Period of Study: Early 1900s

Introduction: Sigmund Freud used psychoanalysis with a patient Freud referred to as *Rat Man*. A 29-year-old man came to Freud complaining of various fears, obsessions, and compulsions, or cravings, which had been occurring for approximately six years. These symptoms had prevented the man from completing his university studies and attaining success at work. Freud focused on Rat Man's uncontrollable fantasy in which the man would see his father and girlfriend tied down and being tortured by hungry rats strapped to their flesh.

Hypothesis: Freud's earliest hypothesis was that Rat Man maintained a conflict over whether he should marry his girlfriend or not. Since Rat Man was unable to decide consciously, he resolved this issue through his unconscious mind. These unconscious thoughts produced disturbing pictures in his mind, thus making him unable to carry out daily activities such as school and work. Freud also theorized that past love and hate issues between Rat Man and his father caused the father to be in Rat Man's dreams and fantasies.

Method: Freud began therapy with Rat Man by using a psychoanalytic technique called *free association*. Freud asked Rat Man to free-associate with the word *rats*. Rat Man came up with the word *rates,* referring to installments or money. In an earlier session, Rat Man indicated his girlfriend had little money and his father had always wanted him to marry a wealthy woman. Freud deduced the rat fantasies were related to the father's opposition to Rat Man's girlfriend.

In another instance during therapy, Rat Man described an event relayed to him by his mother, which had taken place when he was around four years of age. Rat Man claimed his mother had told him that as a little boy he had once bitten the nurse who was taking care of his father. Rat Man's father began to beat him immediately after the incident occurred. Rat Man responded to the beatings with a multitude of angry and harsh words directed toward his father. After hearing those words, Rat Man's father never beat him again. Freud suggested that the act of Rat Man biting the nurse was a sexual action. Since his father beat him for indulging in his sexual needs (biting), Rat Man developed a fright of fulfilling his needs for a relationship in fear he would be beaten.

A major breakthrough occurred when Rat Man revealed another fantasy he had been having. In this fantasy, Rat Man was persuaded to marry Freud's daughter. These wishes came directly from Freud himself (according to Rat Man's fantasy). Freud immediately interrupted and stated that Rat Man was replacing the role of his father with Freud. Moments later Rat Man became emotionally enraged at his therapist, and this rage ended with an intense fear that Freud would beat him. This signified a chief discovery. Freud convinced Rat Man he was reliving the event with his father by placing the therapist in the father's role.

Results: Before therapy, Rat Man had never consciously experienced anger toward his father. This anger came out in therapy sessions. To Freud, the rats biting into and destroying Rat Man's father and girlfriend symbolized significant past events: Rat Man biting his first love, or the nurse, and in another essence *biting* his father with angry words. According to Freud, Rat Man's conscious acceptance of the feelings of fear and anger toward his father would lead to a recovery. However, Rat Man was never able to fully enjoy the newly found insights. Shortly after his sessions with Freud, Rat Man was killed in World War I.

Analyzing the Case Study

1. Why did Rat Man seek therapy?

2. What was Freud's strategy in treating Rat Man?

3. Critical Thinking   How did Rat Man demonstrate transference? How did this transference help in therapy?

Cognitive and Behavior Therapies

Reader's Guide

■ Main Idea
Cognitive and behavior therapies help clients develop new ways of thinking and behaving.

■ Vocabulary
- behavior modification
- cognitive therapy
- rational-emotive therapy (RET)
- behavior therapy
- systematic desensitization
- aversive conditioning
- contingency management
- token economy
- cognitive-behavior therapy

■ Objectives
- Describe cognitive therapies and their aims.
- Explain the processes and goals of behavior therapy.

EXPLORING PSYCHOLOGY

Imagine That!
Five times a day for several days, Brooks Workman stopped what she was doing and vividly imagined herself opening a soft drink can. She made a special point of picturing herself bringing the can to her mouth and placing her lips on it. Just as she was about to drink, hordes of roaches poured out of the can and scurried into her mouth, writhing, twitching, and wiggling their feelers.

—from *Toward a Self-Managed Life Style* by R.L. Williams and J.D. Long, 1979

W hy would someone purposefully imagine the scene in the story above? Brooks's behavior was not as strange as it sounds. She was trying to cut down on the number of soft drinks she had each day. To achieve her goal, she used a method to change her behavior known as **behavior modification.** Brooks Workman used behavior modification, also known as behavior therapy, to eliminate an undesirable behavior. In this section we will examine behavior and cognitive therapies.

behavior modification: a systematic method of changing the way a person acts and feels

COGNITIVE THERAPY

The goal of **cognitive therapies** focuses on changing the way people think (Beck, 1991). Basic assumptions that cognitive therapies share are that faulty cognitions—our irrational or uninformed beliefs, expectations, and

cognitive therapy: using thoughts to control emotions and behaviors

Figure 17.7   **Examples of Irrational Thinking**

Albert Ellis (1961) asserted that the irrational ideas we believe stand in the way of achieving lives that are free of anxiety. *How might a RET therapist counter these irrational beliefs?*

Everything I do must be approved and loved by virtually everybody.

I have to be completely competent, totally in control, and successful in everything I do.

It is catastrophic when things are not going the way I want them to go.

My unhappiness is not my fault. People and events over which I have no control are responsible.

Anytime I encounter something that I fear, I need to be consumed with worries and upset about it.

It is easier to avoid life's difficulties and responsibilities than to develop a better system for meeting them.

My life and the people with whom I work should be changed from the way they are.

The best I can do for myself is to relax and enjoy life. Inaction and passivity are the best bet to maximize my own enjoyment.

ways of thinking—distort our behaviors, attitudes, and emotions, and to improve our lives, we need to change our thinking patterns.

In what other ways are cognitive therapies similar? According to some psychologists (Ross, 1977), all of these theories follow one or more of the three principles: disconfirmation, reconceptualization, and insight. *Disconfirmation* means clients may be confronted with evidence that directly contradicts their existing beliefs. In *reconceptualization,* clients work toward an alternative belief system to explain their experiences or current observations. In *insight,* clients work toward understanding how they derived these new or revised beliefs.

Rational-Emotive Therapy

rational-emotive therapy (RET): aimed at changing unrealistic assumptions about oneself and other people

Albert Ellis developed a form of therapy called **rational-emotive therapy (RET)** (1973). Ellis believed that people behave in deliberate and rational ways, given their assumptions about life. Emotional problems arise when an individual's assumptions are unrealistic (see Figure 17.7).

Suppose a man seeks therapy when a woman leaves him. He cannot stand the fact that she has rejected him. Without her, his life is empty and miserable. She has made him feel utterly worthless. He must get her back. Like a spoiled child, the man is demanding that the woman love him. He expects—indeed, insists—that things will always go his way. Given this assumption, the only possible explanation for her behavior is that something is dreadfully wrong, either with him or with her.

What is wrong, in the therapist's view, is the man's thinking. By defining his feelings for the woman as need rather than desire, he—not she—is causing his depression. When you convince yourself that you need someone, you will in fact be unable to carry on without that person. When you believe that you cannot stand rejection, you will in fact fall apart when you encounter rejection. This kind of faulty thinking is based on unreasonable attitudes, false premises, and rigid roles for behaviors.

The goal of rational-emotive therapy is to correct these false and self-defeating beliefs. Rejection is unpleasant, but it is not unbearable. The woman may be very desirable, but she is not irreplaceable. To teach the individual to think in realistic terms, the RET therapist may use a number of techniques. One is role playing so that the person can see how his beliefs affect his relationships. Another technique is modeling to demonstrate other ways of thinking and acting. A third is humor to underline the absurdity of his beliefs. Still another technique is simple persuasion. The therapist may also assign homework to give the man practice in acting more reasonably. For example, the therapist may instruct him to ask women who are likely to reject him out on dates. Why? He will learn that he can cope with things not going his way.

Ellis liked to teach that behaviors are the result of the ABCs. *A* refers to the *Activating* event. *B* is the person's *Belief* system about the event. *C* refers to the *Consequences* that follow. Ellis claimed it is not the event that causes trouble but rather the way a person thinks about the event. In other words, A does not cause C, but instead B causes C (see Figure 17.8).

In therapy, the therapist and client work to change B, the belief. Ellis believes that the individual must take three steps to cure or correct himself. First, he must realize that some of his assumptions are false. Second, he must see that he is making himself disturbed by acting on false beliefs. Finally, he must work to break old habits of thought and behavior. He has to practice, to learn self-discipline, to take risks.

Figure 17.8	Ellis's ABCs

Many cognitive therapists believe that our emotional reactions to situations are the result not of the situations but of our beliefs about the situations or our interpretations of the situations. *On what aspect—A, B, or C—do cognitive therapists focus? Why?*

A
Activating event
(e.g., a criticism)

↓

B
Belief
(e.g., "I must be loved by everyone to be happy")

↓

C
Consequent emotion
(e.g., unhappiness)

Beck's Cognitive Therapy

Aaron T. Beck (1967, 1970) introduced another form of cognitive therapy that is similar to Ellis's rational-emotive therapy. The primary difference in Beck's therapy is the focus on illogical thought processes (see Figure 17.9). Beck has therapists—through using persuasion and logic to change existing beliefs—also encourage clients to engage in actual tests of their own beliefs. For example, if a client believes that "I never have a good time," the therapist might point out that this is a hypothesis, not a fact. The therapist might then ask the client to

Figure 17.9	Beck's Maladaptive Thought Patterns

Beck believed that maladaptive thought patterns cause a distorted view of oneself and one's world, leading to various psychological problems. *What is polarized thinking?*

Maladaptive Thought Patterns	Definition	Example
Overgeneralization	Making blanket judgments about oneself	I'm a failure.
Polarized Thinking	Categorizing information into two categories	Most people don't like me.
Selective Attention	Focusing on only one detail of many	People always criticize me.

Quick Lab

How can you help someone overcome an irrational fear?

Systematic desensitization is most used to help individuals overcome fears and anxieties. Could this technique help someone you know?

Procedure

1. Identify a situation that makes someone you know fearful, or you can make up a fear for an imaginary person.

2. Imagine that you are that person. List all the aspects of the situation that you find frightening and rank them in order from the most frightening to least frightening.

3. As a therapist, apply the systematic desensitization technique to help the person overcome the fear; suggest a step-by-step plan.

Analysis

1. Prepare a flowchart showing the steps you would use to help the individual change his or her behavior.

2. Why do you think this technique is often effective in overcoming irrational fears?

See the Skills Handbook, page 622, for an explanation of designing an experiment.

test the hypothesis by looking at the evidence differently and note the times in her life when she actually did have a good time. The therapist's goal is to demonstrate to the client that her automatic thinking may be incorrect and that things are not as bad as they seem.

Beck's work has been very successful with people who are depressed. He believed that depressed people blame themselves instead of their circumstances. He also believed that depressed people focus on only negative events and ignore the positive events. They make pessimistic projections about the future. Finally, he believed they make negative conclusions about self-worth based on events that are not significant.

The goal of Beck's cognitive therapy is to change the way people think. The therapist's job is to determine the pace and direction of the therapy and to help the client detect negative thinking patterns. Therapists also help the client use more reasonable standards for self-evaluation.

Beck may also have clients do homework assignments to assess the true value of his or her beliefs. They may be asked to engage in behaviors that test these beliefs outside of the office. For example, a person who is not very assertive may be asked to "butt" into a line at the grocery store, to interrupt people who are talking, or to ask someone for a favor.

BEHAVIOR THERAPIES

behavior therapy: changing undesirable behavior through conditioning techniques

In **behavior therapy** there is emphasis on one's behavior rather than one's thoughts, as in cognitive therapy. Rather than spending large amounts of time going into the patient's past or the details of his or her dreams, the behavior therapist concentrates on determining what is specifically troubling in the patient's life and takes steps to change it. The goal of behavior therapy is behavior modification.

The idea behind behavior therapy is that a disturbed person is one who has learned to behave in an undesirable way and that any behavior that is learned can be unlearned. The therapist's job, therefore, is to "reeducate" the patient. The reasons for the patient's undesirable behavior are not important; what is important is to change the behavior. By changing one's behavior, one's thoughts change as well. The person is asked to list concrete examples and behavioral goals. Once these behaviors have been targeted, a program to correct these goals is developed. To bring about such changes, the therapist uses certain conditioning techniques first discovered in animal laboratories.

Counterconditioning

One behavioral technique used by behavior therapists is counterconditioning. This technique pairs the stimulus that triggers an unwanted behavior (such as the fear of snakes) with a new, more desirable behavior. The therapist helps the client reduce anxiety by pairing relaxation with anxiety-producing situations. Counterconditioning is a three-step process: (1) the person builds an anxiety hierarchy with the least feared situation on the bottom and the most feared situation on top, (2) the person learns deep muscle relaxation, (3) the person imagines or experiences each step in the hierarchy while learning to be relaxed. Since it is impossible to maintain both relaxation and anxiety, the idea is to teach the person that the situation does not have to be anxiety producing. Using the anxiety hierarchy, the person progresses through each step after successfully completing the previous one.

Systematic desensitization is a counterconditioning technique used to overcome irrational fears and anxieties the patient has learned (Wolper, 1961). The goal of systematic desensitization therapy is to encourage people to imagine the feared situation while relaxing, thus extinguishing the fear response (see Figure 17.10). For example, suppose a student is terrified of speaking in front of large groups—that, in fact, his stage fright is so tremendous that he is unable to speak when called upon in class. How would systematic desensitization therapy effectively change this person's behavior?

The therapist might have the student make a list of all the aspects of talking to others that he finds frightening. Perhaps the most frightening aspect is actually standing before an audience, whereas the least frightening is speaking to a single other person. The client ranks his fears, from the most frightening on down. Then the therapist begins teaching the patient muscle relaxation. Once he knows how to relax completely, the client is ready for the next step. The client tries to imagine as vividly as possible the least disturbing scene on his list. As he thinks about speaking to a single stranger, the student may feel a mild anxiety. Because the therapist has taught him how to relax, the patient learns to think about the experience without feeling afraid. The basic logic is that a person cannot feel anxious and relaxed at the same time. The therapist attempts to replace anxiety with its opposite, relaxation, through counterconditioning.

systematic desensitization: a technique to help a patient overcome irrational fears and anxieties

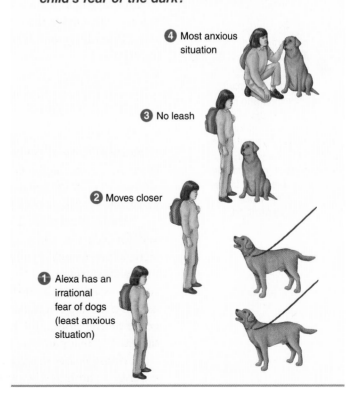

Figure 17.10	**Losing Fears**

Counterconditioning techniques, such as systematic desensitization, are used to help people overcome their irrational fears and anxieties. *What steps might be used to desensitize a child's fear of the dark?*

4 Most anxious situation

3 No leash

2 Moves closer

1 Alexa has an irrational fear of dogs (least anxious situation)

Did You Know?

Virtual-Reality Therapy Some therapists use virtual reality in therapy. They equip their clients with helmets that display a virtual-reality scene. For instance, if you are afraid of heights, your therapist might expose you to a virtual-reality scene in which you are riding a glass elevator to the 74th floor of a building. The therapist can closely monitor your situation and turn off the display or remove your helmet if you become too agitated.

The patient and therapist then progress step-by-step through the list of anxiety-arousing events. The patient reaches a point where he is able to imagine the situations that threaten him the most without feeling anxiety. Now the therapist starts to expose the person to real-life situations that have previously frightened him. Therapy finally reaches the point where the student is able to deliver an unrehearsed speech to a full auditorium.

Flooding refers to another treatment in which a therapist exposes the client to a feared object or situation. For example, let's say that you are deathly afraid of snakes. Your therapist might have you imagine yourself in a room full of snakes or have you hold a snake. This makes your heart rate soar, but it cannot stay that way forever. Eventually your heart rate returns to normal, and you realize that you have survived this test—you have faced your fear. You have begun to overcome your fear.

Behavior therapists also use *modeling* to teach a client to do something by watching someone else do it. For example, when teaching clients how to be assertive, a therapist might demonstrate ways to be assertive. The client watches and then tries to imitate the behavior.

aversive conditioning: links an unpleasant state with an unwanted behavior in an attempt to eliminate the behavior

Aversive Conditioning In **aversive conditioning**, the goal is to make certain acts unpleasant so that they will be avoided. For example, alcoholics can be given medication that will make them sick when they take alcohol. The relearning process involved is to try to associate the aversive (negative) feeling with taking the alcohol and hence reduce its appeal and use. The rate of improvement for this method is about 50 percent, with the "cure" lasting about six months. Thus it is not a solution as much as a good beginning for a number of alcoholics (Ullmann & Krasner, 1969, 1975).

✔ ***Reading Check***
How does aversive conditioning differ from counterconditioning?

Operant Conditioning

Operant conditioning is based on the assumption that behavior that is reinforced tends to be repeated, whereas behavior that is not reinforced tends to be extinguished. In **contingency management** the therapist and patient decide what old, undesirable behavior needs to be eliminated and what new, desirable behavior needs to appear.

contingency management: undesirable behavior is not reinforced, while desirable behavior is reinforced

Arrangements are then made for the old behavior to go unrewarded and for the desired behavior to be positively reinforced. In its simplest form, contingency management consists of the therapist agreeing with the patient: "If you do X, I will give you Y." This form of agreement is similar to systems of reward that people often use on themselves or parents use on children. For instance, a student may say to himself, "If I get a good grade on the exam, I'll treat myself to a great dinner." The reward is contingent (dependent) upon getting a good grade.

Contingency management is used in prisons, mental hospitals, schools, army bases, and with individual patients. In these situations it is possible to set up whole miniature systems of rewards, called **token economies.** For example, psychologists in some mental hospitals select behavior they judge desirable. Patients are then rewarded for these behaviors with "hospital," or token, money. Thus if a patient cleans his room or works in the hospital garden, he is rewarded with token money. The patients are able to cash in their token money for things they want, such as candy or cigarettes, or for certain privileges, such as time away from the ward. These methods are successful in inducing patients to begin leading active lives. They learn to take care of themselves and to take on responsibility instead of having to be cared for constantly.

token economy: desirable behavior is reinforced with valueless objects or points, which can be accumulated and exchanged for various rewards

COGNITIVE-BEHAVIOR THERAPY

Many therapists combine aspects of cognitive and behavior therapies. **Cognitive-behavior therapy** focuses on setting goals for changing a client's behavior and then, unlike other behavior therapies, placing more emphasis on changing the client's interpretation of his or her situation. This type of therapy is aimed at trying to help clients differentiate between serious, real problems and imagined or distorted problems. A cognitive-behavior therapist might work with a client to change her behavior by monitoring her behaviors and thought patterns, setting progressively difficult goals to meet, reinforcing positive changes, substituting positive thoughts for negative thoughts, and practicing new behaviors in a safe setting. Many self-help programs use this approach. For example, you might begin a program of developing positive self-esteem by using these techniques. Cognitive-behavior therapies are becoming increasingly widespread and have proven effective for treating a wide range of symptoms.

cognitive-behavior therapy: based on a combination of substituting healthy thoughts for negative thoughts and beliefs and changing disruptive behaviors in favor of healthy behaviors

SECTION **3** Assessment

1. **Review the Vocabulary** How does cognitive therapy differ from behavior therapy?

2. **Visualize the Main Idea** In a diagram similar to the one below, list and describe rational-emotive therapy techniques.

```
        ⬭           ⬭
          (Rational-Emotive Therapy Techniques)
        ⬭           ⬭
```

3. **Recall Information** How does aversive conditioning work?

4. **Think Critically** Sheila was not picked to be a basketball captain in gym class. She thought the gym teacher didn't pick her because Sheila is short. Sheila became angry with the teacher and acted rudely in gym class. Explain this scenario using what psychologist Albert Ellis calls the *ABC*s.

5. **Application Activity** Your friend is afraid of water and will not even go near a pool. Construct a plan for using systematic desensitization to help your friend overcome this irrational fear.

Biological Approaches to Treatment

Reader's Guide

■ Main Idea

Biological approaches to treatment rely on methods such as medications, electric shock, and surgery to help clients.

■ Vocabulary

- drug therapy
- antipsychotic drugs
- antidepressants
- lithium carbonate
- antianxiety drugs
- electroconvulsive therapy (ECT)
- psychosurgery
- prefrontal lobotomy

■ Objectives

- Explain biological approaches to treatment.
- Give examples of treatment medicines and their effects on patients.

EXPLORING PSYCHOLOGY

Medical Miracles?

Susan A. has spent most of her adult life fighting with people—her parents, her neighbors, her co-workers, and her husband. The 39-year-old Seattle woman has suffered bouts of depression and bulimia, abused drugs and alcohol, and twice tried to kill herself. She once sought relief in an antidepressant called doxepin, but she didn't like the way it made her feel.

Two years ago her therapist, Dr. Michael Norden, suggested she try a new drug called Prozac. She did. Within a month, Susan had given up psychotherapy in favor of school and a full-time job. She had also given up tranquilizers and street drugs. "I feel 1,000%," she said in a written note. "I actually like Mom and Dad now, I'm well liked at work, I don't ruminate on the negatives, I don't have murderous rages, my marriage is five times better."

—from "The Promise of Prozac" by G. Cowley, in *Newsweek*, March 26, 1990

People with ear infections are given antibiotics, and within about 10 days, most infections are gone. Could the same approach be used for people with psychological problems? According to Susan A.'s testimonial, the drug Prozac seemed to alleviate her psychological problems. Some experts believe that biological therapies, such as medications, should be reserved for people who fail to respond to psychotherapy. Other experts believe that a combination of psychotherapy and biological therapy is the answer for many patients.

BIOLOGICAL THERAPY

It is not possible for therapists to help all people with the therapies described so far in the chapter. The various "talking" and "learning" therapies have been aimed primarily at patients who are still generally capable of functioning within society.

Biological approaches to treatment assume there is an underlying physiological reason for the disturbed behavior, the faulty thinking, and the inappropriate emotions the person displays. Biological therapy uses methods such as medication, electric shock, and surgery to help people with psychological disorders.

Since these treatments are medical in nature, physicians or psychiatrists must administer them. Psychologists cannot prescribe drugs or administer biological treatments, but they may help decide whether a biological approach to treatment is appropriate for a particular patient.

Figure 17.11 Starting Biological Therapy

The patient is meeting with her doctor to discuss her treatment and evaluate how she is doing and what should happen next. *When would a psychiatrist suggest that a patient try medications?*

Drug Therapy

The most widely used biological therapy for psychological disorders is **drug therapy.** Drug therapy involves four main types of medications: antipsychotic drugs, antidepressant drugs, lithium, and antianxiety drugs. All the medications used in drug therapy can be obtained only with a prescription and after extensive testing. It is important to note that when patients undergoing drug therapy stop taking the medication, their symptoms may reappear. Often, drugs treat only the symptoms; drug therapy does not remove the causes of the disorder.

drug therapy: biological therapy that uses medications

Antipsychotic Drugs   For a long time the most common method of helping dangerous or overactive schizophrenic patients was physical restraint—the straitjacket, wet-sheet wrapping, and isolation. Doctors calmed the patient by means of psychosurgery or electroconvulsive shock (discussed later).

Today patients with schizophrenia are usually prescribed **antipsychotic drugs.** These drugs have helped schizophrenics stay out of mental institutions. Many patients with schizophrenia who take these drugs improve in a number of ways: they become less withdrawn, become less confused and agitated, have fewer auditory hallucinations, and are less irritable and hostile (Cole, 1964). One theory of schizophrenia proposes that when a person's dopamine neurotransmitter system somehow becomes overactive, that person develops schizophrenia. These medicines inhibit dopamine receptor sites. Drugs like chlorpromazine (such as Thorazine)

antipsychotic drugs: medication to reduce agitation, delusions, and hallucinations by blocking the activity of dopamine in the brain; tranquilizers

Homelessness: A Legacy of Deinstitutionalization

Homelessness is a major problem in the United States, and it is likely that you come into contact with the homeless at least occasionally. When you do, chances are good that you may be observing a person with a psychological disorder.

It is estimated that 33 percent of the homeless are mentally ill, overlapping partially with 33 percent of the homeless estimated to be severely addicted (Rossi, 1990). This seems to be a direct result of deinstitutionalization.

Since the introduction of antipsychotic drugs in the 1950s, the number of patients confined to mental institutions has steadily dropped. Unfortunately, most antipsychotic drugs do not cure disorders. Rather, they merely control the more obvious symptoms of psychological disorders so that patients are no longer dangerous. Thus, there is no longer any reason to keep these people institutionalized.

Many patients who have been released from institutions often find it impossible to hold steady jobs or to live on their own. In this way, the noble goal of deinstitutionalization has contributed to the problem of homelessness and has affected all our lives. Most communities lack efficient systems for aiding these people.

and haloperidol (such as Haldol) block or reduce the sensitivity of dopamine receptors. Clozapine (such as Closaril) decreases dopamine activity and increases the serotonin level, which inhibits the dopamine system. While these drugs reduce the symptoms of schizophrenia, there can be unpleasant side effects, such as muscular rigidity, impaired coordination, and tremors.

Antidepressant drugs Another class of drugs, called **antidepressants,** relieves depression. These drugs are also used for cases of anxiety, phobias, and obsessive-compulsive disorders. Serotonin and norepinephrine imbalances accompany depression. Monoamine oxidase (MAO) inhibitors, such as Nadril, elevate the levels of neurotransmitters. Tricyclicantidepressants, such as Elail, increase levels of these neurotransmitters by preventing the "reuptake" of these transmitters into the axon terminals. Antidepressants may have unpleasant side effects, such as dizziness, fatigue, forgetfulness, and weight gain. Selective serotonin reuptake inhibitors (SSRI), such as those in Prozac, work the same way but target the neurotransmitter serotonin.

antidepressants: medication to treat major depression by increasing the amount of one or both of the neurotransmitters noradrenaline and serotonin

lithium carbonate: a chemical used to treat mood swings of bipolar disorder

antianxiety drugs: medication that relieves anxiety and panic disorders by depressing the activity of the central nervous system

Lithium Carbonate The chemical **lithium carbonate** is widely used to return manic-depressive people to a state of equilibrium in which extreme mood swings disappear. While all of the other medicines described here are synthetic, lithium is a natural chemical element that controls levels of norepinephrine. Lithium can cause side effects if it is not administered under proper medical supervision. The finding that lithium salts reduce the symptoms of someone with a bipolar disorder, more so than those with a unipolar depression, suggests to researchers that these may be two different illnesses (Pokorny & Prein, 1974).

Antianxiety Drugs Commonly known as sedatives or mild tranquilizers, **antianxiety drugs** are used to reduce excitability and cause drowsiness. The barbiturates, then Miltown (meprobamate), and eventually the benzodiazepines have been very popular prescriptions in recent decades. At one time Valium was the most popular prescription drug in the country. Now several benzodiazepines—including Xanax (alprazolam)—have joined it among the 50 most prescribed drugs for panic attacks and agoraphobia.

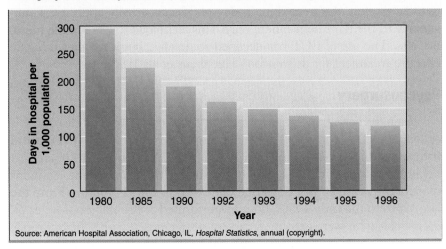

Figure 17.12   Deinstitutionalization

Over the past three decades the national policy has been one of deinstitutionalization. Deinstitutionalization refers to the release of patients from mental hospitals. These patients rejoin the community to attempt to lead independent lives. *How has the number of days patients spend in mental hospitals changed since 1980?*

Source: American Hospital Association, Chicago, IL, *Hospital Statistics*, annual (copyright).

While these drugs are effective for helping normal people cope with difficult periods in their lives, they are also prescribed for the alleviation of various anxiety-based symptoms, psychosomatic problems, and symptoms of alcohol withdrawal. The major effect of Valium, Librium, and Miltown is to depress the activity of the central nervous system by stimulating the action of the neurotransmitter GABA (gamma-aminobutyric acid).

If antianxiety drugs are taken properly, the side effects are few and consist mainly of drowsiness. However, prolonged use may lead to dependence, and heavy doses taken along with alcohol can result in death. These drugs do reduce anxiety but the best use seems to be not for chronic anxiety but for dealing with acute (one-time) anxiety (Mellinger, Balter, & Uhlenhuth, 1985).

Reading Check
What is the major effect of antianxiety drugs?

Electroconvulsive Therapy

"Shock treatment," as **electroconvulsive therapy (ECT)** is commonly called, has proved extremely effective in the treatment of severe depression, although no one understands exactly how it works (Kalinowsky, 1975). It involves administering, over several weeks, a series of brief electrical shocks of approximately 70–150 volts for 0.1–1.0 seconds. The shock induces a convulsion in the brain similar to an epileptic seizure that may last up to a minute.

Many people often consider ECT a barbaric treatment. As administered in the past, it was a brutal treatment. Often the brain seizure caused by the shock treatment would cause muscular contractions so intense that the patient's bones would break. As it is now applied, electroconvulsive therapy entails very little discomfort for the patient. Prior to treatment, the

electroconvulsive therapy (ECT): an electrical shock is sent through the brain to try to reduce symptoms of mental disturbance patient is given a sedative and injected with a muscle relaxant to alleviate involuntary muscular contractions and prevent physical injury. Even with these improvements, however, electroconvulsive therapy is a drastic treatment and must be used with great caution. Many people experience some memory problems after receiving this treatment. When ECT is applied bilaterally—with the electric current running across both of the brain's hemispheres—the patient may lose memory for events occurring one to two days before the treatment. Today physicians usually apply ECT unilaterally to the right hemisphere only. This technique results in little memory loss. The use of ECT has declined somewhat, but it remains a highly effective treatment for depression (Thienhaus et al., 1990).

Psychosurgery

psychosurgery: surgery that destroys part of the brain to make the patient calmer and freer of symptoms

prefrontal lobotomy: a radical form of psychosurgery in which a section of the frontal lobe of the brain is severed or destroyed

Brain surgery that is performed to treat psychological disorders is called **psychosurgery.** The most common operation—**prefrontal lobotomy**—involves destruction of the front portion of the brain, just behind the forehead. This part of the brain, the frontal lobe, contains most of the nerve connections that control a person's emotions. From the late 1930s to the early 1950s, doctors performed prefrontal lobotomies on individuals who were extremely violent or diagnosed with schizophrenia, depression, bipolar disorder, and obsessive-compulsive disorder. The practice of prefrontal lobotomies decreased significantly, though, when newly developed drugs offered alternative treatments in the mid-1950s. At the same time, mounting evidence appeared that showed that lobotomized patients showed an inability to plan. Furthermore, once-destroyed brain tissue never restores itself, so the effects are permanent. Patients may become apathetic and less creative after surgery. If the wrong area of the lobe is destroyed, the person can become more violent and unmanageable. Today the use of psychosurgery is controversial and rare.

SECTION 4 Assessment

1. **Review the Vocabulary** Describe how antipsychotic drugs, antidepressants, and antianxiety drugs work as therapy.

2. **Visualize the Main Idea** In a graphic organizer similar to the one below, list and explain the biological approaches to treatment.

Biological Approaches to Treatment

3. **Recall Information** Why is psychosurgery controversial? Why is it used?

4. **Think Critically** Describe a situation in which you believe a therapist would suggest biological therapy involving psychosurgery for a patient.

5. **Application Activity** Imagine that you have been asked to give a talk about the biological approaches to psychological problems. Create an outline for your speech.

Summary and Vocabulary

People who suffer from emotional problems often seek therapy from mental health professionals. The help these professionals provide is called psychotherapy.

Section 1 | What Is Psychotherapy?

Main Idea:
Psychotherapy is a general term for the several approaches used by mental health professionals to treat psychological disorders.

- Mental health professionals who have been trained to deal with the psychological problems of others include counseling and clinical psychologists, psychiatrists, and social workers.
- An important function of psychotherapy is to help people realize that they are responsible for their own problems and that they are the only ones who can really solve these problems.

Section 2 | Psychoanalysis and Humanistic Therapy

Main Idea:
Psychoanalysis is an analysis of the conscious and unconscious mind based on the theories of psychiatrist Sigmund Freud. Humanistic therapy helps people reach their full potential.

- A main goal of a psychoanalyst is to help make patients aware of the unconscious impulses, desires, and fears that are causing their anxiety.
- Humanistic psychology has given rise to several approaches to psychotherapy known as client-centered therapy.
- Client-centered therapists believe that psychological problems arise when the true self becomes lost and the individual comes to view himself or herself according to the standards of others.

Section 3 | Cognitive and Behavior Therapies

Main Idea: Cognitive and behavior therapies help clients develop new ways of thinking and behaving.

- Cognitive therapists focus on changing the way people think.
- Behavior therapists concentrate on determining what is specifically troubling with a patient's life and taking steps to change it.

Section 4 | Biological Approaches to Treatment

Main Idea:
Biological approaches to treatment rely on methods such as medications, electric shock, and surgery to help clients.

- Biological approaches to treatment assume there is an underlying physiological reason for the disturbed behavior, faulty thinking, and inappropriate emotions an individual displays.
- Drug therapy involves four main types of medications: antipsychotic drugs, antidepressant drugs, lithium, and antianxiety drugs.
- Electroconvulsive therapy is a drastic treatment and must be used with great caution.
- Psychosurgery involves destroying part of the brain to free the patient of symptoms.

Chapter Vocabulary

psychotherapy (p. 486)
eclectic approach (p. 487)
placebo effect (p. 488)
empathy (p. 489)
group therapy (p. 489)
psychoanalysis (p. 494)
insight (p. 494)
free association (p. 494)
resistance (p. 494)
dream analysis (p. 495)
transference (p. 495)
humanistic therapy (p. 496)
client-centered therapy (p. 496)
nondirective therapy (p. 496)
active listening (p. 497)
unconditional positive regard (p. 497)
behavior modification (p. 499)
cognitive therapy (p. 499)
rational-emotive therapy (RET) (p. 500)
behavior therapy (p. 502)
systematic desensitization (p. 503)
aversive conditioning (p. 504)
contingency management (p. 504)
token economy (p. 505)
cognitive-behavior therapy (p. 505)
drug therapy (p. 507)
antipsychotic drugs (p. 507)
antidepressants (p. 508)
lithium carbonate (p. 508)
antianxiety drugs (p. 508)
electroconvulsive therapy (ECT) (p. 509)
psychosurgery (p. 510)
prefrontal lobotomy (p. 510)

PSYCHOLOGY Online

Self-Check Quiz
Visit the *Understanding Psychology* Web site at
psychology.glencoe.com and click on **Chapter 17—
Self-Check Quizzes** to prepare for the Chapter Test.

Reviewing Vocabulary

**Choose the letter of the correct term or concept
below to complete the sentence.**

a. eclectic approach
b. empathy
c. insight
d. free association
e. active listening
f. unconditional positive
regard

g. systematic
desensitization
h. aversive conditioning
i. antipsychotic drugs
j. lithium carbonate

1. Some psychotherapists use a(n) _____ to
therapy, using many different methods.
2. Patients with schizophrenia are often treated
with _____.
3. A technique in which people are urged to imagine a feared situation in order to extinguish the
fear is called _____.
4. In a communication technique called _____,
the client-centered therapist tries to echo back
the feelings the client has expressed.
5. _____, or people's understanding of their
unconscious motives, is the first step toward
gaining control over their behavior.
6. An effective psychotherapist has _____,
or a capacity for warmth and understanding.
7. In a technique called _____, individuals
learn to associate negative feelings with the
behavior they want to avoid.
8. Talking about everything that comes to mind is
called _____.
9. Client-centered therapy is conducted in an atmosphere of emotional support called _____.
10. _____ is often used to bring manic-
depressive people to a state of equilibrium.

Recalling Facts

1. How do self-help groups help people deal with
problems?
2. What is the goal of psychoanalysis? What does
the therapist do to achieve this goal?
3. Using a diagram similar to the one below,
describe the main techniques of client-centered
therapy.

4. What steps does rational-emotive therapy
expect the client to take to solve his or her
problems?
5. Identify the effects of antipsychotic drugs, antidepressants, and antianxiety drugs.

Critical Thinking

1. **Making Inferences** One technique that client-
centered therapists use is active listening. What
does this technique involve? Do you think active
listening might be effective in improving day-to-
day communication between people? Explain.
2. **Demonstrating Reasoned Judgment** Do you
agree with Albert Ellis that it is not the event in
a person's life that causes trouble but rather the
way a person thinks about the event? Explain.
3. **Evaluating Information** Make a list of a few
fears that you have. Rank them from least fearful to most fearful. Do you think any of your
fears are based on conditioning? Describe a
method of counterconditioning that you think
would remove the fear or make it less intense.
4. **Making Comparisons** What do you think are
the major differences between psychoanalysis
and behavior therapy?
5. **Analyzing Information** Do you think psychosurgery should ever be used to treat psychological problems? Why?

Psychology Projects

1. What Is Psychotherapy? Attend an open meeting of one of the following self-help support groups: Alcoholics Anonymous, Alanon, Alateen, Smokenders, Narcotics Anonymous, Weight Watchers, or Overeaters Anonymous. Go with a classmate so that you can share your observations and experiences. Notice and report to the class on the ways in which the group provides support for people.

2. Humanistic Therapies Find out about two other types of client-centered therapies: existential therapies and transactional analysis. What are the basic beliefs? Summarize your research and report your findings in an essay or brief presentation to the class.

3. Behavior Therapies Operant conditioning is based on the assumption that reinforced behavior tends to be repeated. Behavior therapy often involves a system of rewards called token economies. Propose a token economy that could be used in your school. Describe what rewards would be used and what behavior they would reinforce.

4. Biological Approaches to Treatment Go to your local library or video store to find a movie that portrays mental illness. You might view *One Flew Over the Cuckoo's Nest* or *Awakenings*. Describe and classify some of the patients' symptoms and the kinds of treatments that were administered. Describe the effectiveness of the treatments in a written report.

Technology Activity

Search the Internet for sites that provide online psychotherapy services. Find out what types of problems are generally addressed in these sites. Report your findings in a written report.

Psychology Journal

Reread the recommendations for treatment that you wrote in your journal. How do the techniques you suggest resemble the therapies described in this chapter? Answer this question in your journal.

Building Skills

Interpreting a Graph Review the graph below, then answer the questions that follow.

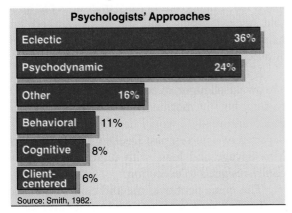

Psychologists' Approaches

Eclectic	36%
Psychodynamic	24%
Other	16%
Behavioral	11%
Cognitive	8%
Client-centered	6%

Source: Smith, 1982.

1. What percentage of psychologists uses behavior therapies? Client-centered therapies?

2. Which type of psychotherapy is used by the greatest percentage of psychologists? Why do you think this is so?

3. Psychodynamic therapy (or short-term dynamic psychotherapy) is an approach that is similar to psychoanalysis. Why do you think more therapists practice psychodynamic therapy rather than classical psychoanalysis?

4. How popular do you think biological approaches are? Why do you think so? Investigate this question and report your findings to the class.

Practice and **assess** key social studies skills with **Glencoe Skillbuilder Interactive Workbook CD-ROM, Level 2.**

See the Skills Handbook, page 628, for an explanation of interpreting graphs.

In the novel *The Bell Jar*, nineteen-year-old Esther Greenwood wins a dream assignment on a New York fashion magazine, but she quickly finds herself sinking into despair. In this excerpt, Esther receives electroshock therapy at Belsize hospital after attempting to commit suicide. This novel is largely autobiographical—poet-author Sylvia Plath ended her own life a month after the book's publication in 1963.

Reader's Dictionary

alcove: a small recessed section of a room

electrotherapy: treatment or therapy that uses electricity; electroconvulsive therapy (ECT)

pallid: lacking sparkle or liveliness

THE BELL JAR

BY SYLVIA PLATH

The nurse rapped on my door and, without waiting for an answer, breezed in.

It was a new nurse—they were always changing—with a lean, sand-colored face and sandy hair, and large freckles polka-dotting her bony nose. For some reason the sight of this nurse made me sick at heart, and it was only as she strode across the room to snap up the green blind that I realized part of her strangeness came from being empty-handed.

I opened my mouth to ask for my breakfast tray, but silenced myself immediately. The nurse would be mistaking me for somebody else. New nurses often did that. Somebody in Belsize must be having shock treatments, unknown to me, and the nurse had, quite understandably, confused me with her.

I waited until the nurse had made her little circuit of my room, patting, straightening, arranging, and taken the next tray in to Loubelle one door farther down the hall.

Then I shoved my feet into my slippers, dragging my blanket with me, for the morning was bright, but very cold, and crossed quickly to the kitchen. The pink-uniformed maid was filling a row of blue china coffee pitchers from a great, battered kettle on the stove. . . .

"There's been a mistake," I told the maid, leaning over the counter and speaking in a low, confidential tone. "The new nurse forgot to bring me in my breakfast tray today."

I managed a bright smile, to show there were no hard feelings.

"What's the name?"

"Greenwood. Esther Greenwood."

"Greenwood, Greenwood, Greenwood." The maid's warty index finger slid down the list of names of the patients in Belsize tacked upon the kitchen wall. "Greenwood, no breakfast today."

I caught the rim of the counter with both hands. . . .

I strode blindly out into the hall, not to my room, because that was where they would come to get me, but to the alcove. . . .

I curled up in the far corner of the alcove with the blanket over my head. It wasn't the shock treatment that struck me, so much as the bare-faced treachery of Doctor Nolan. I liked Doctor Nolan, I loved her, I had given her my trust on a platter and told her everything, and she had promised, faithfully, to warn me ahead of time if ever I had to have another shock treatment.

If she had told me the night before I would have lain awake all night, of course, full of dread and foreboding, but by morning I would have been composed and ready. I would have gone down the hall between two nurses, past DeeDee and Loubelle and Mrs. Savage and Joan, with dignity, like a person coolly resigned to execution.

The nurse bent over me and called my name.

I pulled away and crouched farther into the corner. The nurse disappeared. I knew she would return, in a minute, with two burly men attendants, and they would bear me, howling and hitting, past the smiling audience now gathered in the lounge.

Doctor Nolan put her arm around me and hugged me like a mother.

"You said you'd *tell* me!" I shouted at her through the dishevelled blanket.

"But I *am* telling you," Doctor Nolan said. "I've come specially early to tell you, and I'm taking you over myself."

I peered at her through swollen lids. "Why didn't you tell me last night?"

"I only thought it would keep you awake. If I'd known . . ."

"You *said* you'd tell me."

"Listen, Esther," Doctor Nolan said. "I'm going over with you. I'll be there the whole time, so everything will happen right, the way I promised. I'll be there when you wake up, and I'll bring you back again."

I looked at her. She seemed very upset.

I waited a minute. Then I said, "Promise you'll be there."

"I promise."

Doctor Nolan . . . led me down a flight of stairs into the mysterious basement corridors that linked, in an elaborate network of tunnels and burrows, all the various buildings of the hospital.

The walls were bright, white lavatory tile with bald bulbs set at intervals in the black ceiling. Stretchers and wheelchairs were beached here and there against the hissing, knocking pipes that ran and branched in an intricate nervous system along the glittering walls. I hung on to Doctor Nolan's arm like death, and every so often she gave me an encouraging squeeze.

Finally, we stopped at a green door with Electrotherapy printed on it in black letters. I held back, and Doctor Nolan waited. Then I said, "Let's get it over with," and we went in.

The only people in the waiting room besides Doctor Nolan and me were a pallid man in a shabby maroon bathrobe and his accompanying nurse. . . .

"Do you want to sit down?" Doctor Nolan pointed at a wooden bench, but my legs felt full of heaviness, and I thought how hard it would be to hoist myself from a sitting position when the shock treatment people came in.

"I'd rather stand."

At last a tall, cadaverous woman in a white smock entered the room from an inner door. I thought that she would go up and take the man in the maroon bathrobe, as he was first, so I was surprised when she came toward me. . . .

Through the slits of my eyes, which I didn't dare open too far, lest the full view strike me dead, I saw the high bed with its white, drumtight sheet, and the machine behind the bed, and the masked person—I couldn't tell whether it was a man or a woman—behind the machine, and other masked people flanking the bed on both sides.

Miss Huey helped me climb up and lie down on my back.

"Talk to me," I said.

Miss Huey began to talk in a low, soothing voice, smoothing the salve on my temples and fitting the small electric buttons on either side of my head. "You'll be perfectly all right, you won't feel a thing, just bite down. . . ." And she set something on my tongue and in panic I bit down, and darkness wiped me out like chalk on a blackboard.

Analyzing the Reading

1. What is the setting of this excerpt?
2. How does Esther realize that she is scheduled for a shock treatment that morning?
3. **Critical Thinking** Describe Esther's relationship with Doctor Nolan. Does Esther trust the doctor? Why do you think so?

UNIT 7

Social Psychology

Contents

The Japanese ▶ stock exchange

How and why do we interact with others the way we do? *Social psychology* is an area of psychology in which we first study and seek to explain our own and others' thoughts, feelings, perceptions, and behaviors. Then we study how we are influenced by the presence of and interactions with one another. How do we form impressions? Why do prejudices exist? Why do we perceive social situations the way we do? Social psychologists examine these issues.

Individual Interaction

PSYCHOLOGY JOURNAL

Why do people choose to interact with certain people and not with others? How do you communicate with others? In your journal, keep a log for several days of whom you communicate with and how you communicate. For example, do you use only verbal communication, or do your friends or parents realize what you are feeling by the look on your face? ■

PSYCHOLOGY
Online

Chapter Overview
Visit the *Understanding Psychology* Web site at psychology.glencoe.com and click on **Chapter 18—Chapter Overviews** to preview the chapter.

Interpersonal Attraction

Reader's Guide

■ Main Idea
We depend on others to survive. We are attracted to certain people because of factors such as proximity, reward values, physical appearance, approval, similarity, and complementarity.

■ Vocabulary
- social psychology
- social cognition
- physical proximity
- stimulation value
- utility value
- ego-support value
- complementarity

■ Objectives
- Discuss why we need friends.
- List and explain the factors involved in choosing friends.

EXPLORING PSYCHOLOGY

Alone and Safe?

The . . . story concerns a relative of a friend, who is an extremely wealthy industrialist. He, too, wanted to retire someplace safe from the congestion and crime of Europe. He bought a small island in the Bahamas, built a splendid estate, and surrounded himself with armed guards and attack dogs. At first he felt safe and comfortable, but soon worries began to appear. Were there enough guards to protect him in case his wealth attracted criminals to loot the island? Yet if he strengthened the guards, wouldn't he become increasingly weaker, more dependent on his protectors? In addition, the gilded cage soon became boring; so he fled back to the anonymity of a big city.

—from *The Evolving Self: A Psychology for the Third Millennium* by Mihaly Csikszentmihalyi, 1993

Is it possible to isolate ourselves to remain safe—and also remain happy? As the man in the excerpt above found out, isolation has a price. Being with other people may not be safe, *but* it is often preferable. That is why we choose friends. This topic is the concern of **social psychology**—the study of how our thoughts, feelings, perceptions, and behaviors are influenced by our interaction with others. **Social cognition,** a subfield of social psychology, is the study of how we perceive, store, and retrieve information about these social interactions. Social psychologists might ask: Why did we choose the friends we have? What attracted us to

social psychology: seeks to explain how our thoughts, feelings, perceptions, and behaviors are influenced by interactions with others

social cognition: focuses on how we perceive, store, and retrieve information about social interactions

Student Web Activity
Visit the *Understanding Psychology* Web site at psychology.glencoe.com and click on **Chapter 18— Student Web Activities** for an activity on individual interaction.

them in the first place? Every day we are making judgments about others based on our perceptions of who they are. Then, when we interact with these people, we must adjust our judgments to explain their behavior and ours.

WHY YOU NEED FRIENDS

During infancy we depend on others to satisfy our basic needs. In this relationship we learn to associate close personal contact with the satisfaction of basic needs. Later in life we seek personal contact for the same reason, even though we can now care for ourselves.

Being around other human beings—interacting with others—has become a habit that would be difficult to break. Moreover, we have developed needs for praise, respect, love and affection, the sense of achievement, and other rewarding experiences. These needs, acquired through social learning, can only be satisfied by other human beings (Bandura & Walters, 1963).

Anxiety and Companionship

Social psychologists are interested in discovering what circumstances intensify our desire for human contact. It seems that we need company most when we are afraid or anxious, and we also need company when we are unsure of ourselves and want to compare our feelings with other people's.

Psychologist Stanley Schachter (1959) decided to test the old saying "Misery loves company." His experiment showed that people suffering from a high level of anxiety are more likely to seek out company than are those who feel less anxious. He arranged for a number of college women to come to his laboratory. One group of women was greeted by a frightening-looking man in a white coat who identified himself as Dr. Gregor Zilstein of the medical school. Dr. Zilstein told each woman that she would be given electric shocks to study the effect of electricity on the body. He told the women, in an ominous tone, that the shocks would be extremely painful. With a devilish smile, he added that the

| Figure 18.1 | **Solitary and Social Animals** |

All newborn animals depend on others to fulfill basic biological needs. While snakes are solitary animals, some animals such as elephants and humans remain highly social even after they become self-sufficient. *Why do we need friends?*

shocks would cause no permanent skin damage. For obvious reasons, this group of women was referred to as the high-anxiety group. The doctor was friendly to the other group and told them that the shocks would produce only ticklish, tingling sensations, which they might even find pleasant. These women formed the low-anxiety group.

Zilstein told each participant that she would have to leave the laboratory while he set up the equipment. He then asked each woman to indicate on a questionnaire whether she wished to wait alone in a private room or with other participants in a larger room. Most women in the low-anxiety group chose to wait alone. The majority of high-anxiety women, however, preferred to wait with others. Thus, the experiment demonstrated that high anxiety tends to produce a need for companionship (see Figure 18.2).

Comparing Experiences and Reducing Uncertainty

People also like to get together with one another to reduce their uncertainties about themselves. For example, when you get tests back, you probably ask your friends how they did. You try to understand your own situation by comparing it to other people's. You learn your strengths and weaknesses by asking: Can other people do it, too? Do they do it better or worse? Many individuals use the performance of others as a basis for self-evaluation. According to this theory, one of the reasons why the women in the shock experiment sought company was to find out how they should respond to Dr. Zilstein. Should they feel fear or anger, or should they take the whole thing in stride? One way to get this information was to talk to others.

Schachter conducted another experiment to test this idea. It was essentially the same as the Dr. Zilstein experiment, but this time all the women were made anxious. Half of them were then given the choice between waiting alone and waiting with other women about to take part in the same experiment. The other half were given the choice between waiting alone and passing the time in a room where students were waiting to see their academic advisers.

As you might expect, the women who had a chance to be with other women in the same predicament seized the opportunity. These women wanted to compare their dilemma with others. Yet most of the women in the second group chose to spend the time alone rather than with the unconcerned students. As the experimenter put it, "Misery doesn't love just any kind of company; it loves only miserable company."

Other researchers have shown that the more uncertain a person is, the more likely he or she is to seek out other people. Like Schachter, Harold Gerard and J.M. Rabbie (1961) recruited volunteers for an experiment. When the volunteers arrived, some of them were escorted to a booth and attached to a machine that was supposed to measure emotionality. The machine was turned on, and the participants were able to see not only their own ratings but also the ratings of three other participants. In each case the dial for the participant registered 82 on a scale of 100; the dials for the other participants registered 79, 80, and 81. (As you have undoubtedly guessed, the machine was rigged.) A second group of participants was

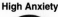

Figure 18.2 Schachter's Results

These graphs show the results of Schachter's experiment about the effects of anxiety on affiliation. *Which group was more likely to seek company? Why?*

Low Anxiety   High Anxiety

22   10   20   12

■ Number of women who chose to be alone or did not care

■ Number of women who chose to affiliate

attached to a similar machine and shown their own ratings but not those of other participants. A third group was not given any information about themselves or other participants in the experiment. When asked whether they wanted to wait alone or with other participants, most of the people in the first group chose to wait alone. They had seen how they compared to others and felt they were reacting appropriately. Most of the participants in the other two groups, who had no basis for evaluating themselves, however, chose to wait with other people.

Friendship also offers support in trying times. Friends may serve as mediators if you have problems with another person. Friends are there to react to your ideas. In your social network, friends are your connections to a broad array of available support.

Yet, as we will see, predicting the effects of friendship can be quite complex. In Karen Rook's study (1987), she found that having friends who offer support helped reduce very high stress. On the other hand, friends were no significant help in dealing with average amounts of stress. Perhaps, most surprisingly, the support of friends actually hindered people's ability to deal with low levels of stress. Rook theorizes that reviewing smaller problems again and again with your friends may actually increase your sensitivity to those problems.

Reading Check
How do friends reduce uncertainty?

HOW YOU CHOOSE FRIENDS

Most people feel they have a great deal of latitude in the friends they choose. Easy transportation, telephones, and the spare time available to most Americans would all seem to ease communication among them and, therefore, to permit them a wide range of individuals from whom to choose companions, friends, and lovers. In fact, we rarely venture beyond the most convenient methods in making contact with others.

Proximity

Would it surprise you to learn that one of the most important factors in determining whether two people will become friends is **physical proximity**—the distance from one another that people live or work? In general, the closer two individuals are geographically to one another, the more likely they are to become attracted to each other. Yet it is more than just the opportunity for interaction that makes the difference.

Psychologists have found that even in a small two-story apartment building where each resident was in easy reach of everyone else, people were more likely to become close friends with the person next door than with anyone else (see Figure 18.3). Psychologists believe that this is a result of the fears and embarrassments most people have about making contact with strangers. When two people live next door to one another, go to the same class, or work in the same place, they are able to get used to one another and to find reasons to talk to one another without ever having to seriously risk rejection. To make friends with someone you do not see routinely is much more difficult. You have to make it clear that you are interested and thus run the risk of making a fool of yourself—either because

physical proximity: the nearness of one person to another person the other person turns out to be less interesting than he or she seemed at a distance or because that person expresses no interest in you. Of course, it may turn out that both of you are very glad someone spoke up.

Reward Values

Proximity helps people make friends, but it does not ensure lasting friendship. Sometimes people who are forced together in a situation take a dislike to one another that develops into hatred. Furthermore, once people have made friends, physical separation does not necessarily bring an end to their relationship. What are the factors that determine whether people will like each other once they come into contact?

One reward of friendship is stimulation. A friend has **stimulation value** if he or she is interesting or imaginative or can introduce you to new ideas or experiences. A friend who is cooperative and helpful—who seems willing to give his or her time and resources to help you achieve your goals—has **utility value.** A third type of value in friendship is **ego-support value:** sympathy and encouragement when things go badly, appreciation and approval when things go well. These three kinds of rewards—stimulation, utility, and ego support—are evaluated consciously or unconsciously in every friendship. A man may like another man because the second man is a witty conversationalist (stimulation value) and knows a lot about gardening (utility value). A woman may like a man because he values her opinions (ego-support value) and because she has an exciting time with him (stimulation value). By considering the three kinds of rewards that a person may look for in friendship, it is possible to understand other factors that affect liking and loving.

stimulation value: the ability of a person to interest you in or to expose you to new ideas and experiences

utility value: the ability of a person to help another achieve his or her goals

ego-support value: the ability of a person to provide another person with sympathy, encouragement, and approval

Physical Appearance

A person's physical appearance greatly influences others' impressions of him or her. People feel better about themselves when they associate with people whom others consider desirable. In the same way, we often consider those with physical beauty to be more responsive, interesting, sociable, intelligent, kind, outgoing, and poised (Longo & Ashmore, 1995). This is true of same-sex as well as opposite-sex relationships. Physical attractiveness influences our choice of friends as well as lovers.

In one study (Dion, Berscheid, & Walster, 1972), participants were shown pictures of men and women of varying degrees of physical attractiveness and were asked to rate their personality traits. The physically attractive people were consistently viewed more positively than the less attractive ones. They were seen as more sensitive, kind, interesting, strong, poised, modest, and sociable, as well as more sexually responsive. It

| Figure 18.3 | Proximity and Friendship |

A set of apartments such as this was used in a study of friendship choice. It was found that the fewer doors there were between people, the more likely they were to become friends. *How does physical proximity affect your choice of friends?*

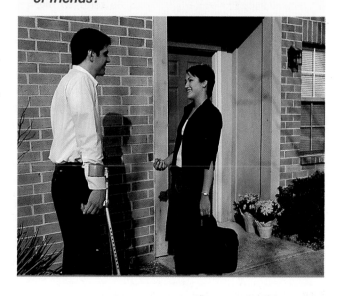

Figure 18.4 **Standards of Beauty**

Standards of physical attractiveness vary widely internationally. These photos are of people considered beautiful from Kenya, Japan, and Bali. *Do you believe that your ideal of physical beauty is dependent on your culture? Explain.*

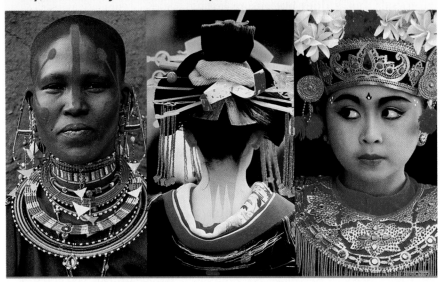

seems, therefore, that although we have heard that "beauty is only skin deep," we act as if it permeates one's entire personality.

People who do not meet society's standards for attractiveness are often viewed in an unfavorable light. Research has shown that obese adults are often discriminated against when they apply for jobs. Even children are targets of prejudice (see Figure 18.5). An unattractive child is far more likely to be judged "bad" or "cruel" for an act of misbehavior than is a more attractive peer (Dion, Berscheid, & Walster, 1972).

Interestingly, psychologists have found that both men and women pay much less attention to physical appearance when choosing a marriage partner or a close friend than when inviting someone to go to a movie or a party. Yet neither men nor women necessarily seek out the most attractive member of their social world. Rather, people usually seek out others whom they consider their equals on the scale of attractiveness (Folkes, 1982).

Approval

Another factor that affects a person's choice of friends is approval. All of us tend to like people who agree with and support us because they make us feel better about ourselves—they provide ego-support value.

Some studies suggest that other people's evaluations of oneself are more meaningful when they are a mixture of praise and criticism than when they are extreme in either direction. No one believes that he or she is all good or all bad. As a result, one can take more seriously a person who sees some good points and some bad points. When the good points come first, hearing the bad can make one disappointed and angry at the person who made them. When the bad points come first, the effect is opposite.

Similarity

People tend to choose friends whose backgrounds, attitudes, and interests are similar to their own. Often, husbands and wives have similar economic, religious, and educational backgrounds.

There are several explanations for the power of shared attitudes. First, agreement about what is stimulating, worthwhile, or fun provides the basis for sharing activities. People who have similar interests are likely to do more things together and to get to know one another better.

Second, most of us feel uneasy around people who are constantly challenging our views, and we translate our uneasiness into hostility or avoidance. We are more comfortable around people who support us. A friend's agreement bolsters our confidence and contributes to our self-esteem. In addition, most of us are self-centered enough to assume that people who share our values are basically decent and intelligent.

Finally, people who agree about things usually find it easier to communicate with each other. They have fewer arguments and misunderstandings, and they are better able to predict one another's behavior and thus feel at ease with each other (Carli, Ganley, & Pierce-Otay, 1991).

Figure 18.5   Subject to Prejudice

In one experiment, women were shown photographs of children participating in a variety of antisocial behaviors. The adults tended not only to see the behaviors committed by the unattractive children as more antisocial but to also attribute a more negative moral character to these children than to the attractive ones (Dion et al., 1972). *Why are we attracted to good-looking people?*

Complementarity

Despite the power of similarity, an attraction between opposite types of people—**complementarity**—is not unusual. For example, a dominant person might be happy with a submissive mate. Still, most psychologists agree that similarity is a much more important factor. Although the old idea that opposites attract seems reasonable, researchers continue to be unable to verify it (Swann et al., 1994).

complementarity: the attraction that often develops between opposite types of people because of the ability of one to supply what the other lacks

SECTION 1   Assessment

1. **Review the Vocabulary**   Explain the differences among stimulation value, utility value, and ego-support value.

2. **Visualize the Main Idea**   Using a diagram similar to the one below, list and describe the factors involved in choosing friends.

Factors Involved in Choosing Friends

3. **Recall Information**   Is the saying "misery loves company" accurate? Explain.

4. **Think Critically**   There is a saying stating that "beauty is only skin deep." Do you think it is true? Do people act as if it is true? Explain.

5. **Application Activity**   Go to a greeting card store and examine several types of cards to send to important people in your life. In a brief essay analyze the following question: What factors of interpersonal attraction do the cards emphasize?

Case Studies

What You See Is What You Get?

Period of Study: 1992

Introduction: Even though people are taught that "looks aren't everything" and "beauty is in the eye of the beholder," these beliefs do not always seem to be upheld within American society. For many years psychologists have disputed whether the importance of physical appearance is a learned concept, from such influences as television or magazines, or has a biological explanation. One consistency found is that physical attractiveness becomes less important as individuals mature.

There have been many studies focusing on the link between physical attractiveness and the behavior of individuals. In 1972 researchers (Dion, Berscheid, & Walster) administered a test to college students by showing them photographs of people with varying physical appearances. The college students would then describe a type of personality for each photograph. Other researchers (Stephan & Langlois, 1984; Karraker & Stern, 1990) researched feelings and perceptions by adults on the "cuteness" of an assorted group of newborn infants. In 1977 research was performed comparing the annual salaries of men and women of like qualifications versus contrasting physical appearance (Dipboye, Arvey, & Terpstra). The results from all of these studies were similar: physical attractiveness was a key factor.

Hypothesis: Alan Feingold set out to study and compare personality traits of those individuals who were considered to be physically attractive with those who were not considered physically attractive. Feingold wanted to disprove the myth that attractive or good-looking individuals could possess superior personality traits.

Method: Defining the attractiveness of individuals for this type of research is not simple. There are far too many ways in which people can be classified within these two categories. Much of this revolves around the personal preference of others. Feingold combined the results of numerous studies dealing with this issue.

Results: Feingold's research indicated no significant relationships between physical attractiveness and such traits as intelligence, leadership ability, self-esteem, and mental health. For reasons unknown, results seem to be reported and discussed more from the studies in which physical attractiveness dominates. Yet in actuality, Feingold's research indicated those type of results occurred far less. Perhaps relaying the cases in which physical attractiveness prevails shows humans that we still can be superficial when judging other people as a whole. Although Feingold found no relationship between physical attractiveness and distinguished personality traits, he did discover tendencies within the two defined groups. He discovered that those individuals who are considered attractive generally are more comfortable in social settings and are less likely to be lonely and anxious. They seem to be more socially skilled than their counterparts. Therefore, what seems to be important is how we define physical attractiveness and our perceptions of the personalities of those attractive people.

Analyzing the Case Study

1. What connection between personality and physical attractiveness did Feingold set out to study?

2. What connections between physical attractiveness and personality did Feingold discover?

3. Critical Thinking Do you think physical beauty influences a person's personality? Explain.

Reader's Guide

■ Main Idea
We explain the behavior of others by making judgments about them. Our judgments are influenced by our perceptions of others.

■ Vocabulary
- primacy effect
- stereotype
- attribution theory
- fundamental attribution error
- actor-observer bias
- self-serving bias
- nonverbal communication

■ Objectives
- Explain how we use first impressions and schemas.
- Describe several factors that influence how we interpret others' behavior.

EXPLORING PSYCHOLOGY

First Meeting

We told a waitress that we had come to see Mr. Malcolm X. . . . In a moment Malcolm appeared at the rear door. His aura was too bright and his masculine force affected me physically. A hot desert storm eddied around him and rushed to me, making my skin contract, and my pores slam shut. He approached, and all my brain would do for me was record his coming. I had never been so affected by a human presence. . . .

"Ladies, *Salaam aleikum.*" His voice was black baritone and musical. Rosa shook hands, and I was able to nod dumbly. Up close he was a great red arch through which one could pass to eternity. His hair was the color of burning embers and his eyes pierced. . . .

—from *The Heart of a Woman* by Maya Angelou, 1981

Maya Angelou, a writer, remembers her first impression of 1960s Black Muslim leader Malcolm X. What influenced her first impression of Malcolm X? Based on what she knew and her own thoughts and feelings, Angelou instantly appraised him.

We often cannot explain our own behaviors. How then do we explain the behavior of others? It takes people very little time to make judgments about one another. From one brief conversation or even by watching a person across a room, you may form an impression of what someone is like, and first impressions influence the future of a relationship. If a person seems interesting, he or she becomes a candidate for future interaction. A person who seems to have nothing interesting to say—or too much to say—does not. We tend to be sympathetic toward someone who seems shy, to expect a lot from someone who impresses us as intelligent, and to be wary of a person who strikes us as aggressive.

Forming an impression of a person is not a passive process in which certain characteristics of the individual are the input and a certain impression is the automatic outcome. If impressions varied only when input varied, then everyone meeting a particular stranger would form the same impression of him or her. This, of course, is not what happens. One individual may judge a newcomer to be "quiet," another may judge the same person to be "dull," and still another person may think the person "mysterious." These various impressions lead to different expectations of the newcomer and to different patterns of interaction with him or her.

FIRST IMPRESSIONS

Imagine that it is the first time you are meeting someone. How do you treat that person? Why? Your first impression of someone is usually based on that person's physical appearance (see Figure 18.6). You instantly make certain judgments based on how he or she looks. For example, if you meet a well-dressed woman in an office building, you might assume that she is a well-paid corporate executive. Should you meet a waiter in a local restaurant, you might assume that he does not make as much money as the corporate executive. You might interact with these people differently, just as you might interact differently with people of different genders, races, or socioeconomic classes.

These initial judgments may influence us more than later information does (Belmore, 1987). For example, one researcher invited a guest lecturer to a psychology class. Beforehand, all the students were given a brief description of the visitor. The descriptions were identical in all traits but one. Half the students were told that the speaker was rather cold; the other half was told that he was very warm. After the lecture, the researcher asked all the students to evaluate the lecturer. Reading their impressions, you would hardly know that the two groups of students were describing the same person. The students who had been told he was cold saw a humorless, ruthless, self-centered person. The other students saw a relaxed, friendly, concerned person. Changing one adverb and one adjective—substituting "rather cold" for "very warm"— had a dramatic effect on the students' perception of the lecturer. This process illustrates a **primacy effect.** The students interpreted the last neutral words in terms of the first one, giving it greater—or primary— impact. Thus, to be warm and determined was perceived as dedicated; to be cold and determined was perceived as rigid. It also affected their behavior. Students in the "warm group" were warm themselves, initiating more conversations with the speaker than did the students in the other group (Kelley, 1950).

primacy effect: the tendency to form opinions on others based on first impressions

What was your first impression of your teacher? Did that first impression ever change? These impressions sometimes become a self-fulfilling prophecy—that is, the way you act toward someone changes depending on your impression of him or her, and this in turn affects how that person interacts with you. For instance, suppose you showed up on the first day of class in a terrible mood. During the class period, you did not really pay attention to the lecture and even made a few jokes in class. Your teacher immediately labeled you as the class troublemaker and, therefore, did not treat you as an atten-

Figure 18.6   Are You Attracted to These People?

Are you drawn to the people in these photos, or is your impression less favorable? Your answer depends in large part on the schemas you have developed. *How do we use our schemas of people?*

tive and good student. You may have responded to that treatment by not studying nor caring about your grade in class. In reality, you may be a great student; you just had a bad day on the first day of class and now cannot seem to please your teacher. On many occasions we take first impressions into account. For example, when you first start dating someone, you try to look nice. When going for a job interview, you dress well.

Schemas

Why do we form impressions about people? Forming impressions about others helps us place these people into categories. The knowledge or set of assumptions that we develop about any person or event is known as a *schema*. We develop a schema for every person we know. When you meet someone who seems unusually intelligent, you may assume she is also active, highly motivated, and conscientious. Another person in the group may have an altogether different "theory" about highly intelligent people—that they are boring, boastful, unfriendly, and the like. Whatever the person does provides "evidence" for both theories. You are impressed by how animated she becomes when talking about her work; the other person does not care for how little attention she pays to other people. Both of you are filling in gaps in what you know about the person, fitting her into a type you carry around in your head.

Sometimes we develop schemas for people we do not know but have heard about. Schemas can influence and distort our thoughts, perceptions, and behaviors. Think of a person you like. If you pass that person in the hallway and he smiles, that smile looks friendly to you. Now think of a person whom you mistrust or do not really like. If that person smiles at you in the hallway, you may not interpret the smile as friendly but instead think of it as a guilty or fake smile.

We develop schemas for people and events. The schemas associated with people are judgments about the traits people possess or the jobs they

Reading Check
How do first impressions help us form schemas?

perform. Schemas about events consist of behaviors that we associate with certain events. For example, we know that we can yell and cheer at the basketball game but that we should be quiet and subdued at funerals.

What is the purpose of developing these schemas? With your schemas you are able to explain a person's past behavior and to predict his future behavior. Schemas allow us to organize information so that we can respond appropriately in social situations.

stereotype: a set of assumptions about people in a given category often based on half-truths and nontruths

attribution theory: a collection of principles based on our explanations of the causes of events, other people's behaviors, and our own behaviors

Stereotypes   Sometimes we develop schemas for entire groups of people. You may have schemas for men, women, Asian Americans, African Americans, or certain religious groups. Such schemas are called stereotypes. A **stereotype** is a set of assumptions about an identifiable group of people. The belief that males are dominant and independent or that females are nurturing and emotional are examples. Stereotypes may contain positive or negative information, but primacy effects may cause stereotypes to bias us. If stereotypes influence our information about people, they may become self-fulfilling prophecies (Hamilton & Sherman, 1989).

Schemas are useful because they help us predict with some degree of accuracy how people will behave. Without them, we would spend considerable energy observing and testing people to find out what they are like, whether we want to pursue a relationship with them, and so on. Like stereotypes, if the assumptions we make about people from our first impressions do not change as we get to know them better, then we are guilty of harboring prejudice.

ATTRIBUTION THEORY

You are waiting at a traffic light. Somebody behind you honks and gestures frantically for you to get out of the way. Not sure what is happening, you move your car—slowly, so they will not think you are a push-over—to allow the driver to pull even with you. As he does, the driver looks across at you and says, "Thanks. My wife's in labor. We're in a hurry!"

If you are like most of us, you feel foolish, but everyone has moments like that. You were facing a situation that many social psychologists study—trying to interpret and explain people's behavior by identifying what caused the behavior (Jones, 1990). The focus of study in this circumstance is called **attribution theory** (Heider, 1958), an analysis of how we interpret and understand other people's behavior. When you first heard the horn, you undoubtedly attributed the man's pushiness to personal characteristics—often called *internal attributions.* Once he thanked you and gave a

More About...

Shyness

Studies show that about 40 percent of adults are shy (Henderson & Zimbardo, 1996). Shyness is a feeling of distress that results from feeling awkward in social situations and from fearing rejection. People may feel shy in front of authoritative figures, in one-on-one dating scenarios, with strangers, or with groups of people. Shyness is really a form of excessive self-focus. The shy person is preoccupied with his or her own thoughts, feelings, or physical reactions.

Shy people differ from others in how they attribute their own successes and failures. Whereas most people demonstrate the self-serving bias—taking credit for success and blaming failures on external causes—shy people reverse this bias and blame themselves for failure and externalize the causes of success. For example, whereas Roger may credit his strength and skill for winning a tennis match, shy Jackie may attribute her win to luck or to her opponent's poor performance.

Psychologists may treat shyness by exposing the patient to feared situations and teaching the patient how to control anxiety. In addition, psychologists may lead a patient to restructure his or her negative thoughts into positive affirmations.

valid reason for his urgency, your analysis immediately changed to credit his behavior to the needs of his wife—often called *external attributions*. Internal attributions are also known as *dispositional*, while external attributions are sometimes referred to as *situational*.

Typically, we use shortcuts to attribute behavior; that is, we explain our own behavior in terms of external attributions, but—as in the example at the traffic light—we attribute others' behavior to internal attributions. That represents what psychologists call a **fundamental attribution error** (Ross, 1977). This is a common occurrence.

This factor is also called the **actor-observer bias** (Jones & Nisbett, 1972). How we interpret another's behavior depends just as much on how we perceive it as on what it is—that is, we are the "actor" when we try to explain our own behavior but an "observer" when we try to explain someone else's behavior (see Figure 18.7). For example, a person who performs an action (the actor) attributes the action to the situation—"I am smiling because it is a beautiful day." However, another person who sees the same action (the observer) is likely to attribute it to the actor's internal characteristics—"She is smiling because she is a cheerful person."

What causes actor-observer bias? Some psychologists propose that we realize that our own behavior changes from situation to situation, but we may not believe the same is true of others. The point is that we all actively perceive other people's actions. What we conclude about other people depends not only on what they do but also on our interpretations. This is true not just when we deal with individuals but also when we react to groups.

When there is glory to be claimed, we often demonstrate another form of error called a **self-serving bias.** In victory, we are quick to claim personal responsibility (internal attribution); in defeat, we pin the blame on circumstances beyond our control (external attribution). For example, if we receive an A on the test, we attribute our good grade to our hard work and intelligence. When we get a D on the test, however, we blame a biased test for our poor performance. In this way we try to keep ourselves in the best possible light.

NONVERBAL COMMUNICATION

Central to the development and maintenance of a relationship is the willingness to communicate aspects of yourself to others. Communication involves at least two people: a person who sends a message and a person who receives it. The message sent consists of an idea and some emotional component. Messages are sent verbally and nonverbally. "I like to watch you dance" is a verbal message, while a warm smile is an example of **nonverbal communication.**

Although most people are aware of what they are saying verbally, they are often unaware of their nonverbal messages. They are more aware of the nonverbal messages when they are on the receiving end of them. You have probably heard someone say, "It doesn't matter," speaking in a low voice and looking away; the unspoken message is "My feelings are hurt." You do not need to be told in so many words that a friend is elated or depressed,

fundamental attribution error: an inclination to attribute others' behavior to internal causes (dispositional factors) but to attribute our own behavior to external factors (situational factors)

actor-observer bias: tendency to attribute one's own behavior to outside causes rather than to a personality trait

self-serving bias: a tendency to claim success is due to our efforts, while failure is due to circumstances beyond our control

nonverbal communication: the process through which messages are conveyed using space, body language, and facial expression angry or pleased, nervous or content. You sense these things. People communicate nonverbally not only through facial expressions but also through their use of space and body language (posture and gestures).

The way you carry your body also communicates information about you. This is your *body language*. If you stand tall and erect, you convey the impression of self-assurance. If you sit and talk with your arms folded and legs crossed—a closed body position—you communicate that you are protecting yourself. When you unfold your arms and stretch out, your open body position may be saying that you are open to people.

Although the use of body language is often unconscious, many of the postures we adopt and gestures we make are governed by *social rules*. These rules are very subtle. Touching, for example, has rules—not just where, but who (Duncan, 1969). Your teacher or boss is much more likely to touch you than you are to touch him or her. Touching is considered a privilege of higher status.

| Figure 18.7 | **Actor-Observer Bias** |

Our eyes point outward, away from ourselves, so that when we watch someone else perform an action we focus on the actor. When we perform an action, we see the surrounding environment, so we attribute behavioral causes to the situation. *Why then do we attribute internal, or dispositional, causes to others' actions?*

SECTION 2 Assessment

1. **Review the Vocabulary** Explain the errors some people make when using shortcuts to attribute behavior.

2. **Visualize the Main Idea** Using a diagram similar to the one below, list and describe the two components of attribution theory.

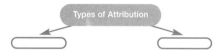

Types of Attribution

3. **Recall Information** What are *social rules?* Give an example of such a rule.

4. **Think Critically** Rate the following situations as external or internal attributions: (a) Your friend helped you wash your car because she is nice. (b) Your friend helped you wash your car because she wanted to impress your parents, who were watching. (c) Your friend helped you wash your car because she owed you a favor.

5. **Application Activity** Use information found in the library, on the Internet, or through personal interviews to find examples of nonverbal communication in other cultures. Be prepared to show at least two such examples to the class.

Personal Relationships

Reader's Guide

■ Main Idea
People experience different types of love and relationships throughout their lives.

■ Vocabulary
• generational identity

■ Objectives
• Describe sources of parent-adolescent conflict.
• Describe different types of love.

EXPLORING PSYCHOLOGY

Raising Your Family

They had been so sweet when they were little. Granny wished the old days were back again with the children young and everything to be done over. It had been a hard pull, but not too much for her. When she thought of all the food she had cooked, and all the clothes she had cut and sewed, and all the gardens she had made—well, the children showed it. There they were, made out of her, and they couldn't get away from that. Sometimes she wanted to see John again and point to them and say, "Well, I didn't do so badly, did I?"

—from *The Jilting of Granny Weatherall* by Katherine Anne Porter, 1930

In the story above, Granny Weatherall looks back on her life—a life of raising and loving children. The relationships you have with your grandparents, parents, guardians, and others will influence and enrich your life. Your personal relationships with others bring meaning and substance to your everyday experiences.

PARENT-CHILD RELATIONSHIPS

Noted psychologists, including Erik Erikson, believed that early and persistent patterns of parent-child interaction could influence people's later adult expectations about their relationships with the significant people in their lives. If a young infant's first relationship with a caregiver is

Figure 18.8 | **Parent-Child Relationships**

Parenting styles vary among different families and different ethnic groups. *Do you think adolescents all over the world experience the same types of conflicts with their parents? Explain.*

generational identity: the theory that generations tend to think differently about certain issues because of different formative experiences

loving, responsive, and consistent, the child will develop a trust in the ability of other people to meet his or her needs. This trusting, in turn, will encourage the person to be receptive to people. On the other hand, a child who has experienced unresponsive, inconsistent, or unaffectionate care in infancy will most likely be more wary or mistrustful of other people. Within the parent-child relationship, we learn how to manipulate others to have our needs met. A parent is likely to satisfy the wishes of a child who acts "good," that is, who does what the parent asks. The child may also learn to get attention by pouting or having temper tantrums.

As children develop and form relationships with people outside their family, they apply what they have learned about relationships. As a result of childhood experiences, an individual might, for example, believe that the only way to establish and maintain good relationships with friends is always to say what pleases them rather than speak the truth.

Your parents influence the quality of your adult relationships in other ways. They provide you with your first model of a marital relationship. As you watched your mother and father interacting with each other as husband and wife, you were most likely forming some tentative conclusions about the nature of relationships. Later on, you might use their example as a guide in selecting a future mate or in evaluating your relationships. If your parents have a happy marriage, you will most likely seek to duplicate it by imitating their patterns. Sadly, the reverse may also be true. Evidence suggests that being part of a violent family in childhood increases the likelihood that someone will perpetuate that mode of behavior against his or her children and spouse (Rice, 1993).

Sources of Parent-Adolescent Conflict

In our society, parent-child conflict may develop during adolescence. Adolescence may be a period of inner struggles—goals versus fear of inability to accomplish them, desire for independence versus the realization that they are "only human." The adolescent thus needs parents who are sure of themselves, their identities, and their values. Such parents serve not only as models but also as sources of stability in a world that has become complicated and full of choices.

Each generation has a **generational identity.** This refers to a simple fact: adolescents and their parents tend to think differently about some things. Why does this happen? You are part of a generation that is distinct from others. Your generation has shared formative experiences that are different from those of other generations. For example, whereas conflicts such as the Vietnam War and political upheavals such as the civil rights movement shaped other generations' ideas, situations such as economic uncertainty, the prevalence of divorce, technological innovations, or a decreased sense of security may shape your generation's views. It is important to note that different generational identities do not automatically lead to conflict. The conflicts that adolescents experience with their parents may result from a changing parent-child relationship, as well as from different ideologies and concerns.

LOVE RELATIONSHIPS

While most people say that they love their parents, their friends, and maybe even their brothers and sisters, they attach a different meaning to love when referring to a boyfriend, girlfriend, or spouse. Love means different things to different people and within different relationships.

Love and Marriage

The idea of love without marriage is no longer shocking. The fact that a couple is developing a close and intimate relationship or even living together does not necessarily mean that they are contemplating marriage. The idea of marriage without love, however, remains unpopular to most Americans. Marrying for convenience, companionship, financial security, or *any* reason that does not include love strikes most of us as impossible or at least unfortunate.

This, according to psychologist Zick Rubin (1973), is one of the main reasons it is difficult for many people to adjust to love and marriage. Exaggerated ideas about love may also help explain the growing frequency of divorce. Fewer couples who have "fallen out of love" are staying together for the sake of the children or to avoid gossip than did in the past. Let us begin at the beginning, though, with love.

Profiles In Psychology

Sigmund Freud
1856–1939

"Martha is mine, the sweet girl of whom everyone speaks with admiration, who despite all my resistance captivated my heart at our first meeting, the girl I feared to court and who came toward me with high-minded confidence, who strengthened the faith in my own value and gave me new hope and energy to work when I needed it most."

It has been said that a person in love does not see his or her lover as others do. Freud obviously viewed his wife Martha Bernays in a unique manner. Freud believed that we saw the lover as our ideal, and the more dissatisfied with ourselves we are, the more we needed a lover to make up for our weaknesses, and the more inclined we were to idealize our lover.

Why do we do this? Freud believed that whenever we make a choice—such as choosing a lover—we are governed by hidden mental processes of which we are unaware and over which we have no control.

Freud's contributions to psychology are controversial. Although his ideas greatly influenced the development of the field of psychology, critics claim that Freud saw people as foolish, weak, and self-deluded. But it may be better to view people as basically good, though injured.

Love Reflecting on almost two decades of studies, one psychologist (Hatfield, 1988) identified two common types of love. *Passionate love* is very intense, sensual, and all-consuming. It has a feeling of great excitement and of intense sexuality, yet there is almost an element of danger—that it may go away at any moment. In fact, it does usually fade in any romance. When passionate love subsides, it may grow into *companionate love,* which includes friendship, liking someone, mutual trusting, and wanting to be with them. Companionate love is a more stable love, which includes the commitment and intimacy identified by Robert Sternberg (1988). There are other views of love, however.

Some years ago Zick Rubin surveyed University of Michigan student volunteers. Couples who had been going together for anywhere from a few weeks to six or seven years filled out questionnaires about their feelings toward their partners and their same-sex friends. The answers enabled Rubin to distinguish between liking and loving.

Liking is based primarily on respect for another person and the feeling that he or she is similar to you. Loving is rather different. As Rubin wrote, "There are probably as many reasons for loving as there are people who love. In each case there is a different constellation of needs to be gratified, a different set of characteristics that are found to be rewarding, a different ideal to be fulfilled" (Rubin, 1973). Looking beyond these differences, however, Rubin identified three major components of romantic love: *need* or *attachment, caring* or *the desire to give,* and *intimacy.*

People in love feel strong desires to be with the other person, to touch, to be praised and cared for, to fulfill and be fulfilled. That love is so often described as a longing, a hunger, a desire to possess, a sickness that only one person can heal, suggests the role need plays in romantic love.

Equally central is the desire to give. Love goes beyond the cost-reward level of human interaction. It has been defined as "the active concern for the life and growth of that which we love" (Fromm, 1956) and as "that state in which the happiness of another person is essential to our own" (Heinlein, in Levinger & Snoek, 1972). This kind of love is very altruistic, very giving. Without caring, need becomes a series of self-centered, desperate demands; without need, caring is charity or kindness. In love, the two are intertwined.

Need and caring take various forms, depending on individual situations. What all people in love share is intimacy—a special knowledge of each other derived from uncensored self-disclosure. Exposing your "true self" to another person is always risky. It does not hurt so much if a person rejects a role you are trying to play, but it can be devastating if a person rejects the secret

Figure 18.9   Different Types of Love

It is easy to think of love in a narrow context and consider only the sexual relationship that exists between a man and a woman. This view, however, omits the kinds of love that exist between children and grandparents, between people and their pets, between siblings and friends, and so on. *Why are caring and need important in love?*

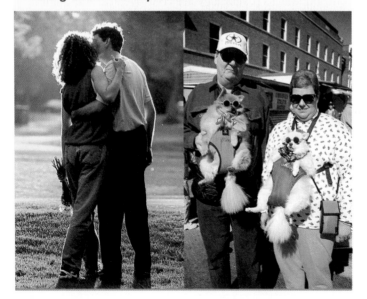

longings and fears you ordinarily disguise or keep hidden. It hurts deeply if he or she uses that private information to manipulate you. This is one of the reasons why love so often brings out violent emotions—the highs and lows of our lives.

Rubin conducted a number of experiments to test common assumptions about the way people in love feel and act. He found that couples who rated high on his "love scale" did, indeed, spend more time gazing into each other's eyes (while waiting for the experimenter) than other couples did. He was unable, however, to prove that lovers sacrifice their own comfort for that of their partners.

Perhaps the most interesting discoveries in "love research" concern the differences between men and women. Rubin found that most couples were equal on the love scale: the woman expressed the same degree of love for her partner as he did for her. Women, however, tended to *like* their boyfriends—to respect and identify with them—more than their boyfriends liked them. Women also tended to love and share intimacies with their same-sex friends more often than men did with theirs.

This is not surprising. As Rubin suggested, women in our society tend to specialize in the social and emotional dimensions of life. The revelation that men carry out more romantic gestures than women, however, is surprising, though perhaps it should not have been. At a time when women usually worked at home, whom they married basically determined their style of living. Now earning power is no longer such a powerful concern. With more than half of all married women working outside the home, both men and women contribute to family finance, and with that comes the ability to perform more romantic gestures. In fact, two psychologists (Fehr & Russell, 1991) reported that women are no longer different from men as to how romantic they are or their ability to participate equally in widely varying forms of passionate or companionate love.

A follow-up questionnaire, sent a year after Rubin's original study, indicated that when both a man and a woman express their interest in each other, the relationship is likely to progress—that is, they become more intimate and committed to each other. What is the implication of this finding? Love is not something that happens *to* you; it is something you seek and create.

Reading Check
What is the difference between passionate and companionate love?

Triangular Theory of Love Love comes in many sizes and shapes. A theory that accounts for the many forms of love has been proposed by Robert Sternberg (1986). Sternberg's triangular theory of love contends that love is made up of three parts: intimacy, passion, and commitment. The various combinations of these parts account for why love is experienced in many different ways (see Figure 18.10).

Using Sternberg's model, we can see how different kinds of love are made of different degrees of intimacy, passion, and commitment. The "love at first sight" felt on a first date has a lot of passion but little commitment, whereas the love felt by a couple celebrating their fiftieth wedding anniversary has much intimacy and commitment but probably less passion.

What traits are important in a potential marriage partner?

About 90 percent of adults in the United States eventually marry. How do they decide which person is right for them?

Procedure

1. Ask at least 10 of your classmates and friends to identify two qualities they consider essential in a potential mate.

2. Separate the results into responses from females and those from males. Tally the results in a chart.

Analysis

1. What three traits did females consider most important in a potential partner? Males?

2. Based on the information in the chapter regarding love and marriage, do you think the traits listed by the people you surveyed are ones that are likely to result in a successful marriage? Explain.

See the Skills Handbook, page 622, for an explanation of designing an experiment.

Marriage   A couple decides to make a formal and public commitment to each other. They marry. Will they "live happily ever after"? Their chances are good if they come from similar cultural and economic backgrounds, have about the same level of education, and practice (or fail to practice) the same religion. Their chances are better still if their parents were happily married, they had happy childhoods, and they maintain good relations with their families. All of these are good predictors of marital success. Two principles tend to govern behavior leading to successful marriages: endogamy and homogamy.

Endogamy identifies the tendency to marry someone who is from one's own social group. Marriages are more likely to be successful when we marry someone similar to us (Buss, 1985). In addition, *homogamy* identifies our tendency to marry someone who has similar attributes, including physical attractiveness, age, and physique, to our own. A common observation is that people who marry tend to look similar to one another. It is now suspected that social processes operate that tend to cause this matching to happen. At a dance held at the University of Minnesota a number of years ago, a computer randomly matched students. Physical attractiveness was the best predictor of the likelihood that two randomly matched people would continue dating (Walster et al., 1966).

Marital Problems and Divorce   In general, healthy adjustment to marriage seems to depend on three factors: whether the couple's needs are compatible, whether the husband's and wife's images of themselves coincide with their images of each other, and whether they agree on what the husband's and wife's roles in the marriage are.

External factors may make it impossible for one or both to live up to their own role expectations. A man who is unemployed cannot be the good provider he wants to be and may take out his frustrations on his family, who constantly reminds him of this. A woman trying to hold a job and raise a family in a slum tenement may have trouble keeping clean the kitchen with a broken sink, providing good meals for her family, or keeping her children safe.

Often couples just grow apart: the husband becomes totally engrossed in his work or in a hobby; the wife, in her career, children, or community affairs. Let us suppose they are unable or unwilling to fill each other's needs and role expectations through accommodation or compromise. Perhaps they cannot face their problems. For whatever reasons, they decide on divorce. What then?

In many ways, adjusting to divorce is like adjusting to death—the death of a relationship. Almost inevitably, divorce releases a torrent of emotions: anger (even if the person wanted a divorce), resentment, fear, loneliness, anxiety, and above all the feeling of failure. Both individuals are suddenly thrust into a variety of unfamiliar situations. A man may find himself cooking for the first time in years; a woman, fixing her first leaky faucet. Dating for the first time in 5 or 10 years can make a formerly married person feel like an adolescent. Friends may feel they have to choose sides. Some divorcing people may find it unsettling to think of giving up on a marriage or being unattached and free to do whatever they like. One of the biggest problems may be time—the free time a person desperately wanted but now has no idea how to fill.

All of this adds up to what Mel Krantzler (1973) calls "separation shock." Whatever the circumstances, most divorced people go through a period of mourning that lasts until the person suddenly realizes that he or she has survived. This is the first step toward adjusting to divorce. Resentment of his or her former spouse subsides. The pain left over from the past no longer dominates the present. The divorced person begins calling old friends, making new ones, and enjoying the fact that he or she can base decisions on his or her own personal interests. In effect, the divorcee has begun to construct a new identity as a single person.

| Figure 18.10 | Triangular Theory of Love |

Intimacy refers to the feeling part of love—as when we feel close to another. Passion is love's motivating aspect—feeling physically aroused and attracted to someone. Commitment is the thinking component—when we realize that a relationship is love and we desire to maintain that relationship over time. *What is consummate love?*

Romantic Love
Intimacy + Passion
(lovers physically and emotionally
attracted to each other but
without commitment, as in a
summer romance)

Liking
Intimacy Alone
(true friendships without passion
or long-term commitment)

Infatuation
Passion Alone
(passionate, obsessive love at
first sight without intimacy or
commitment)

INTIMACY   PASSION

Consummate Love
Intimacy + Passion + Commitment
(a complete love consisting of all three
components—an ideal difficult to attain)

Companionate Love
Intimacy + Commitment
(long-term committed friendship
such as marriage in
which the passion has faded)

COMMITMENT

Empty Love
Commitment Alone
(decision to love each other
without intimacy or passion)

Fatuous Love
Passion + Commitment
(commitment based on passion
but without time for intimacy to
develop; shallow relationship
such as a whirlwind courtship)

Children and Divorce   Adjusting to divorce is usually far more difficult for children than for their parents. First, rarely do the children want the divorce to occur: the conflict is not theirs, but their parents'. Second, while the parents may have good reasons for the separation, the children (especially very young children) are unlikely to understand those reasons. Third, the children themselves rarely have any control over the outcome of the divorce. Such decisions as whom they live with and how frequently they will be able to see the separated parent are out of their hands. Finally, children, especially young ones, cannot muster as much emotional maturity as their parents to help them through such an overwhelming experience.

A child of parents who divorce may exhibit behaviors ranging from being visibly upset to depression to rebellion. The longevity of these behaviors may be determined by "the harmony of the parents' ongoing relationship, the stability of the child's life, and the adequacy of the caregiving arrangement"(Berger, 1994).

Adolescents experience special problems as a result of their parents' divorce, because their developmental stage already involves the process of breaking family ties. When that separation takes place before the adolescent is ready to play his or her own hand in it, the experience can be terribly unsettling. As one young person said, "[It was] like having the rug pulled out from under me" (Wallerstein & Kelly, 1974).

Like their parents, most children do eventually come to terms with divorce. They learn to put some distance between themselves and their parents' conflict, and they learn to be realistic about the situation and make the best of it. Adjustment is made easier when parents take special care to explain the divorce and allow children to express their feelings. Divorce is becoming a problem with which more and more children will have to cope.

SECTION 3   Assessment

1. **Review the Vocabulary**   What is generational identity?

2. **Visualize the Main Idea**   Using an outline similar to the one below, explain why children may have difficulty adjusting to their parents' divorce.

I. Adjusting to Divorce
A. _____
B. _____
C. _____
D. _____

3. **Recall Information**   What is the difference between endogamy and homogamy? Explain.

4. **Think Critically**   In what ways are liking and loving different? Explain.

5. **Application Activity**   Have you heard the phrase "love at first sight"? Write a paragraph explaining what you think this phrase means. Include what psychologists might say about the meaning of this phrase.

Summary and Vocabulary

CHAPTER 18

Psychologists have provided insights into why people choose to interact with some people and not with others. They also have provided insights into why people want to be around other people.

Section 1 — Interpersonal Attraction

Main Idea: We depend on others to survive. We are attracted to certain people because of factors such as proximity, reward values, physical appearance, approval, similarity, and complementarity.

- Social psychologists have discovered that people need company most when they are afraid or anxious or when they are unsure of themselves and want to compare their feelings with other people's.
- The closer two individuals are geographically to one another, the more likely they are to become attracted to each other.
- Friendships provide three rewards—stimulation, utility, and ego support.

Section 2 — Social Perception

Main Idea: We explain the behavior of others by making judgments about them. Our judgments are influenced by our perceptions of others.

- Forming impressions about others helps us place these people into categories.
- We form first impressions of people based on schemas.
- When people develop schemas for entire groups of people, they are developing stereotypes.
- People often try to interpret and explain other people's behavior by identifying what caused the behavior.
- Communication in a relationship consists of both verbal and nonverbal communication.

Section 3 — Personal Relationships

Main Idea: People experience different types of love and relationships throughout their lives.

- Children apply what they have learned from their parent-child relationships to relationships with others.
- There are two common types of love: passionate love and companionate love.
- Robert Sternberg contends that love is made of three parts: intimacy, passion, and commitment.
- People tend to marry someone who is from their own social group and who has similar attributes.
- The success of a marriage seems to depend on three factors: whether the couple's needs are compatible, whether the husband's and wife's images of themselves coincide with their images of each other, and whether they agree on what the husband's and wife's roles in the marriage are.
- Parents and their children may have difficulty adjusting to divorce.

Chapter Vocabulary

social psychology (p. 519)
social cognition (p. 519)
physical proximity (p. 522)
stimulation value (p. 523)
utility value (p. 523)
ego-support value (p. 523)
complementarity (p. 525)
primacy effect (p. 528)
stereotype (p. 530)
attribution theory (p. 530)
fundamental attribution error (p. 531)
actor-observer bias (p. 531)
self-serving bias (p. 531)
nonverbal communication (p. 531)
generational identity (p. 534)

Self-Check Quiz
Visit the *Understanding Psychology* Web site at
psychology.glencoe.com and click on **Chapter 18—
Self-Check Quizzes** to prepare for the Chapter Test.

Reviewing Vocabulary

Choose the letter of the correct term or concept below to complete the sentence.

a. social cognition
b. physical proximity
c. stimulation value
d. utility value
e. complementarity
f. stereotype

g. attribution theory
h. self-serving bias
i. nonverbal communication
j. generational identity

1. A friend who is able to give you his or her time and resources to help you achieve your goal has _____.
2. Waving at someone to get his or her attention is an example of _____.
3. A(n) _____ is an exaggerated set of assumptions about an identifiable group of people.
4. _____ refers to the distance from one another that people live or work.
5. The study of how people perceive, store, and retrieve information about social interactions is called _____.
6. Claiming personal responsibility for positive occurrences and blaming circumstances beyond our control for negative occurrences is called a(n) _____.
7. The tendency for members of different generations to think differently about things refers to the _____.
8. An analysis of how we interpret and understand other people's behavior is called _____.
9. A friend who wants to try new experiences has _____.
10. An attraction between opposite types of people is called _____.

Recalling Facts

1. What is the most important factor in determining the start of a friendship? Why is this an important factor?
2. In general, are you likely to choose as a friend a person who is similar to you or a person who complements your strengths and weaknesses?
3. If you want people to think that you are smart, should you try to do your best on the first, second, or last test in a class? Why?
4. Using a diagram similar to the one below, identify Rubin's three major components of romantic love.

Rubin's Major Components
of Romantic Love

5. Identify three factors upon which marital happiness depends.

Critical Thinking

1. **Evaluating Information** Think of people with whom you are friends. Which rewards do you get from these friendships?
2. **Analyzing Concepts** We may think that stereotyping does not influence us. Watch a television program about (a) a detective, (b) an African American family, (c) a white family, and (d) an independent woman. What character traits does each have? Are these stereotypes?
3. **Making Inferences** People sometimes are accused of saying one thing but meaning another. Do you think people's nonverbal communication sometimes conflicts with their verbal communication? Explain.
4. **Synthesizing Information** Pretend someone has just asked you, "How do I know if I'm in love?" How would you respond?
5. **Applying Information** What do you think could be done to slow the rise in the divorce rate?

CHAPTER 18 Assessment

Psychology Projects

1. **Interpersonal Attraction** Prepare a "want ad" in which you "advertise" for a friend. Include the main characteristics you look for in a friend in the advertisement.

2. **Social Perception** In an essay, support or refute the following common-sense sayings with information you learned from the chapter:
   "Birds of a feather flock together."
   "Opposites attract."
   "Familiarity breeds contempt."
   "Beauty is only skin deep."
   "Absence makes the heart grow fonder."

Technology Activity

Several sites on the Internet are designed to help parents and teenagers deal with conflicts. Find these Web sites and evaluate the suggestions they offer.

Psychology Journal

Some people claim that nonverbal communication is a more accurate indicator of an individual's true feelings than verbal communication. Others disagree. Write an essay that argues both sides of the issue.

Building Skills

Interpreting a Chart Ten thousand people from different countries in the world were surveyed about the characteristics they look for in a mate. The results are listed in the chart below (1 is most important, while 18 is least important). Review the chart, then answer the questions that follow.

Practice and **assess** key social studies skills with **Glencoe Skillbuilder Interactive Workbook CD-ROM, Level 2.**

See the Skills Handbook, page 628, for an explanation of interpreting charts.

Rank Ordering of Desired Characteristics in a Mate						
	China		South Africa Zulu		United States	
	Males	Females	Males	Females	Males	Females
Ambition and industriousness	10	5	8	7	11	6
Chastity (no prior sexual intercourse)	3	6	13	18	17	18
Dependable character	6	7	3	1	3	3
Desire for home and children	2	2	9	9	9	7
Education and intelligence	8	4	6	6	5	5
Emotional stability and maturity	5	1	1	2	2	2
Favorable social status or rating	14	13	17	14	14	14
Good cook and housekeeper	9	11	2	15	13	16
Good financial prospect	16	14	18	13	16	11
Good health	1	3	5	4	6	9
Good looks	11	15	14	16	7	13
Mutual attraction—love	4	8	10	5	1	1
Pleasing disposition	13	16	4	3	4	4
Refinement, neatness	7	10	7	10	10	12
Similar education	15	12	12	12	12	10
Similar political background	17	17	15	17	18	17
Similar religious background	18	18	16	11	15	15
Sociability	12	9	11	8	8	8

Source: Feldman, Robert. *Understanding Psychology.* Boston: McGraw-Hill College, 1999.

1. From which countries were the respondents?

2. In which country were males and females most in agreement about the kinds of characteristics they looked for in a mate?

3. Which characteristic ranked the lowest among both males and females in the three countries included on the chart? How do you explain this?

PSYCHOLOGY JOURNAL

Think of the groups to which you belong—your family, your friends, the band, a sports team, and so on. What effect do these groups have on how you think, act, and feel? Pick one group to which you belong and, in your journal, describe any influences this group has over you. ■

PSYCHOLOGY Online

Chapter Overview
Visit the *Understanding Psychology* Web site at psychology.glencoe.com and click on **Chapter 19—Chapter Overviews** to preview the chapter.

Group Behavior

■ Main Idea

A group—a collection of people who interact, share common goals, and influence how members think and act—is unified by the attitudes and standards members share and by their commitment to them.

■ Vocabulary

- group
- task functions
- social functions
- norms
- ideology
- social facilitation
- social inhibition
- group polarization
- groupthink
- sociogram

■ Objectives

- Define and explain different types of groups.
- Describe the interactive patterns within groups.

EXPLORING PSYCHOLOGY

Greasers Versus Socs

Anyway, I went on walking home, thinking about the movie, and then suddenly wishing I had some company. Greasers can't walk alone too much or they'll get jumped, or someone will come by and scream "Greaser!" at them, which doesn't make you feel too hot, if you know what I mean. We get jumped by the Socs. I'm not sure how you spell it, but it's the abbreviation for the Socials, the jet set, the West-side rich kids. It's like the term "greaser," which is used to class all us boys on the East Side.

—from *The Outsiders* by S.E. Hinton, 1989

In the passage above, S.E. Hinton's character Ponyboy tells his story, a story marked by the rivalry between two groups—the Socs and the Greasers. The differentiation between these groups influences Ponyboy's life to a great degree. What groups influence your life? Why?

WHAT ARE GROUPS?

What do the St. Stanislaus Parish Bowling Team, the AARP (American Association of Retired Persons), and country music's Dixie Chicks have in common? Each can be classified as a group. A **group** is a

group: a collection of people who have shared goals, a degree of interdependence, and some amount of communication

Figure 19.1 **Team Work**

Whether or not the members of this surgical team get along outside the operating room does not matter. Their main purpose is to do a certain job. *What are the features that groups share?*

collection of people who interact, share common goals, and influence how members think and act. In general, the features that distinguish a group from an aggregate (a nongroup) are interdependence, shared goals, and communication. People who congregate but do not interact are not considered a group but rather an aggregate. For example, a group of people waiting for Bus No. 2 to arrive on the corner of 4th Avenue and 33rd Street is not a group but just a collection of people. (If, however, a car screamed to a stop in front of them, almost hitting them, they would become a group by talking and asking questions.) *Interaction* is the key factor in forming a group. Several people who *interact* form a group.

Interdependence

To be classified as a group, a collection of people must demonstrate interdependence. Interdependence occurs when any action by one member will affect or influence the other members. For instance, in groups of athletes, entertainers, or roommates, each member has a certain responsibility to the rest of the group, and if he or she does not fulfill it, the other members will be affected. For the athletes, the consequence may be losing the game; for the entertainers, a bad show; for the roommates, a messy apartment. A person may be the group leader, the decision maker, the one who is the listener, or so on. If the person does not fulfill his or her role, the rest of the group is affected.

In small groups, members usually have a direct influence on one another: one member communicates directly with another. In larger groups, the influence may be indirect. The interdependence between you and the president of the United States is not a result of personal contact. Nevertheless, one of the things that makes the people of the United States a group is that the president's actions affect you and that your actions, together with those of many other Americans, affect the president.

Whether it is boys or girls engaged in a neighborhood tug-of-war contest, a football team preparing for the big game, or a NASA launch team spread around the world, communication is crucial to the functions of a group. In some cases, the communication is directed outward as a declaration of group membership, such as when a member of the band wears a T-shirt or jacket with the school's logo or name.

In other instances, the communication is internal, intended primarily for group members to announce group activities. Direct communication aids members' feelings of belonging. It increases the likelihood that group members will respond differently to one another than to those who do not belong to the group. It encourages debate among members regarding goals and increases members' feelings of commitment to group goals through processes of communication.

Shared Goals

Group members become interdependent because they share common goals. Groups are usually created to perform tasks or to organize activities that no individual could handle alone. Members of a consumer group, for example, share the common goal of working for consumer protection. Members of ethnic and religious groups desire to perpetuate a common heritage or set of beliefs.

The purposes groups serve are of two general kinds: **task functions,** those directed toward getting some job done; and **social functions,** those directed toward filling the emotional needs of members. In most groups, task and social functions are combined naturally and cannot be separated easily, although one dominates in any given group.

Political parties, teams of surgeons, and crews of construction workers are all task-oriented groups. Although social interactions occur within each of these groups, their main purpose is to complete a project or achieve some change in the environment. Social functions are emphasized in more informal, temporary groups. When people take walks together, attend parties, or participate in conversations, they have formed a group to gain such social rewards as companionship and emotional support. Yet again, every group involves both task and social functions.

task functions: activities directed toward getting a job done

social functions: responses directed toward satisfying the emotional needs of members

HOW GROUPS ARE HELD TOGETHER

The factors that work to hold groups together—that increase the group's *cohesiveness*—include the attitudes and standards they share and their commitment to them.

norms: shared standards of behavior accepted by and expected from group members

Norms

Unwritten rules that govern the behavior and attitudes of group members are called **norms.** They include rules—shared beliefs about the correct way to behave and what to believe. For example, there are rules about how to behave at home, at school, and at an amusement park. There are rules about what to say and how to communicate with brothers, sisters, parents, and friends. Would you use the same words and expressions with both your friends and your parents? Most people would not. These rules are not necessarily like rigid laws. They may be more like tendencies or habits, but group members are expected to act in accordance with group norms and are punished in some way if they do not. If a student consistently sneaks to the front of the lunch line, her friends would not hesitate to say something about it. Strangers might point and grow angry—simply because she violated a norm that you wait in line

Figure 19.2	Why Do We Join Groups?

Psychologists have proposed various reasons why we join groups. *For what reason would you join a task-oriented group?*

They satisfy our need to belong.

We must compare ourselves to others who are similar to us.

We must compare our experiences with those of others who are similar to us.

We use group members as standards against which to evaluate ourselves.

Groups reduce our uncertainty.

Group members may offer us support in trying times.

Groups provide us with companionship.

Groups provide comfort and lessen our anxiety.

Groups help us accomplish things that we could not do alone.

Figure 19.3   **Group Norms**

Social norms can be formal or informal. Formal norms are rules such as traffic laws. Informal norms are unwritten rules such as greeting friends and shaking your opponents' hands at the end of a game. *What norms might be important to a group organized according to social functions?*

ideology: the set of principles, attitudes, and defined objectives for which a group stands

after the people who arrived before you. Thus, the punishment may take the form of coldness or criticism from other group members. If the norm is very important to the group, a member who violates it may endure a more severe social reaction or may be excluded from the group.

Ideology

For a group to be cohesive, members must share the same values. In some cases, people are drawn together because they discover they have common ideas, attitudes, and goals—that is, a common **ideology**. In other instances, people are attracted to a group because its ideology provides them with a new way of looking at themselves and interpreting events, and a new set of goals and means for achieving them. The National Organization for Women (NOW), for example, has provided a focal point for resistance to discrimination on the basis of gender. The AARP (American Association of Retired Persons) lobbies for the rights of older people and retirees. Leaders, heroes and heroines, rallies, books and pamphlets, slogans, and symbols all help popularize an ideology, win converts, and create feelings of solidarity among group members.

Commitment

One factor that increases individual commitment is the requirement of personal sacrifice. If a person is willing to pay money, endure hardship, or undergo humiliation to join a group, he or she is likely to continue with it. For example, some groups in high school require initiation rites in order to join the group. College students who undergo embarrassing initiation rites to join sororities or fraternities tend to develop a loyalty to the group that lasts well beyond their college years. Cohesiveness will be high if members are committed to their group. During your first year of high school, you also go through initiation rites. Seniors may tell new students about elevators that do not exist, stairwells that are blocked, or directions that lead to the wrong place.

Another factor that strengthens group commitment is participation. When people actively participate in group decisions and share the rewards of the group's accomplishments, their feeling of membership increases—they feel that they have helped make the group what it is. For example, social psychologists have compared groups of workers who participate in decisions that affect their jobs with other workers who elect representatives to decision-making committees or workers who are simply told what to do. Those who participate have higher morale and accept change more readily than do the other workers (Coch & French, 1948). Other studies have highlighted the importance of supportive managers in maintaining

PSYCHOLOGY
Online

Student Web Activity
Visit the *Understanding Psychology* Web site at psychology.glencoe.com and click on **Chapter 19— Student Web Activities** for an activity on group behavior.

such worker involvement (Locke, Latham, & Erez, 1988).

The processes that hold a group together must work both ways. The individual must be responsive to the norms of the group, subscribe to its ideology, and be prepared to make sacrifices to be part of it. The group must also respond to the needs of its members. It cannot achieve cohesiveness if its norms are unenforceable, if its ideology is inconsistent with the beliefs of its members, or if the rewards it offers do not outweigh the sacrifices it requires.

TYPES OF GROUPS

Social psychologists are interested in what happens between groups of people. Groups can be differentiated by in-groups and out-groups and primary and secondary groups. When a group's members identify with their group, they are referred to as the *in-group*. The *out-group* includes everyone who is not a member of the in-group. The out-group may be rejected by and hostile to the in-group.

A *primary* group is a group of people who interact daily face-to-face. Because of the frequency of these interactions, some situations may become emotionally charged. For example, you see your family members every day. You eat, sleep, and have fun with them, and you also fight with them. A *secondary* group is a larger group of people with whom you might have more impersonal relationships. For example, your psychology class is a secondary group.

PSYCHOLOGY and You — Social Norms

Visual behavior illustrates the effects of norms on our behavior. When you are passing someone in the hallway whom you do not know, you have two choices: to speak or not to speak. If you say hello, nod, or otherwise acknowledge the other person and they respond, then what? If you decide not to speak, then what?

In both instances, when you are 10 to 18 feet in front of the person, accepted social rules are that you divert your eyes to the right. You develop an intense interest in a bulletin board you have looked at a hundred times or you look at the ceiling or the floor.

If you continue looking at the person until your head is turned 90 degrees, it would be considered "pushy." If you turned and continued viewing a member of the opposite gender as he or she (and you) continued walking down the hallway, it would border on sexual harassment.

In an elevator, it is customary for riders to redistribute the floor space more or less equally each time someone gets on or off. These norms are the unwritten "rules of the road" that govern our social behavior.

✓ Reading Check
Name a primary and a secondary group with which you are involved.

SOCIAL FACILITATION VERSUS SOCIAL INHIBITION

Do you perform better or worse in front of a crowd? Have you heard of the "home team advantage"? This is another term for social facilitation. **Social facilitation** refers to the tendency to perform better in the presence of a group. At times, however, you may perform poorly in front of crowds. This is an example of **social inhibition.** Social facilitation and social inhibition may occur because the presence of a crowd increases one's drive or arousal.

Psychologist Robert Zajonc (1965) noticed that social facilitation seemed to occur when participants performed simple or well-learned tasks, whereas social inhibition occurred when participants performed more

social facilitation: an increase in performance in front of a crowd

social inhibition: a decrease in performance in front of a crowd

Figure 19.4) **Performance Factors**

Some people perform better in front of crowds, and others do not. Whether you show social facilitation or social inhibition depends on your past experience, the task at hand, and the crowd itself. *When might social inhibition occur?*

complex tasks or tasks that involved unfamiliar factors to the participants. So, in effect, how you perform in front of a crowd depends on what you are doing. For example, if you are an expert tennis player but a novice piano player, you may perform better in front of others while playing tennis but poorly in front of others when you are trying to play a rendition of *Heart and Soul.*

The effect of a crowd on your behavior may also be a reflection of your concern about being evaluated. For example, you may play an excellent game of tennis in front of your friends and parents, but your performance may slip while playing in front of college recruiters.

INTERACTIONS WITHIN GROUPS

Providing an individual with values and a sense of identity is only one aspect of the group's meaning to him or her. The particular role he or she plays in the group's activities is also important. Each group member has certain unique abilities and interests, and the group has a number of different tasks that need to be performed. The study of the roles various members play in the group and how these roles are interrelated is the study of *group structure.*

There are many aspects to group structure: the personal relationships between individual members, such as liking relationships and trusting relationships; the rank of each member on a particular dimension, such as power, popularity, status, or amount of resources; and the roles various members play. A *role* is behavior expected of an individual because of his or her membership in a particular group. Thus, when your class meets, someone has the role of teacher, and others have the role of students. Is someone a student leader in your class? Does someone always remain silent? Is another person always making jokes? Each of us has *multiple roles* that shift as we merge with different groups. Occasionally, we may find ourselves in *role conflict,* such as if you switch schools and your old school plays your new school in football.

Decision Making

Most groups must make decisions. For example, you and your friends must decide what to do Saturday night. Jurors must decide whether a defendant is guilty or not guilty. A president's advisory committee must determine the proper solution to a company crisis. Group polarization and groupthink are two processes of group decision making.

group polarization: theory that group discussion reinforces the majority's point of view and shifts group members' opinions to a more extreme position

Group Polarization Have you ever expressed an opinion and discussed it with a group of friends? How did the discussion affect the strength of your opinion? According to **group polarization,** if you discuss an opinion with a group of people and a majority of the members argue for one side of the issue, the discussion typically pushes the majority to a more extreme view than they held before the discussion (see Figure 19.5). What occurs is that the majority's point of view is reinforced. The repetition of the same arguments results in stronger attitudes in support of the majority's view. (If opinions of a group are equally split on an issue before a discussion, though, the group discussion usually results in compromise.)

For example, say you think that bikers should wear helmets. One afternoon at lunch, the subject of bikers and helmets comes up. Most of your friends also believe that bikers should wear helmets. As your group discusses the issue, you and your friends use examples and your own reasoning to argue the point. You come away from the discussion feeling very strongly about the issue—much more strongly than before the discussion. You feel that it should be mandatory for bikers to wear helmets.

Groupthink Throughout history, government leaders have sometimes made poor decisions. When John F. Kennedy became president of the United States in 1961, he faced the problem of Fidel Castro, the Communist leader of Cuba. Castro formed a close alliance with the Soviet Union, and this alliance threatened the security of the United States. Kennedy ordered a secret invasion of Cuba to overthrow Castro. The invasion at the Bay of Pigs failed miserably, making Kennedy's administration look weak and bringing the world close to nuclear war. Why did Kennedy make this ill-fated decision? Kennedy and his administration were the victims of groupthink.

When groups emphasize sticking together and fail to adequately appraise alternative courses of action, they are guilty of **groupthink.** When engaged in groupthink, groups do not make the best decisions. Group members may refrain from criticizing one another, and they may not discuss opposing viewpoints or critically evaluate the situation.

While discussing the Bay of Pigs invasion, Kennedy's advisers failed to critically examine Kennedy's decision to invade. Instead, they

groupthink: poor group decision making that occurs as a result of a group emphasizing unity over critical thinking

Figure 19.5 Group Polarization

Each triangle represents the opinion of one individual. Before the group discussion, individuals are divided in the content and strength of their opinions. After the group discussion, individuals' opinions move toward a more extreme version from their initial opinions. *Why do opinions become more extreme during group polarization?*

Before group discussion

After group discussion

Source: Peter Gray, *Psychology*, 1999.

Figure 19.6 The *Challenger* Explosion

The decision to launch the *Challenger* U.S. space shuttle in below-freezing weather in January 1986 was the result of groupthink. Managers ignored the engineers' warnings about the dangers of launching. In full view of people on the ground and millions more on television, the space shuttle exploded just after its launch. *How can groups prevent groupthink?*

sociogram: a diagram that represents relationships within a group, especially likes and dislikes of members for other members

sought to please the president and present a unified front. Several hundred members of the invading force at the Bay of Pigs lost their lives as a result of the decision.

How to Improve Group Decision Making Groups can avoid bad decision making and improve the quality of their decisions. Leaders should avoid strongly advocating their own views and, instead, encourage group discussion. During discussion, group members should hear all viewpoints and challenge one another's views. Minority viewpoints should be expressed and discussed. Also, group members should focus on the task—the issue to be discussed or the problem to be resolved. Group members should not focus on group unity when making decisions; however, they should focus on keeping the lines of communication open and gathering enough information to make an unbiased decision.

Communication Patterns

When studying groups, social psychologists use a technique called the **sociogram** to analyze group structure. All members of a group are asked to name those people with whom they would like to interact on a given occasion or for a specific purpose, those they like best, and so on. For example, the members may be asked with whom they would like to go to a party, to discuss politics, to spend a vacation, or to complete a task. Their choices can then be diagrammed, as shown in Figure 19.7. Sociograms can help psychologists predict how that individual is likely to communicate with other group members. Another way to discover the structure of a group is to examine the communication patterns in the group—who says what to whom and how often.

One experiment on communication patterns was conducted by Harold Leavitt in 1951. He gave a card with several symbols on it to each person in a group of five. Leavitt put each person in a separate room or booth and allowed the members to communicate only by written messages. In this way he was able to create the networks shown in Figure 19.8. Each circle represents a person, and the lines represent open channels. Participants placed in each position could exchange messages only with the person to whom they were connected by channels.

The most interesting result of this experiment was that the people who were organized into a "circle" were the slowest at solving the problem but the happiest at doing it. In this group everyone sent and received a large number of messages until someone solved the problem and passed the information on. In the "wheel," by contrast, everyone sent a few messages to one center person, who figured out the answer and told the rest what it was. These groups found the solution quickly, but the people on the outside of the wheel did not particularly enjoy the job.

Following the experiment, the members in each group were asked to identify the leader of their group. In the centralized groups (wheel, Y, and chain), the person in the center was usually chosen as the group leader.

In the circle network, however, half the group members said they thought there was no real leader, and those who did say there was a leader disagreed on who that leader was. Thus a centralized organization seems more useful for task-oriented groups, whereas a decentralized network is more useful in socially oriented groups.

Leadership

All groups, whether made up of students, workers, Girl Scouts, or politicians, have leaders. A leader embodies the norms and ideals of the group and represents the group to outsiders. Within the group, a leader initiates action, gives orders, makes decisions, and settles disputes. In short, a leader is one who has a great deal of influence on the other members.

Leadership may be defined in several ways. Most of us think of leadership as a *personality trait*. To an extent, this is true. One psychologist (Stogdill, 1974) identified leadership as being an aspect of personality—the ability to get people to comply. It can be thought of as skills in social influence or persuasion or simply as social power. It has been found that leaders tend to be better adjusted, more self-confident, more energetic and outgoing, and slightly more intelligent than other members of their group (Gibb, 1969). Other researchers (Blake & Mouton, 1985) proposed a different model. They argue that leaders are concerned to some degree with both output (that is, the task) and the welfare of the people. Each dimension is separate, and any leader can be at any level on either dimension. A leader deeply concerned with both output and welfare would likely develop a team management program so that workers contribute to the group's goals. A leader concerned solely with output would stress obedience, and a leader whose primary concern was the worker might create a stress-free atmosphere with a friendly organization. A leader who cared little for output or welfare might encourage workers to do the minimum to keep things functioning (Blake & McCanse, 1991).

Another way to think of leadership is as the *end product of the reinforcements of the group* being led (Berry & Houston, 1993). In this way, leadership is simply the center or focus of group action, an instrument for achieving the group's goal or a result of group interaction (Stogdill, 1974). In this sense, the nature of the group in part determines who will lead. Different circumstances call for different kinds of leaders. A group that is threatened by internal conflict requires a leader who is good at handling people, settling disputes, and soothing tempers. A group that has a complex task to perform needs a leader with special experience to set goals and plan strategies for achieving them (Fiedler, 1969).

Another kind of leadership is called a *transformational leadership*. This leadership produces large-scale organizational change by changing the goals of group members and deepening their commitment. Transformational leaders are charismatic, they provide individualized attention to group members, and they are able to enthuse and intellectually stimulate group members. Charisma refers to a leader's persuasive powers. This, in turn, is based on the followers' perceptions of the leader's talents and expertise. When a leader is charismatic, followers trust the correctness

Figure 19.7 Sociograms

In these sociograms, the blue arrows indicate admiration that is not returned, and the black arrows indicate a two-way friendship. The more a person is liked, the higher in the pattern he or she appears. The pattern of the bottom group shows a hierarchical structure. *Who are the leaders in the bottom group?*

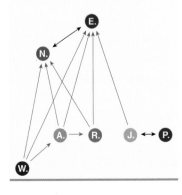

Figure 19.8 Leavitt's Communication Network System

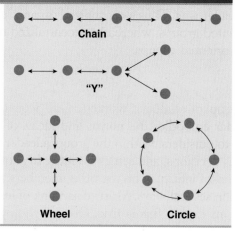

Each dot represents a person. The lines represent open channels. Participants could exchange messages only with the person to whom they were connected by channels. *What were Leavitt's findings regarding centralized organizations?*

Chain

"Y"

Wheel

Circle

of the leader's views, obey the leader willingly, feel affection for the leader, and are motivated to perform at peak levels. Presidents Franklin D. Roosevelt and John F. Kennedy have been called charismatic leaders.

Leadership Styles The three leadership styles are authoritarian, laissez-faire, and democratic. An *authoritarian* leader makes all the decisions and assigns tasks to group members. These leaders are focused on completing tasks and compliance to group goals. Authoritarian leaders, such as Laurent Kabila of the Democratic Republic of the Congo, tell other group members what to do and demand obedience. A *laissez-faire* leader is only minimally involved in a group's decision making. This leader encourages the group to make its own decisions. Under this type of leadership, groups do not actively pursue group goals, and group members make all the decisions. When leading a discussion, your teacher may be a good example of a laissez-faire leader—one who encourages group members to explore their own ideas. A *democratic* leader encourages group members to come to decisions through consensus. These leaders are often viewed as supportive but not good decision makers. Democratic leaders, such as those in the U.S. Congress, try to build a consensus among group members.

SECTION 1 Assessment

1. **Review the Vocabulary** Explain how groups organized for task functions differ from those organized for social functions. Give an example of a task and social group to which you belong.

2. **Visualize the Main Idea** Using a graphic organizer similar to the one below, identify and describe the three styles of leadership.

3. **Recall Information** What is the difference between an in-group and an out-group? Give an example of each group.

4. **Think Critically** When might a group benefit from a laissez-faire style of leadership? When might a group benefit from authoritarian leadership?

5. **Application Activity** Describe an activity that you did in the past month in front of a crowd. How did you perform? Analyze why you performed this way in a brief report.

Conformity and Obedience

Reader's Guide

■ Main Idea
You may engage in behavior because of direct or indirect group pressure or in response to orders given by authorities.

■ Vocabulary
- conformity
- obedience

■ Objectives
- Identify ways that groups can influence an individual's behavior.
- Explain why most people tend to obey authority figures.

EXPLORING PSYCHOLOGY

Why Are They Running?

Suddenly someone began to run. It may be that he had simply remembered, all of a moment, an engagement to meet his wife, for which he was now frightfully late. Whatever it was, he ran east on Broad Street (probably toward the Maramor Restaurant, a favorite place for a man to meet his wife). Somebody else began to run, perhaps a newsboy in high spirits. Another man, a portly gentleman of affairs, broke into a trot. Inside of ten minutes, everybody on High Street, from the Union Depot to the Courthouse was running. A loud mumble gradually crystallized into the dread word "dam." "The dam has broke!" The fear was put into words by a little old lady in an electric car, or by a traffic cop, or by a small boy: nobody knows who, nor does it now really matter.

—from "The Day the Dam Broke" in *My Life and Hard Times* by James Thurber, 1933

The above passage is a good example of people conforming to group pressures. Why did they run? They ran because everyone else was running. Most of these individuals did not make a decision based on their own reasoning; rather, they conformed to a group decision—to run.

GROUP PRESSURE TO CONFORM

Have you ever come home and surprised your parents by wearing the latest fad in clothing? Possibly the conversation that followed went something like this:

"How can you go around looking like that?"

"But everyone dresses like this."

Psychologist Solomon Asch (1952) designed what has become a classic experiment to test conformity to pressure from one's peers. **Conformity** involves any behavior that you engage in because of direct or indirect group pressure. He found that people may conform to other people's ideas of the truth, even when they disagree. The following is what you would have experienced if you had been a participant in this experiment.

You and six other students meet in a classroom for an experiment on visual judgment. You are shown a card with one line on it. You are then shown another card containing three lines and are asked to pick the one that is the same length as the first line. One of the three is exactly the same length and is easy to determine. The other two lines are obviously different (see Figure 19.9). The experiment begins uneventfully. The participants announce their answers in the order in which they are seated in the room. You happen to be sixth, and one person follows you. On the first comparison, every person chooses the same matching line. The second set of cards is displayed, and once again the group is unanimous. The discriminations seem simple and easy, and you prepare for what you expect will be a rather boring experiment.

On the third trial, there is an unexpected disturbance. You are quite certain that line 2 is the one that matches the standard. Yet the first person in the group announces confidently that line 1 is the correct match. Then the second person follows suit, and he, too, declares that the answer is line 1; so do the third, fourth, and fifth participants. Now it is your turn. You are suddenly faced with two contradictory pieces of information: the evidence of your own senses tells you that one answer is clearly correct, but the unanimous and confident judgments of the five preceding participants tell you that you are wrong.

The dilemma persists through 18 trials. On 12 of the trials, the other group members unanimously give an answer that differs from what you clearly perceive to be correct. It is only at the end of the experimental session that you learn the explanation for the confusion. The six other participants were all actors, and they had been instructed to give incorrect answers on those 12 trials (see Figure 19.10).

How do most participants react to this situation? Asch found that almost one-third of his 50 participants conformed at least half the time. These conformers he called the "yielders." Most yielders explained to Asch afterward that they knew which line was correct but that they yielded to group pressure to not appear different from the others. Asch called those who did not conform "independents." (About 25 percent of the participants were independents.) They gave the correct answer despite group pressure. Why so much conformity? According to one

conformity: acting in accordance with some specified authority

Figure 19.9	Asch's Experiment

These two cards were shown to participants in one trial of Asch's experiment on conformity. The participants' task was to determine whether the length of the standard line matches the length of the comparison lines. The actual discrimination is easy. *What was the purpose of Asch's experiment?*

Standard Line   Comparison Lines

Figure 19.10   Should He Conform?

These photographs were taken during Asch's experiment on conformity. Participant 6 is the only real participant, and the others are collaborators with the experimenter. The participant listens to the others express identical judgments that differ from his own. He is in a dilemma: Does he express the judgment he knows to be correct and risk being different from the group, or does he conform to the group's judgment? *Why does Participant 6 find himself in a dilemma? What were Asch's findings?*

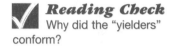

theory, most children are taught the overriding importance of being liked and of being accepted. Conformity is the standard means of gaining this approval.

Reading Check
Why did the "yielders" conform?

Why Do People Conform?

One of the most important findings of Asch's experiment was that if even one person among the first five failed to conform to the group's judgment, the participant was able to stick to his own perceptions. It seems that it is hardest to stand alone. Later researchers have shown that under some conditions, a minority view can come to win over the larger group (Moscovici, 1985). By disagreeing with the majority view, a person can actually reduce the pressure that others feel to conform. A minority dissenter may also serve an informational purpose by making others question whether the majority view is actually right. When people hear a dissenting opinion, they are more likely to examine the issue more closely, which can lead to a better solution.

In Asch's experiment, participants conformed—they responded to match the other group members' responses, yet they might not have actually changed their beliefs that the lines matched. This is an example of *compliance.* Compliance occurs when we give in to social pressure in our public behavior; however, we do not actually change our private beliefs.

A method of gaining compliance is the *foot-in-the-door technique.* This occurs when you get a person to agree to a relatively minor request. This minor request, which the participant is likely to agree with, is really a set-up for a major request. For example, a car salesperson might get you into the showroom by saying, "Just come in, and we'll run a few numbers—no obligation." Once you are in the showroom, though, you

How do we conform to group norms?

Norms are formalized rules for how members of groups should behave. They can exert strong influences on other members' behaviors. How do people react when group norms are not adhered to?

Procedure

1. Think of a norm that regulates what an individual should or should not do in a given situation. (Examples include standing a certain distance from a person when talking, not talking during a movie, or wearing certain types of clothing for given situations.)

2. Design and act out an experiment in which you do not adhere to the norm.

Analysis

1. What were the general reactions of other group members to you not adhering to the particular norm?

2. How did other people's reactions make you feel?

3. Do you think norms are always useful? Can they be harmful? Why do you think so?

See the Skills Handbook, page 622, for an explanation of designing an experiment.

obedience: a change in attitude or behavior brought about by social pressure to comply with people perceived to be authorities

are more likely to develop the attitude that "I need that car." Whereas initially, your commitment was minor, later you commit more intensely.

There are several factors that increase conforming behavior in people. The factors include:

- belonging to a group that emphasizes the role of groups rather than individuals
- the desire to be liked by other members of the group
- low self-esteem
- social shyness
- lack of familiarity with a task
- group size (Conformity increases as the size of the group grows, up to at least eight people. At that point, conformity is not affected.)
- cultural influences

OBEDIENCE TO AUTHORITY

The influence other people have on your attitudes and actions is considerable. Sometimes this influence is indirect and subtle, and at other times it is quite direct. People may simply tell you what to believe and what to do. Under what conditions do you obey them?

Everyone in this society has had experiences with various authorities, such as parents, teachers, police officers, managers, judges, clergy, and military officers. **Obedience,** or behavior in response to orders given by these authorities, can be either useful or destructive. For instance, obeying the orders of a doctor or firefighter in an emergency would be constructive. Psychologists are more interested, however, in the negative aspects of obedience. They know from cases in history such as German Nazism and American atrocities in Vietnam that individuals frequently obey irrational commands. In fact, people often obey authority even when obedience goes against their conscience and their whole system of morality.

The Milgram Experiment

Psychologist Stanley Milgram conducted the most famous investigation of obedience in 1963 (see Figure 19.12). Milgram set up the experiment as follows. Two participants appeared for each session. They were told that they would be participating in an experiment to test the effects of punishment on memory. One of the participants was to be the "teacher" and the other, the "learner." In reality, the learner was not a volunteer participant; he was Milgram's accomplice. The teacher was to read into a microphone a list of words to be memorized by the learner, who would be in a nearby room. If the learner failed to recite the list back correctly, the teacher was to administer an electric shock. The alleged purpose of the experiment was to test whether the shock would have any effect on learning. In actuality, however, Milgram wanted to discover how far the teacher would follow his instructions and how much shock he would be willing to give a fellow human being. (Milgram surveyed a group of psychology students before the experiment. All respondents predicted that only very few participants would be willing to shock the learner.)

As the experiment began, the learner continually gave wrong answers, and the teacher began to administer the prescribed shocks from an impressive-looking shock generator. The generator had a dial that ranged from 15 volts, which was labeled "Slight Shock," to 450 volts, which was labeled "Danger: Severe Shock." After each of the learner's mistakes, the teacher was told to increase the voltage by one level. The teacher believed that the learner was receiving these shocks because he had seen the learner being strapped into a chair in the other room and had watched electrodes being attached to the learner's hands. In reality, however, the accomplice was receiving no shocks at all from the equipment.

As the experiment progressed, the learner made many mistakes, and the teacher was instructed to give increasingly severe shocks. At 300 volts the learner pounded on the wall in protest and refused to provide any further answers. At this point the experimenter instructed the participant to treat the absence of an answer as a wrong answer and to continue the procedure. The experiment ended either when the maximum 450 volts was administered or when the teacher refused to administer any more shocks. If at any point the teacher indicated that he wanted to stop, the experimenter calmly told him to continue: "Whether the learner likes it or not, you must go on until he has learned all the word pairs correctly."

Sixty-five percent of the participants delivered the full range of shocks. These participants were not sadists. Many of them showed signs of extreme tension and discomfort during the session, and they often told the experimenter that they would like to stop. Despite these feelings, most continued to obey the experimenter's commands. They were ordinary people—salespeople, engineers, and postal workers—placed in an unusual situation.

What accounts for this surprisingly high level of obedience? Part of the answer is that the experimenter represents a legitimate authority. People assume that such an authority knows what he is doing, even when his instructions seem to run counter to their own standards of moral behavior.

THE FAR SIDE By GARY LARSON

Laboratory peer pressure

Figure 19.11 **Going With the Group**

Conforming to a group has practical explanations. If you see people running out of a building, you may assume that they know something you do not—that the building is on fire, for example. *What are other reasons for conforming with a group?*

Figure 19.12   Milgram's Experiment

(a) In Milgram's experiment on obedience, the "learner" is connected to the shock apparatus. (b) Milgram explains the procedure to the "teacher." (c) This participant refuses to administer shocks any further and angrily rises in protest. (d) Milgram explains the truth about the experiment. (© 1965 by Stanley Milgram. From the film *Obedience.* Distributed by New York University Film Library.) *Why did many participants continue to administer shocks to the learner?*

Milgram's participants could have walked out at any time—they had nothing to lose by leaving. Nevertheless, social conditioning for obeying legitimate authorities is so strongly ingrained that people often lack the words or the ways to do otherwise. Simply getting up and leaving would have violated powerful unwritten rules of acceptable social behavior.

Milgram's experiment is important because it questions so many different aspects of psychology. The experiment, though, raised questions about the ethics of some psychological experiments. How would you feel if you had been one of Milgram's participants? How would you feel if you had been deceived into engaging in hurtful behavior? Since the experiment, the APA has changed the ethical standards for experiments. Today all experiments, especially those that have potential to cause psychological harm, are carefully screened by research committees. These committees propose ways to eliminate or limit potential harm to experiment participants.

The Zimbardo Experiment

One Sunday summer morning, a siren shattered the silence, awakening Tommy Whitlow. As Tommy opened his eyes, a police cruiser pulled up, screeching its tires to a halt. The police arrested Tommy, charging him with a felony. They informed him of his rights, frisked and handcuffed him, and placed him in the police vehicle. At the station, police fingerprinted and booked Tommy. They then blindfolded him and led him to the Stanford County Prison. Once he was there, guards stripped him naked and sprayed him down with a disinfectant. He was ordered to wear a beige smock uniform with his identification number patched on the front. Police arrested eight other students that morning as well.

Tommy and the other students were actually participants in another experiment that caused ordinary people to act in extraordinary ways. Philip Zimbardo and his colleagues (Haney & Zimbardo, 1975) performed the experiment. Tommy and the other volunteers had answered a newspaper ad—they had no idea that they would be "arrested."

Zimbardo randomly divided the male volunteers into two groups: "prisoners" and "prison guards." He sent both groups to live in a simulated "prison" set up in the basement of a Stanford University building. He gave the guards instructions to maintain order. Within two days, most of the guards had become intoxicated with power, and they acted cruelly toward the prisoners, often without reason. The guards expected the prisoners to follow the rules without question. If the prisoners did not follow the rules, they lost the privilege to read or write letters. As the prisoners disobeyed more rules, the punishments increased. Sometimes the guards subjected the prisoners to embarrassment, humiliation, and mindless tasks such as push-ups and washing toilets with their bare hands.

At the same time, the prisoners began showing signs of extreme stress, often acting subdued and depressed. Sometimes the prisoners refused to follow the rules. They yelled back at the guards, made negative comments about the jail, and later became passive from defeat. Some of the prisoners became angry and disillusioned, while others developed psychological

More About...

Collectivism

Many Americans value individualism—a focus on defining oneself in individual terms and giving priority to personal goals. Other societies, though, focus on collectivism—defining oneself in terms of the groups to which one belongs and giving priority to the groups' goals. Individuals in collective societies, such as those in Africa, Asia, and Central and South America, work to control their behaviors and maintain harmonious relationships with others. These individuals are encouraged to be dependent on and submissive to the values of the group. People from collectivist cultures have different priorities and thus have different strategies in how they resolve conflicts and deal with others.

Figure 19.13　Other Cultures

Some cultures, such as the Mexican culture, place greater emphasis on the group rather than the individual. Individuals are viewed as part of the family and society and must work hard to maintain harmonious relationships with others. *How do you think the American culture views individuals' roles in groups?*

Figure 19.14 **Obeying Orders**

Military pilots do not witness the consequences of their actions. They identify and kill their enemies simply by targeting a blip on a radar screen. *Why might it be easier to obey if you are shielded from the consequences of your actions?*

illnesses and rashes. The emotional reactions were so extreme that experimenters ended the planned two-week experiment after only six days. It seems that the prison environment was much stronger than individual personalities. Although the participants in this experiment were emotionally mature and stable (according to tests administered before the experiment), the roles these individuals adopted changed the way they acted. There may be other situations in everyday life that cause us and those around us to act in ways we do not expect.

In follow-up interviews, none of the participants reported any lasting effects. Some of the participants had difficulty understanding how powerful the experiment had become. The experiment not only changed the ethical standards of experimentation in psychology but it also demonstrated the power that situations can have in changing how we feel, think, and behave. The social situation of being in the prison changed the rules, roles, and expectations of the students (Zimbardo, 1975).

Why Do People Obey? Why did the Germans obey Adolf Hitler's commands to commit genocide during World War II? Why do cult members sometimes consent to their leaders' orders to commit suicide? After all, these leaders' commands are clearly unreasonable, right? Psychologists have proposed that people learn to obey authority figures. Throughout our lives, we obey parents, doctors, teachers, and religious leaders. Throughout our lives, we also have learned to follow orders. We follow traffic rules, school rules, and parental rules. However, we are more likely to follow these rules when the authority figure is actually present.

SECTION 2 Assessment

1. **Review the Vocabulary** Give an example of a way you show conformity.

2. **Visualize the Main Idea** Duplicate and complete the chart below, describing the Asch experiment.

   The Asch Experiment

Hypothesis:	
Method:	
Results:	

3. **Recall Information** How is compliance related to conformity? Explain.

4. **Think Critically** Do you think that conforming to a group is always a negative thing to do? Explain.

5. **Application Activity** Try this experiment with your family or group of friends. Stare at the ceiling continuously for a time. Do other people start to look up at the ceiling also? Why or why not? Explain the principles behind this experiment.

Your Stripes or *Your Morality*

Period of Study: 1994

Introduction: Lawrence Rockwood, a captain in the United States Army, had served in the army for close to 20 years when he was ordered to lead a force of troops into Haiti. (A military government had come to power in Haiti. U.S. troops provided stability while the democratically elected government regained power.) Through the mission, President William J. Clinton intended to stop brutal crimes imposed on the Haitian people. Confident and eager about his mission, Rockwood strongly advocated human rights for people all over the world. Rockwood did not know, however, that his mission would clash intensely with his morals.

Hypothesis: Similar to the studies conducted by Asch and Milgram, the hypothesis was that when faced with pressure to conform, an individual would conform to the group or an authority.

Method: Immediately upon arrival in Haiti, U.S. leaders changed the mission from "stopping brutal crimes" to "forced protection," or keeping American troops safe from harm. Commanders ordered Captain Rockwood to survey local Haitian prisons and report on the conditions there. Rockwood found and reported horrible conditions in these prisons. Guards mistreated and tortured prisoners. Rockwood discovered that one of the prisons had about 30 inmates housed in one small cell and that one man had been confined in a position so long that portions of his skin had rotted off.

Outraged at these conditions, Captain Rockwood petitioned for special operations units to enter the prisons and enforce the rules and regulations involving prisoners of war. A senior officer listened to Rockwood's pleas. The officer recommended that special operations investigate the prisons. Special operations turned down the request.

This refusal prompted Rockwood to take matters into his own hands. Knowing his military career would be put on the line by way of court-martial, Rockwood disobeyed direct orders, climbed the outer fence of his base, and proceeded to a Haitian prison where he demanded to evaluate each prisoner. Four hours later, a United States major arrived at the prison and ordered Rockwood to leave. When Rockwood resisted, troops forced him out of the prison.

Army psychiatrists evaluated Rockwood twice and found him sane. The army then charged him with disobeying direct orders. In Rockwood's own defense, he stated, "I am more sensitive to human rights concerns than the average officer."

Results: In 1995 the Army court-martialed Rockwood for his actions. The Army sentenced Rockwood to dismissal—equal to a dishonorable discharge—despite his perfect military record and stripped him of some pay and allowances. All of this occurred because Rockwood chose not to conform to the extreme pressures placed upon him by the military. He made the moral decision to come to the aid of his fellow human beings. Many people question the power the United States military possesses in making each and every soldier conform to and obey the ideology of each armed forces branch, no matter what the cost. The case of Captain Lawrence Rockwood and his squashed crusade for human rights demonstrates the power of an individual to resist conformity.

Analyzing the Case Study

1. Why did Rockwood refuse to conform to group pressure?

2. Does this case study support the findings of Milgram and Asch? Explain.

3. Critical Thinking Under what circumstances might Rockwood have obeyed his orders? Do you think that conformity depends upon the situation or the person? Or both? Explain your answer.

Reader's Guide

■ Main Idea

Conflicts between groups are a fact of everyday life because groups influence how individuals perceive and respond to situations.

■ Vocabulary

- aggression
- catharsis
- altruism
- diffusion of responsibility
- bystander effect
- social loafing
- deindividuation

■ Objectives

- Explain causes of group conflict and cooperation.
- Summarize how group dynamics promote or restrain altruism and aggression.

EXPLORING PSYCHOLOGY

Watching From Above

This was the evening of April 29, 1992. The Los Angeles Riots were erupting below us. . . .

I peered though my side-window as the copter continued to circle in a steep bank. I could see the traffic was moving through the intersection below us. I watched as various cars whipped in a U-turn around to avoid the ominous chaos ahead. There were clusters of people milling around. They were throwing rocks and bottles at passing cars. There were no police officers around, just an unruly mob venting hate on innocent motorists who happened to find themselves in the wrong place at the wrong time.

—from *News at Ten: Fifty Years With Stan Chambers* by Stan Chambers, 1994

In April 1992, the media released footage of four white police officers beating an African American motorist. When 12 jurors found the police officers not guilty of the beating, mob violence erupted in South Central Los Angeles. That violence continued for several days and fed on itself, resulting in 55 deaths and $1 billion in damages.

What causes group violence? Why did some people in Los Angeles harm others? Would they have committed those same lawless acts in a different and calmer atmosphere?

AGGRESSION

Any behavior that is intended to cause physical or psychological harm is called **aggression.** It seems that our society is being torn apart by increasing violence and aggression. What causes humans to act in ways that harm others? Psychologists have proposed several theories to explain aggression.

Biological Influences

Some animals are naturally aggressive. For instance, you might know that when injured, some otherwise friendly dogs become vicious. This violent response is an innate biological reaction. Psychologists have proposed that humans also have innate biological factors that cause aggression. Neurotransmitters, such as serotonin, influence a person's aggressive behavior. When a person has too much serotonin in the brain, he or she may experience violent outbursts.

Studies on mice indicate that mice whose genes have been altered so that their brains lack serotonin receptors attack other mice quicker and with more intensity than other mice (Shih, 1996). Psychologists, though, warn against labeling aggression as caused by only biological factors.

Cognitive Factors

Psychologist Albert Bandura proposes that children learn aggressive behavior by observing and imitating their parents. Bandura suggested that we watch models perform and then imitate the models' behavior. His social learning theory also proposes that aggressive behavior may be reinforced in several ways. Parents who use aggression to discipline their children may be teaching their children to use aggression.

The media—television, movies, video games, and music—may also be teaching aggressive behavior to children. By 18 years of age, the average American has witnessed an estimated 200,000 acts of violence on television alone (American Academy of Pediatrics, 1995). As children witness media violence, they grow "immune" to the horror of violence, gradually accept violence as a way to solve problems, imitate the violence they observe, and identify with certain characters whether they are victims or victimizers.

Personality Factors

Certain personality traits, such as impulsiveness and having little empathy, combined with favoring domination can turn a person into a bully. Aggressive people also may be arrogant and egotistical. People often strike out at others to affirm their sense of superiority (Baumeister, Smart, & Boden, 1996). Can psychologists predict violent behavior based on personality factors? Usually past experience is the best predictor. An aggressive child usually becomes an aggressive adult.

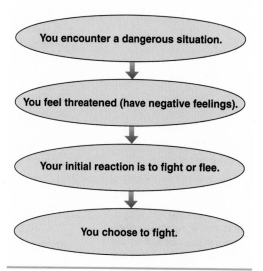

Figure 19.15   A Model of Aggression

This is just one model of aggression. Psychologists have proposed various biological, cognitive, and environmental factors that influence a person's response to the fight-or-flight dilemma. *What leads to aggression in this model?*

> You encounter a dangerous situation.
>
> You feel threatened (have negative feelings).
>
> Your initial reaction is to fight or flee.
>
> You choose to fight.

aggression: behavior intended to do physical or psychological harm to others

Environmental Factors

Sometimes something provokes you and you become violent. Maybe your friend borrowed something without telling you. Maybe another driver refused to let you merge into traffic. Psychologists explain acts of violence that arise from such situations with the *frustration-aggression hypothesis*. This is the idea that frustration or a failure to obtain something expected leads to aggression. The hypothesis, though, fails to note that frustration does not always lead to aggressive behavior. For instance, if your friend trips and falls into you, knocking a soda out of your hands, you may not feel angry once you realize that it was an accident.

Leonard Berkowitz (1989) proposed a modified frustration-aggression hypothesis. Berkowitz proposes that frustration leads to aggression only in certain instances. For example, when a stranger bumps into you, you may strike that person if you have done so before or if the person does not intimidate you. However, you will probably not strike that person if you have never been in a fight or have had bad experiences with fighting.

CONTROLLING AGGRESSION

catharsis: releasing anger or aggression by letting out powerful negative emotions

Aggression, then, is a combination of biological, cognitive, personality, and environmental factors. Knowing this, how do we limit and control aggression? One method is through catharsis. **Catharsis** involves releasing anger or aggression by expressing powerful negative emotions. For instance, when you are angry, you should "get it off your chest." This might mean talking to a friend, playing a tough game of soccer, or kicking a toy animal for a while. Unfortunately, critics of catharsis believe that any expression of aggression is negative. They point out that expressing your aggression may lead to more aggression.

Other strategies of controlling aggression include punishing children for violent behavior and cutting down on the violence they observe. Excessive punishment, though, may trigger aggressive behavior. People can also be taught to control their aggression. Aggressive behavior can be controlled by teaching people to accept frustrations and move on and to react to disappointments in ways other than violence. If people do not view violence as an option, then they will not resort to violence.

GROUP CONFLICT VERSUS COOPERATION

Conflicts between groups are a fact of everyday life: some level of hostility can exist between women and men, young and old, workers and bosses, African Americans and whites, Catholics and Protestants, and students and teachers. Why do these conflicts exist, and why do they persist? Let us consider the findings of a group of psychologists (Sherif & Hovland, 1961) who

Did You Know?

American Violence Social psychologists blame our culture for the increasing amount of violence. They say that social changes have left people feeling isolated and disconnected. The American culture encourages self-centeredness and violence. Arnold Goldstein of the Center for Research on Aggression at Syracuse University commented, "We are a nation whose role models, presidents, and leaders on Wall Street have set the tone for the country—I'm going to get mine" (Benson & Roehlkepartain, 1993).

created a boys' camp to study intergroup relations. The camp at Robber's Cave offered all the usual activities, and the boys had no idea that they were part of an experiment.

From the beginning of the experiment, the boys were divided into two groups. The boys hiked, swam, and played baseball only with members of their own group, and friendships and group spirit soon developed. After a while the experimenters (working as counselors) brought the groups together for a tournament. The psychologists had hypothesized that when these two groups of boys were placed in competitive situations, where one group could achieve its goals only at the expense of the other, hostility would develop. They were right.

Although the games began in a spirit of good sportsmanship, tension mounted as the tournament continued. Friendly competition gave way to name calling, fistfights, and raids on enemy cabins. The psychologists had demonstrated the ease with which they could produce unity within the two boys' groups and hatred between them. The experimenters then tried to see what might end the conflict and create harmony between the two groups. They tried to bring the groups together for enjoyable activities, such as a movie and a good meal. This approach failed. The campers shoved and pushed each other, threw food and insults, and generally used the opportunity to continue their attacks.

Next, the psychologists deliberately invented a series of "emergencies" so that the boys either would have to help one another or lose the chance to do or get something they all wanted. For instance, one morning someone reported that the water line to the camp had broken. The boys were told that unless they worked together to find the break and fix it, they would all have to leave camp. By afternoon, they had jointly found and fixed the damage. Gradually, through such cooperative activities, intergroup hostility and tensions lessened. Friendships began to develop between individuals of the opposing groups, and eventually the groups began to seek out occasions to mingle. At the end of the camp period, members of both groups requested that they ride home together on the same bus.

The results of this experiment were striking. A group of boys from identical backgrounds had developed considerable hostility toward each other, simply because they were placed in competition. The crucial factor in eliminating group hostility was cooperation.

The question of conflict is not confined just to small groups. It applies to large communities, too, but then the possibility of a *social trap* is greater. A social trap occurs when individuals in a group decide not to cooperate. Instead, they act selfishly and create a bad situation for all. An

More About...

Gangs

The Federal Bureau of Investigation (FBI) estimates that there are 400,000 active gang members in the United States. In about 700 cities across the nation, these gangs are harming the communities in which they operate (Office of International Criminal Justice, 1999). Police departments have identified three types of gangs.

Social gangs are relatively permanent groups that hang out in a specific location. Members often engage in organized group activities. Members may hold the norms and values of society in general. *Delinquent gangs* are organized around the principle of monetary gain. Members depend on one another to carry out planned activities. The leader is usually the most skilled member at stealing. *Violent gangs* are organized to obtain emotional gratification from violent activities. Members spend their time carrying out violent acts. Leaders are usually emotionally unstable—they have a need to control others. Group members overestimate the importance and power of their group, and there may be violence within the group (Austin Police Department Gang Suppression Unit, 1999).

Anyone may become a victim of gang violence. Gang members are constantly recruiting members, focusing on younger and younger recruits. Many delinquent and violent gang members become career criminals. How do we stop the spread of gangs? We must teach children self-control and how to deal appropriately with problems. Citizens should get involved in and promote community gang resistance programs.

illustration of the social trap can be seen in the way Americans have responded to the problems of pollution. We know that automobile exhaust pollutes the air. We know that one way to reduce air pollution is to carpool or use public transportation. Yet the driver who commutes 30 miles a day alone and who knows that he or she is polluting the air thinks: "Yes, I know my car exhaust is bad, but I am only one person. If I stop driving, it won't make any difference." As long as we fall into that social trap, we continue to destroy our environment.

Psychologists have been exploring ways to overcome social traps such as this one. One approach is to use laws to bring about behavior changes, such as the law requiring special exhaust systems in cars. Other ways to change people's behavior is to educate them concerning the issues and to communicate the idea that "Yes, you do make a difference." By publicizing the problems and solutions and organizing groups to act, individuals begin to believe that what they do does have an impact, and their actions are reinforced by the group. In this way, people find it more beneficial to cooperate than to act in a purely selfish manner.

ALTRUISM

altruism: helping others, often at a cost or risk, for reasons other than rewards

Altruism means helping another, often with a risk to oneself, for reasons other than the expectation of a reward. Consider the following scene: You are walking on a crowded street and suddenly hear a scuffle off to the side. You turn to see a man trying to rip a woman's purse from her grasp. Everyone else just keeps on walking past the scuffle. What do you do? Whether you help or not may depend on the diffusion of responsibility.

Diffusion of Responsibility

Sometimes when several people are faced with a common problem and there is no opponent, they may not even see themselves as a group. There have been many famous examples of muggings, rapes, and murders that were committed in public while a large group of people watched without intervening or calling for help.

Psychologists have tried to find out why these people did not act by studying artificial crises. In one experiment, college students were asked to participate in a discussion of personal problems. They were asked to wait in separate rooms. Some were told that they would be communicating with only one other person, and others were given the impression that they would be talking with as many as five other people. All communication, the psychologist told each student, was to take place over microphones so that everyone would remain anonymous and thus would be able

Figure 19.16   Us Versus Them

Intergroup conflict results when a group no longer sees the enemy as individual humans and thus can treat them indecently. This occurred in Bosnia-Herzegovina in the late 1990s. *How does intergroup hostility develop?*

to speak more freely. Each person was to talk in turn.

In reality, there were no other people—all the voices the participants heard were on tape. As the discussion progressed, the participant heard one of the other participants go into what sounded like an epileptic seizure. The victim began to call for help and make choking sounds. The experimenters found that 85 percent of the people who thought they were alone with the victim came out of their room to help him. Of those who believed there were four other people nearby, however, only 31 percent did anything to help.

The experimenters suggested that this behavior was the result of **diffusion of responsibility.** In other words, because several people were present, each participant assumed someone else would help. The researchers found that in experiments where people could see the other participants, the same pattern emerged. In addition, bystanders reassured one another that it would not be a good idea to interfere. The **bystander effect** occurs when a person refrains from taking action because of the presence of others. These findings on diffusion of responsibility suggest that the larger the crowd or group of bystanders, the more likely any given individual is to feel that he or she is not responsible for whatever is going on (Darley & Latané, 1968).

Another influence that inhibits action is the tendency to minimize the *need* for any response. To act, you must admit that an emergency exists. You may not know exactly what is going on when you hear screams or loud thumps upstairs. You are likely to wait before risking the embarrassment of rushing to help where help is not needed or wanted. It is easier to persuade yourself that nothing needs to be done if you look around and see other people behaving calmly. Not only can you see that they think nothing is wrong but you also can see that not doing anything is entirely proper. You are able to minimize the need to act and shift any responsibility to those around you. Both the presence of a leader and being familiar with the person needing help, however, increase the likelihood and speed of help being offered. The same is true of *knowing* what kind of help is required, seeing the correct form of assistance being modeled, or expecting future interactions with the person needing help. These situations increase the chances that assistance will be offered when it is most needed (Baron & Byrne, 1991).

Social Loafing Your evaluations of a situation also may lead to social loafing. **Social loafing** occurs when you allow your contributions to the group to slack off because you realize that individual contributions

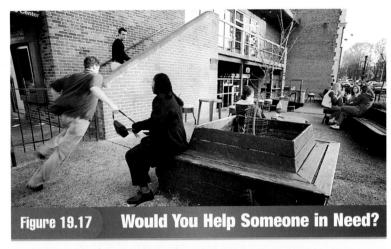

Figure 19.17 Would You Help Someone in Need?

Whether we offer assistance to someone in need depends on several factors, including what other witnesses are doing. *How does diffusion of responsibility affect our behavior in such situations?*

diffusion of responsibility: the presence of others lessens an individual's feelings of responsibility for his or her actions or failure to act

bystander effect: an individual does not take action because of the presence of others

social loafing: the tendency to work less hard when sharing the workload with others are not as apparent and easily measured in a group setting. When you are a member of a large group, for example, you may feel a reduced sense of accountability.

Deindividuation When people act as individuals, obey their consciences, and are concerned with self-evaluation, we think of them as *individualistic*. When **deindividuation** occurs, people lose their sense of self and follow group behaviors. The deindividuated person acts without thinking about self and goes along with the group. Why did normally pleasant people violently throw bottles and rocks at innocent people during the Los Angeles riots? Researchers believe that being in a crowd may reduce feelings of guilt or self-awareness that one ordinarily feels. People in crowds are anonymous—there is little chance of pinpointing who threw the rock and of being identified.

Social pressure can affect us in positive ways, too. Most people care deeply about what others think of them. This can be a powerful source of pressure for individuals to do what others believe they should do. Have you ever refrained from saying or doing something mean because you wanted others to think highly of you? Maybe you went out of your way to act compassionately while others witnessed your actions. In 1999 Microsoft Corporation Chairman Bill Gates made the largest private charitable contribution in history by donating $3.3 billion to two of his foundations. The money will support initiatives in education and world public health and will provide computer technology to libraries in low-income communities. In 1997 CNN founder Ted Turner gave a $1 billion charitable donation to the United Nations. It is difficult to say whether these charitable acts resulted from social pressure, but social influence may have played a role.

deindividuation: individuals behave irrationally when there is less chance of being personally identified

---

SECTION 3 Assessment

1. **Review the Vocabulary** How does diffusion of responsibility affect individuals in a group?

2. **Visualize the Main Idea** Using a graphic organizer similar to the one below, compare and contrast aggression and altruism.

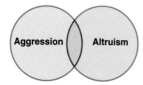

3. **Recall Information** What is deindividuation, and how does it occur?

4. **Think Critically** Do you think that most students work harder on projects they must complete alone for a grade or on team projects in which no individual grades are given? Explain your reasoning.

5. **Application Activity** Keep an "anger" diary for a week. In it include descriptions of several fight-or-flight situations that you experience or observe. Did any of the episodes lead to violence? Why or why not?

Summary and Vocabulary

People belong to many groups for a variety of reasons. Groups can affect the way individuals behave in different situations.

Section 1 Group Behavior

Main Idea: A group—a collection of people who interact, share common goals, and influence how members think and act—is unified by the attitudes and standards members share and by their commitment to them.

- To be classified as a group, a collection of people must demonstrate interdependence.
- Groups serve two general purposes: task functions and social functions.
- To be part of a group, an individual must be responsive to the norms of the group, subscribe to its ideology, and be prepared to make sacrifices in order to be part of it.
- Groups can be differentiated by in-groups and out-groups and primary and secondary groups.
- Research has shown that social facilitation seems to occur when participants perform simple tasks, whereas social inhibition seems to occur when participants perform more complex tasks.
- Group polarization and groupthink are two processes of group decision making.

Section 2 Conformity and Obedience

Main Idea: You may engage in behavior because of direct or indirect group pressure or in response to orders given by authorities.

- Psychologists believe that people conform to gain approval.
- Compliance occurs when an individual gives in to social pressure in his or her public behavior but does not actually change private beliefs.
- Psychologists believe that people conform because they learn to obey authority figures and to follow orders and rules.

Section 3 Conflict and Cooperation

Main Idea: Conflicts between groups are a fact of everyday life because groups influence how individuals perceive and respond to situations.

- Aggression is a combination of biological, cognitive, personality, and environmental factors.
- Psychologists have found that the larger the crowd or group of bystanders, the more likely any given individual is to feel that he or she is not responsible for whatever is going on.
- Social loafing occurs when people allow their contributions to the group to slack off because they realize that individual contributions are not as apparent and easily measured in a group setting.
- When deindividuation occurs, people lose their sense of self and follow group behaviors.

Chapter Vocabulary

group (p. 545)
task functions (p. 547)
social functions (p. 547)
norms (p. 547)
ideology (p. 548)
social facilitation (p. 549)
social inhibition (p. 549)
group polarization (p. 550)
groupthink (p. 551)
sociogram (p. 552)
conformity (p. 556)
obedience (p. 558)
aggression (p. 565)
catharsis (p. 566)
altruism (p. 568)
diffusion of responsibility (p. 569)
bystander effect (p. 569)
social loafing (p. 569)
deindividuation (p. 570)

Self-Check Quiz
Visit the *Understanding Psychology* Web site at
psychology.glencoe.com and click on **Chapter 19—
Self-Check Quizzes** to prepare for the Chapter Test.

Reviewing Vocabulary

Choose the letter of the correct term or concept below to complete the sentence.

a. ideology
b. social facilitation
c. social inhibition
d. group polarization
e. conformity
f. obedience
g. aggression
h. catharsis
i. bystander effect
j. deindividuation

1. _____ occurs when the majority's point of view is reinforced and an extreme view dominates.
2. A behavior that is intended to cause physical or psychological harm is called _____.
3. A group with a common _____ shares a set of principles, attitudes, and defined objectives for which the group stands.
4. _____ involves any behavior that an individual engages in because of direct or indirect group pressure.
5. The tendency to perform poorly in front of a group is known as _____.
6. _____ occurs when people lose their sense of self and follow group behaviors.
7. Punching a pillow to release anger is a form of _____.
8. The tendency to perform better in the presence of a group is known as _____.
9. _____ is behavior in response to orders given by authorities.
10. The _____ occurs when a person refrains from taking action because of the presence of others.

Recalling Facts

1. Using a diagram similar to the one below, identify the characteristics of a group.

2. What factors work to hold a group together? What factors increase the commitment of a person to the group?
3. Why do people conform?
4. How does the cognitive theory explain aggression?
5. What are two factors that inhibit individual action within a group setting?

Critical Thinking

1. **Evaluating Information** Choose a person in your community whom you consider to be a leader. What qualities does this person have that make him or her a leader? How does the person demonstrate the characteristics of leadership?
2. **Analyzing Concepts** Do you think it is possible for an individual to never have to conform to a group? Why do you think so?
3. **Demonstrating Reasoned Judgment** Which psychological theory discussed in the chapter do you think best explains the reasons for aggression? Provide reasons for your opinion.
4. **Applying Concepts** Do you think knowing the causes of aggression is important in finding ways to help reduce violence in society? Why do you think so?
5. **Synthesizing Information** Think about what you have learned from your reading and classroom discussions about altruistic or helping behavior. How might it be possible to increase altruistic behavior in people? What factors might prevent this from occurring?

Psychology Projects

1. Group Behavior Groupthink occurs when group discussions stress agreement rather than critical thinking. The Bay of Pigs invasion was one example of groupthink. Research other historical events that were the result of groupthink, such as Watergate or the *Challenger* disaster. Find out the background of these events and how groupthink contributed to the outcomes. Present your findings in an oral report.

2. Conformity and Obedience Research examples of extreme group conformity and obedience. You might find out about David Koresh and the Branch Davidians or Jimmy Jones and the Jonestown cult. Research the general characteristics of the people who joined the groups and the reasons given for the leaders' ability to command such obedience. Share your findings in a documentary report or presentation.

3. Conflict and Cooperation Create an illustrated, captioned poster that provides strategies for teenagers to use to control aggression. Display your poster in the classroom.

Technology Activity

Think of a cause or an issue about which you feel strongly. Use the library and the Internet to find task-oriented groups that address this cause or issue. Find the E-mail address of the organization and send an E-mail to find out more about the group's goals and the ways that you might become involved. Share the information you collected, your sources, and any E-mail responses with the class.

Psychology Journal

Reread the journal entry you wrote at the beginning of the chapter. Using what you have learned, select one group to which you belong and describe it. Answer the following questions: What is the purpose of the group? What kind of group is it? Why do you belong to it? Do you conform to any ideals of the group? Why? What might happen if you did not conform to the group's ideals or norms?

Building Skills

Interpreting a Graph Milgram was upset about the willingness of his participants to obey an authority. In later experiments, he tried to find ways to reduce obedience. He found that distance between the teacher and the learner had an effect. The graph at right shows the percentage of "teachers" who obeyed orders at three different physical distances. Review the graph, then answer the questions below.

1. What percentage of teachers obeyed orders when they could only hear the learner?

2. What happened to the percentage of teachers who obeyed orders when they were in the same room and could see the learner? When they were asked to touch the learner?

3. What reasons can you give for the differences in the percentage of participants obeying authority in the three physical distances illustrated in the graph?

Practice and **assess** key social studies skills with **Glencoe Skillbuilder Interactive Workbook CD-ROM, Level 2.**

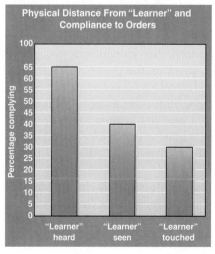

Physical Distance From "Learner" and Compliance to Orders

Percentage complying

100, 65, 60, 55, 50, 45, 40, 35, 30, 25, 20, 15, 10, 5, 0

"Learner" heard "Learner" seen "Learner" touched

See the Skills Handbook, page 628, for an explanation of interpreting graphs.

Shirley Jackson tells a terrifying tale of a town of people picking numbers for their annual lottery. Read this excerpt from the fictional story, written in 1948, to find out what happens to the person who selects the paper with the black spot.

Reader's Dictionary

daintily: done in a delicate or graceful way

defiantly: showing willingness to fight or resist

THE LOTTERY

BY SHIRLEY JACKSON

After that, there was a long pause, a breathless pause, until Mr. Summers, holding his slip of paper in the air, said, "All right, fellows." For a minute, no one moved, and then all the slips of paper were opened. Suddenly, all the women began to speak at once, saying, "Who is it?" "Who's got it?" "Is it the Dunbars?" "Is it the Watsons?" Then the voices began to say, "It's Hutchinson. It's Bill," "Bill Hutchinson's got it."

"Go tell your father," Mrs. Dunbar said to her older son.

People began to look around to see the Hutchinsons. Bill Hutchinson was standing quiet, staring down at the paper in his hand. Suddenly, Tessie Hutchinson shouted to Mr. Summers, "You didn't give him time enough to take any paper he wanted. I saw you. It wasn't fair!"

"Be a good sport, Tessie," Mrs. Delacroix called, and Mrs. Graves said, "All of us took the same chance."

"Shut up, Tessie," Bill Hutchinson said.

"Well, everyone," Mr. Summers said, "that was done pretty fast, and now we've got to be hurrying a little more to get done in time." He consulted his next list. "Bill," he said, "you draw for the Hutchinson family. You got any other households in the Hutchinsons?"

"There's Don and Eva," Mrs. Hutchinson yelled. "Make *them* take their chance!"

"Daughters draw with their husbands' families, Tessie," Mr. Summers said gently. "You know that as well as anyone else."

"It wasn't *fair*," Tessie said. . . .

"How many kids, Bill?" Mr. Summers asked formally.

"Three," Bill Hutchinson said. "There's Bill, Jr., and Nancy, and little Dave. And Tessie and me."

"All right, then," Mr. Summers said. "Harry, you got their tickets back?"

Mr. Graves nodded and held up the slips of paper. "Put them in the box, then," Mr. Summers directed. "Take Bill's and put it in."

"I think we ought to start over," Mrs. Hutchinson said, as quietly as she could. "I tell you it wasn't *fair*. You didn't give him time enough to choose. *Everybody* saw that."

Mr. Graves had selected the five slips and put them in the box, and he dropped all the papers but those onto the ground, where the breeze caught them and lifted them off.

"Listen, everybody," Mrs. Hutchinson was saying to the people around her.

"Ready, Bill?" Mr. Summers asked, and Bill Hutchinson, with one quick glance around at his wife and children, nodded.

"Remember," Mr. Summers said, "take the slips and keep them folded until each person has taken one. Harry, you help little Dave." Mr. Graves took the hand of the little boy, who came willingly with him up to the box. "Take a paper out of the box, Davy," Mr. Summers said. Davy put his hand into the box and laughed. "Take just *one* paper," Mr. Summers said. "Harry, you hold it for him." Mr. Graves took the child's hand and removed the folded paper from the tight fist and held it while little Dave stood next to him and looked up at him wonderingly.

"Nancy next," Mr. Summers said. Nancy was twelve, and her school friends breathed heavily as she went forward, switching her skirt, and took a slip daintily from the box. "Bill, Jr.," Mr. Summers said, and Billy, his face red and his feet overlarge, nearly knocked the box over as he got a paper out. "Tessie," Mr. Summers said. She hesitated for a minute, looking around defiantly, and then set her lips and went up to the box. She snatched a paper out and held it behind her.

"Bill," Mr. Summers said, and Bill Hutchinson reached into the box and felt around, bringing his hand out at last with the slip of paper in it.

The crowd was quiet. A girl whispered, "I hope it's not Nancy," and the sound of the whisper reached the edges of the crowd.

"It's not the way it used to be," Old Man Warner said clearly. "People ain't the way they used to be."

"All right," Mr. Summers said. "Open the papers. Harry, you open little Dave's."

Mr. Graves opened the slip of paper and there was a general sigh through the crowd as he held it up and everyone could see that it was blank. Nancy and Bill, Jr., opened theirs at the same time, and both beamed and laughed, turning around to the crowd and holding their slips of paper above their heads.

"Tessie," Mr. Summers said. There was a pause, and then Mr. Summers looked at Bill Hutchinson, and Bill unfolded his paper and showed it. It was blank.

"It's Tessie," Mr. Summers said, and his voice was hushed. "Show us her paper, Bill."

Bill Hutchinson went over to his wife and forced the slip of paper out of her hand. It had a black spot on it, the black spot Mr. Summers had made the night before with the heavy pencil in the coal-company office. Bill Hutchinson held it up, and there was a stir in the crowd.

"All right, folks," Mr. Summers said. "Let's finish quickly."

Although the villagers had forgotten the ritual and lost the original black box, they still remembered to use stones. The pile of stones the boys had made earlier was ready; there were stones on the ground with the blowing scraps of paper that had come out of the box. Mrs. Delacroix selected a stone so large she had to pick it up with both hands and turned to Mrs. Dunbar. "Come on," she said. "Hurry up."

Mrs. Dunbar had small stones in both hands, and she said, gasping for breath, "I can't run at all. You'll have to go ahead and I'll catch up with you."

The children had stones already, and someone gave little Davy Hutchinson a few pebbles.

Tessie Hutchinson was in the center of a cleared space by now, and she held her hands out desperately as the villagers moved in on her. "It isn't fair," she said. A stone hit her on the side of the head.

Old Man Warner was saying, "Come on, come on, everyone." Steve Adams was in the front of the crowd of villagers, with Mrs. Graves beside him.

"It isn't fair, it isn't right," Mrs. Hutchinson screamed, and then they were upon her.

Analyzing the Reading

1. What was the "lottery"?
2. What are the villagers' attitudes toward the lottery?
3. **Critical Thinking**   Why do you think these people participate in this event? Do you think the pressures from the crowd or community have any influence on participation? Explain.

CHAPTER 20

Attitudes and Social Influence

PSYCHOLOGY JOURNAL

Write a definition of prejudice in your journal. In addition, list at least four examples of prejudiced thinking. ∎

PSYCHOLOGY Online

Chapter Overview
Visit the *Understanding Psychology*
Web site at psychology.glencoe.com
and click on **Chapter 20—Chapter
Overviews** to preview the chapter.

Attitude Formation

Reader's Guide

■ Main Idea
Our attitudes are the result of conditioning, observational learning, and cognitive evaluation. Our attitudes help us define ourselves and our place in society, evaluate people and events, and guide our behavior.

■ Vocabulary
- attitude
- self-concept

■ Objectives
- Trace the origin of attitudes.
- Describe the functions of attitudes.

EXPLORING PSYCHOLOGY

An Attitude of Disbelief

On July 20, 1969, Astronaut Neil Armstrong emerged from a space capsule some 250,000 miles from Earth and, while millions of television viewers watched, became the first man to set foot upon the moon. Since that time other astronauts have experienced that same monumental unique experience in space, yet there are in existence today numerous relatively intelligent, otherwise normal humans who insist it never happened—that the masses have been completely deluded by some weird government hoax—a conspiracy of monumental proportions! There is even a well-publicized organization in England named "The Flat Earth Society," which seriously challenges with interesting logic all such claims of space travel and evidence that the earth is round.

—from *Story of Attitudes and Emotions* by Edgar Cayce, 1972

What do you accept as fact? What do you call products of fantasy? Your attitudes can lead you to believe that something is fact when it is really imaginary or that something is not real when it really is fact. An **attitude** is a predisposition to respond in particular ways toward specific things. It has three main elements: (1) a belief or opinion about something, (2) feelings about that thing, and (3) a tendency to act toward that thing in certain ways. For example, what is your attitude toward the senators from your state? Do you *believe* they are doing a good job? Do you *feel* you trust or distrust them? Would you *act* to vote for them?

attitude: predisposition to act, think, and feel in particular ways toward a class of people, objects, or an idea

WHERE ATTITUDES COME FROM

We have very definite beliefs, feelings, and responses to things about which we have no firsthand knowledge. Where do these attitudes come from? Attitudes are formed through conditioning, observational learning, and cognitive evaluation.

Conditioning

Classical conditioning (discussed in Chapter 9) can help you form attitudes automatically (see Figure 20.1). When a new stimulus (the conditioned stimulus) is paired with a stimulus that already causes a certain reaction (the unconditioned stimulus), the new stimulus begins to cause a reaction similar to the one caused by the original stimulus. For instance, scientist Ivan Pavlov's dog had a positive attitude toward meat (he liked to eat it). When Pavlov paired the meat with the ringing of the tuning fork, the dog formed a positive attitude toward the sound of the tuning fork. So when Pavlov's dog heard the sound of the tuning fork, he wagged his tail and salivated. We also acquire attitudes through operant conditioning—we receive praise, approval, or acceptance for expressing certain attitudes or we may be punished for expressing other attitudes.

Cognitive Evaluation

Sometimes we develop attitudes toward something without stopping to think about it. For example, if our friend feels strongly about politics and uses many statistics or big words when speaking about a specific political issue, we may agree with her simply because she sounds like she knows what she is talking about. If we do this, we have used a heuristic, a mental shortcut to form an attitude.

However, we may sit down and systematically think about an issue that affects us directly. For example, if your friend speaks strongly about State College and its credentials, you may not simply accept her

Figure 20.1 **Attitude Formation Through Classical Conditioning**

Suppose you meet Jane. Jane seems to enjoy making comments that embarrass you. After a few encounters with Jane, even the sound of her voice upsets you. So you learn to avoid her. *What factors were paired to produce your avoidance response?*

argument. You may list and evaluate the pros and cons of State College versus State University when you are selecting the college to attend. This matter is important, and you do not want to rely on shortcuts.

Other Sources

Your attitudes are shaped by other forces. You may develop your attitudes by watching and imitating others—through observational learning. These forces are at work when you interact with others. For example, you may adopt your parents' political views or dress very much like your friends do. The culture in which you grew up, the people who raised you, and those with whom you associate all shape your attitudes. You also learn many of your attitudes through direct experience. For instance, once you drive the new BMW, you may develop a favorable attitude toward it.

Culture Culture influences everything from our taste in food to our attitudes toward human relationships and our political opinions. For example, most (if not all) Americans would consider eating grubs, curdled milk spiced with cattle blood, or monkey meat disgusting. Yet in some parts of the world these are considered delicacies.

The list of culturally derived attitudes is endless. Indeed, it is only by traveling and reading about other ways of life that we discover how many of the things we take for granted are *attitudes,* not facts.

Parents There is abundant evidence that all of us acquire many basic attitudes from our parents (see Figure 20.2). How else would you account for the finding that a high percentage of elementary schoolchildren favor the same political party as their parents? As adults, more than two-thirds of all voters continue to favor the political party their parents supported. Parental influence wanes as children get older, of course.

Peers It is not surprising that parental influence declines as children get older and are exposed to many other sources of influence. In a now classic study, Theodore Newcomb (1943) questioned and requestioned students at Bennington College in Vermont about their political attitudes over a period of four years. Most of the young women came from wealthy, staunchly conservative families. In contrast, most Bennington faculty members were outspoken liberals. Newcomb found that many of the students were "converted" to the liberal point of view. In 1936, 54 percent of the juniors and seniors supported Franklin D. Roosevelt and the New Deal over the conservative Republican candidate Alf Landon. Newcomb contacted the participants of his study 25 years after they had graduated and found that most had maintained the attitudes

Did You Know?

The Exposure Effect One determinant of attitudes is the mere exposure effect—the more frequently people encounter an object or idea, the more favorably they evaluate it. You may have experienced this by listening to a song over and over again and growing to like that song. Candidates for political office use this effect by constantly advertising during political campaigns.

Figure 20.2 **Learning Attitudes**

Children are skilled at detecting their parents' attitudes. Often children learn to react in the same way as their parents to various events or things. *How do we develop attitudes through observational learning?*

Quick Lab

How similar are your views to your parents' views?

Studies have shown that parents are an important source of many of our basic attitudes and beliefs. What is the degree of similarity between your parents' views and your views on selected issues?

Procedure

1. Generate a list of 10 statements about social issues, such as political affiliation, nuclear energy, mandatory retirement, equal pay, and paternity leave.

2. Develop a questionnaire based on these issues in which a person can respond by agreeing or disagreeing with the statements. Use a five-point scale ranging from 1 (strongly agree) to 5 (strongly disagree) to rate your opinions.

3. Complete the questionnaire and ask your parents to do the same.

Analysis

1. Analyze your parents' responses. On what issues did you agree and disagree?

2. Why do you think your parents have been influential in shaping some of your attitudes and not others?

See the Skills Handbook, page 622, for an explanation of designing an experiment.

self-concept: how we see or describe ourselves; our self-perceptions

they had acquired in college. One reason was that they had chosen friends, spouses, and careers that supported liberal values (Newcomb et al., 1967). People tend to adopt the likes and dislikes of groups whose approval and acceptance they seek.

FUNCTIONS OF ATTITUDES

Why do we have attitudes? How do they help us function and interact with others? Attitudes help us evaluate our own beliefs and values to define ourselves, interpret the objects and events we encounter, and determine how to act in given situations.

Attitudes as a Self-Defining Mechanism

Ask a friend to describe herself. How does she do it? Along with a physical description, she may include her attitudes, or values, about certain things. For example, she may claim that she likes helping others, tries to be a good student, or is a strong supporter of equal rights. These attitudes help her define who she is. They refer to what she considers right or wrong and establish her goals. These attitudes make up her self-concept. Our **self-concept** refers to how we see or describe ourselves. If you have a positive self-concept, you will tend to act and feel optimistically and constructively; whereas if you have a negative self-concept, you will tend to act and feel pessimistically or self-destructively.

Social groups as well as individuals hold attitudes. People living in the same conditions and who frequently communicate with one another have attitudes in common because they are exposed to the same information and may have formed as a group partly because of their similar attitudes.

Attitudes as Cognitive Guidelines and Guides to Action

Our attitudes serve as guidelines for interpreting and categorizing people, objects, and events. Attitudes also guide us to behave in certain ways (see Figure 20.3). In effect, attitudes guide us toward or away from particular people, objects, and events. For instance, we may link negative feelings with walking in unlit and dirty alleyways or we may link positive feelings with friendly and happy people. These attitudes tell us to avoid the former and approach the latter.

Sometimes, though, our attitudes are not consistent with our behaviors. For example, although we may disagree with littering, we may throw a candy wrapper on the ground. Your behavior may reflect your attitudes

Figure 20.3   **A Theory of Planned Behavior**

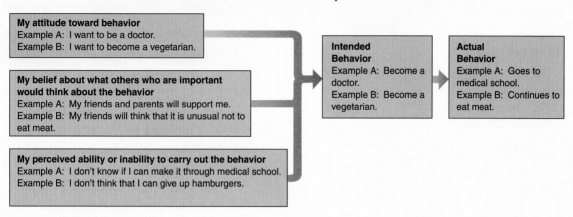

Psychologists have proposed a theory that three factors determine a person's behavior. The strength or weakness of each of these three factors explains why certain people behave differently despite shared attitudes (Ajzen, 1991; Sheppard, Hartwick, & Warshaw, 1988). *What factors other than attitude determine a person's behavior?*

My attitude toward behavior
Example A: I want to be a doctor.
Example B: I want to become a vegetarian.

My belief about what others who are important would think about the behavior
Example A: My friends and parents will support me.
Example B: My friends will think that it is unusual not to eat meat.

My perceived ability or inability to carry out the behavior
Example A: I don't know if I can make it through medical school.
Example B: I don't think that I can give up hamburgers.

Intended Behavior
Example A: Become a doctor.
Example B: Become a vegetarian.

Actual Behavior
Example A: Goes to medical school.
Example B: Continues to eat meat.

more strongly, though, depending on why you have formed a certain attitude. Many psychologists argue that the attitudes that most strongly predict behavior are those that are acquired through direct experience. For example, if you disagree with eating meat because when you have eaten it before you felt sick, the smell and sight of meat may automatically remind you of this negative attitude, so you do not eat meat. If you disagree with eating meat because of strictly moral reasons, however, you may not automatically remember your attitude when you smell and see meat. So, although attitudes do play a role in determining behavior, when and under what circumstances certain attitudes affect our behavior may vary.

Reading Check
How do our attitudes help us organize our reality?

SECTION 1 Assessment

1. **Review the Vocabulary**   What are the three elements of an attitude?

2. **Visualize the Main Idea**   Using a diagram similar to the one below, list and describe the functions of attitudes.

Functions of Attitudes

3. **Recall Information**   How does one's culture influence one's attitudes?

4. **Think Critically**   How can attitudes help keep us out of dangerous situations?

5. Application Activity   Investigate how advertisers use classical conditioning to influence our attitudes. Bring an example of such an advertisement to class and, in a brief report, analyze the advertiser's technique.

SECTION 2 Attitude Change and Prejudice

Reader's Guide

■ Main Idea
Attitudes are formed through compliance, identification, and internalization. Attitudes may be changed as a result of cognitive dissonance.

■ Vocabulary
- compliance
- identification
- internalization
- cognitive dissonance
- counterattitudinal behavior
- self-justification
- self-fulfilling prophecy
- prejudice
- discrimination

■ Objectives
- Cite the sources of attitude change.
- Describe prejudice and its relationship to stereotypes and roles.

EXPLORING PSYCHOLOGY

Can You Figure It Out?

I met my friend the test pilot, who had just completed an around-the-world flight by balloon. With the pilot was a little girl of about two.

"What's her name?" I asked my friend, whom I hadn't seen in five years and who had married in that time.

"Same as her mother," the pilot replied.

"Hello, Susan," I said to the little girl.

How did I know her name if I never saw the wedding announcement?

—from "Steve's Primer of Practical Persuasion and Influence" [Web site], 1996

Did you figure out the answer to the thought problem above? You see, the author knew the name of the little girl because the test pilot was a woman—the little girl's mother. Thus the mother and daughter share the same first name. You may have had trouble coming up with the answer because you assumed that the test pilot was male. Also, we usually do not expect women to name their daughters after themselves. If you had trouble with this thought problem, you were the victim of cognitive consistency—that is, you tried to fit this new situation into your existing assumptions. You made a prejudgment about the situation that prevented you from considering all the possibilities.

ATTITUDE CHANGE

Having suggested where attitudes come from, we can now look at how they develop. The three main processes involved in forming or changing attitudes are compliance, identification, and internalization (Kelman, 1961).

If you praise a certain film director because everyone else does, you are complying. If you find yourself agreeing with everything a friend you particularly admire says about the director, you are identifying with your friend's attitudes. If you genuinely like the director's work and, regardless of what other people think, regard it as brilliant, you are expressing an internalized attitude.

Compliance

One of the best measures of attitude is behavior. If a man settles back into his chair after dinner, launches into a discussion of his support of the women's rights movement, then shouts to his wife—who is in the kitchen washing the dishes—to bring more coffee, you probably would not believe what he had been saying. His actions speak louder than his words. Yet the same man might hire women for jobs he has always considered "men's work" because the law requires him to do so. He also might finally accept his wife's going to work because he knows that she, their children, and many of their friends would consider him old-fashioned if he did not. People often adapt their actions to the wishes of others to avoid discomfort or rejection and to gain support. This is called **compliance.** Under such circumstances, social pressure often results in only temporary compliance, and attitudes do not really change. Later in this chapter, however, we shall see that compliance can sometimes affect one's beliefs.

compliance: a change of behavior to avoid discomfort or rejection and gain approval

Identification

One way in which attitudes may really be formed or changed is through the process of **identification.** Suppose you have a favorite uncle who is everything you hope to be. He is a successful musician, has many famous friends, and seems to know a great deal about everything. In many ways you identify with him and copy his behavior. One night, during an intense conversation, your uncle asks you why you do not vote. At first, you feel defensive and argumentative. You contend that it does not matter, that your vote would not make a difference. As you listen to your uncle, however, you find yourself starting to agree with him. If a person as knowledgeable and respectable as your uncle believes it is important to vote, then perhaps you should, too. Later you find yourself eager to take part in the political process. You have adopted a new attitude because of your identification with your uncle.

Identification occurs when a person wants to define himself or herself in terms of a person or group and therefore adopts the person's or group's attitudes and ways of behaving. Identification is different from compliance because the individual actually believes the newly adopted views. Yet because these attitudes are based on emotional attachment to another person or group rather than the person's own assessment of the issues, they are fragile. If the person's attachment to that person or group fades, the attitudes may also weaken.

Previously, you read that adolescents move away from peer groups and toward independence as they grow older. If this is true, do attitudes stabilize with age? Two psychologists (Krosnick & Alwin, 1989) studied

identification: seeing oneself as similar to another person or group and accepting the attitudes of another person or group as one's own the political and social attitudes of groups of people of various ages over an extended period. Those in the 18 to 25 age group were the most likely to change their attitudes; those age 34 and older held attitudes that were essentially stable. So as identification with peer groups declines through late adolescence and into adulthood, attitudes become more stable.

Internalization

internalization: incorporating the values, ideas, and standards of others as a part of oneself

The wholehearted acceptance of an attitude is **internalization.** The attitude becomes an integral part of the person. Internalization is most likely to occur when an attitude is consistent with a person's basic beliefs and values and supports his or her self-image. The person adopts a new attitude because he or she believes it is right to do so—not because he or she wants to be like someone else.

Internalization is the most lasting of the three sources of attitude formation or change. Your internalized attitudes will be more resistant to pressure from other people because your reasons for holding these views have nothing to do with other people. They are based on your own evaluation of the merits of the issue. A Bennington student put it this way: "I became liberal at first because of its prestige value; I remain so because the problems around which my liberalism centers are important. What I want now is to be effective in solving problems" (Newcomb, 1943).

As this example suggests, compliance or identification may lead to the internalization of an attitude. Often the three overlap. You may support a political candidate in part because you know your friends will approve, in part because someone you admire speaks highly of the candidate, and in part because you believe his or her ideals are consistent with your own.

✔ *Reading Check*
Which attitudes are the most stable and long-lasting—those formed by compliance, identification, or internalization?

COGNITIVE CONSISTENCY

Many social psychologists have theorized that people's attitudes change because they are always trying to get things to fit together logically inside their heads. This is called *cognitive consistency* (see Figure 20.4). Holding two opposing attitudes can create great conflict in an individual, throwing him or her off balance. A doctor who smokes and a parent who is uncomfortable with children have one thing in common: they are in conflict.

According to Leon Festinger (1957), people in such situations experience cognitive dissonance. **Cognitive dissonance** is the uncomfortable feeling that arises when a person experiences contradictory or conflicting thoughts, beliefs, attitudes, or feelings. To reduce dissonance, it is necessary to change one or both of the conflicting attitudes.

cognitive dissonance: the uncomfortable feeling when a person experiences contradictory or conflicting thoughts, attitudes, beliefs, or feelings

People get rid of dissonance in several ways. First, some people just deny the dissonance. They pretend it did not happen. When faced with information on the health hazards of smoking, a smoker simply treats the information as nonsense—propaganda by antismoking groups. Some people attempt to evade dissonance by avoiding situations or exposure to information that would create conflict. For example, they may make a point of subscribing to newspapers and magazines that uphold their political attitudes, of surrounding themselves with people who share the same ideas, and of attending only those speeches and lectures that support their views. It is not surprising that such people get quite upset when a piece of conflicting information finally does get through. Some people change their attitude and/or reevaluate the event. Because the new information they received does not agree with their old attitude, they revise their attitude. The smoker might consider the research on the dangers of smoking and make an attempt to quit smoking. The process of dissonance reduction does not always take place consciously, but it is a frequent and powerful occurrence.

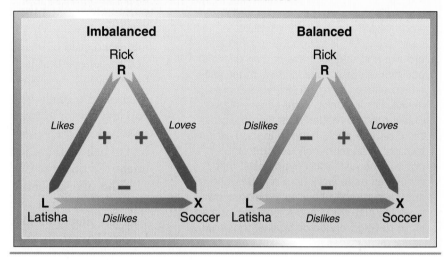

Figure 20.4   Balance Theory

According to the balance theory, people are inclined to achieve consistency in their attitudes by balancing their beliefs and feelings about an object, person, or event against their attitudes about other people. When someone we care about strongly disagrees with us, an uncomfortable state of imbalance occurs. *What do you think we do when we become involved in a state of imbalance?*

ATTITUDES AND ACTIONS

Social psychologists have discovered several interesting relationships between attitudes and actions. Obviously, your attitudes affect your actions: if you like Fords, you will buy a Ford. Some of the other relationships are not so obvious.

Doing Is Believing

It turns out, for example, that if you like Fords but buy a Chevrolet for some reason (perhaps you can get a better deal on a Chevy), you will end up liking Fords less. In other words, actions affect attitudes.

In many instances, if you act and speak as though you have certain beliefs and feelings, you may begin to *really* feel and believe this way. This phenomenon is called **counterattitudinal behavior,** and it is a method of reducing cognitive dissonance. For example, people accused of a crime have confessed to crimes they did not commit. They confessed to relieve the pressure; but having said that they did the deed, they begin to believe that they really *are* guilty.

One explanation for this phenomenon comes from the theory of cognitive dissonance. If a person acts one way but thinks another, he or she will experience dissonance. To reduce the dissonance, the person will

counterattitudinal behavior: the process of taking a public position that contradicts one's private attitude

The Just-World Bias

When watching some movies, we expect the evil character to get punished. Sometimes we may even hear ourselves saying, "He'll get what he deserves." Psychologists label this tendency the *just-world bias* (Lerner, 1980). We need to believe that life is fair, that the world is orderly, and that we have control over our environment, because to think otherwise would cause too much cognitive dissonance. For instance, if we believe life is unfair, then no matter what we do, something terrible could happen to us. That thought is an extremely uncomfortable notion. The just-world hypothesis, then, motivates us to work hard and be good to ensure our survival and well-being. However, the just-world hypothesis may cause us to develop prejudice against those who suffer misfortunes or mistreatment.

To maintain our belief that life is fair, we reason that those who are worse off than we are somehow deserve their lot. We blame the victim. For example, we may say that the woman who was robbed last night should not have been walking alone at night.

self-justification: the need to rationalize one's attitude and behavior

self-fulfilling prophecy: a belief, prediction, or expectation that operates to bring about its own fulfillment

have to change either the behavior or the attitude. A similar explanation is that people have a need for **self-justification**—a need to justify their behavior.

In an experiment that demonstrated these principles, participants were paid either $1 or $20 (roughly $5 and $100 in today's currency) to tell another person that a boring experiment in which they both had to participate was really a lot of fun. Afterward, the experimenters asked the participants how they felt about the experiment. They found that the participants who had been paid $20 to lie about the experiment continued to believe that it had been boring. Those who had been paid $1, however, came to believe that the experiment had actually been fairly enjoyable. These people had less reason to tell the lie, so they experienced more dissonance when they did so. To justify their lie, they had to believe that they had actually enjoyed the experiment (Festinger & Carlsmith, 1959).

The phenomenon of self-justification has serious implications. For example, how would you justify to yourself that you had intentionally injured another human being? In another psychological experiment, participants were led to believe that they had injured or hurt other participants in some way (Glass, 1964). The aggressors were then asked how they felt about the victims they had just harmed. It was found that the aggressors had convinced themselves that they did not like the victims of their cruelty. In other words, the aggressors talked themselves into believing that their defenseless victims had deserved their injury. The aggressors also considered their victims to be less attractive after the experiment than before—their self-justification for hurting another person was something like "Oh, well, this person doesn't amount to much, anyway."

Self-Fulfilling Prophecy

Another relationship between attitudes and actions is rather subtle but extremely widespread. It is possible, it seems, for a person to act in such a way as to make his or her attitudes come true. This phenomenon is called a **self-fulfilling prophecy.** Self-fulfilling prophecies can influence all kinds of human activity. Suppose you believe that people are basically friendly and generous. Whenever you approach other people, you are friendly and open. Because of your smile and positive attitude toward yourself and the world, people like you. Thus your attitude that people are friendly produces your friendly behavior, which in turn causes people to respond favorably toward you. Suppose you turn this example around. Imagine that you believe people are selfish and cold. Because of your negative attitude, you tend to avert your eyes from other people, to act gloomy, and to appear rather unfriendly. People think your actions are strange, and consequently, they act coldly toward you. Your attitude has produced the kind of behavior that makes the attitude come true (Fiske & Taylor, 1991).

PREJUDICE

Prejudice means, literally, prejudgment. Prejudice means deciding beforehand what a person will be like instead of withholding judgment until it can be based on his or her individual qualities. To hold stereotypes about a group of people is to be prejudiced about them. Prejudice is not necessarily negative—men who are prejudiced against women are often equally prejudiced in favor of men, for example.

prejudice: preconceived attitudes toward a person or group that have been formed without sufficient evidence and are not easily changed

Stereotypes and Roles

Prejudice is strengthened and maintained by the existence of stereotypes and roles. A *stereotype* is an oversimplified, hard-to-change way of seeing people who belong to some group or category. Racial groups, scientists, women, and the rich, for example, often have been seen in certain rigid ways rather than as individuals. A *role* is an oversimplified, hard-to-change way of acting. Stereotypes and roles can act together in a way that makes them difficult to break down. For example, many whites once had a stereotype of minority racial groups, believing them to be irresponsible, superstitious, or unintelligent. Whites who believed this expected members of the racial group to act out a role that was consistent with a stereotype. Members of the racial group were expected to be submissive, deferential, and respectful toward whites, who acted out the role of the superior, condescending parent. In the past, many people accepted these roles and looked at themselves and each other according to these stereotypes. In the past several decades, however, many people have worked to step out of these roles and drop these stereotypes, and to some extent they have been successful.

Patricia Devine (1989) proposed a model to explain the relationships between stereotypes and prejudice. She theorizes that if a specific stimulus is encountered, it automatically activates your stereotype mechanism. For example, if you see an old man or woman, it activates your stereotype of old people. Devine suggests that what separates prejudiced from nonprejudiced people is their ability to inhibit negative attitudes. If you can do so, your response will be nonprejudiced; if you cannot restrain your negative beliefs, you will behave in a prejudiced manner.

Illusory Correlation

An illusory correlation occurs when we see relationships that match our set beliefs while ignoring other relationships. For example, suppose that you believe that all women are bad drivers. You can name several instances in which you recall witnessing a female driver do something irresponsible while behind the wheel. However, you ignore all the times you have seen bad male drivers. If you notice a female driving well, you claim that this is a chance happening—this female driver is an exception to all other female drivers. In this way you maintain your (inaccurate) stereotype of bad female drivers.

Another psychologist, Thomas Pettigrew, suggests that in situations where members of a dominant and a deferential group can be identified, each group may play a role that fosters and maintains its respective position. A member of a dominating group, for example, will speak first, interrupt more often, and talk louder and longer. A member of the deferential group will show courtesy and concern for the dominant member and do more listening and less interrupting.

Prejudice and Discrimination

There are many possible causes for prejudice. Prejudice can be based on social, economic, or physical factors. Psychologists have found that people may be prejudiced against those less well-off than themselves—these people seem to justify being on top by assuming that anyone of lower status or income must be inferior. People who have suffered economic setbacks also tend to be prejudiced—they blame others for their misfortune. Prejudice also arises from "guilt by association." People who dislike cities and urban living, for example, tend to distrust people associated with cities. Also, people may be prejudiced in favor of those they see as similar to themselves and against those who seem different. Whatever the original cause, prejudice seems to persist. One reason is that children who grow up in an atmosphere of prejudice conform to the prejudicial norm. That is, they are encouraged to conform to the thoughts and practices of their parents and other teachers.

Prejudice, which is an attitude, should be distinguished from **discrimination,** the unequal treatment of members of certain groups. It is possible for a prejudiced person not to discriminate. He or she may recognize his or her prejudice and try not to act on it. Similarly, a person may discriminate, not out of prejudice, but in compliance with social or economic pressures.

discrimination: the unequal treatment of individuals on the basis of their race, ethnic group, age, gender, or membership in another category rather than on the basis of individual characteristics

SECTION 2 Assessment

1. **Review the Vocabulary**   Describe the relationship between attitudes and behavior in counterattitudinal behavior, self-justification, and self-fulfilling prophecy.

2. **Visualize the Main Idea**   Using a diagram similar to the one below, list and describe the three main processes involved in forming or changing attitudes.

Processes of Forming/Changing Attitudes

3. **Recall Information**   How do stereotypes and roles strengthen prejudice?

4. **Think Critically**   How do theories of cognitive dissonance explain why certain people may be attracted to some information while they avoid other information? Explain.

5. Application Activity   List 10 makes and models of cars (such as Saturn SL2, Honda Civic) and ask 15 people to choose from a wide range of adjectives (such as serious, reliable, dishonest) that best describes someone who drives that type of car. Analyze the results of your survey to see if people are stereotyped by the cars they drive.

Feelings vs. Actions

Period of Study: 1934

Introduction: In 1934 Richard LaPiere conducted a study designed to evaluate a person's feelings and actions with situations regarding race. He studied the social attitudes of individuals and examined the connection between an individual's real behavior and an individual's symbolic behavior. *Symbolic behavior* refers to a person stating how he or she would react in any given situation without it actually occurring. With this idea in mind, LaPiere set out to test individuals' symbolic racial responses compared with their actual racial responses.

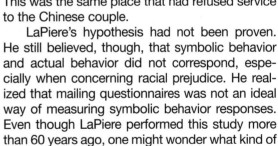

Hypothesis: LaPiere came up with the idea of studying racial behavior when he traveled across the United States to conduct research on a different topic with his wife and a young Chinese student. During the 1930s, much racial prejudice targeted Asian Americans. LaPiere and his traveling companions became the targets of prejudice in many situations. Therefore, LaPiere hypothesized that when dealing with the issue of race, people's actions do not always coincide with what they profess as their beliefs.

Method: LaPiere needed a control variable for his experiment. LaPiere chose the unusual control variable of a Chinese husband and wife. The Chinese couple, along with LaPiere, traveled along the Pacific coast. The couple visited various restaurants, attempted to check in to hotels, and frequented other public service businesses. LaPiere went where the couple went but distanced himself from them and recorded significant data. LaPiere focused on how the couple was treated, if they were served, if they were asked to leave, and

other important information. It took just under three years to complete this part of the experiment.

Next LaPiere sent questionnaires to the establishments that the Chinese couple had visited. The straightforward questionnaires simply inquired if that establishment would provide services to a Chinese husband and wife. To ensure that the opinions of those establishments were not affected by the Chinese couple's visit, LaPiere also sent a number of questionnaires to other businesses in that Pacific coast region. LaPiere received back 51 percent of the surveys.

Results: Of the 251 establishments patronized by the Chinese couple, only one denied them service because of their race. Compared with the questionnaires LaPiere had sent, the symbolic behaviors and actual behaviors of those establishments seemed to correlate remarkably. Only one establishment admitted that it would not serve a Chinese couple. This was the same place that had refused service to the Chinese couple.

LaPiere's hypothesis had not been proven. He still believed, though, that symbolic behavior and actual behavior did not correspond, especially when concerning racial prejudice. He realized that mailing questionnaires was not an ideal way of measuring symbolic behavior responses. Even though LaPiere performed this study more than 60 years ago, one might wonder what kind of results a study similar to LaPiere's would produce today.

Analyzing the Case Study

1. What is the difference between symbolic behavior and actual behavior? Explain.

2. What was LaPiere's hypothesis?

3. Critical Thinking If LaPiere performed this experiment today, do you think that his results would be the same? Why or why not?

Persuasion

■ Main Idea

Persuasion is a direct attempt to influence attitudes. We evaluate when, where, and how a message is presented, as well as the message itself, when determining the credibility of the message.

■ Vocabulary

- persuasion
- boomerang effect
- sleeper effect
- inoculation effect
- brainwashing

■ Objectives

- Describe the factors involved in the communication process.
- Explain the different types of persuasion processes.

EXPLORING PSYCHOLOGY

Why Do Kids Love McDonalds?

By switching the channel on a Saturday morning, a child can watch "Ronald McDonald" in up to a dozen, colorful, fast-paced commercials *each hour;* perhaps this is one reason why the chain sells so many billions of hamburgers.

—from *The Social Animal* by Elliot Aronson, 1995

Advertisers use persuasion to encourage consumers to buy their products. McDonalds uses at least one method of persuasion—familiarity. Most American kids know what McDonalds is; most American kids have seen a McDonalds commercial or advertisement. What methods of persuasion lure you?

PERSUASION

persuasion: the direct attempt to influence attitudes

Persuasion is a direct attempt to influence attitudes. At one time or another everyone engages in persuasion. When a smiling student who is working her way through college by selling magazine subscriptions comes to the door, she attempts to persuade you that reading *Newsweek* or *Sports Illustrated* will make you better informed and give you lots to talk about at parties. Parents often attempt to persuade a son or daughter to conform to their values about life. Similarly, some young people try to persuade their parents that all their friends' parents are buying them home computers. In each case, the persuader's main hope is that by changing the other person's attitudes, he or she can change that person's behavior as well.

The Communication Process

Enormous amounts of time, money, and effort go into campaigns to persuade people to change their attitudes and behavior. Some succeed on a grand scale, while others seem to have no effect. One of the most difficult questions social psychologists have tried to answer is this: What makes a persuasive communication effective?

The communication process can be broken down into four parts. The *message* itself is only one part. It is also important to consider the *source* of the message, the *channel* through which it is delivered, and the *audience* that receives it.

The Source How a person sees the source, or originator, of a message may be a critical factor in his or her acceptance or rejection of it. The person receiving the message asks himself or herself two basic questions: Is the person giving the message trustworthy and sincere? Does he or she know anything about the subject? If the source seems reliable and knowledgeable, the message is likely to be accepted (see Figure 20.5).

Suppose, for example, that you have written for your English class a paper criticizing a short story. A friend who reads the paper tells you about an article that praises the story and asks you to reconsider your view. The article was written by Agnes Stearn, a college student. You might change your opinion, or you might not. Suppose your friend tells you the same critique was written by Stephen King. Chances are that you would begin to doubt your own judgment. Three psychologists tried this experiment. Not surprisingly, many more students changed their minds about a piece of writing when they thought the criticism was written by a famous writer (Aronson, Turner, & Carlsmith, 1963).

A person receiving the message also asks this: Do I like the source? If the communicator is respected and admired, people will tend to go along with the message, either because they believe in his or her judgment or because they want to be like him or her. This identification phenomenon explains the frequent use of athletes in advertisements. Football players and Olympic champions are not (in most cases) experts on deodorants, electric razors, or milk. Indeed, when an athlete endorses a particular brand of deodorant on television, we all know he or she is doing it for the money. Nevertheless, the process of identification makes these sales pitches highly effective (Wu & Shaffer, 1987).

However, attempts to be friendly and personal can backfire. When people dislike the individual or group delivering a message, they are likely to respond by taking the opposite point of view. This

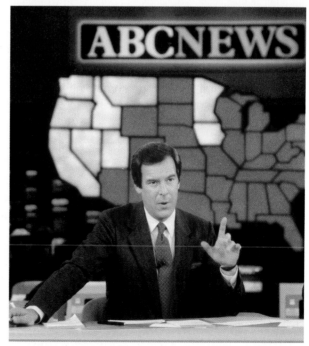

Figure 20.5   The Source

National newscasters, such as Peter Jennings, appear attractive, honest, and credible. We are likely to believe sources that seem trustworthy and are attractive. *What is the identification phenomenon?*

boomerang effect: a change in attitude or behavior opposite of the one desired by the persuader

is known as the **boomerang effect.** For example, the sales of a product may go down after the well-known spokesperson for the product is arrested for breaking the law, or the well-intentioned comments of a politician may offend certain groups and, thereby, damage his popular appeal.

The Message Suppose two people with opposing viewpoints are trying to persuade you to agree with them. Suppose further that you like and trust both of them. In this situation, the message becomes more important than the source. The persuasiveness of a message depends on the way in which it is composed and organized as well as on the actual content.

There are two ways to deliver a message. The *central route for persuasion* focuses on presenting information consisting of strong arguments and facts—it is a focus on logic. The *peripheral route for persuasion* relies on emotional appeals, emphasizing personal traits or positive feelings.

Should the message arouse emotion? Are people more likely to change their attitudes if they are afraid or angry or pleased? The answer is yes, but the most effective messages combine emotional appeal with factual information and argument. A moderately arousing message typically causes the largest shift of opinion. Similarly, a message that deviates moderately from the attitudes of the target audience will tend to move that audience furthest. A communication that overemphasizes the emotional side of an issue may boomerang. The peripheral route sometimes arouses fear (see Figure 20.6). If the message is too upsetting, people may reject it. For example, showing pictures of accident victims to people who have been arrested for drunken driving may convince them not to drive when they have been drinking. Yet if the film is so bloody that people are frightened or disgusted, they may also stop listening to the message. On the other hand, a communication that includes only logic and information may miss its mark because the audience does not relate the facts to their personal lives.

When presenting an argument, is it more effective to present both sides of an issue or only one side? For the most part, a two-sided communication is more effective because the audience tends to believe that the speaker is objective and fair-minded. A slight hazard of presenting opposing arguments is that they might undercut the message or suggest that the whole issue is too controversial to make a decision about.

People usually respond positively to a message that is structured and delivered in a dynamic way. A communication that is forceful to the point of being pushy, however, may produce negative results. People generally resent being pressured. If listeners infer from a message that they are being left with no choice but to agree with the speaker's viewpoint, they may reject an opinion for this reason alone.

Figure 20.6   Appealing to Your Fears

Advertisements, such as this, are effective only if you believe the danger is real and if you believe that you can do something to reduce the danger. *Is this an example of a central or peripheral route for persuasion?*

The Channel   Where, when, and how a message is presented also influences the audience's response. In general, personal contact is the most effective approach to an audience. For example, in one study in Ann Arbor, Michigan, 75 percent of voters who had been contacted personally voted in favor of a change in the city charter. Only 45 percent of those who had received the message in the mail and 19 percent of those who had seen only ads in the media voted for the change (Eldersveld & Dodge, 1954).

As we saw earlier, however, personal contact may boomerang: people may dislike the communicator or feel that they are being pressured. Besides, you can reach a great many more people through mailings and radio and television broadcasts than you can in person.

There is some evidence that television and films are more effective media of persuasion than printed matter. People tend to believe what they see and hear with their own senses (even if they know the information has been edited before it is broadcast). In one experiment, 51 percent of people who had watched a film could answer factual questions about the issue in question—compared to 29 percent of those who had seen only printed material. In addition, more of the people who had viewed the film altered their viewpoints than did people who had read about the issue (Hovland, Lumsdaine, & Sheffield, 1949). The most effective channel also depends in part on the audience.

The Audience   The audience includes all those people whose attitudes the communicator is trying to change. Being able to persuade people to alter their views depends on knowing who the audience is and why they hold the attitudes they do. Suppose, for example, you are involved in a program to reduce the birthrate in a population that is outgrowing its food supply. The first step would be to inform people of various methods of birth control as well as how and where to obtain them. That people know how to limit their families, however, does not mean that they will do so. To persuade them to use available contraceptives, you need to know why they value large families. In some areas of the world, people have as many children as they can because they do not expect most babies to survive early childhood. In this case, you might want to tie the family-planning campaign to programs of infant care. In some areas, children begin working at odd jobs at an early age and bring in needed income. In this case, you might want to promote an incentive system for families who limit themselves to two or three children.

If the people are not taking advantage of available means of birth control, you will want to know who is resisting. Perhaps men believe fathering a child is a sign of virility. Perhaps women consider motherhood an essential element of femininity. Perhaps both sexes see parenthood as a symbol of maturity and adulthood (Coale, 1973). Knowing who your audience is and what motivates them are crucial.

Several strategies effectively involve the audience. One strategy that has been studied extensively is the *foot-in-the-door technique,* which involves first making a very small request that someone is almost sure to agree to and then making a much more demanding request (Dillard, 1991). In one

PSYCHOLOGY Online

Student Web Activity
Visit the *Understanding Psychology* Web site at psychology.glencoe.com and click on **Chapter 20—Student Web Activities** for an activity on attitudes and influence.

✓ ***Reading Check***
How does the foot-in-the-door technique differ from the door-in-the-face technique?

experiment, two researchers (Freedman & Fraser, 1966) asked residents of Palo Alto, California, for permission to place a small sign reading "Be a Safe Driver" in a window of their homes. Two weeks later, another person asked residents for permission to stake a large "Drive Carefully" sign in the front yard. Nearly 56 percent of those who had agreed to the first request also agreed to the second request. However, only 17 percent of the residents who heard only the second request but not the first agreed to put the sign in their yard.

Another strategy is sometimes called the *door-in-the-face technique*. It works like this: To encourage people to agree to a moderate request that might otherwise be rejected, you make a major request—likely to be rejected. When it is, you follow up immediately with a more minor request. For example, you might ask a friend, "I'm helping my parents move this weekend. Would you come over and help us Saturday and Sunday until we're done?" "No? Well, then, could you come over Saturday morning and just help me move our grand piano?" You have a much higher likelihood of success on the second request following the first than if you had made only the second request.

Models of Persuasion

As discussed earlier, a message leads to thinking, but how much and at what depth are determined both by the message and the needs of the person receiving it. Two different levels of activity are possible—central route processing (when the recipient thoughtfully considers the issues and arguments) and peripheral route processing (characterized by considering other cues rather than the message itself). Another model of persuasion is the heuristic model (Chaiken, 1987). A *heuristic* is a rule of thumb or a shortcut that may lead to but does not guarantee a solution (see Figure 20.7).

The heuristic model proposes two ways in which attitudes may be changed. If an individual is not interested in an issue under discussion, he or she is likely to rely on heuristic processing, a very casual, low-attention form of analyzing evidence. In this kind of processing, the recipient tunes in to the peripheral aspects of the message—the likability of the source, the number of arguments, and the tone of voice.

On the other hand, if the recipient is deeply interested or curious about the topic of a message, the likely result is sometimes called systematic processing, or central route processing. Advertisers use heuristics to get you to buy their products. For instance, they may sprinkle their ads with numbers and nice-sounding words such as "integrity," employ celebrities to endorse their products, or state that their product is the most popular one.

The Sleeper Effect Changes in attitudes are not always permanent. In fact, efforts at persuasion usually have their greatest impact immediately and then fade away. However, sometimes people seem to reach different conclusions about a message after a period of time has elapsed. This curious **sleeper effect** has been explained in several ways.

One explanation of the delayed-action impact depends on the tendency to retain the message but forget the source. As time goes by, a positive source no longer holds power to persuade nor does a negative

sleeper effect: the delayed impact on attitude change of a persuasive communication source undercut the message. When the source is negative and the memory of the source fades, the message then "speaks for itself" and more people may accept it (Kelman & Hovland, 1953).

The problem is that this requires forgetting one thing and retaining another, with no obvious reason why that should occur. Researchers (Pratkanis et al., 1988) conducted experiments to verify their differential decay hypothesis. They argued that if the message is heard first, followed by a discounting cue (such as a low-credibility source), the two balance each other out—no effect is observed. At the same time, however, the negative aspects of the cue dissipate more rapidly than the impact of the highly elaborated message. It is easier to remember your own position than the details of an argument. If the cue decays rapidly and the argument more slowly, what remains is the effect on an attitude. It may also be that it simply takes time for people to change their minds. As the message "sinks in," attitudes change more.

The Inoculation Effect

What can you do to resist persuasion? Research has shown that people can be educated to resist attitude change. This technique can be compared to an inoculation (McGuire, 1970). Inoculation against persuasion works in much the same way as inoculation against certain diseases. When a person is vaccinated, he is given a weakened or dead form of the disease-causing agent, which stimulates his body to manufacture defenses. Then, if a person is attacked by a more potent form of the agent, his defenses make him immune to infection. Similarly, a person who has resisted a mild attack on his or her beliefs is ready to defend them against an onslaught that might otherwise have been overwhelming.

The **inoculation effect** can be explained in two ways: it motivates individuals to defend their beliefs more strongly, and it gives them some practice in defending those beliefs. The most vulnerable attitudes you have, therefore, are the ones that you have never had to defend. For example, you might find yourself hard put to defend your faith in democracy or in the healthfulness of vegetables if you have never had these beliefs questioned.

Brainwashing

The most extreme means of changing attitudes involves a combination of psychological gamesmanship and physical torture, aptly called **brainwashing.** The most extensive studies of brainwashing have been done on

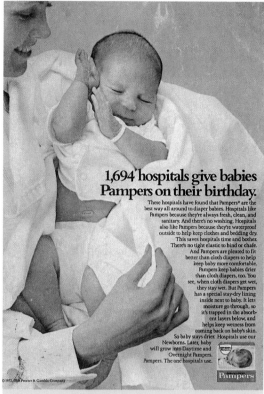

Figure 20.7 **Using Heuristics**

We use heuristics, or shortcuts, to evaluate many messages. This saves us time and energy. *Which heuristic is this advertiser using?*

1. If the message contains many numbers and large words, it must be based on facts.

2. If the message focuses on values I have, it is probably right.

3. Famous or successful people conveying the message are probably right.

4. If most people support this product or believe this, it is probably true.

inoculation effect: developing resistance to persuasion by exposing a person to arguments that challenge his or her beliefs so that he or she can practice defending them

brainwashing: extreme form of attitude change; uses peer pressure, physical suffering, threats, rewards, guilt, and intensive indoctrination

Westerners who had been captured by the Chinese during the Korean War and subjected to "thought reform." Psychiatrist Robert Jay Lifton (1963) interviewed several dozen prisoners released by the Chinese, and from their accounts, he outlined the methods used to break down people's convictions and introduce new patterns of belief, feeling, and behavior.

The aim in brainwashing is as much to create a new person as to change attitudes. So the first step is to strip away all identity and then subject the person to intense social pressure and physical stress. Prison is a perfect setting for this process. The person is isolated from social support, is a number not a name, is clothed like everyone else, and can be surrounded by people who have had their thoughts "reformed" and are contemptuous of "reactionaries." So long as the prisoner holds out, he is treated with contempt or exhorted to confess by his fellow prisoners. He is interrogated past the point of exhaustion and is humiliated and discomfited by being bound at all times, even during meals or elimination. The prisoner is rewarded for cooperating. Cooperation involves confessing to crimes against the people in his former way of life. With every "improvement" in his attitudes, prison life is made a little more pleasant. Finally, by a combination of threat, peer pressure, systematic rewards, and other psychological means, the prisoner comes to believe his confession.

It is difficult to say where persuasion ends and brainwashing begins. Some researchers believe that brainwashing is just a very intense form of persuasion. Drawing this line has become particularly important to the courts—especially in cases such as lawsuits regarding the deprogramming of members of religious cults. A cult is a group of people who organize around a strong authority figure. Cults use influence techniques and deception to attain psychological control over members and new recruits.

SECTION 3 Assessment

1. **Review the Vocabulary** Explain how the boomerang, sleeper, and inoculation effects influence your attitudes.

2. **Visualize the Main Idea** Use a diagram similar to the one below to outline the parts of the communication process.

The Communication Process Involves:

3. **Recall Information** How does brainwashing work? Why is it used?

4. **Think Critically** When evaluating a message that is very important to you, do you rely on systematic processing or heuristics? Explain.

5. **Application Activity** Pretend that you are a car dealer and you are persuading a young couple to purchase an automobile from your dealership. Write a brief script between the dealer and the couple that incorporates aspects of persuasion techniques both might use.

Summary and Vocabulary

Everyone has a variety of opinions, attitudes, and beliefs.
Psychologists study where they come from and how they change.

Section 1 Attitude Formation

Main Idea: Our attitudes are the result of conditioning, observational learning, and cognitive evaluation. Our attitudes help us define ourselves and our place in society, evaluate people and events, and guide our behavior.

- Classical conditioning helps you form attitudes automatically.
- The culture in which you grew up, the people who raised you, and those with whom you associate all shape your attitudes.
- People living in the same conditions and who frequently communicate with one another have attitudes in common because they are exposed to the same information.
- Our attitudes serve as guidelines for interpreting and categorizing people, objects, and events.

Section 2 Attitude Change and Prejudice

Main Idea: Attitudes are formed through compliance, identification, and internalization. Attitudes may be changed as a result of cognitive dissonance.

- People often adapt their actions to the wishes of others to avoid discomfort or rejection and to gain support.
- Identification occurs when a person wants to define himself or herself in terms of a person or group and therefore adopts the person's or group's attitudes and ways of behaving.
- Internalization is the most lasting of the three sources of attitude formation or change.
- People's attitudes change because they are always trying to get things to fit together logically.
- A person's actions can affect his or her attitudes.
- Prejudice means deciding beforehand what a person will be like instead of withholding judgment until it can be based on a person's individual qualities.

Section 3 Persuasion

Main Idea: Persuasion is a direct attempt to influence attitudes. We evaluate when, where, and how a message is presented, as well as the message itself, when determining the credibility of the message.

- The process of communication can be broken down into four parts: the message itself, the source of the message, the channel through which it is delivered, and the audience that receives it.
- The audience may process a message in two ways—by systematically thinking about it or by using heuristics.
- The most effective messages combine moderate emotional appeal with factual information and argument.

Chapter Vocabulary

attitude (p. 577)
self-concept (p. 580)
compliance (p. 583)
identification (p. 583)
internalization (p. 584)
cognitive dissonance (p. 584)
counterattitudinal behavior (p. 585)
self-justification (p. 586)
self-fulfilling prophecy (p. 586)
prejudice (p. 587)
discrimination (p. 588)
persuasion (p. 590)
boomerang effect (p. 592)
sleeper effect (p. 594)
inoculation effect (p. 595)
brainwashing (p. 595)

Self-Check Quiz
Visit the *Understanding Psychology* Web site at
psychology.glencoe.com and click on **Chapter 20—
Self-Check Quizzes** to prepare for the Chapter Test.

Reviewing Vocabulary

Choose the letter of the correct term or concept
below to complete the sentence.

a. attitude   **f.** discrimination
b. compliance   **g.** self-concept
c. identification   **h.** boomerang effect
d. internalization   **i.** sleeper effect
e. self-justification   **j.** brainwashing

1. A(n) _____ is a predisposition to respond
   in particular ways toward specific things.

2. A(n) _____ occurs when people seem to
   reach different conclusions about a message after
   a period of time has elapsed.

3. Justifying one's behavior to reduce cognitive dissonance is called _____.

4. _____ occurs when a person wants to
   define himself or herself in terms of a person or
   group and therefore adopts the person's or
   group's attitudes.

5. Your _____ is how you see or describe
   yourself.

6. The most extreme means of changing attitudes is
   called _____.

7. _____ occurs when a person adapts his or
   her action to the wishes of others to avoid discomfort or rejection and to gain support.

8. A(n) _____ occurs when people dislike the
   individual delivering a message and respond by
   taking the opposite point of view.

9. The unequal treatment of members of certain
   groups is called _____.

10. _____ occurs when a person wholeheart-
    edly accepts an attitude and the attitude becomes
    an integral part of the person.

Recalling Facts

1. In what three ways are attitudes formed?

2. Using a diagram similar to the one below, identify and describe two methods of delivering a
   persuasive message.

3. Which cognitive act are people engaging in
   when they convince themselves that they did
   not like the victim of their aggressive act?

4. What will be the effect on listeners if you use a
   very emotional appeal or if you pressure them to
   adopt your point of view?

5. What is the goal of brainwashing? How does
   brainwashing work?

Critical Thinking

1. **Evaluating Information**   Attitudes come from a
   variety of sources. Using the information in the
   chapter, what source do you think was most
   influential in establishing your attitudes? Why do
   you think so?

2. **Analyzing Information**   There are three processes involved in changing attitudes. Provide examples of an attitude being changed in each of the
   three ways. Explain which process is the most
   lasting process for changing attitudes and why.

3. **Applying Concepts**   What are two ways that
   you can help reduce prejudice in your school or
   community?

4. **Making Inferences**   One of the primary objectives of advertising is to get the viewers or listeners to remember the product. To what extent do
   you think familiarity with brand names influences your choices in the market?

5. **Synthesizing Information**   Think of a recent
   local or national political campaign. Focus on
   the kinds of persuasion techniques used by the
   candidates. How did they use central route processing? Peripheral route processing?

CHAPTER 20 Assessment

Psychology Projects

1. **Attitude Formation** Use a variety of sources to find examples of the ways in which culture influences attitudes. Find out about attitudes in other places of the world and compare those attitudes to ones in this country. Present your findings in an illustrated, captioned poster.

2. **Prejudice** Use magazine and newspaper articles to find out about common stereotypes toward groups such as teenagers and the elderly. Create a cartoon illustrating these stereotypes and provide suggestions for eliminating them.

3. **Persuasion** Choose some issue on which you have a strong opinion. If you were given an unlimited budget, how would you go about persuading people to agree with you? In a written report, describe the sources you would employ, the channels you would use, the content of your message, and the audience you would try to reach.

4. **Attitude Change** Study a recent or ongoing political campaign. What attitudinal change and persuasive strategies are being used? Collect examples of the strategies and report your findings in a brief presentation.

Technology Activity

Locate examples of persuasion techniques used by advertisers on the Internet. Print out pages of the advertisements and explain the techniques used to influence consumers. Evaluate the effectiveness of the advertisements in changing people's attitudes.

Psychology Journal

After reading the chapter and class discussions, would you revise the definition of prejudice that you wrote at the beginning of this chapter's study? In your journal, write a one-page paper explaining whether or not prejudice is unavoidable.

Building Skills

Identifying Cause-and-Effect Relationships Review the advertisement below, then answer the questions that follow.

1. Which function of attitudes does this advertisement illustrate?

2. Do you think this advertisement is an effective persuasive communication tool? Why do you think so?

 Practice and assess key social studies skills with **Glencoe Skillbuilder Interactive Workbook CD-ROM, Level 2.**

See the Skills Handbook, page 624, for an explanation of identifying cause-and-effect relationships.

TIME *REPORTS*

Kids and Race

A new poll shows teenagers, black and white,
have moved beyond their parents' views of race

By **CHRISTOPHER JOHN FARLEY**

RODNEY GULLATTE JR., 17, AN African-American student at Sprayberry High School in Marietta, Ga., was still in middle school when he got his first lesson in racism. It was then that a group of white kids, whom he describes as part of a growing "skinhead" element in his school, began to harass him. After a time Gullatte punched one of the white kids in the face. That earned Gullatte an in-school suspension. Worse, nobody believed him when he explained why he had lashed out. "They kept saying the kid would not say something like that, that stuff like that doesn't happen in the Cobb County public schools," says Gullatte. "But people don't know what really goes on."

What *does* go on? With the number of hate crimes on the rise nationwide, what do today's children really think about the racial chasm that has divided this country since its inception?

The days of Bull Connor, police dogs and fire hoses are long gone, and many would find it comforting to believe that skin color is no longer an issue for kids. Has the newest generation of Americans finally arrived at that melanin-friendly Promised Land? No. But a new TIME/CNN poll of 1,282 adults and 601 teens (ages 12 to 17) has found a startling number of youngsters, black and white, who seem to have moved beyond their parents' views of race. These kids say race is less important to them, both on a personal level and as a social divide, than it is for adults. It must be noted that more than half of both white kids and black still consider racism "a big problem" in America—however, more than a third classify it as "a small problem." Asked about the impact of racism in their own lives, a startling 89% of black teens call it "a small problem" or "not a problem at all." In fact, white adults and white teens are more convinced than black teens that racism in America remains a dominant issue.

Furthermore, black teens are more reluctant than others to blame racism for problems. Indeed, nearly twice as many black kids as white believe "failure to take advantage of available opportunities" is more of a problem for blacks than discrimination. That's especially extraordinary given the fact that 40% of the black teens surveyed believe SATS are loaded against them, and that blacks have to be better qualified than whites to get a job. These responses seem to indicate that black teens believe color barriers exist, but, despite that, they retain an admirably dogged belief in self-determination.

Is this surprising portrait a sign of hope? Or is it just an example of youthful naiveté? Probably both. "One word explains it—experience," speculates sociologist Joe R. Feagin. "You have to be out looking for jobs and housing to know how much discrimination is out there. People doing that are usually over 19." Sure enough, only a quarter of

---

SPEAKING OUT: Teens and Adults See Different Worlds

■ **Which of the following is more of a problem for blacks today?**

TEENS	ADULTS
Failure to take advantage	
of available opportunities	
Whites: 31%	Whites: 52%
Blacks: 58%	Blacks: 51%
Discrimination by whites	
Whites: 47%	Whites: 22%
Blacks: 26%	Blacks: 26%

■ **Is racism a big problem or a small problem?**

TEENS	ADULTS
Big problem	
Whites: 58%	Whites: 64%
Blacks: 62%	Blacks: 78%
Small problem	
Whites: 34%	Whites: 27%
Blacks: 34%	Blacks: 17%

■ **Have you ever been a victim of discrimination because you are black?**

BLACK TEENS	BLACK ADULTS
Yes: 23%	Yes: 53%
No: 77%	No: 45%

■ **Have you ever been a victim of discrimination because you are white?**

WHITE TEENS	WHITE ADULTS
Yes: 16%	Yes: 20%
No: 83%	No: 79%

■ **Will race relations in this country ever get better?**

TEENS	ADULTS
Yes	
Whites: 76%	Whites: 60%
Blacks: 55%	Blacks: 43%

From a telephone poll of 816 white adults, 374 black adults, 301 white teens and 300 black teens taken for TIME/CNN from Sept. 23 to Oct. 2 by Yankelovich Partners Inc. Margins of error are [±]3.4%, 5.1%, 5.6% and 5.6% respectively black teens surveyed said they had been victims of discrimination, whereas half of black adults say they have. For all that, these kids remain astonishingly optimistic: 95% of the black youngsters think they're going on to college, as do 93% of the whites.

But is that gullibility? Or gutsiness? Today's teens have respect for the past, faith in the future—and a distaste for scapegoating that outstrips that of their parents. One of the survey's more

" Teenagers are a mirror of our souls. They speak plainly about things that adults would like to hide. "

notable findings: even though neither black teens nor whites tend to blame racism as a cause of problems facing blacks, they nonetheless support gender- and race-based scholarships in greater numbers than adults.

People don't always level with pollsters; they're notorious in fact for giving answers they believe to be socially acceptable at the expense of revealing their true feelings. But teens are less likely to do that than adults. Sociologist Howard Pinderhughes, author of the new book *Race in the Hood: Conflict and Violence Among Urban Youth*, says, "Teenagers are a mirror of our souls. They speak plainly about things that adults would like to hide. Political correctness isn't an issue to them. You're more likely to get what they think unfiltered." Extensive interviews with children, parents, educators, researchers and law-enforcement officials make clear that the new optimism takes place against a backdrop of a number of new challenges, such as the growing presence of hate groups on the Internet, and old ones, such as interracial dating and ethnic turf wars.

A disinclination to blame problems on racism does not mean a reduced sense of racial identity. Psychologist Beverly Tatum, author of the recently published *Why Are All the Black Kids Sitting Together in the Cafeteria?*, says she often asks her psychology students to complete this sentence: "I am _____." White students tend to answer with personality traits: "I am

friendly," "I am shy," etc. Students of color tend to fill in the blank with their ethnicity: "I am black" or "I am Puerto Rican." The foundation for racial identity, Tatum argues, is constructed in adolescence by peer pressure, societal influences and self-reflection; it is a time when children make choices about who they are.

The attitudes expressed by respondents to the TIME/CNN poll are all the more remarkable given that outside of school, black teens and white teens most often live in separate neighborhoods and sometimes, it seems, on separate planets. Danny, 17, a white Chicago youngster interviewed by TIME, professed to having "more black friends than I do white friends" but also admitted that "we just talk in school" and that he never visits the homes of his black buddies, who tend to live in crime-plagued housing projects.

Danny's situation is not uncommon. While few teens view their neighborhood as dangerous, 40% of black teens reported that they knew someone their age who had been murdered, in contrast to only 15% of white teens. Black teens also feel they don't get a fair shake from the police: one-third of them feel they are at risk of being treated unfairly by cops, while only 1 out of 5 white teens shares that fear.

Three-fourths of the white teenagers polled by TIME/CNN believe race relations will get better, as do more than half of the black teens. "What we're seeing here is a hidden aspect of the black survival process," says Michael Eric Dyson, author of *Race Rules: Navigating the Color Line*. "You imagine a reality better than the one in

which you presently live. I wouldn't call it optimism; it goes too deep. It's hope. Hope goes against everything you see."

One black Newark, N.J., teen interviewed by TIME launched into an ugly tirade about Jews—but many more expressed a sense of catharsis simply to be talking about the racial difficulties they face. On the other hand, white teens interviewed seemed to have more trouble discussing racial issues, and were often unable to even find the words to describe their feelings about ethnicity. According to psychologist Tatum, some parents, particularly white ones, silence their children when racial issues are raised. This is done, sometimes, as part of a well-meaning effort to teach children that such distinctions don't matter. But as a result of such silencing, children are left without answers to their questions and without the social skills to deal with racial issues.

Some youngsters are trying to reach beyond the silence. After Gullatte had his fight with skinheads in his school, he felt he had no one to talk to. He has since joined Group X, a program started in the Cobb County school system in 1993 in which students meet on a semiregular basis and discuss race. Some 450 students are signed up. The meetings, held in groups of about 20, can get emotional. At a recent session, Alison Garcia, 12, stood up, tears in her eyes, and exclaimed, "All Hispanics are not dumb! You don't know me. My father and my uncle were part of the Cherokee tribe, and my uncle had the highest scores in school." Says Gullatte: "What the Group X project did was help me to be able to tell other people about [my experiences] and say what I really feel." It's just talk. But it's a start. ∎

—For the complete text of this article and related articles from TIME, please visit www.time.com/teach

ANALYZING THE ARTICLE

1. Why do kids' views on race relations differ from adults'?
2. **CRITICAL THINKING** Do you believe that race barriers exist in your world? Do you think the adults you know would disagree with you? Explain.

Psychology: Present and Future

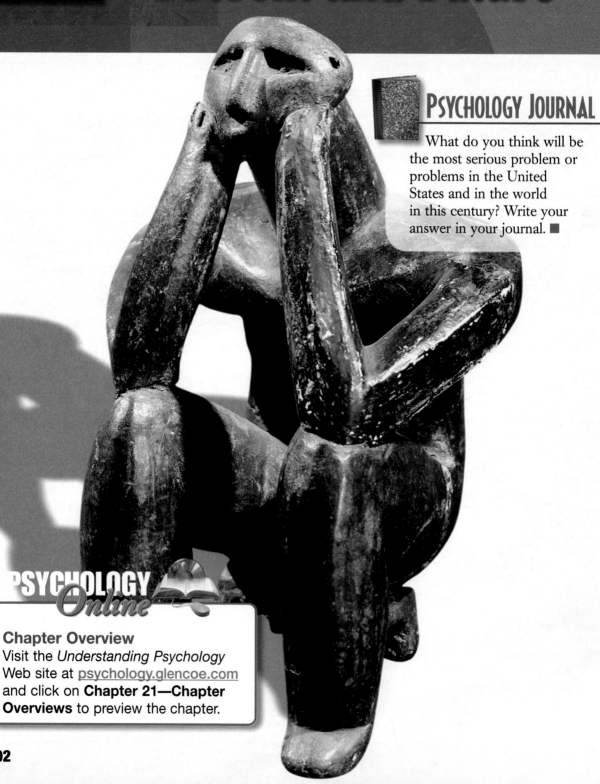

PSYCHOLOGY JOURNAL

What do you think will be
the most serious problem or
problems in the United
States and in the world
in this century? Write your
answer in your journal. ■

PSYCHOLOGY Online

Chapter Overview
Visit the *Understanding Psychology*
Web site at psychology.glencoe.com
and click on **Chapter 21—Chapter
Overviews** to preview the chapter.

Careers in Psychology

Reader's Guide

■ Main Idea
Human behavior plays a key role in many areas of study. Studying psychology can prepare you for many career opportunities.

■ Vocabulary
- crisis intervention program

■ Objectives
- Outline the requirements needed to become a psychologist.
- List several careers available in psychology.

EXPLORING PSYCHOLOGY

Choosing My Destiny

Many of the students at the school had been given intelligence tests and scored at the lowest and most handicapped level. Yet it was evident that these young people had skills that were relevant to their culture. I recall a Down's syndrome child who could beat out complex rhythms on the drum, young women who learned to card and weave rugs from foster grandparents, and Yazzie, our survival artist, who could go for days in very severe weather conditions with little clothing or food and would turn up in a distant town days later seemingly no worse for wear. Obviously, the intelligence tests were missing something that was very important.

—from "Pathways to Change and Development: The Life of a School Psychologist" by Stephen F. Poland, in *Career Paths in Psychology*, edited by Robert J. Sternberg

I n the passage above, author Stephen Poland explains his experiences with teaching a group of mentally handicapped Navajo children. This adventure led him to seek his destiny and his career—becoming a school psychologist.

CAREERS IN PSYCHOLOGY

"What are you going to do when you get out of school?"

"Beats me. My grandparents want me to learn the shoe business and take over when they retire. Mom and Dad want me to think about law as

Figure 21.1 Areas of Expertise of Ph.D. Psychologists

In the past 20 years, the number of people receiving doctorate degrees in the field of psychology has grown by more than 180 percent. *Which area of expertise has enjoyed the greatest growth?*

	1975	1985	1995
Clinical/Counseling/School	35%	44%	50%
Experimental/Comparative/Physiological	17%	17%	16%
Developmental/Child/Social/Personality	14%	14%	13%
Educational	5%	4%	3%
Industrial/Organizational	3%	3%	3%
Other psychology subfields	26%	18%	15%

Source: NSF/SRS Surveys of Doctorate Recipients. Compiled by APA Research Office, May 1999.

a career. I was leaning toward business administration, but my sister just graduated with an M.B.A. I don't want to be just like her. I've got more choices than I can handle."

This conversation is imaginary but typical for juniors and seniors in high school. You do have many options. Because you have spent a period of time studying psychology, it may be beneficial to respond to questions about psychology: What will I do with what I have learned? Was it worth it if this is the only psychology course I ever take? What careers in psychology are open to me? To help you find answers to these questions, this section offers several descriptions of opportunities in psychology careers. The careers described here, though, are only a few in the vast field of psychology and related fields.

What Are Employers Looking For?

Employers are most likely to hire someone who offers special skills. In psychology, as in many other fields, job choices are limited if you have only a high school diploma. Surprisingly, when you have a Ph.D., you also have relatively few choices, but by that time you have chosen to fine-tune your education and experience a specific kind of job—you are a specialist.

Those with a bachelor's degree in psychology may have the most options with the widest array of possible employers. Moreover, psychology is a logical undergraduate major for those planning graduate work in such fields as sociology, social work, law, medicine, or education. Human behavior plays a key role in all of these areas.

Some Career Options

Reading Check
How is psychology both a science and a profession?

Psychology is both a science and a profession. As a science, psychologists study how people perceive, think, feel, and act. In the professional arena, careers that are based on psychological principles seek to predict how people will act; help people modify their behavior; and help organizations, businesses, and communities to change.

crisis intervention program: short-term psychological first aid that helps individuals and families deal with emergencies or highly stressful situations

Crisis Hot Line Adviser

Employer: a large hospital

Can you do it? A person holding this job might even be a senior in high school. For most **crisis intervention programs,** applicants must complete a training program. A county hospital, for instance, might offer such training over three weekends. Following training, a typical assignment would involve two 4-hour shifts a week.

What's involved? Crisis hot line personnel respond primarily to two kinds of problems. One involves the immediate, possibly life-threatening situation that can arise as a result of a personal or family crisis—perhaps an argument or the unexpected death of a loved one. Drug use—whether from withdrawal or overdose—can also bring about an immediate need for help. The other type of problem is the crisis evolving from long-term stress, such as that experienced in the family, on the job, or in a failure to develop one's career. Crises like these are not as threatening but still need to be resolved.

A person handling a hot line will have a list of psychologists and psychiatrists as well as information about a wide array of treatment facilities and programs operating in the vicinity. This job requires being able to calm the caller, identify his or her problem, and help that caller to see the wisdom—once the immediate crisis has been dealt with—of contacting the most appropriate agency for long-term follow-up.

Word Processor Salesperson

Employer: a local computer dealer

Can you do it? People with an interest in psychology are likely to have a higher-than-average interest in behavior—both theirs and others. That interest—even if backed only by a high school diploma—is a vital element of the successful salesperson. One report suggests that the best salespeople are motivated by the need for status, control, respect, routine, accomplishment, stimulation, and honesty. With those needs met, a salesperson—regardless of level of education—will feel happy. A basic understanding of people's driving forces—their needs for achievement, affiliation, and safety—is but one aspect of psychology that would aid someone seeking a career in sales.

What's involved? The key requirement may be experience. One psychologist has suggested that you cannot educate someone to be good in sales, but sensitivity to others can be improved by training. You must also be persistent, skillful at language, able to query prospective customers, and able to relate their needs to those answered by the product you are offering.

Mental Health Assistant

Employer: a senior citizen service center

Can you do it? This is a new career field, usually requiring at least an associate degree. An associate degree is

Try Out a Career in Psychology

As you search the want ads in your local newspaper, you may not see very many entry-level job openings for psychologists. There are jobs, though, that can expose you to psychology-related work. Look for jobs that utilize "people skills" such as communicating or relating to people, "analytical skills" such as figuring out and resolving problems, "writing skills" such as writing logical reports, and "research skills" such as using statistics or tables to analyze issues. These skills are called for in a variety of jobs, such as working for case workers, business managers, probation or corrections officers, and human services.

Profiles In Psychology

Linda L. McCarley

1946–

"Artmaking opens windows to the inner world."

Linda L. McCarley, an art therapist, is founder and director of the Art Therapy Institute in Dallas, Texas. She helps people create drawings, paintings, sculptures, and other art forms that provide a glimpse into their inner world.

How does art therapy work? Have you ever felt better after expressing yourself with music, dance, drama, or art? That is because words may not adequately express some of your deepest feelings or life experiences. Artmaking provides another avenue of self-expression, helps release tension, and is known to be life enhancing. As we can see by studying the images etched on the walls of caves dating back to ancient times, people have always relied upon imagery to express their most significant life experiences. The art made by people throughout history enriches our understanding of those people.

Similarly, art therapists gain an understanding of their clients though the process of making art in therapy. Art therapists set the stage for self-discovery and healing by facilitating their clients' creative expressions.

awarded after a two-year course preparing for paraprofessional occupations in nursing homes, community mental health centers, centers dealing with mental retardation, or even special-education centers for the variously disabled in public schools.

What's involved? Typically supervised by a staff psychologist, an assistant helps with or conducts admission interviews. He or she may be responsible—under supervision—for administering various psychological tests, either to new patients or to assess the progress of those already admitted.

Personnel Director

Employer: a large department store, for example

Can you do it? The successful applicant is likely to have a bachelor's degree in psychology, having concentrated on courses involving interviewing, test construction and interpretation, statistics, and—perhaps surprisingly to you—law. Such a person might also have taken a minor in management courses in a university's College of Business Administration. He or she would stress organizational and quantitative skills. This is not an entry-level job, however. Some prior experience with the employer's policies is a definite requirement.

What's involved? A personnel director may participate in a wide array of activities, depending on the nature and interest of his or her employer. Clearly, the decisions to hire and fire would be this person's responsibility, especially for the support staff in any organization. Such a person might also develop programs to improve or maintain staff skills—in sales, interpersonal sensitivity, or any other skill involved in conducting the company's business.

School Psychologist

Employer: a city school system

Can you do it? A master's degree is a must for this position; an undergraduate major in psychology is desirable. In addition, most school psychologists must be licensed or certified in their state of employment, which involves taking a test.

What's involved? In bigger districts, you might stay in one school, but many school psychologists divide their time among a number of schools. They usually work with children experiencing the normal array of problems in school. A school psychologist might give reading, aptitude, interest, or intelligence tests and must be skillful in interpreting them. At other times he or she might work directly with the children or young adults in school or with the families of those students.

Clinical Psychologist

Employer: yourself (self-employed), government, business, hospital, prison, or nonprofit organization

Can you do it? To use this title in most states requires a Ph.D. (a Doctor of Philosophy) or a Psy.D. (a Doctor of Psychology). The Psy.D. is a degree developed in the 1970s. In a Psy.D. program, a student gains skill in psychotherapy, undergoing intensive training in testing, interviewing, and giving supervised therapy.

What's involved? A practicing clinical psychologist is often self-employed. Thus, required skills include those needed to run any small business, in addition to knowledge of testing and practical experience with the limits and strengths of various forms of therapy. He or she must develop working relations with other clinicians in the area—psychiatrists, medical doctors, and other contacts in local hospitals and mental health facilities. From such sources come the patient/client referrals that are vital to one's success as a psychotherapist.

A typical day might involve 8 to 10 hours in various stages of psychotherapy with different individuals. The hours have to be offered at times when clients are free to visit, so this may not be a traditional 9-to-5 job. Other types of therapy a clinical psychologist might offer are group therapy or consultation with other therapeutic organizations, such as Alcoholics Anonymous. It is also possible, of course, to utilize the same skills as a clinical psychologist in a state-supported mental hospital, a Veterans Administration hospital, or a community mental health center.

Figure 21.2 Consumer Psychology

Consumer psychologists study the processes people go through as they purchase goods and services. Organizations hire them to research and answer questions such as "What do consumers think of us?" "How can we better serve our customers?" *Why might consumer psychologists be involved in employee training?*

More About...

Human Factors Engineering

Human factors engineers, or engineering psychologists, help design machines and equipment such as computer systems, automobiles, office equipment, and household appliances to match human abilities and limitations so the equipment can be operated efficiently and safely. Human factors engineers draw on physics, anatomy, psychology, and sociology as well as contributions from teachers and communications experts to analyze and solve problems. Consider this example: Why is the gas pedal on the right side of your car's floor rather than on the left? The reason is for more efficient use. Most people are right-side dominant and use the gas pedal more than the brake.

Did You Know?

Post-War Psychology The demand for the services of counseling and clinical psychologists always increases dramatically toward the end of a war. This occurred at the end of World War II, the Korean War, the Vietnam War, and the Persian Gulf War. Counseling psychologists are needed to help servicemen and women adjust to civil life, shift war-industry workers, and rehabilitate the wounded and emotionally disturbed war veterans.

Consulting Psychologist

Employer: a management consulting firm

Can you do it? A Ph.D. is required for this job. Such a person might spend graduate school in an industrial/organizational psychology program learning management practices, testing strategies, interpersonal behavioral strategies, and intervention techniques in complex organizations.

What's involved? A consultant—by the very nature of his or her job—must offer an array of skills not normally represented among the full-time employees of companies that hire consultants. Thus, a consultant's job tends to be short term. A consultant might, for instance, advise a company's top management on how to take human performance limits into account in the design of a control board for a nuclear power plant. He or she might be involved in all aspects of the design of an interstate highway—signs, bridges and crossover devices, and lane-flow control.

Future Psychology Career Options

As psychologists in every specialty area meet new challenges, new areas of psychology begin to develop. Often a new area of psychology develops as a result of a merging of other areas. For example, the relatively new area of health psychology combines aspects of physiological, social, counseling, and clinical psychology. Health psychologists focus on the role the psychological functions of an individual play on the health of that individual. A health psychologist might research the origins of obesity and try to find and apply effective treatments. A health psychologist might also deal with how stress is related to illness.

SECTION 1 Assessment

1. **Review the Vocabulary** What types of situations does a crisis intervention program handle?

2. **Visualize the Main Idea** Use a graphic organizer similar to the one below to list a possible psychology career under each discipline.

Careers in Psychology — Medicine — Law — Business

3. **Recall Information** What are most employers seeking in employees?

4. **Think Critically** How might a degree in psychology help you design a popular Web page or market yourself as an up-and-coming actor?

5. **Application Activity** Explore your long-term goals by outlining a possible educational and career path that you might follow. In your outline be sure to indicate your career goal and how you plan to achieve that goal. Explain why you have selected that goal.

Parapsychology

Period of Study: 1882 and 1975

Introduction: Behavior types that seem to deviate from normal behavior are sometimes left unexplained. This area of study is known as *parapsychology*. Parapsychology literally means "alongside psychology." Parapsychology is not considered to be in the mainstream of psychology, but its interesting yet controversial issues have attracted many psychologists and other interested individuals. Parapsychology suggests that humans possess senses other than the known seven: vision, hearing, taste, smell, touch, balance, and body senses. This area is often met with skepticism. Many people do not believe in the possibility of seemingly "supernatural" events. However, there have been some events that psychologists cannot otherwise explain.

Hypothesis: Those who study parapsychological events form hypotheses, which generally conform to consistent ideas about these obscure events. The foundations of these hypotheses are similar because parapsychological concepts cannot easily be studied. Parapsychologists try to eliminate all other scientific explanations for an event.

Method: In 1882 scientists established the first organization to study parapsychology—the Society of Psychical Research—in London. The American version of this society was formed in Boston three years later. These organizations focused on mediumship, or communication with those who have died. As time passed, other phenomena began to be studied, such as telepathy (the ability of people to communicate without using ordinary senses), clairvoyance (the ability to experience an event without physically being there), and psychokinesis (controlling objects with the mind).

Perhaps the greatest example of psychokinesis to date is that of Uri Gellar. Gellar claimed he could bend and break metal objects by using mind control. On many nonscientifically controlled occasions, Gellar did indeed bend and break metal objects without physically touching them. In 1974 psychologists conducted several experiments on Gellar. They filmed these experiments and carefully reviewed them to see if Gellar had used "slight-of-hand" tricks. In one instance, Gellar unbalanced a precision scientific scale. Also, he seemingly bent a steel band that normally requires about 100 pounds of pressure. He accomplished both of these feats without physical contact. Therefore, Gellar represented proof of the existence of parapsychological phenomenon in humans, or did he?

Results: The events surrounding Gellar were highly controversial, but on Gellar's part, they were highly profitable. Gellar began to make appearances in various locations, demonstrating his amazing abilities. In these demonstrations Gellar bent metal spoons or other such objects. Gellar received an invitation to appear on national television and perform his miraculous feats. When it was time to perform his mind control abilities on national television, though, Gellar could not deliver. Gellar claimed that something was blocking his ability to project his mind-controlling thoughts onto the spoons. It was discovered later that before all of his performances, Gellar had access to the objects he was going to manipulate with his mind. On national television, however, Gellar's personal set of objects had been switched with a new set.

One may wonder why we used a failed example to describe the study of parapsychology. We used this example to show how difficult it is to prove the existence of such phenomena. Perhaps in the future, breakthroughs will be made in the study of parapsychology. As for now, skepticism seems to prevail.

Analyzing the Case Study

1. What is parapsychology?
2. What abilities did Gellar claim to have?
3. **Critical Thinking** Do you believe that some people have parapsychological abilities? Why or why not?

Reader's Guide

■ Main Idea
Psychology has made many contributions to society by promoting human welfare, clarifying assessment methods, explaining human behavior, and helping humans better understand their world.

■ Vocabulary
- ACT
- SAT
- forensic psychology
- industrial/organizational psychology
- sports psychology
- visualization
- gerontology

■ Objectives
- Describe psychologists' contributions in everyday life.
- Summarize psychology's challenges for the future.

EXPLORING PSYCHOLOGY

Misinformed
A few years ago, a psychology professor, famous in his field for developing new experimental and statistical methods, got into a taxi. He started a friendly conversation with the driver and when asked what he did for a living, the professor replied that he was a psychologist. "Oh yeah? My sister went to see a psychologist," replied the driver. "She's really a nut-case. Hey wait, can you read my mind? I'd better be careful what I say!" The professor reports that he now replies to such questions by saying that he is a "research scientist."

—from *Opportunities in Psychology Careers* by Charles M. Super and Donald E. Super, 1994

Although most people seem to have an accurate idea of what doctors or lawyers do, many people do not realize what psychologists do. These people probably do not realize, then, the many contributions to life that the science of human behavior has produced.

PSYCHOLOGY'S ROLE IN MENTAL HEALTH

Of all of psychology's contributions, perhaps its most significant is the development of forms of professional helping, including psychotherapy. An early step forward came in the 1790s through the pioneering efforts of Philippe Pinel, a French physician and a founder of psychiatry. Pinel unchained patients who were held in mental wards, some of whom had been restrained for more than 20 years. Pinel argued against the prevailing belief that the mentally ill were possessed by demons. Moreover, he thought mental illness could be treated. Mainly due to his efforts, France became a leader in improving conditions for the mentally ill.

Despite the progress in France, more than half a century passed before similar efforts were exerted in the United States. After discovering that the mentally ill were being jailed along with criminals, teacher and social reformer Dorothea Dix became the chief spokesperson for reform. Her personal crusade in the 1840s aroused interest in the problems of mental illness and led to more enlightened treatment of the mentally ill in Canada and Great Britain, as well as in the United States.

A former mental patient, Clifford Beers became the guiding force in the early growth of the modern mental health movement. Beers's own account of his illness and recovery, *A Mind That Found Itself,* first published nearly 90 years ago, has motivated students, mental health workers, and concerned individuals to promote better psychiatric care in communities, in schools, and in hospitals. The book set into motion Beers's plan to improve conditions. In 1908 Beers founded the Connecticut Society for Mental Hygiene, the first organization of its type. In its charter, the Connecticut Society pledged to eliminate restraints on patients, improve standards of care for the mentally retarded, prevent mental disorders, preserve mental health, and provide information on mental illness to the public.

| Figure 21.3 | Before Psychological Illnesses Were Understood |

Often described as the father of scientific psychiatry, Philippe Pinel argued that the mentally ill required humane treatment, sympathy, and guidance, not the beatings, imprisonment, and ridicule they so often suffered. *Why was Pinel's behavior considered revolutionary?*

PSYCHOLOGY'S ROLE IN TESTING

You probably had your first encounter with a psychologist while in elementary school. Most students are given IQ tests or other tests at an early age. Psychologists have played a leading role in devising and updating these tests, as well as other tests in higher education that assess personal skills. Many of you have taken or will take one or both of the two major standardized college entrance exams: the Scholastic Assessment Test (SAT) and the American College Testing Proficiency Examination Program (ACT). Developed in 1959, the current **ACT** places greater emphasis on scientific concepts and abstract reading skills and less emphasis on factual material than the earlier version. Nearly 1 million high school seniors take the ACT each year. The **SAT,** taken by about 1.2 million high school seniors annually, was redesigned in 1994 to give more weight to abstract thinking skills.

ACT: a standardized test that consists of four academic tests that measure academic development

SAT: a standardized test that is an admission requirement at some colleges; the test measures verbal and mathematical reasoning abilities

PSYCHOLOGY
Online

Student Web Activity
Visit the *Understanding Psychology* Web site at **psychology.glencoe.com** and click on **Chapter 21— Student Web Activities** for an activity about psychology's contributions.

PSYCHOLOGY'S ROLE IN EVERYDAY LIVING

With more than half of all mothers and an even higher percentage of fathers working outside the home, day-care and out-of-home nurturing and learning are significant issues. Researchers note that day care appears to have few negative effects on children and actually promotes development of social skills (Bukatko & Daehler, 1992). Interestingly, children with experience in day care tend to be more assertive and aggressive. Alison Clarke-Stewart (1989) has suggested that this may simply result from the fact that day-care children think at a more advanced level but have not yet developed the social skills with which to implement their plans smoothly.

Harry Harlow's work led to the idea that the attachment of children to their caregivers is made stronger by physical contact. That, in turn, led to the demonstration that breast-feeding versus bottle-feeding really makes no difference in the parent-child attachment. It is the holding, not the feeding, that is important.

Psychologists play a role in designing and assessing tools for learning in a variety of media: for example, their understanding of the principles of learning contributed to the development of the PBS series "Sesame Street." Studies show that almost 60 percent of the preschool children who watch that program at least five times a week can recite the entire alphabet correctly. Originally designed to provide creative ways to educate children with skills required in school—such as spelling, counting, and new words—this program, as the data indicate, has met its goal.

Some of B.F. Skinner's ideas on learning have been implemented into computer software designs. The ideas of feedback, prior knowledge and knowledge of results, and reinforcement play important roles in games as well as educational programs.

The work of many psychologists led to a clearer understanding about challenges facing men and women as they age. As the American population ages, increased understanding of the abilities of the aged is an area in which psychology must make continued contributions.

PSYCHOLOGY TODAY

Contemporary psychology can be grouped into experimental fields and applied fields. Experimental

Figure 21.4	**Then and Now**

Although it is considered a new science, psychology has come a long way. Some of the questions of early psychologists, such as how perception works or why we reason, have been answered. Other questions, such as nature versus nurture, remain the focus of research. *What have psychologists contributed to everyday living?*

Figure 21.5 **Some Significant Dates in the History of Psychology**

The history of psychology reflects the origins of many contemporary psychological issues and questions. *In 1649 René Descartes suggested that the body and soul are separate. How might contemporary psychologists label the "body" and "soul" today?*

B.C.	
170	**170 B.C.** • Claudius Galeno describes the anatomy of the human brain.
0 A.D.	
1600	
	1649 • René Descartes proposes that the body and soul are totally separate.
	1651 • Thomas Hobbes argues in *Leviathan* that all human behavior is the result of physical
1800	processes.
	1848 • Jean-Baptiste Bouillard offers 500 francs to anyone who can show him the brain of a human who suffered from speech disturbance and did not have damage to the left frontal lobe.
	1859 • Karl Marx proposes the idea that social being determines consciousness in *A Contribution to the Critique of Political Economy.*
	1860 • Paul Broca claims that a specific area (left frontal lobe) of the human brain is responsible for speech.
	1879 • Wilhelm Wundt establishes the first psychological laboratory at Leipzig University.
	1884 • William James argues that human behavior can be understood in terms of its purposes or functions.
	1890 • James McKeen Cattell develops first psychological tests for individual differences.
	1891 • American Psychological Association formed at Clark University.
1900	**1901** • Ivan Pavlov discovers the conditioned reflex.
	1905 • Binet-Simon scale, the first intelligence scale, formulated.
	1912 • William Stern develops the intelligence quotient (IQ).
	1913 • John B. Watson advocates behaviorism.
	1920 • Hermann Rorschach develops the inkblot test.
	1930 • Karl Lashley concludes that complex behavior is the result of neural programs in the brain.
	1933 • Lev Vygotsky argues that the human mind is a product of history and culture.
1950	**1951** • Simone de Beauvoir publishes a landmark book on the rights of women (*The Second Sex*).
	1954 • The U.S. Supreme Court rules that racially segregated education is inherently illegal in *Brown* v. *Board of Education,* resulting in many psychological studies of social issues.
	1955 • A federal commission reports that more than 50 percent of the 1,500,000 hospital beds in the U.S. are devoted to patients with mental illness, making mental illness the "greatest single" U.S. health problem.
	1966 • The first federal act to protect animal research subjects is enacted in the United States.
	1971 • B.F. Skinner argues that human behavior is a product of environmental stimuli.
	1980 • It is estimated that 1 of 10 doctorates granted in the United States is in psychology.
1990	**1990s** • Various psychologists argue that behavior is determined by social and cultural influences.
	1995 • First issue of *Psychology, Public Policy, and Law* appears.

psychologists use a variety of scientific methods to study psychological processes. Applied psychologists put knowledge of psychology to work solving human problems. Yet this distinction is not always sharp. Both the experimental and the applied psychologists gather the available evidence and offer the best they find. Both study behavior, and both use similar processes in similar situations. A major difference is that applied psychologists search for immediate solutions; experimental psychologists for long-range answers.

Psi Chi is the national honor society of psychology.

Reading Check
How does the work of experimental and applied psychologists differ?

Current Trends

The American Psychological Association (APA) is a scientific and professional society of psychologists and educators. Founded in 1892, it is the major psychological association in the United States and is made of more than 50 divisions, each representing a specific area, type of work or research setting, or activity. Some divisions are research-oriented, while others are advocacy groups. Together they are a cross section of the diverse nature of psychology.

Beginning in the 1970s, some members expressed dissatisfaction with the direction of the APA. These critics feared that the APA was becoming a professional instead of an academic organization. As a result, a new organization for academic and science-oriented psychologists, the American Psychological Society (APS), was founded in 1988; in five years it had grown to a membership of 15,000. With more than 159,000 members and affiliates, the APA is the world's largest organization of psychologists.

Another organization, Psi Chi—a professional and scientific fraternity—has chapters on many college and university campuses. Members of Psi Chi hold meetings and help orient psychology students to the field.

According to a survey completed by the APA Research Office (1996, 1999), about 43 percent of those who study psychology obtain master's degrees in counseling, 32 percent in clinical psychology, and 15 percent in school psychology. The remaining respondents to the survey obtained their degrees in traditional research and other subfields, such as industrial/organizational psychology, general and educational psychology, and experimental psychology (see Figure 21.6).

The United States Bureau of Labor places psychology among the fastest-growing fields into the twenty-first century. In addition, the number of women in psychology has been increasing rapidly. In the early 1990s, women held 60 percent of the civilian jobs in psychology, and women received more than two-thirds of the bachelor's and master's degrees conferred during that time. Although psychology is still a male-dominated field, the proportion of women in psychology is greater than in most other scientific disciplines (Simonton, 1992).

Ethnic minorities have indeed been a minority in the field of psychology. This trend, however, also seems to be changing. In the past decade, a relatively

| Figure 21.6 | **Employment of Ph.D. Psychologists** |

Psychology is one of the most diverse fields to enter. Almost all psychologists are trained at colleges and universities, and therefore all psychologists are familiar with the academic setting. *Where do most people who obtain Ph.D.s in psychology work?*

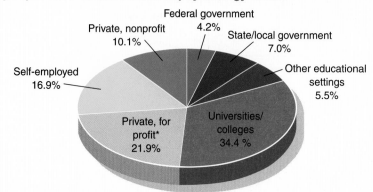

*This category includes businesses and incorporated private practices.

Source: 1997 Survey of Doctorate Recipients, National Research Council and National Science Foundation. Compiled by APA Research Office, March 1999.

larger number of doctorates have been awarded to minority group members. The increasing diversity of the field of psychology is important. As diverse people enter the field, they propose new perspectives on issues of psychology and behavior. Although new perspectives can be controversial, they pave the way for scientific advancement (Super & Super, 1994).

Fields of Psychology

Forensic psychology is a branch of applied psychology that studies and makes practical suggestions about the workings of the law. The work of psychologist Elizabeth Loftus has played a pivotal role (see Chapter 10). Many forensic psychologists study criminal behavior. Still others do work on the reliability of eyewitnesses, the effects on children who appear in court, counseling victims, and the jury selection process. A lawyer-psychologist often has both a Ph.D. and a law degree (Hofer, 1991).

Work and the working environment are the provinces of **industrial/organizational psychology,** or, as the field is often called, organizational psychology (Coutts, 1991). Psychologists in this field apply their findings to help businesses and industries operate more efficiently and humanely through improving methods of selection and training, and developing new organizational and management strategies. Other industrial/organizational psychologists concentrate on such issues as labor-union relations, rules defining harassment, job satisfaction, and worker motivations and incentives.

Sports psychology, a field that developed during the 1980s, is an important part of training for many amateur and professional athletes. Sports psychologists apply the principles of psychology to sports activities. Some focus on maximizing athletic performance through **visualization**— mentally rehearsing the steps of a complete, successful performance— improving concentration or relaxation or reducing negative thoughts that may interfere with performance. Other areas of study include the psychological and physiological benefits of sports participation, violence, ethics in sports, and the design of safe equipment (Durkin, 1991).

The Challenges for Psychology

Social change, urban problems, early learning, psychology and minorities, and the reduction of violence are psychology's challenges today. One way to determine future directions of psychology is by analyzing the trends of age in the population. The average age of the citizens in North America is going steadily upward; there are more people over age 65 in the United States and Canada now than at any time in the history of either country. That creates new problems for psychologists to study and new careers in both research and service. It also suggests a growing field in a specialty such as sports psychology and another in developmental psychology—**gerontology,** the study of aging.

Did You Know?

Funding The United States federal government invests about one twenty-fifth of 1 percent of the national budget in psychological research. The APA and APS send representatives to Capitol Hill to appeal for more support. The government spends painfully little to study the nature of human behavior.

forensic psychology: deals with diagnosis, evaluation, treatment, and testimony regarding the law and criminal behavior

industrial/organizational psychology: deals with the psychology of the workplace

sports psychology: studies athletics and athletic performance

visualization: mentally rehearsing the steps involved in a successful performance or process

gerontology: the study of aging

At the other end of the age spectrum are other factors that may impact future jobs for psychologists. Consider the traditional killers of children—measles, chicken pox, scarlet fever, rheumatic fever, mumps, tuberculosis, and polio. All of these problems—assuming a child has had his or her proper vaccinations—are gone. The top three killers of children through adolescence in our society now are accidents, violence, and drugs. These are not *physiological* problems like our old enemies—they are *psychological* problems. Many of the problems that face society today are behavioral problems—that is, they can be solved only through changing behavior and attitudes.

Where Do You Go From Here?

As you come to the end of this textbook, it is important to consider not only the future of psychology but also how psychology plays a role in your future. Whether you choose further education and a career in psychology or not, you should not stop thinking critically about and seeking to explain your behavior and the behavior of others.

The information presented in this textbook does not represent the absolute truth. Psychology is a science—it is a *process* of trying to understand the world around us. As you encounter articles in newspapers and magazines concerning psychology, try to read them critically. Read the material, think about it, and question it. Analyze the evidence and the author's conclusions. Remember, though, that all conclusions are tentative. Ask yourself: Are there better ways to approach this issue or question? Use what you have learned in this course to determine your own hypotheses and theories and to critically analyze what you read, hear, and experience every day.

SECTION 2 | Assessment

1. **Review the Vocabulary** What do sports psychologists do?

2. **Visualize the Main Idea** Using a graphic organizer similar to the one below, outline the challenges psychologists face.

Challenges for Psychologists

3. **Recall Information** Why must psychologists study aging?

4. **Think Critically** Consider what you have learned in this psychology course. What information will be most useful to you during your lifetime? Why? In what types of situations during your life do you think you will use this information? Explain.

5. **Application Activity** Visit a large bookstore and browse through the titles of books dealing with psychology. What topics seem to be the most popular? Which books seem to be the most helpful? Which books seem most interesting to you? Why? Based on your observations, forecast several topics that could result in a popular psychology book.

Psychology has made many contributions to society in the past. Its place in the future is secure because it helps people resolve issues and problems. The field of psychology is among the fastest-growing into the twenty-first century.

Chapter Vocabulary

crisis intervention program (p. 604)

ACT (p. 611)

SAT (p. 611)

forensic psychology (p. 615)

industrial/organizational psychology (p. 615)

sports psychology (p. 615)

visualization (p. 615)

gerontology (p. 615)

Section 1 Careers in Psychology

Main Idea: Human behavior plays a key role in many areas of study. Studying psychology can prepare you for many career opportunities.

- A bachelor's degree in psychology affords many options with a wide array of possible employers.
- As a profession, careers that are based on psychological principles seek to predict how people will act; help people modify their behavior; and help organizations, businesses, and communities change.

Section 2 Psychology's Contributions

Main Idea: Psychology has made many contributions to society by promoting human welfare, clarifying assessment methods, explaining human behavior, and helping humans better understand their world.

- The most significant contribution of psychology is the development of forms of professional helping, including psychotherapy.
- Psychologists have played a leading role in devising and updating educational testing programs.
- The study of psychology has implications for everyday living, especially in the areas of raising children, improving learning, and understanding the process of aging.
- The common link in careers in psychology is the desire to understand behavior.
- Psychology can be grouped into experimental fields and applied fields.
- Experimental psychologists use a variety of scientific methods to study psychological processes.
- Applied psychologists put knowledge of psychology to work solving human problems.
- According to the United States Bureau of Labor, psychology is among the fastest-growing fields into the twenty-first century.
- The American Psychological Association (APA) is a scientific and professional society of psychologists and educators.
- The American Psychological Society (APS) is an organization for academic and science-oriented psychologists.
- Fields of psychology that have potential for future growth include forensic psychology, industrial/organizational psychology, and sports psychology.
- Many problems that face society today, such as violence, drugs, and AIDS, require behavioral solutions.

CHAPTER 21 Assessment

PSYCHOLOGY Online

Self-Check Quiz
Visit the *Understanding Psychology* Web site at psychology.glencoe.com and click on **Chapter 21— Self-Check Quizzes** to prepare for the Chapter Test.

Reviewing Vocabulary

Choose the letter of the correct term or concept below to complete the sentence.

a. ACT
b. SAT
c. forensic psychology
d. industrial/organizational psychologist
e. sports psychology
f. visualization
g. gerontology
h. crisis intervention program
i. clinical psychologist
j. school psychologist

1. A(n) _____ is often involved in helping businesses operate more efficiently.
2. A(n) _____ may give reading, aptitude, interest, or intelligence tests to middle or high school students.
3. _____ is the study of aging.
4. A(n) _____ is often self-employed, practicing some form of psychotherapy.
5. Athletes sometimes use the process of _____—mentally rehearsing the steps of a successful performance—to reduce negative thoughts that may interfere with performance.
6. Nearly 1 million high school seniors take the _____, which emphasizes scientific concepts and abstract reading skills.
7. About 1.2 million high school seniors take the _____, which was redesigned in 1994 to give more weight to abstract thinking skills.
8. A(n) _____ can respond to an individual's life-threatening situation or long-term stress.
9. A(n) _____ is involved in working on the reliability of witnesses in a court proceeding.
10. An important part of training for many professional athletes is the field of _____.

Recalling Facts

1. Explain what research shows about the effects of day care on children.
2. Explain the projections for the elderly population into the twenty-first century. How does this impact psychology?
3. Using a diagram similar to the one below, list the similarities and differences in the work of applied psychologists and experimental psychologists.

4. List three organizations for psychologists and/or students of psychology.
5. Identify two careers that require a background in psychology and briefly describe the careers.

Critical Thinking

1. **Analyzing Concepts** Define job satisfaction in your own words. Do you think it is possible to measure job satisfaction? Explain.
2. **Evaluating Information** Do college admission tests really predict success in college? Why or why not?
3. **Synthesizing Information** There are many types of mental health professionals. What common characteristics do they all share?
4. **Making Inferences** Name three jobs in psychology that you think will offer good opportunities for employment and explain why. Name three jobs that you think will offer few opportunities and explain why.
5. **Comparing and Contrasting** Compare and contrast the educational requirements and the responsibilities of a crisis hot line adviser, a mental health assistant, and a consulting psychologist.

CHAPTER 21 Assessment

Psychology Projects

1. **Psychology's Contributions** Find out about the historical treatment of psychological problems. You might focus on the treatments used in the Middle Ages and in the early nineteenth century. Share your findings in an oral report.

2. **Psychology Today and in the Future** In recent years, astronauts in the U.S. space program have spent extended time in space in cramped and crowded quarters. A recent field of psychology is space psychology. Psychologists in this field study the behavioral challenges of spaceflight. Find out about this field and the kinds of issues it addresses. Present your findings in an informational pamphlet.

Technology Activity

One of the major contributions of psychology is in the designing and assessing of tools for learning. Find examples of educational computer software. Find out what approach to learning is incorporated in the software—feedback, reinforcement, and so on. Evaluate the effectiveness of the software.

Psychology Journal

Review your journal entry. Do you feel optimistic or pessimistic that those problems can be solved? Why or why not? In what specific ways might psychology help solve these problems? Write answers in your journal.

Building Skills

Interpreting a Graph Job satisfaction—studied by industrial/organizational psychologists—is an issue for many people. Various factors contribute to job satisfaction. Review the graph, then answer the questions that follow.

1. According to this graph, what three job characteristics do most people find important for job satisfaction?

2. With which job characteristic were people most satisfied? Least satisfied?

3. Select an area on the graph. How might an industrial/organizational psychologist help managers and/or employees in this area?

 Practice and **assess** key social studies skills with **Glencoe Skillbuilder Interactive Workbook CD-ROM, Level 2.**

See the Skills Handbook, page 628, for an explanation of interpreting graphs.

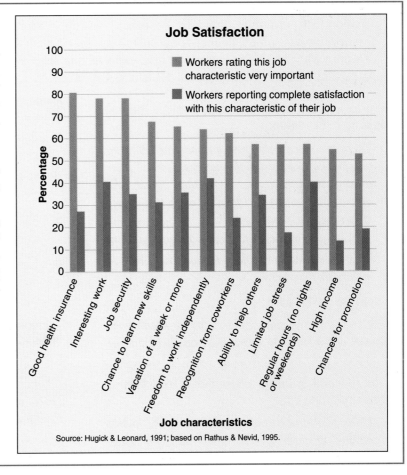

Source: Hugick & Leonard, 1991; based on Rathus & Nevid, 1995.

Skills Handbook

Psychology Skills

Forming a Hypothesis

A researcher in the study of psychology analyzes information and asks a research question. The researcher then forms a **hypothesis,** or an educated guess that answers the research question. A hypothesis allows a person to make sense of unorganized, separate observations and bits of information by permitting them to be placed within a structured and coherent framework. The researcher has some evidence for suspecting a specific answer. The researcher uses the hypothesis to state what he or she expects to find, expressed in such a way that can be proved or disproved.

For example, a researcher may analyze the following information:

There are several different methods for trying to quit smoking. Most people, however, fail at their attempt to quit. Studies show that people who attend "quit smoking" clinics have a better chance of kicking their smoking habit.

Fear tactics, such as describing health hazards, have been used successfully to motivate people to modify their behavior.

The researcher asks:

Can fear tactics, such as describing the health hazards of smoking, be used to increase the number of smokers who sign up for "quit smoking" clinics?

The researcher forms a hypothesis from this research question:

Using fear tactics, such as describing the health hazards of smoking, increases the number of smokers who sign up for "quit smoking" clinics.

Learn the Skill

1. Analyze information to identify a specific problem or question.

2. Use the specific problem or question to form a hypothesis.

3. Test the hypothesis by gathering additional information.

4. Use the additional information to reanalyze the original hypothesis. If necessary, restate the hypothesis.

Apply the Skill

Read the information below. Form a hypothesis using the four steps discussed in *Learn the Skill.*

People who bathe in warm water relax more quickly than if they bathe in cold water.

Some mothers complain that they are unable to calm their babies down in order to get them to sleep.

Interpreting Statistics

Statistics are mathematical processes used to organize, analyze, and summarize data collected by researchers. Interpreting statistics helps us use data to support a generalization or conclusion.

Learn the Skill

There are three things to consider when interpreting statistics—nonrepresentative sample, correlation, and statistical significance.

1. Suppose that a psychologist wants to test the following hypothesis: *Teenagers who eat large breakfasts have high grades.* Since it is impossible to study all teenagers, the researcher must pick a **sample,** or a relatively small population, of students that represents the population of students as a whole. A **nonrepresentative sample** is a sample that does not represent the entire population and, therefore, may affect the results of the study. For example, a sample that includes only females would be a nonrepresentative sample. What information can you learn about the sample by looking at Skills Figure 1?

2. A **correlation** is the association or relationship between the occurrence of two or more events. For example, if data show that students who eat large breakfasts have high grades, this would be a positive correlation. If the data show that students who eat large breakfasts have low grades, this would be a negative correlation. What type of correlation do the statistics in the Skills Figure 1 show?

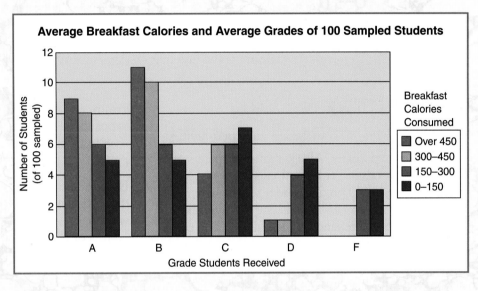

Average Breakfast Calories and Average Grades of 100 Sampled Students

Breakfast Calories Consumed
- Over 450
- 300–450
- 150–300
- 0–150

Skills Figure 1

3. When interpreting statistics, researchers must decide whether the data support a generalization or whether the data are due to chance. The results are called **statistically significant** if the probability that the data support a generalization is 95 percent or higher. Do you think the data in Skills Figure 1 support a generalization or are due to chance? Explain.

Apply the Skill

Develop a survey for which you believe the data might show a correlation. For example, "Do you have a regular exercise routine that you follow?" and "Do you have enough energy to make it through the day?" Pick a representative sample of people and conduct the survey. Organize and interpret your statistics.

Skills Handbook

Designing an Experiment

An **experiment** is a series of carefully planned steps that test a hypothesis. The only way that psychologists can establish cause-and-effect relationships is by performing experiments. Experiments allow the researcher to control the situation and decrease the possibility that something can influence the results. In designing experiments, researchers think in terms of **variables,** or factors or conditions that change or vary. That is, researchers are testing the relationship between two (or more) factors by deliberately producing a change in one factor and observing the effect the change has on the other factor(s). An **independent variable** is the factor that researchers change or alter so they can observe its effects. The **dependent variable** is the one that changes in relation to the independent variable.

Learn the Skill

Use the following steps to design an experiment:

1. Make a hypothesis. All experiments must start with a hypothesis. A **hypothesis** is an educated guess a researcher makes about some phenomenon. The researcher should state the hypothesis in clear, concrete language to rule out any confusion or error in its meaning. To be valid, a hypothesis must be testable by experimentation.

2. Brainstorm a list of ways to test the hypothesis. For example, you may send out a questionnaire, conduct a survey, or conduct a study using samples.

3. Identify the dependent and independent variables that will be measured.

4. From the list created in Step 2, design an experiment to test one variable identified in Step 3.

5. List materials needed for the experiment. This step includes determining the number of participants to be surveyed or tested. Researchers should use two groups of participants in every experiment. The **experimental group** is the group of participants who are exposed to the independent variable. For example, if your hypothesis was that hot temperatures cause aggression in humans, then you would expose the members of the experimental group to hot temperatures and observe their reactions. Members of the **control group** are treated the same as the members of the experimental group in every way except they are not exposed to the independent variable (in this case hot temperatures).

6. Gather the data.

7. Decide how you can graph the results. From the data collected, you will draw a conclusion and make a statement about your results. If your conclusion supports your hypothesis, then you may say that your hypothesis is reliable. (Researchers use statistical procedures to determine if their results are statistically significant, that is, to prove that their results are not due to chance.) If your conclusions did not support your hypothesis, then you would have to make new observations and state a new hypothesis, one that you could also test.

Researchers often repeat experiments many times before they are confident that the answers they found are correct. That is why the results of new studies and experiments are often questioned until other researchers have a chance to repeat the experiments and come up with the same conclusions.

Apply the Skill

Read the hypothesis below. Design an experiment using the steps discussed in *Learn the Skill*.

People exposed to the smell of certain foods prior to eating a meal have a smaller appetite than they would have had if they were not exposed to the smell of the food.

Using the Scientific Method

The **scientific method** is a series of planned steps used to solve problems. It is an objective, logical, and systematic way of collecting data and drawing conclusions. Psychology researchers use the scientific method to try to prevent their own biases from interfering with the research process, with the analyzing of data, and with drawing conclusions.

Researchers **analyze the data** collected in an experiment by looking for patterns and relationships in the data. Analyzing the data leads to **drawing conclusions.** After careful analysis of the data, the researcher asks: Was the hypothesis supported by the data? Was it not supported? Are more data needed? **Inferences** are logical conclusions based on observations and are made after careful analysis of all the data. Inferences are a means to explain or interpret observations.

Researchers also use reasoning to draw conclusions. **Deductive reasoning** involves first considering a number of statements and then drawing a conclusion—reasoning from particular to general. An example of deductive reasoning might be:

Statements: *That woman is a jogger. She is wearing sneakers.* Conclusion: *People who wear sneakers are joggers.*

However, just because someone is wearing sneakers does not necessarily mean that the person is a jogger.

Inductive reasoning involves using past experiences or general rules to decide how probable or possible a certain conclusion is—reasoning from general to particular. An example of inductive reasoning might be:

General rule: *People who jog usually wear sneakers.* Statement: *The woman is a jogger.* Conclusion: *She probably wears sneakers when she jogs.*

Researchers must determine if conclusions based on deductive and inductive reasoning are valid or invalid.

Learn the Skill

The following steps are used in the scientific method:

1. **Question** Ask a question about an observation you have made.

2. **Hypothesis** Make a hypothesis about the observation you have made.

3. **Experiment** Design an experiment to test the hypothesis.

4. **Data** Collect data through observation and organize it into graphic form.

5. **Draw Conclusions** Analyze your data and determine if your hypothesis is true or false.

Apply the Skill

Read the problem below. Use the steps in the scientific method to design a plan to solve this problem.

Robert is having difficulty learning to play the tuba. He is not sure if he learns better practicing by himself, with another tuba player, or with his tuba instructor.

Skills Handbook

Identifying Cause-and-Effect Relationships

When reading information, it is important to determine cause-and-effect relationships in order to understand why an event occurred. A **cause** is the action or situation that produces an event. An **effect** is the result or consequence of an action or situation. The connection between what happens and what makes it happen is known as a **cause-and-effect relationship.**

Learn the Skill

1. Begin by asking questions about why events occur. Look for related problems and actions, since these are likely causes of the event.

2. Look for "clue words" that may help you identify whether one event caused the other. Words or phrases such as *because, led to, brought about, produced, as a result of, so that, for this reason, as a consequence, as an outgrowth, if, since,* and *therefore* indicate cause-and-effect relationships.

3. Identify the outcome or impact of the event or situation. Look for relationships between events. Be sure to check for other, more complex, connections beyond the immediate cause and effect. For example, in a chain of events, an event often becomes the cause of multiple events.

CAUSE→EFFECT (CAUSE)→EFFECT

Takes drugs to reduce stress→Becomes dependent on drugs→Steals to support drug habit

Apply the Skill

Read the passage below and then identify the causes and effects by creating a cause-and-effect diagram. In a paragraph, discuss the immediate effects and possible later effects.

In a recent study of 107 kindergarten students in New York City, [Dr. Carol] Dweck confirmed the notion that negative reactions to failure and criticism start early. Dweck asked the children to role-play a scene in which they pretended to give their teacher a gift they had made. Almost all of them were happy with the gift they gave. But, after the teacher found something wrong with it, nearly half of them decided that the gift they had made was "bad," while the rest of them still considered the gift "good" (Azar, 1996).

Comparing and Contrasting

Oftentimes it is necessary to use comparing and contrasting to understand concepts, to make decisions, or to solve problems. Explain to students that making comparisons is a good way to organize information and extend understanding about the behavior of people. As long as two things share one common quality, they can be compared. To make a comparison, students must examine two or more groups, situations, events, or documents. Then students must identify **similarities,** or ways they are alike, and **differences,** ways they are different. **Comparing** means identifying similarities. **Contrasting** means identifying differences.

Skills Handbook

Learn the Skill

1. Identify what is being compared and contrasted.

2. Determine the purpose for comparing and contrasting. Ask: What do these events or items have in common? What would you compare using these two events or items? What is the purpose of this comparison? What question do you want to answer by comparing the events or items? By answering these questions, you are deciding what items are to be compared.

3. Now you must decide what characteristics will be used to compare the items. Note and list similarities in the characteristics of the items being compared. When comparing items, look for clue words that indicate two things are alike. Such clue words include *all, both, like, as, likewise,* and *similarly.*

4. List differences in the characteristics of the items being compared. When contrasting, look for clue words that show how things differ, such as *different, differ, unlike, however,* and *on the other hand.*

5. At this point you should review the similarities and differences that you have found. Ask: Why are there similarities and differences in these two items? What has caused the differences? Point out information that may have led to the similarities and differences found.

6. Finally, recall the research question or the purpose of comparing the events or items (from Step 2). Ask yourself: Does this comparison answer this research question? How?

Apply the Skill

Research to compare and contrast the beliefs of any two of the following psychologists.

John B. Watson	Wilhelm Wundt	William James
Wolfgang Köhler	Sigmund Freud	Alfred Adler

Distinguishing Fact From Opinion

It is necessary to distinguish between fact and opinion in order to think critically and to make decisions. A **fact** is a statement that can be proved to be false or true and is supported by evidence. For example, the statement *Alcohol is the most widely used and abused drug today; it contributes to 100,000 deaths annually* (McGinnis & Foege, 1993) is a fact because it can be proved. An **opinion** expresses a personal belief, viewpoint, or emotion. For example, the statement *The best method to use to cope with stress is meditation* is an opinion since it cannot be proved and it is not supported with any evidence.

Learn the Skill

The following guidelines will help you distinguish between fact and opinion.

1. When listening to or reading a statement, keep in mind the meanings of *fact* and *opinion*. It is a fact if the statement is supported with evidence. It is an opinion if the statement is not or cannot be supported with evidence.

2. Identify facts by looking for words and phrases that indicate specific information about people, places, events, dates, times, and statistics.

3. Identify opinions by looking for words and phrases such as *I believe, I think, most likely, in my judgment, in my view, may, might, could,* and *seems to me.*

Apply the Skill

Find a newspaper or magazine article about a psychological study. Use the guidelines in *Learn the Skill* to help you identify five statements in the article as being either facts or opinions. Give a reason why each statement is either a fact or an opinion.

Skills Handbook

Using Critical Methods of Inquiry

It is important to use critical methods of inquiry when conducting research. Once you have decided on a topic for your research report, use the library's card catalog or computerized referral service to find suitable reference sources. You might also use the Internet to find information. Resource materials can be accessed through the World Wide Web. Information on the Web is organized according to category and is stored at an address, or *URL*—Universal Resource Locator. Web browsers such as Yahoo! or Netscape help you locate material on the Internet.

Learn the Skill

There is a vast amount of information in libraries and on the Internet. Use the following steps in analyzing sources:

1. Determine if the material is a *primary source*—first-hand information, or a *secondary source*—descriptions or interpretations of events. Primary sources are helpful because they provide a close-up view of research results. Secondary sources are helpful tools because the writer has the advantage of knowing what theories and research results were proved or disproved, thus providing a broad perspective.

2. Read the material to identify main ideas and supporting details. Consider the nature of the material. Is it scientific or is it telling a story?

3. Distinguish fact from opinion. Psychologists often express their beliefs but make sure these beliefs are based on facts.

4. Check for bias or faulty reasoning. Search for evidence presented by the writer that supports the conclusion.

5. If possible, find more than one source to check for accuracy.

6. Consider the origin of the source. Is the writer well-known in the field of psychology? Does the writer have a degree and experience in the subject area?

7. Search for information on the Internet written by a well-known source. Do not use information on the Internet that does not list a source.

Apply the Skill

Select an article from a psychology magazine, journal, or book. Analyze the source by using the steps in *Learn the Skill*.

Organizing and Analyzing Information

Information for research reports must be organized and analyzed. To do this, it is important to know how to classify information you gather as you conduct your research, synthesize information from different sources and mediums, and create an outline of the information as it should appear in the research report.

Learn the Skill

1. **Classifying Information** As you read about your topic, identify information that has similar characteristics. List this information on separate note cards. Label the note cards with categories. Then add facts to the categories as you continue your research.

Remember that when classifying, you are grouping objects or events for a purpose. The purpose could be general such as for ease of finding an item. Once you have classified the material, look for patterns and relationships among the facts. It is at this point that you may make comparisons, draw conclusions, and develop questions or hypotheses for further study.

2. **Synthesizing Information** When using more than one source for a research report, you need to synthesize, or combine, the information. Look for connections and relationships among different sources. You may want to include both primary and secondary sources in your report. Combine the information so that each source adds to the understanding of your topic.

3. **Outlining Information** Outlines are also very useful when researching and writing essays or reports. Use outlines to help clarify and organize your thoughts, to decide what main ideas to include, and to flesh out each main idea with subtopics and supporting details. A good outline summarizes information and shows how ideas and facts are connected. In an outline, information is arranged in three categories: main ideas; subtopics, or parts of each main idea; and supporting details. Outlines begin with broad ideas, followed by more specific ideas. Put your information in order. Determine what information will be part of the introduction, the body, and the conclusion of your report. Use main ideas as headings in your outline. Use supporting details as subheadings under the appropriate headings in your outline.

Apply the Skill

Select a topic for research. Organize and analyze the information you collect using the steps in *Learn the Skill*.

Writing a Research Report/Essay

You will be asked to write research reports and essays in most of the subjects you take in school. There are basic steps to follow when writing research reports or essays.

Learn the Skill

1. Choose a topic and identify your purpose for the research report or essay.

2. Write several main idea questions you want to answer about your topic. Organize these questions into an outline.

3. Conduct research about the topic and take notes.

4. Organize and analyze your information. Classify, synthesize, and outline the information collected.

5. Write a first draft. A research report or essay has an introduction, a body, and a conclusion. The *introduction* explains the purpose of the report or essay. The *body* develops the main ideas of the report or essay. Be sure to use proper transitions between paragraphs in the body. The *conclusion* summarizes your findings.

6. Edit the first draft. Reorganize information, improve sentence structure and transitions, and correct grammar and spelling errors.

7. Write your final report or essay.

Apply the Skill

Write a psychology research report using the steps in *Learn the Skill*.

Skills Handbook

Interpreting Charts, Tables, Graphs, and Diagrams

Data gathered in psychology research are often presented in charts, tables, graphs, and diagrams. These visual representations of data organize the information to make it quicker and easier to read, compare, and contrast.

Charts and tables are divided into columns and rows. The column title usually lists items to be compared. The row headings usually list the specific characteristics being compared among those items. There are three main types of graphs. A **line graph** shows the relationship between two variables. The independent variable usually goes on the x-axis, or the horizontal axis. The dependent variable usually goes on the y-axis, or the vertical axis. A **bar graph** is similar to a line graph, except a bar graph is used to show comparisons between data or to display data that do not continuously change. Thick bars are used instead of dots and lines (see Skills Figure 3). A **circle graph** shows percentages or parts per hundred (see Skills Figure 2). Each section represents part of the whole. A **diagram** is a drawing that shows what something is or how something is done. Diagrams may have several parts that show steps in a process. The parts of a diagram are usually labeled.

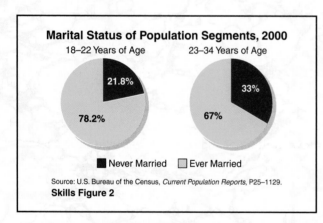

Source: U.S. Bureau of the Census, *Current Population Reports*, P25–1129.
Skills Figure 2

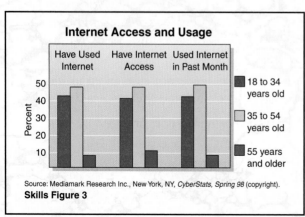

Source: Mediamark Research Inc., New York, NY, *CyberStats, Spring 98* (copyright).
Skills Figure 3

Learn the Skill

1. **Read the title.** The title tells you the purpose of the visual information.

2. **Look for clues.** Study the parts of the visual information. For a chart or table, read the columns and rows to identify what data are being presented. For a line graph or bar graph, read the x-axis and y-axis. For a circle graph, read the sections to find out what parts of a whole are being presented. For a diagram, read the parts that are labeled.

3. **Analyze the information.** Ask yourself questions such as: How do the data, over time, change? What is the relationship of the parts to the whole? What are the steps in the process?

4. **Put the data to use.** Draw conclusions based on the data.

Apply the Skill

Find examples of visual information in your psychology text. Use the steps in *Learn the Skill* to interpret the visuals.

Reading and Making Graphic Organizers

A **graphic organizer** is a type of diagram that shows the relationship among ideas and helps you organize information in a visual context. A graphic organizer can make abstract ideas more concrete and help you better understand the ideas and terms you are studying. A graphic organizer can show the interaction of a series of events, present a hierarchy of procedures, or describe the steps in a process.

Graphic organizers come in many forms. There are network trees, concept webs, events chain maps, cycle concept maps, and others. There may be more than one way to construct a graphic organizer. As you make a graphic organizer, you may realize that there is a better way to show the information on a map. In that case, change the format or how the information is displayed. Graphic organizers can be used to help you review and study information.

The graphic organizer below is a network tree. To read it, begin by reading the term at the top of the network tree that shows the main concept—the nervous system. Next, find the two divisions of the nervous system—central nervous system and peripheral nervous system—that branch out from the main concept. Now look at how the parts of these divisions branch out. Finally, see how the divisions of the autonomic system branch out.

Divisions of the Nervous System

Apply the Skill

Construct a graphic organizer. Choose one of the following main concepts, or choose your own. Use information from your text and the steps in *Learn the Skill* to help you make your graphic organizer.

Learn the Skill

Follow the steps below when creating a graphic organizer.

1. State the main concept.

2. Branch the related concepts from the main concept. Use lines to connect the branches.

3. Continue to branch out more specific details from the related concepts.

4. You may write words on the lines to help explain the relationship of related concepts.

Endocrine System

Classical Conditioning

Processes of Memory

Development of Language

Changes in Old Age

Personality Theory

Glossary

A

absolute threshold the weakest amount of a stimulus that a person can detect half the time (p. 209)

abstinence a choice to avoid harmful behaviors including premarital sex and use of drugs and alcohol (p. 99)

accommodation the process by which a person changes their old methods or schemas to adjust or deal with new situations (p. 71)

achievement test an instrument used to measure the amount of knowledge a person has learned in a given subject or area (p. 360)

acoustic codes when a person tries to remember something by saying it out loud or to themselves repeatedly (p. 274)

acquisition the process by which a conditioned response is established or strengthened (p. 244)

ACT American College Testing Proficiency Examination Program; a standardized test (p. 611)

active listening empathetic listening in which the listener acknowledges, understands, restates, and clarifies the speaker's thoughts and concerns (p. 497)

actor-observer bias the tendency to attribute one's own behavior to outside causes rather than to a personality trait (p. 531)

addiction a self-destructive pattern of drug abuse characterized by an overwhelming and compulsive desire to obtain and use the drug (p. 476)

ageism prejudice or discrimination based on age, especially against the elderly (p. 138)

aggression the initiation of hostile or destructive behavior intended to do physical or psychological harm to others (pp. 119, 565)

agoraphobia extreme fear of being in a public place (p. 457)

algorithm a step-by-step procedure for solving a problem that leads to a solution (p. 299)

altruism unselfishly helping others, often at a cost or risk, for reasons other than rewards (p. 568)

Alzheimer's disease currently an irreversible, incurable condition that destroys a person's ability to think, remember, relate to others, and care for herself or himself (p. 143)

amnesia severe loss or deterioration of memory that occurs after damage to the brain (temporary or permanent) following drug abuse or severe psychological stress (p. 286)

anal stage the stage at which children associate erotic pleasure with the elimination process (p. 82)

androgynous having both male and female characteristics and combining or confusing them (p. 117)

anger a strong feeling of displeasure, resentment, or hostility, with an irate reaction likely to result from frustration (pp. 145, 422)

anorexia nervosa a serious eating disorder where the fear of gaining weight results in prolonged self-starvation and dramatic weight loss (p. 114)

antianxiety drugs a type of medication that relieves anxiety disorders and panic disorders by depressing the activity of the central nervous system (p. 508)

antidepressants a type of medication used to treat major depression by increasing the amount of neurotransmitters believed to be involved in the regulation of emotions and moods (p. 508)

antipsychotic drugs a type of medication used to reduce agitation, delusions, and hallucinations; also called tranquilizers (p. 507)

antisocial personality a personality disorder characterized by a pattern of irresponsibility, shallow emotions, lack of conscience, and violating the rights of others without feeling guilt or remorse (p. 475)

anxiety an unpleasant psychological state characterized by a vague, generalized apprehension or feeling that one is in danger (pp. 422, 456)

applied science discovering ways to use scientific findings to accomplish practical goals (p. 11)

approach-approach conflict a type of conflict situation in which the individual must choose between two positive but mutually exclusive alternatives (p. 414)

approach-avoidance conflict a type of conflict situation in which the individual wants to do something but fears or dislikes it at the same time (p. 415)

aptitude test an instrument used to predict or estimate the probability that a person will be successful in learning a specific new skill or skills in the future (p. 360)

archetype an inherited idea, image, or concept based on the experiences of one's ancestors that shapes one's perception of the world (p. 384)

assimilation the process of fitting objects and experiences into one's schemas to deal with new situations and to understand the environment (p. 71)

asynchrony the condition during adolescence in which the growth or maturation of bodily parts is uneven (p. 96)

attitude a predisposition to act, think, and feel in a particular way toward a class of people, objects, or an idea (p. 577)

attribution theory a collection of principles based on our explanations of the causes of events, other people's behaviors, and our own behaviors (p. 530)

auditory nerve the nerve that carries impulses from the cochlea of the inner ear to the brain, resulting in the sensation of sound (p. 218)

authoritarian family family in which parents attempt to control, shape, and evaluate the behavior and attitudes of children in accordance with a set code of conduct (p. 79)

authoritarian leader a person who makes all the decisions and assigns tasks to group members (p. 554)

autonomic nervous system (ANS) the portion of the peripheral nervous system that controls internal biological functions such as heart rate, breathing, and blood pressure (p. 158)

autonomy the ability to take care of oneself and make one's own decisions independently (p. 437)

Glossary

aversive conditioning a type of counterconditioning that links an unpleasant state with an unwanted behavior in an attempt to eliminate the behavior (p. 504)

aversive control the process of influencing behavior by means of unpleasant stimuli (p. 256)

avoidance-avoidance conflict a type of conflict situation in which the individual must choose between two negative or undesirable alternatives (p. 415)

avoidance conditioning the training of an organism to remove or withdraw from an unpleasant stimulus before it starts (p. 257)

axon a single, threadlike structure within the neuron that extends from and carries signals away from the cell body to neighboring neurons, organs, or muscles (p. 157)

axon terminals small fibers branching out from the end of an axon (p. 157)

B

basic science the pursuit of knowledge about natural phenomena for its own sake (p. 11)

behaviorism the belief that the proper subject matter of psychology is objectively observable behavior and nothing else (p. 387)

behaviorist a psychologist who analyzes how organisms learn or modify their behavior based on their response to events in the environment (p. 20)

behavior modification a systematic application of learning principles to change people's actions and feelings (pp. 263, 499)

behavior therapy a form of therapy that begins with clear, well-defined behavioral goals aimed at changing undesirable behavior through conditioning techniques (p. 502)

binocular depth cues depth cues that depend upon the movement of both eyes (p. 228)

binocular fusion the process of combining the images received from the two eyes into a single, fused image (p. 216)

biofeedback the process of learning to control bodily states with the help of feedback from specialized machines (pp. 194, 434)

bipolar disorder a disorder in which a person's mood inappropriately alternates between feelings of mania (euphoria) and depression (p. 471)

body language an often unconscious but sometimes conscious way of communicating by the way a person carries his or her body to convey an impression (p. 532)

boomerang effect a change in attitude or behavior opposite to the one desired by the persuader (p. 592)

brainwashing the most extreme form of attitude change, accomplished through peer pressure, physical suffering, threats, rewards for compliance, manipulation of guilt, intensive indoctrination, and other psychological means (p. 595)

bulimia nervosa a serious eating disorder in which enormous quantities of food are consumed and then purged by means of laxatives or self-induced vomiting (p. 115)

bystander effect the tendency of a person to be less likely to give aid if other bystanders are present (p. 569)

C

cardinal trait a trait that is so pervasive that the person is almost identified with the trait (p. 400)

career a chosen pursuit, profession, or occupation in which a person works at least a few years (p. 440)

case study an in-depth research method that involves an intensive investigation of one or more subjects (p. 37)

catharsis a psychological process through which anger or aggressive energy is released by expressing or letting out powerful negative emotions (p. 566)

central nervous system (CNS) the part of the nervous system that consists of the brain and spinal cord (p. 156)

central route for persuasion a way to deliver a message by focusing on presenting information consisting of strong arguments and facts (p. 592)

central tendency a number that describes something about the "average" score of a distribution (p. 51)

central trait the trait that best describes a person, such as shy, loyal, friendly, or generous (p. 400)

cerebral cortex the gray mass surrounding the subcortex, which is the information-processing center that controls the higher brain functions, such as reading and problem solving (p. 161)

child abuse inadequate care or acts by a caregiver (physical or emotional abuse) that puts a child in danger, causes physical harm or injury, or involves molestation (p. 80)

chunking combining separate items of information into a larger unit, or chunk, and then remembering chunks of information rather than an individual item (p. 277)

circadian rhythm a regular sequence of biological processes such as temperature and sleep that occurs every 24 hours (p. 186)

classical conditioning a learning procedure in which associations are made between a natural stimulus and a learned, neutral stimulus (p. 241)

client-centered therapy an approach developed by Carl Rogers that reflects the belief that the client and therapist are partners in therapy (p. 496)

climacteric all the psychological and biological changes that occur in a woman between the ages of 45 and 50 (p. 131)

clinical psychologist a psychologist who diagnoses and treats people with emotional disturbances (p. 25)

clique a small, exclusive group of people within a larger group (p. 111)

cognitive having to do with an organism's thinking and understanding (p. 7)

cognitive appraisal the interpretation of an event that helps determine its stress impact (p. 431)

cognitive-behavior therapy a treatment based on a combination of substituting healthy thoughts for negative thoughts and beliefs and changing disruptive behaviors in favor of healthy behaviors (p. 505)

Glossary

cognitive consistency the theory that people's attitudes change because they are always trying to get things to fit together logically inside their heads (p. 584)

cognitive dissonance a state of unpleasant psychological tension that arises when a person experiences contradictory or conflicting thoughts, attitudes, beliefs, or feelings (p. 584)

cognitive learning a form of learning that involves mental processes and may result from observation or imitation (p. 260)

cognitive map a mental picture of spatial relationships or relationships between events (p. 260)

cognitive therapy an approach in which thoughts are used to control emotions and behaviors (p. 499)

cognitivist a psychologist who studies how we process, store, retrieve, and use information and how cognitive processes influence our behavior (p. 20)

cohesiveness the factors that work to hold groups together (p. 547)

collective unconscious the part of the mind that contains inherited instincts, urges, and memories common to all people (p. 384)

community psychologist a psychologist who may work in a mental health or social welfare agency operated by the government or private organization (p. 26)

companionate love a condition associated with trusting and tender feelings for someone whose life is closely bound up with one's own (p. 536)

comparable worth the concept that women and men should receive equal pay for jobs calling for comparable skill and responsibility (p. 441)

complementarity the attraction that often develops between opposite types of people because of the ability of one to supply what the other lacks (p. 525)

compliance a kind of conformity in which there is a change of behavior in order to avoid discomfort or rejection and gain approval (pp. 557, 583)

compulsion an apparently irresistible urge to repeat an act or engage in ritualistic behavior such as hand washing (p. 458)

computerized axial tomography (CAT) an imaging technique in which low levels of X rays are passed through the brain, and a computer measures the amount of radiation absorbed by the brain cells and produces a relatively good image of the brain (p. 167)

concept a way to group objects, events, or characteristics on the basis of some common property they share (p. 296)

conditioned response (CR) a response elicited by the conditioned stimulus; it is similar to the unconditioned response, but not identical in magnitude or amount (p. 242)

conditioned stimulus (CS) a once-neutral event that elicits a given response after a period of training in which it has been paired with an unconditioned stimulus (p. 242)

conditioning a type of learning that involves stimulus-response connections in which the response is conditional on the stimulus (p. 241)

conditions of worth the conditions a person must meet in order to regard himself or herself positively (p. 395)

cones visual receptors that are adapted for color vision, daytime vision, and detailed vision (p. 215)

confabulation the act of filling in memory with statements that make sense but that may be untrue (p. 284)

conflict situation a situation in which a person must choose between two or more options that tend to result from opposing motives (p. 414)

conformity acting in accordance with some specified authority (pp. 111, 556)

consciousness an individual's state of awareness, including a person's feelings, sensations, ideas, and perceptions (p. 183)

conservation according to Piaget, the principle that a given quantity does not change when its appearance is changed (p. 73)

constancy the tendency to perceive certain objects in the same way regardless of changing angle, distance, or lighting (p. 229)

content validity similarity between the items in a test and the information the test is meant to measure (p. 360)

contingencies of reinforcement the occurrence of a reward or punishment following a particular behavior (p. 388)

contingency management a form of behavior therapy in which undesirable behavior is not reinforced, while desirable behavior is reinforced (p. 504)

control group in an experiment, a group of participants that is treated in the same way as the experimental group except that the experimental treatment (the independent variable) is not applied (p. 40)

convergence the process by which your eyes turn inward to look at nearby objects (p. 228)

convergent thinking a way of thinking that depends heavily on symbols, concepts, and rules (p. 297)

conversion disorder a somatoform disorder characterized by changing emotional difficulties into a loss of a specific voluntary body function (p. 461)

correlation the measure of a relationship between two variables or sets of data (p. 39)

correlation coefficient a statistic that describes the direction and strength of the relationship between two sets of variables (p. 52)

counseling psychologist an individual who has a Ph.D. in psychology or education who helps people deal with problems of living (p. 25)

counterattitudinal behavior the process of taking a public position that contradicts one's private attitude (p. 585)

creativity the ability to use information, invent new solutions to problems, or create original and ingenious materials (p. 300)

crisis intervention program a short-term psychological first aid that helps individuals and families deal with emergencies or highly stressful situations (p. 604)

critical period a stage or point in development when certain skills or abilities are most easily learned (p. 75)

cross-sectional studies a research method in which data are collected from groups of participants of different ages and compared so that conclusions can be drawn about differences due to age differences (p. 38)

cultural bias an aspect of an intelligence test in which the wording used in questions and the experiences on which they are based may be more familiar to people of one social group than to another group (p. 356)

D

decay fading away of memory over time (p. 285)

declarative memory memory of facts or events such as scenes, stories, words, conversations, faces, or daily events that can be called forth consciously as needed (p. 279)

decremental model of aging a theory that holds that progressive physical and mental decline is inevitable with age (p. 138)

defense mechanisms certain specific means by which the ego unconsciously protects itself against unpleasant impulses or circumstances (p. 380)

deindividuation individuals behave irrationally when there is less chance of being personally identified (p. 570)

delusions a false belief, as of persecution or grandeur, that a person maintains in the face of contradictory evidence (p. 466)

democratic/authoritative family family in which adolescents participate in decisions affecting their lives (p. 79)

democratic leader a person who encourages group members to come to decisions through consensus (p. 554)

dendrites the branchlike extensions of a neuron that receive impulses from other neurons, muscles, or sense organs and conduct them toward the cell body (p. 157)

denial a defense coping mechanism in which a person refuses to admit that a problem exists (pp. 145, 381, 431)

dependent variable in an experiment, the factor that is being measured that may or may not change when the independent variable is changed (p. 40)

depression a psychological disorder characterized by extreme sadness, an inability to concentrate, and feelings of helplessness and dejection (p. 145)

descriptive statistics the listing and summarizing of data in a practical, efficient way such as through graphs and averages (p. 48)

developmental friendship the type of friendship in which the partners force each other to reexamine their basic assumptions and perhaps adopt new ideas and beliefs (p. 438)

developmental psychologist a psychologist who studies the emotional, physical, cognitive, biological, personal, and social changes that occur as an individual matures (p. 26)

developmental psychology the branch of psychology that studies the emotional, physical, cognitive, biological, personal, and social changes that occur throughout an individual's life cycle (p. 61)

difference threshold the smallest change in a physical stimulus that can be detected between two stimuli (p. 210)

diffusion of responsibility when the presence of others lessens an individual's feelings of responsibility for his or her actions or failure to act (p. 569)

directed thinking a systematic and logical attempt to reach a specific goal, such as a solution to a problem (p. 297)

disconfirmation one of three principles in cognitive therapy where clients may be confronted with evidence that directly contradicts their existing beliefs (p. 500)

discrimination the ability to respond differently to similar but distinct stimuli (p. 244); the unequal treatment of individuals on the basis of their race, ethnic group, age, gender, or membership in another category rather than on the basis of individual characteristics (p. 588)

displacement a defense mechanism that shifts the desires, feelings, or impulses from their proper object to a substitute (p. 383)

dissociative amnesia a dissociative disorder characterized by the inability to recall important personal events or information and usually associated with stressful events (p. 462)

dissociative disorder a disorder characterized by a disruption, split, or breakdown in a person's normally integrated and functioning memory, identity, or consciousness (p. 462)

dissociative fugue a dissociative disorder in which a person suddenly and unexpectedly travels away from home or work and is unable to recall the past (p. 462)

dissociative identity disorder a dissociative disorder in which a person exhibits two or more personality states, each with its own patterns of thinking, perceiving, behaving, and relating in the world (p. 462)

distress the type of stress that stems from acute anxiety or pressure and is damaging or negative (p. 414)

divergent thinking a way of thinking that consists of a free flow of thoughts with no particular plan and depends more on images (p. 297)

door-in-the-face technique a method of gaining compliance by first making an outrageous request and then replying to the refusal with a more reasonable request (p. 594)

double approach-avoidance conflict a situation in which the individual must choose between two or more alternatives, each of which has attractive and unattractive aspects (p. 415)

double-blind experiment an experiment in which neither the experimenter nor the participants know which participants receive which treatment (p. 43)

dream analysis a technique used by psychoanalysts to interpret the content of patients' dreams (p. 495)

drive a condition of arousal or tension produced by a need that motivates an organism toward a goal (p. 315)

drug therapy a form of biological therapy that uses medications (p. 507)

DSM-IV the fourth version of the American Psychiatric Association's Diagnostic and Statistical Manual of Mental Disorders (p. 451)

Glossary

E

echoic memory the sensory register in which traces of sounds are held and may be retrieved within several seconds (p. 275)

eclectic approach an approach to therapy in which the psychotherapist combines techniques and ideas from many different schools of thought (p. 487)

educational psychologist a psychologist who is concerned with helping students learn (p. 26)

ego the part of the personality that is in touch with reality and strives to meet the demands of the id and the superego in socially acceptable ways (p. 380)

egocentric a young child's inability to understand another person's perspective (p. 73)

ego-support value the ability of a person to provide another person with sympathy, encouragement, and approval (p. 523)

eidetic memory the ability to remember with great accuracy visual information on the basis of short-term exposure (p. 284)

elaborate rehearsal a memory device that creates a meaningful link between new information and material that is already known (p. 287)

electroconvulsive therapy (ECT) a radical treatment for psychological disorders in which an electrical shock is sent through the brain (p. 509)

electroencephalograph (EEG) a machine used to record the electrical activity of large portions of the brain (p. 165)

emotion a state of feeling that involves a set of complex reactions to a stimulus involving subjective feelings, physiological arousal, and observable behavior (p. 329)

emotional intelligence the ability to perceive, imagine, and understand emotions and to use that information in decision making (pp. 329, 351)

empathy the capacity for warmth and understanding (p. 489)

encoding placing or storing information such as images, events, or sounds in memory by making mental representations so the nervous system can process it (p. 274)

endocrine system a chemical communication system located throughout the body that uses hormones to send messages through the bloodstream to particular organs of the body (p. 171)

endogamy the tendency to marry someone who is from one's own social group (p. 538)

environmental psychologist a psychologist who studies the effects of the environment on people (p. 27)

episodic memory a memory of a specific experienced event in one's life, including time of occurrence (p. 279)

escape conditioning the training of an organism to remove or terminate an unpleasant stimulus (p. 257)

estrogen one of the major female sex hormones (p. 172)

ethics methods of conduct or standards for proper and responsible behavior (p. 40)

eustress positive stress, which results from motivating strivings and challenges (p. 414)

experimental group the group of participants to which an independent variable is applied (p. 40)

experimental psychologist a psychologist who studies sensation, perception, learning, motivation, and emotion in carefully controlled laboratory conditions (p. 28)

extinction in classical conditioning, the gradual disappearance of a conditioned response because the reinforcement is withheld or because the conditioned stimulus is repeatedly presented without the unconditioned stimulus (p. 245)

extrasensory perception (ESP) a group of psychic experiences that involves perceiving or sending information (images) outside normal sensory processes or channels; includes four general abilities: telepathy, precognition, clairvoyance, and psychokinesis (p. 230)

extrinsic motivation engaging in certain activities or behaviors that either reduce biological needs or help a person obtain external incentives (p. 316)

extrovert an outgoing, active person who directs his or her energies and interests toward other people and things (p. 401)

F

factor analysis a complicated statistical technique used to identify the underlying reasons variables are correlated (p. 401)

family therapy a form of therapy aimed at understanding and improving relationships that have led one or more members in a close social unit to experience emotional suffering (p. 490)

fear the usual reaction when a stressor involves real or imagined danger (p. 422)

fight-or-flight response a state of increased physiological arousal that helps us cope with and survive threatening situations (p. 421)

fixed-interval schedule in conditioning, a schedule of reinforcement in which a specific amount of time must elapse before a response will elicit reinforcement (p. 254)

fixed-ratio schedule in conditioning, a schedule of reinforcement in which a specific number of correct responses is required before reinforcement can be obtained (p. 253)

flexibility the ability to overcome rigidity (p. 301)

flooding therapy for a phobia in which the person is suddenly exposed to the object of the phobia (p. 504)

foot-in-the-door technique a method of gaining compliance by getting a person to agree to a relatively minor request first (pp. 557, 593)

forebrain the largest part of the brain that covers the brain's central core, consisting of left and right hemispheres, which are connected by a wide band of fibers, the corpus callosum (p. 161)

forensic psychology a branch of psychology that deals with diagnosis, evaluation, treatment, and testimony regarding the law and criminal behavior (p. 615)

fraternal twins twins who come from two different eggs fertilized by two different sperm (p. 176)

Glossary

free association a Freudian technique used to examine the unconscious; the patient is instructed to say whatever comes into his or her mind (p. 494)

frequency distribution an arrangement of data that indicates how often a particular score or observation occurs (p. 49)

fully functioning an individual whose person and self coincide (p. 396)

functional fixedness a mental set characterized by the inability to imagine new functions for familiar objects (p. 300)

functionalist a psychologist who studied the function (rather than the structure) of consciousness (p. 16)

fundamental attribution error an inclination to attribute others' behavior to internal causes (dispositional factors) but to attribute our own behavior to external attribution (situational factors) (p. 531)

fundamental needs biological drives or needs that must be satisfied in order to maintain life (p. 326)

G

gate control theory of pain the theory that we can lessen some pains by shifting our attention away from the pain impulses or by sending other signals to compete with the pain signals (p. 221)

gender identity the sex group (masculine or feminine) to which an individual biologically belongs; an individual's subjective sense of being male or female (p. 117)

gender role the sex group (masculine or feminine) with which an individual feels identification; the set of behaviors that society considers appropriate for each sex (p. 117)

gender schema a set of behaviors organized around how either a male or female should think and behave (p. 122)

gender stereotype an oversimplified or distorted generalization about the characteristics of men and women (p. 117)

general adaptation syndrome according to Selye, a series of three stages—alarm, resistance, and exhaustion—that correspond to the three different reactions of the body to stressful situations (p. 421)

generalization in classical conditioning, the tendency for a stimulus that is similar to the original conditioned stimulus to elicit a response that is similar to the conditioned response (p. 244)

generational identity the theory that generations tend to think differently about certain issues because of different formative experiences (p. 534)

generativity the desire in middle age to use one's accumulated wisdom to guide future generations (p. 135)

genes the basic building blocks of heredity (p. 175)

genital stage Freud's fifth and final psychosexual stage during which an individual's sexual satisfaction depends as much on giving pleasure as on receiving it (p. 82)

gerontology the study of aging (p. 615)

Gestalt the experience that comes from organizing bits and pieces of information into meaningful wholes (p. 224)

grammar a set of rules for combining words into phrases and sentences to express an infinite number of thoughts that can be understood by others (p. 66)

grasping reflex an infant's clinging response to a touch on the palm of his or her hand (p. 62)

group a collection of people who have shared goals, a degree of interdependence, and some amount of communication (p. 545)

group polarization the theory that group discussion reinforces the majority's point of view and shifts group members' opinions to a more extreme position (p. 550)

group therapy a form of therapy in which patients work together with the aid of a leader to resolve interpersonal problems (p. 489)

groupthink poor group decision making that occurs as a result of a group emphasizing unity over critical thinking (p. 551)

H

hallucinations a false sensory perception that has no direct external cause (pp. 199, 466)

hallucinogens drugs that often produce hallucinations (p. 200)

hardiness the personality traits of control, commitment, and challenge that help us reduce the stress we feel (p. 432)

hassles common, relatively minor day-to-day stressors (p. 418)

health psychologist a psychologist who studies the interaction between physical and psychological health factors (p. 27)

heredity the genetic transmission of characteristics from parents to their offspring (p. 174)

heritability a measure of the degree to which a characteristic is related to genetic, inherited factors (p. 355)

heuristic a rule-of-thumb, problem-solving strategy that reduces the number of operations or allows us to take shortcuts in solving problems (pp. 299, 594)

hindbrain a part of the brain located at the rear base of the skull that is involved in the basic processes of life such as sleeping, waking, coordinating body movements, and regulating vital reflexes (p. 160)

histogram a graph similar to a bar graph except that histograms show frequency distribution by means of rectangles whose widths represent class intervals and whose areas are proportionate to the corresponding frequencies (p. 50)

homeostasis the tendency of all organisms to correct imbalances and deviations from their normal state (p. 315)

homogamy the tendency to marry someone who has similar attributes, including physical attractiveness, age, and physique, to our own (p. 538)

hormones chemical substances produced by the endocrine glands that carry messages through the body in blood and regulate specific body functions (p. 171)

hospice a type of care for terminally ill patients; an organization that provides such care (p. 147)

Glossary

humanist a psychologist who believes that each person has freedom in directing his or her future and achieving personal growth (p. 20)

humanistic psychology an approach to psychology that is concerned with consciousness, values, and abstract beliefs, including spiritual experiences and the beliefs that people live by and die for (p. 392)

humanistic therapy an approach to psychology that focuses on the value, dignity, and worth of each person and holds that healthy living is the result of realizing one's full potential (p. 496)

hypnosis a state of consciousness resulting from a narrowed focus of attention and characterized by heightened suggestibility (p. 191)

hypnotic analgesia a reduction of pain reported by patients after undergoing hypnosis (p. 194)

hypochondriasis a somatoform disorder characterized by being preoccupied with imaginary ailments (p. 461)

hypothesis an assumption or prediction about behavior or an educated guess about the relationship between two variables that is tested through scientific research (pp. 11, 40)

hysteria more commonly used in Sigmund Freud's time to refer to unexplainable fainting, paralysis, or deafness (p. 461)

I

iconic memory the sensory register that briefly holds mental images of visual stimuli (p. 275)

id in psychoanalytic theory, that part of the unconscious personality that contains our needs, drives, and instincts, as well as repressed material (p. 379)

identical twins twins who develop from one fertilized egg; twins having the same heredity and genes (p. 175)

identification in psychoanalytic theory, the process by which a child adopts the values and principles of the same-sex parent (p. 82); the process of seeing oneself as similar to another person or group and accepting the attitudes of another person or group as one's own (p. 583)

identity crisis a period of inner conflict during which adolescents worry intensely about who they are (p. 105)

ideology the set of principles, attitudes, and defined objectives for which a group stands (p. 548)

illusions perceptions that misrepresent physical stimuli (pp. 229, 436)

image a mental representation of a specific event or object (p. 296)

immune system the body's natural defense system that fights off bacteria, viruses, and other foreign or toxic substances (p. 426)

imprinting inherited tendencies or responses that are displayed by newborn animals when they encounter new stimuli in their environment (p. 75)

incentive environmental factor such as an external stimulus, reinforcer, or reward that motivates our behavior (p. 316)

independent variable in an experiment, the factor that the researcher deliberately controls or manipulates to test its effect on another factor (p. 40)

individualistic when people act as individuals, obey their consciences, and are concerned with self-evaluation (p. 570)

industrial/organizational psychologist a psychologist who uses psychological concepts to make the workplace a more satisfying environment for employees and managers (p. 26)

industrial/organizational psychology a branch of psychology that deals with the psychology of the workplace (p. 615)

inferential statistics numerical methods used to determine whether research data support a hypothesis or whether results were due to chance (p. 53)

inferiority complex a pattern of avoiding feelings of inadequacy and insignificance rather than trying to overcome their source (p. 385)

in-group group members who identify with their group (p. 549)

initiation rites a ceremony or ritual in which an individual is admitted to a new status or accepted into a new position (p. 94)

innate part of a person's biological inheritance (p. 330)

inoculation effect a method of developing resistance to persuasion by exposing a person to arguments that challenge his or her beliefs so that he or she can practice defending them (p. 595)

insight the sudden realization or understanding of the solution to a problem (pp. 301, 494)

insomnia a sleep disorder characterized by recurring problems in falling asleep or staying asleep (p. 187)

instincts innate tendencies that determine behavior (p. 314)

intellectualization a coping mechanism in which the person analyzes a situation from an emotionally detached viewpoint (p. 431)

intelligence the ability to acquire new ideas and new behavior, learn from experience, and adapt to new situations (p. 348)

intelligence quotient (IQ) standardized measure of intelligence based on a scale in which 100 is defined as average (p. 352)

interest test an instrument designed to measure a person's preferences, attitudes, and interests (p. 361)

interference the process that occurs when new information appears in short-term memory and replaces what was already there (p. 286)

internalization the process of incorporating the values, ideas, and standards of others as a part of oneself (p. 584)

intimacy the component of love associated with feeling close and connected to someone (p. 536)

intrinsic motivation engaging in certain activities because they are personally rewarding or because they fulfill our beliefs and expectations (p. 316)

introspection a method of self-observation in which participants report on their thoughts and feelings (p. 16)

introvert a reserved, withdrawn person who is more preoccupied with his or her inner thoughts and feelings than in what is going on around him or her (p. 401)

J

just noticeable difference (JND) the smallest increase or decrease in the intensity of a stimulus that a person is able to detect (p. 210)

K

kinesthesis the sense that provides information about the position and movement of individual body parts (p. 222)

L

laissez-faire leader a person who is only minimally involved in a group's decision making (p. 554)

language a system of communication that involves using rules to make and combine symbols in ways that produce meaningful words and sentences (p. 304)

language-acquisition device (LAD) innate brain structures that include inborn mechanisms that guide a person's learning of the unique rules of his or her native language (p. 306)

latency stage the fourth stage of Freud's psychosexual development at which sexual desires are pushed into the background and the child becomes involved in exploring the world and learning new skills (p. 82)

latent content refers to the hidden meanings represented symbolically in a dream (p. 495)

latent learning learning that is not demonstrated by an immediate, observable change in behavior (p. 260)

lateral hypothalamus (LH) the part of the hypothalamus that produces hunger signals (p. 320)

learned helplessness a condition in which repeated attempts to control or influence a situation fail, resulting in the belief that the situation is uncontrollable and that any effort to cope will fail (p. 261)

learning a relatively permanent change in behavior that results from experience (p. 241)

lens a flexible, transparent oval structure in the eye that changes its shape to focus light on the retina; the lens is attached to muscles that adjust the curve of the lens, which in turn adjusts the focus (p. 215)

linguistic relativity the idea that a person's language influences his or her thoughts (p. 308)

lithium carbonate a chemical used to treat mood swings of bipolar disorder (p. 508)

lobes the different regions into which the cerebral cortex is divided (p. 162)

longitudinal study research method in which data are collected about a group of participants over a number of years to assess how certain characteristics change and remain the same during development (p. 38)

LSD (lysergic acid diethylamide) an extremely potent psychedelic drug that produces hallucinations (p. 200)

M

magnetic resonance imaging (MRI) an imaging technique that passes nonharmful frequencies through the brain; a computer measures the interaction with brain cells and transforms this interaction into an incredibly detailed image of the brain (or body) (p. 167)

maintenance rehearsal a system for remembering that involves repeating information to oneself without attempting to find meaning in it (p. 276)

major depressive disorder a severe form of depression marked by at least two weeks of continually being in a bad mood, having no interest in anything, and getting no pleasure from activities (p. 470)

manifest content what a person remembers about a dream (p. 495)

marijuana a psychoactive drug whose primary ingredient is THC (tetrahydrocannabinol) and produces an altered state of consciousness when smoked or ingested (p. 198)

maturation the internally programmed growth of a child that occurs as a result of automatic, genetically determined signals (p. 64)

mean the arithmetic average of all the individual measurements in a distribution (p. 51)

median the score that divides a distribution of rank-ordered observations in half; the middle score (p. 51)

meditation a systematic narrowing of attention on an image, thought, bodily process, or external object with the goal of clearing one's mind and producing relaxation (pp. 195, 434)

memory the storage and retrieval of what has been learned or experienced (p. 274)

menarche a female's first menstrual period (p. 96)

menopause the biological event in which a woman's production of sex hormones is sharply reduced (p. 131)

mental set the tendency to approach a new problem in a way that has been successful in the past (p. 299)

metacognition the awareness of one's own cognitive process (p. 297)

midbrain the smallest division of the brain above the pons that integrates sensory information and relays it upward (p. 161)

mnemonic devices techniques of memorizing information by forming vivid associations or images, which facilitate recall and decrease forgetting (p. 288)

mode the most frequent score in a distribution of observations (p. 51)

modeling the process of learning behavior through observation and imitation of others; copying behavior (pp. 262, 504)

monocular depth cues depth cues produced by signals from a single eye (p. 227)

Glossary

morpheme the smallest unit of meaning in a given language, such as a prefix or suffix (p. 305)

motion parallax the apparent movement of stationary objects relative to one another that occurs when the observer changes position (p. 228)

motivation various physiological and psychological factors that activate behavior and energize and direct that behavior toward a goal (p. 314)

motive to avoid success a theory that suggests that some people are (or were) raised with the idea that being successful in all but a few careers is odd and unlikely (p. 325)

Munchausen's syndrome a disorder in which an individual develops great sensitivity to emotional pain and will use any method possible to avoid feeling it (p. 464)

myelin sheath a tubelike white fatty substance that insulates the axons and enables rapid transmission of neural impulses (p. 157)

N

narcolepsy a condition characterized by suddenly falling asleep or feeling very sleepy during the day (p. 188)

naturalistic observation a research method in which the psychologist observes the subject in a natural setting and without manipulation or control on the part of the observer (p. 37)

need a biological or psychological requirement for the well-being of an organism (pp. 314, 536)

negative correlation a relationship between two variables in which one variable increases as the other variable decreases (p. 39)

negative reinforcement increasing the strength of a given response by removing or preventing a painful stimulus when the response occurs (p. 256)

neurons the long, thin cells that constitute the structural and functional unit of nerve tissue along which messages travel to and from the brain (p. 157)

neurotransmitters the chemicals released by neurons, which determine the rate at which other neurons fire (p. 158)

neutral stimulus a stimulus that does not initially elicit a response (p. 242)

nightmares unpleasant dreams that contain frightening and anxiety-producing images (p. 188)

night terrors sleep disruptions that occur during Stage IV of sleep, involving screaming, panic, or confusion that is seldom remembered (p. 188)

nondirective therapy the free flow of images and ideas, occurring with no particular goal (p. 496)

nonverbal communication conveying messages using space, body language, and facial expression (p. 531)

normal curve a graph of frequency distribution shaped like a symmetrical, bell-shaped curve; a graph of normal distribution (p. 51)

norms standards of comparison for test results developed by giving the test to large, well-defined groups of people (p. 346); shared standards of behavior accepted by and expected from group members (p. 547)

O

obedience a change in attitude or behavior brought about by social pressure to comply with people perceived to be authorities (p. 558)

objective test a forced-choice test designed to study personality characteristics in which a person must select one of several answers (p. 364)

object permanence a child's realization that an object exists even when he or she cannot see, hear, or touch it (p. 72)

observational learning learning by observing and imitating the behavior of others (pp. 262, 389)

obsession a recurring thought or image that seems to be beyond control (p. 458)

obsessive-compulsive disorder an anxiety disorder consisting of obsessions and compulsions (p. 458)

olfactory nerve the nerve that transmits information about odors from the nose to the brain (p. 220)

operant conditioning a form of learning in which a certain action is reinforced or punished, resulting in corresponding increases or decreases in the likelihood that similar actions will occur again (p. 250)

optic nerve the nerve that carries impulses from the retina to the brain (p. 215)

optimist a person whose thoughts lead him or her to believe and expect that good things will happen (p. 433)

oral stage Freud's first stage of psychosexual development, in which infants associate erotic pleasure with the mouth (p. 82)

out-group everyone who is not a member of the in-group (p. 549)

ovaries the female sex glands (p. 172)

overgeneralization a common error during language acquisition in which children apply a grammatical rule to cases where it should not be used (p. 68)

overjustification effect when people are given more extrinsic motivation than necessary to perform a task, their intrinsic motivation declines (p. 317)

P

panic a feeling of sudden, helpless terror (p. 457)

panic disorder an anxiety disorder characterized primarily by recurrent and unexpected panic attacks (p. 457)

parapsychology the study of behavior types that seem to deviate from normal behavior and are sometimes left unexplained; also literally means "alongside psychology" (p. 609)

passionate love a condition that is associated with continuously thinking about a loved one and accompanied by warm sexual feelings and powerful emotional reactions (p. 535)

percentile system a system for ranking test scores that indicates the ratio of scores lower and higher than a given score (p. 346)

perception the organization and interpretation of sensory information into meaningful experiences (p. 208)

peripheral nervous system (PNS) a network of nerves branching out from the spinal cord that conduct information from the bodily organs to the central nervous system and take information back to the organs (p. 156)

peripheral route for persuasion a way to deliver a message by relying on emotional appeals, emphasizing personal traits or positive feelings (p. 592)

permissive/laissez-faire family family in which children have the final say; parents are less controlling and have a nonpunishing, accepting attitude toward children (p. 79)

personal construct theory George Kelly's theory that our processes are psychologically channelized by the ways in which each of us anticipates events (p. 396)

personality all the consistent, stable, enduring, and unique ways in which the behavior of one person differs from that of others (p. 375)

personality disorders maladaptive or inflexible ways of dealing with others and one's environment (p. 475)

personality test an instrument used to measure a person's traits, behaviors, and unobservable characteristics and to identify problems (p. 363)

persuasion the direct attempt to influence attitudes (p. 590)

pessimist a person whose thoughts lead him or her to believe and expect that bad things will happen (p. 433)

phallic stage in this stage, Freud's third psychosexual stage, children associate sexual pleasure with their genitals (p. 82)

phobia an intense and irrational fear of a particular object or situation (p. 456)

phoneme an individual sound that is the basic structural element of language (p. 305)

physical proximity the physical nearness of one person to another person (p. 522)

physiological having to do with an organism's physical needs (pp. 7, 616)

pituitary gland the center of control of the endocrine system that hangs directly below the hypothalamus and secretes a large number of hormones (p. 171)

placebo effect a change in a participant's illness or behavior that results from a belief that the treatment will have an effect rather than from the actual treatment (pp. 45, 488)

positive correlation a relationship between variables in which one variable increases as the other variable also increases (p. 39)

positive regard viewing oneself in a positive light due to positive feedback received from interaction with others (p. 395)

positive reinforcer a stimulus that increases the likelihood that a response will occur again (p. 251)

positron emission tomography (PET) an imaging technique used by psychologists to see which areas of the brain are being activated while performing tasks (p. 167)

posthypnotic suggestion a suggestion made during hypnosis about performing a particular behavior in response to a predetermined cue that influences the participant's behavior afterwards (p. 193)

post-traumatic stress disorder disorder in which victims of catastrophes or other traumatic events experience the original event in the form of dreams or flashbacks (pp. 423, 459)

preattentive process a method for extracting information automatically and simultaneously when presented with stimuli (p. 213)

precocious puberty premature puberty (p. 100)

predictive validity ability of a test's scores to predict real-world performance (p. 345)

prefrontal lobotomy a radical form of psychosurgery in which a section of the frontal lobe of the brain is severed or destroyed (p. 510)

prejudice preconceived, unjustifiable, and usually negative attitude toward a person or group that has been formed without sufficient evidence (p. 587)

primacy effect the tendency to form opinions about others based on first impressions (p. 528)

primary appraisal one's immediate evaluation of a situation (p. 416)

primary group a group of people who interact daily face-to-face (p. 549)

primary-recency effect the theory that we are better able to recall information presented at the beginning and end of a list (p. 277)

primary reinforcer a stimulus, such as food or water, that is naturally rewarding and satisfying and requires no learning on the part of the subject to become pleasurable (p. 252)

proactive interference a forgetting process in which information that we learned earlier blocks or disrupts the retrieval of related new information (p. 286)

procedural memory memory of learned skills and procedures that does not require conscious recollection (p. 279)

progesterone a female sex hormone (p. 172)

progressive relaxation an exercise performed by lying down comfortably and tensing and releasing the tension in each major muscle group in turn (p. 434)

projection unconsciously transferring one's own undesirable attitudes, feelings, or thoughts to others (p. 382)

projective test an unstructured test of personality in which a person is asked to respond freely, giving his or her own interpretation of various ambiguous stimuli (p. 366)

prototype a representative example of a concept (p. 296)

psychiatry a branch of medicine that deals with mental, emotional, or behavioral disorders (p. 25)

psychoactive drugs chemicals that affect the nervous system and result in altered consciousness or awareness, influence sensations and perceptions, and modify moods and cognitive processes (p. 197)

Glossary

psychoanalysis a form of therapy aimed at making patients aware of their unconscious motives so that they can gain control over their behavior and free themselves of self-defeating patterns (p. 494)

psychoanalyst a psychologist who studies how unconscious motives and conflicts determine human behavior (p. 19)

psychobiologist a psychologist who studies how physical and chemical changes in our bodies influence our behaviors (p. 21)

psychological the emotional and behavioral characteristics of an individual or group (p. 616)

psychological dependence a strong, repetitive desire for use of a drug to such an extent that a person feels nervous and anxious without it (p. 476)

psychological needs urges to belong and to give and receive love and urges to acquire esteem through competence and achievement (p. 326)

psychologist a scientist who studies the mind and behavior of humans and animals (p. 25)

psychology the scientific, systematic study of behaviors and mental processes (p. 9)

psychophysics the study of the relationships between sensory experiences and the physical stimuli that cause them (p. 208)

psychosocial development life periods in which an individual's goal is to satisfy desires associated with social needs (p. 83)

psychosocial hunger factors external cues that affect eating (p. 321)

psychosurgery surgery that destroys part of the brain to make the patient calmer and freer of symptoms (p. 510)

psychotherapy a general term for the application of psychological principles and techniques for any treatment used by therapists to help troubled individuals overcome their problems and disorders (p. 486)

puberty the period of sexual maturation; the end of childhood and the point when reproduction is first possible (p. 95)

pupil the opening in the iris that regulates the amount of light entering the eye (p. 215)

R

random sample a sample group of a larger population selected in such a way that each subject within the population has an equal chance of being selected (p. 37)

range the lowest score in a distribution subtracted from the highest score (p. 52)

rational-emotive therapy (RET) a confrontational cognitive form of therapy aimed at changing unrealistic assumptions about oneself and other people (p. 500)

rationalization a process whereby an individual seeks to explain an often unpleasant emotion or behavior in a way that will preserve his or her self-esteem (pp. 102, 381)

reaction formation a defense mechanism by which the ego unconsciously replaces an unacceptable feeling or urge with its opposite (p. 382)

recall the type of memory retrieval in which a person reconstructs previously learned material without the aid of or with very few external cues (p. 283)

recognition the type of memory retrieval in which a person is required to identify an object, idea, or situation as one he or she has or has not experienced before (p. 283)

recombination mentally rearranging the elements of a problem in order to arrive at an original solution (p. 301)

reconceptualization one of three principles in cognitive therapy where clients work toward an alternative belief system to explain their experiences or current observations (p. 500)

reconstructive memory memory that has been simplified, enriched, or distorted, depending on an individual's experiences and attitudes (p. 284)

regression a defense mechanism in which an individual retreats to an earlier stage of development or pattern of behavior in order to deal with a threatening or stressful situation (p. 383)

reinforcement a stimulus or event that follows a response and increases the likelihood that the response will be repeated (p. 251)

reliability the ability of a test to give the same results under similar conditions (p. 344)

REM sleep a stage of sleep characterized by rapid eye movements, a high level of brain activity, a deep relaxation of the muscles, and dreaming behind closed eyelids (p. 186)

replicate to repeat a research study to confirm the results of the original study (p. 40)

representational thought the intellectual ability of a child to picture something in his or her mind (p. 72)

repression the exclusion from conscious awareness of a painful, unpleasant, or undesirable memory (pp. 286, 381)

resistance in psychoanalysis, the reluctance of a patient either to reveal painful feelings or to examine long-standing behavior patterns (p. 494)

response chain the learned reactions that follow one another in sequence, each reaction producing the signal for the next (p. 256)

resynthesis the process of combining old ideas with new ones and reorganizing feelings in order to renew one's identity (p. 439)

retina the light-sensitive innermost coating of the back of the eye that contains the rods, cones, and neurons that process visual stimuli (p. 215)

retinal disparity a binocular cue for perceiving depth based on the differences between the images stimulating each eye (p. 216)

retrieval the process of obtaining information that has been stored in memory (p. 274)

retroactive interference the hampering of recall of learned material by the recall of other material learned more recently (p. 286)

rods visual receptor cells in the retina that are sensitive to light but not color, allowing us to see in dim light but to see only black, white, and shades of gray (p. 215)

role behavior expected of an individual because of his or her membership in a particular group (pp. 550, 587)

role taking an important aspect of children's play that involves assuming adult roles, thus enabling the child to experience different points of view firsthand (p. 84)

rooting reflex an infant's response in turning toward the source of touching that occurs anywhere around his or her mouth (p. 62)

rule a statement of relation between concepts (p. 297)

S

sample the small group of subjects, out of the total number available of a target population, that a researcher studies (p. 36)

SAT Scholastic Assessment Test; a standardized test (p. 611)

scatterplot a graph of scores that demonstrates the direction of the relationship between two variables (p. 53)

schema an idea or mental framework a person uses to organize and interpret information and make sense of the world (pp. 71, 284, 529)

schizophrenia a group of severe psychotic disorders characterized by confused and disconnected thoughts, emotions, behavior, and perceptions (p. 466)

scientific method a general approach to gathering information and answering questions so that errors and biases are minimized (p. 12)

seasonal affective disorder (SAD) a pattern of depressive symptoms that cycle with the seasons, typically beginning in fall or winter (p. 472)

secondary group a larger group of people with whom you might have impersonal relationships (p. 549)

secondary reinforcer a stimulus such as money that increases the probability of a response because of its association with a primary reinforcer (p. 252)

secondary traits transient or less consistent traits found in individuals, such as food and music preferences (p. 400)

self one's experience or image of oneself, developed through interaction with others (p. 395)

self-actualization the humanist term for realizing one's unique potential (pp. 392, 449)

self-actualization needs the pursuit of knowledge and beauty or whatever else is required for the realization of one's unique potential (p. 326)

self-concept how we see or describe ourselves; our self-perceptions (p. 580)

self-efficacy a person's view of their ability to succeed (p. 390)

self-fulfilling prophecy a belief, prediction, or expectation that operates to bring about its own fulfillment (pp. 42, 586)

self-help group a type of therapy in which a group of individuals share a common problem and meet to discuss it without the active involvement of professional therapists (p. 490)

self-justification the need to rationalize one's attitude and behavior (p. 586)

self-serving bias the tendency to view one's successes as stemming from internal factors and one's failures as stemming from external factors (p. 531)

semantic codes ways in which a person tries to remember something by making sense of it, such as associating a letter with a word (p. 274)

semantic memory a type of declarative memory consisting of factual knowledge of language, including its rules, words, and meanings (p. 279)

semantics the study of meaning in language (p. 305)

senile dementia a collective term to describe decreases in mental abilities experienced by some people after the age of 65 (p. 142)

sensation the stimulation of sensory receptors and the transmission of sensory information to the brain (p. 208)

sensory memory very brief memory storage immediately following initial reception of a stimulus (p. 274)

separation anxiety distress that is sometimes experienced by infants when they are separated from their primary caregivers (p. 76)

set-point the weight around which your day-to-day weight tends to fluctuate (p. 321)

shaping technique of operant conditioning in which the desired behavior is "molded" by first rewarding any act similar to that behavior and then requiring closer and closer approximations to the desired behavior before giving the reward (p. 255)

short-term dynamic psychotherapy a shortened version of psychoanalysis in which the therapist uses a direct and more active approach in identifying and resolving problems (p. 496)

short-term memory memory that is limited in capacity to about seven items for a short period of time (p. 276)

signal-detection theory the study of people's tendencies to make correct judgments, misses, and false alarms in detecting the presence of stimuli (p. 212)

single-blind experiment an experiment in which the participants are unaware of which participants received the treatment (p. 43)

sleep apnea a sleep disorder in which a person stops breathing for intervals of 10 seconds or longer, wakes up briefly, resumes breathing, and returns to sleep (p. 187)

sleeper effect the delayed impact on attitude change of a persuasive communication (p. 594)

sleepwalking walking or carrying out behaviors while still asleep (p. 188)

social cognition a subfield of social psychology that focuses on cognitive processes and how we perceive, store, and retrieve information about social interactions (p. 519)

social facilitation an increase in performance in front of a crowd (p. 549)

social functions responses directed toward satisfying the emotional needs of members (p. 547)

Glossary

social inhibition a decrease in performance in the presence of a crowd (p. 549)

socialization the process of learning the rules of behavior of the culture within which an individual is born and will live (p. 81)

social learning form of learning in which the organism observes, explores, and imitates the behavior of others (p. 259)

social learning theory theory that individuals develop by interacting with others (p. 107)

social loafing the tendency for people to work less hard when sharing the workload with others than when they are working alone (p. 569)

social psychology a broad field of psychology that seeks to explain how our thoughts, feelings, perceptions, and behaviors are influenced by interactions with others (p. 519)

social support information that leads someone to believe that he or she is cared for, loved, respected, and part of a network of communication and mutual obligation (p. 428)

social trap a situation that occurs when individuals in a group decide not to cooperate (p. 567)

sociogram a diagram that represents relationships within a group, especially likes and dislikes of members for other members (p. 552)

somatic nervous system (SNS) the division of the peripheral nervous system that controls voluntary movement of skeletal muscles (p. 158)

somatoform disorder a psychological disorder marked by a pattern of recurring physical symptoms for which there is no apparent physical cause (p. 461)

source trait according to Cattell, an underlying trait that can be considered to be at the core of personality (p. 401)

spermarche a period during which males achieve first ejaculation (p. 96)

spinal cord the bundle of nerves within the spine that runs down the length of the back and transmits most messages back and forth between the body and brain (p. 156)

spontaneous recovery the reappearance of an extinguished conditioned response after some time has passed (p. 245)

sports psychology a branch of psychology that studies athletics and athletic performance (p. 615)

stagnation a discontinuation of development and a desire to recapture the past, characteristic of some middle-aged people (p. 135)

standard deviation a measure of variability that describes an average distance of every score from the mean of the scores (p. 52)

state-dependent learning the idea that we recall information more easily when we are in the same physiological or emotional state or setting as when we originally encoded the information (p. 284)

statistically significant effect that has a low probability of having arisen by chance (p. 54)

statistics the branch of mathematics concerned with summarizing and making meaningful inferences from collections of data (p. 48)

stereotype a set of assumptions about people in a given category, either positive or negative, often based on half-truths and nontruths (pp. 530, 587)

stimulation value the ability of a person or participant to interest or expose another to new ideas and experiences (p. 523)

stimulus any aspect of or change in the environment to which an organism responds (p. 208)

storage the process of placing encoded information into relatively permanent mental storage for later recall (p. 274)

stranger anxiety the fear of strangers that infants commonly display (p. 76)

stratified sample a sample group of a larger population in which subgroups within the larger population are represented proportionally (p. 37)

stress a person's physical and mental perception of his or her inability to cope with a certain tense event or situation (p. 413)

stressor an event or situation that produces stress (p. 414)

stress reaction the body's response to a stressor (p. 414)

structuralist a psychologist who studied the basic elements that make up conscious mental experiences (p. 16)

sublimation the process of redirecting sexual impulses into learning tasks (p. 82); redirecting a forbidden desire into a socially acceptable desire (p. 383)

subliminal messages brief auditory or visual messages that are presented below the absolute threshold so that their chance of perception is less than 50 percent (p. 226)

subliminal perception the ability to notice stimuli that affect only the unconscious mind (p. 227)

superego according to Freud, the part of the personality that is the source of conscience and inhibits the socially undesirable impulses of the id (p. 380)

surface trait according to Cattell, a characteristic that can be observed in certain situations (p. 401)

survey a research method in which information is obtained by asking many individuals a fixed set of questions about their attitudes or behavior (p. 38)

symbol an abstract unit of thought that represents an object or quality (p. 296)

synapse the gap that occurs between the axon terminals of the sending neuron and the dendrites of the receiving neuron (p. 157)

syntax the set of language rules that govern how words can be combined to form meaningful phrases and sentences (p. 305)

systematic desensitization a counterconditioning technique used by behavior therapists to help a patient overcome irrational fears and anxieties (p. 503)

Glossary

T

task functions activities directed toward getting a job done (p. 547)

telegraphic speech the kind of verbal utterances offered by young children in which articles, prepositions, and parts of verbs are left out, but the meaning is usually clear (p. 67)

testes the male sex gland (p. 172)

testosterone the male sex hormone that stimulates the growth of genital organs and the development of secondary sexual characteristics (p. 172)

thalamus a structure of the brain that relays messages from the sense organs to the cerebral cortex (p. 161)

thanatology the study of dying and death (p. 144)

theory a set of assumptions used to explain why something is the way it is and happens the way it does (p. 11)

therapy treatment of behavioral, bodily, or psychological disorders (p. 485)

thinking mental activity that involves changing and reorganizing of the information stored in memory in order to create new information (p. 296)

thyroid gland the gland in the endocrine system that produces several hormones, including thyroxine (p. 171)

token economy form of conditioning in which desirable behavior is reinforced with valueless objects or points that can be accumulated and exchanged for privileges or other rewards (pp. 264, 505)

tolerance the reaction of the body and brain to regular drug use, whereby a person needs an increased amount in order to produce the original effect (p. 476)

trait an aspect of personality with a tendency to react to a situation in a way that remains stable over time (p. 398)

transference process of feeling toward an analyst or therapist the way a patient feels or felt toward some other important figure in his or her life (p. 495)

triarchic theory Robert Sternberg's theory of intelligence that proposes that intelligence can be divided into three ways of processing information (p. 350)

two-factor theory Charles Spearman's theory of intelligence that proposes that two factors contribute to an individual's intelligence (p. 349)

U

unconditional positive regard the perception that individuals' significant others value them for what they are, in their entirety, which leads the individuals to grant themselves the same unconditional positive regard (pp. 396, 497)

unconditioned response (UCR) an organism's automatic (or natural) reaction to a stimulus (p. 242)

unconditioned stimulus (UCS) an event that elicits a certain predictable response without previous training (p. 242)

unconscious according to Freud, the part of the mind that holds mostly unacceptable thoughts, wishes, feelings, and memories of which we are unaware but that strongly influences conscious behaviors (p. 379)

uninvolved parents parents who are typically very self-centered in their child rearing, seemingly uncommitted to their role, and quite distant from their children (p. 79)

uplifts small, positive events that make a person feel good (p. 419)

utility value the ability of a person or participant to help another achieve his or her goals (p. 523)

V

validity the ability of a test to measure what it is intended to measure (p. 345)

variable in an experiment, any factor that is measured or controlled and is capable of change (p. 40)

variable-interval schedule a schedule of reinforcement in which changing amounts of time must elapse before a response will obtain reinforcement each time (p. 255)

variable-ratio schedule schedule of reinforcement in which an unpredictable number of responses is required before reinforcement can be obtained each time (p. 254)

variance a measure of difference, or variance within two distributions (p. 52)

ventromedial hypothalamus (VMH) the part of the hypothalamus that causes one to slow down or stop eating altogether if stimulated (p. 321)

vestibular system three semicircular canals located in the inner ear that provide the sense of balance (p. 220)

visual codes a way a person tries to remember something by keeping a mental picture in his or her mind (p. 274)

visualization mentally rehearsing the steps involved in a successful performance or process (p. 615)

W

Weber's law a psychophysics law stating that the larger or stronger a stimulus, the larger the change required for an observer to notice a difference (p. 211)

withdrawal the symptoms that occur after a person discontinues the use of a drug to which he or she has become addicted (p. 477)

working memory a system that processes and works with current information; also called short-term memory (p. 278)

Italicized page numbers refer to illustrations. Preceding the page number, abbreviations refer to a chart (c), photograph or other picture (p), graph (g), cartoon (crt), painting (ptg). Quoted material is referenced with the abbreviation (q) before the page number.

SUBJECT INDEX

Index

Index

Index

NAME INDEX

Index

References

A

AAA Foundation for Traffic Safety. (1997). *Road Rage: How to Avoid Aggressive Driving*. New York: AAA Foundation for Traffic Safety.

Abramson, L.Y., Seligman M., & Teasdale, J.D. (1987). Learned helplessness in humans: Critique and reformulation. *Journal of Abnormal Psychology, 87,* 49–74.

Adler, A. (1959). *What Life Should Mean to You*. New York: Putnam. (paper).

Ahrens, R. (1954). Beitrag zur Entwicklung des Physiognomie-und Mimiker-kennens. Z. exp. angew. Psychol., 2, 412–454.

Ainsworth, M.D.S. (1989). Attachments beyond infancy. *American Psychologist,* 44, 709–716.

Ainsworth, M.D.S., & Bowlby, J. (1991). An ethnological approach to personality development. *American Psychologist,* 46, 333–341.

Ajzen, I. (1991). The theory of planned behavior. *Organizational Behavior and Human Decision Processes, 50,* 179–211.

Allgeier, A.R. (1983). Sexuality and gender roles in the second half of life. In A.R. Allgeier & N. McCormick (Eds.), *Changing Boundaries*. Palo Alto, CA: Mayfield.

Allport, G. (1937). *Personality: A Psychological Interpretation*. New York: Henry Holt.

_____. (1954). *The Nature of Prejudice*. Garden City, NY: Doubleday. (paper).

_____. (1961). *Pattern and Growth in Personality*. New York: Holt, Rinehart and Winston.

_____. (Ed.). (1965). *letters from Jenny*. New York: Harcourt, Brace & World.

American Academy of Pediatrics. (1995). Media violence policy statement. Retrieved September 2, 1999 from the World Wide Web: http://www.aap.org/

American Demographics. (1997). Longer lives mean longer marriages. Retrieved August 16, 1999 from the World Wide Web: http://www.demographics.com/

American Foundation for Suicide Prevention. (1999). Suicide facts. Retrieved July 2, 1999 from the World Wide Web: http://www.afsp.org

American Humane Association. (1999). Answers to common questions about child abuse and neglect. Retrieved June 2, 1999 from the World Wide Web: http://www.americanhumane.org/

American Psychiatric Association. (1993). APA online public information: The insanity defense. Retrieved July 9, 1999 from the World Wide Web: http://www.psych.org/public_info/insani~1.htm

_____. (1994). *Diagnostic and Statistical Manual of Mental Disorders* (4th ed.). Washington, DC.

American Psychological Association. (1993). 1993 Profile of APA Membership. Washington, DC.

_____. (1996). *Master's, Specialist's, and Related Degrees Employment Survey*. Washington, DC: Author.

_____. (1999). APA research office–Survey reports. Washington, DC: Author. Retrieved September 15, 1999 from the World Wide Web: http://research.apa.org/reports.html

American Psychological Association, Commission on Violence and Youth. (1993). Violence & youth: Psychology's response (Vol. 1) [Summary Report]. Washington, DC: Author.

Antelman, S.M., & Szechtman, H. (1975). Tail pinch induces eating in sated rats which appears to depend on nigrostriatal dopamine. *Science, 189,* 731–733.

Archer, J. (1997). On the origins of sex differences in social behavior: Darwinian and non-Darwinian accounts. *American Psychology, 52,* 1383–1384.

Arkoff, A. (1968). *Adjustment and Mental Health*. New York: McGraw-Hill.

Aronson, E., Turner, J., & Carlsmith, M. (1963). Communicator credibility and communicator discrepancy as determinants of opinion change. *Journal of Abnormal and Social Psychology, 67,* 31–36.

Asch, S. (1940). Studies in the principles of judgments and attitudes: Determination of judgments by group and ego standards. *Journal of Social Psychology, 12,* 433–465.

_____. (1952). *Social Psychology*. New York: Prentice-Hall.

_____. (1956). Studies of independence and conformity: A minority of one against a unanimous majority. *Psychological Monographs, 70,* Whole No. 416.

_____. (1965). Effects of group pressure upon the modification and distortion of judgments. In J. Proshansky & B. Seidenberg. (Eds.), *Basic Studies in Social Psychology,* (pp. 393–401). New York: Holt, Rinehart and Winston.

Atkinson, J.W. (Ed.). (1958). *Motives in Fantasy, Action, and Society*. New York: Van Nostrand Reinhold.

Austin Police Department Gang Suppression Unit. (1999). Basic gang facts. Retrieved September 2, 1999 from the World Wide Web: http://www.austingangbusters.org/

Averill, J. (1983). Studies on anger and aggression: Implications for theories of emotion. *American Psychologist, 38,* 1145–1160.

Axsom, D., Yates, S., & Chaiken, S. (1987). Audience response as a heuristic cue in persuasion. *Journal of Personality and Social Psychology, 53,* 30–40.

Ayer, E.H. (1998). *Everything You Need to Know About Stress*. New York: The Rosen Publishing Group, Inc.

Azar, B. (1996, June). Schools the source of rough transitions. *APA Monitor,* 14.

B

Bahrick, H.P., Bahrick, P.O., & Wittinger, R.P. (1974, December). Those unforgettable high school days. *Psychology Today.*

Baillergeon, R., Graber, M., Decops, J., & Black, J. (1990). Why do young infants fail to search for hidden objects? *Cognition,* 36, 255–284.

Baltes, P.P., & Schaie, K.W. (1977). Aging and IQ: The myth of the twilight years. In S.H. Zarit (Ed.), *Readings in Aging and Death: Contemporary Perspectives.* New York: Harper & Row.

Baltrusch, H.J., Stangel, W., & Titze, I. (1991). Stress, cancer, and immunity: New developments in biopsychosocial and psychoneuroimmunologic research. *Acta Neurologica, 13,* 315–327.

Bandura, A. (1964). The stormy decade: Fact or fiction? *Psychology in the Schools, 1,* 224–231.

_____. (1965). Influence of models' reinforcement contingencies on the acquisition of imitative responses. *Journal of Personality and Social Psychology, 1,* 589–595.

_____. (1971). Analysis of modeling processes. In A. Bandura (Ed.), *Psychological Modeling: Conflicting Theories,* (pp. 1–62). Chicago: Aldine-Atherton.

_____. (1977). *Social Learning Theory*. Englewood Cliffs, NJ: Prentice-Hall.

_____. (1986). *Social Foundations of Thought and Action: A Social Cognitive Theory*. Englewood Cliffs, NJ: Prentice-Hall.

Bandura, A., & Walters, R.H. (1963). *Social Learning and Personality Development*. New York: Holt, Rinehart and Winston.

References

Barber, T.X. (1965). Measuring 'hypnotic-like' suggestibility with and without 'hypnotic induction': psychometric properties, norms, and variables influencing response to the Barber suggestibility scale (BSS). *Psychological Reports, 16,* 809–844.

Baron, R.A., & Byrne, D. (1991). *Social Psychology: Understanding Human Interaction* (6th ed.). Boston: Allyn and Bacon.

Bartoshuk, L. (1989). Taste: Robust across the life span? *Annals of the New York Academy of Sciences, 561,* 65–75.

Bartoshuk, L., Fast, K., Karrer, T.A., Marino, S., Price, R.A., & Reed, D. (1992). PROP supertasters and the perception of sweetness and bitterness. *Chemical Senses, 17,* 594 (Abstract).

Baumeister, R.F., Smart, L., & Boden, J.M. (1996). Relation of threatened egotism to violence and aggression: The dark side of high self-esteem. *Psychological Review, 103,* 5–33.

Baumrind, D. (1971). Current patterns of parental authority. *Developmental Psychology Monographs, 4* (1), Pt. 2.
_____. (1973, February). Will a day care center be a child development center? *Young Children, 28,* 154–169.

Beck, A.T. (1967). *Depression: Causes and Treatment.* Philadelphia: University of Pennsylvania Press.
_____. (1970). Cognitive therapy: Nature and relation to behavior therapy. *Behavior Therapy, 1,* 184–200.

Beebe-Center, J.G. (1949). Standards for the use of Gust scale. *Journal of Psychology, 28,* 411–419.

Belmore, S.B. (1987). Determinants of attention during impression formation. *Journal of Experimental Psychology: Learning, Memory, and Cognition, 13,* 480–489.

Belsky, J. (1984). The determinants of parenting: A process model. *Child Development, 55,* 83–96.

Bem, D.J. (1970). *Beliefs, Attitudes and Human Affairs.* Belmont, CA: Brooks/Cole.

Bem, S.L. (1975, September). Androgyny vs. the little lives of fluffy women and chesty men. *Psychology Today, 8,* 59–62.
_____. (1981). Gender schema theory: A cognitive account of sex typing. *Psychological Review, 88,* 354–364.
_____. (1983). Gender schema theory and its implications for child development: Raising gender-aschematic children in a gender-schematic society. *Signs, 8,* 598–616.

_____. (1985). Androgyny and gender schema theory: A conceptual and empirical integration. In T.B. Sonderegger (Ed.), *Nebraska Symposium on Motivation: Psychology and Gender.* Lincoln, NE: University of Nebraska Press: 179–266.
_____. (1993). *The Lenses of Gender: Transforming the Debate on Sexual Inequality.* New Haven, CT: Yale University Press.

Benson, H. (1975). *The Relaxation Response.* New York: Avon.

Benson, P.L., & Roehlkepartain, E. Youth violence in Middle America. Retrieved September 7, 1999 from the World Wide Web: http://www.ncrel.org/

Berger, K.S. (1994). *The Developing Person Through the Life Span* (3rd ed.). New York: Worth Publishers.

Bergin, A.E. (1971). The evaluation of therapeutic outcomes. In A.E. Bergin & S.L. Garfield (Eds.), *Handbook of Psychotherapy and Behavior Change: An Empirical Analysis.* New York: Wiley.

Berkowitz, L. (1962). *Aggression: A Social Psychological Analysis.* New York: McGraw-Hill Book Company.
_____. (1989). Frustration-aggression hypothesis: Examination and reformulation. *Psychological Bulletin, 106,* 59–73.

Berman, M.E., Tracy, J.I., & Coccaro, E.R. (1997). The serotonin hypothesis of aggression revisited. *Clinical Psychology Review, 17,* 651–665.

Berndt, T.J. (1992). Friendship and friends' influence in adolescence. *Current Directions in Psychological Science, 1,* 156–159.

Berry, L.M., & Houston, J.P. (1993). *Psychology at Work: An Introduction to Industrial and Organizational Psychology.* Madison, WI: WCBrown and Benchmark Publishers.

Biernat, M., & Wortman, C.B. (1991). Sharing of home responsibilities between professionally employed women and their husbands. *Journal of Personality and Social Psychology, 60,* 844–860.

Bischof, L. (1969). *Adult Psychology.* New York: Harper & Row.

Bjorkqvist, K., Lagerspetz, K., & Kaukiainen, A. (1992). Do girls manipulate and boys fight? Developmental trends in regard to direct and indirect aggression. *Aggressive Behavior, 18,* 117–127.

Blake, R.R., & McCanse, A.A. (1991). *Leadership Dilemmas: Grid Solutions.* Houston, TX: Gulf Publishing Company.

Blake, R.R., & Mouton, J.S. (1985). *The Managerial Grid III: The Key to Leadership Excellence* (3rd ed.). Houston, TX: Gulf Publishing Company.

Block, R., & Ghoneim, M. (1993). Effects of chronic marijuana use on human cognition. *Psychopharmacology, 110* (1–2), 219–228.

Bootzin, R.R. (1975). *Behavior Modification and Therapy: An Introduction.* Cambridge, MA: Winthrop.

Bornstein, R.F. (1989). Subliminal techniques as propaganda tools: Review and critique. *Journal of Mind and Behavior, 10,* 231–262.

Bouchard, T.J., Jr., & McGue, M. (1981). Familial studies of intelligence: A review. *Science, 212,* 1055–1059.

Bowlby, J. (1960–1961). Separation anxiety: A critical review of the literature. *Journal of Child Psychology and Psychiatry, 1,* 251–269.
_____. (1965). *Child Care and Growth of Love* (2nd ed.). Baltimore: Penguin.
_____. (1973). *Attachment and Loss: Vol. 2 Separation: Anxiety and Anger.* New York: Basic Books.

Brady, J.V. (1958, October). Ulcers in 'executive' monkeys. *Scientific American, 199,* 95–100.

Brett, J.F., Brief, A.P., Burke, M.J., George, J.M., & Webster, J. (1990). Negative affectivity and the reporting of stressful life events. *Health Psychology, 9,* 57–68.

British Columbia Schizophrenia Society. (1997). Schizophrenia: Youth's greatest disabler. Retrieved July 2, 1999 from the World Wide Web: http://www.mentalhealth.com/book/

Briton, N., & Hall, J. (1995). Beliefs about female and male nonverbal communication. *Sex Roles, 32,* 79–90.

Brooks-Gunn, J., & Peterson, A.C. (1983). *Girls at Puberty: Biological and Psychosocial Perspectives.* New York: Plenum Press.

Brown, R. (1973). A First Language: *The Early Stages.* Cambridge, MA: Harvard University Press.

Buck, L., & Axel, R. (1991). A novel multigene family may encode odorant receptors: A molecular basis for odor recognition. *Cell, 65,* 175–187.

Budzynski, T.H., et al. (1973). EMG biofeedback and tension headache: A controlled outcome study. *Psychosomatic Medicine, 35,* 484–496.

Bukatko, D., & Daehler, M.W. (1992). *Child Development: A Topical Approach.* Boston: Houghton-Mifflin Company.

Bureau of Labor Statistics. (1997, September). Developments in women's labor force participation. Howard V. Hayghe, *Monthly Labor Review.*

Buss, D.M. (1985). Human mate selection. *American Scientist, 73,* 47–51.

C

Campbell, D. (1992). *CISS* (Campbell Interest and Skill Survey). NCS.

Cann, A., Sherman, S.J., & Elkes, R. (1975). Effects of initial request size and timing of a second request on compliance: The foot-in-the-door and the door-in-the-face. *Journal of Personality and Social Psychology, 32,* 774–782.

Cannon, W.B. (1929). *Bodily Changes in Pain, Hunger, Fear and Rage.* Appleton, NY.

Caplan, R.D., Cobb, S., French, J.R.P., van Harrison, R., & Pinneau, R. (1975). *Job Demands and Worker Health: Main Effects and Occupational Differences.* Washington, DC: National Institute for Occupational Safety and Health.

Carey, S. (1978). The child as word learner. In M. Halle, J. Bresnan, & G.A. Miller (Eds.), *Language Theory and Psychological Reality.* Cambridge, MA: MIT Press.

Carli, L.L., Ganley, R., & Pierce-Otay, A. (1991). Similarity and satisfaction in roommate relationships. *Personality and Social Psychology Bulletin, 17,* 419–426.

Carlsson, A. (1988). The current status of the dopamine hypothesis of schizophrenia. *Neuropsychopharmacology, 1,* 179–186.

Carson, R.C., & Butcher, J.N. (1992). *Abnormal Psychology and Modern Life* (9th ed.). New York: HarperCollins Publishers.

Carson, R.C., & Sanislow, C.A., III. (1992). The schizophrenias. In H.E. Adams & P.B. Surkur (Eds.), *Comprehensive Handbook of Psychopathology* (2nd ed.). New York: Plenum.

Carsten, J.M., & Spector, P.E. (1987). Unemployment, job satisfaction, and employee turnover: A meta-analytic test of the Muchinsky model. *Journal of Applied Psychology, 72,* 374–381.

Carter, E.A., & McGoldrick, M. (1988). Overview: The changing family life cycle; A framework for family therapy. In E.A. Carter & M. McGoldrick (Eds.), *The Changing Family Cycle: A Framework for Family Therapy* (2nd ed.). New York: Gardner Press.

Cartwright, R. (1993). Who needs their dreams? The usefulness of dreams in psychotherapy. *Journal of the American Academy of Psychoanalysis, 8 (4),* 539–547.

Ceci, S.J. (1991). How much does schooling influence general intelligence and its cognitive components? A reassessment of the evidence. *Developmental Psychology, 27,* 703–722.

Centers for Disease Control. (1988). Fact sheet: Youth risk behavior trends from CDC's 1991, 1993, 1995, and 1997 Youth Risk Behavior Surveys. Retrieved September 7, 1999 from the World Wide Web: http://www.cdc.gov/nccdphp/dash/yrbs/trend.htm.

Chaiken, S. (1987). The heuristic model of persuasion. In M.P. Zanna, J.M. Olson, & C.P. Herman (Eds.), *Social Influence: The Ontario Symposium* (Vol 5), (pp. 3–39). Hillsdale, NJ: Lawrence A. Eribaum.

Chamberlain, K., & Zika, S. (1990). The minor events approach to stress: Support for the use of daily hassles. *British Journal of Psychology, 81,* 469–481.

Chand, I.P., Crider, D.M., & Willets, F.K. (1975). Parent-youth disagreement as perceived by youth: A longitudinal study. *Youth and Society, 6,* 365–375.

Chang, E.C. (1996). Cultural differences in optimism, pessimism, and coping: Predictors of subsequent adjustment in Asian American and Caucasian American college students. *Journal of Counseling Psychology, 43,* 113–123.

Cherry, F., & Deaux, K. (1978). Fear of success versus fear of gender-inappropriate behavior. *Sex Roles, 4,* 97–102.

Children's Defense Fund. (1997). *The State of America's Children: Yearbook 1997.* Washington, DC: Author.

Chomsky, N. (1957). *Syntactic Structures.* The Hague: Mouton.

Chukovsky, K. (1963). *From Two To Five.* Berkeley: University of California Press.

Clarke-Stewart, K.A. (1989). Infant day care: Maligned or malignant? *American Psychologist, 44,* 266–273.

Coale, A.J. (1973). The demographic transition reconsidered. *In International Population Conference,* Liège.

Cobb, S. (1976, September-October). Social support as a moderator of life stress. *Psychosomatic Medicine, 38,* 300–314.

Cobb, S., & Rose, R. (1973). Hypertension, peptic ulcers, and diabetes in air traffic controllers. *Journal of the American Medical Association, 224,* 489–492.

Coch, L., & French, J.R.P., Jr. (1948). Overcoming resistance to change. *Human Relations, 1,* 512–532.

Cohen, A., Glass, D., & Phillips, S. (1977). Environment and Health. In H.E. Freeman, S. Levine, & L.G. Reeder (Eds.), *Handbook of Medical Sociology.* Englewood Cliffs, NJ: Prentice-Hall.

Cohen, A.R. (1964). *Attitude Change and Social Influence.* New York: Basic Books.

Cohen, S. (1988). Psychosocial models of the role of social support in the etiology of physical disease. *Health Psychology, 7,* 269–297.

Cohen, S., Evans, G., Krantz, D., & Stokols, D. (1983). Physiological, motivational, and cognitive effects of aircraft noise on children: Moving from the laboratory to the field. *American Psychologist, 35,* 231–243.

Cohen, S., Glass, D., & Singer, J. (1973). Apartment noises, auditory discrimination and reading ability in children. *Journal of Experimental Social Psychology, 9,* 407–422.

Cohen, S., & Lezak, A. (1977). Noise and inattentiveness to social cues. *Environment and Behavior, 9,* 559–572.

Cohen, S., Tyrrell, D.A., & Smith, A.P. (1991). Psychological stress and susceptibility to the common cold. *New England Journal of Medicine, 325,* 606–612.

Colby, A., Kohlberg, L., Gibbs, J., & Lieberman, M. (1983). A longitudinal study of moral judgment. *Monographs of the Society for Research in Child Development, 48,* 1–124.

Coles, R. (1971). Life in Appalachia: The case of Hugh McCaslin. In G. Armstrong (Ed.), *Life at the Bottom,* (pp. 26–42). New York: Bantam.

Collins, J. (1998, October 19). Seven kinds of smart. *Time.*

Compas, B.E., Hinden, B.R., & Gerhardt, C.A. (1995). Adolescent development: Pathways and processes of risk and resilience. *Annual Review of Psychology, 46,* 265–293.

Costa, P.T., Jr., McCrae, R.R., & Dye, D.A. (1991). Facet scales for agreeableness and conscientiousness: A revision of the NEO personality inventory. *Personality and Individual Differences, 12,* 887–898.

Coutts, L.M. (1991). The organizational psychologist. In R. Gifford (Ed.), *Applied Psychology: Variety and Opportunity.* Boston: Allyn and Bacon.

Czeisler, C.A., Duffy, J.F., Shanahan, T.L., Brown, E.N., Mitchell, J.F., Rimmer, D.W., Ronda, J.M., Silva, E.J., Allan, J.S., Emens, J.S., Dijk, D., & Kronauer, R.E. (1999). Stability, precision, and the near-24-hour period of the human circadian pacemaker. *Science, 284,* 2177–2181.

References

D

Damasio, A.R. (1994). *Descartes' Error: Emotion, Reason, and the Human Brain*. New York: G.P. Putnam's Sons.

Darley, J.M., & Latané, B. (1968). Bystander intervention in emergencies: Diffusion of responsibility. *Journal of Personality and Social Psychology, 8,* 377–383.

Darwin, C. (1967). *The Expression of Emotions in Man and Animals*. Chicago: University of Chicago Press. (Original work published 1872).

Dasen, P.R., & Heron, A. (1981). Cross-cultural tests of Piaget's theory. In H. Triandis (Ed.), *Handbook of Cross-Cultural Psychology. Vol. 4: Developmental Psychology*. Boston: Allyn and Bacon.

Davis, K. (1985, February). Near and dear: Friendship and love compared. *Psychology Today, 19,* 22–30.

Davison, G.C., & Neale, J.M. (1996). *Abnormal Psychology* (6th ed.). New York: John Wiley & Sons.

De Bono, E. (1968). *New Think: The Use of Lateral Thinking in the Generation of New Ideas*. New York: Basic Books.

Deci, E.L. (1971). Effects of externally mediated rewards on intrinsic motivation. *Journal of Personality and Social Psychology, 18,* 105–115.

Deci, E.L., & Ryan, R.M. (1987). The support of autonomy and the control of behavior. *Journal of Personality and Social Psychology, 53,* 1024–1037.

Delgado, J.M.R. (1969). *Physical Control of the Mind*. New York: Harper & Row.

Delongis, A., Folkman, S., & Lazarus, R.S. (1988). The impact of daily stress on health and mood: Psychological and social resources as mediators. *Journal of Personality and Social Psychology, 54,* 486–495.

Dement, W. (1976). *Some Must Watch While Some Must Sleep*. New York: Norton.

Dement, W., & Wolpert, E. (1958). Relation of eye movements, bodily mobility, and external stimuli to dream content. *Journal of Experimental Psychology, 55,* 543–553.

Dennis, W. (1960). Causes of retardation among institutional children: Iran. *Journal of Genetic Psychology, 96,* 47–59.

———. (1966). Creative productivity between the ages of twenty and eighty years. *Journal of Gerontology, 21,* 1–8.

Deutsch, M., & Collins, M. (1951). *Interracial Housing: A Psychological Evaluation of a Social Experiment*. Minneapolis: University of Minnesota Press.

Devine, P.G. (1989). Stereotypes and prejudice: Their automatic and controlled components. *Journal of Personality and Social Psychology, 56,* 5–18.

Diamond, A. (1985). Development of the ability to use recall to guide action, as indicated by infants' performance on AB. *Child Development, 56,* 868–883.

Dillbeck, M.C., & Ome-Johnson, D.W. (1987). Physiological differences between transcendental meditation and rest. *American Psychologist, 42,* 879–881.

Dion, K.L., Berscheid, E., & Walster, E. (1972). What is beautiful is good. *Journal of Personality and Social Psychology, 24,* 285–290.

Dipboye, R.L., Arvey, R.D., & Terpstra, D.E. (1977). Sex and physical attractiveness of raters and applicants as determinants of resume evaluations. *Journal of Applied Psychology, 62,* 288–294.

Doob, L.W. (1990). Forward. In M.H. Segall, et al. (Eds.), *Human Behavior in Global Perspective: An Introduction to Cross-cultural Psychology*. New York: Pergamon Press.

Downs, A.C. (1990). The social biological constraints of social competency. In T.P. Gullotta, G.R. Adams, & R.R. Montemayor, *Developing Social Competency in Adolescence*. Newbury Park, CA: Sage.

Dubas, J.S., Graber, J.A., & Peterson, A.C. (1991). A longitudinal investigation of adolescents' changing perceptions of pubertal timing. *Developmental Psychology, 27,* 580–589.

Duncan, S. (1969). Nonverbal communication. *Psychological Bulletin, 72,* 118–137.

Duncker, K. (1945). On problem solving. (L.S. Lees, trans.). *Psychological Monographs, 58,* (270).

Durkin, J. (1991). The sports psychologist. In R. Gifford (Ed.), *Applied Psychology: Variety and Opportunity*. Boston: Allyn and Bacon.

Dutton, D.G., & Aron, A.P. (1974). Some evidence for heightened sexual arousal under conditions of high anxiety. *Journal of Personality and Social Psychology, 30,* 510–517.

E

Edwards, J.N., & Brauburger, M.B. (1973). Exchange and parent-youth conflict. *Journal of Marriage and the Family, 35,* 101–107.

Ekman, P. (1984). Expression and the nature of emotion. In K.R. Scherer & P. Ekman (Eds.), *Approaches to Emotion*. Hillsdale, NJ: Erlbaum.

———. (1985). *Telling Lies: Clues to Deceit in the Marketplace, Politics, and Marriage*. New York: W.W. Norton & Company.

Ekman, P., Friesen, W.V., & Ellsworth, P. (1972). *Emotion in the Human Face: Guidelines for Research and an Integration of Findings*. Elmsford, NY: Pergamon.

Ekman, P., Levenson, R., & Friesen, W. (1983). Autonomic nervous system activity distinguishes among emotions. *Science, 221,* 1208–1210.

Eldersveld, S., & Dodge, R. (1954). Personal contact or mail propaganda? An experiment in voting turnout and attitude change. In D. Katz, et al. (Eds.), *Public Opinion and Propaganda,* (pp. 532–542). New York: Dryden Press.

Elkin, I., et al. (1989). National institute of mental health treatment of depression collaborative research program: General effectiveness of treatments. *Archives of General Psychiatry, 46,* 971–982.

Elkind, D. (1984). *All Grown Up and No Place to Go*. Reading, MA: Addison-Wesley.

———. (1985). Egocentrism redux. *Developmental Review, 5,* 218–226.

Ellis, A. (1973). Rational-emotive therapy. In R. Corsini (Ed.), *Current Psychotherapies,* (pp. 167–206). Itasca, IL: Peacock.

Eppley, K.R., Abrams, A.I., & Shear, J. (1989). Differential effects of relaxation techniques on trait anxiety: A meta-analysis. *Journal of Clinical Psychology, 45,* 957–974.

Erickson, M.F., Egeland, B., & Pianta, R. (1989). The effects of maltreatment on the development of young children. In D. Cicchetti, et al. (Eds.), *Child Maltreatment: Theory and Research on the Causes and Consequences of Child Abuse and Neglect,* (pp. 647–684). New York: Cambridge University Press.

Erikson, E. (1950). *Childhood and Society*. New York: Norton.

———. (1968). *Identity: Youth and Crisis*. New York: Norton.

Eysenck, H.J. (1952). The effects of psychotherapy: An evaluation. *Journal of Consulting Psychology, 16,* 319–324.

———. (1966). *The Effects of Psychotherapy*. New York: International Science Press.

———. (1970). *The Structure of Human Personality*. London: Metheun.

———. (1990). Biological dimensions of personality. In L.A. Pervin (Ed.), *Handbook of Personality Theory and Research,* (pp. 244–276). New York: Guilford Press.

F

Fall, G.S. (1904). *Adolescence*. New York: Appleton.

References

Fantz, R.L. (1961). The origins of form perception. *Scientific American, 204,* 66–72.

Fehr, B., & Russell, J.A. (1991). The concept of love viewed from a prototype perspective. *Journal of Personality and Social Psychology, 60,* 425–438.

Feingold, A. (1992). Good-looking people are not what we think. *Psychological Bulletin, 111,* 304–341.

Feist, J. (1985). *Theories of Personality.* New York: Holt, Rinehart and Winston.

Festinger, L., (1957). *A Theory of Cognitive Dissonance.* Stanford, CA: Stanford University Press.

Festinger, L,. & Carlsmith, J.M. (1959). Cognitive consequences of forced compliance. *Journal of Abnormal and Social Psychology, 58,* 203–210.

Fiedler, F.E. (1969). Style or circumstance: The leadership enigma. *Psychology Today, 2,* 38–43.

Fischer, K.W. (1973). *Piaget's Theory of Learning and Cognitive Development.* Chicago: Markham.

Fisher, S., & Greenberg, R.P. (1977). *The Scientific Credibility of Freud's Theories and Therapy.* New York: Basic Books.

Flavell, J.H. (1963). *The Developmental Theory of Jean Piaget.* New York: Van Nostrand.

Flavell, J.H., Green, F., & Flavell, E. (1995). Young children's knowledge about thinking. *Monographs of the Society for Research in Child Development, 60* (1, Serial No. 243).

Folkes, V.S. (1982). Forming relationships and the matching hypothesis. *Personality and Social Psychology Bulletin, 8,* 631–636.

Forsen, A. (1991). Psychosocial stress as a risk for breast cancer. *Psychotherapy and Psychosomatics, 55,* 176–185.

Foulkes, D. (1966). *The Psychology of Sleep.* New York: Scribner's.

Fox, L.J. (1966). Effecting the use of efficient study habits. In R. Ulrich, T. Stachnik, & J. Mabry (Eds.), *Control of Human Behavior,* Vol. 1 Glenview, IL: Scott, Foresman.

Frankl, V. (1970). *Man's Search for Meaning: An Introduction to Logotherapy.* New York: Clarion.

Franklin, B. (1818; reprinted in 1949). *The Autobiography of Benjamin Franklin.* As cited in Gray, 1999. Berkeley: University of California Press.

Freedman, J.L. (1975). *Crowding and Behavior.* San Francisco: Freeman.

Freedman, J.L., & Fraser, S.C. (1966). Compliance without pressure: The foot-in-the-door technique. *Journal of Personality and Social Psychology, 4,* 195–202.

Freud, E.L. (Ed.) (1960). *Letters of Sigmund Freud.* New York: Dover Publications, Inc.

Freud, S. (1943). *A General Introduction to Psychoanalysis.* (J. Riviere, trans.). Garden City, NY: Garden City Publishing.

_____. (1949). *An Outline of Psychoanalysis.* (J. Strachey, ed. and trans.). New York: Norton. (Original work published 1940).

_____. (1965). *The Interpretation of Dreams,* (3rd English ed.). (P.A. Fried & J. Strachey, eds. and trans.). New York: Avon Books.

Friedman, M., & Rosenman, R.H. (1974). *Type A behavior and your heart.* New York: Knopf.

Friedman, M., & Ulmer, D. (1984). *Treating Type A Behavior–and Your Heart.* New York: Alfred A. Knopf.

Friman, P.C., Allen, K.D., Kerwin, M.L.E., & Larzelere, R. (1993). Changes in modern psychology: A citation analysis of the Kuhnian displacement thesis. *American Psychologist, 48,* 658–664.

Fromm, E. (1947). *Man for Himself: An Inquiry Into the Psychology of Ethics.* New York: Holt, Rinehart and Winston.

_____. (1956). *The Art of Loving.* New York: Harper & Row.

Furstenberg, F.F., & Cherlin, A.J. (1991). *Divided Families: What Happens to Children When Parents Part.* Cambridge, MA: Harvard University Press.

Furth, H. (1969). *Piaget and Knowledge.* Englewood Cliffs, NJ: Prentice-Hall.

G

Galanter, M. (1990). Cults and zealous self-help movements: A psychiatric perspective. *American Journal of Psychiatry, 147,* 543–551.

Galton, F. (1869). *Hereditary Genius: An Inquiry into Its Laws and Consequences.* London: Macmillan.

Garcia, J., & Koelling, R.A. (1966). The relation of cue to consequence in avoidance. *Learning. Psychonomic Science, 4,* 123–124.

Gardner, H. (1983). *Frames of Mind: The Theory of Multiple Intelligences.* New York: Basic Books.

Gardner, R.A., & Gardner, B.T. (1969). Teaching sign language to a chimpanzee. *Science, 1965,* 644–672.

Garrod, A. (1992). *Adolescent Portraits.* Needham Heights, MA: Allyn & Bacon, Inc.

Gerard, H.B., & Rabbie, J.M. (1961). Fear and social comparison. *Journal of Abnormal and Social Psychology, 62,* 586–592.

Gerst, M.S. (1971). Symbolic coding processes in observational learning. *Journal of Personality and Social Psychology, 19,* 9–17.

Gesell, A., & Thompson, H. (1929). Learning and growth in identical twin infants. *Genetic Psychological Monograph, 6,* 1–124.

Gibb, C. (1969). Leadership. In G. Lindsey & E. Aronson (Eds.), *The Handbook of Social Psychology, Vol. 4,* (2nd ed.). Reading, MA: Addison-Wesley.

Gibson, E.J., & Walk, R.D. (1960). The "visual cliff." *Scientific American, 202,* 64–71.

Gilligan, C. (1977). In a different voice: Women's conceptions of self and morality. *Harvard Educational Review, 47,* 481–517.

_____. (1982). *In a Different Voice: Psychological Theory and Women's Development.* Cambridge, MA: Harvard University Press.

Gilligan, C., & Attanucci, J. (1988). Two moral orientations: Gender differences and similarities. *Merrill-Palmer Quarterly, 34,* 223–237.

Ginsburg, H., & Opper, S. (1969). *Piaget's Theory of Intellectual Development: An Introduction.* Englewood Cliffs, NJ: Prentice-Hall.

Gladwin, T. (1964). Culture and logical process. In N. Goodenough (Ed.), *Explorations in Cultural Anthropology: Essays in Honor of George Peter Murdoch.* New York: McGraw-Hill.

Glass, D.C. (1964). Changes in linking as a means of reducing cognitive discrepancies between self-esteem and aggression. *Journal of Personality, 32,* 531–549.

Gollaher, D. (1995). *Voice for the Mad: The Life of Dorothea Dix.* New York: The Free Press.

Goodenough, F.L. (1932). Expression of the emotions in a blind-deaf child. *Journal of Abnormal and Social Psychology, 27,* 328–333.

Goodman, B. (1994). *When the Body Speaks Its Mind: A Psychiatrist Probes the Mysteries of Hypochondria and Munchausen's Syndrome.* New York: G.P. Putnam's Sons.

Gottesman, I.I. (1991). *Schizophrenia Genesis: The Origins of Madness.* New York: W.H. Freeman.

Gottesman, I.I., & Shields, J. (1982). *Schizophrenia: The Epigenetic Puzzle.* Cambridge, England: Cambridge University Press.

Gough, H. (1987). *California Psychological Inventory: Administrator's Guide.* Palo Alta: Consulting Psychologists Press.

References

Grambs, J.D. (1989). *Women Over Forty: Visions and Realities* (Rev. ed.). New York: Springer.

_____. (1990). *MMPI–2: Assessing Personality and Psychopathology.* New York: Oxford University Press.

Gray, Paul. (1999, January 11). Cursed by eugenics. *Time.*

Gray, Peter. (1999). *Psychology.* New York, New York: Worth Publishers.

Green, D.M., & Swets, J.A. (1996). *Signal Detection Theory and Psychophysics.* New York: Wiley.

Greenblatt, M., et al. (Eds.). (1965). *Drugs and Social Therapy in Chronic Schizophrenia.* Springfield, IL: Charles C. Thomas.

Gregory, R.L. (1970). *The Intelligent Eye.* New York: McGraw-Hill, (paper).

Guilford, J.P. (1959). *Personality.* New York: McGraw-Hill.

Gura, T. (1997). Obesity sheds its secrets. *Science, 275,* 751–753.

Gustavson, C.R., et al. (1974). Coyote predation control by aversive conditioning. *Science, 184,* 581–583.

H

Haber, R.N. (1970). How we remember what we see. *Scientific American, 222,* 104–112.

Hall, C.S. (1954). *A Primer of Freudian Psychology.* Cleveland: World, (paper).

Hall, C.S., & van de Castle, R.L. (1966). *The Content Analysis of Dreams.* New York: Appleton-Century-Crofts.

Hall, E.T. (1959). *The Silent Language.* Garden City, NY: Doubleday.

_____. (1966). *The Hidden Dimension.* Garden City, NY: Doubleday.

Hall, E.T., & Hall, M. (1990). *Understanding Cultural Differences.* Yarmouth, ME: Intercultural Press, Inc.

Hamilton, D.L., & Sherman, S.J. (1989). Illusory correlations: Implications for stereotype theory and research. In D. Bar-Tal, et al. (Eds.), *Stereotyping and Prejudice: Changing Conceptions.* New York: Springer-Verlag.

Haney, C., & Zimbardo, P. (1975). The socialization into criminality: On becoming a prisoner and guard. In J.L. Trapp & F.L. Levine (Eds.), *Law, Justice and the Individual in Society: Psychological and Social Issues.* New York: Holt, Rinehart and Winston.

Harkins, E.B. (1978). Effect of empty nest transition on self-report of psychological and physical well-being. *Journal of Marriage and the Family, 40,* 549–556.

Harlow, H.F. (1949). The formation of learning sets. *Psychological Review, 56,* 51–65.

_____. (1961). The development of affectional patterns in infant monkeys. In B.M. Foss (Ed.), *Determinants of Infant Behavior,* (pp. 75–100). New York: Wiley.

Harlow, H.F., & Zimmerman, R.R. (1959). Affectional responses in the infant monkey. *Science, 140,* 421–432.

Harris, B. (1979). Whatever happened to little Albert? *American Psychologist, 34,* 151–160.

Harris, C.S. (1978). *Fact Book on Aging: A Profile of America's Older Population.* Washington, DC: National Council on the Aging.

Harris, J.R. (1998). *The Nurture Assumption: Why Children Turn Out the Way They Do.* New York: The Free Press.

Harris, M.J., Milich, R., Corbitt, E.M., Hoover, D.W., & Brady, M. (1992). Self-fulfilling effects of stigmatizing information on children's social interactions. *Journal of Personality and Social Psychology, 63,* 41–50.

Harrison, R.V. (1976). Job demands and worker health: Person-environment misfit. *Dissertation Abstracts International, 37,* 1035.

Hartup, W.W. (1970). Peer interaction and Social organization. In P.H. Mussen (Ed.), *Carmichael's Manual of Child Psychology, Vol. 3.* New York: Wiley.

Hassett, J. (1978). *A Primer of Psychophysiology.* San Francisco: Freeman.

Hatfield, E., & Walster, G. (1981). *A New Look at Love.* Reading, MA: Addison-Wesley.

Hathaway, S.R., & McKinley, J.C. (1940). A multiphasic personality schedule (Minnesota): I. construction of the schedule. *Journal of Psychology, 10,* 249–254.

Havighurst, R.J. (1972). *Developmental Tasks and Education* (3rd ed.). New York: McKay.

Hays, W.L. (1963). *Statistics for Psychologists.* New York: Holt, Rinehart and Winston.

Hebb, D.O. (1974). What psychology is about. *American Psychologist, 29,* 71–79.

Heider, F. (1958). *The Psychology of Interpersonal Relationships.* New York: John Wiley.

Herrnstein, R. (1971). I.Q. *Atlantic, 228,* 43–64.

Herron, J. (1976, March). Southpaws: How different are they? *Psychology Today,* 50–56.

Hess, E.H. (1958). 'Imprinting' in animals. *Scientific American, 198,* 81–90.

_____. (1972). 'Imprinting' in a natural laboratory. *Scientific American, 227,* 24–31.

Hess, R., & Torney, J. (1967). *The Development of Political Attitudes in Children.* Chicago: Aldine.

Higgins-Trenk, A., & Gaite, A.J.H. (1971). Elusiveness of formal operational thought in adolescents. *Proceedings of the Seventy-ninth Annual Convention of the American Psychological Association.*

Hilgard, E.R. (1965). *Hypnotic Susceptibility.* New York: Harcourt Brace Jovanovich.

_____. (1986). *Divided Consciousness: Multiple Controls in Human Thought and Action* (expanded ed.). New York: Wiley-Interscience.

_____. (1987). *Psychology in America: A Historical Survey.* New York: Harcourt Brace Jovanovich.

Hiroto, D.S. (1972). Locus of control and learned helplessness. *Journal of Experimental Psychology, 102,* 187–193.

Hofer, P. (1991). The lawyer-psychologist. In R. Gifford (Ed.), *Applied Psychology: Variety and Opportunity.* Boston: Allyn and Bacon.

Hoffman, B. (1962). *The Tyranny of Testing.* New York: Collier, (paper).

Holden, C. (1980). Identical twins reared apart. *Science, 207,* 1323–1328.

Holland, G.A. (1973). Transactional analysis. In R. Corsini (Ed.), *Current Psychotherapies,* (pp. 353–400). Itasca, IL: Peacock.

Hollon, S.D., & Beck, A.T. (1986). Cognitive and cognitive-behavioral therapies. In S.L. Garfield & A.E. Bergin (Eds.), *Psychotherapy and Behavior Change* (3rd ed.). New York: Wiley.

Holmes, D. (1991). *Abnormal Psychology.* New York: HarperCollins Publishers.

Holmes, D.L., & Morrison, F.J. (1979). *The Child: An Introduction to Developmental Psychology.* Monterey, CA: Brooks/Cole.

Holmes, D.S., & Roth, D.L. (1988). Effects of aerobic exercise on cardiomuscular activity during psychological stress. *Journal of Psychosomatic Research, 32,* 469–474.

Holmes, T.H., & Rahe, R.H. (1967). The social readjustment scale. *Journal of Psychosomatic Research, 11,* 213.

Honig, W.H. (Ed.). (1966). *Operant Behavior: Areas of Research and Application.* New York: Appleton-Century-Crofts.

Horn, J.L. (1982). The aging of human abilities. In *Handbook of Developmental Psychology,* (pp. 847–870). Englewood Cliffs, NJ: Prentice Hall.

Horner, M.S. (1970). Femininity and successful achievement: A basic inconsistency. In J. Bardwick, et al. (Eds.), *Feminine Personality and Conflict.* Belmont, CA: Brooks/Cole.

_____. (1972). Towards an understanding of achievement-related conflicts in women. *Journal of Social Issues, 28,* 157–175.

Horney, K. (1937). *The Neurotic Personality in Our Time.* New York: Norton.

Horrocks, J.E., & Benimoff, M. (1967). Isolation from the peer group during adolescence. *Adolescence, 2,* 41–52.

_____. (1981). *Work Stress and Social Support.* Reading, MA: Addison-Wesley.

Horrocks, J.E., Landis, K.R., & Umberson, D. (1988). Social relationships and health. *Science, 241,* 540–545.

Hovland C., Lumsdaine, A., & Sheffield, F. (1949). *Experiments on Mass Communication.* Princeton, NJ: Princeton University Press.

Hovland, C., & Sears, R. (1940). Minor studies of aggression: Correlation of lynching with economic indices. *Journal of Psychology, 9,* 301–310.

Hrushesky, W. (1994 July/August). Timing is everything. *The Sciences,* 32–37.

Hubel, D.H., & Wiesel, T.N. (1962). Receptive fields, binocular interaction, and functional architecture in the cat's visual cortex. *Journal of Physiology, 160,* 106–154.

Hull, C. (1943). *Principles of Behavior: An Introduction to Behavior Theory.* New York: Appleton-Century-Crofts.

Hunt, M. (1993). *The Story of Psychology.* New York: Doubleday.

Huston, A., et al. (1981). Communicating more than content: Formal features of children's television programs. *Journal of Communication, 31,* 32–48.

Huston, A., Watkins, B.A., & Kunkel, D. (1989). Public policy and children's television. *American Psychologist, 44,* 424–433.

Hyde, J., & Linn, M. (1988). Gender differences in verbal ability: A meta-analysis. *Psychological Bulletin, 104,* 53–69.

I

Inhelder, B. (1969). Memory and intelligence in the child. In D. Elkind & J.F. Flavell (Eds.), *Studies in Cognitive Development,* (pp. 337–364). New York: Oxford University Press.

Inhelder, B., & Piaget, J. (1964). *The Early Growth of Logic in the Child.* New York: Harper & Row.

Itard, J.M.G. (1894). *The Wild Boy of Aveyron.* New York: Appleton-Century-Crofts.

Izard, C.E. (1971). *The Face of Emotion.* New York: Appleton-Century-Crofts.

_____. (1972). *Patterns of Emotions: A New Analysis of Anxiety and Depression.* New York: Academic Press.

J

Jackson, R., Creemers, J., Ohagi, S., Raffin-Sanson, M., Sanders, L., Montague, C., Hutton, J., & O'Rahilly, S. (1997). Obesity and impaired prohormone processing associated with mutations in the human prohormone convertase 1 gene. *Nature Genetics, 16,* 303–306.

James, W. (1890). *Principles of Psychology.* New York: Holt, Rinehart and Winston.

John, O.P. (1990). The big five factor taxonomy: Dimensions of personality in the natural language and in questionnaires. In L.A. Pervin (Ed.), *Handbook of Personality Theory and Research,* (pp. 67–100). New York: Guilford Press.

Johnson, L.D. (1992). *Summary of the 1991 Drug Study Results,* press release. Ann Arbor, MI: Institute for Social Research, University of Michigan.

Jones, E.E. (1990). *Interpersonal Perception.* New York: W.H. Freeman.

Jones, E.E., & Davis, K.E. (1965). From acts to dispositions: The attribution process in person perception. In Leonard Berkowitz (Ed.), *Advances in Experimental Social Psychology,* Vol. 2, (pp. 219–266). New York: Academic Press.

Jones, E.E., & Nisbett, R.E. (1972). The actor and the observer: Different perceptions of the cause of behavior. In E.E. Jones, et al. (Eds.), *Attribution: Perceiving the Causes of Behavior.* Morristown, NJ: General Learning Press.

Jones, M.C. (1924). The elimination of children's fears. *Journal of Experimental Psychology, 29,* 383–390.

_____. (1965). Psychological correlates of somatic development. *Child Development, 36,* 899–911.

Jones, M.C., Albert, P., & Watson, J.B. (1974). *American Psychologist,* (August), 581–583.

Jouvet, M. (1967). The stages of sleep. *Scientific American, 216,* 62–72.

Jung, C.G. (1963). *Memories, Dreams, Reflections.* (A. Jaffe, Ed., R. & C. Winston, Trans.). New York: Pantheon.

K

Kalat, J.W. (1992). *Biological Psychology* (4th ed.). Belmont, CA: Wadsworth Publishing Company.

_____. (1999). *Introduction to Psychology.* Belmont, CA: Wadsworth Publishing Company.

Kaplan, B. (Ed.). (1964). *The Inner World of Mental Illness.* New York: Harper & Row, (paper).

Kaplan, H.I., & Saddock, B.J. (1985). *Modern Synopsis of Comprehensive Textbook of Psychiatry* (4th ed.). Baltimore: Williams & Wilkins.

Karasek, R., & Theorell, T. (1990). *Healthy Work: Stress, Productivity, and the Reconstruction of Working Life.* New York: Basic Books.

Karraker, K.H., & Stern, M. (1990). Infant physical attractiveness and facial expression: Effects on adult perception. *Basic and Applied Psychology, 11,* 371–385.

Kelley, H.H. (1950). The warm-cold variable in first impressions of persons. *Journal of Personality, 18,* 431–439.

_____. (1967). Attribution theory in social psychology. In D. Levine (Ed.), *Nebraska Symposium on Motivation, Vol. 15,* (pp. 192–238). Lincoln, NE: University of Nebraska Press.

Kelley, G.A. (1958). The theory and technique of assessment. *Annual Review of Psychology, 9,* 323–352.

_____. (1991). *The Psychology of Personal Constructs, Volume One: A Theory of Personality.* London: Routledge.

Kelman, H.C. (1961). Processes of opinion change. *Public Opinion Quarterly, 21,* 57–78.

Kelman, H.C., & Hovland, C.I. (1953). 'Reinstatement' of the communicator in delayed measurement of opinion change. *Journal of Abnormal and Social Psychology, 48,* 327–335.

Kendrick, D. (1987). Gender, genes, and the social environment. In F.L. Denmark & M.A. Pauldi (Eds.), *Psychology of Women: A Handbook of Issues and Theories.* Westport, CT: Greenwood Press.

Kessler, R.C., & McRae, J.A. (1981). Trends in the relationship between sex and psychological distress. *American Sociological Review, 46,* 443–452.

Kimmel, D.C. (1980). *Adulthood and Aging* (2nd ed.). New York: Wiley.

Kissin, B. (1986). *Conscious and Unconscious Programs in the Brain.* New York: Plenum Press.

Klapper, J.T. (1960). *The Effects of Mass Communications.* New York: Free Press.

Kleitman, N. (1960, November). Patterns of dreaming. *Scientific American, 203,* 82–88.

_____. (1963). *Sleep and Wakefulness* (rev. ed.). Chicago: University of Chicago Press.

Klüver, H., & Bucy, P.C. (1937). Psychic blindness and other symptoms following bilateral temporal lobectomy in rhesus monkeys. *American Journal of Physiology, 119,* 532–535.

Koffka, K. (1963). *Principles of Gestalt Psychology*. New York: Harcourt Brace Jovanovich.

Kohlberg, L. (1968, September). The child as moral philosopher. *Psychology Today, 2,* 25–30.

_____. (1969a). The development of children's orientations toward a moral order: I. sequence in the development of moral thought. *Vita Humana, 6,* 11–33.

_____. (1969b). Stage and sequence: The cognitive-developmental approach to socialization. In D.A. Goslin (Ed.), *Handbook of Socialization Theory and Research*. Chicago: Rand-McNally.

Kohlberg, L., & Kramer, R. (1969). Continuities and discontinuities in child and adult moral development. *Human Development, 12,* 93–120.

Kohlberg, L., & Tunel, E. (1971). *Research in Moral Development: The Cognitive-Developmental Approach*. New York: Holt, Rinehart and Winston.

Kohler, W. (1976). *The Mentality of Apes*. New York: Liveright.

Kolata, G. (1993, February). Does brain exercise work? *Reader's Digest, 142,* 108–110.

Krantzler, M. (1973). *Creative Divorce*. New York: Evans.

Krosnick, J.A., & Alwin, D.F. (1989). Aging and susceptibility to attitude change. *Journal of Personality and Social Psychology, 57,* 416–425.

Kübler-Ross, E. (1969). *On Death and Dying*. New York: Macmillan.

L

Lachman, S. (1996). Processes in perception: Psychological transformations of highly structured stimulus material. *Perceptual and Motor Skills, 83,* 411–418.

Lakoff, R. (1973). Language and women's place. *Language and Society, 2,* 45–79.

Lange, C.G., & James, W. (1922). *The Emotions*. (K. Dunlap, Ed., I.A. Haupt, Trans.). Baltimore: Williams & Wilkins.

Lashley, K.S. (1929). *Brain Mechanisms and Intelligence*. Chicago: University of Chicago Press.

Lau, R.R., & Russell, D. (1980). Attributions in the sports pages. *Journal of Personality and Social Psychology, 39,* 29–38.

Lauer, J., & Lauer, R. (1985). Marriages made to last. *Psychology Today, 16, (6),* 22–26.

Lazarus, R.H. (1993). From psychological stress to the emotions: A history of changing outlooks. *Annual Review of Psychology, 44,* 1–21.

Lazarus, R.S., DeLongis, A., Folkman, S., & Gruen, R. (1985). Stress and adaptational outcomes: The problem of confounded measures. *American Psychologist, 40,* 770–779.

Lazarus, R.S., et al. (1965). The principle of short-circuiting of threat: Further evidence. *Journal of Personality, 3,* 622–635.

Learman, L.A., Avorn, J., Everitt, D.E., & Rosenthal, R. (1990). Pygmalion in the nursing home: The effects of caregiver expectations on the patient outcomes. *Journal of the American Geriatrics Society, 38,* 797–803.

Leavitt, H.J. (1951). Some effects of certain communication patterns on group performance. *Journal of Abnormal Social Psychology, 46,* 38–50.

Lerner, M.J. (1980). *The Belief in a Just World: A Fundamental Delusion*. New York: Plenum Press.

Levinson, D.J. (1978, May 1). Living with dying. *Newsweek,* 52–61.

_____. (1986). A conception of adult development. *American Psychologist, 41,* 31.

Levinson, D.J., Darrow, C.M., Klein, E.G., Levinson, M.H., & McKee, B. (1978). *The Seasons of a Man's Life*. New York: Alfred A. Knopf.

Levy, J. (1985, May). Right brain, left brain: Fact and fiction. *Psychology Today.*

Levy, S. (1997, May 5). Man vs. machine. *Newsweek.*

Lichtman, A., Dimen, K., & Martin, B. (1995). Systematice or intrahippocampal cannabinoid administration impairs spatial memory in rats. *Psychopharmacology, 119,* 282–290.

Liebert, R.M., & Spiegler, M.D. (1994). *Personality: Strategies and Issues* (7th ed.). Pacific Grove: Brooks/Cole.

Lifton, R.J. (1963). *Thought Reform and the Psychology of Totalism: A Study of Brainwashing in China*. New York: Norton. (paper).

Locke, E.A., Latham, G.P., & Erez, M. (1988). The determinants of goal commitment. *Academy of Management Review, 13,* 23–29.

Loftus, E. (1974). Reconstructing memory: The incredible eyewitness. *Psychology Today, 8, 7,* 116–119.

_____. (1979). *Eyewitness Testimony*. Cambridge, MA: Harvard University Press.

_____. (1980a). Trial by data: Psychological research as legal evidence. *American Psychologist, 35,* 270–283.

_____. (1980b). *Memory: Surprising New Insights Into How We Remember and Why We Forget*. Reading, MA: Addison-Wesley.

Loftus, E., & Loftus, G.R. (1980). On the performance of stored information in the human brain. *American Psychologist, 35,* 409–420.

Loftus, E., & Palmer, J.C. (1974). Reconstruction of automobile destruction: The influence of the wording of a question. *Journal of Verbal Learning and Verbal Behavior, 13,* 585–589.

Longo, L.C., & Ashmore, R.D. (1995). The looks-personality relationship: Global self-orientations as shared precursors of subjective physical attractiveness and self-ascribed traits. *Journal of Applied Social Psychology, 25,* 371–398.

Loranger, A.W., Prout, C.T., & White, M.A. (1961). The placebo effect in psychiatric drug research. *Journal of the American Medical Association, 176 (11),* 920–925.

Lorayne, H., & Lucas, J. (1974). *The Memory Book*. New York: Ballantine. (paper).

Lorenz, K.Z. (1972). *Studies in Animal and Human Behavior,* trans. by Robert Martin, 2 vols. Cambridge, MA: Harvard University Press.

Lovaas, O.I., et al. (1967, August). Establishment of imitation and its use for the development of complex behavior in schizophrenic children. *Behavior Research and Therapy, 5,* 171–181.

Lovaas, O.I., Koegel, R.L., Simmons, J.Q., & Long, J.S. (1973). Some generalizations and follow-up measures on autistic children in behavior therapy. *Journal of Applied Behavior Analysis, 6* (1973): 131–165.

Lubin, B., Larsen, R.M., & Matarazzo, J.D. (1984). Patterns of psychological test usage in the United States: 1935–1982. *American Psychologist, 39,* 451–454.

Luce, G.G., & Segal, J. (1966). *Sleep*. New York: Coward, McCann & Geoghegan.

Luria, A.R. (1968). *The Mind of a Mnemonist*. New York: Basic Books.

Lykken, D.T. (1974). Psychology and the lie detector industry. *American Psychologist, 29,* 725–739.

_____. (1988). Detection of guilty knowledge: A commitment on Forman and McCauley. *Journal of Applied Psychology, 73,* 303–304.

M

Maccoby, E.E. (1992). The role of parents in the socialization of children: An historical overview. *Developmental Psychology, 28,* 1006–1017.

Maccoby, E.E., & Martin, J. (1983). Socialization in the context of the family. In P. Mussen & E.M. Hetherington (Eds.), *Handbook of Child Psychology: Socialization, Personality, and Social Development, Vol. 4* (4th ed.). New York: Wiley.

Maccoby, E.E., & Masters, J.C. (1970). Attachment and dependency. In P.H. Mussen (Ed.), *Manual of Child Psychology, Vol. 2,* (pp. 159–260). New York: Wiley.

MacKay, C. (1932). *Extraordinary Popular Delusions and the Madness of Crowds.* New York: Farrar, Straus & Giroux.

Madison, P. (1969). *Personality Development in College.* Reading, MA: Addison-Wesley.

Marcia, J.E. (1966). Development and validation of ego identity status. *Journal of Personality and Social Psychology, 3,* 551–558.

Marlatt, G., & Rohsenow, D. (1981, December). The think-drink effect. *Psychology Today, 15,* 60–70.

Maslow, A.H. (1970). *Motivation and Personality* (rev. ed.). New York: Harper and Row.

Masters, W.H., & Johnson, V.E. (1970). *Human Sexual Inadequacy.* Boston: Little, Brown.

Matlin, M.W. (1993). *The Psychology of Women* (2nd ed.). Fort Worth, TX: Harcourt Brace Jovanovich.

Matthews, K., Scheier, M., Brunson, B., & Carducci, B. (1989). Why do unpredictable events lead to reports of physical symptoms? In T.W. Miller (Ed.), *Stressful Life Events.* Madison, CT: International Studies Press.

May, R. (1969). *Existential Psychology* (2nd ed.). New York: Random House.

_____. (1977). *The Meaning of Anxiety.* Rev. ed. New York: Norton.

Mayer, J.D., & Salovey, P. (1997). What is emotional intelligence? In P. Salovey & D. Sluyter (Eds.), *Emotional Development and Emotional Intelligence: Implications for Educators.* New York: Basic Books.

McCarley, R.W. (1978, December). Where dreams come from: A new theory. *Psychology Today, 12,* 54–65.

McClelland, D.C. (1958). Risk taking in children with high and low need for achievement. In J.W. Atkinson (Ed.), *Motives in Fantasy, Action, and Society,* (pp. 306–321). Princeton, NJ: Van Nostrand.

_____. (1965). Need achievement and entrepreneurship: A longitudinal study. *Journal of Personality and Social Psychology, 1,* 389–392.

McClelland, D.C., et al. (1953). *The Achievement Motive.* New York: Appleton-Century-Crofts.

McClelland, D.C., & Harris, T.G. (1971, January). To know why men do what they do: A conversation with David C. McClelland. *Psychology Today, 4,* 35–39.

McCoy, K. (1982). *Coping With Teenage Depression.* New York: Mosby.

McDougall, W. (1908). *Social Psychology.* New York: Putnam.

McGinnis, J., & Foege, W. (1993). Actual causes of death in the United States. *Journal of the American Medical Association (JAMA), 270,* 2208.

McGuire, W.J. (1970, February). A vaccine for brainwash. *Psychology Today, 3,* 36–39, 62–64.

McIntosh, D.N. (1996). Facial feedback hypothesis: Evidence, implications, and directions. *Motivation and Emotion, 20,* 121–147.

McMillan, J., Clifton, A., McGrath, D., & Gale, W. (1977). Woman's language: Uncertainty or interpersonal sensitivity and emotionality? *Sex Roles, 3,* 545–560.

Mead, M. (1935). *Sex and temperament in three primitive societies.* New York: William Morrow & Co.

_____. (1973). *Coming of Age in Samoa : A Psychological Study of Primitive Youth for Western Civilization.* New York: William Morrow & Co.

Mediascope National Television Violence Study (NTVS). (1996). Studio City, CA: Mediascope, Inc.

Mednick, M., & Thomas, V. (1993). Women and the psychology of achievement: A view from the eighties. In F.L. Denmark & M.A. Paludi (Eds.), *Psychology of Women: A Handbook of Issues and Theories.* Westport, CT: Greenwood Press.

Mellinger, G.D., Balter, M.B., & Uhlenhuth, E.H. (1985). Insomnia and its treatment: Prevalence and correlates. *Archives of General Psychiatry, 42,* 225–232.

Melzack, R., (1990). Phantom limbs and the concept of a neuromatrix. *Trends in Neurosciences, 13,* 88–92.

Melzack, R., & Wall, P.D. (1965). Pain mechanisms: A new theory. *Science, 150,* 971–979.

Miedzian, M. (1991). *Boys Will Be Boys: Breaking the Link Between Masculinity and Violence.* New York: Doubleday.

Milgram, S. (1964). *Obedience to Authority.* New York: Harper & Row.

_____. (1965). Some conditions of obedience and disobedience to authority. *Human Relations, 18,* 56–76.

_____. (1970). The experience of living in cities. *Science, 167,* 1461–1468.

_____. (1974). *Obedience to Authority.* New York: Harper and Row.

Miller, G.A. (1956). The magical number seven, plus or minus two: Some limits on our capacity for processing information. *Psychological Review, 63,* 81–97.

Miller, G.R., & Schneider, R. (1970). The use of a token system in Project Headstart. *Journal of Applied Behavior Analysis, 3,* 213–220.

Miller, N.E. (1944). Experimental studies of conflict. In J. Hunt (Ed.), *Personality and the Behavior Disorders.* New York: Ronald Press.

Miller, S., & Seligman, M. (1982). The reformulated model of helplessness and depression: Evidence and theory. In N. W. Newfield (Ed.), *Psychological Stress and Psychopathology.* New York: McGraw-Hill.

Miskhin, M., Saunders, R., & Murray, E. (1984). Further evidence that amygdala and hippocampus contribute equally to recognition memory. *Neuropsychologia, 22,* 785–796.

Montague, C., Farooqi, I., Whitehead, J., Soos, M., Rau, H., Wareham, C., Sewter, C., Digby, J., Mohammed, S., Hurst, J., Cheetham, C., Earley, A., Barnett, A., Prins, J., & O'Rahilly, S. (1997). Congenital leptin deficiency is associated with severe early-onset obesity in humans. *Nature, 387,* 903–908.

Morris, C.G. (1990). *Contemporary Psychology and Effective Behavior* (7th ed.). New York: HarperCollins Publishers.

_____. (1996). *Psychology: An Introduction.* Upper Saddle River, New Jersey: Prentice Hall.

Moscovici, S. (1985). Social influence and conformity. In G. Lindsay & E. Aronson (Eds.), *Handbook of Social Psychology* (3rd ed.). New York: Random House.

Motley, M.T. (1985). Slips of the tongue. *Scientific American, 253,* 116–127.

Mowrer, O.H., & Mowrer, M. (1938). Enuresis: A method for its study and treatment. *American Journal of Orthopsychiatry, 8,* 436–459.

Muchinsky, P.M. (1993). *Psychology Applied to Work* (4th ed.). Pacific Grove, CA: Brooks/Cole Publishing Company.

Mulligan, T., & Moss, C.R. (1991, February). Sexuality and aging in male veterans: A cross-sectional study of interest, ability, and activity. *Archives of Sexual Behavior, 20,* 17–25.

Murray, H.A. (1943). *Thematic Apperception Test manual.* Cambridge, MA: Harvard University Press.

Murray, H.A., et al. (1934). *Exploration in Personality.* New York: Oxford University Press.

References

Mussen, P.H. (1980). *Essentials of Child Development and Personality*. Philadelphia: Harper & Row.

Myers, D.G. (1983). *Social Psychology*. New York: McGraw-Hill.

N

Narajano, C., & Ornstein, R. (1971). *On the Psychology of Meditation*. New York: Viking.

Nathan, P.E., & Harris, S.L. (1975). *Psychopathology and Society*. New York: McGraw-Hill.

National Center for Education Statistics. (1997). Statistical analysis report: Fathers' involvement in their children's schools, October. Retrieved September 15, 1999 from the World Wide Web: http://nces.ed.gov/pubs98/fathers/

National Task Force on the Prevention and Treatment of Obesity. (1994). Weight cycling. *Journal of the American Medical Association, 272,* 1196–1202.

Neher, A. (1991). Maslow's theory of motivation: A critique. *Journal of Humanistic Psychology, 31,* 89–112.

Neugarten, B., et al. (1963). Women's attitudes toward the menopause. *Vita Humana, 6,* 140–151.

New York Times. (1958, May 19). Huxley fears new persuasion methods could subvert democratic procedures, 45.

———. (1983, April 17). Parents on the brink of child abuse get crisis aid. 1, 29.

Newcomb, T. (1943). *Personality and Social Change*. New York: Dryden Press.

Newcomb, T., et al. (1967). *Persistence and Change: Bennington College and Its Students After 25 Years*. New York: Wiley.

Nolen-Hoeksema, S. (1987). Sex differences in unipolar depression: Evidence and theory. *Psychological Bulletin, 101,* 259–282.

O

Oakes, P.J., & Turner, J.C. (1990). Is limited information processing capacity the cause of social stereotyping? *European Review of Social Psychology, 9,* 147–152.

O'Donnell, S.A. (1999). Breathe your way out of an asthma attack. *Prevention, 51,* 36.

Offer, D., & Offer, J. (1975). *From Teenage to Young Manhood*. New York: Basic Books.

Offer, D., & Schonert-Reichl, K.A. (1992). Debunking the myths of adolescence: Findings from recent research. *Journal of the American Academy of Child and Adolescent Psychiatry, 31,* 1003–1013.

Office of International Criminal Justice. (1999). Gangs: Public enemy number one. Retrieved September 2, 1999 from the World Wide Web: http://oicj.acsp.uic.edu/

Olds, J., & Olds, M.E. (1965). Drives, rewards and the brain. In F. Barron, et al. (Eds.), *New Directions in Psychology II*. New York: Holt, Rinehart and Winston.

O'Leary, A. (1990). Stress, emotion, and human immune function. *Psychological Bulletin, 108,* 363–382.

Orne, M.T. (1959). The nature of hypnosis: Artifact and essence. *Journal of Abnormal and Social Psychology, 58,* 277–299.

P

Palmore, E. (1977). What can the USA learn from Japan about aging? In S.H. Zarit (Ed.), *Readings in Aging and Death: Contemporary Perspectives*. New York: Harper & Row.

Paludi, M.A. (1984). Psychometric properties and underlying assumptions of four objective measures of fear of success. *Sex Roles, 10,* 765–781.

Parke, R., & Lewis, N. (1980). The family in context: A multilevel interactional analysis of child abuse. In R.W. Henderson (Ed.), *Parent-Child Interaction: Theory, Research and Prospect*. New York: Academic Press.

Parke, R., & Slaby, R. (1983). Aggression: A multilevel analysis. In P.H. Mussen & M.E. Hetherington (Eds.), *Handbook of Child Psychology. Vol. 14. Socialization, Personality and Social Development* (4th ed.). New York: Wiley.

Pavlov, I.P. (1927). *Conditioned Reflexes*. (G.V. Anrep, Trans.). London: Oxford University Press.

Payne, W.A., Hahn, D.B., & Pinger, R.R. (1991). *Drugs: Issues for Today*. St. Louis, MO: Mosby-Year Book, Inc.

Peachey, J.E., & Naranjo, C.A. (1983). The use of disulfiram and other alcohol-sensitizing drugs in the treatment of alcoholism. *Research Advances in Alcohol and Drug Problems, 7,* 397–431.

Pearlson, G.D., Kim, W.S., Kubos, K., Moberg, P., Jarayam, G., Bascom, M., Chase, G., Goldfinger, A., & Tune, L. (1989). Ventricle-brain ratio, computed tomographic density, and brain area in 50 schizophrenics. *Archives of General Psychiatry, 46.*

Pellegrini, A.D. (1987). Rough and tumble play: Developmental and educational significance. *Educational Psychologist, 22,* 23–43.

Penfield, W. (1969). Consciousness, memory, and man's conditioned reflexes. In K.H. Pribram (Ed.), *On the Biology of Learning*. New York: Harcourt Brace Jovanovich.

Perls, F., Hefferline, R.F., & Goodman, P. (1965). *Gestalt Therapy*. New York: Dell.

Perris, C. (1982). The distinction between bipolar and unipolar affective disorders. In E.S. Paykel (Ed.), *Handbook of Affective Disorders*. New York: Guilford Press.

Peterson, A.C. (1988). Adolescent development. *Annual Review of Psychology, 39,* 583–607.

Petty, R.E., & Cacioppo, J.T. (1986). The elaboration likelihood model of persuasion. In L. Berkowitz (Ed.), *Advances in Experimental Social Psychology, Vol. 19*, (pp. 123–205). New York: Academic Press.

Pfungst, O. (1911). *Clever Hans*. New York: Holt.

Piaget, J. (1926). *The Language and Thought of the Child*. London: Routledge & Kegan Paul.

Piaget, J., & Inhelder, B. (1969). *The Development of Physical Number Concepts in Children: Maintenance and Atomism*. Stuttgart, Germany: Ernst Klett.

Pines, M. (1970, November 29). Infants are smarter than anybody thinks. *The New York Times Magazine.*

———. (1981, September). The civilizing of Genie. *Psychology Today,* 28–34.

Plomin, R. (1990). The role of inheritance in behavior. *Science, 248,* 183–188.

Plomin, R., Owen, M.J., & McGuffin, P. (1994). The genetic bias of complex human behaviors. *Science, 264,* 1733–1739.

Plotnick, R. (1999). *Introduction to Psychology*, (5th ed.). Belmont, CA: Wadsworth Publishing Company.

Pokorney, A.D., & Prein, R.F. (1974). Lithium in treatment and prevention of affective disorder. *Diseases of the Nervous System, 35,* 327–333.

Pope, H., & Yurgelun-Todd, D. (1996). The residual cognitive effects of heavy marijuana use in college students. *Journal of the American Medical Association, 275,* 521–527.

Pressy, S.L. (1926). Experiments looking toward fundamental changes in instructional methods in professional courses for teachers. *Studies in Education, 15,* 45–49.

Prevent Child Abuse America. (1996). The relationship between domestic violence and child abuse. Retrieved August 16, 1999 from the World Wide Web: http://www.childabuse.org/

References

Q

Quinn, R., Seashore, S., Kahn, R., Mangione, T., Campbell, D., Staines, G., & McCullough, M. (1971). *Survey of Working Conditions*. Washington, DC: U.S. Government Printing Office.

R

Rahe, R.H. (1975). Life changes and near-future illness reports. In L. Levi (Ed.), *Emotions: Their Parameters and Measurement*. New York: Raven Press.

Raichle, M.E. (1994). Visualizing the mind. *Scientific American, 270,* 58–64.

Ray, O., & Ksir, C. (1993). *Drugs, Society, & Human Behavior* (6th ed.). St. Louis: Mosby-Year Book, Inc.

Reid, D.W., Haas, G., & Hawkings, D. (1977). Locus of desired control and positive self-concept of the elderly. *Journal of Gerontology, 32,* 441–450.

Reinisch, J., & Beasley, R. (1990). *The Kinsey Institute New Report on Sex*. New York: St. Martin's Press.

Reisman, D., Glazer, N., & Denney, R. (1953). *The Lonely Crowd*. New Haven, Conn.: Yale University Press, (paper).

Reisman, J., & Shorr, S. (1978). Friendship claims and expectations among children and adults. *Child Development, 49,* 913–916.

Reppucci, N.D., & Saunders, J.T. (1974). Social psychology of behavior modification. *American Psychologist, 29,* 649–660.

Reynolds, G.S. (1968). *A Primer of Operant Conditioning*. Glenview, IL: Scott, Foresman.

Rhine, J.B. (1964). *Extra-Sensory Perception*. Boston: Branden.

Rhine, L.E. (1961). *Hidden Channels of the Mind*. New York: Apollo, (paper).

Rhoads, K. (1997). Cults: Questions & answers. Retrieved August 16, 1999 from the World Wide Web: http://www.influenceatwork.com/

Rice, F.P. (1990). *The Adolescent: Development, Relationships, and Culture* (6th ed.). Boston: Allyn & Bacon, pp. 434–441.

———. (1992a). *The Adolescent: Development, Relationships, and Culture* (7th ed.). Boston: Allyn & Bacon, pp. 410–419.

———. (1992b). *Human Development: A Life-Span Approach*. Englewood Cliffs, NJ: Prentice Hall.

———. (1993). *Intimate Relationships, Marriages, and Families* (2nd ed.). Mountain View, CA: Mayfield Publishing Company.

———. (1995). *Human Development: A Life-Span Approach*. Englewood Cliffs, NJ: Prentice Hall.

Rice, K.G., Cunningham, T.J., & Young, M.B. (1997). Attachment to parents, social competence, and emotional well-being: A comparison of black and white late adolescents. *Journal of Counseling Psychology, 44 (1),* 89–101.

Richman, A.L., Miller, P.M., & Le Vine, R.A. (1992). Cultural and educational variations in maternal responsiveness. *Developmental Psychology, 28,* 614–621.

Rierden, J., Koff, E., & Stubbs, M. (1988). Gender, depression, and body image in early adolescents. *Journal of Early Adolescence, 8,* 109–117.

Rodin, J., & Salovey, P. (1989). Health psychology. *Annual Review of Psychology, 40,* 533–579.

Roediger, H.L., III. (1990). Implicit memory: Retention without remembering. *American Psychologist, 45,* 1043–1056.

Roethlisberger, F.J., & Dickson, W.J. (1939). *Management and the Worker*. Cambridge, MA: Harvard University Press.

Rogers, C. (1951). *Client-centered Therapy*. Boston: Houghton Mifflin.

———. (1961). *On Becoming a Person*. Boston: Houghton Mifflin.

Rogers, C.R. (1977). *On Personal Power: Inner Strength and Its Revolutionary Impact*. New York: Delacorte.

———. (1980). *A Way of Being*. Boston: Houghton Mifflin.

Rogers, D. (1977). *The Psychology of Adolescence* (3rd ed.). Englewood Cliffs, NJ: Prentice-Hall.

———. (1979). *The Adult Years: An Introduction to Aging*. Englewood Cliffs, NJ: Prentice-Hall.

Rokeach, M. (1971). Long-range experimental modification of values, attitudes, and behavior. *American Psychologist, 26,* 453–459.

Rook, K.S. (1987). Social support versus companionship: Effects on life stress, loneliness, and evaluations by others. *Journal of Personality and Social Psychology, 52,* 1132–1147.

———. (1990). Parallels in the study of social support and social strain. *Journal of Social and Clinical Psychology, 9,* 118–132.

Rosenfeld, M. (1998, March 26). Reexamining the plight of young males. *Washington Post.*

Rosenhan, D., & Seligman, M. (1984). *Abnormal Psychology*. New York: W.W. Norton and Company.

Rosenthal, R. (1966). *Environmental Effects in Behavioral Research*. New York: Appleton-Century-Crofts.

Rosenthal, R., & Rosnow, R.L. (Eds.). (1969). *Artifact in Behavioral Research*. New York: Academic Press.

Ross, L. (1977). The intuitive psychologist and his shortcomings. In L. Berkowitz (Ed.), *Advances in Experimental Social Psychology, Vol. 10.* New York: Academic Press.

Rossi, P.H. (1990). The old homeless and the new homelessness in historical perspective. *American Psychologist, 45,* 954–959.

Roth, D.L., & Holmes, D.S. (1987). Influence of aerobic exercise training and relaxation training on physical and psychologic health following stressful life events. *Psychosomatic Medicine, 49,* 355–365.

Rubin, Z. (1970). Measurement of romantic love. *Journal of Personality and Social Psychology, 16,* 265–273.

———. (1973). *Liking and Loving*. New York: Holt, Rinehart and Winston.

Russell, J. (1994). Is there universal recognition of emotion from facial expression? A review of the cross-cultural studies. *Psychological Bulletin, 115,* 102–141.

S

Salk, L. (1962). Mother's heartbeat as an imprinting stimulus. *Transactions of the New York Academy of Sciences, 24,* 753–763.

Samuelson, R. (1997, January 22). The two-earner myth. *Washington Post.*

Sarason, I.G., & Sarason, B.R. (1980). *Abnormal Psychology* (3rd ed.). Englewood Cliffs, NJ: Prentice-Hall.

Sarbin, I., (1979). Hypnosis and psychopathology: Replacing old myths with fresh metaphors. *Journal of Abnormal Psychology, 88,* 506–526.

Sarbin, I., & Coe, W. (1972). *Hypnosis: A Social Psychological Analysis of Influence Communication*. New York: Holt, Rinehart and Winston.

Savage-Rumbaugh, E.S. (1990). Language acquisition in a nonhuman species: Implications for the innateness debate. *Developmental Psychology, 26,* 599–620.

———. (1998, January 19). Cited in S. Begley, Aping language. *Newsweek.*

Savage-Rumbaugh, E.S., Murphy, J., Sevcik, R., Brakke, K., Williams, S., & Rumbaugh, D. (1993). Language comprehension in ape and child. *Monographs of the Society for Research in Child Development, 58*(3–4).

References

Savage-Rumbaugh, E.S., Sevcik, R., Brakke, K., & Rumbaugh, D. (1992). Symbols: Their communicative use, communication, and combination by bonobos (Pan paniscus). In L.P. Lipsitt & C. Rovee-Collier (Eds.), *Advances in Infancy Research, Vol. 7,* (pp. 221–278). Norwood, NJ: Ablex.

Scarf, M. (1980). *Unfinished Business: Pressure Points in the Lives of Women.* New York: Ballentine Books.

Schachter, S. (1959). *The Psychology of Affiliation.* Stanford, CA: University Press.

_____. (1971). *Emotion, Obesity, and Crime.* New York: Academic Press.

_____. (1978). Second thoughts on biological and psychological explanations of behavior. In L. Berkowitz (Ed.), *Cognitive Theories in Social Psychology.* New York: Academic Press.

Schachter, S., & Singer, J. (1962). Cognitive, social, and physiological determinants of emotional state. *Psychological Review, 69,* 379–399.

Schaie, W.K., & Strother, C. (1968). A cross-sectional study of age changes in cognitive behavior. *Psychological Bulletin, 70,* 671–680.

Schlegal, A., & Barry, H. (1991). *Adolescence: An Anthropological Inquiry.* New York: Free Press.

Schneider, K. (1984). The cognitive basis of task choice in preschool children. *Advances in Motivation and Achievement, 3,* 57–72.

Schreiber, F.R. (1973). *Sybil.* New York: Warner.

Schulman, J., et al. (1973, May). Recipe for a jury. *Psychology Today, 6,* 37–44.

Schultes, R.E. (1976). *Hallucinogenic Plants.* New York: Golden Press.

Schwartz, A.N., & Peterson, J.A. (1979). *Introduction to Gerontology.* San Francisco: Holt, Rinehart and Winston.

Sears, D.O., Peplau, L.A., & Taylor, S.E. (1991). *Social Psychology* (7th ed.). Englewood Cliffs, NJ: Prentice-Hall.

Seeland, I.B., Klagsbrun, S.C., DeBellis, R., Kutscher, A.H., Avellanet, C., & Dennis, J. (Eds.). (1991). *The Final 48 Hours: Observations on the Last Days of Life.* Philadelphia: The Charles Press.

Seigel, R.K. (1977, October). Hallucinations. *Scientific American, 237,* 132–140.

Seligman, M.E.P. (1975). *Helplessness.* San Francisco: Freeman.

_____. (1991). *Learned Optimism.* New York: Alfred A. Knopf.

Selye, H. (1956). *The Stress of Life.* New York: McGraw-Hill.

_____. (1974). *Stress Without Distress.* Philadelphia: Lippincott.

_____. (1976). *Stress in Health and Disease.* Woburn, MA: Butterworth.

_____. (1982). History and present status of the stress concept. In L. Goldberger & S. Breznitz (Eds.), *Handbook of Stress: Theoretical and Clinical Aspects.* New York: Free Press.

Selye, H., & Cherry, L. (1978, March). On the real benefits of eustress. *Psychology Today, 11,* 60–70.

Sexton, V., & Hogan, J.D. (Eds.). (1992). *International Psychology: Views From Around the World.* Omaha: University of Nebraska Press.

Shapiro, D. (1973). Preface. In D. Shapiro, et al. (Eds.), *Biofeedback and Self-Control 1972.* Chicago: Aldine-Atherton.

Shaver, P. (1976). Questions concerning fear of success and its conceptual relatives. *Sex Roles, 2,* 305–320.

Sheehy, G. (1976). *Passages.* New York: Dutton.

Shepard, R.N., & Metzler, J.N. (1971). Mental rotation of three-dimensional objects. *Science, 171,* 701–703.

Sheppard, B.H., Hartwick, J., & Warshaw, P.R. (1988). The theory of reasoned action: A meta-analysis of past research with recommendations for modifications and future research. *Journal of Consumer Research, 15,* 325–343.

Shih, J.C. (1996, June 6). Of mice and mayhem. Cited in T. Monmaney, *Los Angeles Times,* B–2.

Simons, R.L., Whitbeck, L.B., Conger, R.D., & Wu, C.I. (1991). Intergenerational transmission of harsh parenting. *Developmental Psychology, 27,* 159–171.

Singer, J., & Singer, D. (1983). Psychologists look at television: Cognitive, developmental, personality and social policy implications. *American Psychologist, 38,* 826–834.

Singer, M.T. (1979, January). Coming out of the cults. *Psychology Today, 12,* 72–82.

Sizemore, C.C., & Pittillo, E.S. (1977). *I'm Eve.* Garden City, NY: Doubleday Books.

Skinner, B.F. (1961). *The Behavior of Organisms.* New York: Appleton-Century-Crofts.

_____. (1962). *Walden Two.* New York: Macmillan. (Original work published 1948.)

_____. (1971). *Beyond Freedom and Dignity.* New York: Knopf.

_____. (1974). *About Behaviorism.* New York: Knopf.

_____. (1983). Intellectual self-management in old age. *American Psychologist, 38,* 239–244.

Smalley, S.L. (1991). Genetic influences in autism. *Psychiatric Clinics of North America, 14,* 125–139.

Smith, D. (1982). Trends in counseling and psychotherapy. *American Psychologist, 37,* 802–809.

Smith, M.L., & Glass, G.V. (1977). Meta-analysis of psychotherapy outcome studies. *American Psychologist, 32,* 752–760.

Snellgrove, L. (1967). *Psychological Experiments and Demonstrations.* New York: McGraw-Hill.

Solomon, R.L., & Corbit, J.D. (1974). An opponent-process theory of motivation. *Psychological Review, 81,* 119–145.

Snyder, H. (1988). Juvenile arrest rates for all crimes, 1981–1997. Adapted from Snyder, H., *Juvenile Arrests 1997.* Washington, DC: Office of Juvenile Justice and Delinquency Prevention. *OJJDP Statistical Briefing Book.* Retrieved August 3, 1999 from the World Wide Web: http://ojjdp.ncjrs.org/ojstatbb/qa007.html

Spearman, C. (1904). "General intelligence" objectively determined and measured. *American Journal of Psychology, 15,* 201–293.

Sperling, G. (1960). The information available in brief visual presentations. *Psychological Monographs, 74,* no. 11.

Spirduso, W.W., & MacRae, P.G. (1990). Motor performance and aging. In J.E. Birren & K.W. Schaie (Eds.), *Handbook of the Psychology of Aging* (3rd ed.). San Diego, CA: Academic Press.

Squire, L.R. (1987). *Memory and Brain.* New York: Oxford University Press.

Stephan, C.W., & Langlois, J.H. (1984). Baby beautiful: Adult attributions of infant competence as a function of infant attractiveness. *Child Development, 55,* 576–585.

Stephens, R., Roffman, R., & Simpson, E. (1994). Treating adult marijuana dependence: A test of the relapse prevention model. *Journal of Consulting and Clinical Psychology, 62 (1),* 92–99.

Stern, G., McCants, T., & Pettine, P. (1982). Stress and illness: Controllable and uncontrollable events' relative contributions. *Personality and Social Psychology Bulletin, 8,* 140–145.

Sternberg, R. (1985). *Beyond IQ: A Triarchic Theory of Human Intelligence.* New York: Cambridge University Press.

_____. (1986). A Triangular Theory of Love. *Psychological Review, 93,* 119–135.

_____. (1988). *The Triangle of Love: Intimacy, Passion, Commitment.* New York: Basic Books.

Stogdill, R.M. (1974). *Handbook of Leadership: A Survey of Theory and Research.* New York: Free Press.

Stroebe, M., et al. (1992). Broken hearts or broken bonds: Love and death in historical perspective. *American Psychologist, 47,* 1205–1212.

Sulloway, F.J. (1996). *Born to Rebel: Birth Order, Family Dynamics, and Creative Lives.* New York: Pantheon Books.

Super, C.M., & Super, D.E. (1994). *Opportunities in Psychology Careers.* Chicago, IL: VGM Career Horizons, a division of the NTC Publishing Group.

Swann, W.B., Stein-Seroussi, A., & Gleiser, R.B. (1992). Why people self-verify. *Journal of Personality and Social Psychology, 62,* 392–401.

Szasz, T. (1966). *The Myth of Mental Illness.* New York: Harper and Row, Publishers; Dell.

T

Tanner, J.M., Whitehouse, R.H., & Takaishi, M. (1966). Standards from birth to maturity for height, weight, height velocity, and weight velocity for British children, 1965, Parts I and II. *Archives of Disease in Childhood, 41.*

Taylor, S.E. (1991). *Health Psychology* (2nd ed.). New York: McGraw-Hill.

Teigen, K. (1994). Yerkes-Dodson: A law for all seasons. *Theory and Psychology, 4*(4), 525–547.

Terman, L.M. (1916). *The Measurement of Intelligence.* Boston: Houghton Mifflin.

_____. (1973). *Stanford-Binet Intelligence Scale: Manual for the Third Revision.* Form L-M. Boston: Houghton Mifflin.

Terman, L.M., & Merrill, M.A. (1937). *Measuring Intelligence.* Boston: Houghton Mifflin.

Thomas, A., Chess, S., & Birch, H.G. (1968). *Temperament and Behavior Disorders in Children.* New York: New York University Press.

Thurstone, L.L. (1938). *Primary Mental Abilities.* Chicago: University of Chicago Press.

Treisman, A.M. (1964). Verbal cues, language, and meaning in selective listening. *American Journal of Psychology, 77,* 206–219.

Trotter, R. (1983, August). Baby face. *Psychology Today, 17,* 15–20.

Tulving, E. (1972). Episodic and semantic memory. In E. Tulving & W. Donaldson (Eds.), *Organization of Meaning.* New York: Academic Press.

Turner, P., & Gervai, J. (1995). A multidimensional study of gender typing in preschool children and their parents: Personality, attitudes, preferences, behavior, and cultural differences. *Developmental Psychology, 31,* 759–772.

U

United States Census Bureau. (1998). Nearly 70 percent of elderly widows live alone, according to U.S. Census Bureau. Washington, DC: U.S. Bureau of the Census. Retrieved September 27, 1999 from the World Wide Web: http://www.census.gov

University of Michigan's Survey Research Center. (1998). Monitoring the future. Retrieved July 19, 1999 from the World Wide Web: http://www.isr.umich.edu http://www.psych.org/public_info/insani~1.htm

V

Valvo, A. (1971). *Sight Restoration After Long-Term Blindness: The Problems and Behavior Patterns of Visual Rehabilitation.* New York: American Foundation for the Blind.

Vernon, P.E. (1987). The demise of the Stanford Binet scale. *Canadian Psychology, 28,* 251–258.

Vokey, J.R., & Read, J.D. (1985). Subliminal messages, between the devil and the media. *American Psychologist, 40,* 1231–1239.

W

Wadden, T.A., & Stunkard, A.J. (1987). Psychopathology and obesity. *Annals of the New York Academy of Science, 499,* 55–65.

Wade, C., & Cirese, S. (1991). *Human Sexuality* (2nd ed.). San Diego, CA: Harcourt Brace Jovanovich.

Wald, G. (1964). The receptors of color vision. *Science, 145,* 1007–1016.

Wallerstein, J., & Kelly, J. (1974). The effects of parental divorce: The adolescent experience. In J. Anthony & C. Koupernik (Eds.), *The Child in His Family: Children at Psychiatric Risk,* (pp. 479–505). New York: Wiley.

Walster, E., Aronson, V., Abrahams, D., & Rottman, L. (1966). Importance of physical attractiveness in dating behavior. *Journal of Personality and Social Psychology, 4,* 508–516.

Warden, C.H. (1997). Gene heats up obesity research. Cited in R. Plotnick, *Science News, 151,* 142.

Waterson, E. J., & Murray-Lyon, I.M. (1990). Preventing alcohol related birth damage: *A Review. Social Science and Medicine, 30,* 349–364.

Watkinson, B. (1990). 36- and 48-month neurobehavioral follow-up of children prenatally exposed to marijuana, cigarettes, and alcohol. *Development and Behavioral Pediatrics, 11,* 49–58.

Watson, D.L., & Tharp, R.G. (1972). *Self-directed Behavior: Self-modification for Personal Adjustment.* Monterey, CA: Brooks/Cole.

Watson, J.B. (1970). *Behaviorism.* New York: Norton. (Original work published 1924.)

Watson, J.B., & Rayner, R. (1920). Conditioned emotional reactions. *Journal of Experimental Psychology, 3,* 1–14.

Wechsler, D. (1974). *Wechsler Intelligence Scale for Children Revised.* New York: Psychological Corp.

_____. (1981). *Manual for the Wechsler Adult Intelligence Scale Revised.* New York: Psychological Corp.

Weiss, D.J., & Vale, C.D. (1987). Adaptive testing. *Applied Psychology: An International Review, 36.*

Weiss, J.M. (1971). Effects of coping behavior in different warning-signal conditions on stress pathology in rats. *Journal of Comparative and Physiological Psychology, 77,* 1–13.

_____. (1972). Influence of Psychological Variables on Stress-Induced Pathology. In *Physiology, Emotion and Psychosomatic Illness (Ciba Foundation Symposium 8).* New York: American Elsevier.

White, B.L. (1969). Child development research: An edifice without a foundation. *Merrill-Palmer Quarterly of Behavior and Development, 15,* 49–79.

White, R. (1959). Motivation reconsidered: The concept of competence. *Psychological Review, 66,* 297–333.

_____. (1964). *The Abnormal Personality.* New York: Ronald.

_____. (1966). *Lives in Progress: A Study of the Natural Growth of Personality* (2nd ed.). New York: Holt, Rinehart and Winston.

Whorf, B. (1956). *Language, Thought, and Reality.* New York: Wiley.

Williamson, J.B., Evans, L., & Munley, A. (1980). *Aging and Society.* New York: Holt, Rinehart and Winston.

Wilson, E.O. (1975). *Sociobiology: A New Synthesis.* Cambridge, MA: Harvard University Press.

References

Wilson, T.D., Kraft, D., & Dunn, D.S. (1989). The disruptive effects of explaining attitudes: The moderating effects of knowledge about the attitude object. *Journal of Experimental Social Psychology, 25,* 379–400.

Wispe, L., & Drambarean, N. (1953). Physiological need, word frequency, and visual duration thresholds. *Journal of Experimental Psychology, 46,* 25–31.

Wolfe, J.B. (1936). Effectiveness of token-rewards for chimpanzees. *Comparative Psychological Monographs, 12,* 5.

Wolman, B.B. (Ed.). (1965). *Handbook of Clinical Psychology.* New York: McGraw-Hill.

_____. (Ed.). (1973). *Handbook of General Psychology.* Englewood Cliffs: NJ: Prentice-Hall.

Woods, S.C. (1991). The eating paradox: How we tolerate food. *Psychological Review, 98,* 488–505.

Woolfolk, R.L. (1975). Psychophysiological correlates of meditation. *Archives of General Psychiatry, 32,* 1326–1333.

Wu, C., & Shaffer, D.R. (1987). Susceptibility to persuasive appeals as a function of source credibility and prior experience with the attitude object. *Journal of Personality and Social Psychology, 4,* 195–202.

Y

Yarrow, L.J., & Goodwin, M.S. (1973). The immediate impact of separation reactions of infants to a change in mother figures. In L.J. Stone, T.J. Smith, & L.B. Murphy (Eds.), *The Competent Infant.* New York: Basic Books.

Young, A., Stokes, M., & Crowe, M. (1984). Size and strength of the quadricep muscles of old and young women. *European Journal of Clinical Investigation, 14,* 282–287.

Z

Zajonc, R.B. (1965). Social facilitation. *Science, 149,* 269–274.

Zajonc, R.B., & Markus, G.B. (1976). Birth order and intellectual development. *Psychological Review, 82,* 74–88.

Zigler, E., & Muenchow, S. (1992). *Head Start: The Inside Story of America's Most Successful Educational Experiment.* New York: Basic Books.

Zigler, E., Styfco, S.J., & Gilman, E. (1993). The national Head Start Program for disadvantaged preschoolers. In E. Zigler & S.J. Styfco (Eds.), *Head Start and Beyond: A National Plan for Extended Childhood Intervention.* New Haven, CT: Yale University Press.

Zimbardo, P.G. (1975). On transforming experimental research into advocacy for social change. In *Psychology and Life* (10th ed.). Glenview, IL: Scott, Foresman.

_____. (1997, May). What messages are behind today's cults? *APA Monitor.*

Zimbardo, P., & Gerrig, R. (1999). *Psychology and Life.* New York: Longman.

Acknowledgments and Credits

Acknowledgments

From AN ANTHROPOLGIST ON MARS by Oliver Sacks Copyright © 1995 by Oliver Sacks Reprinted by permission of Alfred A. Knopf, Inc., a Division of Random House, Inc.

Photo Credits

COVER Henk Dawson

xii file photo; **xiv** (l)SuperStock, (r)file photo; Jeff Isaac Greenberg/Photo Researchers; **2–3** SuperStock; **4** S. Purdy Matthews/Tony Stone Images; **6** Angelo Hornak/CORBIS; **8** SuperStock; **11** Archivo Iconografico, S.A./CORBIS; **13** Harry J. Przekop/Medichrome/The Stock Shop; **15** North Wind Picture Archive; **17** (t)Archives of the History of American Psychology/The University of Akron, (b)Reprinted by permission of Sidney Harris; **18** (l)SuperStock, (r)First Image **19** Archives of History of American Psychology/The University of Akron; **25** (l)Gabe Palmer/The Stock Market, (r)First Image; **31** CALVIN AND HOBBES ©1999 Bill Watterson. Reprinted with permission of UNIVERSAL PRESS SYNDICATE. All rights reserved; **34** Neil Leslie/Photonica; **36** Bios (M. Gunther)/Peter Arnold, Inc.; **45** Arthur Beck/The Stock Market; **46** Archives of the History of American Psychology/The University of Akron; **58** Courtesy Edward Hodgetts; **59** (tl, bl)Courtesy Edward Hodgetts, (r)Alix Parson; **60** Doug Martin; **63** Aaron Haupt; **66 67** Enrico Ferorelli; **69 72** First Image; **73** Archives of the History of American Psychology/The University of Akron; **76** (t)Nina Leen/Time Life Syndication, (b)Martin Rogers/Tony Stone Images; **79** Michele Burgess/The Stock Market; **81** Elizabeth Hathon/The Stock Market; **84** (l)Tony Stone Images, (r)Robert Essel/The Stock Market; **89** Ross Products Division/Abbott Laboratories; **92** SuperStock; **94** Dugald Bremner/Tony Stone Images; **97** Jeff Zaruba/The Stock Market; **98** Lynn Johnston Productions, Inc./Dist. By United Feature Syndicate, Inc.; **102** Terry Vine/Tony Stone Images; **106** Ted Streshinsky/CORBIS; **108** CORBIS; **111** Lynn Johnston Productions, Inc./Dist. By United Feature Syndicate, Inc.; **112 114 118** SuperStock; **119** K.M. Westermann/CORBIS; **120** Cathy Guisewite/Universal Press Syndicate; **127** Frank Siteman/Tony Stone Images; **128** Mark Gamba/The Stock Market; **132** (l)Liaison Agency, (r)First Image; **134** First Image; **138** Lynn Johnston Productions, Inc./Dist. By United Feature Syndicate, Inc.; **139** Ariel Skelley/The Stock Market; **143** Biophoto Associates/Photo Researchers **145** Reuters/Ken Ross/Archive Photos; **146** David Hiser/Tony Stone Images; **147** Pete Saloutos/The Stock Market; **148** Pugliano/Liaison Agency; **153** Anatomyworks/Custom Medical Stock Photo; **154** Photo Researchers; **157** Biophoto Associates/Photo Researchers; **159** (l)SuperStock, (tr br)Adam Hart-Davis/Science Photo Library/Photo Researchers; **164** Svenskt Pressefoto/Archive Photos; **166** Science Photo Library/Photo Researchers; **168** The Stock Shop/Medichrome; **173** Arnulf Husmo/Tony Stone Images; **176** Roy Morsch/The Stock Market; **182** Reza Estakhrian/Tony Stone Images; **189** Art Resource, NY; **192** North Wind Picture Archive; **195** The Newark Museum/Art Resource, NY; **196** Charles Gupton/The Stock Market; **200** Icon Images; **201** David R. Frazier Photography; **206** Cordon Art, B.V.; **209** Archives of the History of American Psychology/The University of Akron; **218** Lester V. Bergman/CORBIS; **228** (l)Craig Aurness/CORBIS, (r)SuperStock; **230** Kenneth Rogers/CORBIS; **231** Baron Wolman/Woodfin Camp & Associates;

232 Lightstone/CORBIS; **237** Lien/Nebauer Photography/Liaison Agency; **240** SuperStock; **244** The Far Side ©1993 FARWORKS, INC. Used by permission. All rights reserved; **245** Culver Pictures; **249** Courtesy Professor Benjamin Harris/University of Wisconsin-Parkside; **252** Nina Leen/Life Magazine ©Time Inc.; **255** J. Sekowski; **256** Mark A. Johnson/The Stock Market; **256** Lew Long/The Stock Market; **258** CALVIN AND HOBBES ©1999 Bill Watterson. Reprinted with permission of UNIVERSAL PRESS SYNDICATE. All rights reserved; **260** Reprinted by permission of Sidney Harris; **263 265 272** First Image; **278** PhotoDisc, Inc.; **281** Mitch York/Tony Stone Images; **285** Courtesy Elizabeth Loftus, Ph.D./University of Washington; **286** Reprinted by permission of Sidney Harris; **288–289** David Stoecklein/The Stock Market; **291** file photo; **294** Matt Meadows; **300** First Image; **303 306** AP/Wide World Photos; **312** KS Studio; **315** Courtesy the Harlow Primate Laboratory; **317** Roger Ball/The Stock Market; **318** Bernd Kappelmeyer/FPG; **321** Courtesy Dr. Neil E. Miller, Yale Dept. of Psychology; **326** Gail Meese/Meese Photo Research; **330** (l)VCG/FPG; (r)file photo; **331** Courtesy Dr. Paul Ekman; **340** Ernst Grasser/Tony Stone Images; **342** Gail Meese/Meese Photo Research; **344** Geoff Butler; **348** David Hiser, Photographers/Aspen; **350** Courtesy Dr. Howard Gardner; **353** Jose L. Pelaez/The Stock Market; **358** Don Mason/The Stock Market; **360** Ted Rice; **366** Will & Demi McIntyre/Photo Researchers; **367** PhotoDisc, Inc.; **371** THE FAR SIDE, FARWORKS, INC. Used by permission. All rights reserved; **374** Scott Cunningham; **376** Matt Meadows; **377** Cathy Guisewite/Universal Press Syndicate; **381** Gabe Martin; **384 385** CORBIS; **386** (l)Hugh Sitton/Tony Stone Images, (r)AFP/CORBIS; **388** Reprinted by permission of Sidney Harris; **392** Ralph Morse/Life Magazine/Time Inc.; **393** CORBIS; **394** PEANUTS reprinted by permission of United Feature Syndicate, Inc.; **395** Time Life Syndication; **397** Don Smetzer/Tony Stone Images; **399** The New Yorker Collection, 1977 Henry Martin from cartoonbank.com. All Rights Reserved; **404** Michael Shay/FPG; **407** The New Yorker Collection, 1991 Mick Stevens from cartoonbank.com. All Rights Reserved; **409** Tristen Paviot/Tony Stone Images; **410–411** Reza Estakhrian/Tony Stone Images; **412 414** file photo; **421** Nicholas Devore, Photographers/Aspen; **422** (t)Liaison Agency, (bl)First Image, (br)Gail Meese/Meese Photo Research; **423** Evan Agostini/Liaison Agency; **424** Liaison Agency; **426** Prof. S.H.E. Kaufman & Dr. J.R. Golecki/Science Photo Library/Photo Researchers; **428 436** file photo; **439** Penny Tweedie/Tony Stone Images; **440** United Feature Syndicate, Inc.; **446** Shadow/Photonica; **448** Ian O'Leary/Tony Stone Images; **449** David Hiser/Tony Stone Images; **451** CORBIS; **453** SuperStock; **456** Charles Gupton; **459** Bryan McBurney/Liaison Agency; **461** PEANUTS reprinted by permission of United Feature Syndicate, Inc.; **463** Courtesy The Jerry Naylor Company/North Media Group; **464** ChiselVision/The Stock Market; **467** Paul Brown/Photo Researchers; **468** First Image; **469** Courtesy Ms. Edna Morlok; **471** Robert Essel/The Stock Market; **477** Oscar Burriel/Latin Stock/Science Photo Library/Photo Researchers; **484** Nobuo Kuwahara/Photonica; **486 487** North Wind Picture Archive; **490 491** file photo; **495** H. Sakuramoto/Photonica; **496** The New Yorker Collection, 1977 Lee Lorenz from cartoonbank.com. All Rights Reserved; **498** Tom McHugh/Photo Researchers; **507** Cliff Moore; **515** StudiOhio; **516–517** Paul Chesley, Photographers/Aspen; **518** Matt Meadows; **520** (l)Lynn M. Stone, (c)Stan Osolinski/FPG, (r)Don Smetzer/Tony Stone Images; **523** First Image; **524** (l)Art Wolfe/Tony Stone Images, (c)Nicholas DeVore/Tony Stone Images,

Acknowledgments and Credits

(r)Art Wolfe/Tony Stone Images; **525** Jose L. Pelaez/The Stock Market; **526** Mitchell Gerber/CORBIS; **529** (l)Ken Chernus/FPG, (c)Ralf Gerard/Tony Stone Images, (r)Gail Meese/Meese Photo Research; **532** (l)Richard Price/FPG, (r)Carl Schneider/FPG; **534** Nicholas DeVore/Tony Stone Images; **535** Archive/Photo Researchers; **536** (t)Telegraph Colour Library/FPG, (bl)Ronnie Kaufman/The Stock Market, (br)Gail Meese/Meese Photo Research; **544** Lori Adamski Peek/Tony Stone Images; **546** Phil Schermeister, Photographers/Aspen; **548** Bruce Ayres/Tony Stone Images; **550** Nicholas Devore, Photographers/Aspen; **552** Liaison Agency; **557** William Vandivert; **559** The Far Side ©1984 FARWORKS, INC. Used by permission. All rights reserved; **560 561** file photo; **562** Keystone/Hulton Getty; **563** First Image; **568** ZOOM 77 Stringer/Wide World Photos; **569 575** First Image; **576** Michal Heron/The Stock Market; **579** Jim Erickson/The Stock Market; **589** Joe Sohm/The Stock Market; **591** Robert Maass/CORBIS; **592** Liaison Agency; **595 599** Gaslight Ad Archives; **602** Erich Lessing/Art Resource, NY; **606** Courtesy Linda Lea McCarley; **607** Ed Lallo/Liaison Agency; **609** First Image; **611** North Wind Picture Archive; **612** (l)North Wind Picture Archive, (r)Jeff Isaac Greenberg/Photo Researchers; **614** First Image.